The Era of Interactive Media

Jesse S. Jin • Changsheng Xu • Min Xu

The Era of Interactive Media

Jesse S. Jin
University of Newcastle
Callaghan, NSW, Australia

Changsheng Xu
Chinese Academy of Science
Beijing, P.R. China

Min Xu
University of Technology
Sydney Broadway, NSW, Australia

ISBN 978-1-4899-8565-1 ISBN 978-1-4614-3501-3 (eBook)
DOI 10.1007/978-1-4614-3501-3
Springer New York Heidelberg Dordrecht London

Softcover reprin t of the hardcover 1st edition 2013

Printed on acid-free paper

Springer is part of Springer Science+Business Media (www.springer.com)

Preface

Pacific-Rim Conference on Multimedia (PCM) is a major annual international conference organized as a forum for the dissemination of state-of-the-art technological advances and research results in the fields of theoretical, experimental, and applied multimedia analysis and processing. It brings together researchers, developers, and educators in the field of multimedia from around the world. Since the first PCM was held in Sydney in 2000, it had been held successfully around the Pacific Rim, including Beijing in 2001, Hsinchu in 2002, Singapore in 2003, Tokyo in 2004, Jeju in 2005, Zhejiang in 2006, Hong Kong in 2007, Tainan in 2008, Bangkok in 2009, and Shanghai in 2010. After 10 years, PCM came back to Sydney in 2011.

PCM 2011 was the 12th conference in this highly successful and increasingly influential series and was held from 20 to 22 December 2011 at University of Technology, Sydney, Australia. The technical program featured opening keynote addresses, invited plenary talks, tutorials, and technical presentations of refereed papers. This year, we received 113 submissions and accepted 59 papers for oral presentations. The papers were carefully peer-reviewed. The accept rate of PCM 2011 was 52%. Papers in this volume covered a range of pertinent topics in the field including face detection, recognition, and synthesis; video coding and transmission; audio, image, and video quality assessment; audio and image classification; stereo image and video analysis; object detection, action recognition, and surveillance; visual analysis and retrieval; watermarking and image processing and applications.

PCM 2011 could never have been successful without the support of ARC Network in Enterprise Information Infrastructure (EII) and University of Technology, Sydney (UTS). We would also like to thank all the committee members, the keynote speakers, and the tutorial speakers. Our thanks must go to the reviewers who generously spent their time and provided valuable comments. And at the end, we would like to thank all the authors for submitting their work to PCM 2011.

NSW, Australia	Jesse S. Jin
Beijing, China	Changsheng Xu
NSW, Australia	Min Xu

Organization

General Chairs

- Jesse Jin, Newcastle, Australia
- Yong Rui, MSRA, Microsoft, USA
- Xiaofang Zhou, UQld, Australia

Local Organising Chairs

- Massimo Piccardi, UTS, Australia
- Sean He, UTS, Australia
- Maolin Huang, UTS, Australia

Honorary Chairs

- Thomas Huang, UIUC, USA
- Gerard Medioni, USC, USA
- Shih-Fu Chang, Columbia, USA

Program Chairs

- Ernest Edmonds, UTS, Australia
- Heng Tao Shen, UQld, Australia
- Changsheng Xu, CAS, China

Organising Committee

Panel Chairs

- Svetha Venkatesh, Curtin
- Anthony Maeder, UWS
- David Taubman, UNSW

Tutorial Chairs

- Mohan Kankanhalli, NUS
- Manzur Murshed, Monash
- Phoebe Chen, Deakin

Publication Chairs

- Suhuai Luo, Newcastle
- David Tien, CSU

Special Session Chairs

- Ishwar Sethi, Oakland
- Tao Mei, MSRA, Microsoft
- Richard Xu, CSU

Publicity Chairs

- Edward Chang, Google, USA
- Sameer Singh, Loughborough
- Mark Liao, ISAS, Taiwan
- Shuqiang Jiang, CAS, China
- Stephan Chalup, Newcastle
- Zheng-Jun Zha, NUS, S'pore
- Supot Nitsuwat, KMU, Thailand

Technical Committee Members

Bo Geng, Peking University, China
Cees Snoek, University of Amsterdam, Netherlands
Dong Liu, Columbia University, USA
Fei Wu, Zhejiang University, China
Gang Hua, IBM T.J. Watson Research Center, USA
Homer Chen, National Taiwan University, Taiwan
Hong Lu, Fudan University, China
Jialie Shen, Singapore Management University, Singapore
Jian Cheng, Institute of Automation, Chinese Academy of Sciences, China
Jie Shao, University of Melbourne, Australia
Jing Liu, Institute of Automation, Chinese Academy of Sciences, China
Jinhui Tang, Nanjing University of Science and Technology, China
Jinqiao Wang, Institute of Automation, Chinese Academy of Sciences, China
Jizheng Xu, Microsoft.com
Kemal Ugur, Nokia Research
Kuan-Ta Chen, Academia Sinica, Taiwan
Lexing Xie, Australian National University, Australia

Ling-Yu Duan, Peking University, China
Marco Bertini, University of Florence, Italy
Margrit Gelautz, Vienna University of Technology
Meng Wang, National University of Singapore
Nicu Sebe, Universtiy of Trento Italy
Qi Tian, University of Texas at San Antonio, USA
Qingshan Liu, Rutgers University, USA
Qionghai Dai, Tsinghua University, China
Ravindra Guntur, National University of Singapore
Richang Hong, Hefei University of Technology, China
Roger Zimmermann, National University of Singapore
Ruigang Yang, University of Kentucky
Shin'ichi Satoh, National Institue of Informatics, Japan
Shuicheng Yan, National University of Singapore
Shuqiang Jiang, Chinese Academy of Sciences
Tao Mei, Microsoft Research Asia, China
Xiangyang Xue, Fudan University, China
Xiao Wu, Southwest Jiaotong University, China
Xiaokang Yang, Shanghai Jiaotong University
Xinbo Gao, Xidian University, China
Yan Liu, Hong Kong Polytechnic University, China
Yantao Zheng, Institute for Infocomm Research, Singapore
Yao Zhao, Beijing Jiaotong University, China
Yi Yang, Carnegie Mellon University, USA
Yugang Jiang, Fudan University
Zhengjun Zha, National University of Singapore
Zhong Wu, Microsoft, USA
Zi Huang, University of Queensland, Australia

Contents

Audio, Image and Video Quality Assessment

Audio and Image Classification

Stereo Image and Video Analysis

Visual Analysis and Retrieval

Watermarking and Image Processing

Applications

Best Papers and Runner-ups

Image Re-Emotionalizing

Mengdi Xu, Bingbing Ni, Jinhui Tang, and Shuicheng Yan

Abstract In this work, we develop a novel system for synthesizing user specified emotional affection onto arbitrary input images. To tackle the subjectivity and complexity issue of the image affection generation process, we propose a learning framework which discovers emotion-related knowledge, such as image local appearance distributions, from a set of emotion annotated images. First, emotion-specific generative models are constructed from color features of the image super-pixels within each emotion-specific scene subgroup. Then, a piece-wise linear transformation is defined for aligning the feature distribution of the target image to the statistical model constructed from the given emotion-specific scene subgroup. Finally, a framework is developed by further incorporation of a regularization term enforcing the spatial smoothness and edge preservation for the derived transformation, and the optimal solution of the objective function is sought via standard non-linear optimization. Intensive user studies demonstrate that the proposed image emotion synthesis framework can yield effective and natural effects.

Keywords Re-emotionalizing • Linear piece-wise transformation • GMM

M. Xu (✉) • S. Yan
National University of Singapore, Vision and Machine Learning Lab, Block E4, #08-27, Engineering Drive 3, National University of Singapore, 117576 Singapore
e-mail: g0900224@nus.edu.sg; eleyans@nus.edu.sg

B. Ni
Advanced Digital Sciences Center, 1 Fusionopolis Way, Connexis North Tower 08-10, 138632 Singapore
e-mail: bingbing.ni@adsc.com.sg

J. Tang
Nanjing University of Science and Technology, School of Computer Science, Xiao Ling Wei 200, Nanjing, 210094 China
e-mail: jinhuitang@mail.njust.edu.cn

J.S. Jin et al., *The Era of Interactive Media*,
DOI 10.1007/978-1-4614-3501-3_1,

1 Introduction

Images may affect people into different emotions. For example, a photo taken in a rainy day looking at a dark street will usually give one a feeling of sadness; while a picture of a sunshine beach will mostly make people delighted.

Throughout the decade, the multimedia research community has shown great interest in affective retrieval and classification of visual signals (digital media). Bianchi-Berthouze [2] proposed an early Emotional Semantic Image Retrieval (i.e., ESIR) system known as *K-DIME*. In *K-DIME*, individual models for different users are built using neural network. In [8], Itten's color contrast theory [16] is applied for feature extraction. Wang et al. [23] also developed emotion semantic based features for affective image retrieval, while other works, such as [14] and [24], used generic image processing features (e.g., color histograms) for image emotion classification. In [25], Yanulevskaya et al. applied Gabor and Wiccest features, which are combined with machine learning techniques, to perform emotional valence categorization. Cho [6] developed a human–computer interface for interactive architecture, art, and music design. The studies [13] and [22] focused on affective content analysis for movies clips. More recently, some affective image data sets [17] were proposed for affective image classification. Inspired by the empirical concepts from psychology and art theory, low-level image features, such as color, texture, and high-level features (composition and content), are extracted and combined to represent the emotional content of an image for classification tasks. The authors also constructed an image dataset which contains a set of artistic photographs from a photo sharing site and a set of peer rated abstract paintings.

Beyond these emotion analysis efforts, one question naturally rises: could we endow a photo (image) with user specified emotions? An effective solution to this problem will lead to many potential interesting multimedia applications such as instant online messengers and photo editing softwares. This new function, illustrated in Fig. 1, can help the inexperienced users create professional emotion-specific photos, even though they have little knowledge about photographic techniques. Nevertheless, this problem has rarely been studied. Not surprising, image emotion synthesis is a difficult problem, given that: (1) the mechanism of how image affect the human being's feeling evolves complex biological and psychological processes and the modern biology and psychology studies have very limited knowledge on it. Thus, mathematical modeling of this mechanism is intractable; and (2) human being's affection process is highly subjective, i.e., the same image could affect different people into different emotions. Although to develop an expert system like computational model is intractable, we believe that these problems could be alleviated by a learning-based approach. It is fortunate that we can obtain a large number of emotion-annotated images from photo sharing websites such as *Flickr.com*. From a statistical point of view, images within each emotional group must convey some information and common structures which determine its affective property. Therefore, if the underlying

Fig. 1 Objective of the proposed work: emotion synthesis. Given an input image, our system can synthesize any user specific emotion on it automatically

cues that constitute an emotion-specific image can be mined by a learning framework, they can be further utilized for automatic image emotion synthesis.

Our proposed solution is motivated by the recent advances in utilizing web data (images, videos, meta-data) for multimedia applications [18, 5]. First, an emotion-specific image dataset is constructed by collecting Internet images and annotating them with emotion tags by Amazon's Mechanic Turk [1]. Training images within each emotion group are clustered into different scene subgroups according to their color and texture features. Then these images are decomposed into over-segmented patch (super-pixel) representations and for each emotion + scene group, a generative model (e.g., Gaussian Mixture Models) based on the color distribution of the image segments is constructed. To synthesize some specific emotion onto an input image, a piece-wise linear transformation is defined for aligning the feature distribution of the target image with the statistical model constructed from the source emotion + scene image subgroup. Finally, a framework is developed by further incorporation of a regularization term enforcing the spatial smoothness and edge preservation for the derived transformation, and the objective function is solved by gradient descent method. Extensive user studies are performed to evaluate the validity and performance of the proposed system.

2 Related Works

Several works have been done for image color transformation [4, 12, 19, 21]. In [19], Reinhard et al. presented a system that transfers color by example via aligning the mean and standard deviation of the color channels in both input and reference images. However, user input is required to perform the preferred color transformation. Other works focused on non-photorealistic rendering (i.e., image stylization) which communicates the main context of an image and explores the rendering effect of the scene with the artistic styles, such as painting [11, 26], cartoon [15] etc. Typically, the target exemplar style image is selected manually [4].

Our work is distinctive with these works: first, most of the previous works focused on only color transformation without any semantic knowledge transfer, however, our work directly synthesizes affective property onto arbitrary images, which is hardly investigated throughout literature; second, our proposed system is fully automatic which requires no human interactions, however, most of the previous methods require either users' manual selection of certain painting parameters [11] or users' specification of specific example images [4].

3 Learning to Emotionalize Images

In this section, we first discuss our emotion-specific image dataset construction; then we introduce the statistical modeling of the image emotion related features and propose an emotion transfer model for synthesizing any user specified emotion onto the input images.

3.1 Dataset Construction

A training image dataset that contains emotion specific images is constructed. In this work, we mainly consider landscape images (for other categories of images, the same method applies). In [27], the International Affective Picture System (IAPS) was developed and used as emotional stimuli for emotion and attention investigations. Note that we do not use the dataset provided in [17] since most of the images in [17] are artistic photographs or abstract paints, which are not appropriate for training emotion-specific models for real images such as landscape photos. A subset from the NUS-WIDE [7] image dataset, which is collected from web images, is selected as our training dataset. To obtain emotion annotations, we adopt the interactive annotation scheme by Amazon *Mechanical Turk*. The web users are asked to annotate the images into *eight* emotions, including *Awe, Anger, Amusement, Contentment, Sad, Fear, Disgust, Excitement* by Mechanical Turk. We only accept the annotations which are at least agreed by *three* (out of *five*) users, resulting about 5, 000 emotion specific images. As mentioned, we only choose landscape photos, e.g., beach, autumn, mountain, etc. as our training set. Exemplar images are shown in Fig. 2 and the statistics of the resulting image dataset are shown in Table 1. From Table 1, we can observe that only a few landscape images are labeled as disgust or fear, thus we only consider *four* types of emotions, including two positive emotions (i.e., *Awe* and *Contentment*) and two negative emotions (e.g., *Fear* and *Sad*).

3.2 Emotion-Specific Image Grouping

One can observe that even within each emotion group, image appearances may have large variations. Therefore, to develop a single model for each emotion image class is not reasonable. To cope with this problem, we first divide each

Fig. 2 Exemplar emotion-specific images of our dataset. The exemplar images are from *Contentment, Awe, Fear and Sad*, respectively

Table 1 Statistics of our constructed emotion annotated image dataset

	Amuse.	Anger	Awe	Content.	Disgust	Excite.	Fear	Sad	Sum
NUS-WIDE-Subset	115	199	**1,819**	**1,643**	24	201	**238**	**627**	4,866

Values in bold face show the size of chosen emotion sets.

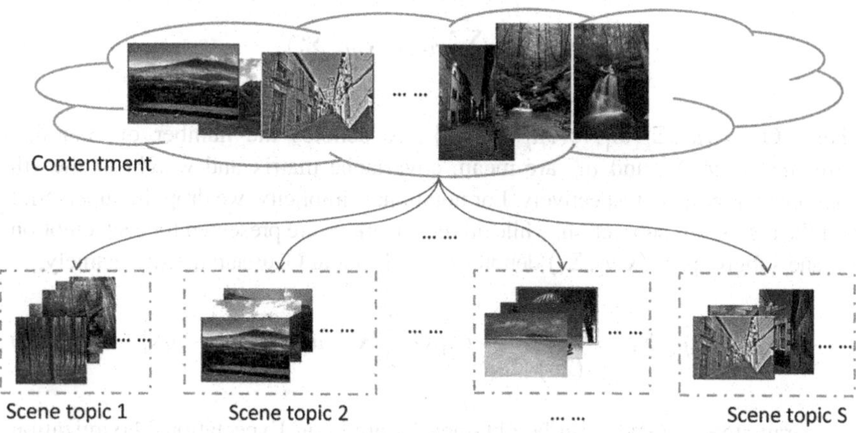

Fig. 3 Example results of the image grouping process. The image set annotated with the emotion *contentment* is grouped into several scene subgroups

emotion-specific image set into several subsets such that the images within the same subgroup share similar appearances and structures. Then computational model is constructed for each of these image sub-groups. Similar with [5], first we decompose each image into a set of over-segmented image patches (i.e., superpixels) by [10], then color (color moment) [20] and texture features (HOG) [9] are extracted and quantized by the bag-of-words model. Note that color and texture are complementary to each other in measuring image patch characteristics. Finally we cluster the images into several scene subgroups by K-means. An illustration of the image grouping result is given in Fig. 3. One can observe that within each scene subgroup, the images' appearances are quite similar. We can also note that different scene subgroups belong to different landscape types such as *beach, autumn, mountain*, etc.

3.3 Image Emotion Modeling

Emotion specific information is implicit within each emotion + scene subgroup. To uncover this information for our emotion synthesis task, we use generative models, i.e., Gaussian mixture models (GMM), for modeling the statistics of the image patch (segment) appearances within each emotion + scene image subgroup. We denote $\mathbf{x}$ as the appearance feature (i.e., a 3D vector of R, G, B values) of an image patch segmented by [10]. Then each image is regarded as a bag of image segments. The reason for using this simple image features (i.e., RGB color space) is that it is simple and direct for color transformation, which has been extensively demonstrated by previous works such as [19, 21]. We further denote that there are C emotion + scene image subgroups.

For each image subgroup $c \in \{1, 2, \ldots C\}$, we utilize GMM to describe the patch feature distribution, which is given as follows:

$$p(\mathbf{x}|\Theta^c) = \sum_{k=1}^{k} \omega_k \mathcal{N}(\mathbf{x}|\mu_k^c, \Sigma_k^c), \tag{1}$$

where $\Theta^c = \{\mu_1^c, \Sigma_k^c, \omega_1^c, \ldots, \mu_k^c, \Sigma_k^c, \omega_k^c\}$. K denotes the number of Gaussian components. μ_k^c, Σ_k^c and ω_k^c are mean, covariance matrix and weight of the kth Gaussian component, respectively. For notational simplicity, we drop the superscript c for the rest of this subsection, while all the equations are presented for each emotion + scene subgroup. $\mathcal{N}(\mathbf{x}|\mu_k, \Sigma_k)$ denotes the uni-modal Gaussian density, namely,

$$\mathcal{N}(\mathbf{x}|\mu_k, \Sigma_k) = \frac{1}{(2\pi)^{\frac{d}{2}}|\Sigma_k|^{\frac{1}{2}}} \exp\{-\frac{1}{2}(\mathbf{x} - \mu_k)^T \Sigma_k^{-1}(\mathbf{x} - \mu_k)\}. \tag{2}$$

The parameters of GMM can be obtained by applying Expectation-Maximization (EM) approach.

After EM, we can obtain the estimated GMM parameters $\{\Theta^1, \Theta^2, \cdots, \Theta^C\}$, where each Θ^c characterizes the feature distribution of a specific emotion + scene subgroup.

3.4 Learning-Based Emotion Synthesis

We first classify the input image into the image subgroup within the target emotion group. This can be achieved by first over-segmenting the input image and forming bag-of-words representation based on the color and texture features; then the nearest neighbor image in the target emotion group is found by computing the Euclidean distance of the histogram representations between the input image and the training images, and the scene label of the nearest database image is selected to be the scene label of the input image, denoted as c.

As studied in [21, 19], color (contrast, saturation, hue, etc.) can convey emotion related information. We therefore perform emotion synthesis via applying linear mapping on the RGB color space for the target image. Instead of performing global mapping for the entire image as in [21], we propose the following piece-wise linear mapping for each segment (super-pixel or patch) of the target image as,

$$f_i(\mathbf{x}) = P_i\mathbf{x} + \Delta\mathbf{x}. \tag{3}$$

Equivalently, we can augment P, $\mathbf{x}$ with an additional constant values, i.e., $\widetilde{\mathbf{x}} = [\mathbf{x}^T, 1]^T$, $\widetilde{P} = [P, \Delta\mathbf{x}]$ as,

$$f_i(\mathbf{x}) = \widetilde{P}_i\widetilde{\mathbf{x}}. \tag{4}$$

For notational simplicity, we use P, $\mathbf{x}$ to represent $\widetilde{P}, \widetilde{\mathbf{x}}$ for the rest of this subsection. Here, $\mathbf{x}$ denotes the appearance feature of one super-pixel (image segment). P_i denotes the mapping function for operating the i-th image segment (super-pixel). These image patches are super-pixels which are obtained by using [10]. Note that every pixel within the same super-pixel (image segment) shares the same mapping function f_i. The goal of our synthesis process is to obtain the set of appropriate linear mapping functions for the entire target image (suppose we have M image segments), namely, $\mathcal{P} = \{P_1, ..., P_M\}$. The objective of emotion synthesis can be expressed as,

$$\max_{\mathcal{P}} (\mathcal{F}_1 + \mathcal{F}_2), \tag{5}$$

The objective formulation contains two parts. The first part is a regularization term, which enforces the smoothness of the transformation and also maintains the edges of the original image. $\mathcal{F}_1$ can be expressed as:

$$\begin{aligned}\mathcal{F}_1 = &- \sum_{i,j\in N(a)} \omega_{ij}^a \|P_i\mathbf{x}_i - P_j\mathbf{x}_j\|_2^2 + \lambda \sum_{i,j\in N(s)} \omega_{ij}^s \|P_i\mathbf{x}_i - P_j\mathbf{x}_j\|_2^2 \\ &- \sum_{i,j\in N(c)} \|P_i - P_j\|_F^2,\end{aligned} \tag{6}$$

where

$$\begin{aligned}N(a) &= \{i,j|i,j \in N(c), \|\mathbf{x}_i - \mathbf{x}_j\|_2^2 \le \theta_1\}, N(s) \\ &= \{i,j|i,j \in N(c), \|\mathbf{x}_i - \mathbf{x}_j\|_2^2 \ge \theta_2\}.\end{aligned} \tag{7}$$

Here, $N(c)$ denotes the spatial neighborhood, i.e., two super-pixels i and j are adjacent. θ_1 and θ_2 are the color difference thresholds. ω_{ij}^a and ω_{ij}^s are the weighting coefficients, which are defined as follows:

$$\omega_{ij}^a \propto \exp(-\|\mathbf{x_i} - \mathbf{x_j}\|_2^2/a), \omega_{ij}^s \propto 1 - \exp(-\|\mathbf{x_i} - \mathbf{x_j}\|_2^2/a). \tag{8}$$

Here, θ_1, θ_2, λ and a are set to be optimal empirically. We can note from this prior that: (1) The first term ensures that original contours in the target image will be preserved by enforcing that originally distinctive neighborhood segments present distinctive color values in the transformed image; (2) The second term encourages smooth transition from image segments to near-by segments.

The second part of the framework is the emotion fitting term, which is expressed as:

$$\mathcal{F}_2 = \log\left(\prod_{i=1}^{M} p(\mathcal{I}|P_i)\right) = \log\left(\prod_{i=1}^{M} p(\mathbf{x}_i|\Theta^c)\right). \tag{9}$$

Here $p(\mathbf{x} \mid \Theta^c)$ is the trained GMM model for emotion+scene subgroup c, $\mathbf{x}_i$ is the color vector of the ith image segment. We can note that this term encourages the distributions of the target image to move towards the statistical model of the training data. Finally the cost function is denoted as:

$$\begin{aligned}\mathcal{F} &= \mathcal{F}_1 + \mathcal{F}_2\\ &= -\sum_{i,j\in N(a)} \omega_{ij}^{a}\|P_i\mathbf{x}_i - P_j\mathbf{x}_j\|_2^2 + \lambda \sum_{i,j\in N(s)} \omega_{ij}^{s}\|P_i\mathbf{x}_i - P_j\mathbf{x}_j\|_2^2\\ &\quad - \sum_{i,j\in N(c)} \|P_i - P_j\|_F^2 + \sum_i \log\left(\sum_k \mathcal{N}_k\right).\end{aligned} \tag{10}$$

Note that Eq. (10) is nonlinear and complex. Therefore, to optimize the cost function, we adopt Newton's method with linear constraints, which can guarantee local optimum [3], as:

$$\max_{\mathcal{P}} \mathcal{F}, s.t. 0 \preceq P_i\mathbf{x} \preceq 255, \forall i = 1, 2, \cdots, M, \tag{11}$$

where $\preceq$ denotes component-wise inequality constraints. These constraints ensure that the resulting color value is within appropriate range. Our method is schematically illustrated in Fig. 4.

4 Experiments

In this section, we will introduce our experimental settings, user studies along with discussions. As mentioned in the previous sections, during the pre-processing stage, training images within each emotion group are segregated into several scene subgroups (subclasses) based on the distributions of the image super-pixels' HOG and color moment features. For each subclass, we train a GMM to describe the

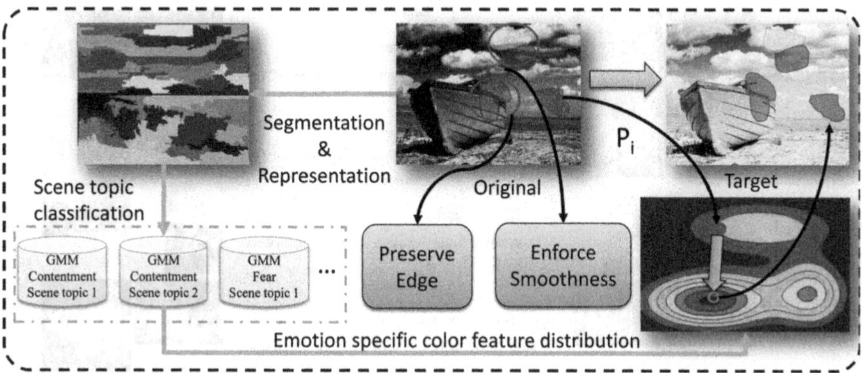

Fig. 4 The learning-based emotion synthesis scheme

distribution of super-pixels' color information. Given an arbitrary input image, in the emotion synthesis phase, we first assign it to the nearest scene subclass based on the HOG and color moment bag-of-words representation. Then our task is to obtain a mapping function which can optimize Eq. (11). Since our probability function is non-convex, we can easily get trapped in a local optimum. Therefore, a good initial mapping matrix is crucial. To get a proper initialization, we firstly assign patch (super-pixel) j to the nearest Gaussian component center μ_i. After that, a pseudo inverse is performed as $P^i_{inv} = x_j^{\dagger} u_i$, here $\mathbf{x}_j$ denotes mean color feature value of image patch j. The linear multiplier transformation part of the initial mapping matrix becomes, $P^i_{ini} = \lambda I + (1 - \lambda)P^i_{inv}$. Here I is the identity matrix. In our experiment, we set $\lambda = 0.8$ empirically. With a good initialization, we can mostly obtain a good mapping matrix using standard non-linear optimization algorithms such as Newton's method.

In our experiment, we choose 55 images from the NUS-WIDE dataset which serve as the testing images while the others construct the training image set. We compare our proposed method with the color transfer method proposed in [19], which directly aligns the mean and standard deviation of the color distribution between the source (reference) and the target image. The target image is mapped with the reference image chosen from the emotion + scene subclass by nearest neighbor assignment (in terms of the HOG and color moment based bag-of-words representation).

The comparative user studies are conducted as follows. Firstly, the transformed images of both methods are presented to the participants in pairs (with the left-right order randomly shuffled). Participants are asked to decide whether these image can express the specified target emotion. We also consider the naturalness of the synthesized images, since the naturalness will significantly affect the image quality. In this sense, the participants are also asked to compare which image of the same pair is more natural. In particular, participants are asked to give a judgement that whether the left image is Much Better, Better, Same, Worse, Much Worse than right one.

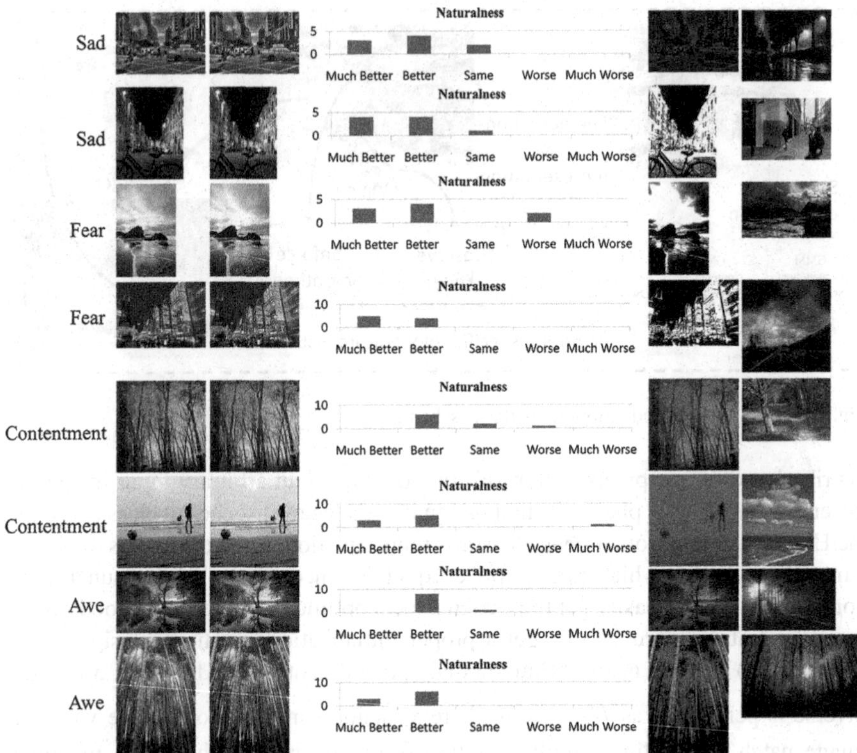

Fig. 5 Example results of the image emotion synthesis. Each row, from *left* to *right*, show the original image, synthesized image using our method, naturalness evaluation bar, color transfer result and reference image in color transfer. The *middle bars* show statistics of user's responses which indicate based on naturalness whether synthesizing result (*left*) is Much Better, Better, Same, Worse, Much Worse than the result from color transfer method (*right*). For better viewing, please see in x2 resolution and in color pdf file

In our user study, 9 participants are asked to judge the image's naturalness, and 20 participants with ages ranging from 20 to 35 years old are asked to judge whether these images can express the target emotion. The statistics of the results for the user study are illustrated in Fig. 6 in terms of the naturalness. We also show several example results in Fig. 5 for both our method and the color transfer method.

In Fig. 6, yellow bars show the number of participants voting for each type of the ratings. We can observe that the images resulting from our method are more natural to the audience than the ones from the color transfer method. This could be explained by the fact that the statistic modeling using GMM is more generative and robust, while the exemplar image based color transfer might sometimes lead to over-fitting. Figure 6 and Table 2 show that in most cases images which are synthesized using our method outperform the color transfer results in terms of the accuracies of emotion synthesis. Figure 5 further shows that our results are more

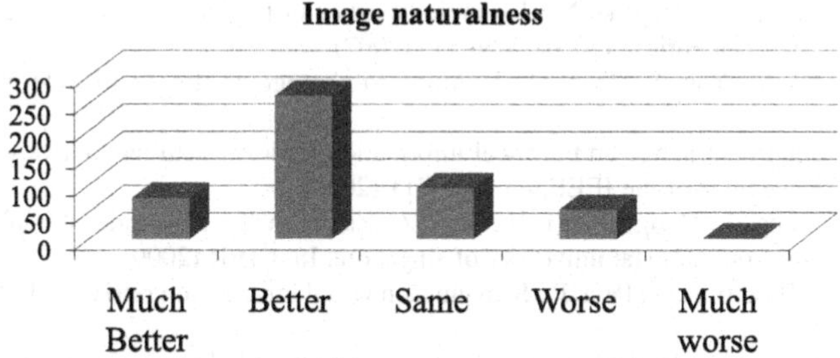

Fig. 6 The statistics from our user studies. The *bar* shows the summation of user's feedback based on naturalness, i.e. whether the result of our method is Much Better, Better, Same, Worse, Much Worse than the result of color transfer

Table 2 Perceptibility comparison of each emotion set

	Awe	Contentment	Fear	Sad	Average
Baseline	0.4375	0.3600	0.4833	0.3788	0.4082
Our method	0.6250	0.6550	0.6100	0.7904	0.7045

natural than color transfer based results. As can be seen, color transfer based results rely on reference images. Therefore, if the color distribution of reference image is too far from the target image, the transformed result will be unnatural, e.g., trees in the last example look red which are not realistic. However, our statistical learning based method do not have such a problem.

5 Conclusions

In this work, we developed a learning based image emotion synthesis framework which can transfer the learnt emotion related statistical information onto arbitrary input images. Extensive user studies well demonstrated that the proposed method is effective and the re-emotionalized images are natural and realistic.

Acknowledgements This research is done for CSIDM Project No. CSIDM- 200803 partially funded by a grant from the National Research Foundation (NRF) administered by the Media Development Authority (MDA) of Singapore. This work is partially supported by Human Sixth Sense Project, Illinois@Singapore Pte Ltd.

References

1. https://www.mturk.com/mturk/welcome
2. Bianchi-Berthouze, N.: K-dime: an affective image filtering system. TMM 10, 103–106 (2003)
3. Boyd, S., Vandenberghe, L.: Convex Optimization. Cambridge University Press (2004)

4. Chang, Y., Saito, S., Nakajima, M.: Example-based color transformation of image and video using basic color categories. TIP 16, 329–336 (2007)
5. Cheng, B., Ni, B., Yan, S., Tian, Q.: Learning to photograph. In: ACM MM. pp. 291–300 (2010)
6. Cho, S.B.: Emotional image and musical information retrieval with interactive genetic algorithm. In: Proceedings of the IEEE. pp. 702–711 (2004)
7. Chua, T.S., Tang, J., Hong, R., Li, H., Luo, Z., Zheng, Y.T.: Nus-wide: A real-world web image database from national university of singapore. In: CIVR (2009)
8. Colombo, C., Bimbo, A.D., Pala, P.: Semantics in visual information retrieval. TMM 6, 38–53 (1999)
9. Dalal, N., Triggs, B.: Histograms of oriented gradients for human detection. In: CVPR. pp. 886–893 (2005)
10. Felzenszwalb, P., Huttenlocher, D.: Efficient graph-based image segmentation. IJCV 59, 167–181 (2004)
11. Guo, Y., Yu, J., Xu, X., Wang, J., Peng, Q.: Example based painting generation. CGI 7(7), 1152–1159 (2006)
12. Gupta, M.R., Upton, S., Bowen, J.: Simulating the effect of illumination using color transformation. SPIE CCI 111, 248–258 (2005)
13. Hanjalic, A.: Extracting moods from pictures and sounds: towards truly personalized tv. IEEE Signal Processing Magazine 23, 90–100 (2006)
14. Hayashi, T., Hagiwara, M.: Image query by impression words-the iqi system. TCE 44, 347–352 (1998)
15. Hong, R., Yuan, X., Xu, M., Wang, M., Yan, S., Chua, T.S.: Movie2comics: A feast of multimedia artwork. In: ACM MM. pp. 611–614 (2010)
16. Itten, J.: The art of color: the subjective experience and objective rationale of color. John Wiley, New York (1973)
17. Machajdik, J., Hanbury, A.: Affective image classification using features inspired by psychology and art theory. In: ACM MM. pp. 83–92 (2010)
18. Ni, B., Song, Z., Yan, S.: Web image mining towards universal age estimator. In: ACM MM. pp. 85–94 (2009)
19. Reinhard, E., Ashikhmin, M., Gooch, B., Shirley, P.: Color transfer between images. CGA 21 (2001)
20. Stricker, M., Orengo, M.: Similarity of color images. In: SPIE. pp. 381–392 (1995)
21. Thompson, W.B., Shirley, P., Ferwerda, J.A.: A spatial post-processing algorithm for images of night scenes. Journal of Graphics Tools 7, 1–12 (2002)
22. Wang, H.L., Cheong, L.F.: Affective understanding in film. TCSVT 16, 689–704 (2006)
23. Wang, W.N., Yu, Y.L., Jiang, S.M.: Image retrieval by emotional semantics: A study of emotional space and feature extraction. In: IEEE International Conference on Systems, Man and Cybernetics. pp. 3534–3539 (2006)
24. Wu, Q., Zhou, C., Wang, C.: Content-based affective image classification and retrieval using support vector machines. Affective Computing and Intelligent Interaction (2005)
25. Yanulevskaya, V., van Gemert, J.C., Roth, K., Herbold, A.K., Sebe, N., Geusebroek, J.M.: Emotional valence categorization using holistic image features. In: ICIP (2008)
26. Zhang, X., Constable, M., He, Y.: On the transfer of painting style to photographic images through attention to colour contrast. In: Pacific-Rim Symposium on Image and Video Technology. pp. 414–421 (2010)
27. Lang, P.J., Bradley, M.M., Cuthbert, B.N.: International affective picture system (IAPS): Affective ratings of pictures and instruction manual. In: Technical Report A-8. University of Florida, Gainesville, FL.(2008)

Thesaurus-Assistant Query Expansion for Context-Based Medical Image Retrieval

Hong Wu and Chengbo Tian

Abstract While medical image retrieval using visual feature has poor performance, context-based retrieval emerges as a more easy and effective solution. And medical domain knowledge can also be used to boost the text-based image retrieval. In this paper, UMLS metathasaurus is used to expand query for retrieving medical images by their context information. The proposed query expansion method is with a phrase-based retrieval model, which is implemented based on Indri search engine and their structured query language. In the phrase-based retrieval model, original query and syntax phrases are used to formulate a structured query. The concepts detected from the original query and their hyponyms are used to append query, and added to the structured query. Both phrases and medical concepts are identified with the help of the MetaMap program. Our approach was evaluated on ImageCLEFmed 2010 dataset, which contains more than 77,000 images and their captions from online medical journals. Several representations of phrase and concept were also compared in experiments. The experimental results show the effectiveness of our approach for context-based medical image retrieval.

Keywords Medical image retrieval • Query expansion • Phase-based model • UMLS • MetaMap

1 Introduction

With the progress of digital imaging technologies, a large number of medical images have been generated by hospitals and medical centers in recent years [1]. These visual data play an increasingly important role in diagnosis, treatment

H. Wu (✉) • C. Tian
School of Computer Science and Engineering, University of Electronic Science and Technology of China, 611731 Chengdu, P. R., China
e-mail: hwu@uestc.edu.cn; tianchengbo@gmail.com

J.S. Jin et al., *The Era of Interactive Media*,
DOI 10.1007/978-1-4614-3501-3_2,

planning and education [2], and are integrated into PACS, published as online collections or in the online content of journals. These large volumes of image data produce a strong need for effective medical image retrieval systems.

Traditional medical image retrieval relies on manual image annotation, which cannot meet the rapid growth in the amount of medical images. And content-based image retrieval has limited retrieval performance due to the semantic gap problem. In ImageCLEFmed 2010 campaign [3], the MAP of the best content-based run was only 0.0091. Thus, context-based image retrieval emerges as a more easy and effective solution. In context-based medical image retrieval, the text information that describes the images is extracted from medical reports or medical articles, and used to retrieve images. And the image retrieval problem is transformed to a text retrieval problem.

Text retrieval has been studied for decades, and a lot of methods have been proposed. Among them, query expansion is a technique to overcome the mismatch problem between query terms and documents terms. Query expansion enriches the query by its related terms and makes the expanded query a better match with the relevant document. For biomedical information retrieval, researchers have proposed to expand query with domain specific thesauri and ontologies such as MeSH [4] and UMLS [5]. Current query expansion methods either add synonyms of the original query terms [6–8], or expand terms that are hypernyms/hyponyms of the original query terms [9]. Besides, the retrieval performance is also affected by some other important factors, such as the retrieval model used, and how the expanded terms are integrated into the ranking function. Current query expansion methods were different in these factors, and got inconsistent results.

In this work, we proposed a thesaurus-assistant query expansion method with a phrase-based retrieval model. To relax the term independent assumption used by most retrieval systems, a phrase-based model is implemented based on Indri search engine and its structured query language, and different phrase definitions and representations are investigated. For query expansion, the query text is map to UMLS concepts by MetaMap [10], and mapped concepts and their hyponyms are used to expand query. Different representations for concept are also explored. The proposed methods were evaluated with the collection, queries and relevance judgments of the ad-hoc retrieval task in ImageCLEFmed 2010.

The structure of the paper is as follows. Section 2 introduces some previous works on query expansion with biomedical knowledge. Section 3 describes our phrase-based model and thesaurus-assistant query expansion. The experiments and their results are presented in Sect. 4, and the conclusions are given in Sect. 5.

2 Previous Works

The mismatch problem between query terms and documents terms leads to low retrieval accuracy. This is more prominent for domain specific retrieval, since general user may lack the domain knowledge, and their vocabulary might not match well with the vocabulary used in the professional literature. Query expansion is a technique to overcome the mismatch problem by adding related terms to the query and making it closer to the relevant documents vectors. Query expansion mainly includes three kinds of approaches: global analysis, local analysis, and knowledge based approach. In domain specific area, many research works focused on utilizing domain knowledge to expand query.

For biomedical information retrieval, some works have been studied on query expansion using domain thesauri and ontologies such as MeSH and UMLS, but their results were inconsistent. Srinivasan [11] used a statistical thesaurus to add MeSH term to query, and achieved improvement on average precision. Aronson and Rindflesch [6] used UMLS for query expansion and their method outperformed the baseline method. Hersh et al. proposed to expand query with synonym, hierarchical, and related terms as well as term definitions from UMLS Metathesaurus [9]. But all types of their query expansion strategies resulted in degraded performances. Liu and Chu [12] focused on scenario-specific queries, and proposed a knowledge-based query expansion method that exploited UMLS to append query with terms specifically relevant to the query's scenarios. Their method achieved improvement in retrieval performance. Lu et al. [13] studied query expansion with MeSH on the TREC Genomics Track data, and also got improvement. Mu and Lu's recent work [14] proposed four query expansion strategies based on UMLS and evaluated on TREC Genomic Track 2006 data set, but their results were negative. In recent years, there has been also some works on query expansion with domain knowledge for multi-model information retrieval or context-based image retrieval, mainly with ImageCLEF track data. With conceptual indexing model, Diem et al. [15] expanded both queries and documents based on *is-a* semantic relation in UMLS, and achieved notable improvement. Díaz-Galiano et al. [16] proposed to expand query with MeSH terms and improved the performances of not only the text-based retrieval system but also the textual and visual combined retrieval system. In ImageCLEF2008, they compared query expansion with MeSH and UMLS. The query expansion with MeSH got good results, but that with UMLS obtained worse results than the baseline.

Our method is similar to Aronson and Rindflesch's work [6]. Their work in fact used a phrase-based model, also used structured query and extracted medical concepts with MetaMap. But there are many differences between the two works. Our method expands query with not only the mapped concepts but also their child concepts, while their method only uses the mapped concepts. And we also compared different representations for phrase and concept in experiments. They used the corpus index by human-assigned MeSH terms and ran experiments on INQUERY system [17], while we used a corpus composed of context information of medical images, and conducted experiments on Indri search engine [18]. Different from most other query expansion methods for medical image retrieval, our method uses a phrase-based retrieval modal, and the expanded terms are unequally combined with original query representation.

3 Phrase-Based Retrieval Model and Query Expansion

Most traditional information retrieval approaches adopted unigram models which assume independence between terms. Recently, a number of retrieval approaches have been attempted to utilize phrase in retrieval models to improve the retrieval performance. Some works [19–24] explored the use of statistical phrases such as n-grams or proximity-based phrases, and other works [25–29] studied the utility of various kinds of syntactic phrases. Some of these works got promising results in their experiments.

To utilize phrase in information retrieval, there're three steps: (1) Identify phrases in query text, (2) Identify these phrases in document, (3) Combine phrase with individual word in ranking function. The abovementioned methods are different in some of these steps, and exhibit different effectiveness. In this work, the first step is performed with the help of MetaMap, and the last two steps are implemented based on Indri search engine [18] and its structured query language. Indri is a scalable search engine that inherits the inference net framework from InQuery and combines it with language modeling approach to retrieval.

3.1 Phrase Identification

In our approach, phrase identification is conducted with the help of MetaMap [10] which is a tool to map biomedical text to concepts in the UMLS Metathesaurus. MetaMap first parses the text into phrases, and then performs intensive variant generation on each phrase. After that, candidates are retrieved from the Metathesaurus to match the variants. Finally, the candidates are evaluated by a mapping algorithm, and the best candidates are returned as the mapped concepts.

In this study, the concept mapping is restricted to three source vocabularies: MeSH, SNOMED-CT, and FMA. And two phrase identification strategies are explored. One is to use the phrases produced by the early step in MetaMap program, and filter out the unwanted words in them, such as preposition, determiner etc. Another is to consider the individual word or sequence words which mapped to UMLS concept as a phrase.

3.2 Phrase Representation

After identifying phrase in query text, the query phrases would be recognized again within documents. Many phrase identification techniques only look at contiguous sequences of words. But, the constituent words of a query phrase might be several words apart, and even with different order when used in a document. Fortunately, this problem can be easily solved by using operators in Indri query language. The new query can be formulated with the special operators to provide more exact information about the relationship of terms than the original text query. Here, we introduce some operators which are used for representing phrase.

- Ordered Window Operator: #$N(t_1 \ldots t_n)$ or #od$N(t_1 \ldots t_n)$

The terms within an ordered window operator must appear orderly in the document with at most $N-1$ terms between adjacent terms (e.g. t_i and t_{i+1}) in order to contribute to the document's belief score.

- Unordered Window Operator: #uw$N(t_1 \ldots t_n)$

The terms contained in an unordered window operator must be found in any order within a window of N words in order to contribute to the belief score of the document.

For example, the phrase "congestive heart failure" can be represented as #1(congestive heart failure), which means that the phrase is recognized in a document only if the three constituent words are found in the right order and no other words between them. It can also be represented as #uw6(congestive heart failure), which means that the phrase is recognized in a document only if the three constituent words are found in any order within a window of six words.

There are also some other operators related to our works. They are introduced as follows.

- Combine Operator: #combine $(t_1 \ldots t_n)$

The terms or nodes contained in the combine operator are treated as having equal influence on the final result. The belief scores provided by the arguments of the combine operator are averaged to produce the belief score of the #combine node.

- Weight Operator: #weight $(w_1 t_1 \ldots w_n t_n)$

The terms or nodes contained in the weight operator contribute unequally to the final result according to the corresponding weight (w_i). The belief scores provided by the arguments of the weight operator are weighted averaged to produce the belief score of the #weight node. Taking #weight(1.0 dog 0.5 train) for example, its belief score is 0.67 log(b(dog)) + 0.33 log(b(train)).

3.3 *Phrase-Based Retrieval Model*

When utilizing phrase in information retrieval, phrase term should be combined with word term in ranking function. Simply, we can use one ranking function for word term, another for phrase term, and the final ranking function is weight sum of them.

$$F(Q,D) = w_1 f_1(Q,D) + w_2 f_2(Q,D) \tag{1}$$

where Q and D stand for query and document respectively. $f_1(Q,D)$ is the ranking function for word term, and $f_2(Q,D)$ for phrase term. The weights w_1 and w_2 can be tuned by experiment.

With Indri search engine, this ranking function can be implemented easily with a structured query and the inference network model. For example, the topic 2 in ad-hoc track of imageCLEFmed 2010 is:

"A microscopic image of Acute Myeloid Leukemia"

With the second phrase identification strategy, the phrases are "microscopic" and "acute myeloid leukemia". The query can be formulated as following,

#weight(0.9 combine(A microscopic image of Acute Myeloid Leukemia)
0.1 #combine(microscopic #uw9(acute myeloid leukemia)))

The first #combine() in the structured query corresponds to $f_1(Q,D)$, and the second one corresponds to $f_2(Q,D)$, while w_1 is 0.9 and w_2 is 0.1.

3.4 *Thesaurus-Assistant Query Expansion*

After the original query text is mapped to concepts in UMLS, the query can be expanded with the mapped concept terms, their synonyms, hierarchical or related terms. Since the query terms of ordinary users tend to be general, we use the preferred names of the mapped concepts and their direct children to expand query. The added terms are not necessarily important as the original ones, so weight can also be introduced, and the new ranking function is,

$$F(Q,D) = w_1 f_1(Q,D) + w_2 f_2(Q,D) + w_3 f_3(Q,D) \tag{2}$$

and $f_3(Q,D)$ is the ranking function for concepts, and w_3 is the corresponding weight. Concepts can be represented in the same way as phrases.

To expand query with the mapped concept and their direct children, the preferred names of these concepts are normalized and redundant names are erased. Taking the topic 2 for example, the expanded query can be as following,

#weight(0.5 #combine(A microscopic image of Acute Myeloid Leukemia)
0.3 #combine(microscopic #uw9(acute myeloid leukemia))
0.2 #combine(#uw6(granulocytic sarcoma) #uw6(basophilic leukemia)
#uw6(eosinophilic leukemia) #uw9(acute myeloid leukemia)))

4 Experiments

ImageCLEFmed is a medical image retrieval task within ImageCLEF campaign. The dataset from the ad-hoc retrieval task of ImageCLEFmed 2010 [3] was used for our experiments. It contains more than 77,000 images from articles published in Radiology and Radiographics, together with the text of the captions and a link to

Table 1 Retrieval performances for different phase-based methods

Method (phrase/operator)		MAP	P@10
Baseline		0.2907	0.4187
p1	#3	0.3031(0.9,0.1)	0.4375
	#uwN ($N = 2n$)	**0.3040** (0.9,0.1)	**0.4375**
	#3_#uwN ($N = 2n$)	0.3028 (0.8,0.1,0.1)	0.4375
p2	#3	0.3005 (0.9,0.1)	0.4437
	#uwN ($N = 3n$)	**0.3033** (0.6,0.4)	0.4375
	#3_#uwN ($N = 3n$)	0.3031 (0.6,0.1,0.3)	**0.4437**

the html of the full text articles. The image captions were used as the context information in this study. The experiments were based on the 16 short queries and the ground-truth of the retrieval task. The retrieval performance was measured using MAP and p@10.

We first explored various methods for phrase-based model, which were different in phrase identification strategy and query formulation. Tow phrase identification strategies were tested. The first is represented as "p1" which using the filtered phrases identified in the early step of MetaMap program, and the second is represented as "p2" which using the word sequence as a phrase which mapped to a concept. We explored three different representations for phrase, #*N*(), #uw*N*(), and the combination of them. For #*N*(), we tested #1() and #3(), and experiments indicated #3() was better for both p1 and p2. For #uw*N*(), we set $N = k*n$, where n is the number of terms within the operator, and k is a free parameter. We tested $k = 2$, 3, 4, and found that $N = 2n$ was the best for p1, and $N = 3n$ was the best for p2. These best settings were also used for the combination case. The weights within the weight operator were tuned by experiment to maximize MAP with the constraint that sum of them equals to one.

The experimental results of the phrase-based method and baseline are listed in Table 1, and bold indicates the best result for a given setting. The baseline was to use the raw query to search on Indri. The numbers in bracket behind the MAP values are the weights for different parts of the structured query. From the results, we can see that the MAPs of all phrase-based retrieval is better than that of baseline, and the best phrase-based retrieval method can improve the MAP by 4.6% to 0.3040. It also indicates that the first phrase identification method are superior than the second one for phrase-based retrieval, and #uw*N*() is the best representation for phrase in both p1 and p2. The best settings were also used in the later experiment.

Our second phase of experiment was to compare two types of query expansions, expansion with the mapped concepts only and together with their child concepts, and also explore different query formulations. We chose #combine() or #uw*N*() to represent concept, and tested three query formulations, represented as QE1, QE2, and QE3. In all cases, raw query was combined with phrase and concept. For QE1, phrase was represented with #3() and concept with #combine(). For QE2, phrase was represented with #uw*N*() and concept with #combine(). And for QE3, both phrase and concept were represented with #uw*N*(). When using #uw*N*() to

Table 2 Retrieval performances for different query expansion methods

	QE with concepts		QE with concepts and hyponyms	
Method	MAP	P@10	MAP	P@10
QE1_p1	0.3031 (0.8,0.1,0.1)	0.4250	0.3168 (0.3,0.3,0.4)	0.4187
QE2_p1	0.3040 (0.8,0.1,0.1)	0.4250	**0.3188** (0.3,0.3,0.4)	0.4375
QE3_p1	**0.3052** (0.8,0.1,0.1)	**0.4375**	0.3082 (0.7,0.1,0.2)	**0.4562**
QE1_p2	0.3086 (0.6,0.2,0.2)	0.4500	0.3174 (0.6,0.2,0.2)	**0.4687**
QE2_p2	0.3105 (0.6,0.2,0.2)	0.4562	**0.3175**(0.6,0.2,0.2)	0.4562
QE3_p2	**0.3115** (0.6,0.2,0.2)	**0.4688**	0.3098 (0.5,0.3,0.2)	0.4500

represent phrase, we set $N = 2n$ for p1 and $N = 3n$ for p2. Since phrase of p2 corresponds to concept, we set $N = 3n$ when using #uw$N$() to represent concept. We also compared the two phrase identification strategies, and finally got 12 query expansion methods based on different combinations. The experimental results of these methods are listed in Table 2. The method QE1_p1 uses QE1 formulation and the first phrase identification method. When expanding query with only the mapped concepts, it simulates the method of Alan and Rindflesch [5], and its results are given with underline.

For query expansion with only the mapped concepts, the QE3 formulation gets the best MAPs and p@10s with both phrase identification strategies respectively. And it achieves the best with p2 at MAP of 0.3115, which is 7.2% above the baseline. For query expansion with the mapped concepts and their hyponyms, the QE2 formulation gets the best MAPs with both phrase identification strategies, and the best is with p1 at 0.3188. The best MAP is 9.7% above the baseline, and 5.2% above Alan and Rindflesch's method. The experimental results indicate query expansion with phrase-based model can further improve the retrieval performance, and query expansion with hyponyms is better than expansion with only the mapped concepts.

5 Conclusion

For medical retrieval, general users may lack the domain knowledge needed to choose the right query terms. This makes the vocabulary mismatch problem more prominent than for general information retrieval. In this paper, we have proposed a knowledge-based query expansion method to improve context-based image retrieval. In our method, UMLS metathesaurus is used to expand query in a phrase-based retrieval model. Our experimental results show the effectiveness of the phrase-based model and thesaurus-assistant query expansion.

In future work, we will explore other semantic relations in UMLS to expand query, test other retrieval model such as unigram models, and test our method on other dataset.

Acknowledgements This research is partly supported by the National Science Foundation of China under grants 60873185 and the Open Project Program of the National Laboratory of Pattern Recognition (NLPR).

References

1. Robb, R.A.: Biomedical Imaging, Visualization, and Analysis. Wiley-Liss Publisher (1999)
2. Müller, H., Michoux, N., Bandon, D., Geissbuhler, A.: A Review of Content-Based Image Retrieval Systems in Medical Applications-Clinical Benefits and Future Directions. International Journal of medical Informatics, 73, 1–23 (2004)
3. Müller, H., Kalpathy-Cramer, J., Eggel, I., Bedrick, S., Kahn Jr., C.E. and Hersh, W.: Overview of the CLEF 2010 Medical Image Retrieval Track. In: the Working Notes of CLEF 2010, Padova, Italy, (2010)
4. Nelson, S.J., Johnston, D., Humphreys, B.L.: Relationships in Medical Subject Headings. In: Relationships in the Organization of Knowledge, Kluwer Academic Publishers, New York, pp. 171–184 (2001)
5. Bodenreider, O.: The Unified Medical Language System (UMLS): Integrating Biomedical Terminology. Nucleic Acids Research, 32, 267–270 (2004)
6. Aronson, A.R., Rindflesch, T.C.: Query Expansion Using the UMLS Metathesaurus. In: the 1997 AMIA Annual Fall Symposium, pp. 485–489 (1997)
7. Guo, Y., Harkema, H., Gaizauskas, R.: Sheffield University and the TREC 2004 Genomics Track: Query Expansion Using Synonymous Terms. In: the Thirteenth Text REtrieval Conference, pp. 753–757 (2004)
8. Plovnick, R.M., Zeng, Q.T.: Reformulation of Consumer Health Queries with Professional Terminology: A Pilot Study. Journal of Medical Internet Research, 6(3), (2004)
9. Hersh, W.H., Price, S., Donohoe, L.: Assessing Thesaurus-Based Query Expansion Using the UMLS Metahesaurus. In: the AMIA Annual Symposium 2000, pp. 344–348 (2000)
10. Aronson, A.R.: Eective Mapping of Biomedical Text to the UMLS Metathesaurus: the MetaMap Program. In: the AMIA Symposium 2001, pp. 17–21. (2001)
11. Srinivasan, P.: Query Expansion and MEDLINE. In: Informaiton Processing and Management. 32(4), 431–443 (1996)
12. Liu, Z., Chu, W.W.: Knowledge-Based Query Expansion to Support Scenario-Specific Retrieval of Medical Free Text. In: the 2005 ACM Symposium on Applied Computing, pp. 1076–1083 (2005)
13. Lu, Z., Kim, W., Wilbur, W.: Evaluation of Query Expansion Using MeSH in PubMed. Information Retrieval. 12, 69–80 (2009)
14. Mu, X., Lu, K.: Towards Effective Genomic Information Retrieval: The Impact of Query Complexity and Expansion Strategies. Journal of Information Science. 36(2), 194–208 (2010)
15. Le, D.T.H., Chevallet, J., Thuy, D.T.B.: Thesaurus-Based Query and Document Expansion in Conceptual Indexing with UMLS: Application in Medical Information Retrieval. In: 2007 I.E. International Conference on In Research, Innovation and Vision for the Future, pp. 242–246 (2007)
16. Díaz-Galiano, M.C., Martín-Valdivia, M.T., Ureña-López, L.A.: Query Expansion with a Medical Ontology to Improve a Multimodal Information Retrieval System. Computers in Biology and Medicine, 39, 396–403 (2009)
17. Callan, J.P., Croft, W.B., Harding, S.: The INQUERY Retrieval System. In: the 3rd International Conference on Database and Expert Systems Applications, pp. 347–356 (1992)
18. Strohman, T., Metzler, D., Turtle, H., Croft, W. B.: Indri: A Language Model-Based Search Engine for Complex Queries. In: the International Conference on Intelligence Analysis, (2005)

19. Fagan, J.L.: Automatic Phrase Indexing for Document Retrieval. In: ACM SIGIR'87, pp. 91–101 (1987)
20. Mitra, M., Buckley, C., Singhal, A., Cardie, C.: An Analysis of Statistical and Syntactic Phrases. In: RIAO'97, pp. 200–214 (1997)
21. Miller, D.R.H., Leek, T., Schwartz, R.M.: A Hidden Markov Model Information Retrieval System. In: ACM SIGIR'99, pp. 214–221 (1999)
22. Gao, J., Nie, J., Wu, G., Cao, G.: Dependence Language Model for Information Retrieval. In: ACM SIGIR'04, pp. 170–177 (2004)
23. Metzler, D., Croft, W.B.: A Markov Random Field Model for Term Dependencies. In: ACM SIGIR'05, pp. 472–479 (2005)
24. Tao, T., Zhai, C.: An Exploration of Proximity Measures in Information Retrieval. In: ACM SIGIR'07, pp. 295–302 (2007)
25. Lewis, D.D., Croft, W.B.: Term Clustering of Syntactic Phrases. In: ACM SIGIR'90, pp. 385–404 (1990)
26. Strzalkowski, T., Perez-Carballo, J., Marinescu, M.: Natural Language Information Retrieval: Trec-3 Report. In: TREC'1994, pp. 39–54 (1994)
27. Zhai, C.: Fast Statistical Parsing of Noun Phrases for Document Indexing. In: ANLP'97, pp. 312–319 (1997)
28. Kraaij, W., Pohlmann, R.: Comparing the Effect of Syntactic vs. Statistical Phrase Indexing Strategies for Dutch. In: ECDL'98, pp. 605–617 (1998)
29. Arampatzis, A., Van derWeide, T.P., Koster, C.H.A., Van Bommel, P.: Linguistically Motivated Information Retrieval. In: Encyclopedia of Library and Information Science. pp. 201–222, Marcel Dekker, New York (2000)

Forgery Detection for Surveillance Video

Dai-Kyung Hyun, Min-Jeong Lee, Seung-Jin Ryu, Hae-Yeoun Lee, and Heung-Kyu Lee

Abstract In many courts, surveillance videos are used as important legal evidence. Nevertheless, little research is concerned with forgery of surveillance videos. In this paper, we present a forgery detection system for surveillance videos. We analyze the characteristic of surveillance videos. Subsequently, forgeries mainly occur to the surveillance videos are investigated. To identify both RGB and infrared video, Sensor Pattern Noise (SPN) for each video is transformed by Minimum Average Correlation Energy (MACE) filter. Manipulations on the given video are detected by estimating scaling factor and calculating correlation coefficient. Experimental results demonstrate that the proposed scheme is appropriate to identify forgeries of surveillance video.

Keywords Sensor pattern noise • Surveillance videos • Forgery detection

1 Introduction

In many courts recently, surveillance videos are used as important legal evidence. These surveillance videos can be easily forged using video editing tools such as Premier, Vegas, etc. Moreover, the forger might replace the whole video taken by the surveillance camera with another video. In the event that forged surveillance videos are used as court evidence, it may potentially cause severe problems and mistakenly convict the wrong person. Therefore, it is important to detect surveillance video forgery.

D.-K. Hyun (✉) • M.-J. Lee • S.-J. Ryu • H.-K. Lee
Department of CS, Korea Advanced Institute of Science and Technology (KAIST), 291 Daehak-ro, Yuseong-gu, Daejeon, Republic of Korea
e-mail: dkyun@mmc.kaist.ac.kr; mjlee@mmc.kaist.ac.kr; sjryu@mmc.kaist.ac.kr; hklee@mmc.kaist.ac.kr

H.-Y. Lee
Department of Computer Software Engineering, Kumoh National Institute of Technology, Sanho-ro 77, Gumi, Gyeongbuk, Republic of Korea
e-mail: haeyeoun.lee@kumoh.ac.kr

J.S. Jin et al., *The Era of Interactive Media*,
DOI 10.1007/978-1-4614-3501-3_3,

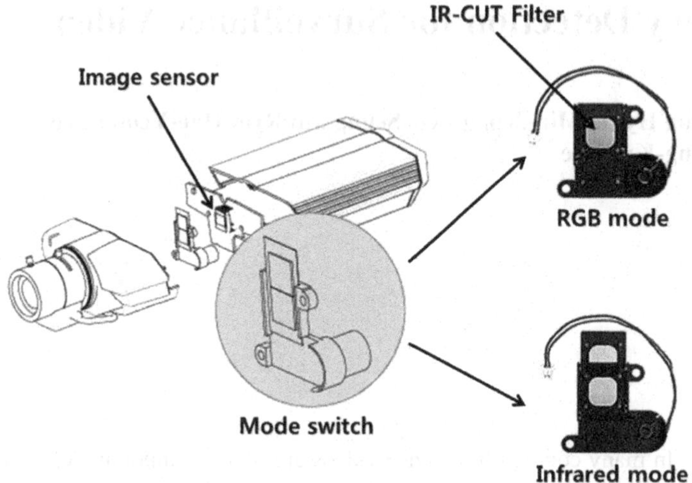

Fig. 1 The structure of surveillance camera

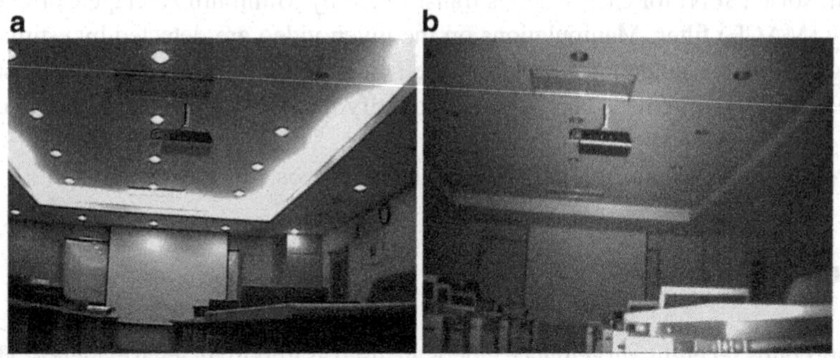

Fig. 2 Different mode of surveillance camera: (**a**) RGB video mode, and (**b**) Infrared video mode

In order to achieve integrity of videos taken by surveillance cameras, first of all, structural difference between surveillance camera and general camcorder should be considered. The main difference of the devices is that the surveillance camera provides both RGB and infrared mode. Figure 1 depicts mode changing mechanism of a common surveillance camera. The surveillance camera records an RGB video or an infrared video by switching IR-CUT filter with additional post-processing. By the result, when the surveillance camera is on the infrared mode as seen in Fig. 2(b), intensity and saturation of the image are relatively degraded compared with the scene on the RGB mode as seen in Fig. 2(a). Therefore, the forensic method should compensate for the image quality degradation of infrared video.

Moreover, manipulations mainly occur to the surveillance video should also be uncovered to detect the forgeries related to the surveillance cameras. In this

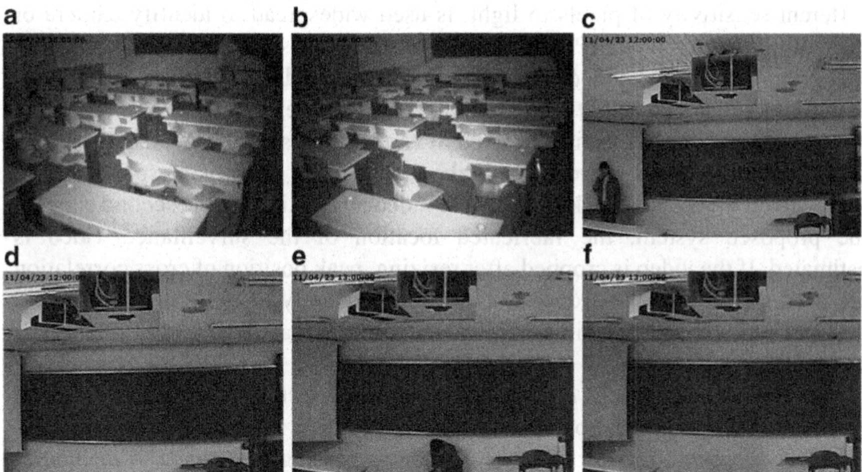

Fig. 3 Example of forgeries: (**a**) Video taken at a criminal place, (**b**) Video taken at another place, (**c**) Video taken at a criminal place, (**d**) Upscale-cropped video, (**e**) Video taken at a criminal place, and (**f**) Partially manipulated video

perspective, three types of representative manipulations named video alternation, upscale-crop forgery, and partial manipulation need to be concerned:

1. Video alternation refers to the fabrication of evidence by switching a surveillance video taken at a criminal place with surveillance video that was taken at another place. Figure 3(a) is a video taken at criminal place and Fig. 3(b) is a video taken at another place at the same time. If the police asks for the video of criminal place as court evidence, the culprit can present the video taken at another place instead of criminal place to conceal his crime. In Fig. 3(b), it is difficult to find any differences excluding the desk arrangement, which changes every day. Therefore, it is difficult to verify that the given video was taken at criminal place with only the information provided by the video.
2. Upscale-crop forgery refers to upscaling the given video and then cropping it in order to conceal time information or criminal evidence. Figure 3(d) is produced by upscale-crop forgery of Fig. 3(c). To manipulate the time information and conceal the crime, Fig. 3(c) is slightly enlarged followed by cropping time and the culprit out. Finally, new time information is re-written on the forged image.
3. Partial manipulation refers to the fabrication by falsifying parts of a video to forge time information or criminal evidence. As explained above, the criminal evidence can be edited to forge the evidence. Instead of cropping out the forged part, the evidence in Fig. 3(e) can be precisely removed as seen in Fig. 3(f).

To detect above mentioned forgeries for surveillance cameras, we propose an improved sensor pattern noise (SPN) representation method by using Minimum Average Correlation Energy (MACE) filter [8]. The SPN, which is generated by different sensitivity of pixels to light, is used widespread to identify camera or camcorder. Even though SPN from an RGB video has same form compared with that from an infrared video, the SPN of infrared video is weaken by various conditions such as low light and post-processing. Therefore, the SPN is amplified by the MACE filter. By using extracted SPN, the proposed system detects forgery of surveillance videos in two steps. In the first step, we identify the source device of the given video and check if there was video alternation. In the second stage of the proposed system, the fabricated location of the surveillance video is estimated. If the video is cropped after resizing, peak position of cross correlation are used to estimate the cropped region. Subsequently, if the video is partially manipulated, the partial similarity of the SPN is calculated to estimate the manipulated region.

The rest of this paper is constructed as follows. Section 2 summarizes related literatures. A proposed source surveillance camera identification method is introduced in Sect. 3. After that, we explain forged region estimation method in Sect. 4. Experimental results are then exhibited in Sects. 5 and 6 concludes.

2 Related Works

A number of forgery detecting techniques for digital videos have been developed. Wang et al. exposed digital forgery by exploiting static and temporal artifacts of double MPEG compression [9]. Their technique determined whether a video was resaved after original recording. Kobayashi et al. detected suspicious regions in static scenes of a given video based on inconsistency in noise level functions [6]. They introduced a probabilistic model providing the inference of noise level function. Hsu et al. proposed an approach for locating forged regions in a video using correlation of noise residue [4]. They modeled the distribution of correlation of temporal noise residue in a forged video as a Gaussian Mixture Model (GMM) and then estimated the parameters using Expectation-Maximization (EM) algorithm. However, it is difficult for these techniques to be applied directly to surveillance videos since they do not consider forgeries easily occurred to surveillance applications. On the contrary, Goljan et al. presented a digital camera identification method robust to scaling [3]. Since they calculated the similarity for all scaling factors in the expected range, complexity of their method was relatively high. Chen et al. suggested a camcorder identification scheme using SPN [1]. To enhance the performance, they removed the periodic codec noise. However, the noise elimination also weaken the energy of SPN. Thus, in case of infrared videos, which have weaker SPN energy than RGB videos, their method shows low identification accuracy. Therefore, in the following section, we describe the proposed source camcorder identification method which satisfies most of requirements for the surveillance camera.

3 Surveillance Camera Identification Method

In this section, we identify a source surveillance camera of a given video. Figure 4 depicts the whole procedure of alternated video detection method. First, the reference SPN (RSPN) is extracted from a surveillance camera. Then the RSPN is transformed to the form of MACE filter to enhance the detection accuracy of both RGB and infrared video. Simultaneously, test SPN (TSPN) is extracted from a suspected video. Since the suspected video may have undergone scaling, the proposed method estimates scaling factor before extracting TSPN from the suspected video. After that, the TSPN is resized by the estimated scaling factor. Finally, the peak-to-correlation-energy (PCE) ratio [7] is calculated from the output of the cross-correlation between two SPNs. If the PCE is greater than the predefined threshold τ_{pce}, it is determined that the suspected video was taken by the tested surveillance camera. In the following subsections, we describe MACE filter and how the scaling factor is estimated.

3.1 Minimum Average Correlation Energy Filter

The correlation plane[1] calculated by normalized-cross-correlation (NCC) is easily distorted by noise as seen in Fig. 5{a}. Thus, Chen et al. method removed codec noise before calculating the correlation plane [1]. However, their method weaken the energy of the SPN. Thus, in case of infrared videos, their method reveals low identification accuracy as mentioned before. Therefore, to increase the detection accuracy, we calculate the correlation plane by MACE filter [8].

The MACE filter is made for not only minimizing the energy of correlation plane but also ensuring a sharp correlation peak at the origin. Here, we describe the RSPN as a column vector **r** of dimensionality d equal to the number of the pixels in the RSPN, i.e.,

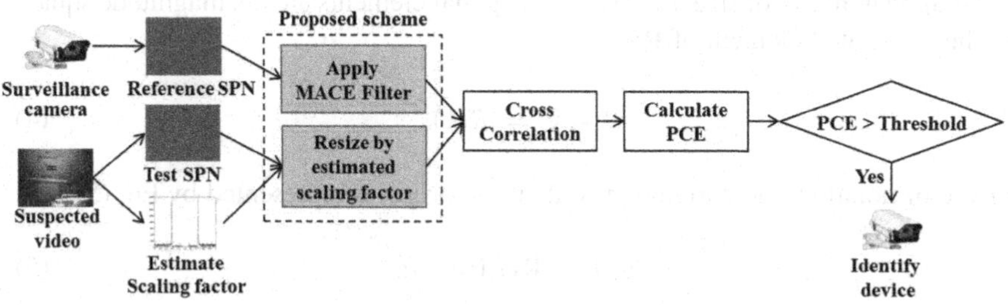

Fig. 4 Proposed surveillance camera identification procedure

[1] We adopt "correlation plain" which is originated in the field of optical filtering [5].

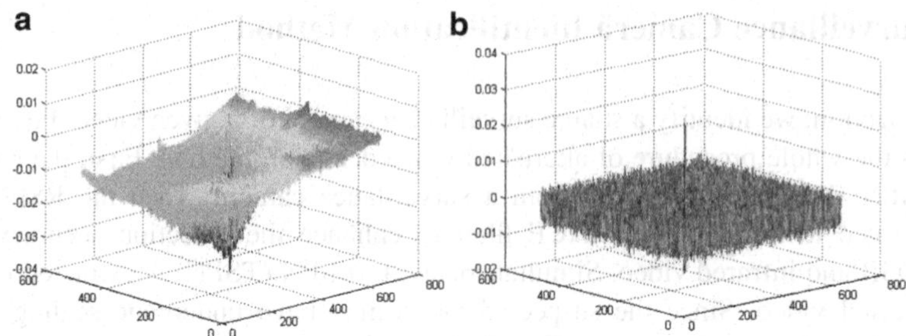

Fig. 5 Correlation plan calculated by two videos extracted from the same camera: (**a**) Correlation plane calculated by NCC (PCE = 3.41), and (**b**) Correlation plane calculated by MACE filter (PCE = 287.33)

$$\mathbf{r} = [r(1), r(2), ..., r(d)]^T. \quad (1)$$

We denote the correlation function of $r(n)$ with the filter $h(n)$ by $g(n)$:

$$g(n) = r(n) \otimes h(n). \quad (2)$$

If $G(k)$ is the DFT of the correlation function, the energy of the correlation plane is

$$E = \sum_{n=1}^{d} |g(n)|^2 = (1/d) \sum_{k=1}^{d} |H(k)|^2 |R(k)|^2,$$

where H(k) and R(k) is the DFT of h(k) and r(k), respectively. When arranging Eq. (3) as the vector form, it is as

$$\mathbf{E} = \mathbf{H}^{+}\mathbf{DH}, \quad (3)$$

where the superscript + denotes the conjugate transpose of a complex vector, and **D** is a diagonal matrix of size $d \times d$ whose diagonal elements are the magnitude square of the associated element of **R**:

$$D(k,k) = |R(k)|^2. \quad (4)$$

In vector notation, the correlation peak at the origin is represented by Eq. (5),

$$g(0) = \mathbf{RH}(0) = u, \quad (5)$$

where u is the user specified value.

In order to find correlation filter **H** that satisfies to minimizing Eq. (3) and satisfying Eq. (5), we use Lagrange multipliers. The correlation filter H given by

$$\mathbf{H} = \mathbf{D}^{-1}\mathbf{R}(\mathbf{R}^{+}\mathbf{D}^{-1}\mathbf{R})^{-1}u. \tag{6}$$

The proposed algorithm transforms the RSPN to the form of Eq. (6), and gets the correlation plane by calculating cross-correlation between the resized TSPN and the transformed RSPN. After that, we calculate PCE in the correlation plane as follows.

$$PCE = \frac{CP(i_{peak}, j_{peak})^2}{\sum_{i,j} CP(i,j)^2} \tag{7}$$

where CP is the correlation plane and (i_{peak}, j_{peak}) are the peak positions in the correlation plane. Figure 5(b) is the correlation plane calculated by the MACE filter. It shows that the PCE calculated by the MACE filter is higher than that calculated by NCC.

3.2 Scaling Factor Estimation

Unlike Goljan's method [3] that calculates the similarity for all scaling factors within the specified range, the proposed scheme estimates the scaling factor by using statistical characteristics which occur during the resizing process, and then calculates the similarity by the estimated scaling factor. We adopted the periodicity in the variance of the second derivative signal suggested in [2] to estimate the scaling factor.

The scaling factor is estimated in three steps. The first step is to compute the second derivative of each row of the frame. Suppose the frame is represented as $p(i, j)$, then the second derivative of each row is computed as follows.

$$s_p(i,j) = 2p(i,j) - p(i,j+1) - p(i,j-1) \tag{8}$$

Then, the magnitudes of the rows of second derivative signals are averaged together to form a pseudo-variance signal $v_p(j)$.

$$v_p(j) = \sum_{i=0}^{R} \left| s_p(i,j) \right| \tag{9}$$

Finally, the discrete Fourier transform (DFT) of $v_p(j)$ is examined for peaks, and the corresponding frequencies of the peak location f_p are used to determine scaling factor $\hat{N}$.

$$\hat{N} = \frac{1}{f_p} \tag{10}$$

After calculating scaling factor in each video frame, we choose the scaling factor which occurs the most frequently among them. Then, TSPN is resized by this scaling factor.

4 Forgery Region Estimation Algorithm

In the second step of the proposed system, the forged location is estimated. More specifically, the scheme retrieve cropped region for upscale-crop forgery or localize partially manipulated region.

4.1 Cropped Region Estimation

The peak position of a given correlation plane is equal to the left top point of cropped region. This fact is used to detect the cropped region. If the estimated scaling factor is $\hat{N}$, the position of the peak is (x_l, y_t), and the size of test video is $R \times C$, the right down point of the cropped region (x_r, y_d) is calculated as follows.

$$(x_r, y_d) = \left(x_l + \frac{1}{\hat{N}} \times C, y_t + \frac{1}{\hat{N}} \times R\right) \tag{11}$$

4.2 Partially Manipulated Region Estimation

If the surveillance video is partially manipulated, the manipulated region will have weak energy of SPN or not be synchronized with the RSPN. Thus, the corresponding correlation coefficient may have a very small value. To detect partially manipulated region, a given RSPN and TSPN is divided into overlapped sub-block with block size B, and then the correlation coefficient of each block is calculated. After that, the block with the smaller coefficient value than the threshold which is empirically set as 0.3 is estimated as partially manipulated region.

5 Experimental Results

We conducted experiments with eight surveillance cameras. With the videos taken by these surveillance cameras, we extracted SPN. Particularly, a blue-sky video for each camera is taken to make corresponding RSPN. Furthermore, we prepared

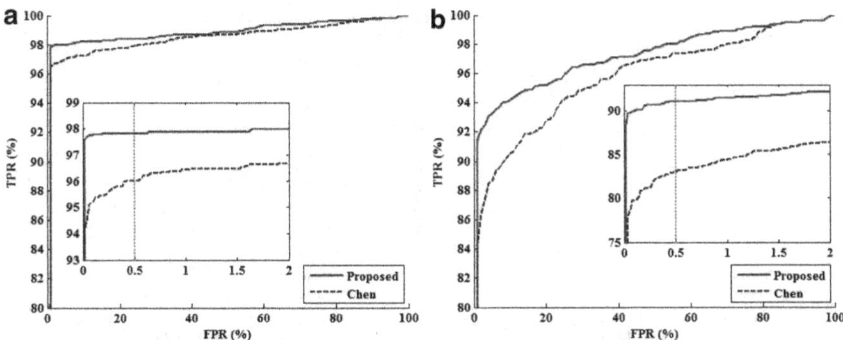

Fig. 6 ROC curves for the proposed and Chen's method: (**a**) ROC curves for RGB videos, and (**b**) ROC curves for infrared videos

totally 480 high quality videos including various indoor and outdoor scenes to extract TSPN. (240 RGB videos and 240 infrared videos) All the videos are taken with resolution of 640 ×480, frame rate of 10 Hz, MPEG4 (xvid) with 8 Mb/s, and 30 s recoding time. Other conditions such as white balance, sharpness, contrast, etc., are automatically set.

5.1 *Source Camera Identification Test*

In order to measure the identification accuracy of the proposed method, we resized 480 videos in increments of 0.1 from 1.0 to 1.8 by bilinear interpolation kernel. The center of the scaled videos are then cropped to make size of 640 ×480 videos. We carried out the proposed method for every test video and calculated the identification rate according to each scaling factor. We also compared the proposed method with Chen's method [1].

To decide identification threshold τ_{pce}, we calculated PCE values among RSPNs which represent each surveillance camera and TSPNs from every test video. Figure 6 depicts ROC curves compiled from all the pairs with different τ_{pce}. From the results, τ_{pce} was determined as 30.56 at which false positive rate (FPR) was 0.5%. Moreover, the ROC curves indicate that the proposed algorithm is indeed more robust to false alarms than Chen's method.

Figure 7 depicts identification rate at FPR $= 0.5\%$ for each scaling factor. The bigger scaling factor, the smaller region is cropped from the video. Eventually, the energy of SPN became smaller. Even in the proposed algorithm, the identification rates were dropped as the scaling factors were increased. However, the proposed method showed better performance compared with Chen's algorithm. Particularly in the case of scaling factor 1.8 for infrared videos, which have the weakest SPN energy, the proposed method showed more than 15% better performance than Chen's method.

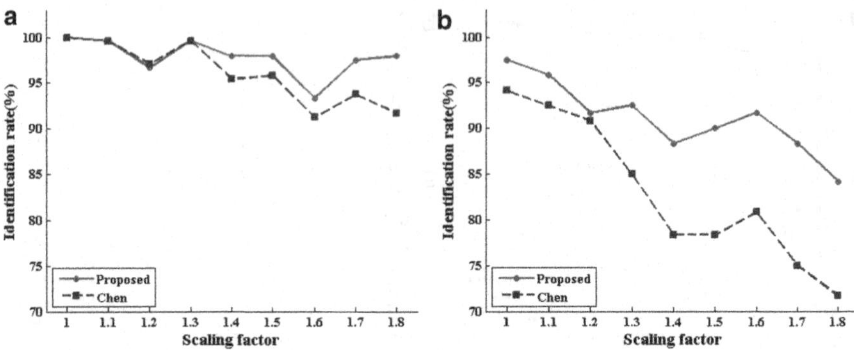

Fig. 7 Identification accuracy at FAR = 0.5%: (**a**) RGB videos, and (**b**) Infrared videos

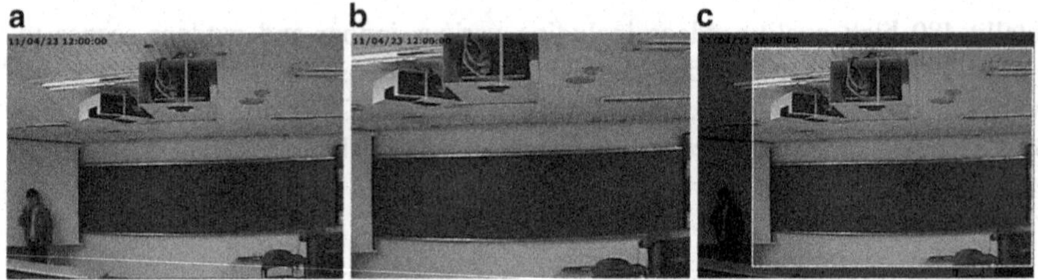

Fig. 8 Detection of cropped region: (**a**) Original video (**b**) Upscale-cropped video (**c**) Estimated cropped region (*encircled in white*) in the original video

5.2 Cropped Region Estimation Test

In this experiment, we tested the performance of cropped region estimation algorithm. We manipulated 480 videos with scaling factor of 1.2, followed by cropping to 640 × 480 at random position. With these videos, we estimated cropped region in the original videos. The average error between actual coordinates and estimated coordinates for x and y of upper-left point were 0.2 and 0.3 pixel, respectively. Figure 8 shows the detected cropped region in the original video. It shows that the proposed method is capable to estimate the cropped region very accurately.

5.3 Partially Manipulated Region Estimation Test

In this experiment, we carried out the partially manipulated region estimation algorithm. We manipulated 480 videos with scaling factor of 1.2, followed by cropping to 640 × 480 at center position. After that, we copied a part of the videos with size of 80 × 80, then randomly pasted it into the same videos. With these

Fig. 9 Detection of partially manipulated region (TPR = 71.42%, FPR = 1.09%): (**a**) Original video, (**b**) Partially manipulated video, and (**c**) Estimated region (manipulated region is *encircled in white*, whereas estimated region is painted in *gray*)

videos, we estimated partially manipulated region and measured True Positive Rate (TPR) and False Positive Rate (FPR). TPR and FPR are defined as

$$TPR = \frac{(Forged\ Region\ \cap\ Detected\ Region)}{Detected\ Region} \times 100\,[\%] \tag{12}$$

$$FPR = \frac{(Detected\ Region\ -\ Forged\ Region)}{Forged\ Region^{c}} \times 100\,[\%]. \tag{13}$$

The average rate of TPR and FPR for 480 images were 79.86% and 0.45%, respectively. Figure 9 shows experimental results for the elaborately forged video in which the culprit was removed by partial manipulation. Through the experiment, the accuracy of proposed method to detect partially manipulated regions was verified.

6 Conclusion

In many courts, surveillance videos are used as important legal evidence. As these surveillance videos can easily be forged, it may cause great social issues. In this paper, we proposed a system which detects surveillance video forgery. The proposed system is composed of surveillance camera identification and forged region detection. The surveillance camera were identified maximumly 15% higher than the existing method. Furthermore, the forged region were detected with high accuracy.

The proposed system estimate the scaling factor by using periodic characteristic of resampling. However, such characteristic does not appear in another interpolation methods such as nearest neighbor interpolation. Thus, in our future work, a method which can identify the source device without estimating the scaling factor will be presented. Furthermore, the features of the video will be analyzed in order to improve the partially manipulated region estimation algorithm.

Acknowledgment This research project was supported by Ministry of Culture, Sports and Tourism (MCST) and from Korea Copyright Commission in 2011, WCU (World Class University) program (Project No: R31-30007), and NRL (National Research Lab) program (No. R0A-2007-000-20023-0) under the National Research Foundation of Korea and funded by the Ministry of Education, Science and Technology of Korea

References

1. Chen, M., Fridrich, J., Miroslav Goljan, J.L.: Source digital camcorder identification using sensor photo response non-uniformity. In: The International Society for Optical Engineering (SPIE) (2007)
2. Gallagher, A.C.: Detection of linear and cubic interpolation in jpeg compressed images. In: Computer and Robot Vision (2005)
3. Goljan, M., Fridrich, J.: Camera identification from cropped and scaled images. In: The International Society for Optical Engineering (SPIE) (2008)
4. Hsu, C.C., Hung, T.Y., Lin, C.W., Hsu, C.T.: Video forgery detection using correlation of noise residue. In: IEEE 10th Workshop on Multimedia Signal Processing (2008)
5. Kerekes, R.A., Kumar, B.V.: Selecting a composite correlation filter design: a survey and comparative study. Optical Engineering 47(6) (2008)
6. Kobayashi, M., Okabe, T., Sato, Y.: Detecting forgery from static-scene video based on inconsistency in noise level functions. IEEE Trans. Information Forensics and Security 5(4), 883–892 (2010)
7. Kumar, B.V.K.V., Hassebrook, L.: Performance measures for correlation filters. Optical Society of America 29(20), 2997–3006 (1990)
8. Mahalanobis, A., Kumar, B.V.K.V., Casasent, D.: Minimum average correlation energy filters. Optical Society of America 26(17), 3633–3640 (1987)
9. Wang, W., Farid, H.: Exposing digital forgeries in video by detecting double mpeg compression. In: Multimedia and Security Workshop (2006)

Digital Image Forensics: A Two-Step Approach for Identifying Source and Detecting Forgeries

Wiem Taktak and Jean-Luc Dugelay

Abstract Digital Image Forensics includes two main domains: source device identification and semantic modification detection. Usually, existing works address one aspect only: either source identification or either image manipulation. In this article, we investigate a new approach based on sensor noise that operates in a two-step sequence: the first one is global whereas the second one is local. During the first step, we analyze noise in order to identify the sensor. We reused the method proposed by Jessica Fridrich et al. with an improvement of it useful when only a limited number of images is available to compute noise patterns. Then, having identified the sensor, we examine more locally, using quadtree segmentation, the noise differences between the pattern noise attached to the sensor and the noise extracted from the picture under investigation in order to detect possible alterations. We assume here that the portion of the image that underwent modifications is relatively small with regards to the surface of the whole picture. Finally, we report tests on the first publically available database (i.e. the Dresden database) that makes possible further comparisons of our algorithm with other approaches.

Keywords Digital image forensic • Image authentication • Forgeries detection • Sensor noise.

W. Taktak (✉)
Department of Multimedia Communication, EURECOM, Sophia Antipolis, France
e-mail: Wiem.Taktak@eurecom.fr

J.-L. Dugelay
2229, Route des Crêtes, 06560, Valbonnem, Sophia Antipolis, France
e-mail: Jean-Luc.Dugelay@eurecom.fr

DOI 10.1007/978-1-4614-3501-3_4,

1 Introduction

In today's digital age, images and videos play a vital role in several applications like video surveillance, news, social networks, etc. In parallel, the availability of powerful image processing tools and the ease with which digital media can be edited without leaving any visual traces have led to the multiplication of fake images [1]. So that, the usage of multimedia data is questionable. To restore the trust towards digital images, digital forensics has become the most important science to check images. It aims at providing tools to support blind investigation. Two main research domains exist under the name of Digital Image Forensics (DIF). The first one is *source device identification* whose objective is to prove that a given picture or video was taken by a specific camera model. The second field is *semantic forgery detection* which aims to discover malicious manipulations denoted as tampering.

In IF (Image Forensics), several techniques can be found [2] which take advantage of traces left at different levels of the image processing pipeline [3]. Among the large set of forensic tools [4,5], techniques that analyze sensor pattern noise were proven to be promising to identify the exact camera source model and also to detect forged region in a given image. Usually, existing works refer to one aspect only, i.e. source identification or image manipulation. Detecting image manipulations is a so challenging task that most of proposed techniques assume to have an a priori knowledge about the type of attack that the picture has undergone (e.g. duplication of an object).

In our work, we consider a method based on sensor noise that operates in two adjoined steps: the first one is global whereas the second one is local. Within the first phase, we reused the method proposed by Jessica Fridrich et al. with some improvements to identify the acquisition device using the sensor noise. Then, given the knowledge of the sensor, we verify in the second phase the correlation level between the sensor pattern and the extracted noise from the picture under investigation in order to detect possible alterations. In our experiment, we use a public database called *Dresden Image Database* [6] in order to provide some more reproducible results with regards to ones in most of previous publications.

This paper is organized as follows: In Sect. 2, we describe the sensor pattern noise and how to extract it using the denoising filter described in the literature [7,8]. Section 3 gives details on our improved process for the image authentication (global step). To check the presence of a forged region (local step), Sect. 4 describes our tampering detection method. In Sect. 5, we report some experimental results. Section 6 concludes this paper and gives some possible future works.

2 Sensor Pattern Noise

2.1 Image Noises

Digital camera records visual information via CMOS or CCD image sensor which measures the light gathered during an exposure. During this imaging process, two pixels may have different intensity even if they represent exactly the same scene

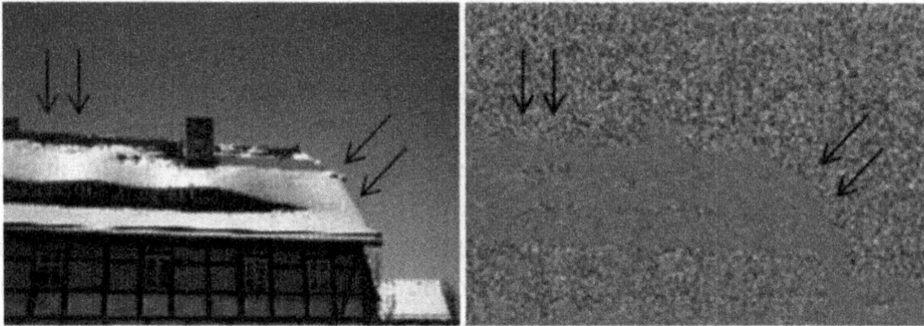

Fig. 1 Edges in the residual noise

with uniform light; this small difference is referred to noise; and this is partly due to some physical sensor imperfections.

In order to better understand the sensor noise in pixel values, one must first understand the main sources of noise [9]. Noise usually comes from three sources: *shot noise* which is caused by random arrival of photons and vary from an image to another one of different scene; *readout noise* which is caused by the amplifier processing chain and is a consequence of the imperfect operation of physical electronic devices and *pattern noise* which is a fundamental trait of the sensor due to variations during fabrication and is a spatial noise that implies that all images acquired with the same camera contain similar noise.

The pattern noise is divided into two components Fixed Pattern Noise (FPN) and Photo Response Non-Uniformity noise (PRNU). The FPN arises from changes in dark currents due to the absence of light during the image acquisition. The PRNU noise which is unique to every sensor describes the difference in pixel responses to uniform light sources; it is also divided into low frequency and Pixel Non Uniformity (PNU) [7]. The PNU noise is the dominant component in the pattern noise caused by physical properties of the sensor and it is nearly impossible to eliminate it. As PNU noise cannot be seen directly, we estimate it by computing the difference between original image and its denoised version. This approximation is called *residual noise*. The denoised image is deduced using a denoising filter.

2.2 Denoising Filter

The implementation of the denoising filter is based on the work proposed in Appendix A of [7] which in turn is based on the work presented in [8]. This denoising algorithm is constructed in the wavelet domain and takes advantage of the Wiener filter method. The purpose of this algorithm is to remove the sensor noise without substantially affecting the image structure e.g. high frequencies.

When generating the residual noise, we observe that edges present in the original image have a significant impact (Fig. 1). As a consequence, the denoising filter cannot discriminate between the high frequencies associated with a residual noise and high frequencies associated with fine details of the picture. This is a problem for images that contain significant amount of textured data i.e. high frequency details.

The extracted sensor noise from an image under investigation is one of the most useful irregularities of the camera component in forensic applications.

According to some properties of the senor noise, we propose a new approach based on sensor pattern noise that operates in two steps: the first one is global (i.e. we use the whole pattern) whereas the second one is local (we use only some part of the pattern). During the first step, we analyze noise in order to identify the sensor for the image authentication. During a second pass of analysis, local this time, we examine differences between the extracted sensor noise from the image under investigation and the reference pattern attached to the just identified sensor in order to check the presence of some modifications.

3 Global Step: Image Authentication

Using the sensor pattern noise, we can easily associate the whole pattern to a biometric trait, which can be used to determine whether the camera that took the picture is the claimed one (genuine) or another one (impostor). As a consequence, the architecture of the image authentication approach using sensor pattern noise is similar to classical protocols used in person recognition (i.e. biometrics). Hence, our proposed approach can operate in two main modes: *identification* and *verification*.

To motivate and illustrate our contributions, let us start by detailing our tool architecture similar to a classical biometric system. More precisely, we proceed as depicted in Fig. 2; the complete methodology is divided primarily into two main steps.

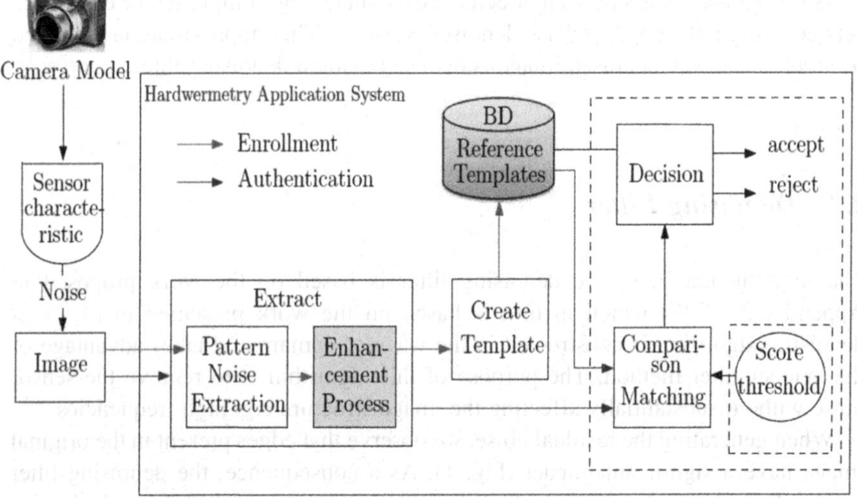

Fig. 2 Hardwermetry application system

The first step which is called *enrollment* includes the generation of the reference pattern noise *RPN* (it is the camera model estimation step). Before the registration of the noise template (i.e. camera fingerprint), we proposed a method to weight each sensor noise pixel in order to enhance the quality of the resulting camera pattern noise.

In the second step which is called *authentication* an extracted pattern from the image under investigation; called residual noise is sent to a matcher that compares it with other existing sensor pattern noises. Afterwards, we can consider this step as a *classification* step which compares the pattern noise of the unknown image with the camera fingerprints retrieved from the database, and computes the similarity score for each possible match (one or more, depending on the operational mode). The final decision is determined by the operational mode: in identification task, cameras are classified from the most to the least probable, whereas in verification, the image source claim is confirmed or rejected.

3.1 Enhancement Process

The PRNU noise is estimated from image in typical viewable formats, such as TIFF or JPEG and its approximation is called residual noise which carries information about the camera brand or model. The residual noise W is estimated using the *de-noising filter* as follows:

$$W_n = x_n - F(x_n) \tag{1}$$

where x_n is the original image, while F is the denoising filter constructed in the wavelet domain.

In this case, we can formally describe this image source identification as follows. At first, we consider having a set of N training images X_k for each camera c_k, $X_k = \{x_{n/}n = 1 \ldots N\}$. This collection X_k serves to generate the reference pattern noise. Hence, for each camera c_k, its model pattern Θ_k is obtained by averaging the N residual noise W extracted from X_k as defined in Eq. (2).

$$\Theta_k = \frac{1}{N} * \sum_{n=1}^{N} W_n \tag{2}$$

In our work, a processing step is performed on the creation of the reference model to improve the identification task and to limit the impact of high frequencies associated with edges and textures. For each camera c_k, its reference pattern Θ_k^* is obtained by averaging the N weighted residual noises $W*$ which are generated using our proposed method (3).

$$\Theta_k^* = \frac{1}{N} * \sum_{n=1}^{N} W_k^* \tag{3}$$

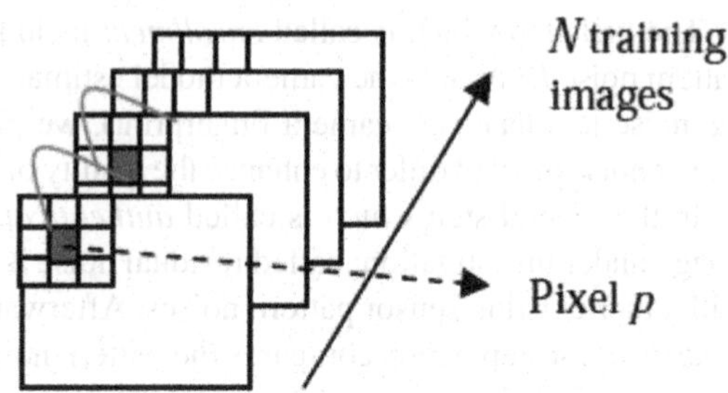

Fig. 3 Identification with reduction of the influence of textured parts of images

Our method consists to associate a weight to each pixel based on local luminance properties. Thus, each pixel value p of the pattern noise served to generate the reference pattern noise can be defined as follows:

$$W_p^* = w_p * W_p \tag{4}$$

where W_p is the initial sensor noise of the pixel p of position (i, j) and w_p is a weight of the underling pixel. The weight w_p of the defined position is computed using its local intensity variance and the intensity variance of the same position for all pixels of training images as described in Fig. 3:

$$w_p = \begin{cases} 1 - \dfrac{\sigma}{\sum\limits_{k=1}^{N} \sigma(k)} & if \ \sum\limits_{k=1}^{N} \sigma(k) \neq 0 \\ 1 & otherwise \end{cases} \tag{5}$$

Where N is the number of training images and σ is the aforementioned intensity variance of the pixel p at position (i, j) defined by Eq. (6).

$$\sigma^2 = \frac{1}{M_w} \sum_{i=1}^{M_w} (y_i - \bar{y})^2 \tag{6}$$

where M_w means the number of pixels inside neighboring windows, y means intensity of the pixel p, and $\bar{y}$ means average intensity of the neighboring pixels. The intensity variance is large in regions that contain a lot of details or edges.

The work described in this subsection intends to avoid the problem of generating the reference pattern noise with areas not smooth enough.

After having obtained all reference patterns, the final step is to measure the degree of similarity between the pattern to check, and reference patterns present in the database. We use the total correlation as the similarity measure in order to find out whether a certain pattern W_n originates from a certain camera c_k. In order to do so, we compute the correlation between the residual noise from the given image and the reference pattern noise and compare it with a predefined threshold, Th_{c_k}, specific for the used camera c_k (i.e. verification).

4 Local Step: Forgeries Detection

With the availability of low-cost photo editing software, digital images can be easily manipulated and altered. It is then possible to change the data represented by an image and create forgeries. Such a manipulation may alter on purpose the perception that users may have about a picture. We may want to detect such fake and altered images if any. This calls for reliable detection algorithms of tampered digital photos. In the literature, we can find several works dealing with this issue [10,11]. A fake image can be generated with different manipulation techniques such as re-sampling, composing, copy-move [11] and so on. In fact, the integrity of a given image is checked to detect the traces of these malicious manipulations.

The aforementioned copy-paste or copy-move technique is one of the most common semantic forgeries. The manipulation of an image using this technique comes to copying and pasting a portion of this image to produce a non-existing object in the scene or to erase an important part of it. In our work, we create some fake images using this technique and we develop a method based on sensor pattern noise to detect these semantic modifications.

4.1 Detection of Semantic Modifications

Based on the knowledge of the source camera of the given fake image (using the results of the previous and global step), we extend our work to trace its altered regions. Our proposed method is based on the fact that modified regions have the lowest matching scores with their corresponding regions in the reference pattern noise than any other region (i.e. not altered). Of course, we assume here that the size of the modified regions is relatively limited with regards to the surface of the whole image in order to prevent a wrong identification at the end of the first step.

Thus, our proposed forgery detection algorithm tests the correlation level between the computed noise of each part of the underling image and its corresponding part of the selected sensor reference noise in order to compute, what we call later, the pre-classification mask (a binary mask). Furthermore, we adopt the quad tree method to segment images.

4.2 Modified Region Search

As written before, since the tampering process changes some properties of the sensor noise pattern, we can distinguish the altered regions from the non-tampered ones by analyzing the block score noise correlation. In fact, we propose a *pre-classification* scheme to determine whether an image has been forged. Hence, our pre-classification system is defined as follows:

$$Class_n = \begin{cases} 0 & |s_n - \bar{s}| \leq th \\ 1 & otherwise \end{cases} \tag{7}$$

where $Class_n$ denotes the classification mask of the nth block. A forged block is referred by the binary digit "1" in the built classification mask (a genuine block is then referred by a "0"). In the condition part of our system, s_n presents the correlation value for the nth block (i.e. correlation between residual noise from the given image and its appropriate reference pattern noise), while $\bar{s}$ is the mean correlation value of the remaining blocks relatively to the considered decomposition level. *th* is a predefined, camera-dependent threshold.

5 Experiments and Results

This section is devoted to validate our approach for tampering detection of fake images with an a priori knowledge of the camera that took it. We will start by presenting the used database on which we run our experiments. We then move to exposing the way we validate the first step of our approach, namely the global step for source camera identification. For that, we get inspired from validation methods used for biometric applications. Hence, our validation will cover the two well known operational modes; namely the identification mode and the verification mode.

The last part of this section is dedicated to the validation of the semantic modification detection part of our proposal.

5.1 Database

To assess the efficiency of our proposal, we need to apply it on real complex textured images taken by different cameras from different models. For that purpose, we need a set of images sufficiently large as well as rich enough in terms of contents. We then selected more than 5,000 photos taken by various cameras, from a public database named *Dresden Image Database* [6]. This *Dresden Image Database* is made available to the research community to mainly benchmark the source camera identification techniques.

Like in the classical biometric domain, the downloaded database is divided into three subsets: the *«Training set»*, the *«Evaluating set»*, and the *«Test set»*. In our experiments, we use the *«Training set»* to build the reference pattern noise for each camera. The *«Evaluating set»* aims to estimate the impostor models (i.e. to

Table 1 List of camera models used in our experiments

Camera model	Senor type	Resolution (Mp)	Picture size
AGFA DC-504	1/ 2,4" CMOS	5	4,032 × 3,024
AGFA DC-733 s	1/ 2,5" CCD	7	3,072 × 2,304
AGFA DC-505x	1/ 2,4" CMOS	5	2,592 × 1,944
AGFA DC-530	1/ 2,4" CMOS	5	4,032 × 3,024
CANON IXUS55	1/ 2,5" CCD	5	2,592 × 1,944
CANON IXUS70	1/ 2,5" CCD	7.1	3,072 × 2,304
CASIO EX-Z150	1/ 3,0" CCD	8.1	3,264 × 2,448
NIKON S710	1/ 2,72" CCD	14.5	4,352 × 3,264
OLYMPUS	1/ 2,5" CCD	10.2	3,872 × 2,592
KODAK M1063	1/ 2,3" CCD	10.3	3,664 × 2,748

compute the Th_{c_k} threshold). The performance of the camera authentication is evaluated using the *«Test set»* subset.

Moreover, we used for our experiments, ten camera models from different companies. Note that we used two KODAK M1063 cameras (KOD-1 and KOD-2) to check the reliability of the identification in case of using two camera devices from the same model and the same brand. Relevant technical specifications of the models of the used cameras are shown in Table 1.

5.2 *Validation of the Global Step*

5.2.1 The Identification Mode

This issue addresses how to determine the camera that most likely took the underling image, among all the considered cameras. Such identification can be achieved by simply assigning the investigated image to the camera whose reference pattern presents the highest correlation with the noise extracted from this photo (i.e. the top 1). As shown in the illustrating sample of Fig. 4, we choose the same scene image taken by cameras from different models, and we tried to link each of them to the specific camera that took it. Note that, for AGFA-504 and AGFA-505 camera models, the present scene is not available.

As shown in the table presented by Fig. 5, the highest correlation values for each image are ranged in the column *Max* (the pink column). Recall that this maximum value corresponds to the maximum of correlation between the extracted noise from the investigated image and the reference pattern noise of each camera. As it is clearly displayed, our approach succeeds on ensuring a perfect match between images and cameras. All the used images are correctly assigned to the source cameras.

As described before, camera source identification method based on sensor pattern noise was first developed by Fridrich et al. [7]. In our work, we adopted this same approach, but with some improvements. As we already explained,

Fig. 4 A set of same scene images taken by different cameras

	N710	A505	A530	A504	A733	C55	C70	CAS	KOD	OLM	Max
Image_N710	0,0053	-0,0026	-0,0036	0	0,0033	0,001	-0,0006	0,0018	-0,0019	-0,0001	0,0053
Image_A530	0,0011	0,0039	0,0079	-0,0023	0,0063	0,0028	0,0049	0,005	-0,0011	0,0032	0,0079
Image_A733	0,0077	-0,0002	0,0029	0,0018	0,0166	0,001	0,0036	0,0049	-0,0038	0,0060	0,0166
Image_C55	0,0092	0,0072	0,0057	0,0012	0,0045	0,0112	-0,0002	0,0054	0,0009	0,0027	0,0112
Image_C70	-0,0007	0,0005	0,0038	-0,0012	0,0001	-0,0023	0,0041	-0,0025	0,0007	0,0011	0,0041
Image_CAS	0,0049	0,0033	0,0027	-0,0019	0,0044	0,0003	0,0024	0,0217	-0,0036	0,0034	0,0217
Image_KOD	0,0033	0,0063	-0,0035	0,0003	0,008	0,0002	-0,0013	-0,0022	0,0068	-0,0029	0,0068
Image_OLM	0	-0,0002	0,0017	0,0035	0,0015	0,0038	-0,0013	0,0028	-0,0034	0,0061	0,0061

Fig. 5 Table of correlation values of the eight mentioned images

our improved method is able to create a more accurate reference noise pattern even with a small number of training images, as it will be shown later. Figure 6 presents a comparison between the two approaches. For that purpose, we tested a large number of images with different scenes taken by different source cameras. The matching scores between the mean residual noise of the considered images and the reference patterns of the aforementioned ten cameras, generated from the use of 100 training photos are equivalent for both approaches. We can observe that the used source camera is the one presenting the highest correlation match.

Nevertheless, when the number of the training images decreases (if we are in a situation where less than 100 images are available) for generating the reference pattern noise, we can expect that our approach outperforms the original Fridrich's one. Figure 6 presents a comparison between the both approaches using different number of training images (i.e. 10, 20, 50 and 100) to generate the reference pattern noise. We only plotted results of the exact source camera that took these training photos, that is to say, the camera having the highest correlation values. We can clearly see that the smaller the number of training images is, the greater difference

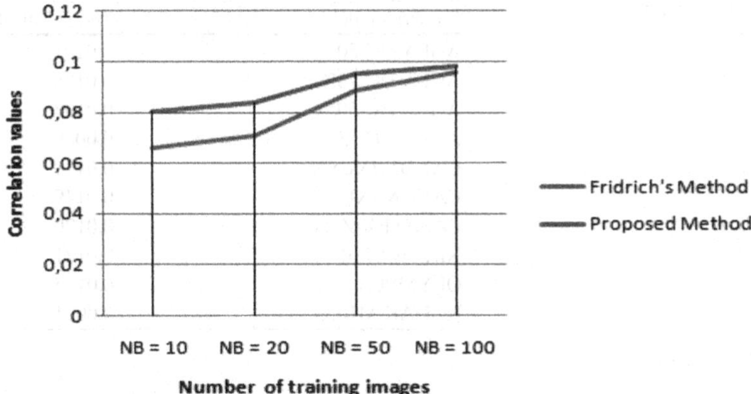

Fig. 6 The smaller the number of training images is, the greater difference between the two approaches we get

between the two approaches we get. Values have been obtained by averaging correlation results from a pool of 20 images.

As a conclusion, we can say that our proposed method correctly identify the source cameras used to take the investigated images. We still need to validate the verification operational mode, which will be the subject of the following section.

5.2.2 The Verification Mode

As written before, we created a subset of the downloaded database, called the *«Evaluating set»*, to generate the impostor scores from which we can deduce thresholds to use in order to take the decision on whether an image is taken by a tested camera or not.

Let a set of cameras *C*. c_k denotes the camera *k* in *C*. As it is known, the evaluating set is composed of a collection of images grouped by cameras taking them. Let *Set*(c_k) the group of images in the evaluating set that was captured by camera c_k. To determine the *Th*(c_k) threshold attached to the camera c_k, we first compute a mean correlation for each camera $c_j \in C$. These mean correlations are made between all the images in *Set*(c_k) and the reference pattern noise of every considered camera c_j respectively. It is obvious that the highest correlation corresponds to the camera c_k since all the remaining cameras are imposters. Our threshold is fixed as the mean value of the two highest imposter correlations. Table 2 summarizes the results we found.

The image source verification aims to highlight if a given image was actually taken by a specific given camera, yes or no. Figure 7 displays the correlation values between 50 residual noises extracted from images taken by a CASIO EX- Z150 camera and all reference noise patterns in the database. We want to check whether our proposal succeeds in the source verification task. Results show that the highest

Table 2 List of camera thresholds

Camera model	$Th(c_k)$ Threshold
AGFA DC-504	0,0101
AGFA DC-733 s	0,0126
AGFA DC-505x	0,0107
AGFA DC-530	0,0089
CANON IXUS55	0,0111
CANON IXUS70	0,0149
CASIO EX-Z150	0,0120
NIKON S710	0,0121
OLYMPUS	0,0115
KODAK M1063	0,0091

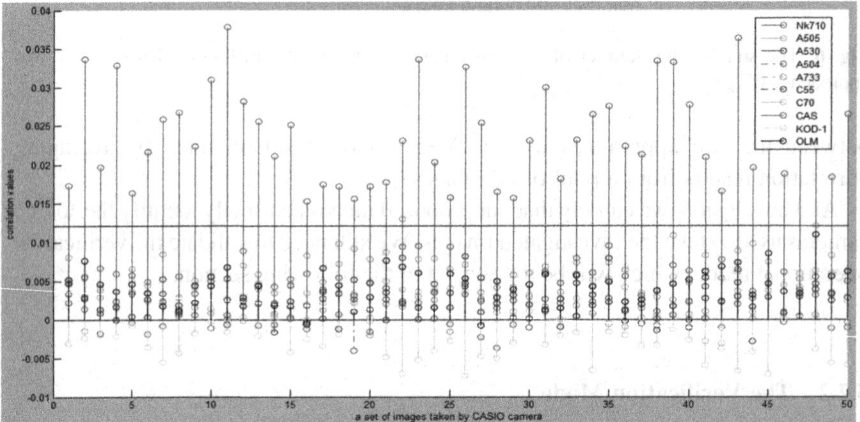

Fig. 7 The correlation between the 10 reference patterns and the residual noises extracted from 50 images by CASIO-EX-Z150 camera model

Table 3 Verification system evaluation (CAR, FAR and FRR)

Camera model	CAR (%)	FAR (%)	FRR (%)
AGFA DC-733 s	96.67	1	3.3
CANON IXUS55	97.37	1.16	2.6
CANON IXUS70	94	0.6	6
CASIO EX-Z150	98	1	2
KODAK M1063	97.34	0	2.66

values are those related to the correlation between the noise residuals of the images captured by this specific camera and its reference pattern noise. All other correlation values are rather close to "0" and far below our genuine camera (CASIO EX-Z150 camera) threshold.

A practical way for presenting the performance of a verification system is to evaluate decision measures. In our case, we checked the source of 750 images from five different camera models (i.e. 150 images per camera). Then, we computed the evaluation measures for each used camera as shown in Table 3. Note that CAR is

Table 4 Distribution of a set of images taken by KOD-1 and KOD-2 on the 10 cameras

Camera model	A504	A530	A505	A733	C55	C70	KOD-1	CAS	N710	OLM
KOD-1	3	5	4	0	2	1	132	1	0	2
KOD-2	15	17	13	6	4	12	62	8	9	4

the correct acceptance rate, FAR is the false acceptance rate and FRR is the false rejection rate. As shown, our proposal is highly efficient since it guarantees very low FAR and FRR rates that do not exceed a maximum of 1.16 and 3.3 respectively, for all the considered cameras.

Recall here that we used two different cameras but from the same brand and exact model (KODAK M1063-1 and KODAK M1063-2). We may want then, to see the ability of our system to distinguish between these two cameras. For that, we propose to train using one camera (i.e. generate the reference pattern noise) and to verify using the other one. Hence, we checked the reliability of the authentication of 150 images taken by both cameras in question. Table 4 presents the obtained results. Note that the used reference pattern noise for Kodak camera is generated using images taken by KODAK M1063-1. As a consequence, we found that for KODAK M1063-1 camera model, the correct acceptance rate is 88% whereas for KODAK M1063-2 camera model is equal to 41,33%. We can conclude that our system is able to overcome such a situation, and fairly distinguish different camera devices even from the same brand and model.

5.3 Validation of the Local Step: The Tampering Detection

As mentioned before, one of the most important problems in digital image forensics is to detect malicious manipulations in a given picture. Hence, once the sensor is identified, we still need to verify the content of the image in order to determine whether if it was affected by some forgeries. This section is devoted to validate this very last step; that is the tampering detection.

First, we started by creating some forged images (TIFF format) on which we based our experiments. All the considered images are taken from the Dresden Image database and were manipulated using the only copy-paste technique (but we do not use such a priori knowledge about the attack in our approach).

Then, and after the identification of the source camera for each image (resulting from the first phase of our proposal), we look for possible regions that have been tampered. More precisely, we locate regions that are locally not compliant with the reference pattern noise. As described in the previous sections, our proposed method was to decompose the underlying residual noise as well as its appropriate camera fingerprint using the quad tree strategy. We then compute the correlation between the respective blocks at the same decomposition level. According to the calculated matching scores, we assume that a region is tampered if it has a small correlation value compared to the average of other correlation values of same decomposition

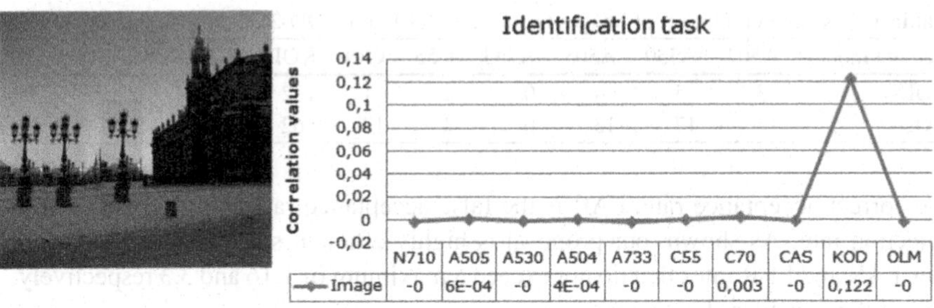

Fig. 8 Global step: camera source identification

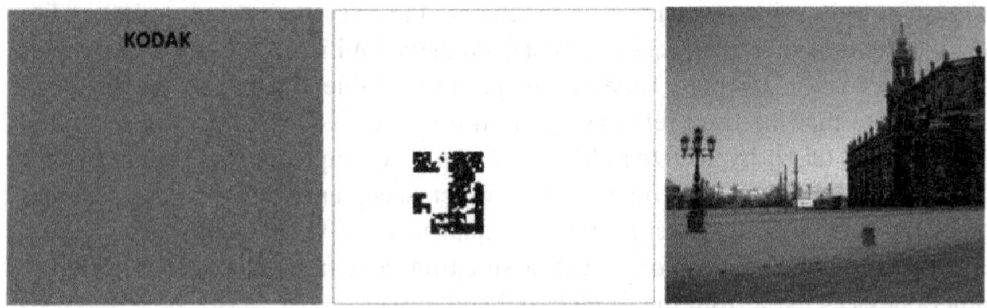

Fig. 9 Local Step: Tampering detection. *Left*: KODAK's reference pattern noise; *middle*: pre-classification mask; *right*: original image

level regions. Results of the application of our system's scheme (two steps) on a given image are shown in Figs. 8 (step 1) and 9 (step 2).

Figure 8 shows the results given by our approach in authenticating the given image. We can see that our application succeeded in pointing out that this photo was taken by the KODAK M1063-1 camera. Using the reference pattern noise of the already deduced source device (result of the first step), we detected the forged part of the image. Figure 9 displays then the camera fingerprint of KODAK M1063-1; the computed pre-classification mask which traces the modified region (i.e. here it is the duplication of the Street lamps) and the original image. We can observe that our system successfully detects the fake parts (the street lamps) clearly represented by the black zone in the output binary mask.

6 Conclusion

As pointed out by several researchers in the digital image forensics, image authentication is one of the most important issues to ensure the reliability of information contained in images and videos.

In this paper we investigated the use of sensor pattern noise to first identify the source camera and then detect malicious modifications of an image under investigation. We therefore proposed an enhanced process for camera reference pattern noise generation that makes it accurate even with a small number of training images. This reference serves to check the source camera by the global correlation detector.

Given the source camera pattern noise, i.e. resulting from the global step; a forged region can be detected based on our tampering detection method; i.e. the local step. This method utilizes the well known quad tree decomposition strategy to make comparison between the computed correlations of respective blocks and finally build a binary mask retracing the altered parts of the investigated image.

Our proposal links the two main topics studied in digital image forensics (namely the source camera identification; i.e. the global step; and the forgery detection; i.e. the local step) in a unique system. Via extensive experiments we demonstrate that our proposed approach provides significant and interesting results.

References

1. http://spectrum.ieee.org/computing/software/seeing-is-not-believing/
2. J. A Redi, W. Taktak and J- L. Dugelay, "Digital image forensics: a booklet for beginners", *Multimedia Tools and Applications, Springer*, pp. 1–30 October 2010
3. J. Adams, K. Parulski and K. Sapulding, "Color Processing in Digital Cameras", IEEE Micro, vol. 18, no. 6, 1998
4. Tran Van Lanh a, Kai-Sen Chong b, Sabu Emmanuel b, Mohan S Kankanhalli «A Survey on Digital Camera Image Forensic Methods. ICME 2007: 16–19
5. A.C. Popescu and H. Farid, "Statistical tools for digital forensics", *International Workshop on Information Hiding*, 2004.
6. T. Gloe and R. Bohme,"The Dresden Image Database for benchmarking digital image forensics," SAC, Sierre, 2010
7. J. Lukáš, J. Fridrich and M. Goljan, "Digital camera identification from sensor pattern noise," *IEEE Transactions on Information Forensics and Security*, vol. 1, no. 2, pp. 205–214, June 2006
8. M.K. Mihcak, I. Kozintsev and A. Tzortis, "Spatially adaptive statistical modeling of wavelet image coefficients and its application to denoising," in Proc. IEEE Int. Conf. Acoustics, speech, and Signal Processing, vol. 6, pp. 3253–3256, Mar 1999
9. Delp E.J, Khanna N, Mikkilineni A.K (2009) «Forensic Camera Classification: Verification of Sensor Pattern Noise Approach». Proceeding of the SPIE international Conference on Security
10. Photo tampering throughout history. http://www.cs.dartmouth.edu/ farid/ research/ digitaltampering/.
11. Jessica Fridrich, David Soukal and Jan Lukas(2003) «Detection of Copy-Move Forgery in Digital Images» Proceedings of Digital Forensic Research Workshop, www.ws.binghamton.edu/fridrich/Research/copymove.pdf

Human Activity Analysis for Geriatric Care in Nursing Homes

Ming-Yu Chen, Alexander Hauptmann, Ashok Bharucha, Howard Wactlar, and Yi Yang

Abstract As our society is increasingly aging, it is urgent to develop computer aided techniques to improve the quality-of-care (QoC) and quality-of-life (QoL) of geriatric patients. In this paper, we focus on automatic human activities analysis in video surveillance recorded in complicated environments at a nursing home. This will enable the automatic exploration of the statistical patterns between patients' daily activities and their clinical diagnosis. We also discuss potential future research directions in this area. Experiment demonstrate the proposed approach is effective for human activity analysis.

Keywords Video analysis • CareMedia • Informedia • Multimedia information systems

1 Introduction

In this section, we briefly discuss the background of our work as well as related work.

1.1 Background

As reported by the U.S. Census, the U.S. population over age 85 will be 14.2 millon by 2040, with 20–50% of them expecting to be placed in a nursing home at some point in their lives [1]. This trend leads to an exponential growth in the need for

M.-Y. Chen (✉) • A. Hauptmann • A. Bharucha • H. Wactlar • Y. Yang
School of Computer Science, Carnegie Mellon University, 5000 Forbes Avenue, Pittsburgh, PA 15213, USA
e-mail: mychen@cs.cmu.edu; alex@cs.cmu.edu; wactlar@cs.cmu.edu; yiyang@cs.cmu.edu

J.S. Jin et al., *The Era of Interactive Media*,
DOI 10.1007/978-1-4614-3501-3_5,

some form of long-term care (LTC) for this segment of the population within the next few decades. In light of these sobering demographic shifts, it is urgent to address the profound concerns that exist about the quality-of-care (QoC) and quality-of-life (QoL) of this frailest segment of the population.

Traditional nursing home health care is performed mainly by nursing staff. In nursing homes, nursing staff members not only provide care for residents' daily lives but also take notes of the activities which may be medically significant. These notes provide important information for doctors to better understand the patients' daily lives and make more accurate diagnoses. Nursing staff members are professionals whose goal is to provide a quality of care that enables residents to maintain the best possible quality of life. Their professional training not only gives them the necessary knowledge to provide health care but also to notice unusual mental and physical behaviors. This makes nursing staff members capable of maintaining high levels QoC and QoL for patients, and also able to provide critical information to assist the treating physicians.

A previous study [2] has shown that a critical element in long-term patient care is an accurate account of the patient's physical, behavioral and psychosocial functioning. However, the United States General Accounting Office (GAO) reported that in 2003 [3], "one in five nursing homes nationwide (about 3,500 homes) had serious deficiencies that caused residents actual harm or placed them in immediate jeopardy... Moreover, GAO found significant understatement of care problems that should have been classified as actual harm or higher... The GAO attributes the underreporting of such problems to: lack of clarity regarding the definition of harm, inadequate state supervisory review of surveys, delays in timely investigation of complaints, predictability of the timing of annual nursing home surveys." On the other hand, without methods to continuously record, monitor and document the care of these residents, it is exceedingly difficult to verify resident-specific data reported by nursing staff and review complaint investigations.

Deficiencies in nursing staff and lack of 24 h supervision require effective computer aided tools to maintain high levels QoC and QoL for nursing home residents. As a way to provide critical health information, surveillance recording has recently been shown to have great potential to help current nursing homes health care [5]. Therefore, it becomes an important research challenge to leverage information technology to automatically analyze surveillance video data of geriatric patients. The CareMedia project, which is a part of the Informedia project at Carnegie Mellon University, is dedicated to developing effective yet practical and efficient tools for recording and analyzing video surveillance data for better nursing home care of geriatric patients.

As indicated in [4], the core technology problems in CareMedia project mainly consist of the following three components:

- Identifying and labeling individuals.
- Tracking people in the captured video streams.
- Analyzing their activities.

1.2 Related Work

Among the problems confronted in our CareMedia research, in this paper we are particularly interested in activities analysis in video streams. In this subsection, we briefly discuss some related work in human activity analysis/recognition in video data. Automatic analysis and understanding of human activities in surveillance video have received much research attention from both industry and academia in recent years. In [7], Hu et al. reviewed the techniques for visual surveillance in dynamic scenes. In [8], Weinland et al. have discussed the recent progress in vision-based methods for action representation, segmentation and recognition. Generally speaking, in a generic automatic human activities analysis system, there are four main components. These are: video recording, feature extraction, action segmentation and activity classification/recognition.

The human activities analysis techniques can be classified into different groups according to different criteria. For example, they can be classified as model-based approaches [9], appearance-based approaches [10] and part-based approaches [11]. In [8], Weinland et al. grouped the activities analysis techniques into two classes, i.e., spatial action representation based techniques [12, 13, 14] and temporal action representation based techniques [15, 16]. While progress in this field has been impressive, further research efforts are still required for geriatric care since the type of video data recorded in real nursing homes are usually complicated, involving many occulsions and partial observations of natural daily activities with multiple people visible.

In this paper, we present our approach of activity analysis in video data recorded in nursing homes. The rest of this paper is organized as follows. In Sect. 2, we briefly present the data collection and feature design. After that, we show the activity analysis results of our approach, followed by discussion and future work.

2 Data Recording and Feature Extraction of Nursing Home Video Dataset

In this section, we present the details about data recording of nursing home video dataset and the human activity analysis approach.

2.1 Video Recording in a Nursing Home

CareMedia aims to leverage information techniques to improve QoC and QoL of geriatric patients. The ultimate goal of CareMedia is to accurately and timely record and predict in an automatic manner the geriatric patients' health status as observed in video surveillance data. As an important component of CareMedia, we need to develop a reliable human activities recognition approach for real world video data

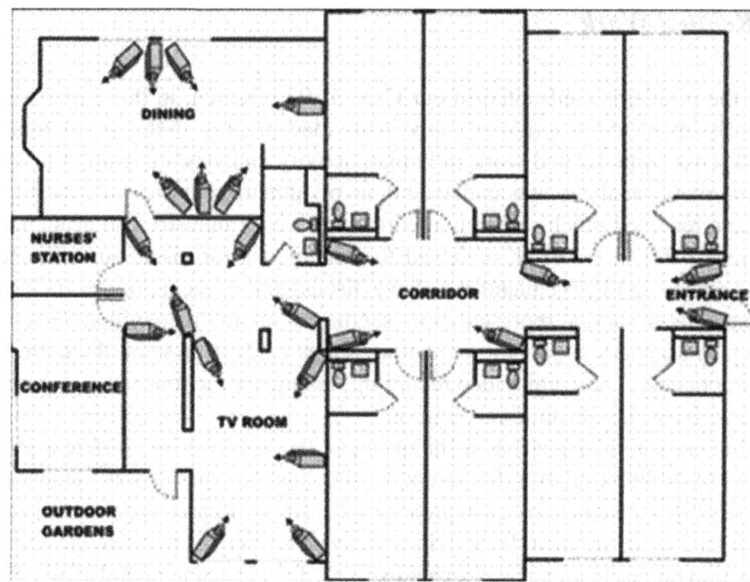

Fig. 1 Camera placement in the nursing home

recorded in nursing homes. To this end, we collected a video surveillance dataset in a nursing home for research purposes. The surveillance system was designed to collect information about patients' daily activities and to provide useful statistics to help doctors' diagnosis.

Figure 1 shows the camera set up in the nursing home. Twenty-three ceiling-mounted cameras were placed in public areas such as the dining room, TV room and hallway. Patients' life was recorded 24 h a day for 25 days. The recording was at 640 × 480 pixel resolution and 30 fps MPEG-2 Format. Over 25 terabytes of video data were recorded, lasting over 13,000 h in total.

2.2 *Feature Extraction*

In this subsection, we show the proposed human activity analysis approach.

MoSIFT Feature for Activity Analysis Feature design plays an important role in activity analysis. Intuitively, motion information is crucial for activity analysis. While the SIFT feature has been shown to be very effective in human activity analysis in previous research [8], it does not account for motion information. To achieve a better performance, we extracted the MoSIFT feature [6] from the recorded video data and then utilize a Bag-of-Words (BoW) approach to quantify them. A classifier is then trained based on this feature for analysis of activities. The overall approach is shown in Fig. 2.

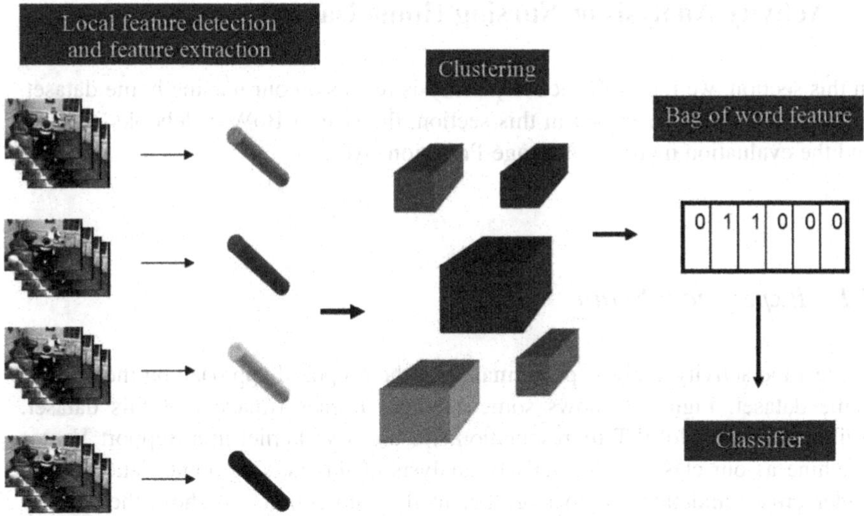

Fig. 2 General framework for human behavior recognition. There are three major stages: (1) feature point detection and MoSIFT descriptor extraction, (2) clustering and bag-of-words representation based on video codebooks, and (3) classification for behavior recognition

Table 1 Activity analysis results (AP) of Hollywood movie dataset. In this table, Laptev's Approach denotes the approach proposed in [11]

Activity	Random results (%)	Laptev's approach (%)	Our approach (%)
AnswerPhone	10.6	13.4	17.5
GetOutCar	6.0	21.9	45.3
HandShake	8.8	18.6	18.9
HugPerson	10.1	29.1	37.9
Kiss	23.5	52.0	49.5
SitDown	13.8	29.1	34.7
SitUp	4.6	6.5	7.5
StandUp	22.6	45.4	44.3
Average	12.5	27.0	32.2

Activity Analysis of Hollywood Movie Dataset For the sake of activity analysis, we propose to use MoSIFT feature with Support Vector Machine as classifier in this section. Next, we conduct preliminary experiment to test the performance of the proposed approach by applying it to Hollywood movie dataset for activity analysis. Hollywood movie dataset is a standard real world video dataset that allows direct comparison to other published work. The results is shown in Table 1. In this experiment, we use Average Precision (AP) as evaluation metric. As in Table 1, we observe that our approach achieves satisfactory results, especially when compared with Laptev's algorithm proposed in [11]. This experiment demonstrates the effectiveness of our approach for general human activity analysis in video data.

3 Activity Analysis of Nursing Home Dataset

In this section, we report the activity analysis results on our nursing home dataset. In the experiments described in this section, the size of BoW codebooks is 1,000 and the evaluation metric is Average Precision (AP).

3.1 Experiment Setup

We test the activity analysis performance of the proposed approach on the nursing home dataset. Figure 3 shows some example frames (images) of this dataset. Building on the MoSIFT representation, we use a χ^2 kernel in a Support Vector Machine as our classifier for activity analysis of this nursing home dataset. Five folder cross-validation was performed. In this subsection, we show the activity analysis of the video data recorded by a particular camera in the dining room, i.e., camera 133. This camera captures patients' activities during lunch and dinner time. In total, we labeled 2,528 activities from the movement category and 4,376 activities from the patients' detailed behavior category.

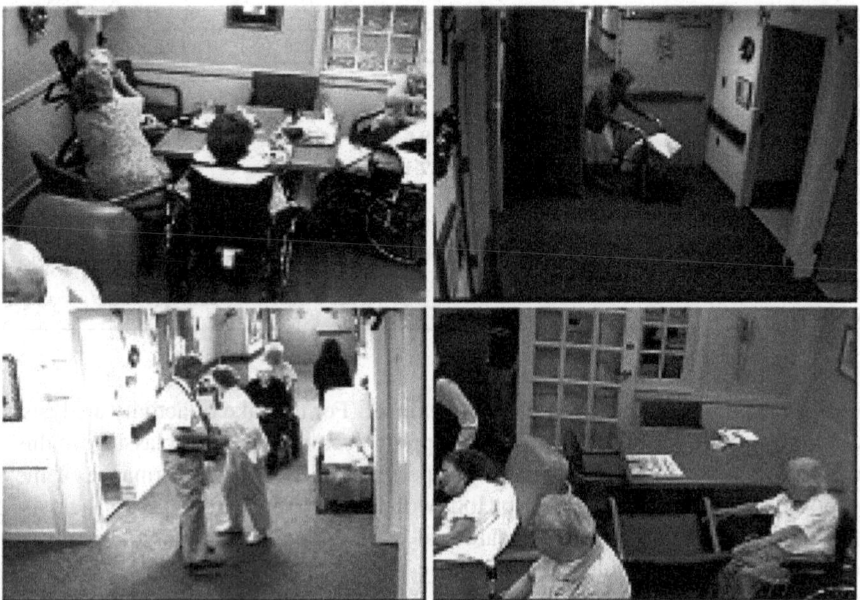

Fig. 3 Some examples of the nursing home video surveillance dataset. Images in the upper row are "Staff activity: Feeding" and "Walking though," respectively. Images in the lower row are "Wheelchair movement" and "Physically aggressive: Pulling or tugging," respectively

Table 2 Activity analysis results (AP) of nursing home dataset recorded by camera 133. In this table, Laptev's Approach denotes the approach proposed in [17]

Activity	Random results (%)	Laptev's approach (%)	Our approach (%)
WalkingThough	36.7	70.0	84.7
WalkingToStandingPoint	22.9	54.2	72.3
StandingUp	3.5	32.8	47.3
SittingDown	3.6	34.4	53.1
ObjectPlacedOnTable	17.8	29.9	51.2
ObjectRemovedFromTable	13.5	36.9	42.9
WheelchairMovement	1.7	18.1	16.8
CommunicatingWithStaff	0.3	1.3	1.8
Average	12.5	34.7	46.3

3.2 *Experiment Results*

Table 2 shows the experimental results on the nursing home dataset recorded by camera 133. We can see from this table that our approach comparatively achieves very good performance, especially when obvious actions occur, e.g., walking, moving objects, etc. This experiment demonstrates that our approach has great potential in geriatric patients activity analysis. Based on these activity analysis results, we are in the process of taking further steps that will ultimately improve the QoC and QoL of the geriatric patients in nursing home. An example of our current research direction is the generation of behavioral logs to facilitate better use of psychotropic medications.

We observe from the experiment that sometimes activities may be wrongly recognized. Even though automated analysis may be errorful, a caregiver reviewing the automatic log can overcome many errors through a direct link back to the original source video. For example, a fall reported by the system can be dismissed as a false alarm when looking at the actual video record. Thus, the caregiver can still review a comprehensive record of important patient activities in a short period of time. Nevertheless, precise recognition of human activities in video data is a long term goal in the community.

4 Discussions and Future Work

The goal of human activity recognition is to identify human behaviors in noisy environments and diverse circumstances, which is a challenging yet important research direction in the field of multimedia, computer vision, machine learning and information retrieval. Beyond automatic human behavior recognition we also want to make progress toward understanding the implications of recognized video observations over weeks or months of time. Based on the activity analysis results, we can create meaningful summaries of the patients' activities and associated changes over multiple days, weeks or even longer periods. In that way, we may expect that the QoC and QoL would be significantly improved by this technique.

To further improve the accuracy of activity analysis, the following research approaches could be pursued:

- Given that a feature is the fundamental element for video analysis, it is important to define and infer discriminative features for activity recognition, e.g., feature design, feature selection [18], codebook learning, subspace learning [19], etc.
- Considering that manually labeling large amounts of training data is time consuming and labor intensive, it is beneficial to employ active learning [21] or leverage unlabeled data [20] for a higher activity recognition accuracy with limited amount of labeled training data.
- Because multiple modalities are usually complementary to each other, it would be helpful to incorporate multiple types of evidence (e.g. audio, multiple views, sensor data) for a more robust performance.

Acknowledgements This material is based upon the work supported in part by the National Institutes of Health (NIH) Grant No. 1RC1MH090021-0110, and in part by the National Science Foundation under Grants IIS-0812465 and CNS-0751185. Any opinions, findings, and conclusions or recommendations expressed in this material are those of the author(s) and do not necessarily reflect the views of the National Institutes of Health and National Science Foundation.

References

1. German, P.S., Rovner, B.W., Burton, L.C., Brant, L.J., and Clark, R.: The role of mental morbidity in the nursing home experience. In: Gerontologist, 32(2):152–158, 1992
2. C. Steele et al.: Psychiatric Consultation in the Nursinig Home. In: Am J. Geriatric Psycbitatry, 147(8):1049–1051, 1990.
3. U. G. A. Office.: Nursing homes: Prevalence of serious quality problems remains unacceptably high, despite some decline. Washington, D.C.: U.S. General Accounting Office, 2003.
4. Hauptmann, A.G., Gao, J., Yan, R., Qi, Y., Yang, J., Wactlar, H.D.: Automated Analysis of Nursing Home Observations, IEEE Pervasive Computing, 3(2)15–21, 2004.
5. Bharucha A., Wactlar H., Stevens S., Pollock B., Dew M., D. Chen, and Atkeson. C., Caremedia: Automated video and sensor analysis for geriatric care. In Proceedings of the Fifth Annual WPIC Research Day, University of Pittsburgh School of Medicine, 2005.
6. Chen, M-Y. and Hauptmann, A, MoSIFT: Recognizing Human Actions in Surveillance Videos. CMU-CS-09-161, Carnegie Mellon University, 2009.
7. Hu, W., Tan, T., Wang, L., and Maybank, S.: A Survey on Visual Surveillance of Object Motion and Behaviors. In: IEEE Transactions of Systems, Man, and Cybernetics, 34(3): 334–352, 2004.
8. Weinland D., Ronfard R., Boyer E.: A survey of vision-based methods for action representation, segmentation and recognition. In: Computer Vision and Image Understanding. 115(2): 224–241, 2011.
9. Bregler, C.: Learning and recognizing human dynamics in video sequences, In CVPR, 1997.
10. Bobick, A.F. and Davis, J.W.: The recognition of human movement using temporal templates. In: IEEE Trans. PAMI, 2001.
11. Laptev I., Marszalek M., Schmid C., and Rozenfeld B.. Learning realistic human actions from movies. In: CVPR, 2008.

12. Blank M., Gorelick L., Shechtman E., Irani M., Basri R..: Actions as spaceCtime shapes, In: ICCV, 2005.
13. Liu J., Ali S., Shah M., Recognizing human actions using multiple features, In: CVPR, 2008.
14. Scovanner P., Ali S., Shah M., A 3-dimensional sift descriptor and its application to action recognition, In: ACM International Conference on Multimedia, 2007.
15. Sminchisescu C., Kanaujia, A. Li Z., Metaxas D.: Conditional models for contextual human motion recognition, In: ICCV, 2005.
16. Schindler K., van Gool L., Action snippets: how many frames does human action recognition require? In: CVPR, 2008.
17. Laptev, I. and Lindeberg, T.: Space-time interest points, In: ICCV, 2003.
18. Yang. Y., Shen. H., Ma Z., Huang Z and Zhou X.: L21-Norm Regularized Discriminative Feature Selection for Unsupervised Learning, In: IJCAI 2011.
19. Nie, F., Xiang, S. and Zhang C.: Neighborhood MinMax Projections, In: IJCAI, 2007.
20. Yang Y., Nie F., Xu D., Luo J., Zhuang Y. and Pan Y.: A Multimedia Retrieval Framework based on Semi-Supervised Ranking and Relevance Feedback. In: IEEE Trans. PAMI, 2011.
21. Wang M., Hua X.: Active Learning in Multimedia Annotation and Retrieval: A Survey. In: ACM Transactions on Intelligent Systems and Technology. 2(2): 10–31, 2011.

Face Detection, Recognition and Synthesis

Multi-Feature Face Recognition Based on 2D-PCA and SVM

Sompong Valuvanathorn, Supot Nitsuwat, and Mao Lin Huang

Abstract Identification and authentication by face recognition mainly use global face features. However, the recognition accuracy rate is still not high enough. This research aims to develop a method to increase the efficiency of recognition using global-face feature and local-face feature with four parts: the left-eye, right-eye, nose and mouth. This method is based on geometrical techniques used to find location of eyes, nose and mouth from the frontal face image. We used 115 face images for learning and testing. Each-individual person's images are divided into three difference images for training and two difference images for testing. The Two-Dimension Principle Component Analysis (2D-PCA) technique is used for feature extraction and the Support Vector Machine (SVM) method is used for face recognition. The results show that the recognition percentage is 97.83%.

Keywords Face recognition • Face feature extraction • Two-dimension principle component analysis (2D-PCA) • Support vector machine (SVM)

S. Valuvanathorn (✉)
Department of Information Thechnology, Faculty of Information Technology, King Mongkut's University of Technology, North Bangkok, Thailand
e-mail: scsompva@hotmail.com

S. Nitsuwat
Department of Mathematics, Faculty of Applied Science, King Mongkut's University of Technology, North Bangkok, Thailand
e-mail: sns@kmutnb.ac.th

M.L. Huang
Mao Lin Huang, Faculty of Engineering and Information Technology, University of Technology, Sydney, Australia
e-mail: maolin@it.uts.edu.au

J.S. Jin et al., *The Era of Interactive Media*,

DOI 10.1007/978-1-4614-3501-3_6,

1 Introduction

Currently, it is necessary to have a security system for each important location. These places require systems which can identify and authenticate person who want to access them. Face recognition system is a system that can identify and authenticate person from both still and moving images. It is a popular application for security places such as airports, banks, immigration department, etc. These places also have Closed-Circuit Television System (CCTV) to record events. When an unusual situation arises, these images will be verified to find the person involved. An important activities processed on these images are indication and identification an individual face. Searching for a face in image by people usually takes a lot of time and manpower which causes reduction of performance and authentication correctness.

Normally, most of face recognition can be implemented on still images and/or video. Research of this field mainly uses global face features. However, the recognition accuracy rate is not high enough. Therefore, this research has developed a method to increase the accuracy of face recognition using both global-face feature and local-face feature with four parts: the left-eye, right-eye, nose and mouth. The main methods used to improve face recognition accuracy are 2D-PCA and SVM. We also compared the performance of face recognition using only global-face feature with those using both global-face feature and local-face feature.

In this paper, Sect. 2 states about related researches in this field. In Sect. 3, Geometric Face Model, 2D-PCA, and SVM are introduced. The proposed face recognition system based on 2D-PCA and SVM is presented in Sect. 4. The experimental results are then shown. Finally, conclusion is given in Sect. 5.

2 Related Research Work

The most popular and well know method used in face recognition is the eigenface-based method, PCA. Recently, the 2D-PCA method has also been used in face recognition which allows better recognition of the PCA. Cheng-Yuan et al. [1] compared results between using PCA with 2D-PCA for face recognition. They used global-face and local-face features by integrating both features with different weightings. The results shown that 2D-PCA performed considerably better than PCA. The integration of both global-face feature and local-face feature gave better recognition accuracy than global-face feature. Radha et al. [2] compared results between using PCA with 2D-PCA for face recognition using only global-face feature. Performance of the 2D-PCA method and processing time were better than the PCA method. Sani et al. [3] focused on SVM classification method for face recognition. Adaptive Multiscale Retinex (AMSR) was also introduced to reduce various lighting conditions before performing the classification task and then compared with the PCA method. The SVM method processing times and performance were better than that of PCA. Le et al. [4] combined 2D-PCA with SVM to face recognition, where 2D-PCA was used for extracting feature vectors, while SVM was used for classification. Bui et al. [5] presented that 2D-PCA method performed significantly better than PCA when they were used with SVM face gender detection method separately to face feature extraction. Jiao et al. [6] focused on the local feature analysis for face recognition by using the methods of the Euclidian metric, angle between vectors and city block distance metric, and concluded that the local feature method performed much better than the global one.

3 Methods and Materials

3.1 Geometric Face Model

Geometric Face Model [7] is another method that can be applied to find location information on the face, using both circular and oval shapes, shown in Fig. 1.

The intersection of a circle and the ellipse on the Y axis is proportional to the position of the eyes, nose and mouth.

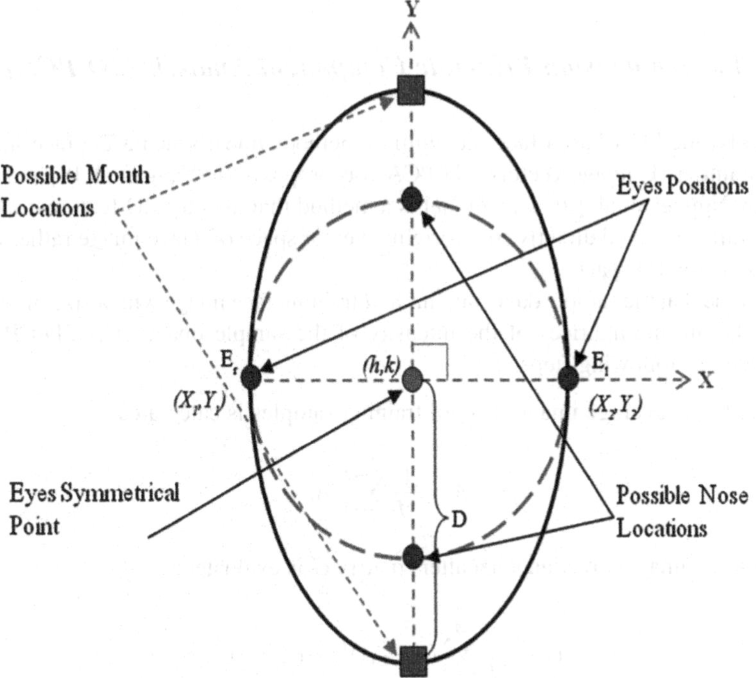

Fig. 1 Geometric face model

- The positions of both eyes (E_r and E_l) are determined from the BioID face database.
- We then calculates the distance between the right-eye (E_r) and left-eye (E_l) as following equation:

$$\overline{E_r E_l} = \sqrt{(X_2 - X_1)^2 + (Y_2 - Y_1)^2} \tag{1}$$

- Next, calculation of the center point (*h, k*) distance between the right-eye and left-eye is calculated as following equation:

$$(h, k) = \left(\frac{(X_2 - X_1)}{2}\right), \left(\frac{(Y_2 - Y_1)}{2}\right). \tag{2}$$

- Points (*h, k*) are the center of a circle. The radius equals to *0.6D* or half the distance between the right-eye and left-eye. The cut-off point on the *Y* axis is the position of the nose. This is possible for the upper or lower points.
- Points (*h, k*) are the midpoint in the ellipse. *D* is radius of major axis and *0.6D* is a radius of minor axis. The cut-off point on the *Y* axis is the position of the mouth. This is possible for the top or bottom point.

3.2 Two-Dimension Principle Component Analysis (2D-PCA)

Normally, the PCA-based face recognition methods transformed a 2D face image sample into a 1D image vectors. 2D-PCA was proposed by Yang et al. [8] and was used by Nguyen et al. [9]. This model is a method that uses the 2D features, which are features obtained directly from original vector space of a face image rather than from a vector 1D space.

Assume that the sample data contains a *M* training face image with a size of *m x n*. $A_1,\ldots,A_M$ are the matrices of the intensity of the sample image. The 2D-CPA is calculated as following steps:

- Firstly, the average image *A* of all training samples is calculated:

$$\bar{A} = \frac{1}{M}\sum\nolimits_1^M A_i \tag{3}$$

- Then the image covariance (scatter) matrix *G* is evaluated:

$$G = \frac{1}{M}\sum_{j=1}^{M}(A_j - \bar{A})^T \times (A_j - \bar{A}) \tag{4}$$

- Next, d orthonormal vectors $X_1, X_2, \ldots, X_d$ corresponding to the d largest eigenvalues of G is computed. $X_1, X_2, \ldots, X_d$ construct a d-dimensional projection subspace. $X_1, \ldots, X_d$ are the d optimal projection axes, such that when projecting the sample images on each axis Xi, the total scatter of the projected images is maximum.
- We then project $A_1, \ldots, A_M$ on each vector $X_1, \ldots, X_d$ to get the principal component vectors:

$$Y_i^j = A_j X_i; i = 1, \ldots, d; j = 1, \ldots, M \tag{5}$$

- When a testing image with 2D intensity matrix B arrives, the principal component vectors of the new image are computed.

$$Y_i^B = BX_i; i = 1, \ldots, d \tag{6}$$

- Next, the Euclidean distance between $(Y_1^B, \ldots, Y_d^B)$ and $(Y_1^j, \ldots, Y_d^j)$ is computed:

$$dist(B, A_j) = \sum_{i=1}^{d} \left\| Y_i^B - Y_i^j \right\|; j = 1, \ldots, M \tag{7}$$

  where $\left\| Y_i^B, \ldots, Y_i^j \right\|_2$ is the Euclidean distance between $Y_i^B, \ldots, Y_i^j$.
- Finally, we use $dist(B,Aj)(j = 1, \ldots, M)$ and a threshold θ to select the label of the testing image.

The dimension d of the subspace in the 2D-PCA has a great impact on the energy of the constructed image. The energy of the constructed image is concentrated on the first small number of component vectors corresponding to the larger eigenvalues. Therefore, choosing the dimension d small is enough to obtain a high accuracy rate for the 2D-PCA.

3.3 Support Vector Machine (SVM)

The SVM is a statistical classification method proposed by Corinna and Vladimir [10] and was used by Sani et al. [3]. It is a popular machine learning algorithm because it can resolve a non-linear classification problem in higher dimensional space with a supporting (Fig. 2) result.

Assume that we have a dataset, which given m as the amount of the labeled training samples, x_i are the training samples while y_i are the targets or labels in N-dimensional space as:

$$\left\{ x_i, y_i \middle| x_i \in R^N, y_i \in \{\mathbf{-1}, \mathbf{1}\}, i = \mathbf{1} \ldots \text{m} \right\}. \tag{8}$$

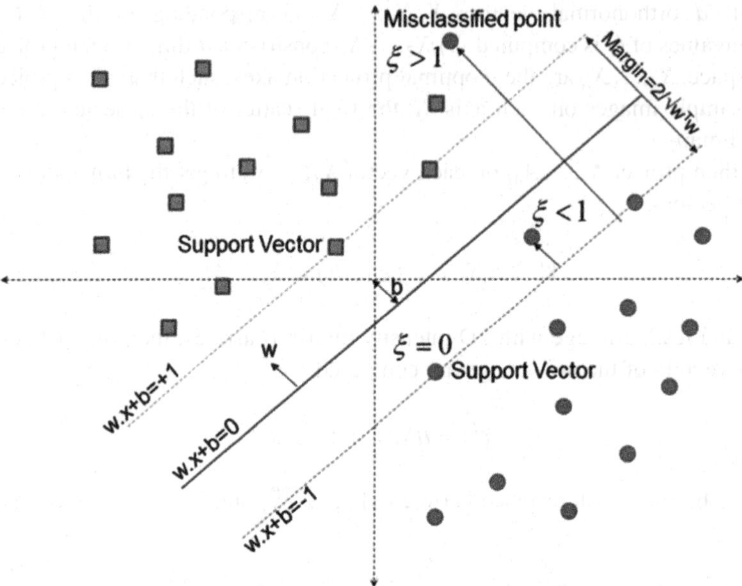

Fig. 2 Basic support vector machine classifier

The results in a linearly severable problem corresponding to a determination function:

$$f(x) = sign((w \cdot x) + b). \tag{9}$$

The set of samples is optimally separated by the hyperplane. If it is separated without error and the margin is maximal, this hyperplane bisects the shortest line between the convex hulls of the two classes. Therefore, it must satisfy the following constrained minimization:

$$Min : \frac{1}{2} w^T w, \; y_i(w \cdot x_i + b) \geq 1. \tag{10}$$

The hyperplane can be created by solving quadratic optimization problem which is the solution of w and expands with $w = \sum_i \alpha_i x_i y_i$ in terms of a subset of training patterns that lie on the margin. These training patterns x_i are called support vectors, which afford the important information of classification problems. Then the decision function is defined as follows:

$$f(x) = sign \sum\nolimits_i \alpha_i y_i (x \cdot x_i) + b. \tag{11}$$

For the linearly non separable case, a modification of previous minimization problem is required to recover the misclassified data points. A new penalizing error variable is introduced; ξas the measurement of infringement of the limitations as follows:

$$Min : \frac{1}{2} w^T w + c \sum_{i=1}^{L} \xi_i, \quad y_i(w \cdot x_i + b) \geq 1 - \xi, \tag{12}$$

where C is used to weight the penalizing parameter ξ_i.

The SVM separate a non-linear separable classification problem by mapping the data into a feature space via a non-linear map. This solution is done by using kernel, K. By using kernel, the non-linear separated samples input space will turn out to be linearly separated after being mapped in feature space. The determination boundaries function for non-linear problems can be formulated as follows:

$$f(x) = \sum_i \alpha_i y_i K(x \cdot x_i) + b. \tag{13}$$

There are a lot of kernel functions for SVM. Any type of kernel can be chosen based on experiments as it depends on the sample data. In our experiments, we selected the linear function kernel due to better recognition performance.

4 Experimentation and Results

This section presents details of our experiment (Fig. 3) and results as follows:

4.1 Preparation for Experiment

In this experiment, we used BioID face database which contains 115 male and female gray-scale images of 23 people. Each person has five different gray-scale images. The resolution of each image is 384 × 286 pixels. Coordinates of eyes have been assigned.

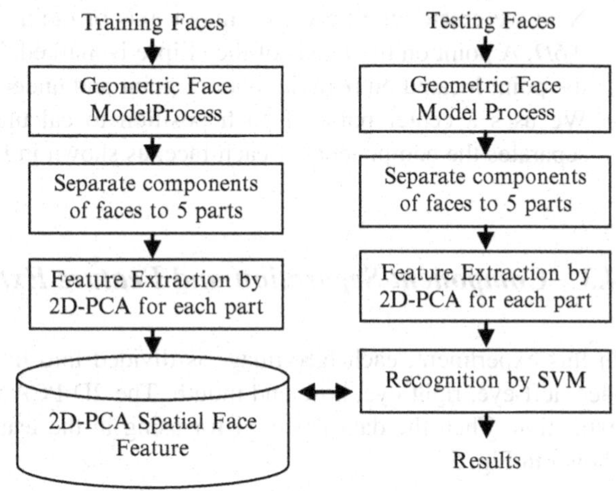

Fig. 3 Block diagram of multi-feature face recognition based on 2D-PCA and SVM

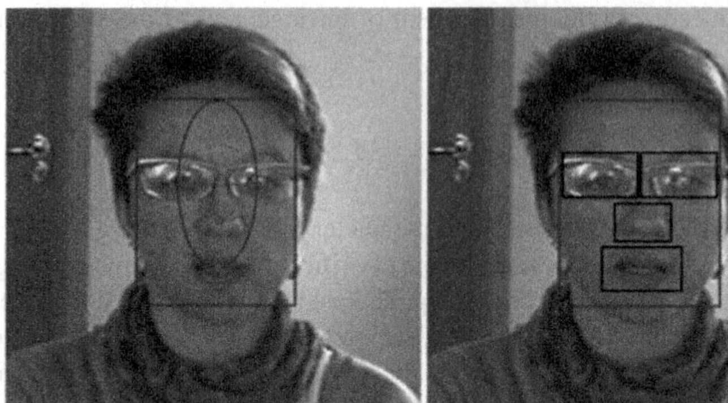

Fig. 4 Calculate the local component of face by geometric face model

Images of the individuals have been taken with varying light intensity, facial expression (open/close eyes, smiling/not smiling), facial details (glasses/no glasses, mustache/no mustache). The histogram equalization process is used for each gray-scale image before conducting the next process.

4.2 Calculate the Local Component of Face

The geometric face model is applied to calculate the position of components of the face: global-face, eyes, nose and mouth as follows:

- We first calculate the midpoint between the positions of both eyes with the Eq. (1).
- We then create a circle with a radius of half the distance between both eyes. The cut-off point on the *Y* axis of the circle is obtained. The position of the nose either on the top or the bottom is then assigned. In this experiment, the frontal face image is used. The bottom point is just the one consideration point.
- Next we create an ellipse with major axis of radius *D* with a master radius of *0.6D*. A point on the *Y* axis of the ellipse is marked. The position of the mouth, the point located on both the bottom point and under the nose is assigned.
- We uses a center point of each position to calculate the region which also separates the components of each face, as shown in Fig. 4.

4.3 Component Separation and Feature Extraction

In this experiment, each face-image is divided into five separate regions: whole face, left-eye, right-eye, nose and mouth. The 2D-PCA method is used for feature extraction. Then the data is stored for using in the learning and testing steps, as shown in Fig. 5.

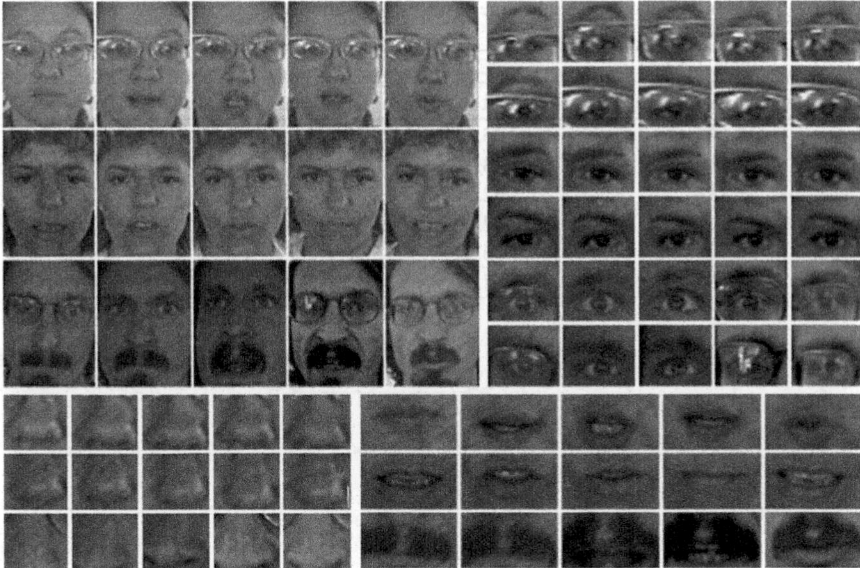

Fig. 5 Example of component of face

4.4 Recognition by SVM

The global-face feature and four parts of the local-face feature are used for training and testing the SVM. For SVM, the number of classes is 23. The data is divided into 3:2 for individual sample, three difference images of individual used for training and two difference images used for testing. Classification is conducted by using the linear function kernel.

We also integrated all parts using the Majority Vote technique to determine the best recognition result. However, there is a possibly of duplicates for majority votes. In this case, firstly, we consider a group of global-face (part of face image) to determine the recognition result. Secondly, groups of right-eye, left-eye are considered, respectively, because the right-eye having the highest recognition performance of local-feature.

4.5 Experiment Results

In this research, there are three techniques used for performance and processing time comparison: Processed Histogram based (PHB) [11], PCA and 2D-PCA. These methods were implemented using the same face database. The results are shown in Table 1.

Table 1 Performance and processing time of face recognition using PHB, PCA and 2D-PCA methods

Global and local face	PHB + SVM		PCA + SVM		2D-PCA+SVM	
	Accuracy (%)	Time (sec.)	Accuracy (%)	Time (sec.)	Accuracy (%)	Time (sec.)
Face	52.17	*0.12*	95.65	*7.35*	95.65	*1.01*
R-eye	47.83	*0.13*	93.48	*1.53*	93.48	*0.34*
L-eye	47.83	*0.13*	82.61	*1.51*	82.61	*0.38*
Nose	41.30	*0.14*	67.39	*1.03*	73.91	*0.33*
Mouth	36.96	*0.12*	56.25	*1.94*	67.39	*0.40*
Whole	54.35	*0.64*	97.83	*13.36*	97.83	*2.46*

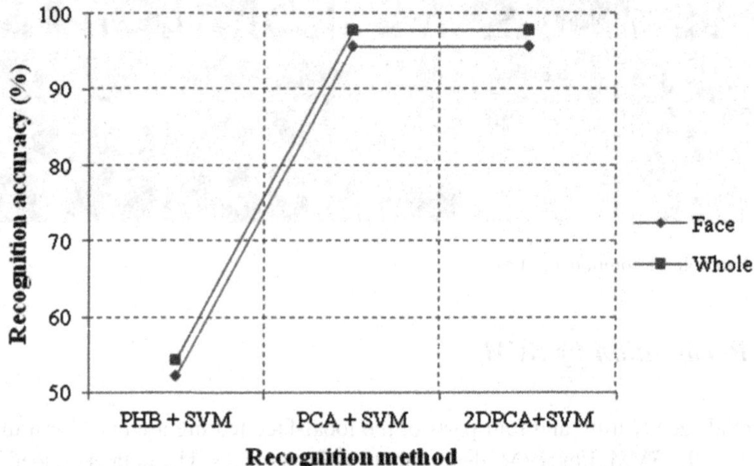

Fig. 6 The graph shows the comparison of various methods of face recognition

From the result in Table 1, the recognition accuracy rate for Global-face feature using the 2D-PCA+SVM method is 95.65% which similar to the PCA+SVM method. While recognition accuracy rate when integrating face, right-eye, left-eye, nose and mouth features and using the 2D-PCA+SVM method increase to 97.83% which similar to the PCA+SVM method, shown in Fig. 6.

5 Conclusion

This research aims to develop a method to increase the efficiency of face recognition using global-face feature and local-face feature. This method is based on geometrical techniques used to find location of eyes, nose and mouth from the frontal face image. When using global-face feature only, recognition accuracy rate of using the PHB, PCA and 2D-PCA methods are 52.17%, 95.56% and 95.56%, respectively. On another hand, in the case that we integrated global-face and local-face features, the recognition accuracy are 54.35%, 97.83% and 97.83%, respectively. Therefore, face recognition using both global and local features increased the performance efficiency.

For considering the processing time, the PHB method used a short time, but the recognition accuracy was low. The PCA and 2D-PCA methods had the same high recognition accuracy rate. However, the 2D-PCA method used less processing time than the PCA method.

References

1. Tang, C.-Y., Lin, Y.-C., Liu, C.-T.: Comparison Between PCA and 2D-PCA for Face Recognition. In: 18th IPPR Conference on Computer Vision, Grapics and Image Processing (CVGIP 2005) 2005, pp. 766–773.
2. Radha, V., Pushpalatha, M.: Comparison of PCA Based and 2DPCA Based Face Recognition Systems. International Journal of Engineering Science and Technology 2 (12), 7177–7182 (2010).
3. Sani, M.M., K.A. Ishak, Samad, S.A.: Classification using Adaptive Multiscale Retinex and Support Vector Machine for Face Recognition System. Journal of Applied Sciences 10, 506–511 (2010).
4. Le, T.H., Bui, L.: Face Recognition Based on SVM and 2DPCA. International Journal of Signal Processing, Image Processing and Patten Recognition 4, No. 3, 85–94 (2011).
5. Bui, L., Tran, D., Huang, X., Chetty, G.: Face Gender Recognition on 2D Principle Component Analysis and Support Vector Machine. In: Fourth International Conference on Network and System Security 2010, pp. 579–582
6. Jiao, F., Gao, W., Chen, X., Cui, G., Shan, S.: A Face Recognition Method Based on Local Feature Analysys. In: The 5th Asian Conference on Computer Vision (ACCV2002), Melbourne, Australia 2002, pp. 1–5
7. Cheddad, A., Mohamad, D., Manaf, A.A.: Exploiting Voronoi diagram properties in face segmentation and feature extraction. Pattern Recognition 41, 3842–3859 (2008).
8. Yang, J., Zhang, D., Frangi, A.F., Yang, J.: Two-dimensional PCA: A new approach to appearance-based face representation and recognition. IEEE Transactions on Pattern Analysis and Machine Intelligence 26(1), 131–137 (2004).
9. Nguyen, N., Liu, W., Venkatesh, S.: Random Subspace Two-Dimensional PCA for Face Recognition. In: Advances in Multimedia Information Processing (PCM 2007) 2007, pp. 655–664.
10. Corinna, C. and V. Vladimir, 1995. Support vector Network. Machine Learning, 20: 273–297.
11. Swain, M.J., Ballard, D.H.: Indexing Via Color Histograms. In: Third International Conference on Computer Vision (ICCV), Dec 4–7 1990, pp. 390–393

Face Orientation Detection Using Histogram of Optimized Local Binary Pattern

Nan Dong, Xiangzhao Zeng, and Ling Guan

Abstract Histogram of optimized local binary pattern (HOOPLBP) is a new and robust orientation descriptor, which is claimed to be content-independent. In this paper, we improved the algorithm by disregarding features of some unwanted pixels. Furthermore, we found out that the minimum range of HOOPLBP is much smaller on human face orientation detection than other content-based images. Then we set up a series of experiments on human face orientation detection and with a general model, we can detect the face orientation with arbitrary degree. Thus the method can be further developed to enhance the present face detection algorithm.

Keywords Orientation detection • Histogram • Face

1 Introduction

Research on human face has drawn a lot of attention in recent years and also achieves a lot of progress. However there are few papers discussing human face orientation detection. Human face orientation detection is an important and difficult task in face related research, especially in face detection. Most recent face detection approaches detect only upright human faces. Some reported that it can detect variable face patterns, rotated up to $\pm 20^\circ$ in image plane [5]. With out tests, the algorithm in [2] can detect faces within $\pm 15^\circ$. However there are lots of images and photos with human faces rotated up to $\pm 180^\circ$. So a face orientation detection method is needed.

Histogram of optimized local binary pattern (HOOPLBP) is a new and robust content-independent orientation descriptor. We proposed the HOOPLBP in [1].

N. Dong (✉) • X. Zeng • L. Guan
Ryerson Multimedia Research Laboratory, Department of Electrical and Computer Engineering, Ryerson University, Toronto, Ontario, Canada
e-mail: gdongnan@gmail.com

J.S. Jin et al., *The Era of Interactive Media*,
DOI 10.1007/978-1-4614-3501-3_7,

It can detect the orientation between different but similar-texture-pattern images. Motivated by that the classic local binary patterns (LBP) [3, 4] is used on face recognition and facial expression recognition, we introduce the HOOPLBP on face orientation detection in this paper. The main contributions of this paper lie in three aspects. First, we improved the algorithm of HOOPLBP by reducing the unwanted features of 0, 90, 180, 270 which will negatively affect the detections. Second, we found out that the HOOPLBP can achieve much better results on human face orientation detection than the orientation detection of other content-based images. The third is that a general face model is built and we can detect the face orientation with arbitrary rotation degree. As far as we know, there are no papers reported to perform this task. Thus the method can be further developed to enhance the present face detection algorithm.

The remaining sections are organized as follows. First we give a short review of the HOOPLBP algorithm in Sect. 2 in which the improvement of HOOPLBP is shown in the last of this section. The experimental setup and results on human face orientation detection are shown in Sect. 3. The conclusion is give in the last section.

2 Histogram of Optimized Local Binary Pattern

Histogram of optimized local binary pattern (HOOPLBP) originates from local binary pattern (LBP). In HOOPLBP, it uses the bit-wise shift times by which it achieves the minimum LBP value as the feature value instead of the minimum LBP value. Through the histogram and optimization, HOOPLBP shows robust and efficient in image orientation detection.

2.1 Gray Scale and Rotation Invariant Local Binary Pattern

The LBP operator was defined as texture descriptor, in which the texture T is defined in a local circle area centered on each pixel of the image:

$$T = t(g_c, g_0, \cdots, g_{p-1}), \tag{1}$$

where g_c is the gray value of the center pixel and $g_p(p = 0, \ldots, P-1)$ correspond to the gray values of P equally distributed pixels around the center pixel on a circle of radius $R(R > 0)$, shown in Fig. 1.

To achieve gray scale invariance, it subtracts the gray value of the center pixel from the circularly symmetric neighborhood $g_p(p = 0, \ldots, P-1)$ and only consider the signs of the differences instead of the exact values, giving:

$$T = t(s(g_0 - g_c), s(g_1 - g_c), \ldots, s(g_{P-1} - g_c)), \tag{2}$$

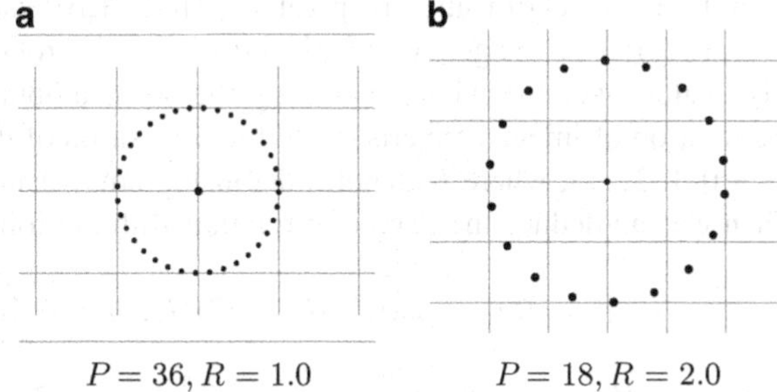

Fig. 1 Circularly symmetric neighbor sets

where

$$s(x) = \begin{cases} 1, & x \geq 0 \\ 0, & x < 0. \end{cases}$$

The LBP operator can form 2^P binary pattern, corresponding to the starting position of the P neighborhoods. To remove the effect of the rotation, we can assign a unique identifier to each rotation invariant local binary pattern, like:

$$LBP_{P,R} = min\{ROR(LBP_{P,R}, i)|i = 0, 1, \ldots, P - 1\}, \tag{3}$$

where $ROR(x, i)$ does a circular bit-wise shift on the binary number x i times.

2.2 Histogram and Feature Extraction

To detect the degree, the times of bit-wise shift i is used as feature value in HOOPLBP, by which LBP achieves the minimum value. For example, pattern 10011000 has the value of i as 5 if we perform circular left shifts and pattern 00010011 has the value of *zero*. The degree of rotation can be deduced with the following formula:

$$Deg = |i_1 - i_2| \times \frac{P}{360}, \tag{4}$$

where i_1 and i_2 denotes the correspondent times of bit-wise shift of the original image and the rotated image. Hence, the difference of i of the same pixel in the original image and the rotated image denotes the degree of the rotation. The precision of the degree is determined by the value P. The greater the value of P is, the more precisions it achieves, and the more accurately the proposed method detects the orientation. If P equals 360, the precision of the degree will be *one* which may be pretty steep for a human.

However it is not viable to locate the same pixel on two images. Furthermore, there's no such matching points between two similar but different images.

Therefore instead of using one pixel, the HOOPLBP uses the histogram computed over a region of image. As mentioned above, the rotation of image changes the LBP value over the whole image by the same amount. It means the degree of the rotation of image converts to the bit-wise shifts of the histogram, like $ROR(H, i|i = 0, 1, 2 \ldots)$, where H denotes the histogram, i denotes the degree of rotation. Then we can deduce the degree of rotation with the following formula:

$$Deg = min\{d(H_1, ROR(H_2, i|i = 0, 1, 2 \ldots))\} \quad (5)$$

where H_1, H_2 denote the histogram of the original image and the rotated image. $d(H_1, H_2)$ is the distance matrix used for the comparison of the histograms.

In our experiments, we use *chi-square* histogram comparison algorithms in which high scores indicate good matches and low scores indicate bad matches, described as follows:

$$d_{chi-square}(H_1, H_2) = \sum_i \frac{(H_1(i) - H_2(i))^2}{H_1(i) + H_2(i)} \quad (6)$$

2.3 Optimization

In image orientation detection, the high precision is needed, like $P = 360$. However, it's a very time-consuming task. An optimization method is provided in [1], which converts numerous calculations of interpolation to solving a quartic equation, that saves us a lot of time.

HOOPLBP is a novel and efficient method. It provides us a method to detect the object orientation. We gave a short review of the key steps of the HOOPLBP. The details can be checked in [1].

2.4 Feature Choice

Figure 2a shows us that the histogram of HOOLBP in Fig. 2b is dominated by the features of 0, 90, 180 and 270. Actually, several experiments with different images demonstrate that all share this common trait. This characteristic negatively influences our detections. In the following of the section, we tried to figure out why these features exist at the histogram and managed to reduce them.

The straightforward thought is that some edge points produce these features. In order to see the pixels which yields these features, we map the features of 0, 90, 180 and 270 back to the pixels in the image and the results are shown at Fig. 3. From the figure, we can see that the pixels which mapped back from the features of 0, 90, 180, 270 are located all over the image. By further analysis of the pixel values and their

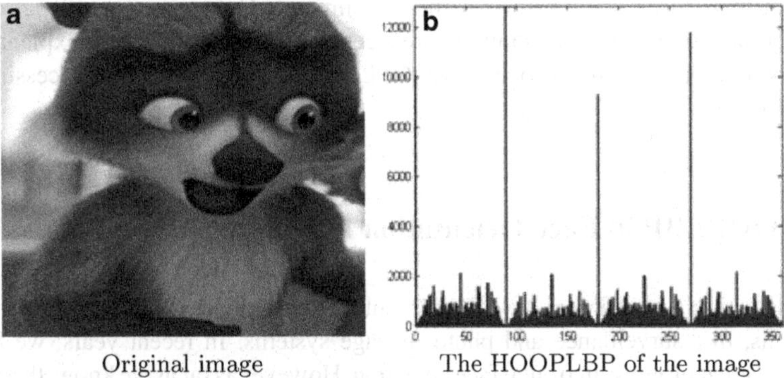

Fig. 2 An image and its HOOPLBP feature

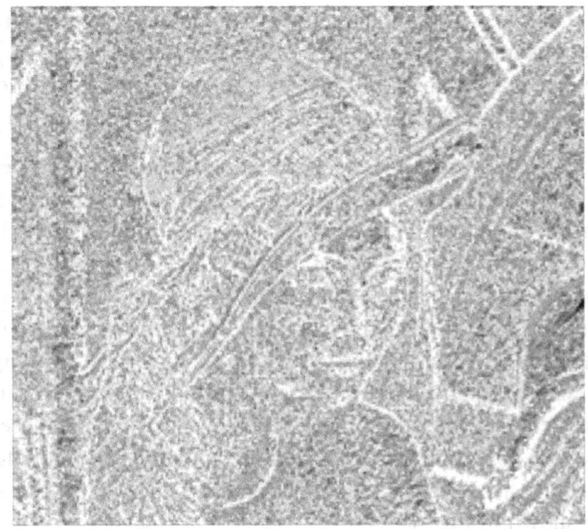

Fig. 3 Pixels which are mapped back from the features of 0, 90, 180, 270 of the HOOPLBP

neighbors, we found out that if the intensity of the pixel equals to the value of any one of its four nearest neighbors, the feature of the pixel tends to be 0, 90, 180 or 270. And only a small amount of the pixels meeting the condition do not yield these features. Thereby, skipping the pixels meeting the condition will improve the HOOPLBP feature without much sacrifice of other pixels.

The theory of the HOOPLBP doesn't expect such unwanted number of features of 0, 90, 180, 270. One explanation could be that how the digital images work produces this feature. The current digital image is presented as rectangles which makes the neighbors along the four directions are special. Furthermore, because of the limitation of sensitivities of the sensors on a charge-coupled device (CCD), values of some of the pixels captured by the CCD are calculated by interpolations which also induces some errors in the raw images. However, it's still an open question and more experimentations are needed to give a complete explanation which will not only help improve the HOOPLBP, but also benefits the processing of digital images.

3 HOOPLBP in Face Orientation Detection

Face detection is a popular field in computer vision. It is a key step in various situations, like surveillance and photo manage systems. In recent years, we have achieved great progress in frontal face detection. However as far as we know, there are few paper reported to detect human faces with arbitrary rotation degree, which it's a common situation in videos and photos. Although they are easily observed by humans, it is difficult for computers. HOOPLBP is a novel method and can helps us detect object orientations with similar features. Human faces, of no matter what races or sex, have a set of similar features, which makes it suitable for applying HOOPLBP to detect the face orientation. In this section, by training a general face model based on the HOOPLBP, our method can successfully detect the orientation of a human face.

1. *Image Data and Experimental Setup* In our experiments, we use The Database of Faces (formerly 'the ORL Database of Faces') [6]. There are ten different images of each of 40 distinct subjects. For some subjects, the images were taken at different times, varying the lighting, facial expressions (open/closed eyes, smiling/not smiling) and facial details (glasses/no glasses). Furthermore, not all the images are shot from the frontal view. Some are taken with some out-of-plane rotation. All the images were taken against a dark homogeneous background with the subjects in an upright, frontal position (with tolerance for some side movement). Based on the original form of the database, we rotated each image every 30°. It means each single image now has 12 duplications with different orientations. The total size of our database is 4, 800. The samples of the database are shown in Fig. 4.

   We further divided the database into two categories for experiments: *category I* and *category II*. Category I includes eight images with 12 orientations of each subject for the first 30 subjects, totally 2, 880. Category II includes the rest of the database, which includes two images with 12 orientations of each subject for the first 30 subjects and all ten images with 12 orientations of each subject for the last *ten* subjects, totally 1,920.
2. *Experimental Plan* Three separate experiments are planed to demonstrate the performance of HOOPLBP in face orientation detection.
   a. Use HOOPLBP to test the face orientation of the same image with different orientations. Compare the result with other content-based images.
   b. Use HOOPLBP to build one model for each orientation using database *category I* and compare the 12 models to test if the models have bit-wise shift relations.

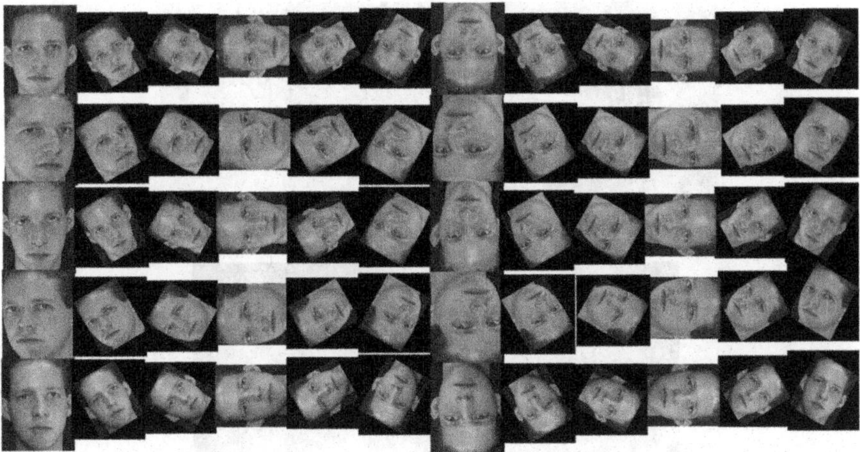

Fig. 4 Samples of the database used in the experiment: one person with different frontal position and 12 orientations

   c. Use HOOPLBP to build one model from *category I* and use it for face orientation detection in *category II* to test the recognition rate.

3. *Experimental Results* In the rest of the section, we present the experimental results according to the experimental plan using the Database of Faces.

   a. In this experiment, we use bisection method to find the minimum range of optimum performance of orientation detection. The example of orientation detection on human face and other content-based images using the content-independent HOOPLBP are shown in Fig. 5. The range lies in around 30° with other content-based images, while the range decreases to less than 5° with human face images. Therefore, HOOPLBP shows better results in face images than others with the same pre-processing techniques and environments.
   b. In this experiment, we use the mean of each orientation of *category I* for each model which are shown in Fig. 6. (The histogram in Fig. 6 are not processed by our proposed algorithm of HOOPLBP in order to show that the features of 0, 90, 180 and 270 are not dominant with facial images. That may be a reason that HOOPLBP performs better with facial images than images with other contents.) It means each model is built from 240 images. From the figure, we can observe the movements of the four waves, 30°/each time, which shows their bit-wise shift relations. The orientation detection rate is 100% among these 12 models. Because we get the models from the means of different images, we can conclude that HOOPLBP is a content-independent orientation descriptor and works very well with human faces.
   c. From the above experiment, the 12 models have close bit-wise shift relations. Therefore we simply use the upright face model as a universal model for this experiment. The HOOPLBP of a normal single face and the histogram after average filter is shown in Fig. 7. The orientation recognition rate with

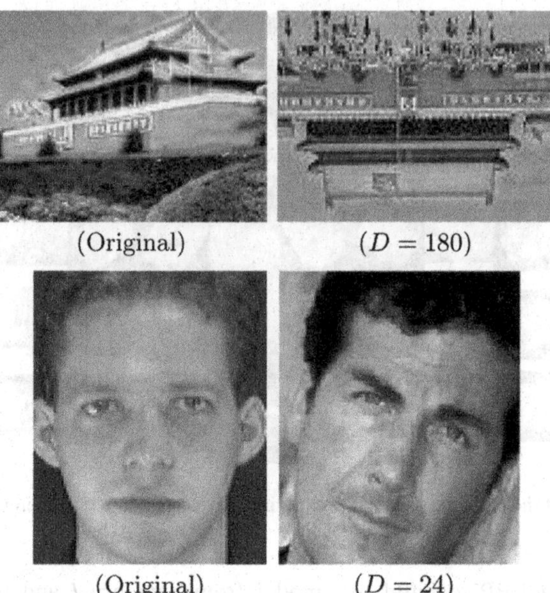

Fig. 5 Examples of content-independent orientation detection using the HOOPLBP. *D* denotes the detected degree by the HOOPLBP

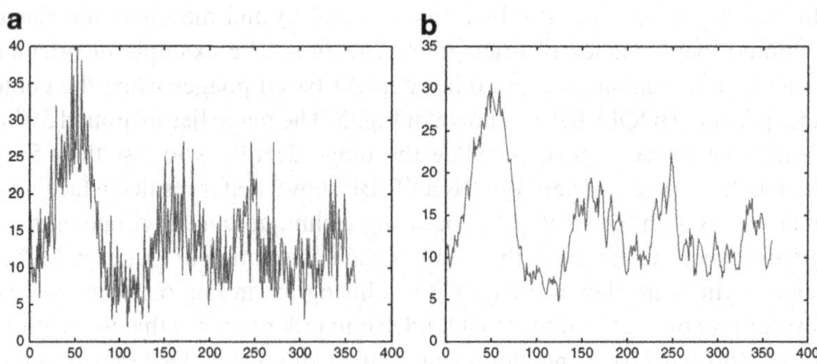

Fig. 6 The HOOPLBP models for 12 orientations. *D* denotes the rotation degree between the model and the upright face model

database *category II* is 66. 67% with 80% upright face orientation recognition rate. We concern about the orientation recognition rate of upright face more, because they can be detected by present face detection approaches. We don't want them be mis-detected by our algorithm. By multiplying $\lambda(0 < \lambda < 1)$ with the *chi-square* value around $0°$, we can increase the orientation recognition rate of upright face without decrease the overall orientation detection rate a lot. When $\lambda = 0.9$, the orientation recognition rate over *category II* is 63. 02% with 90. 62% upright face orientation recognition rate.

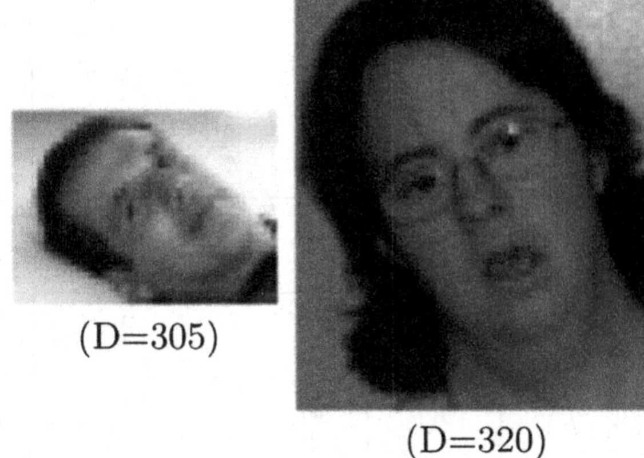

Fig. 7 The HOOPLBP of a normal single face and the feature after average filter

The experiments show a very impressive results, especially the orientation recognition rate with 100% among the models. Considering that the images have differences in the head orientation, the lighting and the scaling and the face details are also various at beard, wrinkles, glasses and expressions, the orientation recognition rate is good enough. From Fig. 7a, the HOOPLBP of a single face contains many high-frequency signals, but the ensemble shows clear indication and very similar with the above models.

Furthermore, the general model we used in the above experiment(c), is not constrained to the ORL database, but can be used in other face images, as shown in Fig. 8. From the experiment, we see that HOOPLBP is not only a scale invariant descriptor, but also can detect face orientation with some out-of-plane rotation.

4 Conclusion

The feature of HOOPLBP is dominated by the unwanted feature values of 0, 90, 180 and 270 which negatively affect the detections. By mapping back from the feature values to their pixels in the image, we analyzed the pixels and their neighbors and we are successful to reduce those features without losing much information from other pixels. However, this set of features are not dominate with facial images, which may explain why the HOOPLBP performs better with facial images. Furthermore, we guess, from another perspective, this help to state why human facial research is a very active and successful area in our society. Then, we set up a set of experiments for the application of human face orientation detection and got very positive and impressive results. Based on LBP, HOOPLBP gets better results in human face images than other content-based images.

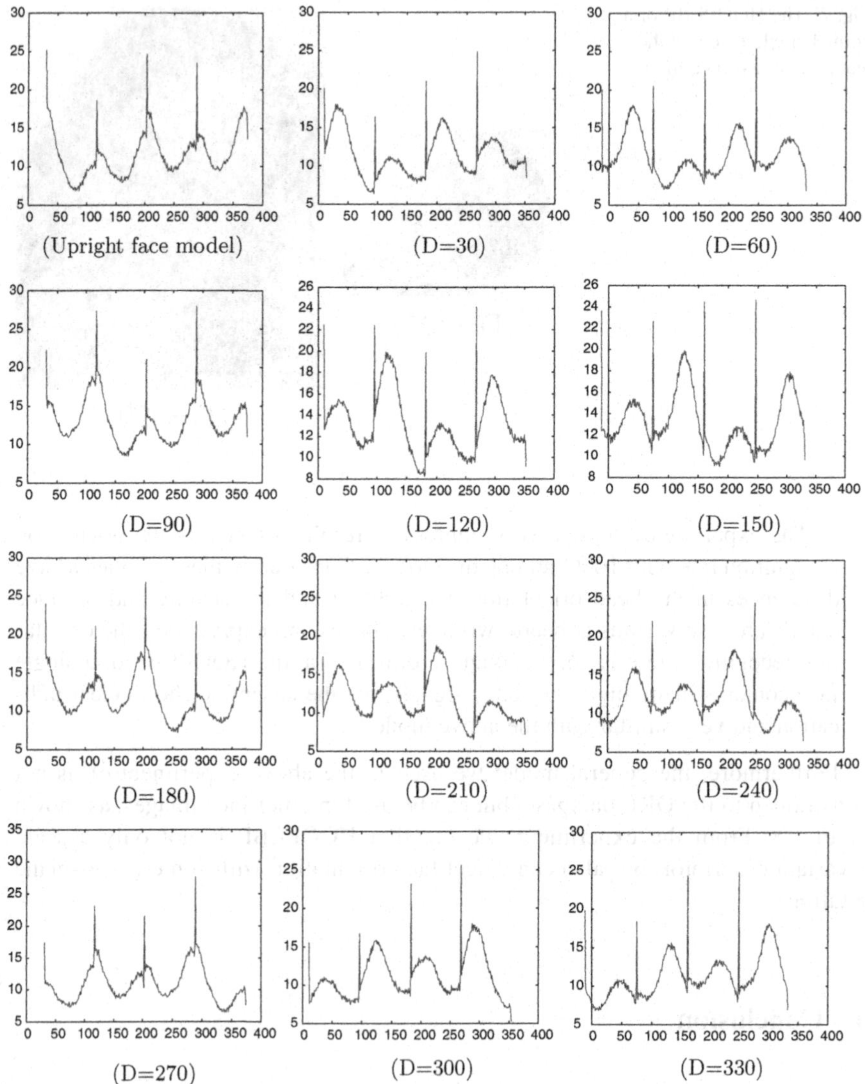

Fig. 8 Orientation detection using the trained general model from the ORL database. D denotes the rotation degree

The algorithm can successfully detect face orientations, rotated up to ±180° in the image plane. In the experiments, we used the ORL database, which contains images taken under various situations, including lights, facial expressions and shooting angle. Without further pre-processing and training, the overall recognition rate can achieve 63. 02% with upright face recognition rate to 90. 62%. The approach is not constrained to the ORL database, but can be used in other face images.

The state-of-the-art face detection system uses either a pyramid searching scheme or a candidate selection based scheme. One advantage of candidate selection based method is fast, which can eliminate most of the non-face regions. In the future, we will propose a hybrid face detection algorithm which integrates the candidate selection phase with our HOOPLBP operation to successfully detect faces with rotation within the plane. The future research will also focus on learning a better model to increase the orientation detection rate and trying to use HOOPLBP in other computer vision fields.

References

1. N. Dong and L. Guan, "Content-free Image Orientation Detection Using Local Binary Pattern", *IEEE International Workshop on Multimedia Signal Processing (MMSP)*, Rio de Janeiro, Brazil, October, 2009.
2. Y. Tie and L. Guan, "Automatic face detection in video sequences using local normalization and optimal adaptive correlation techniques," *Pattern Recognition*, 2008.
3. T. Ojala, M. Pietikainen and T. Maenpaa, "Gray scale and rotation invariant texture classification with local binary patterns," *Lecture Notes in Computer Science*, vol. 1842, pp. 404–420, 2000.
4. T. Ahonen, A. Hadid and M. Pietikainen, "Face description with local binary patterns: Application to face recognition," *IEEE Transactions on Pattern Analysis and Machine Intelligence*, vol. 28, no. 12, pp. 2037, 2006.
5. C. Garcia and M. Delakis, "Convolutional face finder: A neural architecture for fast and robust face detection," *IEEE Transactions on Pattern Analysis and Machine Intelligence*, vol. 26, no. 11, pp. 1408–1423, 2004.
6. F. Samaria and A. Harter, "Parameterisation of a stochastic model for human face identification," in *Applications of Computer Vision, 1994., Proceedings of the Second IEEE Workshop on*, 1994, pp. 138–142.

Fast Eye Detection and Localization Using a Salient Map

Muwei Jian and Kin-Man Lam

Abstract Among the facial features, the eyes play the most important role in face recognition and face hallucination. In this paper, an efficient algorithm for eye detection in face images is proposed. The proposed algorithm is robust to illumination variations, size, and orientation of face images. As the eye region always has the most variations in a face image, our algorithm uses a wavelet-based salient map, which can detect and reflect the most visually meaningful regions for eye detection and localization. Our proposed algorithm is non-iterative and computationally simple. Experimental results show that our algorithm can achieve a superior performance compared to other current methods.

Keywords Eye detection • Salient map • Facial landmarks • Face recognition

1 Introduction

Face recognition has a wide range of applications, and still has many technical and challenging issues to be solved [1]. It has therefore attracted attention from different industrial sectors and from academic researchers of different subject areas, such as pattern recognition, psychology, criminology, machine learning, computer interaction, computer vision, etc. [2]. Over the past several decades, many face recognition approaches have been proposed: Principal Component Analysis (PCA) [3–7] and Linear Discriminant Analysis (LDA) [8–11] are two of the most common approaches, and have always been used as benchmarks for face recognition. However, these typical approaches face recognition algorithms require an accurate position of the two eyes and the mouth for normalization and alignment. The performances of these

M. Jian • K.-M. Lam (✉)
Department of Electronic and Information Engineering, The Hong Kong Polytechnic University, Hung Hom, Kowloon, Hong Kong
e-mail: 10902666r@polyu.edu.hk; enkmlam@polyu.edu.hk

J.S. Jin et al., *The Era of Interactive Media*,
DOI 10.1007/978-1-4614-3501-3_8,

algorithms will degrade if the face images under consideration are not aligned properly. Similarly, most of the face hallucination (or face super-resolution) algorithms [12] also require an accurate alignment of the key facial features.

Most of these face hallucination and face recognition algorithms assume that the face images under consideration have been aligned accurately with respect to the important facial features, such as the eyes and mouth. This assumption makes these algorithms semi-automatic. Most of the existing facial feature detection and localization algorithms [2] cannot work accurately and reliably when the eyes are closed, the faces are rotated, or the face are under a poor lighting condition. This will, in turn, have an adverse effect on the performance of both face hallucination and face recognition algorithms. In real applications, face detection will be performed first in order to locate the positions of faces [13, 14]. Then, facial feature detection is carried out in the detected face region. Based on the detected eye positions or some other facial feature points, the face regions can be normalized and aligned so that an accurate face recognition or hallucination result can be achieved.

A lot of research has been conducted on detecting facial landmarks (such as eyes, mouth, etc.) in face images and video clips. In [15], a template-based approach was proposed to detect and locate the human eyes in a frontal face. This approach has difficulty when the appearance of the features changes significantly, for example, closed eyes, open mouth, etc. Another template-based approach to detecting the eyes and mouth in real images was presented in [18], which is based on matching predefined parameterized templates to an image that contains a face region. Energy functionals are defined, which link the edges, peaks, valleys, etc. of the image intensity to the deformable templates. The minimization of these energy functions requires changing the template parameters iteratively so as to fit an image. The Active Shape Model [17] was proposed in terms of handling shape variations of human faces using statistical models. However, the statistical-shape model is manually designed, and the fitting is also done iteratively. In [19], a corner-detection scheme is first employed to locate possible facial-feature candidates in a head-and-shoulders image, and the approximate positions of the features are estimated by means of average anthropometric measures. Based on the rough positions of the facial features, the eye templates can be initialized and used to localize the eyes more accurately. Many other methods have also been devised for eye detection. A multi-layer perception (MLP) eye finder was proposed by Jesorsky et al. in [30]. In [16], a generalized projection function (GPF) was defined, and the hybrid projection function (HPF) was used to determine the optimal parameters of the GPF for eye detection. Recently, an approach for human-face detection and facial-feature extraction was proposed using a genetic algorithm and the Eigenface technique in [20]. As the genetic algorithm is, in general, computationally intensive, the searching space is limited around the eye regions so that the required runtime can be greatly reduced. In addition, some other state-of-the-art eye-detection approaches have been proposed. A method using pixel-to-edge information was proposed in [31], which employs the length and slope information about the closest edge pixels to detect and locate eyes. In [32], an eye-location algorithm based on the radial-symmetry transform was proposed. A symmetry magnitude map was computed using the transform to identify possible eye candidates. Campadelli et al. [33] proposed a method using the support vector machine and the Haar wavelet coefficients for eye detection. Hamouz et al. [34] proposed a method using Gabor features. A feature-based, affine-invariant method using isophote curvature was proposed by Valenti et al. in [35] for eye localization. Recently, an eye tracking and blink detection system was proposed in [39].

This paper proposes a novel scheme based on a wavelet-based salient map for human eye detection and localization. First, an improved salient-point detector is introduced, which can extract salient points in an image more accurately than existing detectors. Then, the improved salient-point detector is extended for eye detection and localization, but its improvement in this algorithm for the task of human eye detection is not robust. That is because, although the salient-point detector can express the points' variations in the image, there are too many visual salient points in a human face, such as corner points and edges of the eyebrows, eyes, nose, lips and so on. The salient-point detector can locate the visually meaningful points in those corner points and edges, but it is hard to ensure the first two salient points are detected and located in the eyes. Fortunately, it is observed that the regions of the two eyes are always the most varied blocks in a face image. Therefore, in our algorithm, the saliency at a point is calculated as the sum of saliency values inside a rectangular box centered at the point. We can locate some rectangles with maximum saliency values as the possible eye–region candidates. Then, pairs of eye regions will be formed, and then verified using a fitness function to identify the best pair of eyes.

The rest of the paper is organized as follows. In Sect. 2, we introduce the proposed algorithm for human eye detection and localization based on the salient map. Experimental results are presented in Sect. 3. Finally, we conclude the paper in Sect. 4.

2 Human Eye Detection and Localization

2.1 An Improved Salient-Point Detector

Due to the resemblance between multi-resolution filtering and human visual processing, wavelet-transform techniques have successfully been used to analyze spatial-frequency content [21]. An extensive comparison of salient-point techniques can be found in [22–27].

Orthogonal wavelet with a compact support leads to a non-redundant and a complete representation of signals. Using orthogonal wavelet, the wavelet coefficient at each signal point is computed, at scales of 2^j. The wavelet transform can therefore provide information about the variations in a signal at different scales. A local absolute maximum value of the wavelet coefficients at a coarse resolution corresponds to a region with high global variation in the signal. In other words, salient points can be detected by finding a relevant point to represent the global variation by searching coefficients at finer resolutions.

For wavelets with a compact support, a wavelet coefficient, computed as $W_{2^j}f(n)$ where W^{2j} and $f(n)$ are the wavelet function and the signal, respectively, at the scale 2^j is computed with $2^{-j}p$ signal points, where p is the wavelet regularity. We can further investigate the wavelet coefficients at the finer scale 2^{j+1}. At the scale 2^{j+1}, there is a set of the coefficients computed with the same signal points as a coefficient at the scale 2^j. We call these coefficients, $C(W_{2^j}f(n))$, the children of the coefficient $W_{2^j}f(n)$, and they are related as follows:

$$C(W_{2^j}f(n)) = \{W_{2^{j+1}}f(k), 2n \leq k \leq 2n + 2p - 1\}, \tag{1}$$

where $0 \leq n \leq 2^jN$ and N is the length of the signal. The children coefficients $C(W_{2^j}f(n))$ reflect the variations of the 2^jp signal points, and the most salient point should have the wavelet coefficient with the largest absolute value. Salient points can therefore be detected by considering this maximum, and the children are then searched. By applying this process recursively, all the salient points can be identified. The following formulation has been used to compute saliency values for detecting salient points in [22–27]:

$$saliency = \sum_{k=1}^{-j} |C^{(k)}(W_{2^j}f(n))|,\ 0 \leq n \leq 2^jN,\ -\log_2 N \leq j \leq -1. \tag{2}$$

However, the largest absolute values of the wavelet coefficients at different scales have different mean values and ranges. The set of maximum wavelet coefficients at the first level have larger magnitudes than those at the second level, and so on. This result actually follows the wavelet transform theory [21]. In order to extract salient points more accurately, the maximum values at different scales should be normalized. In this paper, we propose an improved salient-point detector as follows:

$$saliency = \sum_{k=1}^{-j} |w(k)C^{(k)}(W_{2^j}f(n))|,\ 0 \leq n \leq 2^jN,\ -\log_2 N \leq j \leq -1, \tag{3}$$

where $w(k)$ is the weight to be assigned to the maximum wavelet coefficients at different scales. The weight $w(k)$ is the reciprocal of the standard deviation of the coefficients, which is defined as follows:

$$\mu_k = \frac{1}{S}\sum_{z=1}^{S} |W_{2^k}f(z)|, \tag{4}$$

$$\sigma_k = \frac{1}{S}\sum_{z=1}^{S} ([W_{2^k}f(z) - \mu_k]^2)^{\frac{1}{2}}, \tag{5}$$

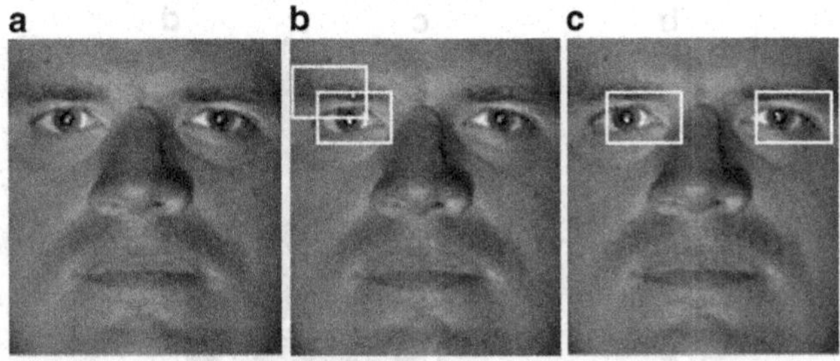

Fig. 1 Comparison of eye detection using different salient-point detectors: (**a**) original image, (**b**) eye detection using the traditional method with the Db4 wavelet and (**c**) eye detection using the improved method with the Db4 wavelet. *White boxes* indicate the detected eye positions

and

$$w(k) = 1/\sigma_k, \tag{6}$$

where $W_{2^k}f(z)$ is an element in the set of maximum coefficients with $0 \leq z \leq S$, and S is the number of maximum wavelet coefficients at k level. In practice, if M salient points are detected in an image, we can set $S = 1.5\,M$. In practice, M can be set at 60.

Our proposed algorithm is applied to three different subbands, namely the horizontal-detail, vertical-detail, and diagonal-detail subbands, denoted as H, V, and D, respectively. The total saliency value of a point is the sum of the weighted saliency values computed from these three subbands. More details on the improved salient-point detector can be found in [[22, 27, 28, 36].

Figure 1 shows a detection result for our improved salient-point detector. As shown in Fig. 1c, the improved salient-point detector can detect the visually meaningful points more accurately. Our previous work in [28] also demonstrates that our improved method can extract salient points more accurately than the transitional methods [22–27].

2.2 *Extension of Salient-Point Detection to Eye Detection and Localization*

As the improved salient-point detection method can extract salient points in images more accurately and effectively, we therefore extend it to the task of eye detection and localization. However, the salient-point detection is not specific to eye detection, so the detection results are inaccurate and not robust. Although the salient-point detector can represent the variations around the points in an image, it is hard to judge whether or not the salient points detected belong to the two eyes.

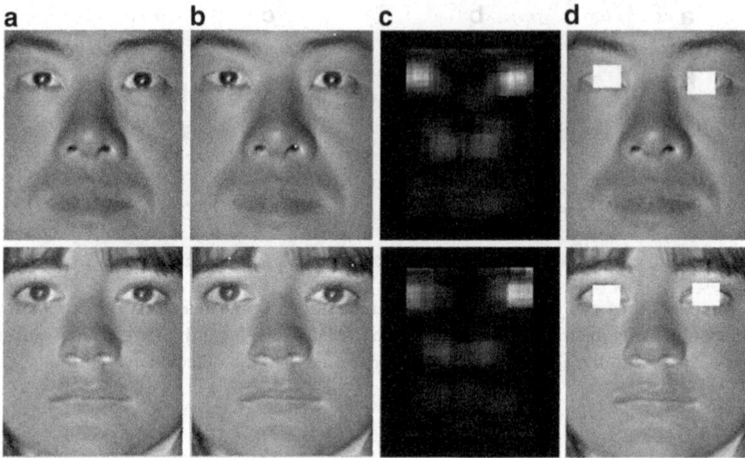

Fig. 2 Results of eye detection and localization with face images pre-processed by illumination normalization: (**a**) the original images, (**b**) using the improved salient-point method with the Db4 wavelet, (**c**) the salient maps, and (**d**) using the proposed region-based salient-detection scheme

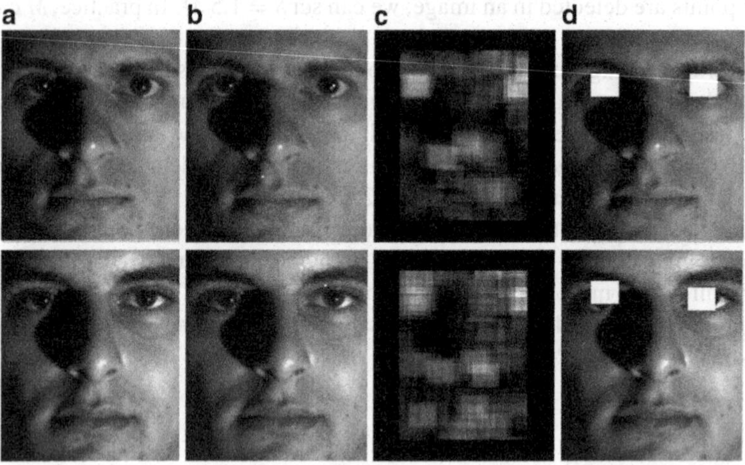

Fig. 3 Results of eye detection and localization without illumination normalization performed: (**a**) the original images, (**b**) using the improved salient-point method with the Db4 wavelet, (**c**) the salient maps, and (**d**) using the proposed region-based salient-detection scheme

Figures 2b and 3b illustrate some examples of eye detection and localization results using the improved salient-point detection method with the Db4 wavelet. It can be seen that a direct use of the improved salient-point detector for eye detection is not effective.

2.3 Eye Detection and Localization Based on the Salient Map

As the two eye regions are the most varied blocks in a face image, many salient points are therefore detected in these regions. In order to detect and locate the eyes, instead of considering salient points, the salient values of the regions are computed. The two blocks in a face image which have the largest total saliency values are identified to be the eye positions.

Define a rectangle region Rect(x, y), whose center coordinates are (x, y), and whose length and width aredenoted as *len* and *wid*, respectively. Consider the wavelet coefficients at the scale 2^j in Rect(x, y), we can further investigate the region at the finer scale 2^{j+1}, where a set of coefficients is computed using the same points at the scale 2^j, i.e. the children in Rect(x, y). These children coefficients reflect the variations inside Rect(x, y), and the most salient Rect(x, y) is the one that has the largest sum of absolute wavelet coefficients at the scale 2^{j+1}.

The algorithm is applied to three different subbands (i.e. H, V, D). If the different rectangles based on different subbands lead to the same position, the sum of the saliency values of the three subbands is computed to form the saliency values. The saliency at (x, y) of the resulting salient map of an image is computed by summing the saliency values inside Rect(x, y). Some positions with maximum saliency values are considered to be candidates for possible eye positions. In our algorithm, 10 rectangular regions, denoted as Rect$_i$(x, y), with maximum saliency values are selected as the eye–region candidates. The total saliency value of the region Rect$_i$(x, y) is denoted as S_i, and the respective saliency values of the horizontal, vertical, and diagonal subbands are denoted as S_i^h, S_i^v, and S_i^d. It is obvious that the eye regions are always the most varied blocks in a face image, and the two eye regions of a face should be similar to each other. Therefore, the following fitness function is defined for a pair of eye-region candidates:

$$fit(i,j) = (S_i + S_j) - \lambda\left(\left|S_i^h - S_j^h\right| + \left|S_i^v - S_j^v\right| + \left|S_i^d - S_j^d\right|\right), \qquad (7)$$

which measures the similarity between the ith and the jth eye-region candidates, as well as the total saliency of the two regions. λ is used to define the importance of the similarity between two eye regions, which is determined empirically. The pair of eye regions which has the largest fitness value will be selected as the two best eye regions in a face.

3 Experiments

Experiments have been conducted to evaluate the effectiveness of our scheme. In each of the experiments, the eye detection and localization algorithm is tested using a wide range of face images and a simple geometric constraint of

Table 1 Detection rates with e $\leq$ 0.25 for Experiment 1 and Experiment 2

Accuracy rate of:	Experiment 1	Experiment 2
The improved salient point method	**1.58%**	**1.05%**
The improved method in this paper	**98.68%**	**90.54%**

considering only the top half of the face images. All the face images are obtained from a face detector, which forms and resizes face images of size 168×196. All the experiments also use the Db4 wavelet with 3 levels of decomposition [21], and set the eye-region size with $len = 25$ and $wid = 21$. By experiments, we found that $\lambda = 5$ can produce a robust and good result. The detection accuracy is measured as follows [30]:

$$e = \max(d_l, d_r)/d_{lr}, \tag{8}$$

where d_l and d_r are the Euclidean distances between the located positions and the corresponding ground-true positions of the left and right eyes, respectively, and d_{lr} is the Euclidean distance between the two eyes of the ground truth. In practice, a quarter of the inter-ocular distance (the distance between the eye center and the corresponding eye corner), i.e. $e \leq 0.25$, is used as a criterion to assess the accuracy.

3.1 *Experiment 1*

In order to test the effectiveness of the proposed method under illumination variations, experiments were carried out using the Yale Face Database B [37] and the extended Yale Face Database B [38], which have been commonly used to evaluate the performances of illumination-invariant face recognition methods. The Yale Face Database B consists of 10 classes, named from yaleB01 to yaleB10. The extended Yale Face Database B contains 28 human subjects, named from yaleB11 to yaleB13, and from yaleB15 to yaleB39. Each subject in these two databases is under 9 poses and 64 illumination conditions. The total number of distinct subjects in the two databases is 38. As the Yale Face Database B provides different illumination conditions of the same person, before performing eye detection and localization, an efficient illumination-normalization method based on [29] was performed. Four images per class were selected randomly, i.e. 38 × 4 = 152 in total, in this experiment. Figure 2c shows the salient maps of the original images, which can effectively reflect the variations around the eye regions. Figure 2d shows some eye-detection results using the proposed approach. Table 1 tabulates the detection accuracy. Based on our region-based scheme, the detection rate with $e \leq 0.25$ is 98.6842%, with illumination normalization used.

3.2 Experiment 2

In this section, we will evaluate the robustness of our proposed schemes when the face images are under different illumination variations. Similar to Experiment 1, the Yale Face Database B and the extended Yale Face Database B [38] are used, but the face images have not been pre-processed by any illumination-normalization operations. The face images named **_P00A-035E-20 and **_P00A + 035E-20 (** represents yaleB01-yaleB13 and yaleB15- yaleB39) were selected in the experiment, i.e. $38 \times 2 = 76$ images in total. Figure 2 shows some detection results. Although the face images used in this experiment have their illumination conditions changed dramatically, Fig. 3 shows that the proposed method can still located the eye region accurately. Table 1 shows that 67 out of 76 face images have the eye positions detected accurately, with $e \leq 0.25$, and the detection rate is 90.54%.

Experiments have demonstrated the effectiveness of our proposed scheme on images under different illumination conditions. Experimental results show that using the improved salient-point detector directly for eye detection and localization achieves a low detection rate; only 1.26% on average. By considering the total saliency inside blocks, the two eyes in a face image can be detected and located accurately, with detection rates of 98.68% and 90.54% when the face images are with and without illumination normalization, respectively.

3.3 Summary and Discussion of the Experimental Results

Experiments have verified the effectiveness of our proposed scheme. Following are some additional advantages of our proposed method:

1. Compared to those statistical-learning-based methods [32–34], our proposed method does not need any training or learning in advance—which usually requires a lot of training samples and is time-consuming.
2. In contrast to the projection-based [16] and template-based approaches [15, 18], our proposed method can locate accurately the eye regions of face images under variations of illumination, pose, facial expression, perspective, and resolution. Since the computation of saliency values considers the saliency from three different directional wavelet subbands. Experiments show that the proposed scheme is insensitive to face orientations and robust to detect the eyes even if the face images are under rotated, tilted or perspective variations.
3. The computational complexity of our proposed method is low: it requires only the computation of a salient map. The computation required is therefore linearly proportional to the image size, so it is suitable for real-time applications.

4 Conclusion

In this paper, we have proposed an efficient algorithm for eye detection in face images. The proposed algorithm can locate eyes accurately for face images under illumination variations, uncontrolled circumstances, with different resolutions and orientations, etc. An improved wavelet-based salient-point detector is employed in our algorithm, which can detect salient points in an image more accurately. We extend this improved salient-point detector to eye detection by considering the total saliency within blocks. Experiment results show that our method can achieve a high detection accuracy level, and its performance is comparable to existing state-of-the-art algorithms. Our method also has the advantages of being non-iterative and computationally inexpensive.

Acknowledgement The work described in this paper was supported by a grant from RGC of the HKSAR, China (Project No. PolyU 5187/11E).

References

1. Viola, P. and Jones, M. J.: Robust real-time face detection. IJCV, 57(2):137–154, 2004.
2. Zhao, W., Chellappa, R., Rosenfeld, A., Phillips, P.J.: Face Recognition: A Literature Survey, ACM Computing Surveys, 2003, pp. 399–458.
3. Kirby, M., Sirovich, L.: Application of the Karhunen-Loeve procedure for the characterization of human faces. IEEE Trans. Patt. Anal. Mach. Intell. 12, 1990.
4. Turk, M., Pentland, A.: Eigenfaces for Recognition, Journal of Cognitive Neurosicence, Vol. 3, No. 1, 1991, pp. 71–86.
5. Turk, M.A., Pentland, A.P.: Face Recognition Using Eigenfaces, Proceedings of the IEEE Conference on Computer Vision and Pattern Recognition, 3–6 June 1991, pp. 586–591.
6. Pentland, A., Moghaddam, B., Starner, T.: View-Based and Modular Eigenspaces for Face Recognition, Proceedings of the IEEE CVPR, 21–23 June 1994,, pp. 84–91.
7. Moon, H., Phillips, P.J.: Computational and Performance aspects of PCA-based Face Recognition Algorithms, Perception, Vol. 30, 2001, pp. 303–321.
8. Etemad, K., Chellappa, R.: Discriminant Analysis for Recognition of Human Face Images, Journal of the Optical Society of America A, Vol. 14, No. 8, August 1997, pp. 1724–1733.
9. Belhumeur, P.N., Hespanha, J.P., Kriegman, D.J.: Eigenfaces vs. Fisherfaces: Recognition using class specific linear projection. IEEE Trans. Patt. Anal. Mach. Intell. 19, 711–720. 1997.
10. Martinez, A.M., Kak, A.C.: PCA versus LDA, IEEE Trans. on Pattern Analysis and Machine Intelligence, Vol. 23, No. 2, 2001, pp. 228–233.
11. Lu, J., Plataniotis, K.N., Venetsanopoulos, A.N.: Face Recognition Using LDA-Based Algorithms, IEEE Trans. on Neural Networks, Vol. 14, No. 1, January 2003, pp. 195–200.
12. Hu, Y., Lam, K.M., Qiu G.P., Shen, T.Z.: From Local Pixel Structure to Global Image Super-Resolution: A New Face Hallucination Framework. IEEE Transactions on Image Processing 20(2):433–445 (2011).
13. MARTINEZ, A.: Recognizing imprecisely localized, partially occluded and expression variant faces from a single sample per class. IEEE Trans. Patt. Anal. Mach. Intell. 24, 748–763, 2002.
14. YANG, M. H., KRIEGMAN, D., AND AHUJA,N.: Detecting faces in images: A survey. IEEE Trans. Patt. Anal. Mach. Intell. 24, 34–58, 2002.
15. HALLINAN, P.W.: Recognizing human eyes. In SPIE Proceedings, Vol. 1570: Geometric Methods In Computer Vision. 214–226, 1991.

16. Zhou, Z.H., Geng, X.,: Projection functions for eye detection. Pattern Recognition 37(5): 1049–1056 (2004).
17. COOTES, T. F., EDWARDS, G. J., AND TAYLOR, C. J.: Active appearance models. IEEE Trans. Patt. Anal. Mach. Intell. 23, 681–685, 2001.
18. YUILLE, A. L., COHEN, D. S., AND HALLINAN, P. W.: Feature extracting from faces using deformable templates. Int. J. Comput. Vis. 8, 99–112, 1992.
19. Lam, K.M., Yan, H.: Locating and extracting the eye in human face images. Pattern Recognition 29(5): 771–779, 1996.
20. Wong, K.W., Lam, K.M., Siu, W.C.: A novel approach for human face detection from color images under complex background. Pattern Recognition 34(10): 1993–2004 (2001).
21. Daubechies, I.: Orthonormal Bases of Compactly Supported Wavelets, Communications on Pure and Applied Mathematics, 1988, Vol. 41, pp. 909–996.
22. Sebe, N., Tian, Q., Loupias, E., Lew, M.S. and Huang, T.S.: Color indexing using wavelet-based salient points. In IEEE Workshop on Content-based Access of Image and Video Libraries,pages 15–19, 2000.
23. Tian, Q., Sebe, N., E., Lew, M.S. and Huang, T.S.: Image retrieval using wavelet-based salient points. Journal of Electronic Imaging, (2001) 835–849.
24. Sebe, N., Lew, M.S.: Salient points for content-based retrieval, in: British Machine Vision Conference (BMVC'01) (2001) 401–410.
25. Sebe, N., Tian, Q., Loupias, E., Lew, M.S. and Huang, T.S.: Evaluation of salient point techniques, in: International Conference on Image and Video Retrieval (CIVR'02) (2002) 367–377.
26. Sebe, N., Lew, M.S.: Comparing salient point detectors, Pattern Recognition Letters 24 (1–3) (2003) 89–96.
27. Sebe, N., Tian, Q., Loupias, E., Lew, M.S. and Huang, T.S.: Evaluation of salient point techniques, Image and Vision Computing, Volume 21, Issues 13–14, 1 December 2003, Pages 1087–1095.
28. Jian, M.W., Dong, Y.J.: Wavelet-Based Salient Regions and their Spatial Distribution for Image Retrieval, 2007 Int. Conf. on Multimedia & Expo,. 2–5 July 2007. pp: 2194–2197.
29. Xie, X., Lam, K.M.: An efficient illumination normalization method for face recognition. Pattern Recognition Letters 27(6): 609–617, 2006.
30. Jesorsky, O., Kirchbergand, K. J. and Frischholz, R.: Robust face detection using the Hausdorff distance. In Audio and Video Biom. Pers. Auth., pages 90–95, 1992.
31. Asteriadis, S., Nikolaidis, N., Hajdu, A., and Pitas, I.: An eye detection algorithm using pixel to edge information. In Int. Symp. on Control, Commun. and Sign. Proc., 2006.
32. Bai, L., Shen, L. and Wang, Y.: A novel eye location algorithm based on radial symmetry transform. In ICPR, pages 511–514, 2006.
33. Campadelli, P., Lanzarotti, R. and Lipori, G.: Precise eye localization through a general-to-specific model definition. In BMVC, 2006.
34. Hamouz, M., Kittlerand, J., Kamarainen, J. K., Paalanen, P., Kalviainen, H. and Matas, J.: Feature-based affine-invariant localization of faces. PAMI, 27(9):1490–1495, 2005.
35. Valenti, R. and Gevers, Th.: Accurate Eye Center Location and Tracking Using Isophote Curvature, IEEE CVPR, Alaska, USA, June 24–26, 2008.
36. Jian, M.W., Dong, J.Y., Ma, J.: Image retrieval using wavelet-based salient regions, Imaging Science Journal, The, Volume 59, Number 4, August 2011, pp. 219–231.
37. Lee, K.C., Ho, J. and Kriegman, D.: Acquiring Linear Subspaces for Face Recognition under Variable Lighting, IEEE Trans. Pattern Anal. Mach. Intell., 2005, vol. 27, no. 5, pp. 684–698.
38. Georghiades, A.S., Belhumeur, P.N. and Kriegman, D.J.: From Few to Many: Illumination Cone Models for Face Recognition under Variable Lighting and Pose, IEEE Trans. Pattern Anal. Mach. Intell., 2001, vol. 23, no. 6, pp. 643–660.
39. Wu, J., Trivedi, M.M.: An eye localization, tracking and blink pattern recognition system: Algorithm and evaluation. TOMCCAP, Volume 6 Issue 2, March 2010.

Eyeglasses Removal from Facial Image Based on MVLR

Zhigang Zhang and Yu Peng

Abstract Eyeglass is a kind of common interfering factor in face recognition and analysis. A statistical learning method is presented to remove eyeglass from an input facial image for this problem. First, training samples are collected from facial images wearing eyeglasses and their corresponding facial images without eyeglasses. Then, a model of multi-variable linear regression is established based on linear correlation assumption between two sets of samples. Finally, the parameters matrix is solved by which the eyeglasses can be removed from an input facial image. Experimental results have demonstrated that the proposed algorithm is efficient and practical. The method is easy to be realized without any auxiliary equipment.

Keywords Multi-variable linear regression • Eyeglasses • Removal

1 Introduction

In recent years, face recognition and analysis have become one of the most active research areas in pattern recognition and computer vision [1,2]. As one of the prerequisite research works, some interfering factors must be removed or pre-processed from input facial images, such as pose, eyeglasses, expression and shadow [3,4]. In most cases, eyeglasses are common occluding objects in facial images, which

Z. Zhang (✉)
School of Information, Xi'an University of Finance and Economics, Xi'an, Shaanxi, PRC

Faculty of Engineering and Information Technology, University of Technology, Sydney, Australia
e-mail: zzg@xaufe.edu.cn

Y. Peng
School of Design, Communication & IT, University of Newcastle, Newcastle, Australia

J.S. Jin et al., *The Era of Interactive Media*,
DOI 10.1007/978-1-4614-3501-3_9,

may greatly affect the recognition performance [5]. Therefore, it is of great importance to analyze removal of eyeglasses for face detection, recognition and synthesis.

In order to solve the problem, some research works have concentrated on removal of eyeglasses. A Morkov chain Monte Carlo method was employed to locate the eyeglasses by searching for the global optimum of the posteriori, then, an example based approach was developed to synthesize an image with eyeglasses removed from the detected and localized face image [6], however, as a prerequisite condition, the position of rimless eyeglasses is hard to detect accurately using this method. In the field of infrared face recognition, a method of region eigenface component compensation based on eigenfaces was proposed to solve eyeglasses interference, in this method, the eyeglasses was detected at first, then, eigenface components can be extracted from infrared face for compensating the following classification, nevertheless, this algorithm was only used for infrared face recognition [7]. Another concept based on synthesis can also be used for the eyeglasses removal, by which some natural looking eyeglassless facial image can be synthesized based on recursive error compensation using principle component analysis reconstruction [8]. More generally, an innovative three dimensional occlusion detection and restoration strategy was presented for the recognition of three dimensional faces partially occluded by unforeseen, extraneous objects, which considers occlusions as local deformations of the face that correspond to perturbations in a space designed to represent non-occluded faces, but the algorithm was built on the basis of three dimension environment [9].

Based on the research works above mentioned, in this paper, a samples statistics method based upon the model of multi-variable linear regression has been adopted to establish a linear relationship between facial images wearing eyeglasses and there corresponding facial images without eyeglasses, then, the parameters matrix can be solved by which the eyeglasses can be removed from an input facial image. Experimental results in this paper demonstrate the practicability and effectiveness of this approach.

2 Model of Multi-Variable Linear Regression

The model of multi-variable linear regression is mainly used to analyze experimental data based on linear correlation assumption [10].

For two sets of variables: X, Y:

$$X = [x_1, x_2, x_i, \ldots, x_s],\ x_i = [x_{i1}, x_{i2}, \ldots, x_{in}]^{\mathrm{T}}$$

$$Y = [y_1, y_2, y_i, \ldots, y_s],\ y_i = [y_{i1}, y_{i2}, \ldots, y_{im}]^{\mathrm{T}} \tag{1}$$

Where X is an n-by-s matrix, and Y is an m-by-s matrix. Normally, n is not equal to m. Suppose that the corresponding linear relationship exists between X and Y.

$$X = LY + \varepsilon. \tag{2}$$

Where ε denotes an error, and L is an n-by-m matrix. If the error is very little and can be ignored, the above equation degenerates into a simple linear model, and it can be described by:

$$X = LY. \tag{3}$$

Thus L can be solved using s pairs of experimental data.

3 Removal of Eyeglasses

Our method consists of several steps: samples normalization, calculation of parameter matrix, and removal of eyeglasses. The first step is essential to remove eyeglasses. For model construction, the corresponding relationship between training samples is quantized as a linear model, from which eyeglasses can be removed from an input facial image wearing eyeglasses through parameter L.

3.1 Normalization of Training Samples

The training samples consists of s sets of facial images. For every set of samples, facial images wearing eyeglasses and their corresponding facial images without eyeglasses are included. They are illustrated in Fig. 1.

Samples normalization includes two aspects: pose and gray. The former can eliminate negative impact caused by rotation, scale and translation, and the latter will reduce the effects due to differences in the distribution of gray. With respect to the gray adjustment, a simple method can be carried out. For example, for sample r,

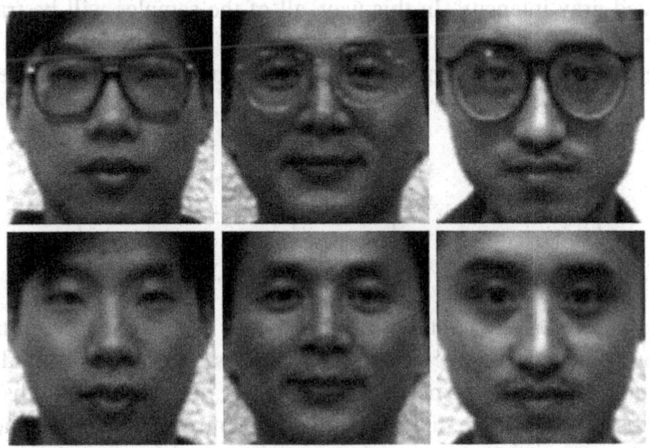

Fig. 1 Training samples

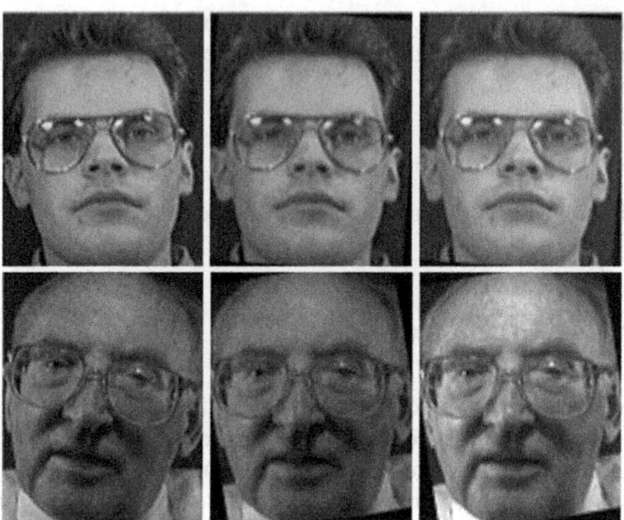

Fig. 2 Normalization of training samples

its mean and variance can reach expected values after the computation using the equations below:

$$R(i,j) = \begin{cases} m_0 + \sqrt{\dfrac{v_0(r(i,j) - m(r))^2}{v(r)}}, r(i,j) > m(r) \\ m_0 - \sqrt{\dfrac{v_0(r(i,j) - m(r))^2}{v(r)}}, else \end{cases} \tag{4}$$

Where *m(r)* and *v(r)* are mean and variance of the sample r respectively, m_0 and v_0 are expected mean and expected variance of the sample r respectively, and *R(i,j)* is the normalized gray intensity. In this way, all of the samples will be transformed into a unified measurement framework, as shown in Fig. 2 below.

Once the above steps are completed, the model of multi-variable linear regression can be constructed by $X = LY$. Mathematically,

$$\begin{bmatrix} x_{11} & x_{21} & \cdot & x_{s1} \\ x_{12} & x_{22} & \cdot & x_{s2} \\ \cdot & \cdot & \cdot & \cdot \\ x_{1n} & x_{2n} & \cdot & x_{sn} \end{bmatrix} = L \times \begin{bmatrix} y_{11} & y_{21} & \cdot & y_{s1} \\ y_{12} & y_{22} & \cdot & y_{s2} \\ \cdot & \cdot & \cdot & \cdot \\ y_{1m} & y_{2m} & \cdot & y_{sm} \end{bmatrix}. \tag{5}$$

Where $x_i = [x_{i1}, x_{i2}, \ldots, x_{in}]^T$ and $y_i = [y_{i1}, y_{i2}, \ldots, y_{im}]^T$ are two column vectors which represent a facial image wearing eyeglasses and its corresponding facial image without eyeglasses respectively. However, the vector lengths of these samples are usually too large. To solve this problem, we can simply the samples further by using some typical approaches such as active shape model etc.

3.2 Solution Method of Model

Recall that L is an n-by-m matrix in (3), and usually n or m is far larger than s, so it is difficult to solve L from (5) directly. To solve this problem, a solution method of model is presented, and its detailed procedure for solving L is described below.

From (5), the largest k eigenvalues of matrix Y^TY can be worked out and denoted by $\lambda_1, \lambda_2, \ldots, \lambda_k$, and the corresponding eigenvectors can also be organized into a matrix $\varphi_k = [p_1, p_2, \ldots, p_k]$. Let Λ_k represent the diagonal matrix $\Lambda_k = diag(\lambda_1, \lambda_2, \ldots, \lambda_k)$. Obviously, their relationships are demonstrated in the following equation.

$$Y^TY\phi_k = \phi_k\Lambda_k. \tag{6}$$

We post-multiply both sides of (6) by Λ_k^{-1}. Then, transpose operation is implemented by:

$$B_k = \phi_k^T = \left[Y^TY\phi_k\Lambda_k^{-1}\right]^T = \left(\Lambda_k^{-1}\phi_k^TY^T\right)Y. \tag{7}$$

Since B_k is an orthogonal matrix, the following equation holds:

$$B_kB_k^T = I. \tag{8}$$

Suppose another equation as bellow:

$$X = L'B_k. \tag{9}$$

Substituting (8) into (9) produces:

$$L' = XB_k^T. \tag{10}$$

By (5), (7), (9) and (10), we can get the following equation:

$$LY = L'\left(\Lambda_k^{-1}\phi_k^TY^TY\right). \tag{11}$$

By further derivation, we can obtain:

$$L = L'\left(\Lambda_k^{-1}\phi_k^TY^T\right). \tag{12}$$

Substituting (10) into (12) produces:

$$L = XB_k^T\left(\Lambda_k^{-1}\phi_k^TY^T\right). \tag{13}$$

Finally, the parameter matrix L can be solved in this way, and the eyeglasses can also be removed from an input facial image by (5). Mathematically,

$$\begin{bmatrix} x_1 \\ x_2 \\ \vdots \\ x_n \end{bmatrix} = L \times \begin{bmatrix} y_1 \\ y_2 \\ \vdots \\ y_m \end{bmatrix}. \tag{14}$$

Where column vector $[y_1, y_2, \ldots, y_m]^T$ represent an input facial image wearing eyeglasses, the synthesized facial image with removed eyeglasses is represented by column vector $[x_1, x_2, \ldots, x_n]^T$.

4 Experiments and Analysis

The experiments have been conducted on the Yale face dataset using the proposed method, and the effectivity of the algorithm is supported by the experimental results. Some examples are illustrated in Fig. 3.

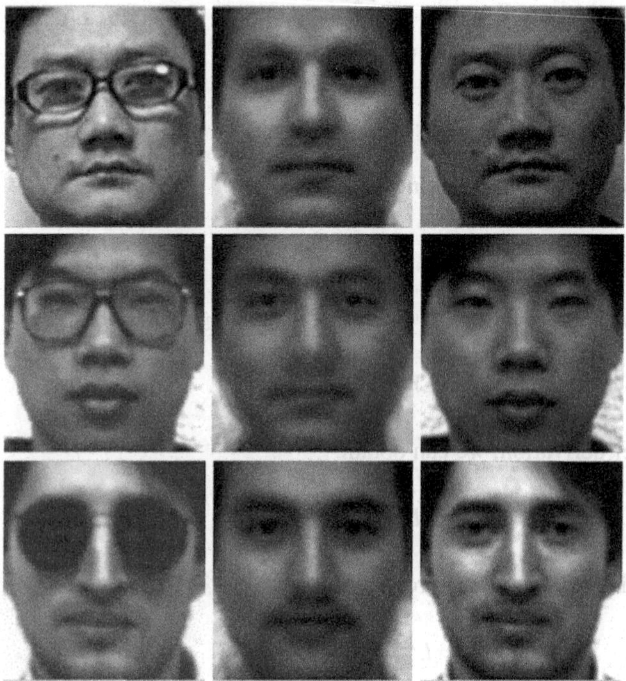

Fig. 3 Experimental results of eyeglasses removal

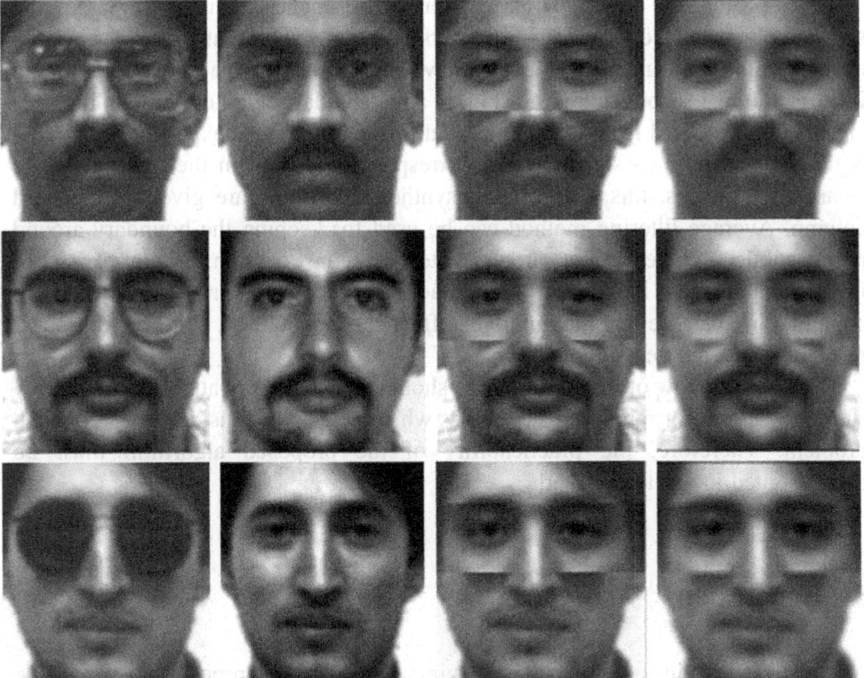

Fig. 4 Experimental results of part synthesis

In Fig. 3, the first column contains three input facial images wearing eyeglasses. Correspondingly, the processed images using this method are shown in the second column. For comparison, the original input facial images without eyeglasses are given in the last column.

By comparison of input facial images and their corresponding processed images, we can see that the proposed algorithm can keep synthesis results subtle relatively. However, the characteristics of training samples have a strong influence on synthesized facial image. As a result, both of the second column images have characteristics of western people obviously, because the majority of training samples from Yale face dataset are western people. In addition, interference of illumination and beard should not be ignored, and it also is a common problem confronting all statistical learning methods.

We can see from the above experimental results, the facial images with removed eyeglasses seem to be blurred, even they aren't realistic facial images compared to the original facial images. In fact, the output facial images are synthesized by use of the statistical learning algorithm, as one of the negative effects, the majority of original characteristics from input images must have been lost during the procedure. Considering our target is no more than removing the eyeglasses from facial images, another improved attempt can be conducted in which only part of the input facial image are synthesized. Some experimental results are illustrated in Fig. 4.

In Fig. 4, the first column contains input facial images wearing eyeglasses, the second column includes corresponding original images without eyeglasses. Based on the synthesized images which we have obtained from the above experiment illustrated in the second column of Fig. 3, a rectangular region only including eyes area can be extracted from the synthesized image in previous experiment, then the region can be used as substitute for corresponding region in the original image wearing eyeglasses, this kind of part synthesized results are given in the third column. Average filtering method can be used for keeping the boundary around region subtle, and their effects are presented in the last column. By comparison of input facial images in column 1 and their corresponding processed images in column 4, we can see that the improved effect can be obtained, but the synthesized results are still not very satisfactory.

Here, the last row of images in Fig. 4 should be given more attentions. This row shows the effect for removing sunglasses which is usually considered as a ticklish problem. Therefore, the practicability of the proposed algorithm must be demonstrated in our future work.

5 Conclusion

A statistical learning method for removing eyeglasses is proposed, in which the eyeglasses can be removed from a single facial image without using any auxiliary equipment, Experimental results demonstrate that this method is easy to be implemented. Nevertheless, there are several shortcomings as shown below.

For computational convenience, parameter ε in formula (2) has been ignored, thus the effect of algorithm should be influenced.

For the heavy workload in collection and normalization of training samples, the quality of samples is unavoidably influenced by subjective factors of operators. Moreover, pose normalization is only available for translation and scaling, so it cannot be applied for space rotation. Thus, the practicability of system may be impacted to a certain extent.

Training samples are collected based on specific group of people for the research subject, therefore, they may provide better overall image quality. But in practical application, the quality of random input facial image will be decreased by some factors, such as noise, image-forming condition etc. In addition, the output facial images which have been removed eyeglasses are processed based on the idea of statistical synthesis, so considering the experimental results as shown in Figs.3 and 4, the facial images removed eyeglasses seem to be significantly blurred compared to the original images, and some of them even does not look like the real faces.

As an algorithm based on statistics, the performance of this method is usually influenced by sampling distribution to a large extent, thus it might be better for set of samples to include all kinds of eyeglasses as much as possible. As a result, the computational cost will increase dramatically.

In terms of similarity between facial images with eyeglasses and their counterpart without eyeglasses, it is hard to find a quantized criteria to measure experimental results, so it can be assessed by vision currently.

For the above-mentioned reasons, future research plans will focus on the following aspects.

With the improvement of sampling method, sample classification based on type of eyeglasses should be adopted to enhance system availability. On the other hand, more research should be carried out for model construction, which has advantages for better stability and reasonability, and will hence improve performance of system further. Finally the photorealistic of synthesized facial images should be updated in which the colored facial image should be included.

Acknowledgments The authors would like to thank Professor Xiangjian He for valuable suggestions.

References

1. Taiping, Z., Yuanyan, T., Bin, F., Zhaowei, S., Xiaoyu, L.: Face Recognition Under Varying Illumination Using Gradientfaces. IEEE Transactions on Image Processing. 11, 2599–2606 (2009)
2. Agarwal, M., Agrawal, H., Jain, N., Kumar, M.: Face Recognition Using Principle Component Analysis, Eigenface and Neural Network. In: 2010 International Conference on Signal Acquisition and Processing, ICSAP '10, pp. 310–314. IEEE Press, Bangalore (2010)
3. Wagner, A., Wright, J., Ganesh, A., Zihan, Z., Yi, M.: Towards A Practical Face Recognition System: Robust Registration and Illumination by Sparse Representation. In: IEEE Conference on Computer Vision and Pattern Recognition, CVPR 2009, pp. 597–604. IEEE Press, Miami USA (2009)
4. Qinfeng, S., Anders, E., Anton, V., Chunhua, S.: Is Face Recognition Really A Compressive Sensing problem?. In: IEEE Conference on Computer Vision and Pattern Recognition, CVPR 2011, pp. 553–560. IEEE Press, Colorado Springs (2011)
5. Meng, Y., Lei Z., Jian Y., David Z.: Robust Sparse Coding for Face Recognition. In: IEEE Conference on Computer Vision and Pattern Recognition, CVPR 2011, pp. 625–632. IEEE Press, Colorado Springs (2011)
6. Chenyu, W., Ce, L., HeungYueng, S., YingQing, X., Zhengyou, Z.: Automatic Eyeglasses Removal from Face Images. IEEE Transactions on Pattern Analysis and Machine Intelligence. 30, 322–336 (2004)
7. Xuerong, C., Zhongliang, J., Shaoyuan, S.: A Method for Solving Eyeglasses Interference in Infrared Face Recognition. Journal of Shanghai Jiaotong University. 3, 113–116 (2006)
8. Cheng, D., Guangda, S.: Eyeglasses Removal from Facial Images for Face Recognition. Journal of Tsinghua University (Science and Technology). 7, 928–930 (2005)
9. Alessandro, C., Claudio, C., Raimondo, S.: Three-Dimensional Occlusion Detection and Restoration of Partially Occluded Faces. Journal of Mathematical Imaging and Vision. 1, 105–119 (2011)
10. Weihua, Z.: The Facial Image Understanding Based on Statistical Model. Master Thesis, (2002)

Video Coding and Transmission

A Multiple Hexagon Search Algorithm for Motion and Disparity Estimation in Multiview Video Coding

Zhaoqing Pan, Sam Kwong, and Yun Zhang

Abstract In single viewpoint video coding, there are many fast block matching motion estimation algorithms proposed, such as three-step search, four-step search, diamond search as well as hexagon-based search and so on. However, experimental analysis show that these algorithms are not suitable for using directly in Multiview View Coding (MVC). Since the increased search range, the larger format of multiview video as well as the correlations between inter-view frames are not considered by these algorithms, they may easy led the block matching search into local minimum, the Rate-Distortion (R-D) performance will degrade dramatically. In this paper, we propose a novel multiple hexagon search algorithm to address this problem. Firstly, according to the original initial search point, four sub-search windows are constructed. Then, the hexagon based search algorithm will be performed respectively in the four sub-search windows. The final result is the best search point with the minimum R-D cost among the best points in the four sub-search windows. In order to trade off the computational complexity and R-D performance, two adaptive early termination strategies are proposed. The experimental results show that the proposed algorithm yields a quite promising coding performance in terms of R-D performance and computational complexity. Especially, the proposed algorithm can work well in multiview video sequences with various motion and disparity activities.

Z. Pan • S. Kwong (✉)
Department of Computer Science, City University of Hong Kong, Hong Kong, China
e-mail: zqpan3@student.cityu.edu.hk; cssamk@cityu.edu.hk

Y. Zhang
Department of Computer Science, City University of Hong Kong, Hong Kong, China

Shenzhen Institutes of Advanced Technology, Chinese Academy of Sciences, Shenzhen 518055, China
e-mail: yunzhang@cityu.edu.hk

J.S. Jin et al., *The Era of Interactive Media*,
DOI 10.1007/978-1-4614-3501-3_10,

1 Introduction

Multiview Video (MVV) is a group of video sequences which are captured simultaneously by more than one cameras with different viewpoints [1, 2]. It is the crucial data format for many multimedia applications, such as free-viewpoint video, free-viewpoint television, three-dimensional television and so on. However, MVV contains vast raw video data since the increased number of cameras. This drawback limits its application in current internet bandwidth. In view of this reason, efficient MVV coding technology is a key factor for its widely application. Recently, the Joint Video Team (JVT) of ITU-T Video Coding Experts Group and ISO/IEC Moving Picture Experts Group (MPEG) propose a MVC standard, which is regarded as an extension of H.264/AVC (Advanced Video Coding) [3, 4, 5]. The excellent coding performance of MVC is at the cost of high computational complexity. Hence, for efficient MVC, a lot of methods have been proposed. These methods can be classified into efficient MVC prediction structure scheme, efficient multi-reference frame selection algorithm, fast mode decision algorithm as well as fast motion and disparity estimation algorithm. P. Merkle et al. propose a hierarchial B picture prediction structure for MVC [6]. This prediction structure has been adopted by JVT and used in Joint Multiview Video Coding (JMVC) which is the reference software of MVC. L. Shen et el. propose a early skip mode decision for MVC, which using the correlations between inter-views [7]. Y. Zhang et al. propose a fast multi-reference frame selection method for HBP prediction structure, which regards there is a high probability for small Macroblock (MB) partition selecting the same reference frame as 16×16 MB partition used [8].

Different from single viewpoint video coding, MVV has tremendous redundancy between inter-view sequences. As a result, Motion Estimation (ME) is extended into two parts in MVC, the traditional ME which aims to exploit the temporal redundancy between consecutive frames and Disparity Estimation (DE) which aims to remove redundancy between inter-view frames, respectively. In single viewpoint video coding, there are a lot of fast ME algorithms proposed, such as Three-Step Search (3SS) [9], Four-Step Search (4SS) [10], Diamond Search (DS) [11] and Hexagon Based Search (HBS) [12]. Among these fast algorithms, HBS can be regarded as the best one, it has admirable performance in reducing the computational complexity while maintaining a quite similar R-D performance with Full Search (FS). However, experimental analysis show that it is not suitable for using directly in MVC. Since the increased search range, the larger format of MVV sequences as well as the correlations between inter-view frames are not considered by HBS, they may easy led the block matching search into local minimum, the R-D performance will degrade dramatically. In this paper, we propose a novel multiple hexagon search algorithm to address this problem. Firstly, according to the original initial search point which is derived by median predictor [14], four sub-search windows are constructed. Then, the HBS [12] will be performed in the four sub-search windows. The final result is the best search point with the minimum R-D cost among the best points in the four sub-search windows. In order to trade off the computational complexity and R-D performance, two adaptive early termination strategies are proposed. The experimental results demonstrate that the proposed algorithm yields a quite promising performance in terms of R-D performance and computational complexity.

The rest of this paper is organized as follows. The hierarchial B picture prediction structure in JMVC is described in Sect. 2. The details of the proposed multiple hexagon search algorithm are given in Sect. 3. Experimental results are shown in Sect. 4. At last, Sect. 5 concludes this paper.

2 Hierarchial B Picture Prediction Structure in JMVC

P. Merkle et al. propose a Hierarchial B Picture (HBP) prediction structure for efficient MVC [6]. This prediction structure has been adopted by JVT and used in the reference software of MVC. Figure 1 shows the MVC-HBP prediction structure. In Fig. 1, the length of Group of Pictures (GOP) equals to eight. S_n represents the n-th camera's view, T_n denotes the n-th frame in temporal direction. In even views (S_0, S_2, S_4 and S_6), only temporal prediction is used. ME is applied to remove the temporal redundancy between consecutive frames in one view. In odd views (S_1, S_3, S_5 and S_7), both

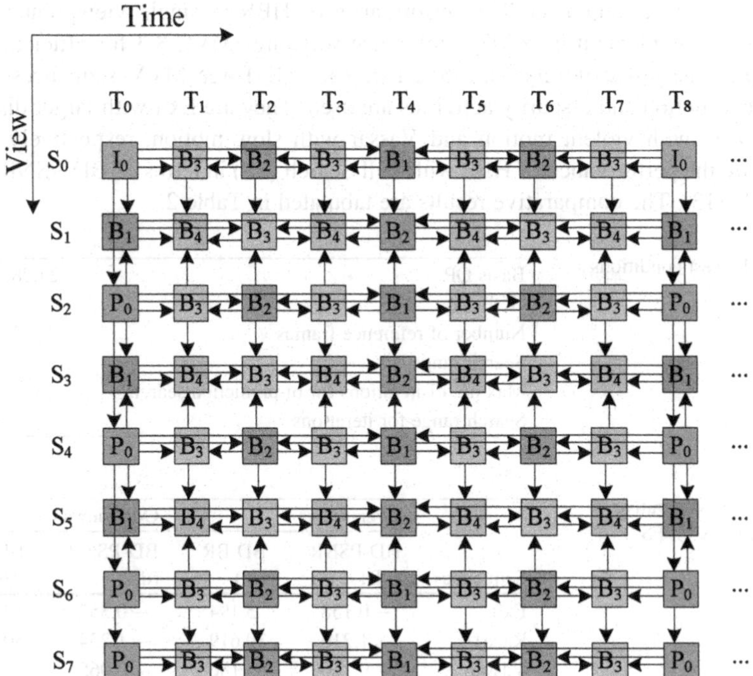

Fig. 1 MVC HBP prediction structure in JMVC

temporal prediction and inter-view prediction are employed. ME is utilized to remove the temporal redundancy. DE is used to remove the redundancy between inter-view frames. Let S_0T_3 and S_1T_3 as an example, S_0T_2 and S_0T_4 are referred for ME of S_0T_3. S_1T_2 and S_1T_4 are referred for ME of S_1T_3, S_0T_3 and S_2T_3 are referred by S_1T_3 for DE.

3 Proposed Multiple Hexagon Search Algorithm

3.1 Motivation

In [12], a HBS algorithm is proposed for fast block matching ME. Firstly, a Larger Hexagon Search Pattern (LHSP) with six points is performed on (0,0). If the best point which is with the minimum R-D cost is the center of LHSP, stop the LHSP search process. Otherwise, recursively repeat the LHSP until the best point locates at the center. Then switch the search pattern from LHSP to the Small Hexagon Search Pattern (SHSP) with four points, the best point among the five checked points is the final search result. Experimental results show that HBS is the best fast block matching ME algorithm among the conventional algorithms, such as 3SS, 4SS, DS. It can locate the best MV with fewer search points, while the R-D performance is not comprised.

Due to the excellent coding performance of HBS in single viewpoint video coding, we implement it in MVC reference software JMVC 8.3 for efficient ME and DE. The test conditions are listed in Table 1. Three MVV sequences with different motion and disparity activities are used. They are Exit with larger disparity, Race1 with violent motion and Vassar with slow motion, respectively. We compare the performance of HBS with Full Search (FS) in terms of BD-PSNR and BD-BR [13]. The comparative results are tabulated in Table 2.

Table 1 Test conditions

Basis QP	24,28,32,36
GOP size	12
Number of reference frames	2
Search range	64
Max no. of iterations for bi-prediction search	4
Search range for iterations	8

Table 2 Comparative results, HBS vs. FS

	Even views		Odd views	
Sequence	BD-PSNR (dB)	BD-BR (%)	BD-PSNR (dB)	BD-BR (%)
Exit	– 0.158	5.194	– 0.357	13.007
Race1	– 1.216	30.619	– 1.234	30.508
Vassar	– 0.116	5.186	– 0.065	2.848
Average	**–0.497**	**13.666**	**–0.552**	**15.454**

From Table 2, we can see that compared to FS, HBS cannot obtain an admirable R-D performance. For even views, PSNR decrease 0.497, Bitrate increase 13.666%, on average. For odd views, 0.552 PSNR decrease and 15.454% Bitrate increase. Especially for the MVV sequences with violent motion, such as Race1, the PSNR and Bitrate change dramatically. Since for video sequences with violent motion activity, HBS will easy drop into local minimum. The comparative results indicate that since the R-D performance decrease seriously, no matter how much computational complexity is saved, HBS algorithm is not suitable for ME and DE in JMVC.

3.2 *Proposed Multiple Hexagon Search Algorithm*

There are two steps in ME and DE process. The first step is to determine a Initial Search Point (ISP). The second step construct a search window based on the ISP, then using a search strategy to locate the best matching block in the search window. The philosophy of fast ME and DE is finding the best matching block with less search points while the R-D performance is not comprised.

Median Predictor (MP) [14] is a popular ISP predictor, which use median vector value of the neighboring blocks of the top, top-right (or top-left), left of the current block. In this paper, we use the value of MP as the Original Initial Search Point (OISP). According to the OISP, a multiple hexagon search algorithm is proposed. Firstly, based on the OISP, four sub-search windows are constructed. Figure 2 shows the proposed four sub-search windows. Then, HBS [12] is performed respectively in the four sub-search windows. The final output is the point which with the minimum R-D cost among the best points in the four search windows.

In Fig. 2, the circle represents the OISP which is obtained by MP. Suppose the OISP with Motion Vector (MV) (x,y). The ISP of the constructed four sub-search windows are (x+Search Range/2, y+Search Range/2), (x – Search Range/2, y+Search Range/2), (x – Search Range/2, y – Search Range/2), (x+Search Range/2, y – Search Range/2), respectively.

Since the increased number of search windows, total computational complexity of ME and DE will increase dramatically. In order to trade off the R-D performance and computational complexity, two adaptive early termination strategies are proposed for the multiple hexagon search algorithm. We analyze the best search point in even and odd views with natural MVV sequences. FS is used for find the distribution information of best search point. The statistical results are tabulated in Table 3. From Table 3, we can see that OISP selected as the best search point in even and odd views occupies larger proportion, about 63.08% and 44.52%, respectively. If they are can be early determined, much more time will be saved. According to the principle that the best point is always center-biased, a early termination strategy is used to early stop the multiple HBS. The early termination strategy performs a SHSP on the OISP, if OISP is the best point which is with the minimum R-D cost among the five checked points, the following HBS will be

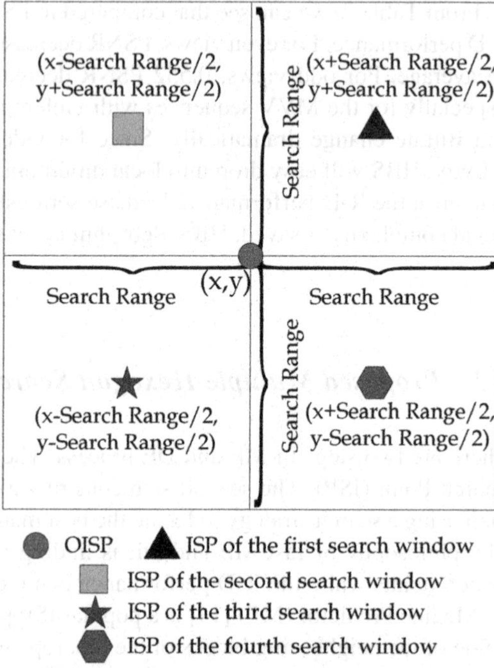

Fig. 2 Proposed four search windows

Table 3 Percentages of OISP is selected as the best search point in even views and odd views

View	Sequence	24 (%)	28 (%)	32 (%)	36 (%)	*Average* (%)
Even views	Exit	75.03	58.91	78.92	81.36	73.56
	Race1	7.40	11.11	18.04	26.48	15.76
	Vassar	90.70	92.38	92.55	92.38	92.00
	Average	57.71	54.13	63.17	66.74	**60.44**
Odd views	Exit	45.72	45.07	53.48	60.69	51.24
	Race1	5.34	9.47	14.86	23.55	13.31
	Vassar	56.05	63.48	69.39	74.25	65.79
	Average	35.70	39.34	45.91	52.83	**43.45**

skipped. Otherwise, the following HBS will be performed. The candidate MVs of SHSP are given by

$$\overrightarrow{MV_{SHSP}} = \{(MV_x, MV_y)|(MV_x, MV_y) = (x \pm 1, y), (x, y \pm 1)\}, \quad (1)$$

where (x, y) denotes the vector of OISP.

The second proposed early termination strategy performs a cross search on OISP, the candidate MVs of cross search are given by

$$\overrightarrow{MV_{CS}} = \{(MV_x, MV_y)|(MV_x, MV_y) = (x \pm 2i, y),\ i = 1, 2, \ldots, s/2; \\ (x, y \pm 2j),\ j = 1, 2, \ldots, s/2\}, \quad (2)$$

Algorithm 1 The proposed multiple hexagon search algorithm

Step 1. OISP prediction. Median predictor is applied to predict the OISP. According to the OISP, four new search windows are constructed. The ISP of these four search windows are (x+Search Range/2, y+Search Range/2), (x-Search Range/2, y+Search Range/2), (x-Search Range/2, y-Search Range/2), (x+Search Range/2, y-Search Range/2), respectively.

Step 2. Perform a SHSP on the OISP to early terminate the multiple hexagon search. If the best point which has the minimum R-D cost among these five checked points is OISP, go to step 10; Else go to Step 3.

Step 3. Perform a cross search on the OISP, record the R-D cost of the best point which is obtained in this search procedure as *RDC*.

Step 4. Perform HBS [12] in the first search window. In this search procedure, we get a best point which is with the minimum R-D cost, record this minimum R-D cost as *MRD1*.

Step 5. Compare *RDC* and *MRD1*, if $MRD1 > RDC$, go to Step 10; Else go to Step?6.

Step 6. Perform HS in the second search window. Record the R-D cost of the best search point in this search window as *MRD2*.

Step 7. Perform HBS in the third search window. Record the R-D cost of the?best search point in this search window as *MRD3*.

Step 8. Perform HBS in the fourth search window. Record the R-D cost of the?best search point in this search window as *MRD4*.

Step 9. Select the smallest one from *MRD1*, *MRD2*, *MRD3*, *MRD4*.

Step 10. Return the vector of the best search point.

where (x, y) represents the vector of OISP. s denotes the search range. In this search procedure, we can get a best point which with the minimum R-D cost, record this minimum R-D cost as *RDC*. After HBS is performed in the first search window, we can obtain a best point, record the R-D cost of this best point as *MRD1*. If $MRD1 > RDC$, the following HBS will be skipped. Otherwise, HBS is performed in the second, third, and fourth search window, respectively.

Finally, the proposed multiple hexagon search algorithm is presented in Algorithm 1.

4 Experimental Results

The proposed algorithm is implemented on MVC reference software JMVC 8.3 to evaluate its efficiency. The test conditions are listed in Table 1. Five MVV test sequences with different motion and disparity activities are used. They are Ballroom with rotated motion and larger disparity, Exit with larger disparity, Flamenco2 with medium motion, Race1 with violent motion as well as Vassar with slow motion, respectively. The format of these five MVV sequences are 640 $\times$480. For each view, 61 frames to be encoded. The hardware platform is Intel Core 2 Duo CPU E5800 @ 3.16 GHz and 3.17 GHz, 4.00 GB RAM with Microsoft Windows 7 64-bit operating system.

Table 4 Summary of encoding results

View	Sequence	Proposed vs. FS BD-PSNR (dB)	BD-BR (%)	TS (%)	Proposed vs. HBS BD-PSNR (dB)	BD-BR (%)	TS (%)
Even views	Ballroom	– 0.097	2.436	– 95.937	0.167	– 3.995	– 61.594
	Exit	– 0.064	2.439	– 96.862	0.093	– 2.971	– 69.203
	Flamenco2	– 0.114	2.373	– 95.385	0.030	– 0.620	– 52.968
	Race1	– 0.298	7.078	– 92.497	1.276	– 24.251	– 26.765
	Vassar	– 0.019	0.960	– 98.159	0.073	– 3.305	– 81.375
	Average	**–0.119**	**3.057**	**–95.768**	**0.328**	**–7.028**	**–58.381**
Odd views	Ballroom	– 0.067	1.752	– 94.096	0.420	– 10.147	– 43.978
	Exit	– 0.080	2.938	– 95.547	0.312	– 10.247	– 55.959
	Flamenco2	– 0.158	2.743	– 94.337	0.857	– 15.015	– 43.154
	Race1	– 0.290	6.838	– 91.857	0.918	– 18.011	– 23.582
	Vassar	– 0.010	0.573	– 96.431	0.033	– 1.573	– 63.158
	Average	**–0.121**	**2.969**	**–94.454**	**0.508**	**–10.998**	**–45.966**

We compare the performance of the proposed algorithm with FS and HBS [12] in terms of BD-PSNR, BD-BR [13] and total encoding time. The comparative results are tabulated in Table 4. TS represents the CPU time saving in encoding process, and defined as

$$TS = \frac{Time_{proposed} - Time_{original}}{Time_{original}} \times 100\%, \tag{3}$$

where $Time_{proposed}$ denotes the total encoding time of the proposed algorithm. and $Time_{original}$ represents total encoding time of FS and HBS, respectively.

From Table 4, we can see that the proposed multiple hexagon search algorithm can obtain significantly better results than FS and HBS algorithm in reducing the encoding time. Compared to FS, for even views, the proposed algorithm can reduce the encoding time up to 95.768% with 0.119 dB PSNR loss and 3.057% Bitrate increase. For odd views, the encoding time is saved by 94.454% with 0.121 dB PSNR loss and 2.969% Bitrate increase. Compared to HBS algorithm, for even views, the proposed algorithm can save the encoding time up to 58.381% with 0.328 dB PSNR increase and 7.028% Bitrate decrease. For odd views, the encoding time is reduced up to 45.966% with 0.508 dB PSNR increase and 10.998% Bitrate decrease. Especially, the proposed algorithm can work well in MVV sequences with various motion and disparity activities, such as Exit with larger disparity, Race1 with violent motion, Ballet with fast motion and small disparity, Vassar with slow motion.

In order to demonstrate the R-D performance of the proposed algorithm, we give the R-D curves of Ballroom with even views and odd views, Race1 with even views

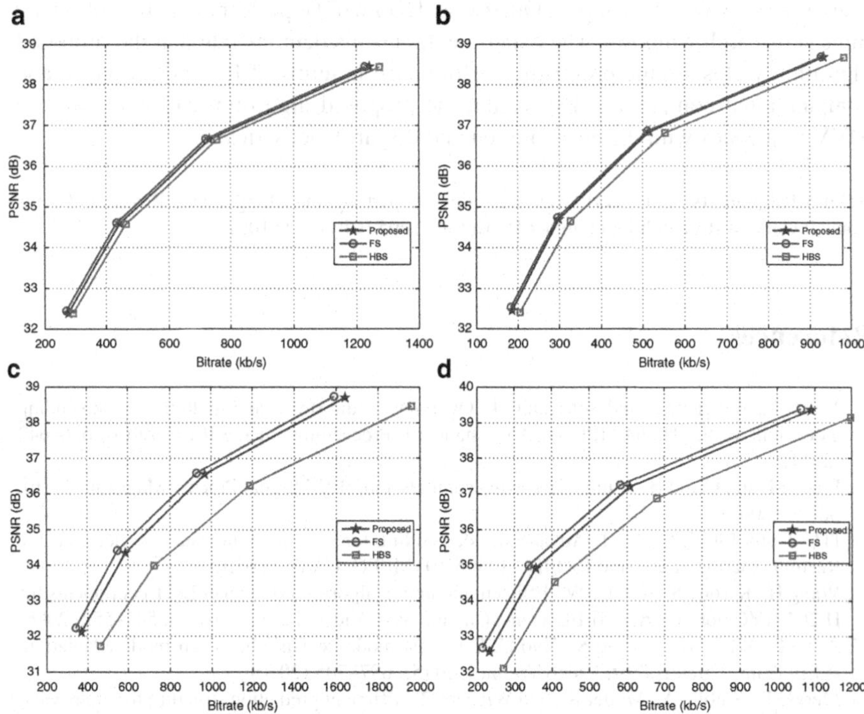

Fig. 3 R-D curves. (**a**) Ballroom (even views). (**b**) Ballroom (odd views). (**c**) Race1 (even views). (**d**) Race1 (odd views)

and odd views in Fig. 3. It can be observed that the proposed algorithm achieves a similar R-D performance with FS, and a quite better R-D performance than HBS.

5 Conclusion

In this paper, we propose a novel multiple hexagon search algorithm for ME and DE in MVC. Firstly, according to OISP which is derived by MP, four sub-searchwindows are constructed. Then, HBS will be performed in the four sub-search windows. The final result is the best search point with the minimum R-D cost among the best point in the four sub-search windows. In order to trade off the computational complexity and R-D performance, two adaptive early termination strategies are proposed. The first early termination strategy performs a four points SHSP on the OISP, if the best point is OISP, the following search will be skipped. Otherwise, the following search strategies will be performed. The second early termination strategy performs a cross search on the OISP, if the R-D cost of the best point in this cross search process is smaller than that in the hexagon based search in the first search window, the following HBS in the second, third, fourth search window will be skipped. Otherwise, HBS will be performed in the following three sub-search windows. The experimental results demonstrate that the proposed algorithm yields a quite promising performance in terms of R-D performance and computational complexity. Especially, the proposed algorithm can work well in MVV sequences with different motion and disparity activities.

Acknowledgements This work was supported in part by the Hong Kong Research Grants Council General Research Fund, under Project 9041495 (CityU 115109).

References

1. Vetro A., Wiegand T. and Sullivan G.J., Overview of the stereo and multiview video coding extensions of the H.264/MPEG-4 AVC standard, Proceedings of the IEEE 99 (4), 626–642 (2011)
2. Flierl M. and Girod B., Multi-view video compression, IEEE Signal Process Magazine 24 (6), 66–76 (2007)
3. ITU-T and ISO/IEC JTC 1, Advanced video coding for generic audiovisual services, ITU-T Recommedation H.264 and ISO/IEC 14496-10 (MPEG-4 AVC) (2010)
4. Wang H., Kwong S., Kok C.-W., Efficient prediction algorithm of integer DCT coefficients for H.264/AVC optimization, IEEE Trans. Circuits Syst. Video Technol. 16 (4), 547–552 (2006)
5. Zhao T., Wang H., Kwong S., Kuo C.-C.J., Fast mode decision based on mode adaptation, IEEE Trans. Circuits Syst. Video Technol. 20 (5), 697–705 (2010)
6. Merkle P., Smolic A., Müller K., and Wiegand T., Efficient prediction structure for multi-view video coding, IEEE Trans. Circuits Syst. Video Technol. 17 (11), 1461–1473 (2007)
7. Shen L., Liu Z., Yan T., Yang Z. and An P., Early skip mode decision for MVC using inter-view correlation, Signal Processing: Image Communication 25 (2), 88–93 (2010)
8. Zhang Y., Kwong S., Jiang G., and Wang H., Efficient multi- reference frame selection algorithm for hierarchical B pictures in multiview video coding, IEEE Trans. Broadcast. 57 (1), 15–23 (2011)
9. Koga T., Iinuma K., Hirano A., Iijima Y. and Lshiguro T., Motion-compensated interframe coding for video conferencing, in: Proceeding of the National Telecommunications Conference, New Orleans, pp. G5.3.1–G5.3.5 (1981)
10. Po L., Ma W, A novel four-step search algorithm for block motion estimation, IEEE Trans. Circuits Syst. Video Technol. 6 (3), 313–317 (1996)
11. Zhu S., Ma K.-K, A new diamond search algorithm for fast block matching motion estimation, in: Proceedings of the International Conference on Information, Communication and Signal Processing, Singapore, pp. 292–296 (1997)
12. Zhu C., Lin X., and Chau L., Hexagon-based search pattern for fast motion estimation, IEEE Trans. Circuits Syst. Video Technol. 12 (5), 349–355 (2002)
13. Bjontegaard G., Calculation of average PSNR differences between RD-curves, Document VCEG-M33, VCEG 13th meeting, Austin, Texas, USA, (2001)
14. Tourapis A., Cheong H.-Y., Topiwala P., Fast ME in JM reference software, Document JVT-P026, 16th meeting: Poznań, PL, (2005)

Adaptive Motion Skip Mode for AVS 3D Video Coding

Lianlian Jiang, Yue Wang, Li Zhang, and Siwei Ma

Abstract Inter-view motion skip mode has been proposed to improve the coding efficiency of multiview video coding (MVC) by reusing the motion information of the referenced views. In this paper, an adaptive motion estimation algorithm for the motion skip mode is proposed for AVS 3D video coding. The proposed algorithm searches the best motion information, by means of adaptive global disparity estimation and a refine search along the horizontal direction, for the purpose of motion-compensated coding. Moreover, the method is applied to sampling-aided scheme for AVS 3D video coding, which encodes the reorganized sequence by merging two downsampled videos. Rate-distortion optimization criterion is employed to find the best motion information. Experimental results demonstrate that the proposed algorithm can substantially improve the coding efficiency.

Keywords 3D • Adaptive motion skip • Disparity vector

1 Introduction

Multiview video is acquired by simultaneously capturing the same scene from different viewpoints. Independently coding of separated videos using a state-of-the-art codec such as H.264/AVC [1], is the most straightforward method, called simulcast. However, there exists considerable redundancy among the neighboring-views. Motion compensation techniques that are well-developed for single-view video compression can be used to temporal prediction. Likewise, disparity compensation techniques can be utilized to reduce inter-view redundancies [2]. Hierarchical B-picture [3] as supported by H.264/AVC syntax was adopted by JVT as the joint multiview view model (JMVM) due to its high coding efficiency [4].

L. Jiang (✉) • Y. Wang • L. Zhang • S. Ma
Institute of Digital Media, Peking University, Beijing, China
e-mail: lljiang@jdl.ac.cn; ywang@jdl.ac.cn; lzhang@jdl.ac.cn; swma@jdl.ac.cn

J.S. Jin et al., *The Era of Interactive Media*,
DOI 10.1007/978-1-4614-3501-3_11,

To further remove the redundancy, several MVC schemes based on the existing video codec have been proposed consequently. In [5], sampling-aide MVC scheme is one of them without significant modification of current video coding standards, which merges two videos from neighboring viewpoints into one video. The AVS video coding standard issued by Audio Video coding Standard (AVS) Workgroup of China has adopted that as one coding profile. To be specific, downsampling is performed for each view prior to the encoding, and decoded frame are upsampled to the original resolution. With the advantage of the lower complexity and overhead, downsampling scheme has been employed into practice.

In order to further take advantage of the temporal and interview correlations, some experiments are conducted in the context of MPEG standardization [6]. During the standardization of MVC, illumination compensation [7] and motion skip [8] are studied for further enhancement. Our algorithm is conducted on the downsampling scheme of AVS and motion skip is likewise crucial for the further coding efficiency.

Motion skip commits itself to removing the redundancy of motion information between neighboring views. Namely, the collocated macroblocks in the neighboring view are characterized by similar coding mode, reference index as well as motion vectors [9]. Therefore, reference to similar information is reasonable. To determine the location of corresponding macroblock, global disparity vector generated by camera geometry is used and a refine search is done for each macroblock.

In [10], the optimal motion information is derived from the inter-view corresponding macroblock with three fixed neighboring macroblocks as candidates. Moreover, fine-granular motion estimation algorithm aims to find the best motion information by enlarging the search area along both horizontal and vertical directions [11].

In general, multiview video is captured by parallel cameras. Hence, the expansion of vertical search area will counteract the improvement to some extent. Furthermore, global disparity is not capable of estimating the exact disparity of distinct macroblocks. As a result, an accurate adaptive global disparity method is proposed in this paper to tackle those problems.

This paper presents a new coding mode for sampling-aided MVC scheme, called adaptive motion skip mode. The remaining section is organized as follow. Section 2 will focus on the sample-aide scheme. Section 3 will devote to the proposed adaptive motion skip mode in detail. Experimental results and analysis are described in Sect. 4. Eventually, Sect. 5 summarizes and concludes the paper.

2 Sampling-Aided Multiview Video Coding Scheme

In this section, we will briefly introduce the sampling-aided MVC framework [5]. Before encoding process, the images of two view sequences are first downsampled into half size in vertical direction, respectively. The two downsampled view

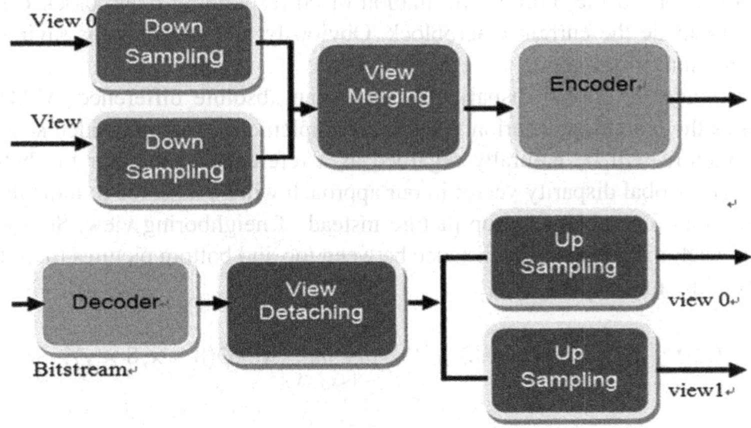

Fig. 1 Proposed sampling-aided encoding scheme

sequence can be merged into a single sequence as the original resolution and encoded with a traditional codec. At the decoder, the decoded video image should first split into two view images and some interpolation methods are employed to recover the original resolution.

Taking an HD sequence for instance, as illustrated in Fig. 1, two sequences both are captured with the format of 1080p (1920 × 1080, progressive). Firstly, two videos are downsampled into the format of 1920 × 540 respectively. Then, videos are merged into a reorganized video by placing one downsampled video above the other downsampled video. Therefore, two halves of reorganized video in a frame are called top picture and bottom picture respectively. At the decoder, the decoded video is detached into two separate videos, which are then upsampled to the original resolution using the same filter as downsampling process.

3 Proposed Adaptive Motion Skip Mode for AVS

3.1 Global Disparity Estimation

With intention of explaining more accurately, we define some symbols as follows:

$I_{top,t}$ stands for the top picture of the reorganized frame at time *t*. Likewise, $I_{bottom,t}$ signifies the bottom picture of the reorganized frame at time *t*.

$MB_{top,t}$ represents a 16 × 16 macroblock in $I_{top,t}$. At the same time, $MB_{bottom,t}$ denotes a 16 × 16 macroblock in $I_{bottom,t}$.

The first step of our proposed mode is similar to the existing motion skip mode in MVC [11].Our approach firstly exploits the displacement between different views, called global disparity, in order to locate the position of corresponding macroblocks. Then the motion information of corresponding macroblock can be reused to encode the current macroblock. Obviously, the advantage is saving the bits for motion information.

To estimate the global disparity vector, mean absolute difference (MAD) is utilized as the matching criterion. Due to the implement in sample-aided scheme, the top picture will be naturally regarded as a reference picture for the bottom picture. The global disparity vector in our approach will be adjusted to indicate the corresponding macroblock in top picture instead of neighboring view. So, global disparity vector is added to the distance between top and bottom pictures to find the corresponding macroblock in $I_{top,t}$.

$$\mathrm{GDV}_{org} = (x_{gdv}, y_{gdv} - N_{half})^T = \underset{-S \le x,y \le S}{arg\ min} \{\mathrm{MAD}(8 \times \mathrm{x}, 8 \times y)\} \tag{1}$$

where S is the search range with 8-pel precision. Empirically, S is defined as 8 × 8-pel. N_{half} is equivalent to the distance between top and bottom pictures.

$$\mathrm{MAD}(x, y) = \frac{1}{(h - y)(w - x)} \sum_{i=0}^{w-x-1} \sum_{j=0}^{h-y-1} |I_{top,t}(i + x, j + y) - I_{bottom,t}(i, j)| \tag{2}$$

where w and h respectively stand for the width and the height of the top and bottom pictures.

Considering the algorithm complexity and feasibility, the precision of the global disparity vector is set to 8-pel in both horizontal and vertical directions [11]. As we know, motion compensation is implemented on the basis of 8 × 8 block in AVS. In order to use the information, composed of reference picture index, up to four motion vectors as well as mbtype, it is reasonable that we adopt 8-pel precision instead of 1-pel precision.

3.2 *Adaptive Motion Skip Mode*

Actually, there is an inherent relationship between depth and disparity. That is to say, if depth of each object in the scene is different, the disparity between corresponding macroblocks within different regions is correspondingly different. Thus, the global disparity is insufficient to represent the optimal disparity for each individual macroblock. For this reason, according to the GDV_{org} previously estimated, the second step is to find the optimal disparity of each $\mathrm{MB}_{bottom,t}$.

Because the reorganized video consists of two neighboring videos captured by parallel cameras, vertical parallax almost equals to zero, which is restricted by camera geometry. It is rational that search window in our algorithm is stretched solely along the horizontal direction rather than both the horizontal and vertical directions in [11].

Consequently, our algorithm uses a horizontal search window generated around the corresponding macroblock. The search window of (5 × 8-pel) includes five search positions. Namely, five candidate macroblocks in the search window provide the motion information that can be reused for current macroblock.

When enforcing coding process, horizontal offset need to be encoded previously in order to inform the decoder of the disparity offset value. The disparity vector D_i of each search point is represented as:

$$D_i = \mathrm{GDV}_{org} + \mathit{offset}_i, \mathit{offset}_i = (\mathit{offset}_{xi}, 0)^T \tag{3}$$

where offset$_i$ is the relative disparity vector based on GDV_{org}.

Considering the following circumstance when several neighboring macroblocks are within the same foreground area, their local disparities will be similar but quite differ from the GDV_{org}. Conceivably, it will increase bit rates to encode them individually.

Based on this comprehension, our approach uses the adaptive global disparity vector to update continually. Apparently, the advantage is reduction of bits for similar offset. When coding macroblocks in the first line, search window is still generated based on GDV_{org}. As long as offset$_i$ is attained for one macroblock, newly generated adaptive global disparity vector will be immediately updated by adding offset$_i$ to it, as follows:

$$\begin{aligned} \mathrm{GDV}_{ada(i,j)} &= \mathrm{GDV}_{org} + \mathit{offset}(i,j) \\ &= \left(x_{org} + \mathit{offset}_i, y_{org} - N_{half}\right) \end{aligned} \tag{4}$$

The subsequent Macroblocks will be directed with the aid of the adaptive global disparity vector, obtained by the above process, as follows:

$$\begin{aligned} \mathrm{GDV}_{ada(i,j)} &= \mathrm{GDV}_{ada(i_{up},j)} + \mathit{offset}(i,j) \\ &= (x_{ada(i_{up},j)} + \mathit{offset}_i, y_{org} - N_{half}) \end{aligned} \tag{5}$$

where $\mathrm{GDV}_{ada(i,j)}$ stands for the updated adaptive global disparity vector of the current macroblock in position *(i,j)* in a frame. Offset *(i,j)* indicates optimum disparity offset of current macroblock. $\mathrm{GDV}_{ada(i,j)}$ signifies adaptive global disparity of $\mathrm{MB}_{UP,j}$, which is the nearest macroblock in *j*th column adopting adaptive motion skip mode.

The reason why updating global disparity vector referring to information of macroblock in the same column rather than row is that via vast statistical data, disparity offset is usually identical along the vertical direction. Therefore, it is reasonable to record the disparity offset and make refinement to it.

Thus, formula (3) is refined as follows:

$$D_i = \mathrm{GDV}_{ada} + \mathit{offset}_i \tag{6}$$

Give the Lagrangian parameter λ_{MODE}, the Lagrangian cost function is employed to determine the optimal candidate macroblock, as follows:

$$J(D_i) = D(M_i) + \lambda_{MODE} R(D_i) \tag{7}$$

where M is the four motion vectors of each candidate $MB_{bottom,t}$ at the *ith* search point, which is composed of four 8 × 8 blocks. M_i are denoted as $\{m_i(x,y) / i = 1, 2, 3, 4\}$. The rate R ($D_i$) is the total bits to encode the whole macroblock. In addition to the residual data, R (D_i) includes the number of bits which are used to encode disparity offset, and the flag which indicates whether $MB_{bottom,t}$ adopts our approach. The distortion D (M_i) is measured by the sum of the squared differences (SSD) between the original macroblock and the reconstructed macroblock, after temporal motion compensation.

Therefore, the optimal motion information M_{opt} for the current macroblock can be acquired and $offset_i$ can be determined as well.When the adaptive motion skip mode achieves better performance than other coding modes, the disparity offset $offset_i$ is transmitted to the decoder for the derivation of the motion information $\mathbf{M}_{opt}$, without need to encode reference index, mbtype as well as motion vectors.

4 Experimental Results and Analysis

The experiments are conducted on the sampling-aided scheme for AVS. Compared with adaptive motion skip mode (AMS), the coding scheme without AMS is tested.

In order to present more results of the proposed algorithm, multiview sequences are included in the evaluation. The number of reference picture is set to 1 and the quantization parameter (QP) is assigned to 36, 40, 44, and 48 separately to maximize coding gains. In addition, the prediction structure of P pictures is applied to temporal prediction and the first 100 frames of each set of the sequences are encoded. The function of context-based adaptive binary arithmetic coding (CABAC) and rate-distortion optimization is enabled. The search range for motion is 32, and the size of the search window for the proposed algorithm is (5 × 8-pel).

The rate-distortion curves for two sequences are illustrated in Fig. 2. Horizontal axis and the vertical axis represent the average bit rate and the average PSNR respectively. BD PSNR and Bit Rate reduction are shown in Table 1. Moreover, in each sequence, the ration of macroblocks,which have chosen our proposed mode, is presented in Table 2. As a result, the coding efficiency is promoted due to the adoption of adaptive motion skip mode.

Apparently, due to the application of Adaptive Motion Skip mode, the coding performance makes significantly advance in contrast to sample-aided scheme for AVS without the aid of our approach. As demonstrated in Table 1, significant coding gains of −4.7362%/0.2842 dB and −4.5602%/0.277466 dB can be achieved for sequences such as Balloons and Kendo respectively.

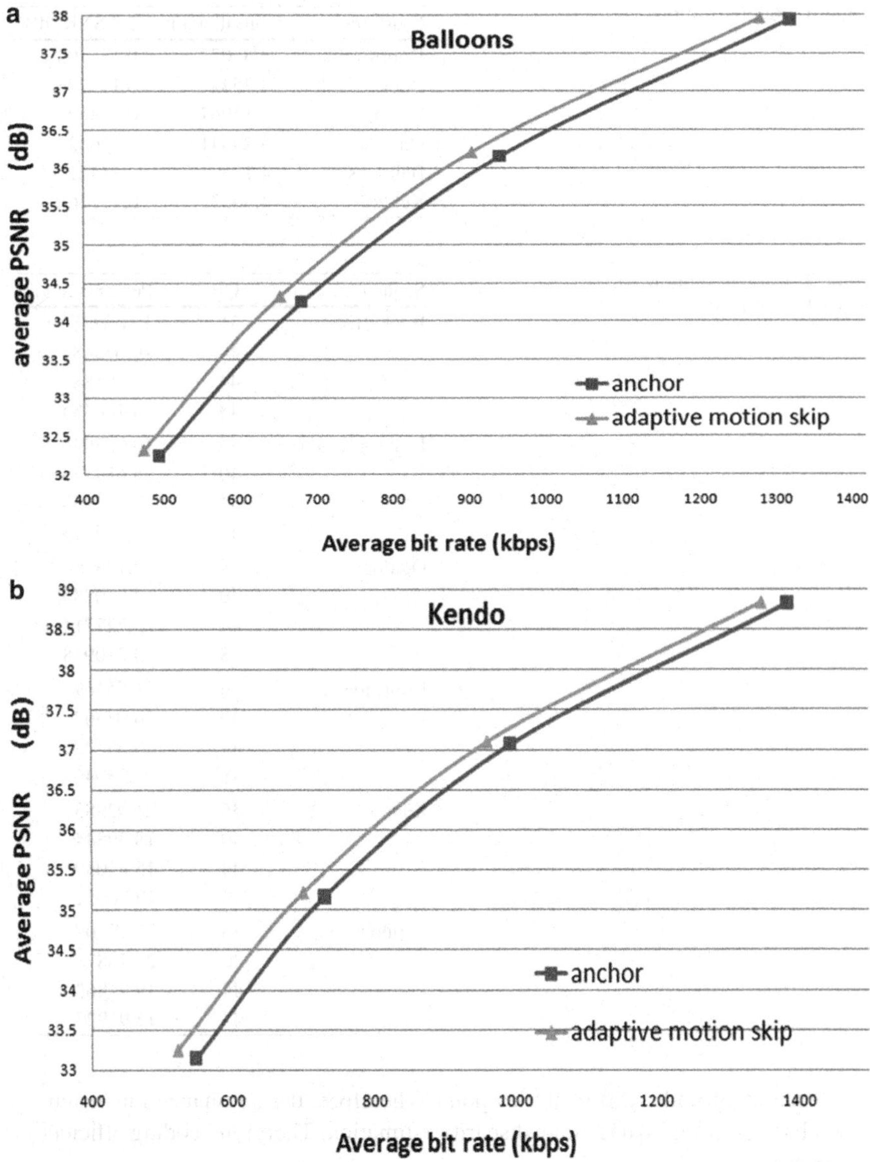

Fig. 2 Rate-distortion curves for (**a**) Balloons, (**b**) Kendo

The reason why Balloons demonstrate best performance is that the sequence is captured by moving camera. In consequence, our approach has advantage over temporal motion compensation on that condition. Outdoor performs worst, since this sequence subjects to severe distinction between neighboring views. As the sequence is captured on outdoor condition, the light condition differs

Table 1 Rate-distortion comparison

Sequence	Δ bitrate (%)	Δ PSNR (dB)
Doorflower	−4.54077	0.176193
Bookarrival	−4.7544	0.195226
Laptop	−4.17967	0.16362
Outdoor	−3.29341	0.12652
Balloons	−4.7362	0.28421
Kendo	−4.5602	0.277466

Table 2 Ratio of motion skipped macroblocks

Sequence	QP	Percentage (%)
Bookarrival	36	12.06901
	40	10.67448
	44	9.39388
	48	8.146484
Leavinglaptop	36	10.05794
	40	8.684245
	44	7.723958
	48	6.695313
Outdoor	36	4.128255
	40	4.240885
	44	3.727214
	48	3.210938
DoorFlowers	36	11.55469
	40	10.04362
	44	8.585286
	48	7.230469
Kendo	36	21.02083
	40	18.39844
	44	15.65039
	48	13.70052
Balloons	36	27.10807
	40	23.73828
	44	19.91862
	48	15.91927

from each other under different viewpoint. Therefore, the luminance mismatch is inevitable, resulting in inaccurate disparity estimation. Therefore, coding efficiency is decreased.

5 Conclusion

This paper presents an adaptive motion skip mode for AVS sample-aided 3D video coding scheme. Conducted on AVS codec, 8-pel precision motion estimation is applied to reorganized video in reference to the top picture of video. Along with variance of local disparity, the method is adaptive and utilizes a predefined offset search window for the purpose of obtaining accurate local disparity. Experimental results show that rate-distortion performance is promoted significantly.

Acknowledgements This work was supported in part by National Science Foundation (60833013,60803068) and National Basic Research Program of China (973 Program, 2009CB320903).

References

1. Advanced video coding for generic audio-visual services, ITU-T Recommendation H.264 & ISO/IEC 14496–10 AVC (2003).
2. M. Flierl, A. Mavlankar, and B. Girod.: Motion and disparity compensated coding for multi-view video, IEEE Transactions on Circuits and Systems for Video Technology (2007).
3. H. Schwarz, D. Marpe, and T. Wiegand.: Analysis of hierarchical B-pictures and MCTF, IEEE International Conference on Multimedia and Exposition (2006).
4. A. Smolic, K. Mueller, N. Stefanoski, J. Ostermann, A. Gotchev, G.B. Akar, G. Triantafyllidis, and A. Koz.:Coding Algorithms for 3DTV-A Survey, IEEE Transactions on Circuits and Systems for Video Technology, 17, 1606–1621(2007).
5. Xin Zhao, Xinfeng Zhang, Li Zhang, Siwei Ma, Wen Gao. Low-Complexity and Sampling-Aided Multi-view Video Coding at Low Bitrate, in Proceedings of IEEE Pacific-Rim Conference International Conference on Multimedia, PCM, Shanghai, China, pp.319–327, 21–24/09/2010
6. Joint Draft 8.0 on Multiview video coding, Joint Video Team (JVT) of ISO/IEC MPEG & ITU-T VCEG/JVT-AB204., 28th Meeting: Hannover (2008).
7. J.-H. Hur, S. Cho, and Y.-L. Lee.:Adaptive local illumination change compensation method for H.264/AVC-based multiview video coding,IEEE Trans. Circuits Syst. Video Technol., vol. 17, no. 11, pp. 1496–1505, Nov. 2007.
8. H.-S. Koo, Y.-J. Jeon, and B.-M. Jeon. (2006, Oct.). MVC Motion Skip Mode, ISO/IEC JTC1/ SC29/WG11 and ITU-T Q6/SG16, Doc. JVTU091.
9. X. Guo and Q. Huang.:Multiview video coding based on global motion model, Lecture Notes Comput. Sci., vol. 3333, pp. 665–672, 2004.
10. H.-S. Song, W.-S. Shim, Y.-H. Moon, and J.-B. Choi. (2007, Jan.).Macroblock Information Skip for MVC, ISO/IEC JTC1/SC29/WG11 and ITU-T Q6/SG16, Doc. JVT-V052.
11. Haitao Yang; Yilin Chang; Junyan Huo.:Fine-Granular Motion Matching for Inter-View Motion Skip Mode in Multiview Video Coding, Circuits and Systems for Video Technology, IEEE Transactions on, vol.19, no.6, pp.887–892, June 2009

Adaptive Search Range Methods for B Pictures Coding

Zhigang Yang

Abstract This paper presents some adaptive search range strategies at both frame and macroblock level for B pictures coding in H.264/AVC. First, a basic frame-level search range scaling strategy is proposed based on the linear motion relationship between P and B pictures, which is only suitable for normal or low motion situation. Then, an improved frame-level adaptive search range scaling (F-ASRS) algorithm is proposed by taking full advantage of intra mode and motion vector statistics. F-ASRS algorithm can precisely detect the global motion degree and adjust the search range of next B picture in advance. The local motion is further studied according to the information of the adjacent previous coded blocks, and then a macroblock-level adaptive search range (MB-ASR) algorithm is proposed. When integrating F-ASRS with MB-ASR, the search area of B pictures can be greatly reduced without any coding performance loss.

Keywords Video coding • Adaptive search range • B pictures • H.264/AVC

1 Introduction

In hybrid video coding, B pictures are encoded using both future and past pictures as references [1]. In H.264/AVC standard, there are usually five prediction modes in B pictures coding, including forward prediction, backward prediction, bi-prediction, direct prediction and intra modes. The usage of direct and bi-prediction modes is able to exploit the temporal correlation efficiently, especially for uncovering areas caused by zooming, non-linear motion etc. B pictures can also be coarsely quantized as B picture does not propagate errors when it is not used as a

Z. Yang (✉)
College of Information and Communication, Harbin Engineering University,
Harbin 150001, China
e-mail: zgyang@hrbeu.edu.cn

J.S. Jin et al., *The Era of Interactive Media*,
DOI 10.1007/978-1-4614-3501-3_12,

reference. In a word, B pictures become a substantial part in video coding in terms of both coding performance and video transmissions.[1]

The computational complexity of B pictures is far higher than that of I and P pictures. In order to accelerate B pictures coding, fast block matching algorithm might be used. However, in hardware implementation, full search (FS) is usually adopted, because the specific hardware is usually designed for pipelines but not for uncertain branch operations. Another efficient way to reduce the computation is search range adjustment for different motion-level video. When FS is adopted, the search range mainly determines the runtime. Furthermore, the processor can only deal with the data which have already been loaded into the high speed cache from outside. Therefore the size of search window also affects the cache hit rate and the data exchange rate between on-chip and extended memory [2]. In one word, a reasonable search range should not only reduce the coding time but also keep the coding performance.

There are two kinds of search range adjustment algorithms; one is at block level, the other is at frame level. Most of the block-level algorithms, like [3–6], use the motion information of the adjacent previous coded blocks to estimate the current block's search range. For example, Hong and Kim [3] proposed a macroblock-level dynamic search range (DSR) algorithm for H.264, and Xu and He [4] further extended the DSR algorithm to a subblock-level algorithm. Although these block-level algorithms use the local motion information to achieve relatively precise control, they are not efficient for hardware implementation because there are serious correlations between the current block and the adjacent previous coded blocks. The frame-level search range adjustment algorithm is more suitable for hardware implementation. Hosur [5] and Yamada et al. [6] have mentioned some frame-level algorithms, but they are combined with other macroblock-level algorithms and can not give a good performance when working separately. Minocha and Shanbhag [7] proposed a frame-level window follower (WF) algorithm, but it would fail in the case of sudden motion changes. Saponara and Fanucci [8] used blocks' SAD values to overcome the limits of the WF algorithm and the improved WF algorithm was adopted in some VLSI hardware design.

The main purpose of the present study is to develop efficient search range adjustment algorithms for B pictures coding based on our previous work [9], in order to reduce the computational complexity as well as to keep the coding performance. The rest of this paper is organized as follows. In Sect. 2, the motion feature in P and B pictures is first studied, and then a basic search range scaling method is introduced. After analyzing the limits of the basic method, an improved frame-level adaptive search range scaling algorithm is presented. In Sect. 3, a MB-level adaptive search range algorithm is proposed. Simulated results are demonstrated in Sect. 4 to show the effectiveness of the proposed algorithms. Finally, the paper is concluded in Sect. 5.

[1] This work was supported in part by the Fundamental Research Funds for the Central Universities under Grant HEUCFR1017.

2 Search Range Scaling

2.1 Basic Search Range Scaling (SRS)

Generally speaking, the motion vectors (MVs) in P pictures are often greater than the MVs in B pictures because the temporal distance between B picture and its forward/backward reference pictures (mainly refer to P pictures) is smaller than the distance between the forward and backward reference pictures. Suppose that there is an object M moving from point A in the forward reference picture to point B in the backward reference picture, and the corresponding position in the current B picture is point C, as shown in Fig. 1. Then

$$\mathrm{CA} : \mathrm{CB} : \mathrm{BA} = \mathrm{tb} : \ -\mathrm{tp} : \mathrm{td} \tag{1}$$

where *tb* and *tp* denote the temporal distance between the current B picture and the forward/backward reference pictures respectively, and *td* denotes the temporal distance between the forward and backward reference pictures. *CA* and *CB* represent the forward/backward MVs of the block in object M in current B picture respectively, and *BA* represents the MV of the block in object M in the backward P picture.

According to (1), a basic search range scaling algorithm for B pictures can be obtained as follows:

$$\begin{array}{l} SR_F = \begin{cases} \lceil SR_{init} \times tb/td \rceil & \text{, for the latest forward reference picture} \\ SR_{init} & \text{, for the other forward reference picture} \end{cases} \\ SR_B = \lceil SR_{init} \times tp/td \rceil \quad \text{, for the latest backward reference picture} \end{array} \tag{2}$$

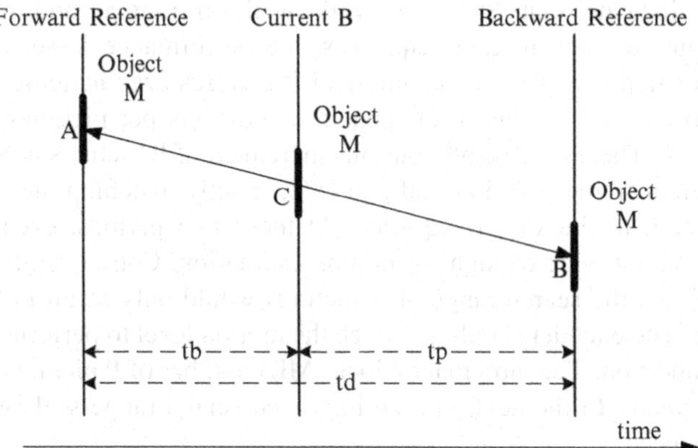

Fig. 1 Diagram of motion relationship in P/B pictures

Table 1 Test conditions

Ref software	H.264/AVC JM10.2	Search range	24
MV resolution	1/4 pixel	ME	Fast full search (FFS)
RDO	OFF	GOP	IBBPBBP
P ref number	2	QP	24,28,32,36
B ref number	1 forward, 1 backward	Loop filter	ON

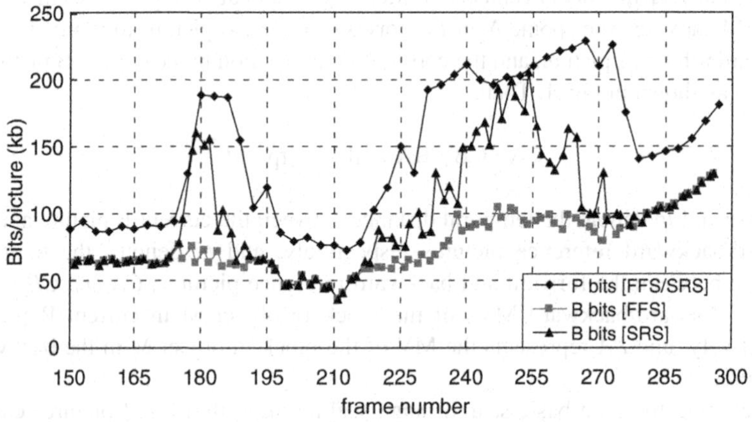

Fig. 2 Bitrate comparisons per picture of SRS and FFS on *stefan* when QP = 24

where SR_F and SR_B denotes the forward and backward search range of B pictures respectively, and SR_{init} denotes the initial (also maximum) search range of P pictures.

Six CIF sequences are selected to evaluate SRS algorithm, including *stefan, foreman, bus, mobile, news*, and *paris*. Test conditions are listed in Table 1. Our experiments indicate that SRS can work well on normal and low motion sequences, but for high motion sequences, the performance losses quite a lot. Especially for *stefan* sequence, the bitrate of B pictures even increases more than 26%. To further analyze this phenomenon, coding bits per picture on *stefan* is shown in Fig. 2. There are two obvious bits increment of B pictures in SRS' curve, which happen at frame 176–191 and 220–278, exactly matching the two periods of sharp motion in the *stefan* sequence. At these two periods, even the initial search range is not wide enough for motion estimation. Consequently still using SRS to cut down the search range of B pictures would only result in bad coding performance. The encoder should prejudge the motion level to perform SRS under the proper condition. The intra macroblock (MB) number of P picture could be an efficient judgment. In the next part, an improved search range scaling algorithm will be introduced.

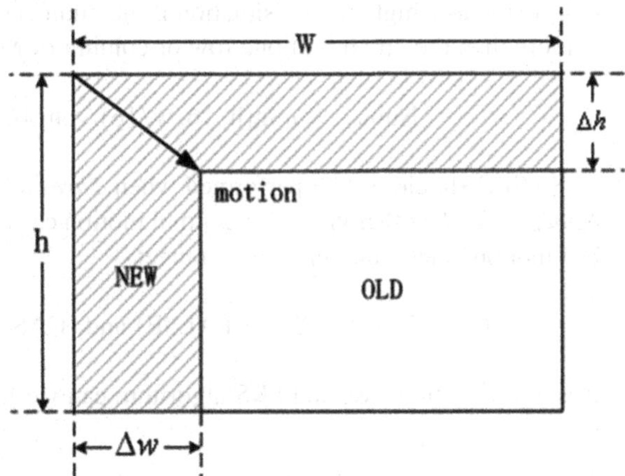

Fig. 3 Demonstration of picture division caused by motion

2.2 *Frame-Level Adaptive Search Range Scaling (F-ASRS)*

2.2.1 Adaptive Threshold Decision

Figure 3 shows a common situation of picture division caused by motion. Some symbols are firstly defined as follows. w and h ($w \geq h$) are the width and height of the picture; Δw and Δh are picture offsets in horizontal and vertical direction caused by the motion. OLD is the remained area from last P picture, and NEW is the new area of the picture caused by the motion. SR_{init} is the initial search range.

Assume that MBs in the NEW area are mostly intra coded because there are probably no reference blocks. Let Num_{intra} denote the number of intra MB, and then the motion is classified into three cases:

1. The motion exceeds double search range:

$$\mathrm{CASE1} = (\Delta \mathrm{w} \geq 2\mathrm{SR_{init}}) \text{ or } (\Delta \mathrm{h} \geq 2\mathrm{SR_{init}})$$

$$\mathrm{Num_{intra}} \geq \mathrm{h}/16 \times \Delta \mathrm{w}/16 + (\mathrm{w} - \Delta \mathrm{w})/16 \times \Delta \mathrm{h}/16 \geq \mathrm{h}/16 \times \lfloor SR_{init}/8 \rfloor = \mathrm{Thd1}$$

   It is a high motion case, therefore SRS should not be performed.

2. The motion is less than double search range but more than search range:

$$\mathrm{CASE2} = (\mathrm{CASE1} = \mathrm{FALSE}) \text{ and } ((\mathrm{SR_{init}} \leq \Delta \mathrm{w} < 2\mathrm{SR_{init}}) \text{or} (\mathrm{SR_{init}} \leq \Delta \mathrm{w} < 2\mathrm{SR_{init}}))$$

$$Num_{intra} < Threshold1, \text{ and}$$
$$\mathrm{Num_{intra}} \geq \mathrm{h}/16 \times \Delta \mathrm{w}/16 + (\mathrm{w} - \Delta \mathrm{w})/16 \times \Delta \mathrm{h}/16 \geq \mathrm{h}/16 \times \lfloor SR_{init}/8 \rfloor = Thd2$$

   In this case, if there is a inter-coded MB in the OLD area, its motion vector (mv_x, mv_y) possibly satisfies that $mv_x \geq SR_{init}$ or $mv_y \geq SR_{init}$. Then it is considered as a high motion situation if the number of this kind of MB (*Num_{mv}*) is more than the number of one row or column of MBs.

$$\mathrm{Num_{mv}} \geq \min(h/16, w/16) \geq h/16 = \mathrm{Thd3}$$

So SRS should not be performed when *Threshold1* $>$ *Num_{intra}* $\geq$ *Thd2* and *Num_{mv}* $\geq$ *Thd3*; otherwise it is a normal motion case and SRS can be performed.

3. The motion is less than the search range:

$$\mathrm{CASE3} = (\mathrm{CASE1} = \mathrm{FALSE})\ \text{and}\ (\mathrm{CASE2} = \mathrm{FALSE}).$$

It is a low motion case and SRS algorithm can work well.

2.2.2 F-ASRS Algorithm

The main idea of F-ASRS algorithm is as follows: create the *Num_{intra}* and *Num_{mv}* statistics after a P picture is coded; prejudge the search range for the next B picture in terms of the three thresholds, *Thd1*, *Thd2*, and *Thd3*, and record the results to two tags, *ForScalable* and *BackScalable*; decide whether to adjust the forward and backward search range according to the prejudgment results before coding the next B picture. The flow chart of F-ASRS algorithm is shown in Fig. 4.

3 Adaptive Search Range

F-ASRS algorithm introduced in Sect. 2.2 is able to judge the whole picture's motion degree and scale the search range at frame level through a group of adaptive thresholds. It is suitable for adapting the search range to the global motion. But it is not efficient to control the search range at frame level when there are lots of local motions in the picture. In this section, a local search range decision method at MB level is discussed and then integrated with F-ASRA algorithm to achieve more efficient search range adjustment strategy for B pictures coding.

3.1 MB-level Adaptive Search Range (MB-ASR) Algorithm

As shown in Fig. 5, E is the current MB under motion estimation and the four (left, up, up-left, and up-right) neighboring blocks are respectively A, B, C, and D with the corresponding MVs (mva_x, mva_y), (mvb_x, mvb_y), (mvc_x, mvc_y), and (mvd_x, mvd_y). SR_{init} is the initial search range and also the maximum search range. Then the MB-level adaptive search range (MB-ASR) algorithm is described as following steps.

Image type

I

P

B

Coding I picture

First frame ?

Y

N

BackScalable = TURE

ForScalable = BackScalable

Coding P picture

Num_{intra}& Num_{mv}Stat.

ForScalable = BackScalable

$Num_{intra} \geq Thd1$?

Y

N

$Num_{intra} \geq Thd2$?

Y

N

$Num_{mv} \geq Thd3$?

Y

N

BackScalable = FALSE

BackScalable = TURE

ForScalable=TRUE&& BackScalable=TRUE ?

Y

N

for latest ref picture

$SR_F = \lceil SR_{init} * tb/td \rceil$

$SR_B = \lceil SR_{init} * tb/td \rceil$

$SR_F = SR_B = SR_{init}$

Coding B picture

Next picture

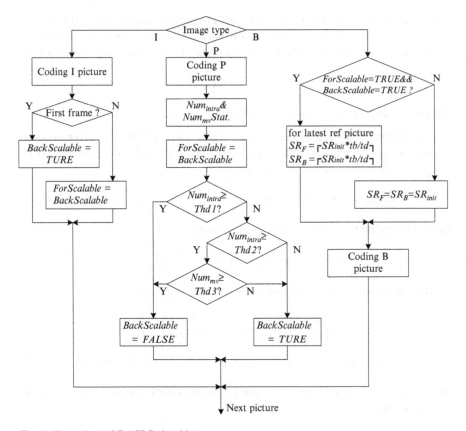

Fig. 4 Flow chart of F-ASRS algorithm

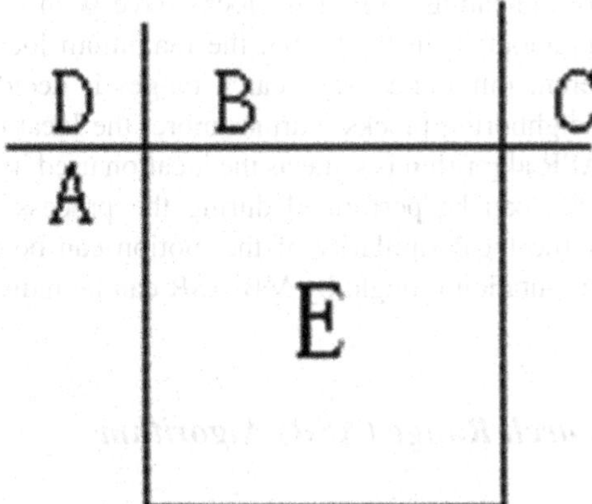

Fig. 5 Reference block location for local search range decision

Step1: Select three blocks A, B, and C and check their availabilities. If C is not available, it is replaced by D. If at most one block is available or at least one block is intra coded among the three blocks, the temporary local search range is written as

$$SR'_{local} = SR_{init} \tag{3}$$

and then go to Step 4; otherwise go to Step 2.

Step2: Determine the maximum absolute value mve_{max} from the given motion vectors of the three blocks selected in Step1. If any block is unavailable, 0 is assigned to its motion vector components.

$$mve_{max} = \max\left(|mva_x|, |mva_y|, |mvb_x|, |mvb_y|, |mvc_x|, |mvc_y|\right) \tag{4}$$

Step3: Determine the temporary local search range as

$$SR'_{locall} = \max(SR_{\min}, (3^{*}mve_{\max} + 1) >> 1) \tag{5}$$

where the local minimum search range SR_{min} is defined as

$$\begin{aligned} SR_{\min} &= (SR_{init} + 4) >> 3 \text{ if sum} = 0 \\ SR_{\min} &= (SR_{init} + 2) >> 2 \text{ if sum} > 0 \end{aligned} \tag{6}$$

$$sum = |mva_x| + |mva_y| + |mvb_x| + |mvb_y| + |mvc_x| + |mvc_y| \tag{7}$$

Step4: The local search range is subject to the initial search range, so it is constrained as

$$[SR_{local} = \min(SR_{local}, SR_{init})] \tag{8}$$

In the Step1, a small number of available blocks mean not enough local motion information, so the search range is not modified; and if one of the adjacent blocks is intra coded, probably indicating no proper blocks have been matched, the maximum search range is adopted. In the Step3, the maximum local search range is $1.5mve_{max}$, and different minimum local search ranges is decided in accordance with movement of neighboring blocks. Further more, the location of neighboring blocks used in MB-ASR algorithm is same as the location used in the motion vector predictor, so MB-ASR can be performed during the process of motion vector prediction. Not only the local similarity of the motion can be made full use of, but also the extra computation brought by MB-ASR can be reduced.

3.2 Adaptive Search Range (ASR) Algorithm

Integrating the frame-level adaptive search range scaling F-ASRS algorithm in Sect. 2.2 with the MB-level adaptive search range MB-ASR algorithm in Sect. 3.1, the final adaptive search range (ASR) algorithm for B pictures is proposed. First, the

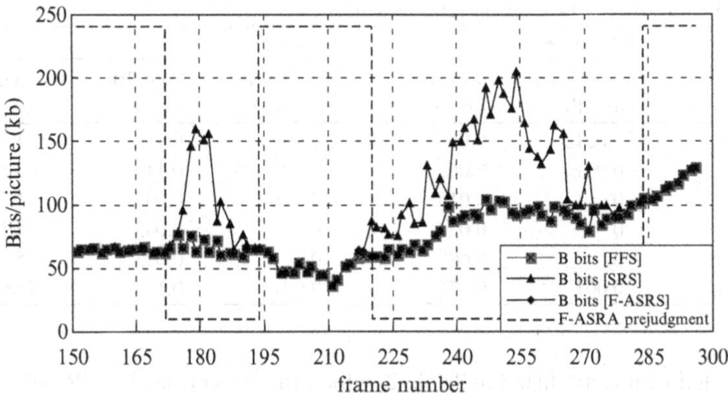

Fig. 6 Bitrate comparisons per picture of F-ASRS, SRS and FFS on *stefan* when QP = 24

global search range $SR_{F\text{-}ASRS}$ is determined at frame level through the F-ASRS algorithm. And then the local search range $SR_{MB\text{-}ASR}$ is decided at MB level through the MB-ASR algorithm. The smaller one is finally chosen to be the new search range SR_{MB} for the current MB, which is

$$[\mathrm{SR}_{MB} = \min(\mathrm{SR}_{\mathrm{F-ASRS}}, \mathrm{SR}_{\mathrm{MB-ASR}})] \tag{9}$$

4 Simulated Results

4.1 Experiments on F-ASRS

In Sect. 2.1, the performance of SRS algorithm on *stefan* sequence has been shown in Fig. 2, and it demonstrates that SRS does not work well on high motion sequences. Since the search range scaling algorithm has been improved, F-ASRS algorithm is applied on *stefan* sequence to do the same experiment as SRS algorithm. The test conditions are listed in Table 1.

Figure 6 shows bitrate comparisons per picture of F-ASRS, SRS and FFS on *stefan* when QP = 24. The dashed line represents F-ASRS prejudgment of the search range and indicates that F-ASRS algorithm can make a right decision whether to scale the search range for each B picture or not.

To evaluate F-ASRS algorithm under difference picture size and different search range, six 720p sequences with 60fps are selected, including *city*, *cyclists*, *harbour*, *night*, *shuttlestart*, and *spincalendar*. The test conditions are: search range 48, QP 27, 30, 35, 40, and the other conditions are same with Table 1.

Table 2 Performance of F-ASRS on 720p sequences

	All pictures		B pictures		
Seq.	Avg. PSNR gain (dB)	Avg. BR saving (%)	Avg. PSNR gain (dB)	Avg. BR saving (%)	Avg. SA saving (%)
City	−0.001	0.062	−0.001	0.11	71.76
Cyclists	−0.001	0.065	−0.001	0.115	52.11
Harbour	0	0.015	0	0.034	71.76
Night	0	0.021	0	0.043	25.12
Shuttlestart	0	0.009	0	0.023	55.98
Spincalendar	0.001	0.071	0.001	0.12	71.61

The detailed results are listed in Table 2, which further verifies F-ASRS algorithm to be efficient for B pictures in both maintaining the picture quality and reducing computational quantity.

4.2 Experiments on ASR

Six CIF sequences with 30fps are selected to evaluate F-ASRS and ASR algorithm, including two high motion sequences *stefan* and *foreman*, two normal motion sequences *bus* and *mobile*, and two low motion sequences *news* and *paris*. The test conditions are listed in Table 1. To evaluate the effectiveness of the proposed algorithms, the search area (SA) saving rate is calculated, which is defined as

$$F_{SA} = \left(1 - \frac{\sum\limits_{dir \in \{F,B\}} \sum\limits_{k=0}^{N-1} (2 \times SR_{dir,k} + 1)^2}{2N \times (2 \times SR_{init} + 1)^2} \right) \times 100\% \quad (10)$$

where *dir* denotes the direction of the reference picture, *k* denotes the index of MB, *N* denotes the total number of MB in a picture, $SR_{dir,k}$ denotes the search range of the *k*th MB in a reference picture, and $(2\times SR_{dir,k}+1)^2$ denotes the SA. To further evaluate the effectiveness of the proposed algorithms, ASR and F-ASRS are compared with dynamic search range (DSR) [3] and window follower (WF) algorithms [8]. DSR algorithm can efficiently adjust the search range at MB level in H.264, and WF is a low-complexity algorithm at both frame and MB level which is often adopted in VLSI hardware design.

Table 3 lists the coding performance of FFS, ASR, F-ASRS, DSR, and WF on two typical sequences, *stefan* and *news*. ASR, F-ASRS, DSR, and WF have the same coding performance compared with FFS, which indicates that these four algorithms can adjust the search range as well as keeping coding efficiency at the same time.

Table 3 Performance comparisons of FFS, ASR, F-ASRS, DSR, and WF

		PSNR (dB)				Bitrate (kbps)			
Seq.	QP	24	28	32	36	24	28	32	36
Stefan	FFS	38.222	35.133	31.855	28.809	2566.1	1507.9	836.96	476.65
	ASR	38.220	35.130	31.851	28.805	2570.5	1513.9	839.16	478.31
	F-ASRS	38.222	35.131	31.854	28.809	2566.0	1510.1	837.36	477.01
	DSR	38.221	35.131	31.852	28.805	2569.9	1510.9	839.08	477.86
	WFA	38.222	35.133	31.854	28.809	2565.6	1507.7	837.25	476.71
News	FFS	40.434	37.918	35.026	32.345	378.25	229.36	139.04	84.17
	ASR	40.433	37.917	35.025	32.345	377.71	229.63	139.29	84.57
	F-ASRS	40.433	37.918	35.026	32.345	377.68	229.23	139.06	84.27
	DSR	40.433	37.918	35.026	32.345	377.92	229.74	139.45	84.60
	WFA	40.433	37.918	35.026	32.345	377.74	229.08	139.05	84.21

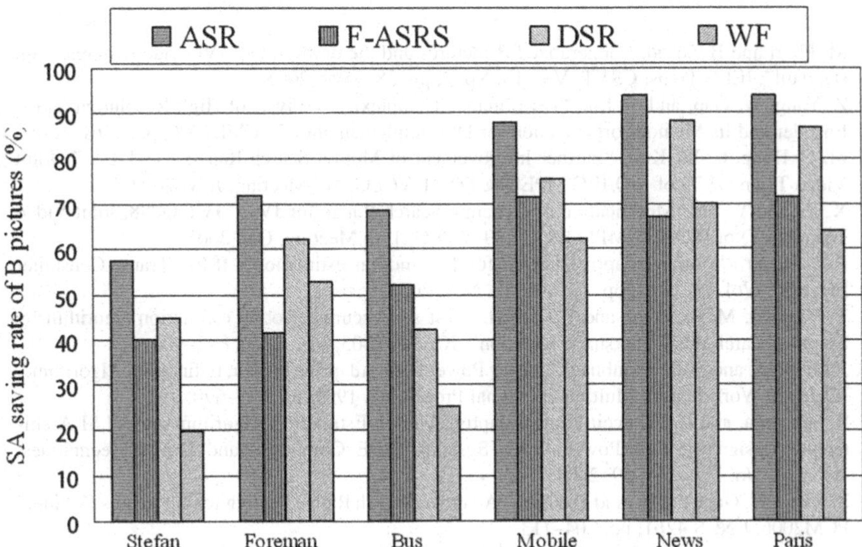

Fig. 7 SA saving rate of B pictures of ASR, F-ASRS, DSR, and WF

SA saving rate of B pictures of ASR, F-ASRS, DSR, and WF is shown in Fig. 7. On the whole, all the four algorithms have high SA saving rate on *news*, *pairs*, and *mobile*, and low SA saving rate on *stefan*; and ASR has the best performance. SA saving rate of ASR on all the six sequences is the highest, from 57.6% (on *stefan*) to 93.9% (on *news*). SA saving rate of F-ASRS is from 39.8% (on *stefan*) to 71.3% (on *pairs*). SA saving rate of DSR is from 42.2% (on *bus*) to 88.2% (on *news*). SA saving rate of WF is from 19.9% (on *stefan*) to 69.8% (on *news*).

5 Conclusion

In this paper, a novel ASR algorithm for B pictures is presented, which can precisely control the search range and efficiently reduce the computational complexity of B pictures while keeping the same coding performance. ASR algorithm includes two parts, F-ASRS and MB-ASR algorithm. F-ASRS algorithm determines the search range at frame level according to the linear motion relationship between P and B pictures, first detecting the global motion degree of P pictures and then prejudging the search range of following B pictures. MB-ASR algorithm modifies the search range at MB level based on the local motion information of the adjacent coded blocks.

References

1. M. Flierl and B. Girod, "Generalized B pictures and the draft H.264/AVC video-compression standard", IEEE Trans. CSVT, Vol. 13, No. 7, pp. 587–597, 2003.
2. Z. Yang, W. Gao, and Y. Liu, "Performance-Complexity Analysis of High Resolution Video Encoder and Its Memory organization for DSP Implementation", ICME2006, pp. 1261–1264.
3. M.-C. Hong, C.-W. Kim. "Further Improvement of Motion Search Range." JVT-D117, Joint Video Team (JVT) of ISO/IEC MPEG & ITU-T VCEG, 4rd Meeting, July, 2002.
4. X. Xu and Y. He. "Modification of Dynamic Search Range for JVT." JVT-Q088, Joint Video Team (JVT) of ISO/IEC MPEG & ITU-T VCEG, 17th Meeting, Oct, 2005
5. P. I. Hosur, "Motion adaptive search for fast motion estimation", IEEE Trans. Consumer Electron., Vol. 49, No.4, pp. 1330–1340, Nov. 2003.
6. T. Yamada, M. Ikekawa, and I. Kuroda, "Fast and accurate motion estimation algorithm by adaptive search range and shape selection", ICASSP2005, Vol. 2, pp. 897–900.
7. J. Minocha, and N. R. Shanbhag. "A Low Power Data-Adaptive Motion Estimation Algorithm." IEEE 3rd Workshop on Multimedia Signal Processing. 1999, pp. 685–690.
8. S. Saponara, and L. Fanucci. "Data-Adaptive Motion Estimation Algorithm and VLSI Architecture Design for Low-Power Video Systems." IEE Computers and Digital Techniques, Vol. 151, No. 1, pp. 51–59, 2004.
9. Z. Yang, W. Gao, Y. Liu, and D. Zhao, "Adaptive Search Range Scaling for B Pictures Coding." PCM2006, LNCS 4261, pp. 704–713.

Replacing Conventional Motion Estimation with Affine Motion Prediction for High-Quality Video Coding

Hoi-Kok Cheung and Wan-Chi Siu

Abstract In modern video coding systems, motion estimation and compensation play an indispensable role among various video compression tools. However, translation motion model is still extensively employed for motion compensation, making the systems not efficient in handling complex inter-frame motion activity including scaling, rotation and various forms of distortion. In this paper, we propose a local affine motion prediction method, which manages to improve the inter-frame image prediction quality using the conventional motion vectors. Our method is characterized with no extra overhead, such that no extra bit has to be sent to the decoder for proper decoding. Experimental results show that our method manages to achieve a maximum average bit rate reduction of 5.75% compared to the conventional inter-frame prediction method using translation only motion compensation techniques, at no cost on quality degradation. Our proposed algorithm is useful for the current video standard, H.264, but is also particularly efficient for large partition size coding modes. For future video compression standards: high-efficiency video coding (HEVC) or the possible H.265, which could include partition sizes of 64 × 64 and 32 × 32, the coding gain should further be boosted by making use of our proposed algorithm.

Keywords Motion vectors • Affine prediction • Motion compensation • Affine motion

H.-K. Cheung • W.-C. Siu (✉)
Centre for Multimedia Signal Processing, Department of Electronic and Information Engineering, The Hong Kong Polytechnic University, Hung Hom, Kowloon, Hong Kong
e-mail: enwcsiu@polyu.edu.hk

J.S. Jin et al., *The Era of Interactive Media*,
DOI 10.1007/978-1-4614-3501-3_13,

1 Introduction

Block based motion estimation (ME) and compensation (MC) [1–4] play an indispensable role in recent coding standard with extra features of variable block-size and multiple references frame motion compensation [5–6]. However, the translational motion model is still being extensively used, which cannot efficiently describe the motion activities of the general video sequences including zooming, rotation and various forms of distortion.

To alleviate this problem, researchers proposed to use some more advanced parametric motion models, including geometric model, affine model and perspective model. Some examples of applications include image registration, static-sprite generation in MPEG-4 Sprite coding [7–10], and global motion compensation [10] in MPEG-4 advanced simple profile, which mainly focus on the global description of the motion field [12–14]. Recently, Kordasiewicz et. al. [15] proposed a post-processing step of applying the affine motion prediction (after all the MVs are computed) to the macroblock level. In this paper, we propose a pre-processing application of local affine motion prediction method to generate a better prediction of the coding MB. Figure 1a,1b show an example of two frames having significant rotation motion activity. Figure 1c shows the prediction of the macroblocks in the current image using conventional ME and MC techniques. There is a significant mis-alignment artefact because conventional MC technique does not allow the reference frame to be rotated. Figure 1d shows a much better prediction produced by our proposed method as we uses affine motion model allowing the reference frame to be rotated. The new prediction is generated to replace the original prediction before mode decision is made (pre-processing application). Therefore, the advantage of our new predictor can be fully considered in the RD optimization process. Our method is also characterized with the fact that no extra bit has to be sent to the decoder.

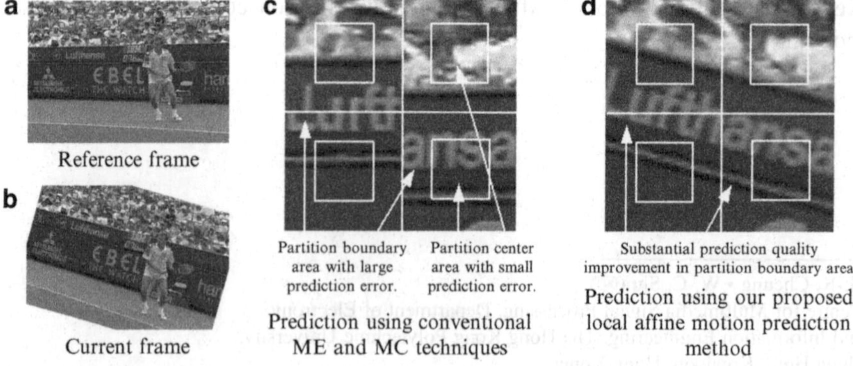

Fig. 1 Example illustrating the capability of our proposed local affine motion prediction method in predicting MBs which has rotation motion activity

2 Proposed Local Affine Prediction Method

In H.264 video coding system, macroblocks (MBs) are coded one by one from left to right and from top to bottom in a raster scan order. Therefore, in general case as shown in Fig. 2, there are four coded MBs (in green colour) close to the coding MB (the MB to be encoded, marked in red colour) and these four coded MBs may provide some local motion information for better description of the local motion activity. However, the conventional coding approach does not fully consider the motion information provided and assumes that all the pixels within the coding MB have identical motion activity represented by a single MV (16 × 16 coding mode, see Fig. 1c). We denote this conventional prediction as MV based prediction. In this paper, we propose a local affine prediction (LAP) method making use of the motion information provided by the four neighbouring coded MBs in addition to the MVs of the coding MB. The proposed method manages to increase the prediction quality for video sequences involving zooming, rotation and various forms of distortion.

The H.264 attempts to code each MB with different coding modes and selects the mode resulting the minimum RD cost. In the proposed system, we focus on applying the LAP method for coding modes with large partition sizes including the SKIP, 16 × 16, 16 × 8 and 8 × 16 modes (mode 0, 1, 2 and 3 respectively). The major reason is that we assume a MV can best represent the motion of the partition centre and conventional MV based prediction can best predict the pixels close to the centre of the partition. Thus, the prediction error is mostly distributed around the boundary of the partition. For small partition cases, the boundary pixels are

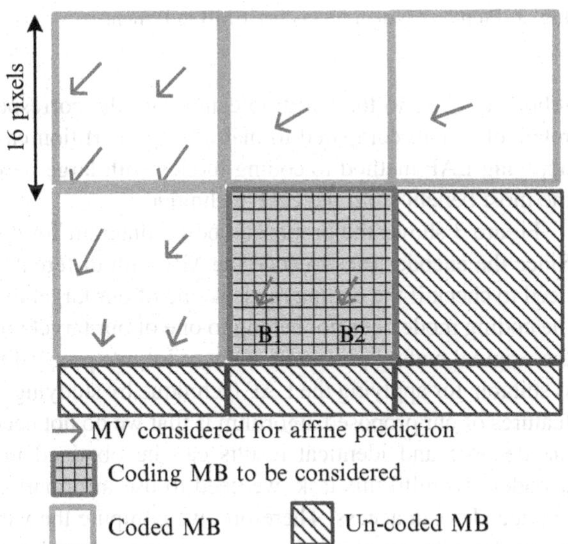

Fig. 2 Diagram illustrating the MVs considered for local affine prediction

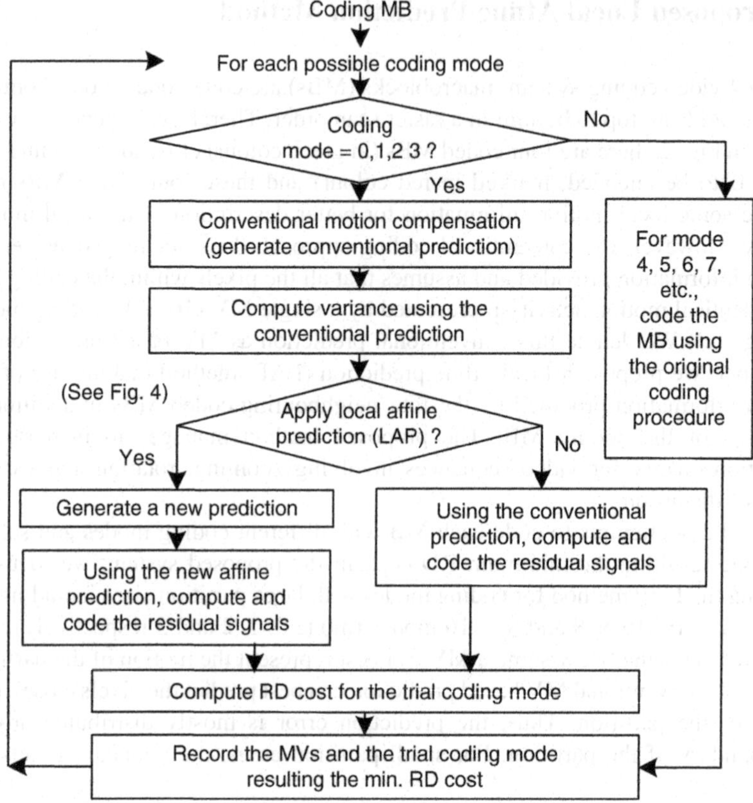

Fig. 3 Proposed system for coding 1 MB in P frame

relatively close to the partition centre and the corresponding prediction errors are relatively small compared to that of large partition cases. Therefore, we focus on applying LAP method to coding modes with large partition sizes which can share the most benefit from the LAP technique.

Figure 3 shows the proposed coding diagram for coding one MB in a P frame. Since the encoder tries to code the MB with different modes, at the first stage, we need to check if the coding mode is one of our target modes (mode 0, 1, 2 and 3). If the coding mode does not belong to one of our target modes, we code the MB using the original coding procedure. Otherwise, we proceed to analyse if the coding MB is suitable for applying the LAP technique by studying the MB variance. One of the features of our proposed algorithm is that we do not need to send extra overheads to the decoder and identical results can be obtained in both the encoder and the decoder. To fulfil this task, we need to use information that both the encoder and the decoder can access. Therefore, we compute the variance of the coding MB by using the MV based prediction generated using the conventional MC technique (identical procedure can also be done in the decoder).

Subsequently, a MB selection process is performed to determine if this particular MB is selected for applying the LAP technique to generate a new prediction replacing the MV based prediction. Identical MB selection process is also performed in the decoder so that the same decision can be made and no overhead bit has to be sent to signal the decision. By a careful selection of MBs, our new affine motion prediction can provide a better prediction compared with the MV based prediction and result a lower RD cost. Therefore, our algorithm can provide a better prediction to coding modes with large partition sizes and increase the chance for the coding system to select the coding modes with large partition sizes. This allows a more efficient video compression.

2.1 MB Selection Process

In our proposed algorithm, not all the MBs are selected to apply the local affine prediction (LAP) method to generate a new prediction. The objective of LAP method is to better describe the motion activity of the pixels within the coding MB so as to allow a better prediction in case object distortion occurs, e.g. object rotation. To achieve a good prediction using the affine prediction technique, we need to consider two issues; (1) the reliability of the MVs, and (2) the smoothness of the local motion field. An accurate motion field can describe the true object motion activity and allow an accurate description of the object deformation. If the MVs cannot truly describe the motion activity, (e.g. a MB from a homogeneous area, the lack of texture information can result in an unreliable (0,0) MV), the resulted affine motion prediction often yields a poor prediction. In this case, it is better to keep using the MV based prediction.

Another issue is the smoothness of the motion field. The five MBs (the coding MB and the four coded MBs) as shown in Fig. 2 may cover two objects having distinct motion activities which result in a motion field discontinuity. The estimated motion activity becomes unreliable and returns a poor prediction. In view of these two considerations, we propose to select MB using four tests: (1) coding MB variance test, (2) motion field discontinuity test, (3) uniform local motion vector field test, and (4) minimum number of selected neighbouring partition test (See Fig. 4). Coding MB, which can pass all the four tests, is selected to apply the LAP method and the resultant prediction is used to replace the MV based prediction.

Test 1: We identify the coding MB which is a boundary MB or MB with coding mode of INTRA category and exclude it from processing. Subsequently, we check if the variance of the coding MB (using the MV based prediction) is smaller than a user provided threshold, Tvar. MBs having variance smaller than the threshold are considered texture-less and we consider LAP technique cannot greatly improve the prediction quality of these MBs. These texture-less MBs are not selected for applying the LAP technique and MV based prediction is used for coding. The typical value for threshold Tvar is 0.4 for CIF sequences and 0.6 for HD sequences.

Fig. 4 MB selection process

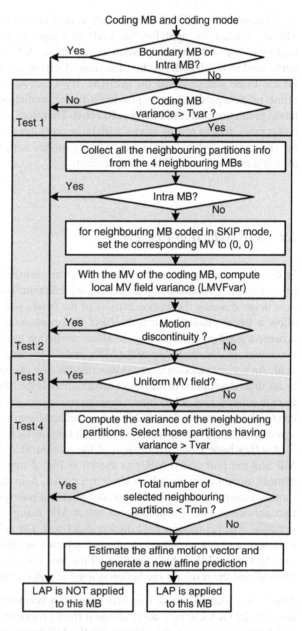

Test 2: The objective of this test is to examine the local motion vector field and identify if there is an abrupt change in motion vector field. We need to collect the neighbouring partitions information of all the partitions within the four neighbouring coded MBs as shown in Fig. 2. (For example in Fig. 2, we have to collect information for the 10 partitions inside the 4 MBs marked with green color). The information includes the motion vector, the coding mode, the partition centre

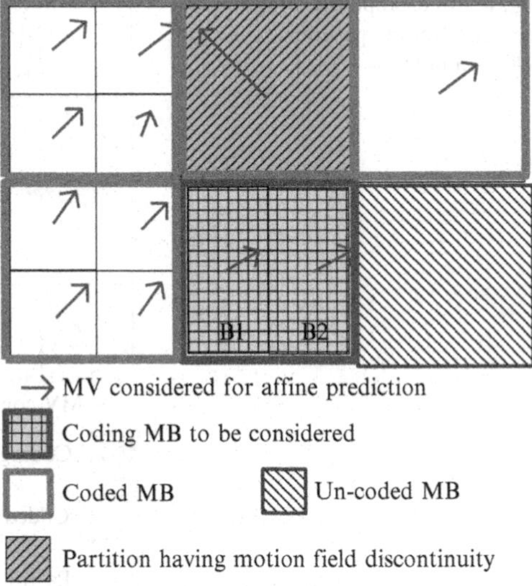

Fig. 5 An example showing an abrupt change in motion vector field

position and the variance of the partition. If any of the four neighbouring coded MBs is coded in INTRA mode, we do not apply the LAP technique to this coding MB as the motion vector field is not reliable for prediction. Otherwise, we compute the local motion vector field variance (LMVFvar) using the MVs of the neighbouring coded partitions and the coding MB. For example, we use all the 12 MVs in Fig. 2 to calculate LMVFvar using the following equation.

$$\text{LMVFvar} = \text{Var(MV.x)} + \text{Var(MV.y)} \tag{1}$$

where Var denotes the variance operator, Var(MV.x) and Var(MV.y) denotes the variance of the x-and y- component respectively of the 12 MVs in Fig. 2 (for instant). If the value of LMVFvar is larger than a threshold Tdis, we consider there is a great variety in the local motion vector field. I.e. the local area may cover two objects having distinct motion activities. Figure 5 shows an example in which the MB marked in blue color has a distinct motion vector from the other motion vectors. In this case, we do not apply the LAP technique to code the coding MB. Otherwise, we proceed to Test 3 for further testing. The typical value for threshold Tdis is 0.9 for CIF sequences and 1.5 for HD sequences.

Test 3: We check for uniform motion vector field (i.e. the MVs of the neighbouring partitions are the same). If all the MVs are the same, only translation motion exists. MV based prediction is good enough for coding the MB and LAP is not applied. In this test, we compare the value of LMVFvar, computed in Test 2, to a threshold Tunif. If the value of LMVFvar is smaller than Tunif, we assume the local motion vector field is nearly uniform and LAP is not applied to this coding MB. Otherwise, we proceed to Test 4 for testing. The typical value for the threshold Tunif is 0.05 for CIF sequences and 0.2 for HD sequences.

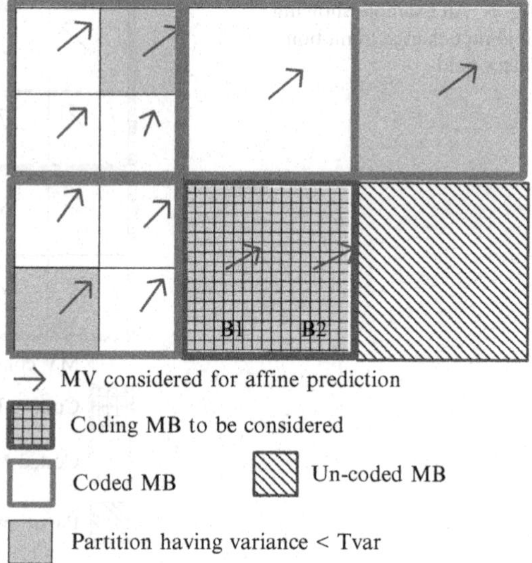

Fig. 6 An example showing the neighbouring partitions selection in test 4

Test 4: Finally, we test if there is sufficient local motion information to estimate affine motion parameters (to be explained in the next session). We first check the variance of each neighbouring coded partition. If the partition variance is smaller than the threshold Tvar, we consider the partition is texture-less and the corresponding MV is unreliable. That particular partition is not selected. Otherwise, the partition is selected and counted. The total number of selected neighbouring partitions is compared to a user provided threshold, Tmin. If the number is smaller than Tmin, we consider there is insufficient local motion field information for LAP technique and that particular coding MB is not selected to apply LAP. Figure 6 shows an example that the partitions marked in orange colour have variance smaller than Tvar and are not selected. Therefore, in this case, we have a total of seven neighbouring partitions selected. As the typical value of Tmin is 2, the coding MB passes this test. For MBs passing the four tests, we proceed to generate a new prediction using the MVs of the coding partitions and the selected neighbouring partitions.

2.2 A New Prediction Generated by LAP Method

For MBs decided to apply the LAP method, we use the affine motion model to model the local motion activity.

$$\begin{pmatrix} x' \\ y' \end{pmatrix} = \begin{pmatrix} a & b & c \\ d & e & f \end{pmatrix} \begin{pmatrix} x \\ y \\ 1 \end{pmatrix} \tag{2}$$

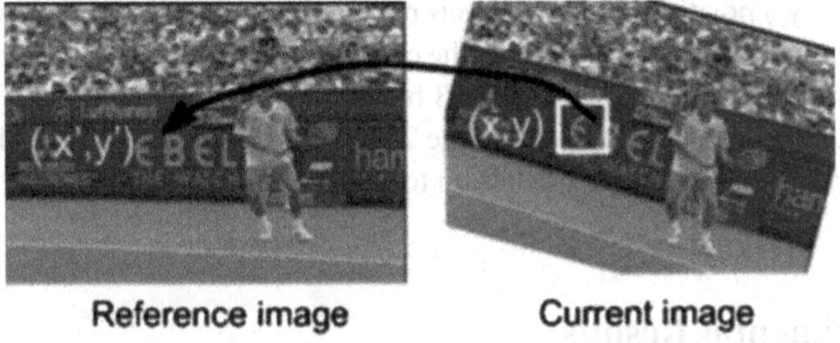

Fig. 7 Warping process to generate a prediction of the current MB

where (x,y) and (x',y') represent a pair of corresponding points denoting a point position in the current and reference frame respectively under affine transformation. The vector (a,b,c,d,e,f) is called affine motion vector which defines the positional mapping between the two images. We assume that a MV can best represent the motion of the partition centre. Thus, to estimate the vector, we make use of the MVs and the partition centres of the coding partitions and the selected neighbouring partitions. Subsequently, the affine motion vector can be estimated by means of least square technique.

For example, using Eq. (2), (x,y) and (x', y') = (x + MV.x, y + MV.y) denote the centre position of a 8 × 8 partition block in the current frame and its corresponding position in the reference frame respectively. Equation (2) can also be rewritten as

$$x' = (x\ y\ 1)\mathbf{V} \text{ and } y' = (x\ y\ 1)\mathbf{W} \tag{3}$$

where $\mathbf{V} = (a\ b\ c)^T$, $\mathbf{W} = (d\ e\ f)^T$ are two unknown vectors to be estimated. Assuming we have N partitions, 2 N equations can be formed and two systems of linear equations can be established.

$$X = \mathbf{BV} \text{ and } \mathbf{Y} = \mathbf{BW} \tag{4}$$

where each row of matrix B and vectors X and Y corresponds to the partition centre coordinates. (For the example shown in Fig. 6, we have nine partitions selected for processing. These nine partitions form nine sets of Eq. (3) and form one set of Eq. (4).) The least square solutions to the two systems are given by

$$\mathbf{V} = \left(\mathbf{B}^T\mathbf{B}\right)^{-1}\mathbf{B}^T\mathbf{X} \text{ and } \mathbf{W} = \left(\mathbf{B}^T\mathbf{B}\right)^{-1}\mathbf{B}^T\mathbf{Y} \tag{5}$$

After estimating the affine motion vector, we can use Eq. (2) to warp the reference frame and generate a new prediction [8, 9]. For example, in Fig. 7, we have a point (x, y) in the current MB to be predicted. We use Eq. (2) to compute the value of (x', y'). Then, we sample the pixel value in the reference frame using the computed (x', y') position. This process is repeated for all the pixels within the MB, regardless of the coding mode used for the coding MB. For example, the coding MB is coded in mode 3 in Fig. 6 with the MB being divided into two 8 × 16 partitions. The warping process is the same for all the 256 pixels within the coding MB. By this means, we can generate a new prediction to replace the MV prediction.

3 Experimental Results

To test the performance of our proposed method in H.264, a number of sequences were tested. In this paper, some testing sequences with typical results are reported including, CIF sequences FlowerGarden (150 frames) and Stefan (300 frames), which involve pronounced perspective distortion and some zooming camera operation; HD sequences Shield (720p, 80 frames), Cactus (1080p, 80 frames) and BlueSky (1080p, 80 frames), which involve significant scaling and rotation camera operations.

We compared the MB prediction quality and the coding efficiency of our proposed system with the original H.264 system, which uses the MV based prediction (ver. 12.2, search range = 32, 1 ref. frame, IPP structure and CABAC). Table 1 shows the summary of the average prediction gain (selected MB average prediction quality gain, denoted as Sel. MB pred. gain), the average bit rate changes and the usage rate (percentage of MBs selected for applying LAP method). We empirically set the values of the thresholds Tvar, Tdis, Tunif and Tmin to optimize the average bit rate reduction for each sequence. In our test, we configured two coding modes for testing: (1) allow only 16 × 16 partition size coding mode, and (2) allow all the possible coding modes to be used for coding each MB. In addition, we also test the coding performance of the proposed system under different frame skip (abbreviated as FS) ratios (For CIF sequences, we tested FS = 0, 1, 2 and 3. For HD sequences, we tested FS = 0, 3, 5 and 9.) and Table 1 only shows some typical results to illustrate the performance difference.

Our proposed method selects appropriate MBs to apply the LAP technique. For the selected MBs, from Table 1, almost all the sequences have prediction quality improvement compared to the MV based prediction. For small frame skip ratio (FS = 0), the prediction gain is low. Meanwhile, for large frame skip ratio (FS = 3 for CIF sequences and FS = 5 for HD sequences), the prediction gain increases up to 1.35 dB (Cactus sequence, FS = 5 and all modes allowed). This can be explained that the frame difference (resulted from rotation, scaling and various forms of distortion) is directly proportional to the frame skip ratio. If the frame difference increases, there is more room for improvement. In some cases with small frame skip ratio, e.g. FS = 0, the prediction quality using the LAP technique is lower than the MV based prediction because there is image quality drop resulted from interpolation process.

In addition to the amount of prediction quality improvement, another important issue affecting the coding performance is the portion of MBs selected applying the

Table 1 Summary of the proposed system coding gain compared with H.264

Sequences	Size	Frame skip	Block sizes	Sel. MB pred. gain (dB)	Usage rate (%)	Δbitrate (%)	Sequences	Size	Frame skip	Block sizes	Sel. MB pred. gain (dB)	Usage rate (%)	Δbitrate (%)
Flower-Garden	CIF	0	16 × 16	**0.05**	11.33	**−1.31**	Cactus	1080p	0	16 × 16	−0.51	1.21	0.99
Flower-Garden	CIF	0	All	**0.62**	9.17	**−0.75**	Cactus	1080p	0	All	**0.08**	0.74	0.71
Flower-Garden	CIF	3	16 × 16	**0.81**	34.90	**−5.75**	Cactus	1080p	5	16 × 16	**1.29**	1.79	**−2.2**
Flower-Garden	CIF	3	All	**1.09**	9.06	**−0.53**	Cactus	1080p	5	All	**1.35**	0.9	**−0.47**
Stefan	CIF	0	16 × 16	−0.27	4.08	0.03	BlueSky	1080p	0	16 × 16	−1.35	0.04	0.03
Stefan	CIF	0	All	**0.2**	2.39	**−0.01**	BlueSky	1080p	0	All	−0.09	0.08	**−0.02**
Stefan	CIF	3	16 × 16	**0.12**	6.55	**−1.22**	BlueSky	1080p	5	16 × 16	**0.25**	10.74	**−1.78**
Stefan	CIF	3	All	**0.35**	4.58	0.40	BlueSky	1080p	5	All	**0.42**	7.24	**−0.72**
Shield	720p	0	16 × 16	−0.98	0.27	1.37							
Shield	720p	0	All	**0.09**	0.66	1.17							
Shield	720p	5	16 × 16	**0.39**	8.88	**−4.4**							
Shield	720p	5	All	**0.82**	8.24	**−2.81**							

LAP technique (usage rate). From Table 1, we found that the MB usage rate is generally higher for CIF sequences than that of the HD sequences. Moreover, as frame skip ratio increases, the usage rate also increases. This can be explained by the complexity of the local motion vector field. For a single 16×16 MB, the relative frame covering area is larger in CIF sequences than that in HD sequences. Therefore, the relative local area covered by 5 MBs as shown in Fig. 2 in CIF sequences is larger than that in HD sequences and there is a higher chance for the covered area to have distortion (CIF sequences). (In other words, CIF sequences have a lower chance to have all the 12 MVs identical in Fig. 2). For HD sequences, due to the relatively less complex local motion vector field nature, it tends to have uniform motion vector field. Therefore, less MBs are selected to apply the LAP technique and it explains the fact that the usage rate for CIF sequences is higher than HD sequences. (This reason also explains that there are more MBs selected to be coded in large partition sizes in HD sequences than that in CIF sequences. See Figs. 11 and 12). As the frame skip ratio increases, the usage rate also tends to increases as the complexity of the local motion vector field increases. However, if the frame skip ratio is too large (e.g. FS = 9 for HD sequences, not shown in Table 1), both the usage rate and the MB prediction gain decreases (similarly, the amount of bit-rate reduction also decreases). It is because the motion estimator can no longer accurately estimate motion and the local motion vector field becomes too complex. If the local motion vector field is too complex, the system classifies the case as area having abrupt change in motion vector field (area covering two or more objects with distinct motion activities) and does not select the MB (not applying the LAP technique). Therefore, we suggest a maximum frame skip ratio of 3 for CIF sequence and 5 for HD sequences for best coding efficiency.

Another observation from Table 1 is that the bit-rate reduction (proposed method compared with H.264) is generally higher for coding system using only 16×16 partition size than the coding system using all seven coding partition sizes. To explain this observation, we need to study the distribution of the coding modes being used in coding MBs and the efficiency of the LAP method in improving the prediction quality for different coding modes. In the following paragraphs, we select sequences FlowerGarden (FS = 3) and Shield (FS = 5) as examples for analysis.

Figures 8, 9 and 10 (Figs. 11 and 12 resp.) show the coding modes distribution for FlowerGarden (Shield resp.) sequence using the reference H.264 coding system and our proposed system. The bars marked in red color indicate the portion of MBs selected to apply the LAP technique. Note that our proposed system only applies the LAP technique to select MBs which are coded in mode 0, 1, 2 or 3 only. From the figures, we can observe that our proposed system manages to increase the number of MBs being coded in mode 1, 2 and 3 compared with the reference H.264 coding system. (For mode 0, there is no MB selected to apply the LAP technique. The major reason is that the regions coded in mode 0 usually have uniform motion vector field and LAP technique is not applied.) This reveals the ability of our proposed LAP technique that it not only increases the prediction quality, but also encourages more MBs to be coded using coding modes with large partition sizes.

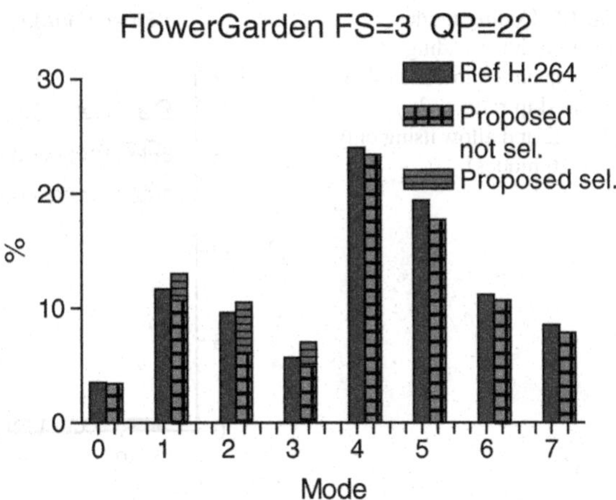

Fig. 8 Coding modes distribution for coding CIF sequence FlowerGarden (frame skip ratio = 3, QP = 22 and allow using all seven coding modes)

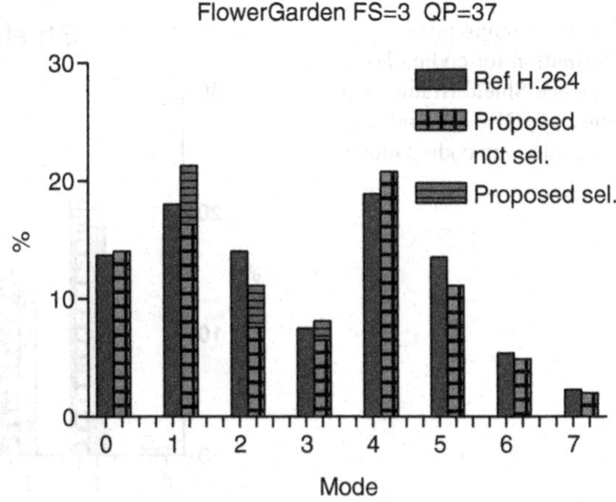

Fig. 9 Coding modes distribution for coding CIF sequence FlowerGarden (frame skip ratio = 3, QP = 37 and allow using all seven coding modes)

Some MBs originally coded in small partition sizes (e.g. mode 4, 5, 6 and 7) are now coded with large partition sizes (mode 1, 2 and 3). This also reveals an additional advantage that the proposed LAP technique manages to save overhead bits. (e.g. there are more overhead bits in coding 16 MVs for a MB coded in mode 7 than that coded in mode 1 which only have 1 MV to be coded. Thus, some overhead bits are saved.) Therefore, a shift in the coding modes distribution towards large partition size modes is an important factor contributing to the average bit-rate reduction. For coding sequences FlowerGarden and Shield (see Figs. 8, 9, 11 and 12), we can see that there is a shift in the coding mode distribution towards the large partition size coding modes. This forms one of the reasons in explaining the bit-rate reduction. Meanwhile, for sequence FlowerGarden being coded with 16×16 partition size only (see Fig. 10), we do not have a significant shift in the coding mode distribution, but there is a significant reduction in bit-rate (a bit-rate reduction of 5.75%, see Table 1). At the same time, we observe that there is

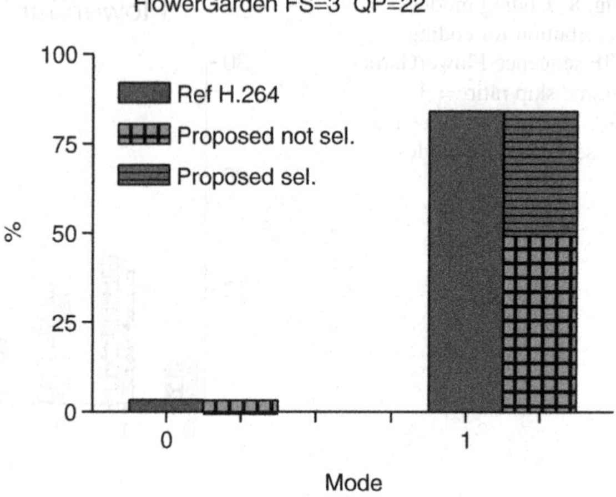

Fig. 10 Coding modes distribution for coding CIF sequence FlowerGarden (frame skip ratio = 3, QP = 22 and allow using only 16 × 16 modes)

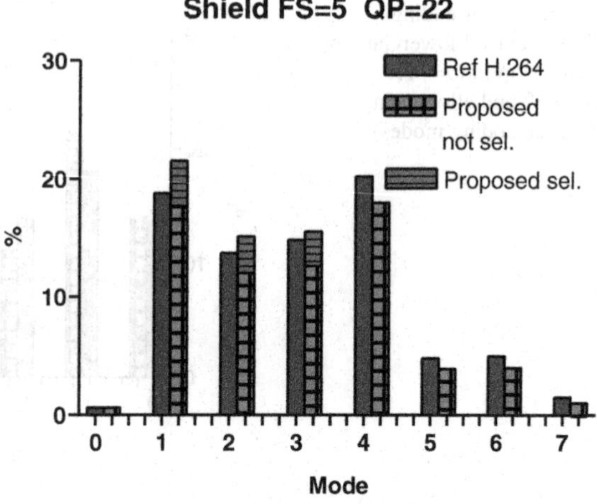

Fig. 11 Coding modes distribution for coding HD sequence Shield (frame skip ratio = 5, QP = 22 and allow using all seven coding modes)

a substantial number of MBs selected to apply the LAP technique in mode 1 (e.g. 34.9% of MB selected, see Fig. 10 and Table 1). In this case, the bit-rate reduction is primarily contributed by the improvement in the prediction quality, in which fewer bits are required to code the prediction error.

Generally speaking, different coding modes have different prediction gain. The major reason is that a MV can best represent the motion activity of the partition center and conventional MV based prediction can most efficiently predict the pixels close to the partition center. Therefore, most of the prediction error distribute around the partition boundary area leaving more room for improvement. Tables 2–5 show some figures about the MBs selected to apply the LAP technique in different modes including: percentage of MBs selected and not selected to apply LAP technique (denoted as "MB sel." and "MB not sel." respectively), the average prediction quality of the selected MBs, average prediction quality improvement

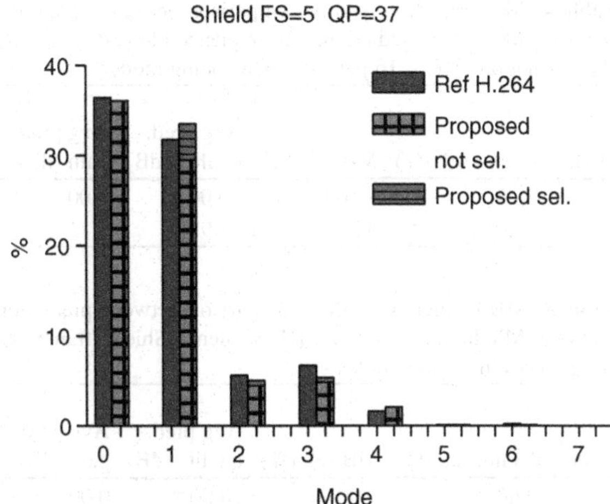

Fig. 12 Coding modes distribution for coding HD sequence Shield (frame skip ratio = 5, QP = 37 and allow using all seven coding modes)

Table 2 MB prediction quality comparison between prediction using LAP technique and conventional MV based prediction: CIF sequence FlowerGarden, frame skip ratio = 3, QP = 22 and allow using all seven coding modes

Mode	MB not sel. (%)	MB sel. (%)	Avg pred. quality (dB)	Avg pred. gain (dB)	Block center pred. gain (dB)	Block boundary pred. gain (dB)
0	3.40	0.00	0.00	0.00	0.00	0.00
1	10.70	2.30	22.80	1.53	0.51	1.82
2	6.00	4.50	22.30	0.54	0.07	0.68
3	4.90	2.10	22.30	1.49	0.54	1.75

Table 3 MB prediction quality comparison between prediction using LAP technique and conventional MV based prediction: CIF sequence FlowerGarden, frame skip ratio = 3, QP = 37 and allow using all seven coding modes

Mode	MB not sel. (%)	MB sel. (%)	Avg pred. quality (dB)	Avg pred. gain (dB)	Block center pred. gain (dB)	Block boundary pred. gain (dB)
0	14.00	0.00	0.00	0.00	0.00	0.00
1	16.30	5.00	21.08	0.94	0.25	1.14
2	7.60	3.50	20.76	0.33	0.02	0.43
3	6.50	1.60	20.84	0.94	0.29	1.13

compared with the MV based prediction, average prediction quality improvement for partition center area and partition boundary area. Figure 13 shows some diagrams illustrating the definition of the partition center area and partition boundary area for coding modes 0, 1, 2 and 3.

Table 4 MB prediction quality comparison between prediction using LAP technique and conventional MV based prediction: CIF sequence FlowerGarden, frame skip ratio = 3, QP = 22 and allow using only 16 × 16 partition size coding mode

Mode	MB not sel. (%)	MB sel. (%)	Avg pred. quality (dB)	Avg pred. gain (dB)	Block center pred. gain (dB)	Block boundary pred. gain (dB)
0	3.20	0.00	0.00	0.00	0.00	0.00
1	49.20	34.90	21.98	1.12	0.29	1.33

Table 5 MB prediction quality comparison between prediction using LAP technique and conventional MV based prediction: HD sequence Shield, frame skip ratio = 5, QP = 22 and allow using all seven coding modes

Mode	MB not sel. (%)	MB sel. (%)	Avg pred. quality (dB)	Avg pred. gain (dB)	Block center pred. gain (dB)	Block boundary pred. gain (dB)
0	0.60	0.00	0.00	0.00	0.00	0.00
1	17.60	3.90	33.74	1.75	0.63	2.07
2	12.00	3.10	33.63	1.41	0.47	1.69
3	12.60	2.90	33.69	1.04	0.36	1.25

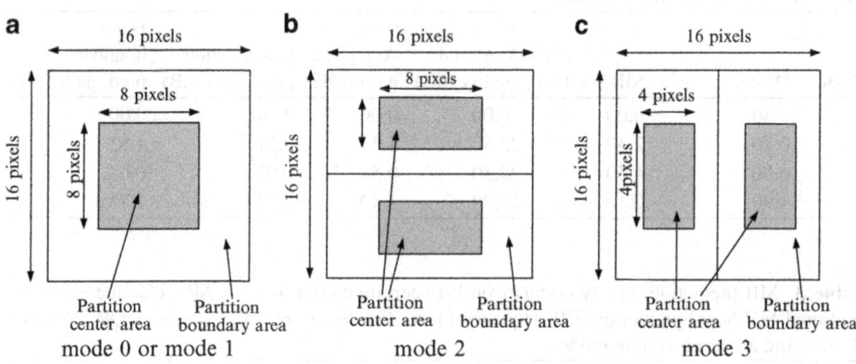

Fig. 13 Diagrams illustrating the partition center area and boundary area for different coding modes

From the tables, we can observe that the average prediction gain for high bit-rate configuration (low QP value of 22) is generally higher than the low bit-rate configuration (high QP value of 37) (compare the "Avg pred. gain" column in Table 2 with that in Table 3. Also compare Table 4 with Table 5). The major reason is that the average reference frame quality is higher at high bit-rate case than low bit rate case. Therefore, in terms of prediction quality improvement, LAP technique can contribute more for high bit-rate application than low bit-rate application. However, at the same time, there are fewer MBs coded with large partition size coding modes (mode 0, 1, 2 and 3) at high bit-rate application than low bit-rate application. (Compare Fig. 8 with Fig. 9 and Fig. 11 with Fig. 12.) Therefore, it is difficult to tell if the proposed LAP technique favors high bit-rate application more

Table 6 MB prediction quality comparison between prediction using LAP technique and conventional MV based prediction: HD sequence Shield, frame skip ratio = 5, QP = 37 and allow using all seven coding modes

Mode	MB not sel. (%)	MB sel. (%)	Avg pred. quality (dB)	Avg pred. gain (dB)	Block center pred. gain (dB)	Block boundary pred. gain (dB)
0	36.10	0.00	0.00	0.00	0.00	0.00
1	29.50	4.00	26.87	0.38	0.07	0.48
2	4.40	0.60	26.80	0.37	0.02	0.49
3	4.80	0.50	26.75	0.19	−0.02	0.26

or not. From our experimental results, we found that the LAP technique roughly benefit both the high and low bit-rate applications equally.

In addition, our proposed LAP technique is more efficient in improving the prediction quality of the partition boundary areas than the partition center areas. (Compare "Block boundary pred. gain" column with "Block center pred. gain" column in Table 2–6.) Furthermore, we can observe that the average prediction gain is the highest for mode 1. This can be explained that the partition size for mode 1 (16×16) is larger than the sizes of mode 2 and 3 (16×8 and 8×16 resp.) and the boundary pixels for 16×16 partition are further away from the partition center than that of 16×8 and 8×16 partitions. Thus, the MV is the least efficiently representing the true motion of the boundary pixels for 16×16 partition and leaving more room for improvement. Meanwhile, the affine motion model used in our proposed LAP method is better in modeling the motion vector field of the boundary pixels and results a higher prediction gain. (The two frames having rotation inter-frame motion shown in Fig. 1 is a good example. In Fig. 1c, the boundary pixels are not well predicted (using MV based prediction) because the MV of the MB does not match the true motion vectors of the boundary pixels. In Fig. 1d, our proposed LAP method better models the motion field and generate a much better prediction. Figure 14 shows the prediction frames in the real coding environment for a sequence with significant rotation inter-frame motion activity. Similar observation can also be found).

Therefore, our proposed LAP technique is more efficient in improving prediction quality of large partition size. To explain the reason for bit-rate reduction, another point of consideration is the number of MBs selected to apply the LAP technique and the MBs are coded in large partition size (mode 1). For example, for the case coding sequence FlowerGarden using only 16×16 partition size, we do not have a shift in the coding mode distribution (see Fig. 10), but we have a significant amount of MBs selected to apply the LAP technique and are coded in mode 1 (34.9%, See Table 4). In this case, we have a bit-rate reduction of 5.75 % (see Table 1) which is solely contributed by the improvement in the prediction quality.

In summary, there are two influencing factors affecting the bit-rate reduction: (1) the amount of shift in the coding modes distribution towards large partition size modes, and (2) the number of MBs selected to apply the LAP technique and are

Fig. 14 (**a**) MV based prediction for frame having significant rotation motion activity (using conventional block based prediction with a single MV). As reference frame cannot be rotated, mis-alignment artefact arises. (**b**) Prediction using proposed LAP technique. Affine motion model allows the reference frame to be rotated to generate a better prediction

Table 7 Comparison of average prediction gain between method proposed by Kordasiewicz et al. [15] and the proposed LAP method

Sequence	MV based pred. (dB)	Pred. gain by Kordasiewicz et al. [15](dB)	Pred. gain by proposed method (dB)
Stefan	25.31	0.203	0.328
Mobile	24.93	0.209	0.292
Foreman	34.3	0.151	0.176

coded with large partition size coding mode like mode 1. From our experience, we found that most of the HD sequences have most of the MBs coded using coding modes with large partition sizes and there is not much shift in the coding mode distribution between the coding statistics of the original H.264 system and our proposed system. Also, the number of MB selected to apply the LAP technique is small. The major reason is that the MB size of 16×16 is relatively small compared with the frame size such that the complexity of the local motion vector field tends to be low (i.e. uniform local motion vector field). Therefore, not much MBs are selected to apply the LAP technique and the bit-rate reduction tends to be small compared with CIF sequences. For CIF sequences, on the contrary, we found most sequences have large (compared with HD sequences) amount of shift in the coding modes distribution towards large partition size modes and a high percentage of MBs are selected to apply the LAP technique. Therefore, the average bit-rate reduction is higher than that of HD sequences.

Table 7 shows the average prediction quality improvement (compared with the MV based prediction) for Kordasiewicz's [15] method and our proposed LAP method. In this test, we restricted the partition size to 8×8 only and modified our proposed method to use 8 neighbouring MBs (similar to [15]) instead of 4 as described in Sect. 2. From the results, our proposed method manages to provide a higher prediction gain than Kordasiewicz's method.

In summary, our proposed LAP method is not only an efficient technique to compensate complex motion activities like zooming, rotation and various forms of distortion, but also a good technique in handling relatively large inter-frame motion activity resulted from frame skipping. For example, our method can be useful for the applications of video transcoding (frame skipping) and hierarchical B frame coding. Another potential application is fast video coding application using only 16×16 partition size (mode 0 and 1) for coding. (I.e. processing time is saved by not trying to code MBs in other modes.) Using our proposed LAP technique, the compression efficiency can be significantly increased (A maximum bit-rate reduction of 5.75% was recorded for using only 16×16 partition size. See Table 1). Although the coding efficiency (using only 16×16 partition size for coding) still cannot exceed the coding performance of the system using all possible coding modes, the coding performance difference between the two systems is significantly reduced.

4 Conclusion

Coping with complex inter-frame motion activity including scaling, rotation and various forms of distortion is a challenging task for coding system using translation only motion estimation and compensation system. In this paper, we propose a local affine motion prediction method, which makes use of the computed motion vectors near the coding MB to generate a better modelled motion field in terms of a set of affine motion vector. With the estimated affine motion vector, a better MB prediction can be produced and it can replace the original MV based prediction to achieve a higher average prediction quality. We propose to apply the proposed technique to coding modes with large partition sizes (mode 0, 1, 2 and 3) which benefits the most from our algorithm. Another advantage of our proposed algorithm is that it manages to encourage more MBs to be coded in coding modes with large partition sizes. This can effectively reduce the bits for coding overheads. (For example, if a MB was coded in mode 1 (16×16 block) instead of mode 7 (16 4×4 blocks), the bits for coding the extra 15 MVs can be saved.) Most importantly, our proposed method does not need to send any extra bits to the decoder for proper decoding. From the experimental results, our proposed method can achieve a maximum average bit rate reduction of 5.75% compared to the conventional MV based prediction. The results showed that our proposed algorithm is useful for H.264 and is particularly high in coding efficiency improvement for large partition sizes. We expect that the coding gain should further be boosted by making use of our proposed algorithm in the future video compression standards including high-efficiency video coding (HEVC) or the possible H.265, which could include partition sizes of 64×64 and 32×32 [1].

Acknowledgements This work is supported by the Centre for Multimedia Signal Processing, Hong Kong Polytechnic University(G-U863) and ASTRI (Hong Kong Applied Science and Technology Research Institute)

References

1. Ugur,K., Andersson, K., Fuldseth, A., et al.: High performance, low complexity video coding and the emerging HEVC standard. In: IEEE Trans. Circuits Syst. Video Technol., vol. 20, no. 12, pp. 1688–1697, IEEE Press, (Dec 2010)
2. Hui, K.C., Siu, W.C., Chan, Y.L.: New adaptive partial distortion search using clustered pixel matching error characteristic. In: IEEE Trans. Image Process., vol. 14, no. 5, pp. 597–607, IEEE Press, (May 2005)
3. Orchard, M.T., Sullivan, G.J.: Overlapped block motion compensation: An estimation-theoretic approach. In: IEEE Trans. Image Process., vol. 3, no. 9, pp. 693–699, IEEE Press, (Sep 1994)
4. Bossen, F., Drugeon, V., Francois, E., et al.: Video coding using a simplified block structure and advanced coding techniques. In: IEEE Trans. Circuits Syst. Video Technol., vol. 20, no. 12, pp. 1667–1675, IEEE Press, (Dec 2010)
5. Wiegand, T., Steinbach, E., Girod, B.: Affine multipicture motion-compensated prediction. In: IEEE Trans. Circuits Syst. Video Technol., vol. 15, no. 2, pp. 197–209, IEEE Press, (Feb 2005)
6. Kim, S-E., Han, J-K., Kim, J-G.: An efficient scheme for motion estimation using multireference frames in H.264/AVC. In: IEEE Trans. Multimedia, vol. 8, no. 3, pp. 457–466, IEEE Press, (June 2006)
7. Smolic, A., Sikora, T., Ohm, J-R.: Long term global motion estimation and its application for sprite coding, content description and segmentation. In: IEEE Trans. Circuits Syst. Video Technol., vol. 9, no. 8, pp. 1227–1242, IEEE Press, (Dec 1999)
8. Cheung, H.K., Siu, W.C.: Robust global motion estimator and novel sprite update strategy for sprite coding. In: IET Image Processing, vol. 1, no. 1, pp. 13–20, IET Press, (March 2007)
9. Cheung, H.K., Siu, W.C., Feng, D., Wang, Z.: Efficient Retinex Based Brightness Normalization Method For Coding Camera Flashes and Strong Brightness Variations Videos. In: Signal Processing: Image Communication, vol. 25, no. 3, pp.143–162, Elsevier Press, Netherlands (March 2010)
10. Cheung, H.K., Siu, W.C., Feng, D., et al.: New block based motion estimation for sequences with brightness variation and its application to static sprite generation for video compression. In: IEEE Trans. Circuits Syst. Video Technol., vol. 18, no. 4, pp. 522–527, IEEE Press, (April 2008)
12. Ye, G., Wang, Y., Xu, J., et al.: A practical approach to multiple super-resolution sprite generation. In: Proc. IEEE 10th Workshop on Multimedia Signal Process., MMSP, pp. 70–75, IEEE Press, (Oct 2008)
13. Su, Y., Sun, M-T., Hsu, V.: Global motion estimation from coarsely sampled motion vector field and the applications. In: IEEE Trans. Circuits Syst. Video Technol., vol. 15, no. 2, pp. 232–242, IEEE Press, (Feb 2005)
14. Luo, J., Ahmad, I., Liang, Y., et al.: Motion estimation for content adaptive video compression. In: IEEE Trans. Circuits Syst. Video Technol., vol. 18, no. 7, pp. pp.900–909, IEEE Press, (July 2008)
15. Kordasiewicz, R.C., Gallant, M.D., Shirani, S.: Affine motion prediction based on translational motion vectors. In: IEEE Trans. Circuits Syst. Video Technol., vol. 17, no. 10, pp. 1388–1394, IEEE Press, (Oct 2007)

Fast Mode Decision Using Rate-Distortion Cost and Temporal Correlations in H.264/AVC

Yo-Sung Ho and Soo-Jin Hwang

Abstract In this paper, we propose a fast mode decision scheme in the H.264/AVC standard. The encoder uses variable block sizes to select the optimal best mode incurring the high computational complexity. Thus, we propose the fast mode decision algorithm to reduce the complexity. Using the rate-distortion cost and temporal correlations, we propose the additional early SKIP and inactive inter/intra mode decision methods in P frames. Experimental results show the proposed method provides about 60% encoding time savings on average without significant performance loss, compared to the H.264/AVC fast high complexity mode. Specifically, we can save the time about 22% and 39% in the intra and inter mode conditions, respectively.

Keywords H.264/AVC • Fast mode decision • Rate-distortion costs (RD cost) correlation for optimal and sub-optimal modes • Temporal correlation

1 Introduction

H.264/AVC is the latest international video coding standard developed by JVT (Joint Video Team) which is the ITU-T Video Coding Experts Group (VCEG) and the ISO/IEC Moving Picture Experts Group (MPEG) [1].

The standard achieves higher compression efficiency than the previous video coding standards with the rate-distortion optimized (RDO) technique for the mode decision. As shown in Fig. 1, H.264/AVC has several candidate modes: SKIP, 16 × 16, 16 × 8, 8 × 16, P8 × 8, intra 4 × 4, and intra 16 × 16 [2]. In the technique, by searching all combinations of the modes for each macroblock exhaustively, we

Y.-S. Ho (✉) • S.-J. Hwang
Gwangju Institute of Science and Technology (GIST), 261 Cheomdan-gwagiro, Buk-gu, Gwangju 500-712, Republic of Korea
e-mail: hoyo@gist.ac.kr; soojin@gist.ac.kr

DOI 10.1007/978-1-4614-3501-3_14, © Springer Science+Business Media, LLC 2013

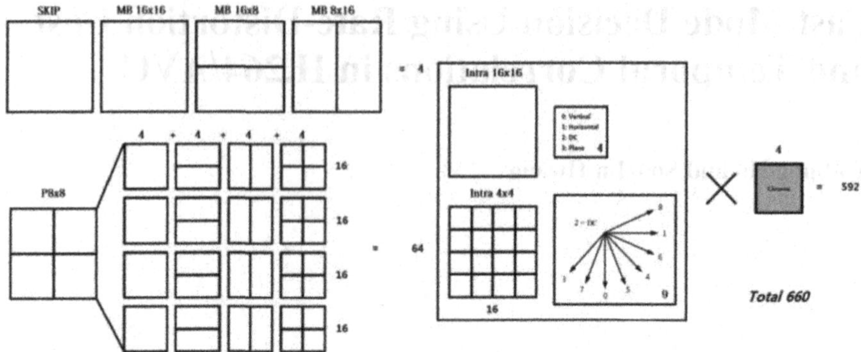

Fig. 1 The maximum number of computing RD cost in the mode decision

can achieve the optimal best coding quality while minimizing the bit rate. However, Fig. 1 more specifically shows that the RDO technique increases complexity and computation load drastically; it has to be calculated 660 times (inter mode: 68 and intra mode: 592) for each macroblock. Since the technique makes H.264/AVC unsuitable for real-time applications, the encoding time reduction is still an issue.

Most fast mode decision algorithms were already proposed using the correlations of spatial, temporal, RD cost, and so on. However, most proposed methods carry out experiments on only simple sequences or are used their own internal variables through several preliminary tests [3,4].

Therefore, we suggest a new approach based on the RD cost and temporal correlations without any internal variables and also experiment with both the simple and complex sequences. In this paper, we propose the fast mode decision method which adopts the additional early SKIP and inactive intra/inter mode conditions based on the correlations of temporal and RD costs between the optimal/sub-optimal best modes.

In the following, we introduce the overview of H.264/AVC mode decision method in Sect. 2. After that, we proposed the fast mode decision algorithm using the RD cost and temporal correlations in Sect. 3; In Sect. 4, we evaluate the experimental results and make analysis. Finally, we make conclusions in Sect. 5.

2 Overview of Mode Decision in H.264/AVC

2.1 Mode Decision Method

Using the RD cost, H.264/AVC decides to select the best mode for each macroblock. The RD costs consist of J_{motion} and J_{mode} [5]. Generally, J_{motion} shows worse performance than J_{mode} in terms of the best mode decision. However, to reduce the complexity, the encoder calculates J_{motion} to determine the best motion vector (*MV*) and reference picture number (*REF*), since J_{motion} does not calculate the actual coding bits but estimates them to reduce the complexity. The smallest of J_{motion} is called the sub-optimal mode. In the J_{motion} equation, it includes the sum of absolute difference (SAD) between the original and reference blocks. These are defined as follows:

$$J_{motion}(MV, REF|\lambda_{motion}) = SAD(s, r(MV, REF)) + \lambda_{motion} \cdot R(MV, REF). \quad (1)$$

$$SAD(s, r(MV, REF)) = \sum_{x \in H, y \in V}^{H,V} |s(x, y) - r(x - m_x, y - m_y)|. \quad (2)$$

where λ_{motion} is the Lagrangian multiplier that depends on the quantization parameters.

In addition, *R(MV, REF)* represents the coding bits used for the coding *MV* and *REF*, *s* and *r* indicate the current and reference blocks, respectively.

To decide the best mode for each macroblock, the encoder calculates the RD cost of each mode and then chooses the smallest one. The RD cost indicates J_{mode}, it is defined as follows:

$$J_{mode}(s, r, M|\lambda_{mode}) = SSD(s, r, M) + \lambda_{mode} \cdot R(s, r, M). \quad (3)$$

$$SSD(s, r, M) = \sum_{x \in H, y \in V}^{H,V} (s(x, y) - r(x - m_x, y - m_y))^2 \quad (4)$$

where M and λ_{mode} represent the macroblock coding mode and the Lagrange multiplier, respectively. Then, *SSD(s, r, M)* and *R(s, r, M)* denote the square of the distortion costs between the original and reconstructed signal, and the number of coding bits associated with the given mode, respectively.

2.2 Early SKIP Conditions

The fast high complexity mode of H.264/AVC JM reference software includes the fast inter mode decision. It is called the early SKIP conditions [1].

- *Reference frame = Previous frame*
- *SKIP MV = 16 × 16 MV*
- *Best motion compensated block size = 16 × 16*
- *Coded block pattern (CBP) = 0*

SKIP mode are encoded without motion and residual information. Hence, it can be reduce the complexity. The early SKIP conditions decide whether the optimal best macroblock mode is SKIP mode or not. When the above conditions are satisfied simultaneously, all remaining encoding parts should be omitted.

3 Proposed Fast Mode Decision Algorithm

3.1 Fast Inter Mode Decision in P Frame

In our proposed fast inter mode decision algorithm, we use two kinds of correlations: the temporal correlation and the RD cost correlation for the optimal/ sub-optimal best modes. In here, the sub-optimal best mode is decided, when the mode has the minimum value of J_{motion}. As shown in Fig. 2, the frequency distribution of SKIP mode is quite higher than other inter modes; in here, the inter modes consist of SKIP, 16 × 16, 16 × 8, 8 × 16, and P8 × 8.

Jang et al. proposed a fast mode decision algorithm which used the correlation between the sub-optimal best mode and the optimal best mode [6]. In this sense, we inactivate the modes rarely selected as the optimal best mode using the sub-optimal mode. For example, when the sub-optimal best mode is 16 × 16 mode, the percentage which the optimal best mode is selected as 8 × 16, 16 × 8 or P8 × 8 mode is low.

Figure 3 shows each inter mode RD costs. It is distinct from each other. Besides, Ri et al. showed that there exists the strong Lagrangian cost correlation between the temporally collocated blocks [3]. As the candidate mode to predict the best mode for the current macroblock, we can use the best mode of the collocated macroblock in the previous frame. Therefore, we propose the additional early SKIP conditions and inactive mode decision methods of the inter modes.

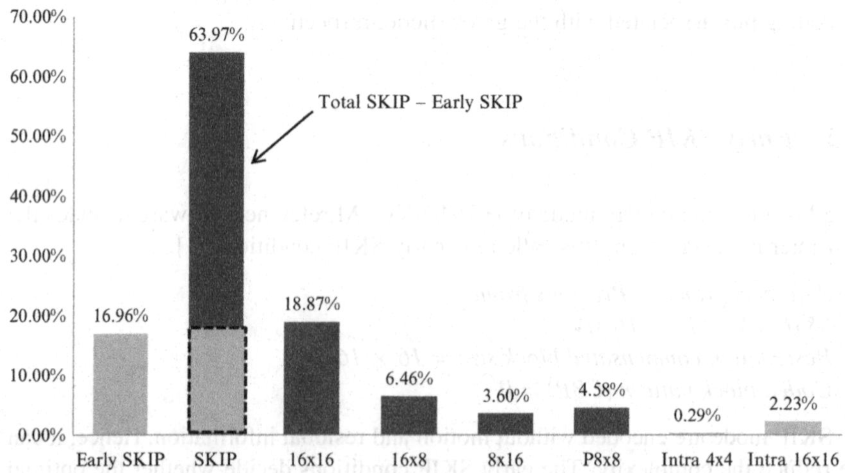

Fig. 2 Optimal best mode distribution in P frames (Sequence: hall_cif.yuv, QP: 27)

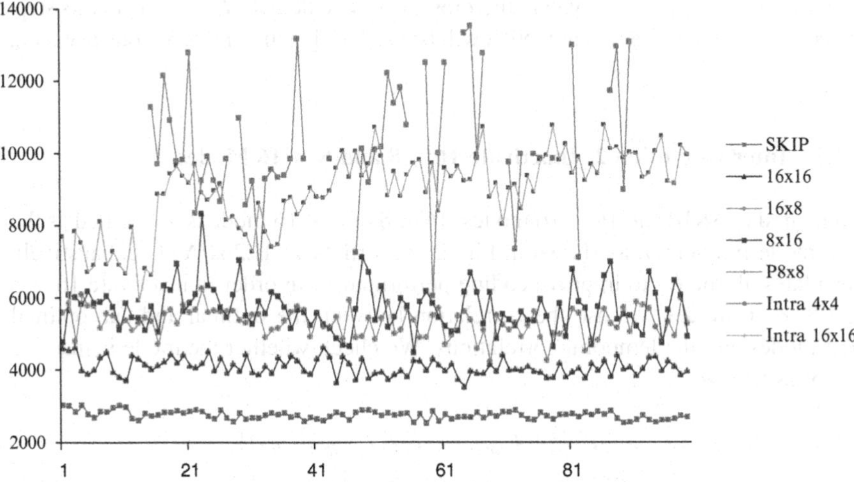

Fig. 3 J_{mode} of each best mode in P frames (Sequence: hall_cif.yuv, QP: 27)

3.1.1 Inter Condition 1: Additional Early SKIP Condition

The early SKIP conditions are used in the fast high complexity mode of the JM reference software; that is to say H.264/AVC omits unnecessary calculations via the early SKIP conditions (in Sect. 2.2). However, the number of SKIP modes by the early SKIP conditions is not sufficiently high percentage compared to the total number of SKIP modes. Figure 2 shows the satisfied percentage of the early SKIP conditions accounts for only one-third of SKIP mode. It means there is still some room for determining SKIP mode. The additional early SKIP conditions as follows.

- $(Reference\ frame = Previous\ frame)\ ]\&\&\ (SKIP\ MV = 16 \times 16\ MV)$
- $\{J_{mode(SKIP)} < avg\_J_{prev-mode(SKIP)}\}\&\&\{prev\_best\_mode(SKIP)\}$

where $J_{mode(i)}$ and $avg\_J_{prev\text{-}mode(i)}$ denote the RD cost in the current macroblock and the average RD cost in the previous frame for the corresponding mode, respectively. $prev\_best\_mode(i)$ represents the best mode of the collocated macroblock in the previous frame according to the mode i.

The first condition comes from the early SKIP conditions in the original JM reference software (in Sect. 2.2), and the second condition is proposed by the temporal correlation. If $J_{mode(\mathrm{SKIP})}$ is less than $avg\_J_{prev\text{-}mode(SKIP)}$ and the collocated macroblock mode is SKIP, we can expect SKIP mode to be selected as the best mode.

The original procedure in H.264/AVC is that $J_{mode(16\times16)}$ is calculated in the fast high complexity mode; and then the encoder calculates J_{mode} for the remaining modes at last. While the encoder check the early SKIP conditions, the encoder already has the $J_{mode(16\times16)}$ value; therefore, we can calculate $J_{mode(SKIP)}$ in this step. It does not give any time saving, but it will be used for inactive P8 × 8 mode decision.

3.1.2 Inter Condition 2: Inactivate 16 × 8 and 8 × 16 Modes

Compared to SKIP and 16 × 16 modes, 16 × 8 or 8 × 16 mode is not settled as the best mode frequently, as shown in Fig. 2. Nevertheless, H.264/AVC exhaustively calculates all modes to improve coding performance. In order to inactivate 16 × 8 and 8 × 16 modes, we use the correlation between the optimal and sub-optimal best modes and the temporal correlations. We check whether the mode is inactive or not as follows:

- $\{(J_{motion(16\times16)} < J_{motion(16\times8)}) || (J_{motion(16\times16)} < J_{motion(8\times16)})\}$
- $\{prev\_best\_mode(SKIP) || prev\_best\_mode(16 \times 16)\}$

where $J_{motion(i)}$ represents J_{motion} value for the corresponding mode i at the current macroblock.

The first condition is based on the RD cost correlation between the sub-optimal and optimal best modes (in Sect. 3.1). The second condition is using the temporal correlation between the current and collocated macroblock modes. We can expect the percentage that 16 × 8 or 8 × 16 mode is determined as the best mode is quite low when the above conditions are satisfied simultaneously.

Therefore, we can inactivate 16 × 8 and 8 × 16 modes according to the above conditions. However, if the proposed condition is not satisfied, we calculate $J_{mode(16\times8)}$ and $J_{mode(8\times16)}$ values at this step. It also does not save any encoding time, but it will be used at the step of the inactive P8 × 8 mode decision.

3.1.3 Inter Condition 3: Inactivate P8 × 8 Mode

The encoding time for the P8 × 8 mode decision is same as that of all other inter modes; it means the complexity is high. As stated in Sect. 3.2, P8 × 8 mode also needs to inactivate if the following condition is satisfied.

$$Minimum\{J_{mode(SKIP)}, J_{mode}(16 \times 16), J_{mode}(16 \times 8), J_{mode}(8 \times 16)\} < avg\_J_{prev-mode(P8\times8)}$$

$J_{mode(i)}$ is already calculated in the previous steps. As shown in Fig. 3, the RD cost distribution of P8 × 8 is higher than those of other inter modes. Based on this feature, when $avg\_J_{prev\text{-}mode(P8\times8)}$ is less than the minimum value of $J_{mode(i)}$, P8 × 8 mode rarely selected as the best mode; in this case, we can inactivate P8 × 8 mode.

3.2 Fast Intra Mode Decision in P Frame

The H.264/AVC standard allows the intra and inter modes in P frames. The intra mode uses the spatial correlation features, whereas the inter mode utilizes the temporal correlations. In general, since P frames contain higher correlation in time than in space, the occurrence frequencies of the intra modes are lower than those of the inter modes, as shown in Fig. 2. Therefore, we should make conditions for inactive intra modes in P frames.

The intra modes consist of intra 4 × 4 and intra 16 × 16 in the baseline profile. Features of these modes are different; first, intra 16 × 16 mode is used in a homogeneous region, whereas intra 4 × 4 mode is determined at a complexity region. Second, the ranges of the RD cost values are quite different. In Fig. 3, $J_{mode(intra\ 4\times4)}$ is quite different from $J_{mode(intra\ 16\times16)}$; $J_{mode(intra\ 4\times4)}$ is much larger than $J_{mode(intra\ 16\times16)}$. Therefore, we propose the distinct ranges which are divided by the decided thresholds.

Most group of picture (GOP) structure is IPPP or IBBB. It means we can estimate the brief distributions of $J_{mode(intra\ 4\times4)}$ and $J_{mode(intra\ 16\times16)}$ via the first I frame. The distributions of each intra mode RD costs in the first I frame are similar to the one in the first P frame. Therefore, we can decide two thresholds: the maximum and minimum thresholds. The maximum and minimum thresholds are decided based on the average RD cost values of intra 4 × 4 and intra 16 × 16, respectively. The selective conditions for inactive intra mode are described as follows.

- $J_{mode(i)} < minimum\ threshold$: inactivate intra 16 × 16 and intra 4 × 4
- $Minimum\ threshold < J_{mode(i)} < maximum\ threshold$: inactivate intra 4 × 4
- $J_{mode(i)} > maximum\ threshold$: inactivate intra 16 × 16

where $i \in \{16 \times 16, 16 \times 8, 8 \times 16\}$, $maximum\ threshold = avg\_J_{mode(intra\ modes)} \times 1.5$,and minimum threshold = $\mathrm{avg\_J}_{\mathrm{mode(intra\ modes)}}/1.5$.

Figure 4 shows the flow chart of the proposed algorithm. As shown in Fig. 4, we determine the maximum and minimum thresholds in I frame using $avg\_J_{mode(intra\ modes)}$; and then, check the conventional and additional SKIP conditions to early terminate the remain mode decision parts, 16 × 8, 8 × 16, and P8 × 8 mode conditions to inactivate with the inter condition 1, 2, and 3 based on the correlation between the optimal and sub-optimal best modes and the temporal correlations. In addition, we decide whether intra 4 × 4 and intra 16 × 16 modes are inactive or not, based on the intra conditions 1 and 2. Finally, we decide the final mode by comparing the RD cost.

4 Experimental Results and Analysis

To evaluate coding performance of the proposed algorithm, the reference software version JM 12.4 was modified [7]. Table 1 indicates the experimental conditions.

We compared coding performance in terms of time saving, bit saving rates, PSNR differences [8]. To evaluate these performance, we use the Eqs. (5)–(7).

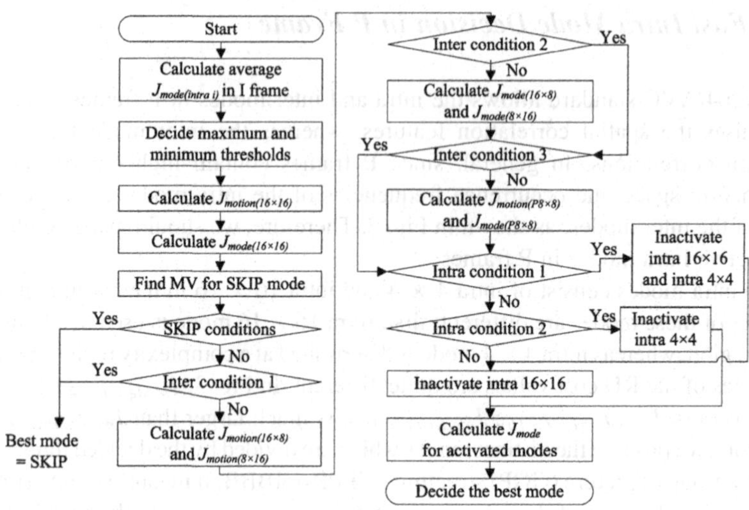

Fig. 4 Flowchart of proposed algorithm

Table 1 Experimental conditions

Classify	Encoder description
RDOptimization	Fast high complexity mode
Encoding frames	100
Quantization parameter	22, 27, 32, 37
The number of reference frames	5

$$\Delta Time(\%) = \frac{Time_{proposed} - Time_{original}}{Time_{original}} \times 100. \quad (5)$$

$$\Delta Bitrates(\%) = \frac{Bitrates_{proposed} - Bitrates_{original}}{Bitrates_{original}} \times 100. \quad (6)$$

$$\Delta PSNR(dB) = PSNR_{proposed} - PSNR_{original}. \quad (7)$$

In order to verify efficiency of each proposed algorithm, our experiment included three sections: intra, inter, and intra + inter modes. Table 2 shows the performance comparison results between the proposed intra/inter mode and the fast high complexity mode decision of H.264/AVC. We can reduce the encoding time approximately 22% and 39%, respectively.

In Table 3, we compare the performances between Jang's algorithm and our inter mode algorithm. The average saving time of Jang's algorithm is faster than our proposed algorithm for inter mode decision, but other performances which are PSNR and bit rate changes are better than Jang's algorithm. Additionally, our

Table 2 Experimental results of each intra/inter mode

		Intra mode			Inter mode		
Sequence	QP	ΔTime (%)	ΔBitrate (%)	ΔPSNR (dB)	ΔTime (%)	ΔBitrate (%)	ΔPSNR (dB)
Mobile	22	−25.54	0.00	−0.01	−38.87	1.56	−0.07
	27	−23.63	−0.02	−0.01	−43.23	1.88	−0.07
	32	−21.70	0.10	−0.01	−46.65	2.05	−0.06
	37	−19.90	0.10	0.00	−49.62	1.34	−0.02
Paris	22	−30.63	0.24	−0.01	−49.48	1.79	−0.07
	27	−25.51	0.29	−0.03	−45.71	2.07	−0.07
	32	−21.09	0.76	−0.01	−43.72	1.75	−0.05
	37	−19.07	0.81	−0.03	−43.59	0.91	−0.05
Flowergarden	22	−22.46	0.01	−0.08	−23.52	0.51	−0.02
	27	−21.59	0.15	−0.06	−24.24	0.53	−0.03
	32	−20.07	0.22	−0.03	−27.13	0.39	−0.05
	37	−17.33	0.05	−0.03	−31.84	−0.56	−0.07
Tempete	22	−26.11	0.69	0.00	−30.19	1.23	−0.04
	27	−24.02	1.06	0.01	−33.63	1.30	−0.03
	32	−21.40	2.40	0.01	−37.38	0.68	−0.04
	37	−19.29	2.05	−0.03	−37.48	−0.30	−0.02
Stefan	22	−23.98	0.50	−0.02	−38.99	1.29	−0.04
	27	−21.85	0.54	−0.03	−41.97	1.89	−0.05
	32	−19.92	0.82	−0.02	−44.80	2.32	−0.04
	37	−17.78	0.80	−0.02	−46.68	0.87	−0.03
Akiyo	22	−24.04	0.17	−0.01	−39.90	0.93	−0.04
	27	−21.40	−0.42	−0.01	−38.88	−0.56	−0.04
	32	−17.98	−0.82	−0.02	−32.08	−1.59	−0.02
	37	−16.22	−0.17	−0.04	−26.01	−0.44	−0.05
Hall	22	−27.79	1.35	0.00	−37.65	0.45	−0.05
	27	−24.94	0.29	−0.04	−48.40	−2.49	−0.06
	32	−19.09	1.75	−0.04	−44.84	−1.24	−0.06
	37	−17.13	1.45	−0.07	−38.12	0.48	−0.01
Container	22	−28.05	0.46	−0.02	−51.11	0.06	−0.07
	27	−23.09	0.49	−0.02	−49.72	−0.54	−0.04
	32	−17.73	0.14	−0.02	−40.15	−1.27	−0.04
	37	−16.52	−0.08	−0.01	−32.14	−1.85	−0.03
Total Average		**−21.78**	**0.51**	**−0.02**	**−39.30**	**0.48**	**−0.04**

algorithm includes the fast intra mode decision scheme. We can get the combined experimental results as shown in Table 4, when we experiment about the fast intra and inter modes simultaneously. It shows the total average of the saving time rate is about 58.86% with negligible BDPSNR and BDBR, compared to the H.264/AVC fast high complexity mode [9]. The average BDBR increases approximately 2.49% and BDPSNR decreases 0.12 dB. Figure 5 shows the rate-distortion curves.

Table 3 Performance comparison between Jang's and our proposed inter mode algorithm

	Proposed inter mode algorithm			Jang's algorithm [6]		
Sequence	ΔTime(%)	ΔBitrate(%)	ΔPSNR()	ΔTime(%)	ΔBitrate(%)	ΔPSNR(dB)
Mobile	−22.69	0.05	−0.01	−18.20	1.52	−0.05
Paris	−24.07	0.53	−0.02	−27.80	3.26	−0.05
Flowergarden	−20.36	0.11	−0.05	−26.03	2.27	−0.02
Stefan	−20.88	0.66	−0.02	−24.56	1.30	−0.04
Akiyo	−19.91	−0.31	−0.02	−31.35	0.66	−0.02
Hall	−22.24	1.21	−0.04	−39.20	1.03	−0.07
Container	−21.35	0.25	−0.02	−33.13	2.04	−0.02
Average	−21.64	0.36	−0.03	−28.61	1.72	−0.04

Table 4 Experimental results of inter + intra modes

		Inter mode and Intra mode				
Sequence	QP	ΔTime(%)	ΔBitrate(%)	ΔPSNR(dB)	BDBR(%)	BDPSNR(dB)
Mobile	22	−63.20	1.57	−0.07	1.82	−0.12
	27	−65.31	−1.24	−0.08		
	32	−66.55	2.26	−0.07		
	37	−66.48	1.21	−0.04		
Paris	22	−66.60	2.04	−0.07	3.63	−0.19
	27	−62.57	2.42	−0.08		
	32	−59.94	2.29	−0.07		
	37	−59.05	1.49	−0.09		
Flowergarden	22	−47.05	0.52	−0.11	1.71	−0.11
	27	−46.20	0.57	−0.08		
	32	−46.07	0.30	−0.09		
	37	−47.81	−0.33	−0.09		
Tempete	22	−56.42	1.86	−0.05	3.20	−0.15
	27	−56.73	2.18	−0.03		
	32	−58.27	2.71	−0.05		
	37	−57.70	3.06	−0.02		
Stefan	22	−62.13	1.77	−0.08	3.92	−0.20
	27	−62.80	2.30	−0.08		
	32	−62.98	3.17	−0.06		
	37	−62.77	2.32	−0.06		
Akiyo	22	−59.84	1.00	−0.04	0.70	−0.03
	27	−57.63	0.00	−0.05		
	32	−49.68	−1.52	−0.05		
	37	−40.93	−0.96	−0.09		
Hall	22	−63.97	1.84	−0.06	3.48	−0.10
	27	−66.75	−1.34	−0.09		
	32	−59.60	0.93	−0.10		
	37	−52.80	2.47	−0.11		
Container	22	−71.30	0.84	−0.07	1.42	−0.05
	27	−68.00	0.43	−0.06		
	32	−57.36	−1.02	−0.05		
	37	−49.78	−1.80	−0.03		
Total Average		**−58.57**	**1.04**	**−0.07**	**2.49**	**−0.12**

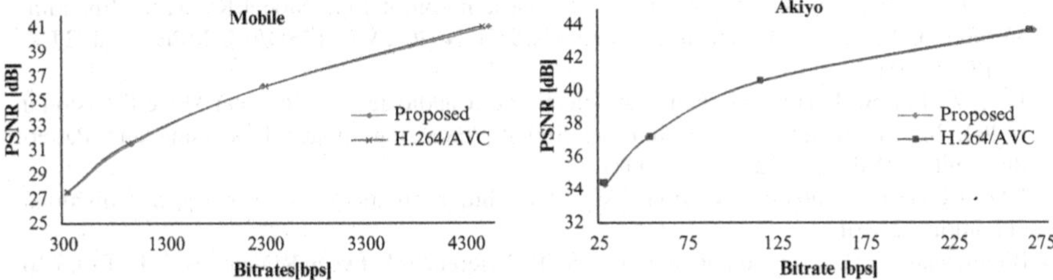

Fig. 5 Rate-distortion curves

5 Conclusion

H.264/AVC has been developed by focusing on coding performance instead of the complexity. For this reason, it is hard to use in real-time applications. One of the abundant computational parts is the mode decision part. Therefore, in this paper, we proposed the fast mode decision algorithm to reduce the encoding time by the additional early SKIP conditions, inactive inter mode (16 × 8, 8 × 16, and P8 × 8), and intra mode conditions (intra 4 × 4 and intra 16 × 16), based on the RD cost correlation for the optimal/sub-optimal best modes and the temporal correlation. From the experimental results, it reduced the encoding time by approximately 60%. However, the PSNR decreased only about 0.07 dB and bit rate increased only about 1%. Also, BDPSNR decreased 0.12 dB and BDBR increased 2.49% compared to the fast high complexity mode on of the H.264/AVC. Furthermore, our proposed algorithm for inter and intra is speeded up approximately 30% and the PSNR and bit rate are better as compare with Jang's algorithm.

Acknowledgement This work was supported by the National Research Foundation of Korea (NRF) grant funded by the Korea government (MEST) (No. 2011-0030822).

References

1. Wiegand, T., Sullivan, G.J., Bjontegaard, G., Luthra, A.: Overview of the H.264/AVC Video Coding Standard. IEEE Transactions on Circuits and Systems for Video Technology, 13(7), pp. 560–576 (2003)
2. Richardson, I.E.G.: H.264 and MPEG-4 Video Compression - Video Coding for Next-generation Multimedia. Wiley. Chichester (2003)
3. Ri, S.H., Ostermann, J.: Fast Inter-Mode Decision in an H.264/AVC Encoder Using Mode and Lagrangian Cost Correlation. IEEE Transactions on Circuits and Systems for Video Technology, 19(2), pp. 302–306 (2009)
4. Pan, L.J. and Ho, Y.S.: Fast Mode Decision Algorithm for H.264 Inter Prediction. IET Electronics Letters, 43(24), pp. 1351–1353 (2007)

5. Lim, K.P., Sullivan, G.J., Wiegand, T.: Text Description of Joint Model Reference Encoding Methods and Decoding Concealment Methods. JVT-N046, JVT of ISO/IEC MPEG and ITU-T VCEG (2005)
6. Jang, W.S., Heo, J., Ho, Y.S.: Efficient Selection of Candidates for Fast Inter Mode Decision in H.264. In: International Symposium on Signal Processing, Image Processing and Pattern Recognition (SIP), pp. 222–225, (2008)
7. JVT Reference Software version JM 12.4,: http://iphome/hhi.de/shehring/tml/download/old_jm/jm12.4.zip.
8. Bjontegaard, G.: Calculation of Average PSNR Differences between RD-curves. ITU-T Q.6/16, Doc. VCEG-M33 (2001)
9. Bjontegaard, G.: Improvement of the BD-PSNR Model. ITU-T Q6/16, Doc. VCEG-AI11, (2008)

Disparity and Motion Activity Based Mode Prediction for Fast Mode Decision in Multiview Video Coding

Dan Mao, Yun Zhang, Qian Chen, and Sam Kwong

Abstract Multiview video coding (MVC) uses exhaustive variable size block mode decision in motion estimation and disparity estimation to improve coding efficiency; however, it causes intensive computational complexity. A fast mode decision algorithm for the non-anchor pictures is proposed to lower computational complexity of MVC. In the proposed algorithm, mode decision is early terminated based on the inter-view mode correlation among neighboring views and motion activity predicted from motion information from checking previous macroblock mode. Experimental results show that the proposed fast mode decision algorithm achieves from 53.67 to 81.75% complexity reduction. Meanwhile, the peak signal-to-noise ratio degradation of the proposed algorithm is 0.046 dB on average and bit rate increases from −2.13% to 0.77%, which are negligible.

Keywords Multiview video coding • Mode decision • Inter-view correlation • Disparity estimation

D. Mao • Q. Chen
Shenzhen Institutes of Advanced Technology, Chinese Academy of Sciences, Shenzhen 518055, China
e-mail: dan.mao@siat.ac.cn; qian.chen@siat.ac.cn

Y. Zhang (✉)
Shenzhen Institutes of Advanced Technology, Chinese Academy of Sciences, Shenzhen 518055, China

Department of Computer Science, City University of Hong Kong, Kowloon, Hong Kong SAR
e-mail: yun.zhang@siat.ac.cn

S. Kwong
Department of Computer Science, City University of Hong Kong, Kowloon, Hong Kong SAR
e-mail: cssamk@cityu.edu.hk

J.S. Jin et al., *The Era of Interactive Media*,
DOI 10.1007/978-1-4614-3501-3_15,

1 Introduction

Multi-view image/video is becoming a reality in the consumer electronics with the development of multimedia technologies and the demand for realistic visual systems [1]. It is widely used in free-viewpoint television [2], 3D television [3] and surveillance systems which can provide a more realistic visual experience. Multi-view video are captured by an array of cameras from different positions and viewing angles. Since all the cameras capture the same world scene, there exits considerable redundancy in the multiview sequence data.

Multi-view Video Coding (MVC) has designed sophisticated mechanisms to compress multi-view video and achieves high compression efficiency. Motion Estimation (ME) and Disparity Estimation (DE) are both utilized to improve coding efficiency. Variable block size macroblock (MB) modes selection, including SKIP, 16×16, 16×8, 8×16, 8×8, 8×8Frext, I16MB, I8MB, and I4MB, are used and the best mode is selected by Rate Distortion (RD) cost comparison. These methods improve MVC RD performance, but at the cost of significant high computational complexity, which hinders MVC technology from real time interactive application [3].

In recent years, various fast algorithms are proposed to reduce the complexity of mode decision. Hu et al. proposed RD cost based mode decision for H.264/AVC [4]. Wang et al. [5] proposed all zero block detection algorithm which was used for early mode decision and ME in H.264/AVC. Zhao et al. [6] proposed probability based mode candidate list for best mode selection. However, they are proposed for traditional mono-view video coding and not so efficient if it is directly applied to MVC since inter-view correlation are not considered. In [7], a fast MB mode selection algorithm is proposed based on the MB mode similarity between texture video and depth video, but this prediction mechanism can only be used in video coding which includes texture videos and associated depth videos of the same scene. A fast inter frame prediction algorithm is proposed in [8] which use the relationship between motion compensation prediction and disparity compensation prediction to decrease the candidate modes. Kuo et al. [9] proposed a fast algorithm by using RD-cost as a factor to decide whether to choose or skipping motion SKIP mode. Such algorithm is high correlated with Quantization Parameter (QP) and video content. In [10–12], MB mode of the current MB is predicted from the mode decision of the corresponding MB in the neighboring view via Global Disparity Vector (GDV). In [13], segmentation information is also adopted to exploit interview correlation. However, the GDV concept assumes a globally unique displacement among inter-views. Unfortunately, this hypothesis is usually not true for toed-in camera arrangement and video with different depth-of-fields. In this paper, we present an efficient inter-view correlation based fast mode decision algorithm for MVC, which exploits inter-view correlation via DE of 16×16 block and achieves higher accuracy than GDV scheme.

2 Observations and Analyses

2.1 Mode Correlation Among Neighboring Views

Since multi-view video is captured by camera array simultaneously from slightly different positions and angles, there is very high inter-view mode correlation between the current view and the neighboring view(s) with respect to content [10]. Figure 1 shows an example of MBs modes correspondence among neighboring views, where the three pictures indicate images of three neighboring views and the red, green and yellow ones stand for the MBs encoded with SKIP, INTER and INTRA mode, respectively. We can see that MB modes distribution among different views is quite similar due to the fact that video content and motion property is similar; however, they have a displacement among views. Generally, the existing related works exploit interview mode correlation using GDV with the assumption of global displacement among images of different views. However, it is not true for the multiview video with different depth-of-field and the video captured by toed-in (arc) camera array [14]. According to Fig. 1, for different depth regions, such as the blue and red rectangle in the center view S_n, we can see that their disparities are not uniform, i.e. $DV_{f,1} \neq DV_{f,2}$, $DV_{b,1} \neq DV_{b,2}$. Therefore, inaccuracy of mode prediction may be caused by using GDV. Similar problem also occurs for video sequences captured by arc arrange sequences.

To improve the accuracy of mode prediction and maintain low complexity, more accurate disparity vectors among views, which is generated from variable block-sizes DE process, are adopted in this paper. MVC performs the variable block-sizes DE process to eliminate inter-view redundancies among views. Through this DE, we can find the corresponding MB which is most like the current MB in the neighboring view(s), as shown in Fig. 1. In the figure, MB_c is the current MB in center view (denoted by S_n), $MB_f(i)$ are the corresponding MB and its neighboring

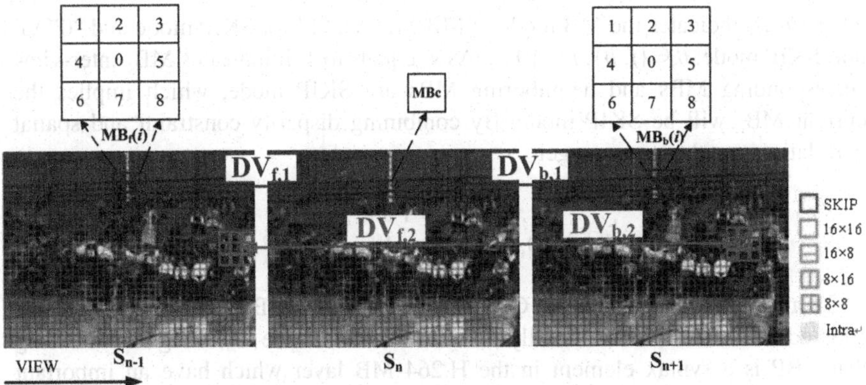

Fig. 1 Example of MBs modes correspondence among neighboring views

MBs found by DE in forward view (denoted by S_{n-1}), and $MB_b(i)$ are the corresponding MB and its neighboring MBs found by DE in backward view (denoted by S_{n+1}). As SKIP mode has largest percentage and with lowest computational complexity according to statistical analysis, we intent to early terminate SKIP mode decision process as early as possible to lower the complexity.

According to the similarity of mode distribution among views, we can see that MB_c is mostly encoded in SKIP mode when corresponding $MB_f(0)$, $MB_b(0)$ in neighboring views are encoded with SKIP mode. However, since the similarity is different for different regions, it is more similar in stationary background regions (red rectangle in Fig. 1) than object regions with fast motion or complicated texture (green or yellow rectangle). We can easily perceive that stationary background regions are mostly encoded in SKIP mode while regions with motion or complicated texture are suitable for other modes. So, the similarity is higher when a MB chooses SKIP mode as its best mode. As a result, a corresponding MB which is SKIP mode can be used to encode the current MB. Because corresponding MB found by DE may exist some deviation, a disparity difference constraint is provided to ensure matching accuracy. Whether they match or not can be presented as

$$r_\theta = \begin{cases} 1, & \text{if} |D_\theta| < D_{Max} \\ 0, & \text{else} \end{cases}, \tag{1}$$

where D_θ is the inter-view disparity in the θ view which is found by 16×16 DE, $\theta \in \{f, b\}$, f represents the forward view (S_{n-1} in Fig. 1) and b represents the afterward view (S_{n+1} in Fig. 1), r_θ represents whether they match (denoted by "1") or not match (denoted by "0"), D_{Max} is the maximum disparity. MB mode also has high spatial correlation. If the corresponding MB and its eight spatial neighbor MBs are all SKIP mode, the current MB is probably SKIP mode. So we calculate an index s_θ as

$$s_\theta = \prod_{i=0}^{8} m_\theta(i) \tag{2}$$

where $m_\theta(i)$ indicates the MB mode of MB $MB_\theta(i)$, "1" for SKIP mode and "0" for non-SKIP mode, $\theta \in \{f, b\}$, $i \in [0,8]$. As s_θ equals to 1, it indicates MB_c inter-view corresponding MBs and neighboring MBs are SKIP mode, which implies the current MB_c will be SKIP mode. By combining disparity constraint and spatial correlation together, we can get

$$k_\theta = \begin{cases} 1, & \text{if}(r_\theta = 1 \text{ and } s_\theta = 1) \\ 0, & \text{else} \end{cases}, \tag{3}$$

To maintain high accuracy, Coded Block Pattern (CBP) information is also adopted since the CBP is usually zero after SKIP mode checking. Considering that CBP is a syntax element in the H.264 MB layer which have an important implication on mode decision [8], finally the enabling of current coding MB choose SKIP as best mode(denoted by Φ) is determined as

Table 1 Statistical analyses of early termination rate for SKIP mode

Multiview video	QP	R_{H}(%)	R_{O} (%)
Vassar	24	97.68	40.86
	28	99.13	70.59
	32	99.74	82.34
	36	99.85	89.08
Exit	24	96.58	37.24
	28	98.80	57.27
	32	98.97	64.57
	36	99.01	72.51
Ballroom	24	97.17	33.25
	28	98.52	46.25
	32	98.82	54.21
	36	98.85	59.63
Ballet	24	97.55	35.90
	28	98.57	46.20
	32	99.05	55.46
	36	99.41	64.85
Average		**98.61**	**56.89**

$$\Phi = \begin{cases} 1, & \text{if}((K_f = 1 \text{ or } K_a \;\; = 1) \text{ and } CBP_{SKIP} = 0), \\ 0, & \text{else} \end{cases} \tag{4}$$

where $\mathrm{CBP_{SKIP}}$ is the value of CBP after SKIP implementation in current coding MB. If Φ equals to 1, the mode selection process is early terminated and the SKIP mode is selected as the best MB mode.

To analyze the efficiency and accuracy of the proposed early termination algorithm, statistical analyses of the early terminate rate are performed, where four typical multi-view test video are used. Table 1 illustrates the statistical results. R_H denotes the hit rate for the proposed early termination method, which means the probability when Φ equals to 1 and the best mode of $\mathrm{MB_c}$ is SKIP mode, i.e. identical to SKIP mode obtained from full mode search. R_O indicates the occurrence rate of Φ equals to 1. Higher R_H means ensuring less RD degradation and higher R_O means more reduction of the computational complexity. As can be seen from the table, R_H is 98.61% and R_O is 56.89% on average. High value of R_H and R_O ensures that our algorithm can reduce computational complexity significantly with unnoticeable RD degradation.

2.2 Correlation Between Temporal Motion Activity and MB Mode

In the mode decision process, ME and DE operation is implemented in modes of 16 × 16, 16 × 8, 8 × 16, 8 × 8 (including 8 × 4, 4 × 8, and 4 × 4) MB partitions; Moreover, each mode requires for searching for multiple temporal

Fig. 2 Relation between motion activity and modes of Ballroom sequence (*Left*: original image, *Right*: corresponding motion activity map)

reference and inter-view reference frames. However, the percentage for a MB to be coded as small block-sizes, such as 8 × 8, 4 × 8 and 4 × 4, is very low, about 5% [12], but these modes consume huge computational complexity in each mode search process. Therefore, our basic idea of this stage is avoid checking those low probability and time consuming block-size modes so as to further speed up the mode decision process.

The small block size MB mode is usually selected in fast motion regions and their difference between motion vector and predictive motion vector is usually non-zero. Also, there is high motion vector correlation between motion activity of large block-size modes which is early searched and small block-size modes later implemented. The motion activity of MB_c with MB mode m, A_m, is defined as

$$A_m = V_m - \hat{V}_m \, , \tag{5}$$

where m stands for different INTER partition modes, $m \in \{16 \times 16, 16 \times 8, 8 \times 8\}$, V_{m} denotes the best motion vector found by using mode m, $\hat{V}_m$ is the predicted motion vector of mode m.

The correlation between motion activity and MB modes is shown in Fig. 2. The left picture is original color image and the right picture is the motion activity map corresponding to the left picture. In the figure, the yellow rectangles represent that $A_{16\times16}$ of the MB is zero after checking SKIP and 16 × 16 mode and the best mode is SKIP or 16 × 16 in full mode search for these MBs. The red ones represent the $A_{16\times16}$ is zero after checking SKIP and 16 × 16 mode search and the best mode of these MBs are not SKIP or 16 × 16, i.e. wrong predicted MBs. The rest MBs represent $A_{16\times16}$ is a non-zero value after SKIP and 16 × 16 mode search. We can see from Fig. 2 that the smooth yellow areas almost cover entire image and the number of red blocks are very small. This correlation between motion activity and mode shows it is effective to early terminate the ME/DE search for smaller MB partition while $A_{16\times16}$ is zero. Accordingly, if the two $A_{16\times8}$ s are all zero after 16 × 8 search, the 8 × 8 mode search process is early terminated and the smaller mode checking is unnecessary. If the $A_{8\times8}$ s are all zero after 8 × 8 search, 8 × 4, 4 × 8, and 4 × 4 modes are skipped.

3 Proposed Disparity and Motion Activity Based Fast Mode Decision for MVC

We propose a fast mode decision including two phases for MVC and it is only optimized for non-anchor hierarchical picture for the inter-view views. The first phase is early SKIP mode termination using inter-view correlation (Step1). The second stage is mode decision based on motion activity (Step2 to Step7). Figure 3 shows the flowchart of the proposed algorithm and its detailed steps are as follow

Step1 Encode current MB with SKIP mode, do 16 × 16 DE to find the corresponding MBs among two inter-view neighboring views, then get the value of Φ according to Eq. (4). If the Φ equals to 1, SKIP mode is chosen as the best mode and go to Step 7, else, go to Step 2.

Step2 Do the 16 × 16 ME, and calculate $A_{16\times16}$. If $A_{16\times16}$ equals to 0, go to Step 6, else go to Step 3.

Step3 Do 16 × 8 and 8 × 16 ME/DE, and calculate $A_{16\times8}$ for each partition. If $A_{16\times8}$ equals to zero go to Step 6, else go to Step 4.

Step4 Do 8 × 8 ME and DE, then and calculate $A_{8\times8}$ for each partition. If $A_{8\times8}$ equals to 0, go to Step 6, else, go to Step 5.

Step5 Do 8 × 4, 4 × 8 and 4 × 4 ME and DE.

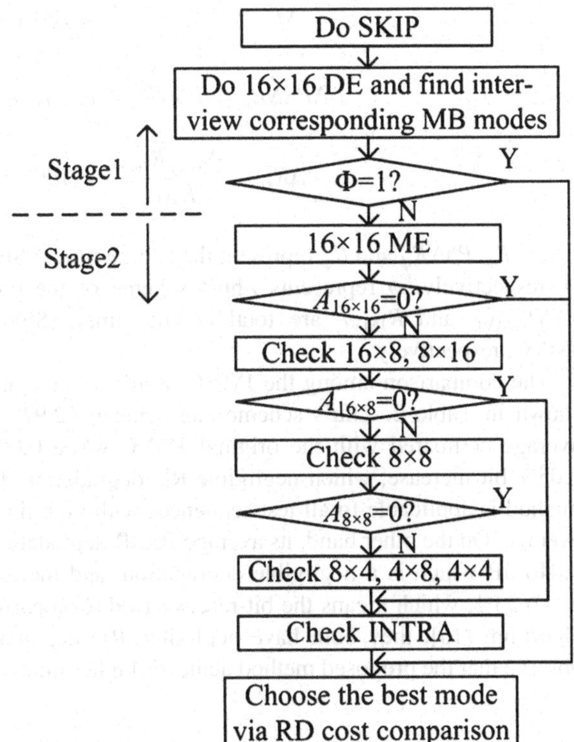

Fig. 3 Flowchart of the proposed fast mode decision algorithm

Step6 Check INTRA modes, including I16MB, I8MB, I4MB and PCM.

Step7 Select the MB mode that yields the minimum RD cost as the best mode. Then, go to Step 1 for next MB.

4 Experimental Results and Analyses

The proposed fast mode decision algorithm is implemented on recent H.264/AVC based JMVC 8.0 reference software. We adopt five multi-view test sequences "Vassar", "Lovebird1", "Dog", "Ballet" and "Breakdancers" and they are with different motion, texture property and camera arrangement, where "Vassar", "Lovebird1", "Dog" are captured by parallel camera array, "Ballet" and "Breakdancers" are captured by arc camera array. In our experiment, fast ME/DE search is enabled and their search range is ±96, and basis QP is 20, 24, 28, and 32. GOP length of is 12, 8 views are encoded and coding performance of three inter-views are compared with the reference JMVC and the state-of-art Zhu's scheme [13]. All tests of the experiment are performed on computer with Pentium Dual-core CPU E5500 in 2.80 GHZ and 2.79 GHZ with 2 GB RAM, operating system is Microsoft Windows XP Professional. The complexity reduction ΔT, Peak Signal-to-Noise Ratio (PSNR) degradation $\Delta PSNR$ and bit-rate increment ΔR, are defined as

$$\Delta T_{\phi} = \frac{T_{JMVC} - T_{\phi}}{T_{JMVC}} \times 100\%, \tag{6}$$

$$\Delta PSNR_{\phi} = PSNR_{\phi} - PSNR_{JMVC}, \tag{7}$$

$$\Delta R_{\phi} = \frac{R_{\phi} - R_{JMVC}}{R_{JMVC}} \times 100\%, \tag{8}$$

where T_{ϕ}, $PSNR_{\phi}$ and R_{ϕ} represent the coding time, PSNR and bitrate of algorithm ϕ, respectively. ϕ represents Zhu's scheme or the proposed algorithm. T_{JMVC}, $PSNR_{\mathrm{JMVC}}$ and R_{JMVC} are total coding time, PSNR and bit-rate of original JMVC, respectively.

The comparison among the JMVC, Zhu's scheme and the proposed scheme is shown in Table 2. Zhu's scheme can achieve 62.92% complexity reduction on average compared with the original JMVC while 0.002 PSNR degradation and 0.05% bit increase, which negligible RD degradation. Furthermore, the proposed method is applicable to all test sequences with high time savings about 74.4% on average. On the other hand, its average PSNR degradation compared JMVC is only 0.046 dB which is a negligible degradation, and the average of bit-rate increase is −0.23%, which means the bit-rate is saved. Comparing our method with Zhu's algorithm [13], they both have negligible RD degradation. In addition, we can observe that the proposed method achieves higher time saving ratio, 11.48% higher

Table 2 Performance comparisons among the proposed algorithm, Zhu's scheme [13] and full mode decision in JMVC

		Zhu's algorithm			Proposed algorithm		
Multi-view video	QP	ΔR (%)	$\Delta PSNR$(dB)	ΔT(%)	ΔR (%)	$\Delta PSNR$(dB)	ΔT(%)
Vassar	24	−0.03	0.000	73.91	−0.07	−0.030	78.73
	28	0.09	−0.001	73.27	0.39	−0.044	80.20
	32	0.06	−0.001	72.48	0.33	−0.019	80.96
	36	−0.04	−0.001	71.74	0.72	−0.012	81.75
Lovebird1	24	−0.01	−0.001	73.66	0.42	−0.054	80.71
	28	0.00	−0.001	71.67	0.17	−0.035	80.54
	32	0.03	0.001	69.12	−0.23	−0.04	80.19
	36	0.05	0.000	67.76	−0.35	−0.028	81.08
Dog	24	−0.01	−0.003	58.67	−0.82	−0.036	74.44
	28	0.15	−0.003	57.73	−1.12	−0.032	75.51
	32	0.14	−0.002	56.49	−1.64	−0.05	76.07
	36	0.15	−0.003	55.24	−1.98	−0.078	76.64
Ballet	24	0.09	0.000	68.55	0.41	−0.029	72.25
	28	−0.04	−0.004	67.62	0.14	−0.046	73.62
	32	0.01	0.000	66.32	0.28	−0.054	74.43
	36	0.18	−0.001	65.23	0.03	−0.085	75.4
Break-dancers	24	−0.07	−0.006	44.94	−0.12	−0.043	53.67
	28	0.02	−0.003	47.46	0.21	−0.057	59.51
	32	0.08	−0.001	47.85	−0.4	−0.068	63.97
	36	0.11	−0.004	48.7	−1.04	−0.089	68.33
Average		**0.05**	**−0.002**	**62.92**	**−0.23**	**−0.046**	**74.40**

on average, than Zhu's scheme. Additionally, as for the proposed algorithm, we can also see that our method can achieves more complexity reduction as QP value increases because a larger QP value will produce more SKIP mode.

For better observation, Fig. 4 illustrates the RD curves and coding time saving for different video sequences. Figure 4a shows that the RD curves of Zhu's scheme, JMVC and proposed algorithm are overlapped, which means the proposed algorithm maintains nearly the same RD performance as original JMVC and Zhu's scheme for all test sequences due to high accuracy of mechanism in mode prediction. Figure 4b shows coding time saving comparison between Zhu's scheme and proposed algorithm, from which we can obviously observe that our method can achieve much more time saving than Zhu's algorithm for all the test video sequences. It is also noticed that the proposed algorithm has great adaptability for different kinds of video sequences, such as the fast motion Breakdancers sequence captured by arc camera array and slow motion Dog by parallel camera array. Also, for Lovebird1 with slow motion, the proposed algorithm achieves 81.08% time saving. For sequences have both fast and slow motion, such as Vassar and Ballet, the encoding time saving ratio is quite stable too.

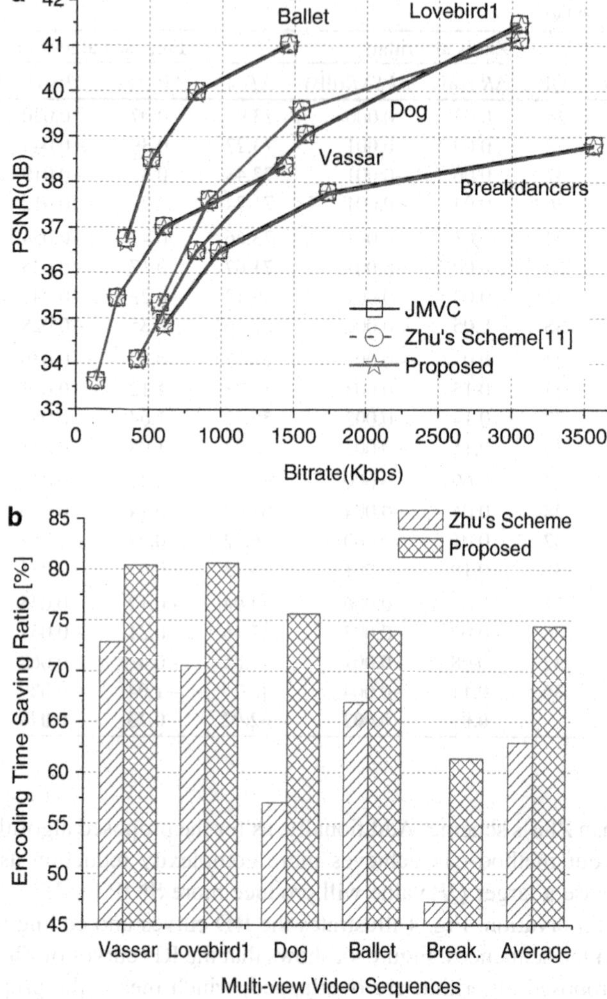

Fig. 4 RD performance and encoding time saving ratio achieved by Zhu's scheme and the proposed scheme. (**a**) RD curves for different multiview video sequences, (**b**) Encoding time saving ratio for different multiview video sequences

5 Conclusions

In this paper, we present an inter-view correlation and motion activity based fast mode decision for MVC. In the first phase, the mode correlation among corresponding MBs in neighboring views is exploited using 16×16 disparity search and it is used for early SKIP mode termination. Then, mode candidates are reduced based motion activity of previous MB mode. Experimental results show the proposed method can reduce 74.4% complexity on average in comparison with JMVC. Compared with Zhu's scheme, the proposed scheme can achieve from 5 to 21% more computational complexity reduction. Meanwhile, the PSNR degradation of the proposed algorithm is 0.046 dB on average and bitrate increases from −2.13 to 0.77%, which are negligible.

Acknowledgments This work was supported by Natural Science Foundation of China (Grant No. 61102088, 61070147), in part by the Hong Kong Research Grants Council General Research Fund, under Project 9041495 (CityU 115109).

References

1. Vetro A., Wiegand T., and Sullivan G.: Overview of the stereo and multiview video coding extensions of the H.264/MPEG-4 AVC standard, in Proc. of the IEEE, 2011, 99(4), 626–642 (2011)
2. Tanimoto M., Tehrani M.P., Fujii T., and Yendo T.: Free-viewpoint TV, IEEE Signal Process. Mag., 28(1), 67–76 (2011)
3. Smolic A., Mueller K., and Stefanoski N.: Coding algorithms for 3DTV-A survey, IEEE Trans. Circuits Syst. Video Technol., 17(11), 1606–1621 (2007)
4. Hu S., Zhao T., Wang H. and Kwong S.: Fast inter-mode decision based on rate-distortion cost characteristics, in Proc. PCM'10, LNCS, 145–155 (2010)
5. Wang H., Kwong S., and Kok C.-W.: An efficient mode decision algorithm for H.264/AVC encoding optimization, IEEE Trans. Multimedia, 9 (4), 882–888 (2007)
6. Zhao T., Wang H., Kwong S., and Kuo C. C.: Fast mode decision based on mode adaptation, IEEE Trans. Circuits Syst. Video Technol., 20(5), 697–705 (2010)
7. Peng Z., Yu M., Jiang G., Shao F., Zhang Y., and Yang Y.: Fast macroblock mode selection algorithm for multiview depth video coding, Chin. Opt. Lett., 8(2), 151–154 (2010)
8. Li X., Zhao D., Ji X., Wang Q., and Gao W.: A fast inter frame prediction algorithm for multi-view video coding, in Proc. ICIP'07, 6(3), 417–420 (2007)
9. Kuo T., Lai Y., and Lo Y.: Fast mode decision for non-anchor picture in multiview video, in Proc. IEEE BMSB'10, 1–5, (2010)
10. Yu M., Peng Z., Liu W., Shao F., Jiang G., and Kim Y.: Fast macroblock selection algorithm for multiview video coding based on inter-view global disparity, in Proc. CISP'08, 1(1), 575–578 (2008)
11. Han D. and Lee Y.: Fast mode decision using global disparity vector for multiview video coding, in Proc. FGCNS'08, 3, 209–213 (2008)
12. Shen L., Yan T., Liu Z., Zhang Z., An P., and Yang L.: Fast mode decision for multiview video coding, in Proc. ICIP'09, 2953–2956 (2009)
13. Zhu W., Tian X., Zhou F., and Chen Y.: Fast inter mode decision based on textural segmentation and correlations for multiview video coding, IEEE Trans. Consumer Electron., 56(3), 1696–1704 (2010)
14. Zhang Y., Jiang G., Yu M., Yang Y., Peng Z. and Chen K.: Depth perceptual region-of-interest based multiview video coding, J. Vis. Comm. Image R., 21(5–6), 498–512 (2010)

Multiple Reference Frame Motion Re-estimation for H.264/AVC Frame-Skipping Transcoding with Zonal Search

Jhong-Hau Jiang, Yu-Ming Lee, and Yinyi Lin

Abstract In this paper we propose an efficient multiple reference frame motion re-estimation for H.264/AVC frame-skipping transcoding. In the proposed algorithm, all information including reference frame number, motion vector etc. in original H.264/AVC-coded videos are reused when the original reference frame is not skipped; while an efficient multiple reference frame motion re-estimation is employed when the reference frame is dropped. The neighboring reference frames around the skipped reference frame are selected for motion re-estimation, and in addition a zonal search method is used for motion re-estimation. The experimental results reveal that average 87% of computation time (corresponding to a speed-up factor of 8) can be saved for the proposed H.264 frame-skipping transcoding algorithm, when compared with fully decoding/encoding procedure. The degradation in the rate-distortion performance is fairly small.

Keywords Multiple reference frame motion estimation • H.264/AVC • Prediction motion vector

1 Introduction

The latest H.264/AVC can significantly achieve better coding performance compared with prior video coding standards [1], due to many advanced techniques, such as variable block sizes mode decision and multiple reference frames motion estimation etc., employed in H.264/AVC. Applications of H.264/AVC become popular and important in multimedia content transfer between networks and devices.

J.-H. Jiang (✉) • Y.-M. Lee • Y. Lin
Department of Communication Engineering, National Central University, Taiwan
e-mail: yilin@ce.ncu.edu.tw

J.S. Jin et al., *The Era of Interactive Media*,
DOI 10.1007/978-1-4614-3501-3_16,

However, because different networks have various formats or bandwidths, the coded video bit stream has to be converted or transcoded to different formats to meet channel requirements.

In video transcoding, there are many schemes such as requantization, frame-skipping and spatial resolution reduction, to reduce overall bit-rates. In this paper we focus on reducing bit-rate to meet an available channel capacity through frame-skipping process. The straightforward method for frame-skipping transcoding is to decode the video stream and re-encode the reconstructed video sequences after frame-skipping. However, the computational complexity of the completely decoding and re-encoding process, referred to as complex cascaded pixel domain transcoding (CCPDT), is very high.

The computation cost can be greatly reduced when the original mode, motion vector information in the skipped frame is reused to encode the non-skipped frame. However, this could lead to a severe degradation in coding performance due to mode and motion vector mis-matched problems. To improve coding performance, many efficient motion re-estimation algorithms, based on original motion vector information, have been recently proposed for frame-skipping transcoding [2, 3] which usually consider single reference frame motion re-estimation. In this paper we suggest an efficient multiple reference frame motion re-estimation algorithm for H.264/AVC frame-skipping transcoding, to reduce computation cost while still maintaining good coding performance.

2 Multiple Reference Frame Selection Scheme for H.264/AVC-Coded Videos

The H.264/AVC encoder provides multiple reference frames motion estimation (MRFME) for both inter and intra mode predictions in the inter frame (P-frame), as Fig. 1 illustrates. In the H.264/AVC reference software baseline encoder, the MRFME process begins from the 16×16 mode to the 4×4 mode in a hierarchical descending order for each MB, with reference frames searched from frame (t-1) to frame (t-N). An H.264/AVC-coded video stream in inter P frames includes not only the coded macroblock type and the coded block pattern, but also the motion vector (MV) for each 4×4 block and the reference frame number for each 8×8 block. The original information is shown in Fig. 2.

As shown in Fig. 1, one important technique in H.264/AVC is the use of multiple reference frames motion estimation (MRFME), and the computational complexity of H.264/AVC increases linearly with the number of reference frames employed. For H.264/AVC frame-skipping transcoding, the original reference frame might not be a skipped frame and in this situation the re-encoding process is not necessary. Instead all information including mode, motion vector (MV) and reference frame could be preserved and reused. This achieves low computational complexity and

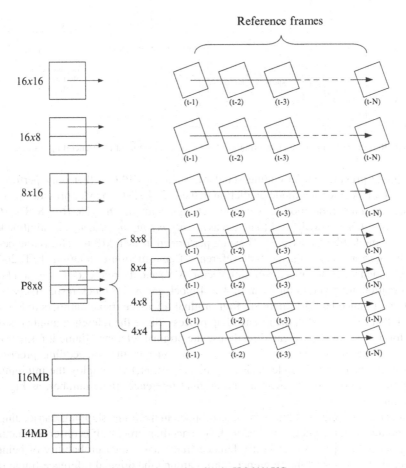

Fig. 1 Multiple reference frame motion estimation in H.264/AVC

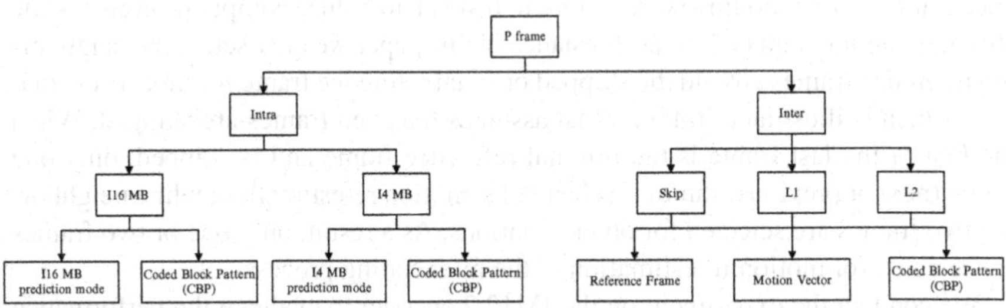

Fig. 2 Information in original H.264/AVC-coded video bit stream

high video quality. For example, consider $N = 5$ and skip even frames, the experiment demonstrates that about 12% (corresponding to the percentage of best reference frames distributed in even positions) of computation time can be saved with negligible performance degradation.

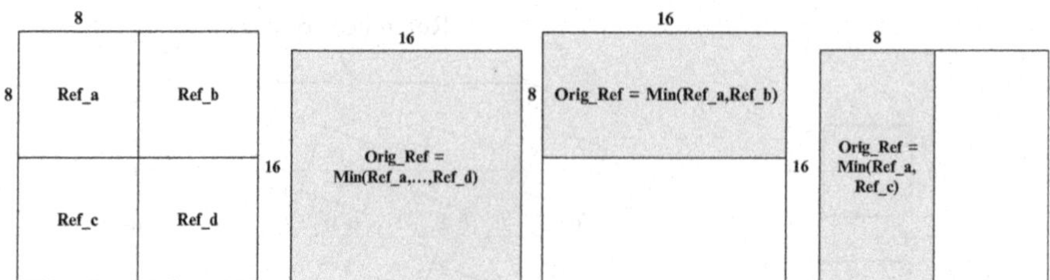

Fig. 3 Reference frame number information for L1-level mode used in re-encoding process

Unlike previous video coding standards such as MPEG-2 that only performs 16×16 mode, the inter mode prediction in the H.264/AVC encoder provides seven modes for inter-frame motion estimation, changing among $16 \times 16, 16 \times 8, 8 \times 16, 8 \times 8, 8 \times 4, 4 \times 8$, and 4×4 (denoted as $m_1, m_2, m_3, m_4, m_5, m_6, m_7$), in addition to the skip mode (denoted as m_0). They are performed in each MB to achieve the best coding performance with multiple reference frame motion estimation. In H.264/AVC-coded video streams the motion vector (MV) and the reference frame number information are given in the form of 4×4 block and 8×8 block respectively.

For a re-encoded MB, there are four original reference frame numbers of 8×8 block that can be used in the re-encoding process. Since the reference number is of the form 8×8 block, we can directly use the original reference frame information for L2-level mode decision (i.e., m_4, m_5, m_6, m_7) in the re-encoding process. However, for L1-level mode decision (i.e., m_1, m_2, m_3) we employ the minimum reference number among them as the original reference frame number, as Fig. 3 illustrates.

When the original reference frame is dropped in the frame skipping transcoding, the motion vector cannot be reused in the re-encoding process. It is observed that in the re-encoding process the best reference frame has a high probability of being selected from neighboring reference frames around the original reference frame in H.264/AVC-coded videos. The observation indicates that performing all N reference frames in re-encoding is not required. Instead, to reduce computation cost while still maintaining high coding performance in this paper we only select the neighboring reference frames around the skipped original reference frame for motion estimation, which is illustrated in Fig. 4 that assumes the even frames are skipped. When the first or the last frame is the original reference frame and is skipped, only one frame (next or previous frame) is selected for motion re-estimation; while neighboring two frames are selected for other situations. As a result, only one or two frames are selected for motion re-estimation in the re-encoding process.

We conduct the experiment on the JM12.2 encoder to evaluate the performance of the neighboring reference frame motion estimation scheme. Eight video sequences are used in our simulations, covering a wide range of motion contents and various formats (QCIF and CIF). The experimental setting is tabulated in Table 1, where the original H.264/AVC-coded video sequence has the first 300 frames in simulations. Each sequence is coded using IPP… structure, i.e., the first frame is

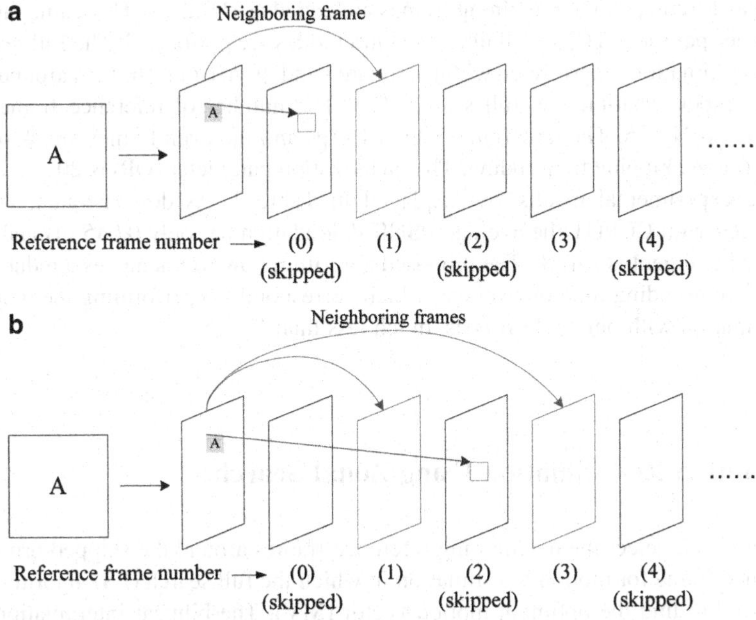

Fig. 4 Neighboring reference frame motion re-estimation scheme. (**a**) Original best reference frame $n = 0$ being skipped. (**b**) Original best reference frame $n = 2$ being skipped

Table 1 Simulation conditions and tested sequences

Profile	Baseline
Total frame	300
Number of reference frames	5
Entropy coding	CAVLC
GOP structure	IPPP
Frame rate	30
RDO	on
Hadamard	on
Resolution	¼ pixel
Search range	33 × 33
Coder version	12.2
Video Resolution	Sequence
QCIF (17 × 144)	Carphone
	Claire
	Foreman
	News
	Container
CIF (352 × 288)	Mobile
	Paris
	Stefan

coded as I frame, all the remaining frames are coded as P frames. The frame rate is 30 frames per second (fps). All inter and intra modes are performed. The full search motion estimation is performed within a square window size of [-16, +16] around the current block position (i.e. full search, FS). The number of reference frames is assumed as N = 5. The new frame rate is 15 fps and the even frames are skipped in the frame-skipping transcoding. The quantization parameter (QP) is 20.

The experimental results are displayed in Table 2. As demonstrated, when compared with CCPDT the average PSNR degradation are only 0.045 dB and the bit-rate increment is 2.42%. The proposed algorithm however achieves a reduction of 74% transcoding time on average, which corresponds to performing the motion re-estimation with only 1.25 frames, much less than $N = 5$.

3 Motion Re-estimation Using Zonal Search

In Sect. 2, we select the neighboring reference frames around the skipped original reference frame for motion re-estimation in which the full search (FS) algorithm is employed to find the optimum motion vector (MV). The bilinear interpolation of the median prediction MV (denoted as $PMV_{default}$) is assumed as the initial search point in the FS. The median PMV is defined as the median value of the MVs in its neighboring MBs in the same frame (left, top and top-right):

$$PMV_{default} = median((MV\_l, MV\_t, MV\_tr) \tag{1}$$

Since the MV information referred to the skipped original reference frame also exists in H.264/AVC-coded video sequences, we can use the MV information to more accurately estimate the PMV in the motion estimation in re-encoding process, in addition to$PMV_{default}$.

Many MV composition (MVC) algorithms to estimate PMV for motion re-estimation in the re-encoding processing have been proposed [2, 3], with the use of original MV information. In [2], the MVC is computed based on the forward dominant vector selection (FDVS) technique which selects one dominant MV out of neighboring macroblocks (MBs) in the skipped original reference frame for MVC computation, as Fig. 5a shows. The dominant MV is defined as the MV of the MB in the skipped original reference frame which has the largest overlapping area. The dominant MV is added to the original MV (which is obtained using align-to-average weighting (AAW) technique [4], denoted as PMV_{AAW}) pointed to the skipped reference frame to compose PMV. The FDVS is shown to be superior to the conventional bilinear interpolation method. To improve FDVS, another technique [3] uses the efficient-FDVS (E-FDVS) with a compensation vector to find a more accurate composed PMV, as illustrated in Fig. 5b. Another drawback of the FDVS technique is that when the overlapping areas of neighboring MBs are very close, the dominant MV might leads to a bad MVC. Another way to improve FDVS for close

Table 2 PSNR loss, bit-rate increment and time saving

		PSNR comparison (dB, Δ(dB))			Bit rate comparison (bps, Δ(%))			Time (ms, Δ)(%))		
QP20	Sequence	CCPDT	NMRFS	Δ(d B)	CCPDT	NMRFS	Δ(%)	CCPDT	NMRFS	Δ(%)
QCIF	Carphone	45.044	44.926	−0.118	564253	592910	5.08	534809	135811	−74.61
	Claire	48.135	48.057	−0.078	147723	150082	1.60	250547	68202	−72.78
	Foreman	43.866	43.792	−0.074	670155	691362	3.16	641559	154843	−75.86
	News	46.884	46.873	−0.0111	309344	311456	0.68	310951	83026	−73.30
CIF	Container	45.313	45.293	−0.020	1495026	1516389	1.43	1800360	417517	−76.81
	Mobile	43.358	43.381	0.023	5750610	5997634	4.30	2516907	697749	−72.28
	Paris	45.817	45.712	−0.105	1819640	1838182	1.02	1357405	369530	−72.78
	Stefan	44.383	44.403	0.020	4880624	4981739	2.07	2513643	601970	−76.05
Avg.				−0.045			2.42			−7431

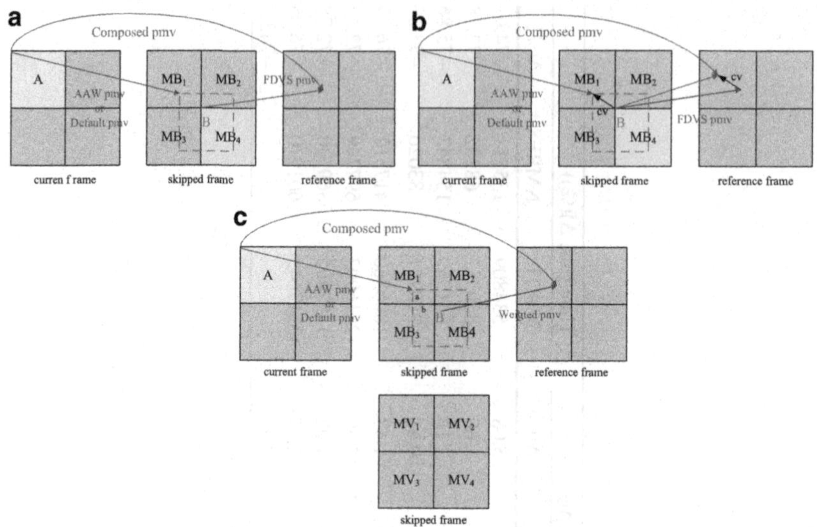

Fig. 5 Motion vector compositions. (**a**) FDVS (**b**) E-FDVS (**c**) WVS

overlapped areas is to use the weighted vector selection (WVS) of all neighboring MBs, as shown in Fig. 5c, with MV given by

$$MV_{WVS} = \frac{ab}{256}MV_1 + \frac{a(16-b)}{256}MV_2 + \frac{(16-a)b}{256}MV_3 + \frac{(16-a)(16-b)}{256}MV_4 \tag{2}$$

In the left neighboring reference frame the PMV or initial search point for motion re-estimation is obtained using bilinear interpolation of PMV_{AAW} or $PMV_{default}$; while using composed PMVs as the initial search point for the right neighboring reference frame. Figure 6 illustrates the motion re-estimation in the re-encoding process. The experiments show that although the composed MV is not optimal, it is very close to the optimum MV. The composed MV is then refined with a small search range window of [−1, +1] for motion re-estimation to improve the coding performance.

There are six MVC methods. Table 3 only summarizes PSNR loss, bit-rate increment and time saving for two MVC methods: $PMV_{AAW} + \text{E} - \text{FDVS}$ and $PMV_{default} + \text{E} - \text{FDVS}$. The average PSNR loss, bit-rate increment and time saving for $PMV_{AAW} + \text{E} - \text{FDVS}$ are 0.064 dB, 2.54% and 89.59% respectively; while 0.105 dB, 6.58% and 89.61% for $PMV_{default} + \text{E} - \text{FDVS}$. As shown, the MVC method using MV information (i.e., $PMV_{AAW} + \text{E} - \text{FDVS}$) achieves much better coding performance than the MVC method using median PMV (i.e., $PMV_{default} + \text{E} - \text{FDVS}$). This is due to the use of the original MV information PMV_{AAW} that gives more accurate motion vector prediction.

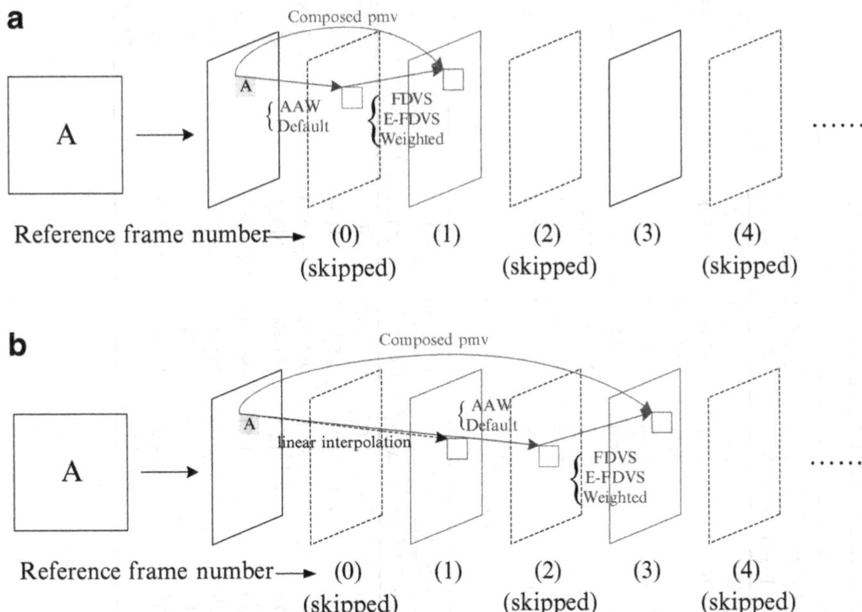

Fig. 6 Motion re-estimation for neighboring reference frames. (**a**) Original best reference frame $n = 0$ being skipped. (**b**) Original best reference frame $n = 2$ being skipped

When compared with Table 2 that uses the FS algorithm, we see that the MVC methods achieve much higher time saving (with 90%) than the FS algorithm (with 74% only), but with slightly higher degradation in coding performance. Similar results for other MVC methods using FDVS and WVS can be also obtained and not shown, but in general with slightly worse coding performance when compared with $PMV_{AAW} + \mathrm{E} - \mathrm{FDVS}$. Since video sequences have varieties of characteristics, the conclusion that $PMV_{AAW} + \mathrm{E} - \mathrm{FDVS}$ achieves the best coding performance is not always true in all situations. For example, we conducted all six MVC methods on foreman video sequence with constant bit-rate of 500 kbps, and the PSNR performance on frame-by-frame basis is shown in Fig. 7. From this figure, we see that all six approaches might be preferable on various frames. For instance, $PMV_{default}+$ WVS obviously achieves the best PSNR on frames from 110 to 115, while $PMV_{default}+$ FDVS and $PMV_{default} + \mathrm{E} - \mathrm{FDVS}$ are preferable for frames between 13 and 27. For frames around 140, the MVC methods using PMV_{AAW} achieve much better coding performance, compared to the methods using $PMV_{default}$. As shown, up to 4 dB coding gain can be obtained.

The PSNR performance shown in Fig. 7 indicate that the video quality can be further improved by using the zonal search (ZS) motion re-estimation with union of the six 1×1 sub-search areas. To improve its coding efficiency, we suggest employing the zonal search (ZS) algorithm to find the optimum MV, in which all

Table 3 PSNR loss, bit-rate increment and time saving for PMV_{AAW}+E-FDVS and $PMV_{default} + \text{E} - \text{FDVS}$

(a) $PMV_{AAW} + \text{E} - \text{FDVS}$

		PSNR comparison (dB, Δ(dB))			Bit rate comparison (bps, Δ(%))			Time (ms, Δ(%))		
QP20	Sequence	CCPDT	AAW+E-FDVS	Δ(dB)	CCPDT	AAW+E-FDVS	Δ(%)	CCPDT	AAW+E-FDVS	Δ(%)
QCIF	Carphone	45.044	44.915	−0.129	564253	600456	6.42	534809	45286	−91.53
	Claire	48.044	44.915	−0.129	564253	600456	6.42	534809	45286	−91.53
	Foreman	43.866	43.805	−0.061	670155	691662	3.21	641559	47385	−92.61
	News	46.884	46.864	−0.020	309344	312802	1.12	310951	40297	−87.04
CIF	Container	45.313	45.271	−0.042	1495026	1517464	1.50	1800360	171625	−90.47
	Mobile	43.358	43.385	0.027	5750610	6018295	4.65	2516907	236472	−90.60
	Paris	45.817	45.728	−0.089	1819640	1843206	1.30	1357405	181827	−86.60
	Stefan	44.383	44.384	0.001	4880624	4919191	0.79	2513643	212531	−91.54
Avg.				−0.064			2.54			−89.59

(b) $PMV_{default} + \text{E} - \text{FDVS}$

		PSNR comparison (d B, Δ(dB))			Bit rate comparison (bps, Δ(%))			Time (ms, Δ(%))		
QP20	Sequence	CCPDT	Default+E-FDVS	Δ(dB)	CCPDT	Defaulat+E-FDVS	Δ(%)	CCPDT	Default+E-FDVS	Δ(%)
QCIF	Carphone	45.044	44.902	−0.142	564253	607518	7.67	534809	45022	−91.58
	Claire	48.135	47.884	−0.251	147723	149952	1.51	250547	34139	−86.37
	Foreman	43.866	43.802	−0.064	670155	726430	8.40	641559	47518	−92.59
	News	46.884	46.730	−0.154	309344	314171	1.56	310951	39921	−87.16
CIF	Container	45.313	45.242	−0.071	1495026	1517560	1.51	1800360	170053	−90.55
	Mobile	43.358	43.370	0.012	5750610	6055859	5.31	2516907	235502	−90.64
	Paris	45.817	45.699	−0.118	1819640	1863810	2.43	1357405	181410	−86.64
	Stefan	44.383	44.334	−0.049	4880624	6065165	24.27	2513643	218526	−91.31
Avg.				−0.105			6.58			−89.61

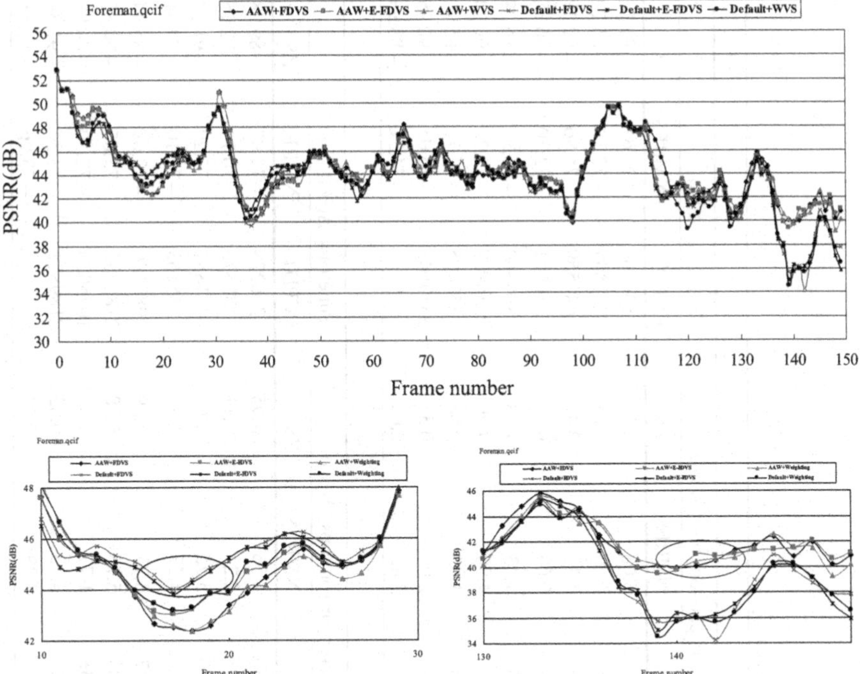

Fig. 7 PSNR on frame-by-frame basis for *foreman* sequence

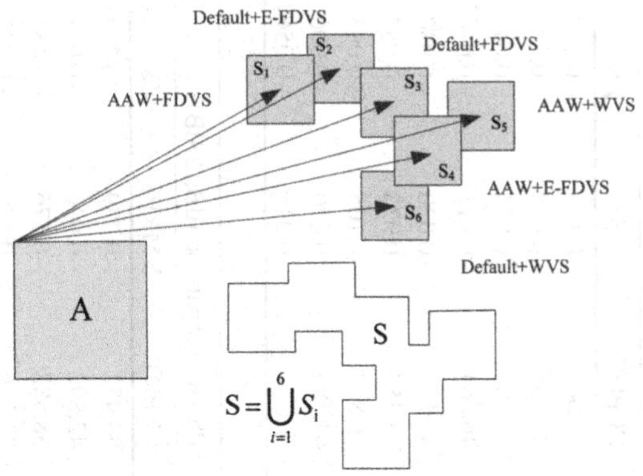

Fig. 8 Zonal search algorithm

six MVC methods are taken into account for motion re-estimation in re-encoding process. A search range of ±1 pixel around these six predictors is then used for refinement. The ZS algorithm is depicted in Fig. 8, where S represents the whole search area, given by. $S = \bigcup_{i=1}^{6} S_i$

Table 4 PSNR loss, bit-rate increment and time saving for full search and zonal search

(a) QP = 20

		PSNR comparison (dB, Δ(dB))			Bit rate comparison (bps, Δ(%))			Time (ms, Δ(%))		
QP20	Sequence	CCPDT	NMRFS	ZS	CCPDT	NMRFS	ZS	CCPDT	NMRFS	ZS
QCIF	Car Phone	45.044	−0.118	−0.107	564253	5.08	5.30	534809	−74.61	−91.05
	Claire	48.135	−0.078	−0.176	147723	1.60	1.53	250547	−72.78	−85.22
	Foreman	43.866	−0.074	−0.042	670155	3.16	2.42	641559	−75.86	−92.17
	News	46.884	−0.011	−0.046	309344	0.68	0.52	310951	−73.30	−86.28
CIF	Container	45.313	−0.020	−0.030	1495026	1.43	1.53	1800360	−76.81	−86.28
	Mobile	43.358	0.023	0.037	5750610	4.30	4.20	2516907	−72.28	−90.24
	Paris	45.817	−0.105	−0.093	1819660	1.02	0.88	1357405	−72.78	−85.90
	Stefan	44.383	0.020	0.006	4880624	2.07	0.37	2513643	−76.05	−90.95
Avg.			−0.045	−0.056		2.42	2.09		−74.31	−88.98

(a) QP = 28

		PSNR comparison (dB, Δ(dB))			Bit rate comparison (bps, Δ(%))			Time (ms, Δ(%))		
QP28	Sequence	CCPDT	NMRFS	ZS	CCPDT	NMRFS	ZS	CCPDT	NMRFS	ZS
QCIF	Car Phone	39.477	−0.239	−0.318	184486	4.56	4.95	396278	−74.97	−89.98
	Claire	42.892	−0.046	−0.051	42013	2.21	2.11	180576	−70.74	−82.15
	Foreman	38.582	−0.176	−0.181	191086	3.25	2.61	481881	−77.29	−91.59
	News	41.266	−0.130	−0.235	110965	1.23	1.45	235563	−72.10	−84.41
CIF	Container	40.484	−0.157	−0.188	249227	3.77	3.89	980126	−72.69	−85.44
	Mobile	36.372	−0.110	−0.104	21121106	5.75	5.58	2180782	−73.65	−90.85
	Paris	39.661	−0.075	−0.059	685138	1.77	1.95	1075926	−72.10	−84.88
	Stefan	37.745	−0.018	−0.084	1885027	3.33	−0.82	2189871	−77.36	−91.39
Avg.			−0.119	−0.153		3.23	2.72		−73.86	−87.58

(a) QP = 36

		PSNR comparison (dB, Δ(dB))			Bit rate comparison (bps, Δ(%))			Time (ms, Δ(%))		
QP36	Sequence	CCPDT	NMRFS	ZS	CCPDT	NMRFS	ZS	CCPDT	NMRFS	ZS
QCIF	Car Phone	34.603	−0.602	−0.648	52214	1.74	3.16	275267	−73.95	−87.50
	Claire	38.809	−0.235	−0.217	13589	−0.67	0.24	115653	−65.94	−75.22
	Foreman	33.746	−0.232	−0.253	61059	1.77	1.70	351898	−77.75	−89.99
	News	35.447	−0.130	−0.074	37083	−0.50	0.70	187878	−71.20	−82.74
CIF	Container	36.113	−0.388	−0.404	59842	2.52	2.70	618100	−68.73	−80.12
	Mobile	30.212	−0.282	−0.283	455971	2.83	3.26	1727737	−76.20	−90.79
	Paris	34.338	−0.203	−0.198	193096	1.96	2.79	797588	−71.09	−82.73
	Stefan	31.485	−0.067	−0.252	553346	1.44	−5.13	1840517	−79.56	−91.44
Avg.			−0.267	−0.291		1.39	1.18		−73.05	−85.07

4 Experimental Results

We implement the proposed zonal search (ZS) algorithm into JM encoder (JM12.2) [5] to evaluate the performance and compare with full search algorithm. The simulation conditions are the same as that given in Table 1, and experimental results for QP = 20, 28 and 36 (representing different bit-rates respectively) are shown in Table 4, which summarize the performance in terms of PSNR loss, bit-rate increment and time saving, in which the neighboring reference frame selections with FS (denoted as NMRFS) and ZS (denoted as ZS) are compared with the fully decoding and encoding (denoted as CCPDT).

As shown when compared with CCPDT, average PSNR loss and bit-rate increment for ZS are 0.17 dB and 2.0% while 0.14 dB and 2.35% for FS. The results reveal that the degradation in coding performance is fairly small, but with average 87% of time saving, as compared to CCPDT. As can be seen, the degradation mainly comes from the neighboring reference frame selection scheme, and the degradation caused by ZS is negligible, as compared to FS.

By comparing Table 3a and Table 4a for the case with QP = 20, we also see that the ZS (with 0.056 dB PSNR loss and 2.09% bit-rate increment) achieves better rate distortion performance than $PMV_{AAW} + \mathrm{E} - \mathrm{FDVS}$ (with 0.064 dB SPNR loss and 2.54% bit-rate increment), but with similar computation time saving (88.98% and 89.59% respectively).

5 Conclusion

In this paper we suggest an efficient multiple reference frame motion re-estimation for H.264/AVC frame-skipping transcoding, in which a neighboring reference frame selection scheme around the skipped reference frame is proposed for motion re-estimation, and in addition a zonal search employing motion vector composition method is used instead of full search. The experimental results reveal that average 87% of computation time (corresponding to a speed-up factor of 8) can be saved for the proposed H.264 frame-skipping transcoding algorithm, when compared with fully decoding/encoding procedure. The degradation in the rate-distortion performance is fairly small (with average 0.17 dB PSNR loss and 2.0% bit-rate increment).

Acknowledgement This work was supported in part by the MediaTek Fellowship and in part by the National Science Council, Taiwan, R.O.C. under Grant Number NSC 99–2221-E-008–010

References

1. Wiegand, T., Sullivan, G.J., Bjontegaard, G., Luthra, A.: Overview of the H.264/AVC video coding standard. IEEE Trans. Circuits Syst. Video Technol., 13, 560–576 (2003)
2. Youn, J., Sun, M. T.: Fast motion vector composition method for temporal transcoding. In: Proc. IEEE ISCAS, 4, pp. 243–246 (1999)
3. Yang, S., Kim, D., Jeon, Y., Jeong, J.: An efficient motion re-estimation algorithm for frame-skipping video transcoding. In Proc. IEEE ICIP, 3, pp. 668–671 (2005)
4. Shen, B., Sethi, I. K., Vasudev, B.: Adaptive motion-vector resampling for compressed video downscaling. IEEE Trans. Circuits Syst. Video Technol., 9(6), 929–936 (1999)
5. JM Reference Software version12.2, [Online], http://iphome.hhi.de/suehring/tml/download/

Frame Layer Rate Control Method for Stereoscopic Video Coding Based on a Novel Rate-Distortion Model

Qun Wang, Li Zhuo, Jing Zhang, and Xiaoguang Li

Abstract Rate control plays an important role in video coding and transmission. In this paper, a novel rate-distortion model has first been proposed to characterize the coding characteristics of stereoscopic video coding, where the weighted average of the left and right viewpoint measured with the video quality metric (VQM) is adopted as the stereoscopic video coding distortion metric, instead of Mean Square Error (MSE). Then a frame layer rate control method for stereoscopic video coding has been presented based on the proposed R-D model. Experimental results demonstrate that, the proposed R-D model can accurately characterize the relationship among coding distortion, coding rate and quantization parameter and the proposed rate control method can efficiently control the output bit rate consistent with the target bit rate while the reconstructed video quality is comparable.

Keywords Stereoscopic video • Video quality metric (VQM) • Rate distortion model • Rate control

1 Introduction

Rate control plays an important role in video coding and transmission. On the one hand, it is an essential component for robust video transmission, especially over time-varying and narrowband channel, where the transmission channels usually have fluctuated bandwidth. Hence, with the rate control technique, we can control the output bit rate according to the channel conditions and buffer size etc. On another hand, rate control is also beneficial to improve the video quality. The compression efficiency of the video encoder and the reconstructed video quality can be greatly improved through optimal bit allocation.

Q. Wang (✉) • L. Zhuo • J. Zhang • X. Li
Signal and Information Processing Laboratory, Beijing University of Technology, Beijing, China
e-mail: wangqun@emails.bjut.edu.cn; zhuoli@bjut.edu.cn; zhj@bjut.edu.cn; lxg@bjut.edu.cn

J.S. Jin et al., *The Era of Interactive Media*,
DOI 10.1007/978-1-4614-3501-3_17, © Springer Science+Business Media, LLC 2013

Source model was first presented by Hang H.M. et al. in 1997 [1], which describes the relationships among the output rate (*R*), coding distortion (*D*) and quantization parameter (*QP*). Source models are also called rate-distortion (R-D) models to characterize the coding performance of the video encoder. Rate-distortion model has been widely used in some applications, such as rate control and rate-distortion optimization techniques, where its accuracy posts direct influence on the accuracy of subsequent operations.

However, due to the randomness and complexity of the video signal, it is very hard to obtain a completely accurate rate-distortion model. Therefore, in the most applications, empirical models are usually built with mathematical analysis on the basis of a large amount of experimental data [1]. The first-order linear model has been used in MPEG-2 TM5 rate control algorithm [2], and the quadratic model has been used in MPEG-4 VM8 algorithm [3]. Compared to the former one, the latter can describe the rate-distortion characteristics of the encoder with more precision, but it achieves at the cost of a much higher computational complexity. TMN8, proposed by Jordi Ribas Cobera et al., has been used in H.263 rate control algorithm, and its R-D model is the combination of the logarithmic model and the quadratic model [4]. Compared with the VM8, TMN8 can control the target rate more precisely to maintain the stability of the buffer, thus it is widely used in low-latency conditions. In high bit rate applications, the quadratic model will result in large estimation error when the quantization step is small, while the exponential model can achieve a better performance of characterizing the relationship of R-Q in this case [5]. The various rate-distortion models discussed above mainly adopt Mean Square Error (MSE) as the coding distortion metric, and they describe the coding rate-distortion characteristics of the 2-D videos.

With recent advances in stereoscopic video coding, the research on rate-distortion model based rate control for stereoscopic videos has attracted high interest over the past years. Generally speaking, the rate-distortion models used for the stereoscopic video coding currently are mostly the improvements of traditional quadratic R-D model. For example, Chen [6] proposed a rate control algorithm for H.264-based Multiview Video Coding (MVC) scheme, which used an independent quarter R-D model for each viewpoint video. Therefore, the algorithm is computationally intensive, complicated to implement, and could achieve low control accuracy. Zhu [7] proposed a frame layer rate control algorithm for stereoscopic video coding, which improved the conventional quadratic R-D model to achieve more accurately rate control.

In this paper, based on MVC encoder, a novel rate-distortion model for stereoscopic video coding is first proposed. In this model, the weighted average VQM of the left and right views is used as the stereoscopic video coding distortion metric, where the weights of VQM of the left and right views are set to 0.7 and 0.3 respectively. From a large amount of experimental data, it can be seen that, for the MVC coding framework, after a logarithmic operation on *R*, a cubic polynomial model could describe the correlation curves well, i.e. *logR* and distortion *D*, as well as *logR* and *QP* well for both I frame and P frame. Therefore, a cubic model is proposed in this paper to characterize the rate distortion characteristics of I frame and P frame. Then a rate control algorithm for stereoscopic video coding at frame layer has been presented based on the proposed R-D model. The experimental results indicate that, the R-D model presented in this paper coincides well with the actual stereoscopic video coding rate-distortion curves and the proposed rate control method can efficiently control the output bit rate.

The rest of this paper is organized as follows. The proposed rate-distortion model for stereoscopic video coding is studied in the Sect. 2. The frame layer rate control method based on the proposed R-D model is presented in the Sect. 3. Section 4 concludes the paper.

2 Proposed Rate-Distortion Model for Stereoscopic Video Coding

2.1 Coding Framework of Stereoscopic Video

In this paper, MVC is used as the coding framework of stereoscopic video. MVC was proposed by ITU-T and MPEG Joint Video Team (JVT) to achieve a high multi-view video coding efficiency. The coding architecture of stereoscopic video coding is shown in Fig. 1 [8]. It can be seen that the stereoscopic video encoder usually

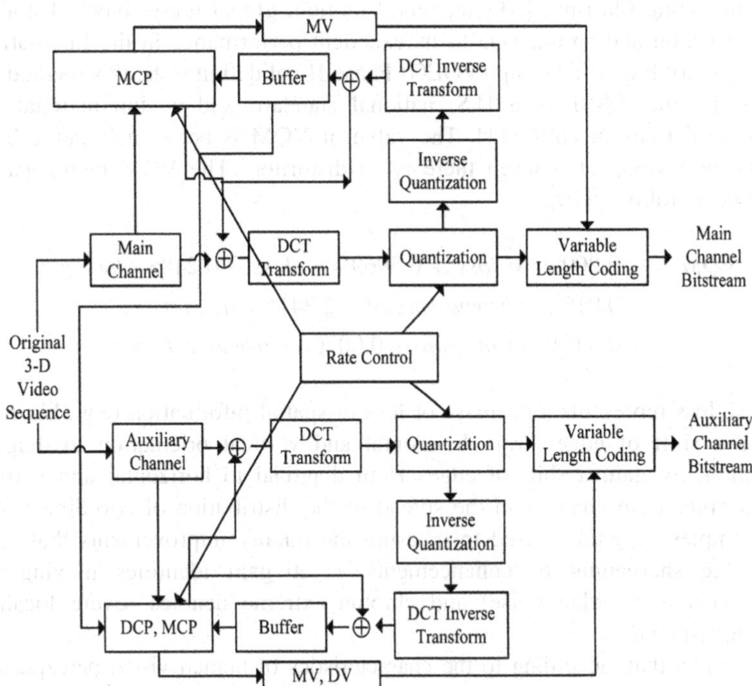

Fig. 1 The coding framework for stereoscopic video coding

adopts the combination of disparity compensated prediction (DCP) and motion compensated prediction (MCP) method to completely remove the redundant information.

2.2 Coding Distortion Measurements of Stereoscopic Video

The coding distortion measurements of the stereoscopic video differ from the traditional 2-D video, as it has two video channels, not only the image distortion is needed to evaluate, but also the depth perception. In [9], the problems of coding distortion measurements of stereoscopic video are investigated to compare the three objective methods commonly used, namely PSNR(Peak Signal to Noise Ratio),VQM (Video Quality Metric) and SSIM (Structural Similarity Index). The comparison results show that VQM can represent both the perceived overall image quality and depth of 3-D video well and has shown a better performance in terms of stereoscopic video coding distortion compared with the traditional PSNR metric.

VQM, which is developed by the Institute of Telecommunication Sciences (ITS) and American National Standard Institute (ANSI), is a standardized objective video quality metric [10]. VQM measures the perceptual effects of video impairments including blurring, jerky/unnatural motion, global noise, block distortion, color distortion and so on. Due to its excellent performance in the International Video Quality Expert's Group (VQEG) Phase II validation tests, this method was adopted by the ANSI as a U.S. national standard and as international ITU Recommendations in 2004 [11]. The value of VQM is between 0 and 100 and gets the best value of 0 when there is no distortion. The VQM metric can be expressed as follows [10]:

$$\begin{aligned} VQM = & -0.2097 * si\_loss + 0.5969 * hv\_loss + 0.2483 * hv\_gain \\ & + 0.0192 * chroma\_spread - 2.3416 * si\_gain \\ & + 0.0431 * ct\_ati\_gain + 0.0076 * chroma\_extreme \end{aligned} \tag{1}$$

where si_loss represents a decrease or loss of spatial information (e.g., blurring); hv_loss a shift of edges from horizontal and vertical orientation to diagonal orientation; hv_gain a shift of edges from diagonal to horizontal and vertical; chroma_spread the changes in the spread of the distribution of two-dimensional color samples. si_gain is used to measure the quality improvements that result from edge sharpening or enhancements, ct_ati_gain identifies moving-edge impairments (e.g., edge noise) and chroma_extreme denotes severe localized color impairments.

It's known that, according to the characteristics of human visual perception, if the right and left views are displayed with different quality and resolutions, the overall 3-D video quality is determined by the view with the better quality and resolution [12].

Table 1 Test sequences and their features

Data set	Sequences	Image property	Camera arrangement
MERL	Ballroom, Exit, Vassar	640 × 480, 25fps (rectified)	Eight cameras with 20 cm spacing; 1D/parallel
KDDI	Race1	640 × 480, 30fps (non-rectified)	Eight cameras with 20 cm spacing; 1D/parallel
KDDI	Flamenco2	640 × 480, 30fps (non-rectified)	Five cameras with 20 cm spacing; 2D/parallel (cross)

Based on this theory, in this paper, we use the weighted average VQM of the left and right views instead of the average VQM as the stereoscopic video coding distortion metric, where the weights are set to 0.7 (left) and 0.3 (right) respectively.

2.3 *The Actual R-D Model for Stereoscopic Video Coding*

MVC coding framework supports two kinds of coding modes, i.e. Intra and Inter mode. The coding structure of I frame and P frame is quite different, thus the coding distortion property also varies. Therefore, we need to set up their own R-D model respectively. For the Intra coding mode, only the adjacent macroblocks of one frame is referenced for prediction, and the coding distortion will not spread to the next frames. While for the Inter coding mode, it usually refers to the previous one or several frames for prediction. Once an error exists, the quantization distortion will be spread from the current frame to the subsequent frames.

In order to analyze the rate distortion characteristics of stereoscopic video encoder, three kinds of 3-D video sequences with different motion characteristics are tested in this paper firstly. One is the sequences with low motion, such as *Vassar,Exit*, another is the sequence with medium motion, such as *Flamenco2, Ballroom*, and the last one high motion, such as *Race1* etc. The test sequences and their features are shown in Table 1.

The Joint Multiview Video Coding (JMVC) reference software version 4.0, which is developed by the Joint Video Team (JVT), is used in this paper to encode each test sequence. For each sequence, 250 frames are chosen for the test, and the frame rate is fixed to 25 frames/s. We take two views from eight views video to test using the weighted average VQM of the left and right views as the coding distortion metric. To measure the R-D characteristics of I frame, the coding structure is set as all I frames. While for P frames, the IPPP...IPPP... coding structures, that is the first frame of each GOP is I frame and the remaining are all P frames, is utilized to measure the R-D characteristics. The GOP size is set as 8 and the QP value as 5, 10, 15...50 respectively for each sequence.

Figure 2 shows the relationship curves of rate vs. distortion, quantization parameter vs. distortion, and rate vs. quantization parameter of I frame for the *Ballroom* sequence, which are simply called *R-D*, *Q-D* and *R-Q* curve respectively.

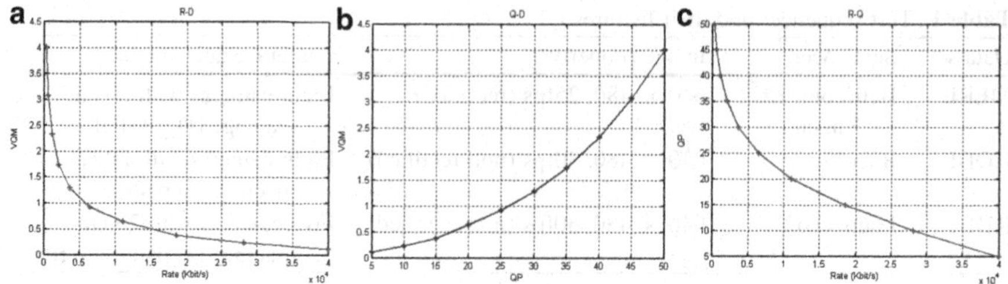

Fig. 2 R-D, Q-D and R-Q curves of Ballroom sequence I frame

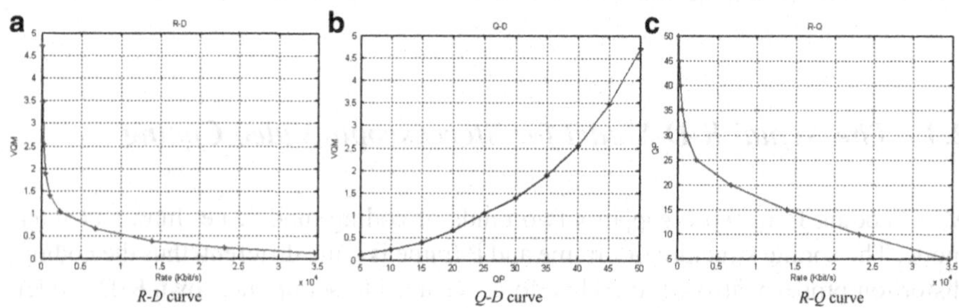

R-D curve *Q-D* curve *R-Q* curve

Fig. 3 R-D, Q-D and R-Q curves of Ballroom sequence P frame

Figure 3 shows the P frame results of *Ballroom* sequence (the other test sequences show a similar trend with *Ballroom*, they are not listed here due to the length limitation of this paper).

From Figs. 2 and 3, it can be seen that a quadratic polynomial model exhibits the best correlation with *Q-D* curve for both I frame and P frame. However, it is difficult to approximate the relationship of *R-D* and *R-Q*.

2.4 The Proposed R-D Model for Stereoscopic Video Coding

We have found through a large number of experiments that if we adopt exponential function directly to fit the R-D and R-Q curves in Figs. 2 and 3, its accuracy is very low and it can lead to the rapid increase of computational complexity. However, if we compute logarithmic operation on *R*, and list the results again in Figs. 4 and 5, we can see clearly that a cubic polynomial model can describe the *logR-D* and *logR-Q* curves well whether for I frame or P frame, which will reduce the computational complexity of the model to a certain extent.

Therefore, considering the trade-offs between the model complexity and accuracy, we characterize the rate distortion characteristics of both I frame and

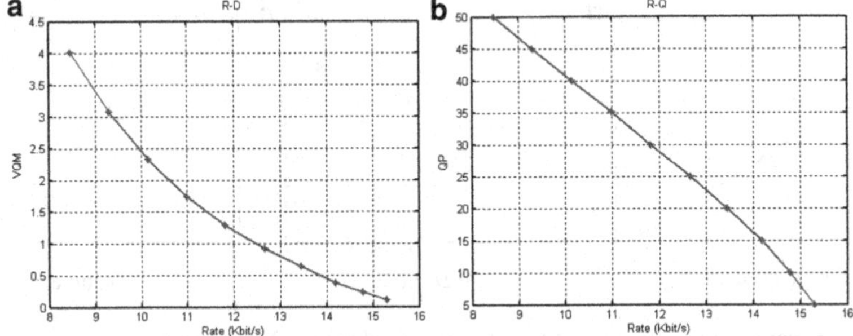

Fig. 4 log(R)-D and log(R)-Q curves of Ballroom sequence I frame

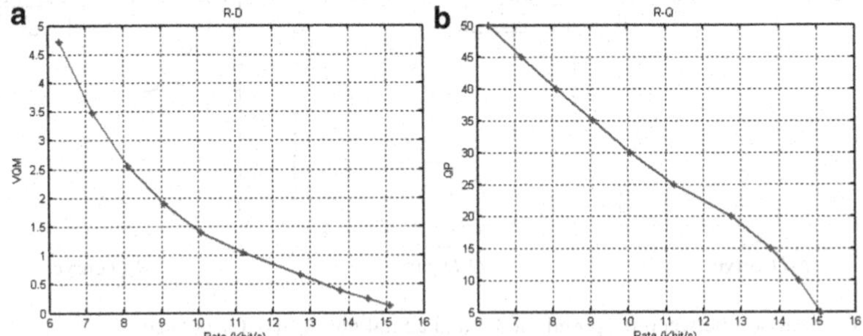

Fig. 5 log(R)-D and log(R)-Q curves of Ballroom sequence P frame

P frame using the same simple cubic model. In this paper, rate-distortion model for stereoscopic video coding has been proposed as follows:

$$\begin{cases} R-D\colon D_p = p_1\log^3(R) + p_2\log^2(R) + p_3\log(R) + p_4 \\ Q-D\colon D_p = p_5QP^3 + p_6QP^2 + p_7QP + p_8 \\ R-Q\colon QP = p_9\log^3(R) + p_{10}\log^2(R) + p_{11}\log(R) + p_{12} \end{cases} \tag{2}$$

where QP is the quantization step, R is the coding rate, D_p is the coding distortion measured using VQM, p_i, $i = 1, 2, \cdots, 12$ are the parameters of the proposed model. The coding performance of the adjacent P frame in one GOP has little difference except when the scene change occurs, hence, we can obtain the model parameters of the current frame utilizing the results of coded frames in the same GOP.

2.5 Experimental Results and Analysis

The accuracy of R-D model is essential for the subsequent rate control and rate distortion optimized applications. Several 3D video sequences are tested

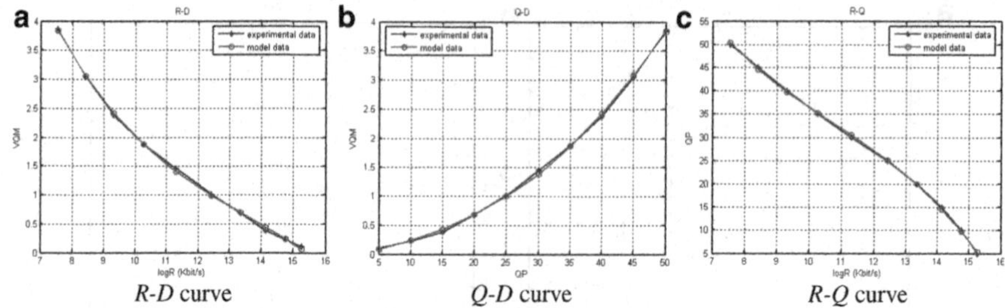

Fig. 6 Comparison between proposed model and actual data of Vassar sequence

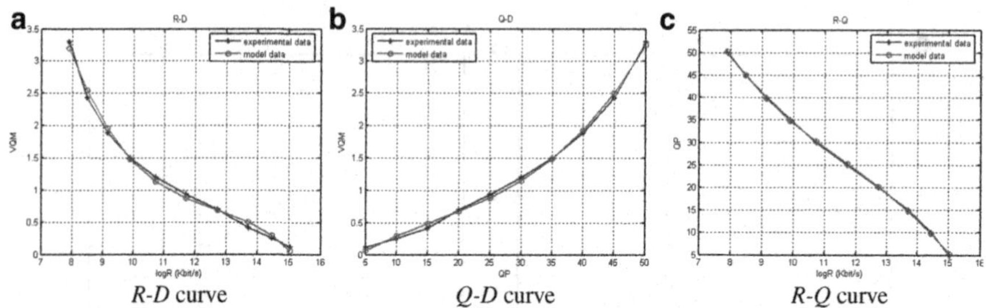

Fig. 7 Comparison between proposed model and actual data of Exit sequence

and compared to validate the accuracy of R-D model presented in this paper. The model of *Vassar* and *Exit* sequence with their actual test data are compared and shown in Fig. 6 and Fig. 7 respectively.

In Figs. 6 and 7, the blue curve represents the results of actual test data, whereas the red curve the model data. From Figs. 6 and 7, it can be seen that the R-D model presented in this paper coincides well with the actual R-D curves, and the model can accurately characterize the relationship among coding distortion, coding rate and quantization parameter. Similar results have been achieved when other sequences were tested.

The computational complexity is another essential factor that should be taken into account for the R-D model. Now we will compare the complexity of the proposed model with the existing R-D model. In [7], Zhu adopted a traditional quadratic R-D model for stereo video coding, where MSE is used as the coding distortion metric. For a picture with M × N size, it will need about 2 × M × N addition operations and M × N multiplication to obtain MSE value. While for the proposed model, VQM is used as the coding distortion metric and VQM value is obtained from a linear combination of the seven parameters as given in Eq. (1). The computational complexity of VQM is high than MSE to a certain extent, however, the accuracy of the proposed model is also greatly improved than the method in [7]. Generally speaking, taken the trade-offs between the model accuracy and computational complexity into account, the proposed model is simple in form and the model accuracy is also greatly improved compared with the state-of-the-art rate-distortion model. The presented R-D model for the stereoscopic video coding in this paper provides a solid foundation for rate control and other operations.

3 Proposed Frame Layer Rate Control Method

The goal of rate control method is to control the output bit rate of the encoder consistent with the target bit rate Under the given target bit rate constraint, the first step is to estimate the quantization parameter (QP) of source encoder according to the proposed model. And then encode the current frame with the estimated QP parameters.

3.1 Experimental Steps

In this paper, a frame layer rate control method is investigated based on the proposed R-D model for the stereoscopic video coding. The basic rate control unit is GOP. For the R-D model based rate control method, the key is to calculate the parameters of the model. Duo to the characteristics of the neighboring frames are very close to each other, the coding statistics of previous coded frames can be utilized to estimate the model parameters of the current frame. Therefore, the method can be implemented with the following steps:

Step 1: Initialization

- Encode the I frame with the preset QP parameters and obtain the output bit number B_I. Set *Encoded_Frame_Num* = 1. Subtract B_I from the target bits B_T and get the remaining bits B_P used for the P frames of GOP.

$$B_P = B_T - B_I \tag{3}$$

where $B_T = \frac{R_{target}}{Frame\_rate} \cdot GOP\_Size$, *GOP_Size* is the GOP size and R_{target} the target bit rate.

- Encode the 1st, 2nd, 3rd and 4th P frames with the preset QP parameters and achieve four sets of data, i.e. (R_1,QP_1), (R_2,QP_2), (R_3,QP_3) and (R_4,QP_4). Set *Encoded_Frame_Num* = 5

Step 2: Determine the QP

- Calculate the target bits B_i of the remaining P frames in the same GOP using the Eq. (4):

$$B_i = \frac{B_p - \sum_{i=1}^{Encoded\_Frame\_Num} R_i}{GOP - Encoded\_Frame\_Num} \tag{4}$$

- Estimate the model parameters of Equation (2) using R_1,QP_1), (R_2,QP_2), (R_3,QP_3) and (R_4,QP_4), then use these model parameters to determine the QP value of the current frame corresponding to the target bits.
- Encode the frame with the achieved QP and obtain the output bit number of the current frame.
- Update *Encoded_Frame_Num* = *Encoded_Frame_Num* +1.

Step 3: Update

- Update the coding data in Equation (2) using the newly output bit number and QP. Use these coding data to estimate the model parameter of the next frame.

Step 4: Loop over frames

- Repeat step 2 and 3 until all the P frames in the current GOP are encoded.

3.2 Experimental Results and Analysis

In order to validate the effectiveness of our proposed rate control method in this paper, we performed experiments over several stereoscopic video test sequences with different motion characteristics. And we compared our proposed method with the fixed QP method of JMVC reference software. In the experiments, we test 250 frames for each sequence, and the frame rate is fixed to 25 frames per second. The coding structure of IPPP. . .IPPP. . .is utilized to encode each GOP. The GOP

Table 2 The difference between the output bit rate and the target bit rate for various video sequences

	Bit rate (kbit/s)		VQM			
Test sequences	Target bit rate	Actual bit rate	JMVC	R-D model	RCE(%)	VQM error
Ballroom	6543.068	6324.1224	0.65964	0.71598	3.346	0.05634
	2123.4784	2112.5580	1.04394	1.06976	0.514	0.02582
	946.044	979.6448	1.39534	1.41635	3.552	0.02101
Exit	4769.2176	4592.6684	0.71671	0.76298	3.702	0.04627
	1145.7196	1175.4584	1.06049	1.08272	2.596	0.02223
	372.3664	365.9608	1.31349	1.33847	1.720	0.02498
Vassar	7177.8368	6873.018	0.69012	0.75355	4.247	0.06343
	1944.4324	1805.6980	1.14576	1.25299	7.135	0.10723
	373.874	381.7824	1.61696	1.65842	2.115	0.04146
Race1	4271.6256	4111.7936	0.56787	0.60208	3.742	0.03421
	2121.6644	2202.5396	0.80411	0.82813	3.812	0.02402
	927.166	949.7148	1.15071	1.16556	2.432	0.01485
Flamenco2	3359.4508	3517.4008	0.56106	0.59032	4.702	0.02926
	1798.9368	1823.2428	0.75477	0.78519	1.351	0.03042
	921.9116	955.1424	1.05668	1.11578	3.604	0.0591

size is set as 15. The rate control error (RCE) is used to measure the accuracy of rate control method:

$$RCE = \frac{|R_{target} - R_{actual}|}{R_{target}} \times 100\% \quad (5)$$

Table 2 illustrates the difference between the target bit rate and the actual output bit rate for various video sequences. From Table 2, it can be seen that the proposed rate control method can efficiently control the output bit rate consistent with the target bit rate while the reconstructed video quality is comparable. The average rate control error is only about 2.99%. The proposed rate control method can be applied in the stereoscopic video coding and transmission applications.

4 Conclusion

In this paper, a novel R-D model for stereoscopic video coding is first proposed using the weighted average VQM of the left and right views as the stereoscopic video distortion metric, where the weights are set to 0.7 and 0.3 respectively. A cubic polynomial model is proposed to describe the correlation curves i.e. $logR$ and distortion D, as well as $logR$ and QP for both I frame and P frame. The experimental results indicate that, the R-D model presented in this paper coincides well with the actual stereoscopic video coding curves. Then a rate control method for stereoscopic video coding at frame layer has been presented based on the proposed R-D model. Experimental results demonstrate that, the proposed rate control method can efficiently control the output bit rate consistent with the target bit rate while the reconstructed video quality is comparable.

Acknowledgements This work is supported by National Natural Science Foundation of China under Grant 61003289, Natural Science Foundation of Beijing under Grant 4102008, Excellent Science Program for the Returned Overseas Scholars of Ministry of Human Resources and Social Security of China.

References

1. H. Hang, J. Chen, "Source model for transform video coder and its application in fundamental theory". IEEE Trans. Circuits Syst. Video Technol., vol.7 (2), pp: 287–298, 1997.
2. ISO/IEC JTC1/SC29/WG11, MPEG-4 test model5[S].1993.
3. ISO/IEC JTC1/SC29/WG11, MPEG-4 Video Verification Model Version 18.0,2001.
4. ITU-T/SG15.Video codec test model, TMN8[S].1997.
5. HE Zhihai, Kim Y K, and Mitra S K, "Low-delay rate control for DCT video coding via ρ domain source modeling[J],"IEEE Transaction on Circuits and Systems for Video Technology, 2001,11(8):928–940.

6. CHEN J L. "Research on Mulit-view Video Coding" [D]. Zhejiang University, Zhejiang, China, 2006.
7. ZHU Z J, LIANG F, et al. "Bit-allocation and rate-control algorithm for stereo video coding". Journal on Communications [J].2007, 28 (7):15–21.
8. ZHU Z J, JIANG G Y, YU M. "Fast disparity estimation algorithm for stereo video coding" [A]. Proceedings of 2002 I.E. Region 10 Conference on Computers, Communications, Control and Power Engineering[C]. Beijing, China, 2002. 285–288.
9. Chaminda T.E.R.Hewage, et al, "Quality Evaluation of Color Plus Depth Map-Based Stereoscopic Video," IEEE Journal of Selected Topics in Signal Processing, VOL,3,NO.2, APRIL 2009:304–318.
10. M. Pinson, S. Wolf, "A new standardized method for objectively measuring video quality," IEEE Transactions on Broadcasting, v. 50, n. 3, pp. 312–322, Sept. 2004.
11. Video Quality Experts Group (VQEG), "Final report from the Video Quality Experts Group on the validation of objective models of video quality assessment, phase II," 2003 VQEG. Available at: www.vqeg.org.
12. S L. B. Stelmach, W. J. Tam, D. Meegan, and A. Vincent. "Stereo image quality: Effects of mixed spatio-temporal resolution," IEEE Trans. Circuits yst. Video Technol., vol. 10, no. 2, pp. 188–193, Mar. 2000.

Hardware Friendly Oriented Design for Alternative Transform in HEVC

Lin Sun, Oscar C. Au, Xing Wen, Jiali Li, and Wei Dai

Abstract Hardware implementation for video coding is gathering more and more focus these days. For intra prediction, the new emerging secondary directional transform is applied after DCT/ICT in the video coding to exploit the potential energy compaction. In this paper, we propose a hardware friendly orientated design flow based on simple difference function which can achieve similar performance as original transform but substitute all low efficient multiplication operations by regular shifting and addition. Especially for the current secondary transform which is rotational transform (ROT), we obtain the hardware friendly ROT (HF_ROT) through our method. Based on the analysis, the proposed method can achieve massive operation reduction if properly design and regular data flow and simple control signal. Simulation results of hardware friendly ROT show that our proposed method can achieve similar performance as the original transform and importantly it is hardware friendly, largely lifting the hardware implemented efficiency. What is more, our proposed method can be applied to other matrix related coding methods.

1 Introduction

Nowadays, video coding becomes more and more important concerning our daily life. One latest step for the video coding standard is H.264/AVC [1, 2] developed by ITU-T and ISO/IEC/MPEG. H.264 provides much better coding efficiency than previous video coding standards such as MPEG1/2/4 [3, 4] and H.261/263 [5, 6] by introducing a number of new tools, including intra prediction based on spatial neighbors and variable block size motion partition in inter prediction. Recently,

L. Sun (✉) • O.C. Au • X. Wen • J. Li • W. Dai
Department of Electronic and Computer Engineering, Hong Kong University of Science and Technology, Clear Water Bay, Kowloon, Hong Kong
e-mail: lsunece@ust.hk; eeau@ust.hk; wxxab@ust.hk; jiali@ust.hk; weidai@ust.hk

J.S. Jin et al., *The Era of Interactive Media*,
DOI 10.1007/978-1-4614-3501-3_18,

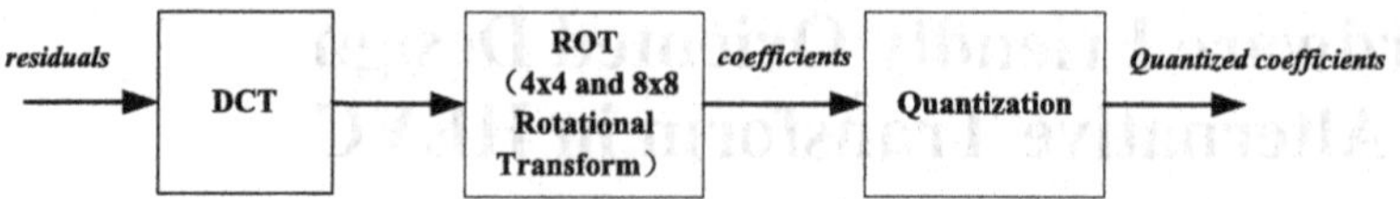

Fig. 1 Forward ROT procedure

ITU-T and ISO/IEC/MPEG have formed a joint collaborative team on video coding (JCT-VC) on next generation video coding standard called High Efficiency Video Coding (HEVC) [7]. For efficient and flexible representation of video content with various resolutions, the new representation introduced in HEVC is based on a concept of coding unit (CU), prediction unit (PU), and transform unit (TU). CU is the basic unit of compression and broadly similar to the concept of macroblock (MB), but much more flexible. PU is the unit of inter/intra prediction and there can be multiple PUs in a single CU. TU is designed for transform and quantization.

Technically, for intra coding, H.264 exploits the spatially adjacent blocks to be predictor in order to reduce the spacial redundancy. After prediction, the residual block is formed by subtracting the prediction block from the current block. In state-of-the-art video coding standard, integer discrete cosine transform (ICT) is applied after obtained residues to exploit the potential residual energy compaction. In H.264/AVC High Profile (HP), a 2-D 8×8 ICT is used adaptively as an alternative to the 2-D 4×4 ICT in H.264/AVC. The 2-D 16×16 ICT for the large macroblock (MB) is presented in [8, 9]. ICT has two advantages for the video coding. Firstly, the algorithm can be accelerated by using the butterfly architecture. Secondly, ICT is generated from the DCT by replacing the real numbered elements of the DCT matrix with integers, so multiplication can be substituted by simple shifting and addition which is beneficial for hardware implementation. However, these methods concentrate on the discrete cosine transform which can not be applied to other transforms.

In order to exploit the potential energy compaction, the secondary transform was proposed to apply after DCT/ICT. Mode dependent directional transform (MDDT) [10] and Rotational Transform (ROT) [7] are the current popular secondary transform implemented in Test Mode under Consideration (TMuC) [11]. MDDT consists of a series of pre-defined separable transforms; each transform is efficient in compacting energy along one of the prediction directions, thus favoring one of the intra modes. ROT is another transform after DCT/ICT which changes the coordinate system of the transform basis and achieves the directional energy compaction. The whole process procedure with ROT is showed in Fig. 1.

In this paper we propose reconfigurable hardware friendly method for the transform based on minimized difference function which can largely reduce the number of operations, balance the performance and the data throughput and finally make the data flow regular. The simple constraint which we propose in this paper will be also helpful for other matrix related hardware orientated designs. Furthermore, the proposed hardware orientated method could achieve the similar rate distortion (RD) performance compared with the original method.

The rest of this paper is organized as follows: Sect. 2 gives the introduction about the new emerging secondary transform and analyzes the drawbacks for hardware implementation. Section 3 proposes our hardware-friendly orientated design scheme and analyzes the difference induced by approximated transform matrix and the original one. Simulation results based on our proposed method according to the test conditions are shown in Sect. 4. Section 5 gives the simple hardware architecture based on the previous design. And Sect. 6 concludes this work.

2 Review of Rotational Transform

2.1 Rotational Transform

Recently, some schemes have been proposed to improve intra coding by applying the secondary transform after ICT/DCT to further exploit the residual energy compaction and can achieve good performance, such as MDDT [10]. Rotational transform [7] is also a secondary transform proposed by Sumsang.

The main idea of ROT is to rotate the coordinate system of the transform basis, instead of direct rotation of the input source. For this purpose, the following matrices are defined as:

$$R_h = R_z(\alpha_1)R_x(\alpha_2)R_z(\alpha_3) \tag{1}$$

$$R_v = R_z(\alpha_4)R_x(\alpha_5)R_z(\alpha_6) \tag{2}$$

where R_x and R_z is compound Given's rotation matrices. R_h and R_v represent the rotation matrices for horizontal and vertical directions with the rotation angles of α_1, α_2, α_3 and α_4, α_5, α_6, respectively. Thus the vertical and horizontal rotational transform matrix R_v can be expressed as $R_v(\alpha_1, \alpha_2, \alpha_3)$ and R_h expressed as $R_h(\alpha_4, \alpha_5, \alpha_6)$.

Then the whole transform process with rotational transform is:

$$m_o = R_v^T D^T m_i D R_h \tag{3}$$

where m_i is input residual matrix, m_o is transformed matrix, D is DCT/ICT matrix, R_h is horizontal ROT matrix, R_v is vertical ROT matrix.

For the TUs of sizes larger than 4 × 4, only 8 × 8 low-frequency blocks are rotated by multiplying ROT matrix. In the implementation, the elements of rotational matrices were scaled by 2^n and rounded to nearest integer. TMuC contains four horizontal and four vertical ROT matrices $R_h{}^i$ and $R_v{}^i$ corresponding to four sets of rotation angles $\alpha_1{}^i$, $\alpha_2{}^i$, $\alpha_3{}^i$, $\alpha_4{}^i$, $\alpha_5{}^i$, $\alpha_6{}^i$, for i = 1,··· ,4. There is no need to store angles α, ··· , α_6, we only use the final scaled integer matrix. For example, one horizontal 4 × 4 ROT matrix is:

$$R_h^1 = \begin{bmatrix} 3736 & -1603 & 48 & 0 \\ 1597 & 3756 & -397 & 0 \\ 112 & 387 & 4073 & 0 \\ 0 & 0 & 0 & 4096 \end{bmatrix} \tag{4}$$

The binarization representation R_{bh}^1 without sign showed in (5):

$$R_{bh}^1 = \begin{bmatrix} 111111000000 & 101100101 & 1010100000 & 0 \\ 1001001011 & 111011001111 & 10110011001 & 0 \\ 111101110 & 10111100101 & 111011000001 & 0 \\ 0 & 0 & 0 & 1000000000000 \end{bmatrix} \tag{5}$$

2.2 Hardware Orientated Analysis

The matrix multiplication process is consisted of two steps. First, each coefficient in the input matrix is multiplied with the transform coefficient at corresponding position and get the temporal result. For example, 4 × 7 is $(100)_b \times (111)_b$ in binary, the temporal result is $(100)_b$, $(1000)_b$ and $(10000)_b$. And then the temporal results is added together to form the final coefficient in output matrix. The multiplication process can be treated as a series of addition and shifting operations, and the operation number is decided by the number of "1" of the multiplicand (coefficient in the transform matrix). The whole system delay is determined by the critical path, that is the operation which need maximum clock cycles. Table 2 shows the number of "1" of the $R_h^1(i, j)$, and the number of corresponding addition and shifting operations. For simplicity, we here assume that shifting and addition both take only one clock cycle. It is easy to observe that it need different clock cycles to computer different temporal results, for example, for the first row of R_h^1, $R_h^1(1, 1)$ need 15 clock cycles and $R_h^1(2, 1)$ need 12 clock cycles but $R_h^1(3, 1)$ only need 4 clock cycles. And if we compute one result in parallel, for example:

$$tem_o(1,1) = P(1,1) * R_h^1(1,1) + P(1,2) * R_h^1(2,1) + P(1,3) * R_h^1(3,1) \tag{6}$$

where $tem_o(1, 1)$ is one of the temporal results at corresponding position (1,1), P is results after DCT/ICT transform. It needs total 15 clock cycles to receive the temporal results. In particularly, $R_h^1(2, 1)$ and $R_h^1(3, 1)$ are waiting while $R_h^1(1, 1)$ is computing. This would significantly decrease the data throughput and increase the power consumption. On the other hand, if we compute the temporal results in a serial mode with re-using identical architecture, the required clock cycles for different transform coefficients are different, this would result in irregular data flow, complex control signal, and low efficient pipeline design (Table 1).

Table 1 $R_h{}^1$ coefficient operations

Matrix	Original binary	Shift num	Adder num	Clock cycles
R(1,1)	111010110011	8	7	15
R(1,2)	11001000011	5	4	9
R(1,3)	110000	2	1	3
R(2,1)	11000111101	7	6	13
R(2,2)	111010101100	7	6	13
R(2,3)	110001101	5	4	9
R(3,1)	1110000	3	2	5
R(3,2)	110000011	4	3	7
R(3,2)	111111101001	9	8	17

3 Proposed Hardware Orientated Design Scheme

Binary is the way of computer, shifting, addition or multiplication. Multiplication is the basic operation for the transform except DCT and ICTs which have suitable structures thus butterfly architecture can be applied to accelerate the algorithm. In hardware architecture, we do not favor multiplier because it will take significant hardware resources and lower data throughput. However, if we just simply binarize the matrix, the hardware implementation is low efficiency as discussed before. In this paper we proposed a hardware-friendly approximation method based on minimized difference function, which makes transform matrix can be easily and regularly implemented by hardware with similar performance compared with original one (Fig. 2).

3.1 Reconfigurable k-Bit Hardware Friendly Approximation

In this section, we propose a hardware-friendly method in which all multiplication operations will be substituted by regular binarization shifting and addition, largely shorten the critical path. In [12], we proposed a mapping method to use shifting operation to replace multiplication, with this method, we can use $A^{'}(i,j)$ to approximate the original coefficient $A(i,j)$:

$$A^{'}(i,j) = 2^n; n = floor\lfloor\frac{\ln A(i,j)}{\ln 2}\rfloor \tag{7}$$

However, based on our simulation results, simply mapping method as in [12] would result in quality drop both in subjective and objective aspects. It is because the difference between approximated coefficients $A^{'}(i,j)$ and the original values $A(i,j)$ are relatively huge. So in this paper, a modified approximation is derived to make

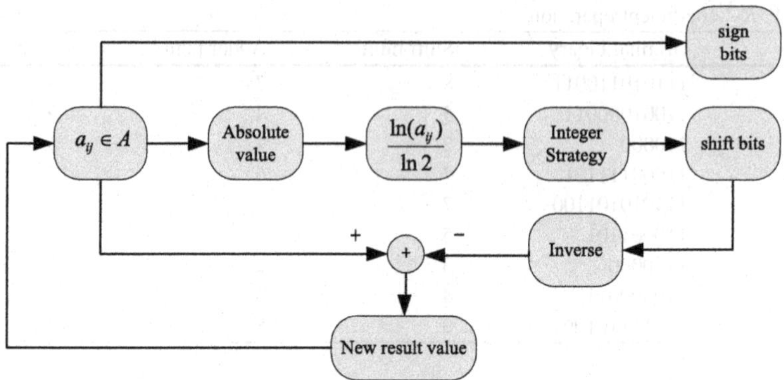

Fig. 2 Proposed minimized difference function with k level pipeline for transform. A is the original matrix and a_{ij} is one matrix coefficient at corresponding position (i, j)

the approximated and the original number as similar as possible. The modified coefficients $A(i, j)'_k$ can be expressed as follows:

$$\begin{aligned}
A(i,j)'_k &= s_1 2^{n_1} + s_2 2^{n_2} \cdots + s_k 2^{n_k};\\
n_1 &= floor\lfloor \frac{\ln\ A(i,j)}{\ln 2} \rfloor,\\
n_2 &= floor\lfloor \frac{\ln\ (A(i,j) - 2^{n_1})}{\ln 2} \rfloor, \cdots\\
n_k &= floor\lfloor \frac{\ln\ (A(i,j) - 2^{n_1} - 2^{n_2} \cdots - 2^{n_{k-1}})}{\ln 2} \rfloor
\end{aligned} \tag{8}$$

where s_k is the sign bit which can be negative or positive and k indicates the number of pipeline level. Here k can be any integer which balances the tradeoff between the RD performance and the data throughput. The whole processing diagram is shown in Fig. 2.

The modified method have some significant advantages. Firstly, all the temporal results require the same clock cycles, which lead to the regular data flow. Secondly, if properly designed the proposed method can largely reduce the number of operations.

After processing, the original non-regular binary shifting matrix become the regular k pipeline level for all the matrix coefficients.

3.2 Approximation Constraints

In this section, we will give a simple constraint for the modified method in order to make the approximated matrix and the original matrix as similar as possible. Let A be the original matrix and the approximated hardware friendly matrix be A', therefore the difference function f_D after hardware orientated approximation is:

$$f_D = \sum_{i=0}^{N-1} \sum_{j=0}^{N-1} |A(i,j) - A_k^{'}(i,j)| \tag{9}$$

Obviously, the difference function f_D is smaller as the k become larger. However, we should not set k a large number for it will decrease the data throughput. In order to balance the performance and the data throughput, we should properly set k. Actually, when the f_D <threshold, it should be regarded that the approximated matrix can largely represent the original one, where the threshold should be different for different matrix. Then we will get the value of k.

4 Software Experimental Results

The simulation results of our proposed method is showed in this section. We also apply our proposed method with k = 4 to the matrix $R_h^{\ 1}$ we illustrate before. After approximation, the original matrix become:

$$R_h^1 = \begin{bmatrix} 3744 & -1604 & 48 & 0 \\ 1596 & 3760 & -396 & 0 \\ 112 & 387 & 4073 & 0 \\ 0 & 0 & 0 & 4096 \end{bmatrix} \tag{10}$$

Now the difference between the approximated matrix with k = 4 and the original one is 15. The new generated one is nearly the same as the original one. Currently, the $R_h^{\ 1}(3,\ 3)$ = $(111111101001)_b$ can be represented by $(1000000000000)_b$ – $(0000000100000)_b$ + $(0000000001000)_b$ + $(0000000000001)_b$. Now the shift number is 4 and the number of adders is 3 which is also the same for other coefficients, while the original number need 9 shiftings and 8 adders. Actually, if the approximated matrix is obtained by our proposed method with k = n, the shifting number for every coefficient is the same n and the number of addition is (n–1) which is regular for the whole processing. Furthermore if we apply the proposed method with k = 5 again, the approximated matrix is just the same as the original.

Now the clock cycles for each coefficient is the same, that is 9 based on our proposed method whit k = 5. Also we compute the numbers of corresponding addition and shifting operations for one pass transform.

From the Table 2, we can see that the proposed method restricts the clock cycles for different coefficients of one pass transform to 9. That means the clock cycles for one corresponding results is the same, it will largely lift the utilization of hardware resources, reduce the complicated control signal and make the data flow regular.

In the implementation, we choose k = 5 for the encoder side and k = 3 for the decoder side balanced the performance and the data throughput based on the constrain to generate the hardware friendly matrix using (8). The text condition

Table 2 Proposed R_h^{1} coefficient operations

Matrix	Original binary	Shift num	Adder num	Clock cycles
R(1,1)	111010110011	5	4	9
R(1,2)	11001000011	5	4	9
R(1,3)	110000	5	4	9
R(2,1)	11000111101	5	4	9
R(2,2)	111010101100	5	4	9
R(2,3)	110001101	5	4	9
R(3,1)	1110000	5	4	9
R(3,2)	110000011	5	4	9
R(3,2)	111111101001	5	4	9

Table 3 Some sequences' simulation results HF_ROT vs. ROT for different test conditions

Sequence	Condition	BD-rate Y	BD-rate U	BD-rate V
BQTerrace 1080p	Intra HE	0.2	0.1	– 0.1
	Intra Loco	0.3	0.3	0.3
	HE	0.1	– 0.6	– 0.6
	Random Loco	0.2	– 0.2	0.3
Vidyo1 720p	Intra HE	0.2	0.1	– 0.1
	Intra Loco	0.3	0.1	0.1
	Random HE	N/A	N/A	N/A
	Random Loco	N/A	N/A	N/A
PeopleOnStreet 2,560 × 1,600	Intra HE	0.3	0.0	0.0
	Intra Loco	0.4	0.2	0.2
	Random HE	0.1	0.0	– 0.1
	Random Loco	0.1	0.0	0.1

satisfies [13] and all the work is based on Tmuc 0.9 [14]. Here we use BDrate [15] to evaluate the results. Here we only test some large sequences using our proposed method, from the Table 3 we could see that the performance of HF_ROT and the original ROT is nearly the same, however, the proposed method achieves the regular data flow and large reduction of complex control signal. From the RD curve of BQTerrace of Intra HE in Fig. 3 we also could see clearly that the two RD curves are almost overlapped with each other and both outstands than the simple hardware friendly ROT (SHF_ROT) proposed in [12].

5 Simple Proposed Hardware Architecture

In this section, we will give a simple hardware architecture according to the proposed design method.

Figure 4(a) shows the block diagram of a single processing element (Single PE). It contains a data register (DR) to store the original value, an multi-shift element (MSE) designed to achieve variable length shifting operation, a sign determination

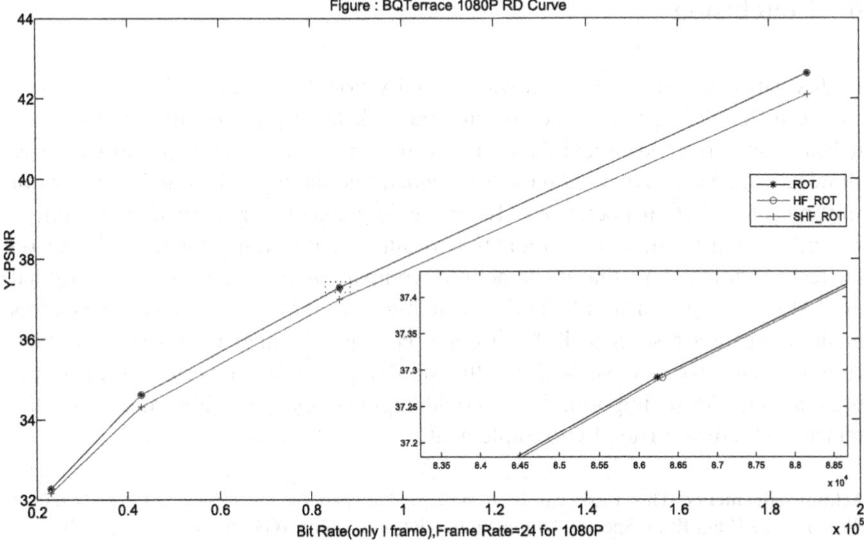

Fig. 3 BQTerrace intra HE: RD curve example of proposed HF_ROT vs. original ROT

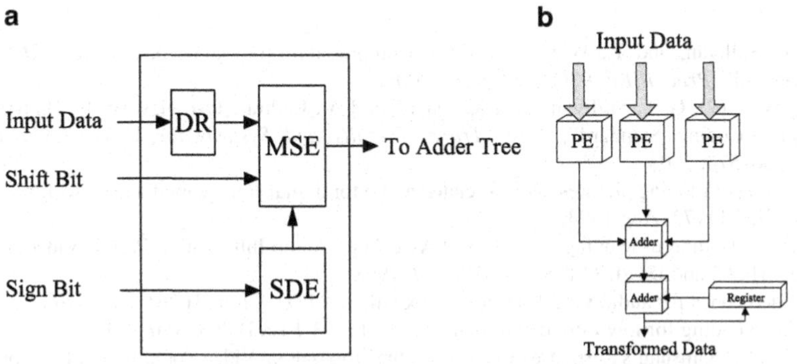

Fig. 4 Simple hardware architecture. (**a**) single PE architecture (**b**) single line or column processing hardware architecture

element (SDE) to determine the sign bit for the shifting. Figure 4(b) shows the block diagram of processing one line or column hardware architecture, since for ROT we only need calculate the first three elements of the line or column, we need three PEs for one line or column. The same operation clock cycle make the hardware implementation high efficiency thanks to the regular design.

6 Conclusion

In this paper, we propose a hardware-friendly orientated design flow based on a simple difference function and reconfigurable k level pipeline approximation to balance the performance and data through put. We also use one special matrix to show its efficiency in making data flow regular and largely reducing the number of shifting and addition operations. Later we implement our method onto current secondary transform, ROT. Simulation results for different sequences based on the test condition show that it can achieve comparable performance as the original one. At last, we give a simple hardware architecture for this design. Of course, this method does not restrict to ROT, it could be apply to other matrix related video coding, which we believe will get the similar if not better performance as the original one. More importantly, it could regulate the data flow and make the transform hardware friendly to implement.

Acknowledgements This work has been supported in part by the Research Grants Council (RGC) of the Hong Kong Special Administrative Region, China. (GRF Project no. 610210).

References

1. G.J., Sullivan, and T., Wiegand, "Video Compression-From Concepts to the H.264/AVC Standard", *Proc. IEEE*, 93(1), pp.18–31, 2005.
2. T., Wiegand, G. J., Sullivan, G., Bjϕtegaard, and A., Luthra, "Overview of the H.264/AVC Video Coding Standard", *IEEE Trans. Circuits and Systems for Video Tech*, 13(7), pp.560–576, 2003.
3. "Coding of moving pictures and associated audio for digital storage media at up to 1.5 Mhr/s." ISO/IEC 11172, Aug 1993.
4. Generic Coding of Moving Pictures and Associated Audio Information Part 2: Video, ITU-T Rec. H.262 and ISO/IEC 13818-2 MPEG-2, 1998
5. "Video codes for audio visual services at px 64kb/s," ITU-T Rec. H.261, Mar 1993.
6. "Video coding for low bitrate communication." ITU-T Rec. H.263, Mar 1996.
7. JCT-VC, "Samsung's Response to the Call for the Proposals on Video Compression Technology", JCTVC-A124, Joint Collaborative Team on Video Coding Meeting, April 2010, Dresden, Germany.
8. S. Ma and C.-C. Kuo, "High-definition video coding with supermacroblocks", *Proc. SPIE Vis. Commun. Image Process*, vol.6508, pp. 650816-1-650816-12, Jan 2007.
9. J. Dong, K. N. Ngan, C. K. Fong and W. K. Cham, "2-d order-16 integer transforms for HD video coding", *IEEE Trans. Circuits Syst. Video Technol.*, 19(10), pp.1462–1474, Oct 2009.
10. Y. Ye and M. Karczewicz, "Improved H.264 intra coding based on bi-directional intra prediction, directional transform, and adaptive coefficient scanning", *IEEE International Conf. Image Process*, San Diego, U.S.A., Oct 2008.
11. JCT-VC,"Test Model under Consideration", JCTVC-B205, Joint Collaborative Team on Video Coding meeting, Geneva, Switzerland, July 2010.
12. X. Wen, O. C. Au, et. al., "Novel RD-optimized VBSME with Matching Highly Data Re-usable Hardware Architecture", *Accepted by Transactions on Circults and Systems for Video Technology*, Sept. 2010.

13. F. Bossen, "Common test conditions and software reference configurations", JCTVC-B300, July, 2010, Geneva, Switzerland.
14. JCT-VC, TMuC-0.9 Reference Software, (https://hevc.hhi.fraunhofer.de/svn/svn_TMuCSoftware/tags/0.9/) and (http://hevc.kw.bbc.co.uk/git/w/jctvc-tmuc.git).
15. G. Bjϕtegaard, "Calculation of average PSNR differences between RD-Curves", ITU-T SG16 Q.6 Document, VCEG-M33, Austin, April 2001.

A New Just-Noticeable-Distortion Model Combined with the Depth Information and Its Application in Multi-view Video Coding

Fengzong Lian, Shaohui Liu, Xiaopeng Fan, Debin Zhao, and Wen Gao

Abstract Traditional video compression methods remove spatial and temporal redundancy based on the statistical correlation. However the final receptor is the human, we can remove the perception redundancy to get higher compression efficiency, by taking use of the properties of human visual system (HVS). Research has simulated the sensitivity of HVS to luminance contrast and spatial and temporal masking effects with the just-noticeable-distortion (JND) model, which describes the perception redundancy quantitatively. This paper proposes a new model named MJND (JND in Multi-view), which explores the property of HVS to stereoscopic masking effect. The proposed model not only contains the spatial and temporal JND, but also includes the JND in depth. The MJND model is then used in macroblock (MB) quantization adjustment and rate-distortion optimization in multi-view video coding (MVC). Compared with the standard MVC scheme without JND, our model can get better visual quality in the case of the same bit rate.

Keywords MJND • Stereoscopic masking effect • MVC

F. Lian (✉) • S. Liu • X. Fan • D. Zhao
School of Computer Science and Technology, Harbin Institute of Technology, Harbin 150001, Heilongjiang, China
e-mail: cleartear@foxmail.com; shliu@hit.edu.cn; fxp@hit.edu.cn; dbzhao@hit.edu.cn

W. Gao
Institute of Digital Media, Peking University, Beijing 100871, China
e-mail: wgao@pku.edu.cn

J.S. Jin et al., *The Era of Interactive Media*,
DOI 10.1007/978-1-4614-3501-3_19,

1 Introduction

Traditional video compression methods mainly remove the spatial and temporal statistical redundancy. A number of image and video coding methods aiming to account for psychovisual properties of the HVS in the quantization and rate allocation problems have been proposed [1–3]. Tang et al. [4] proposed a visual distortion sensitivity model based on the non-uniform spatio-temporal sensitivity property of the HVS. The macroblock (MB) visual distortion sensitivity was achieved by analysis of the motion and textural structure. The MB which can allow more distortion will be allocated less bits, so that the rate of whole video can be reduced accordingly. Extending the method of [4,5] acquired a better model by considering the motion attention, spatial-velocity visual sensitivity and visual masking.

Recently, researchers have proposed a few JND (just-noticeable-distortion) models to describe the sensitivity threshold of HVS quantitatively. Chou and Li [6], Chou and Chen [7], Yang et al. [8], Zhang et al. [9] have studied and applied the JND in image and video compression and transmission. However these JND models are based on the premise that the visual acuity is consistent over the whole image. However, because of the non-uniform density of the sensor cells on the retina, the visual acuity decreases with increased distance or eccentricity from the fixation point. According to this truth, Chen and Guillemot [10] proposed FJND (foveated JND) based on the spatio-temporal JND (STJND). They computed the foveation of the image which contained some fixation points, and made the foveation as the scale factor of the STJND. It should be noted that all of these JND models are studied and applied in images and videos without considering the depth information. However, an existing work [11] has indicate that human also has the perception redundancy to the change of the depth information. Moreover, now the research about the depth map is a very hot topic. To the best of our knowledge, none of existing JND models considers to combine the depth redundancy and spatial and temporal redundancy. Hence, a new JND model should be studied and applied in the stereo scene, such as MVC. The new JND model can make algorithms utilize the depth information more effectively.

This paper proposed a JND model named MJND (JND in Multi-view), which can be used in the stereo, multi-view video coding and other related areas. The model mainly accounts for the perception redundancy of HVS to the depth masking effect. Human can't apperceive the distortion of the depth below a threshold which is called DJND (Depth JND) [11]. Here, the DJND is used as the scale factor for improving the STJND. The proposed MJND model is then applied in the MVC. For each MB, we can get the MB distortion threshold from the MJND and use the threshold to adjust the MB quantization parameters adaptively. The MB which can tolerate more distortion will be allocated a bigger QP, and the saved bits from the previous MB can be allocated to the MB with high sensitivity. Also, the Lagrange multiplier in the rate-distortion optimization is adapted with the MJND so that the MB noticeable distortion is minimized.

The reminder of this paper is organized as follows. The next section presents the MJND model. The use of the MJND model in MVC is presented in Sect. 3. Experimental results and the conclusion are given in Sects. 4 and 5 respectively.

2 MJND Model

As the description in the previous section, this paper proposes a JND model applied in the stereoscopic and MVC scene. The model not only considers the spatial and the temporal visual effect, but also includes the sensitivity of HVS to the change of stereoscopic depth. Therefore, we define the MJND model as a combination of the spatial JND (SJND), temporal JND (TJND), and JND in depth (DJND).

$$MJND(x,y,t) = f(SJND(x,y), TJND(x,y,t), DJND(x,y)) \tag{1}$$

Where $MJND(x,y,t)$ $SJND(x,y)$ $TJND(x,y,t)$ and $DJND(x,y)$ denote MJND, SJND, TJND and DJND, respectively. t is the frame index, (x,y) denote the position of the pixel in an image.

Before introducing the DJND and MJND models, let us review the spatial and temporal JND described in [6] and [7], respectively.

2.1 *Spatial JND Model*

The perceptual redundancy in the spatial domain is mainly due to the luminance contrast and spatial masking effect. Up to now, many JND model have been exploited. In [6,8,10], the models are based on the spatial pixel domain, but [2,3,12,13] based on the DCT and wavelet domain. Chou and Li [6] defined a function to simulate the relation of JND and the luminance contrast and spatial masking effect.

$$SJND(x,y) = \max\{f_1(bg(x,y), mg(x,y)), f_2(bg(x,y))\} \tag{2}$$

where $f_1(bg(x,y), mg(x,y))$ and $f_2(bg(x,y))$ estimate the luminance contrast and spatial masking effect, respectively.

$f_1(bg(x,y), mg(x,y))$ is defined as follow:

$$f_1(bg(x,y), mg(x,y)) = mg(x,y) \times \alpha(bg(x,y)) + \beta(bg(x,y)) \tag{3}$$

Where $mg(x,y)$ is the maximum weighted average of luminance differences derived by calculating the weighted average of luminance changes around the pixel (x, y) in four directions as

$$mg(x,y) = \max_{k=1,2,3,4}\{|grad_k(x,y)|\} \tag{4}$$

0	0	0	0	0
1	3	8	3	1
0	0	0	0	0
-1	-3	-8	-3	-1
0	0	0	0	0

0	0	1	0	0
0	8	3	0	0
1	3	0	-3	-1
0	0	-3	-8	0
0	0	-1	0	0

0	1	0	-1	0
0	3	0	-3	0
0	8	0	-8	0
0	3	0	-3	0
0	1	0	-1	0

0	0	1	0	0
0	0	3	8	0
-1	-3	0	3	1
0	-8	-3	0	0
0	0	-1	0	0

Fig. 1 Matrix G_k. **(a)** G_1. **(b)** G_2. **(c)** G_3. **(d)** G_4

1	1	1	1	1
1	2	2	2	1
1	2	0	2	1
1	2	2	2	1
1	1	1	1	1

Fig. 2 Matrix B

where

$$grad_k(x,y) = \frac{1}{16}\sum_{i=1}^{5}\sum_{j=1}^{5} p(x-3+i, y-3+j) \times G_k(i,j) \quad (5)$$

$G_k(i,j)$ is a direction filter, defined in Fig. 1.

Both $\alpha(bg(x,y))$ and $\beta(bg(x,y))$in Eq. (3) are related with background luminance, forming the following linear relation.

$$\alpha(bg(x,y)) = bg(x,y) \times 0.0001 + 0.115 \quad (6)$$

$$\beta(bg(x,y)) = \mu - bg(x,y) \times 0.01 \quad (7)$$

where $bg(x,y)$denotes the average luminance of the background, calculated by a weighted low-pass filter B (see Fig. 2).

$$bg(x,y) = \frac{1}{32}\sum_{i=1}^{5}\sum_{j=1}^{5} p(x-3+i, y-3+j) \times B(i,j) \quad (8)$$

$f_2(bg(x,y))$ denotes the spatial masking effect, defined as follow:

$$f_2(bg(x,y)) = \begin{cases} T_0 \times \left(1 - \sqrt{\frac{bg(x,y)}{127}}\right) + \varepsilon, & bg(x,y) \leq 127 \\ \gamma \times (bg(x,y) - 127) + \varepsilon, & bg(x,y) > 127. \end{cases} \quad (9)$$

T_0 denotes the visual threshold when the background luminance level is 0. ε is the minimum threshold. This function describes that visual threshold and background luminance are root relation when the background luminance is low, whereas are linear relation. This paper directly uses the values of [10] as the parameters of above functions. T_0, γ, μ and εhave been set to 14, 3/128, 1/4 and 2, respectively.

2.2 Temporal JND Model

Generally, the more the luminance difference of the inter-frame is, the greater the temporal masking effect is. We take use of the model of [7], which is determined by the inter-frame luminance difference and background luminance. So TJND is defined as

$$TJND(x,y,t) = \begin{cases} \max(\tau, \frac{H}{2}\exp(\frac{-0.15}{2\pi}(\Delta(x,y,t)+255)) + \tau), \Delta(x,y,t) \leq 0 \\ \max(\tau, \frac{K}{2}\exp(\frac{-0.15}{2\pi}(255 - \Delta(x,y,t))) + \tau), \Delta(x,y,t) > 0 \end{cases} \quad (10)$$

where H=8, K=3.2, τ=0.8, and

$$\Delta(x,y,t) = \frac{p(x,y,t) - p(x,y,t-1) + bg(x,y,t) - bg(x,y,t-1)}{2}$$

From the above model, the more luminance difference of the inter-frame results in greater visual threshold. H>K denotes that the change of high luminance to low luminance can bring on more masking effect than the change of low luminance to high luminance.

Generally, STJND is defined as follow:

$$STJND(x,y,t) = [SJND(x,y)] \cdot [TJND(x,y,t)] \quad (11)$$

2.3 DJND Model

Traditional JND models only contain the spatial and temporal sensitivity of HVS. In order to exploit more accurate JND model in the stereoscopic scene, we should take use of another property of HVS, which is the masking effect to stereoscopic depth. When the change of depth is below a threshold which is named DJND, HVS could not perceive it. De Silva et al. [11] gets the threshold quantitatively by the experiment.

$$D_{jnd} = \begin{cases} 21 & if \quad 0 \le X(i,j) < 64 \\ 19 & if \quad 64 \le X(i,j) < 128 \\ 18 & if \quad 128 \le X(i,j) < 192 \\ 20 & if \quad 192 \le X(i,j) < 255 \end{cases} \tag{12}$$

where $X(i,j)$ denotes the value of pixel in $(i,j)$of depth image. The depth image can be obtained by two methods. One is exactly formed through the reflection of objects to the camera. The other is coarsely obtained by calculation from two or more images which are taken from different points of view. The depth images of this experiment in this paper are achieved by the former method.

In MJND, we take the DJND model as the scale factor of the STJND model. So the DJND is defined as follow:

$$DJND(x,y) = 1 + D_{jnd}/256 \tag{13}$$

From this equation, the DJND value is greater, the area or the pixel of the image can tolerate more distortion and should be allocated more bits when it is being coded, vice versa.

After obtaining the DJND, we define the MJND model by combining the spatial JND, temporal JND, and the DJND model as

$$MJND(x,y,t) = [SJND(x,y)]^{\xi} \cdot [TJND(x,y,t)]^{\varphi} \cdot [DJND(x,y)]^{\zeta} \tag{14}$$

where ξ, φ and ζ are set to 1s in this paper.

3 An Application of the MJND Model in Multi-view Video Coding

For each MB in MVC, the MB quantization can be adjusted adaptively by using the MJND information of corresponding MB. Moreover, the Lagrange multiplier in the rate-distortion optimization is adapted to achieve the minimum noticeable distortion for the MB.

3.1 Macroblock Quantization Adjustment

In [14], the distortion of MB is defined as

$$D = w\frac{Q^2}{\wedge} \tag{15}$$

where Q denotes the QP of MB, $\wedge$ is a constant, $w$describes the distortion sensitivity of MB. When the w is larger, it denotes that the MB is more sensitive to the distortion, accordingly the QP should be less.

So, when D is invariable, $D_r = w_r\frac{Q_r^2}{\wedge} = D_i = \frac{Q_i^2}{\wedge}$, we can get that

$$Q_i = \sqrt{\frac{w_r}{w_i}}Q_r \tag{16}$$

where w_r= 1, Q_r has been established previously. $w_i$is a sigmoid-like function with respective to MJND values:

$$w_i = \left(a + b\frac{1 + m\exp(-c\frac{s_i - \bar{s}}{\bar{s}})}{1 + n\exp(-c\frac{s_i - \bar{s}}{\bar{s}})}\right)^{-1} \tag{17}$$

From the experiments of [10], a=0.7, b=0.6, m=0, n=1, c=4. s_i denotes the average of MJND in MB_i, and the $\bar{s}$ is the average of MJND in whole image. From the Eq. (17), the MJND of MB is larger, the w_i is smaller. It denotes that this MB is less sensitive to the distortion, hence the QP of the MB is larger.

3.2 Rate-Distortion Optimization

The rate-distortion optimization (RDO) minimizes the Lagrangian cost function for mode selection

$$J_M(M|Q, \lambda_M) = D_M(M|Q) + \lambda_M R_M(M|Q) \tag{18}$$

where D_M and R_M denote the distortion and bit rate of mode M, respectively. M is the set of mode collection and Q is the quantization parameter. λ_M is the Lagrange multiplier. The J_M is convex, we can get the derivative

$$\frac{\partial J_m(M|Q, \lambda_M)}{\partial R_M(M|Q)} = \frac{\partial D_M(M|Q)}{\partial R_M(M|Q)} + \lambda_M = 0 \tag{19}$$

and

$$\lambda_M = -\frac{\partial D_M(M|Q)}{\partial R_M(M|Q)} \quad (20)$$

We substitute the Eq. (15) into Eq. (20), and obtain:

$$\lambda_i = 0.85w_i \times 2^{(Q_i-12)/3} \quad (21)$$

4 Experimental Result

To evaluate the performance of the MJND model, various comparisons and subjective visual quality assessment have been carried out. Firstly, we compare MJND with the traditional STJND model and FJND [10]. Afterward, we apply the MJND model into the multi-view video coding and compare it with the standard scheme JMVM. The objective quality assessments such as PSNR could not match the truth perception of HVS. Accordingly the subjective visual tests are required. This experiment did not make the standard test like the SDSCE (simultaneous double stimulus for continuous evaluation) protocol [15], due to the restrictions of the experimental condition and the new application in MVC. Subjective test results are divided into five classes, which are 5 for imperceptible, 4 for perceptible but not annoying, 3 for slightly annoying, 2 for annoying and 1 for very annoying. The tests have been performed in a laboratory with normal lighting. The display system was a normal LCD screen with resolution of 1440 $\times$ 900. The viewing distance has been set to three times of screen width. Fifteen observers participated in the tests. When testing the stereo effect, the observers need wear the stereoscope glass.

4.1 MJND Test (vs. STJND and FJND)

The test sequences are two views of *ballet* and two views of *bookarrival*, which are all with a resolution of 1024 × 768. When JND values are randomly added or subtracted to the original image, forming a new image. As well known, JND describes the distortion threshold of the image. If the JND values are accurate, the distortion to the new image should not been perceived.

We can use above method to evaluate the different JND models. Generally, when the subjective quality is the same, the value denoted by PSNR of the new image processed by a JND model and original image is less, which indicates that the image could tolerate more noise, and the corresponding JND model can match the perception better. The results of comparisons of different JND models are shown in Table 1. From the table, while keeping the subjective perception of image unchanged, the average PSNR for MJND is least among these JND models, which indicates that the image could tolerate more noise and the MJND model

Table 1 Results of comparisons of varies JND models

Test sequences	Average PSNR (dB) for STJND	Average PSNR (dB) for FJND	Average PSNR (dB) for MJND	Subjective quality
Ballet-view0	35.356585	35.143652	34.777517	5
Ballet-view1	35.777957	35.489426	34.728871	5
Bookarrival-view0	25.360644	25.035229	23.999294	2
Bookarrival-view1	26.526423	23.877150	23.647172	2

describes the perception distortion better. In Fig. 3, the PSNR of distorted frame with MJND noise is 32.74, while 33.00 with FJND noise and 33.23 with STJND noise. This proves the conclusion again.

4.2 *Subjective Tests for MVC Application*

For application, we take use of MJND model to improve the performance of the standard MVC. And the original JMVM-based method in MVC is used for comparison.

The sequences considered in the tests are *ballet* and *bookarrival*, which are both contain 3 views. The frame rate of these sequences is 30 frames/s. The resolution of the sequences is 1024 × 768. The JMVM software version is JMVM 8.0(CVS tag: JMVM_8_0). Each sequence has been coded with hierarchical B and fast motion search of search range of 64. The number of frame to be encoded is 50. Because the JMVM is lack of the rate control, we compare MJND-based method with JMVM-based method in different QPs which result almost the same bit rate. The results of experiment are in Table 2. The detail comparison of local areas between MJND-based and JMVM-based is displayed in Fig. 4.

From the Table 2, under the situation of same bit rate, the PSNR of MJND-based method decreases more than 0.4dB compared with the JMVM-based method. But the subjective quality of MJND-base method is better.

In Fig. 4, there are two column images. The left is from JMVM-based method, and the right is from MJND-based method. From the comparisons of (c) and (d), we can find that the right is better than the left, owing to the RDO with MJND information. The motion estimation is accurate accordingly. (f) is also better than (e), because the border region of texture usually is perceived sensitively. So the region of QP will be smaller, and the quality will be better. However, we find that (g) is better than (h), in contrast to the above two pairs. We analyze that the reason for that is that the region is primarily less sensitive for HVS.

Not only the single view is compared, but also the stereoscopic shaped by two views is compared. We wear the stereoscope glass to watch the stereo effect which is conducted from the two sequences of different views. From the experiment, we can get the same conclusion.

Fig. 3 (**a**) Distorted frame with STJND noise(PSNR is 33.23). (**b**)STJND map(× 4 for display). (**c**) Distorted frame with FJND noise(PSNR is 33.00). (**d**) FJND map(× 4 for display). (**e**) Distorted frame with MTJND noise(PSNR is 32.74). (**f**) MJND map(× 4 for display)

Table 2 Results of MJND applied in multi-video coding

	Bit rate(kbit/s)			PSNR(dB)			Subjective quality	
Test sequences	JMVM	MJND	Delta	JMVM	MJND	Delta	JMVM	MJND
Ballet_view0	158.16	157.64	−0.52	37.99	37.44	−0.55	3	4
Ballet_view1	119.50	120.30	0.80	37.71	37.32	−0.39	3	4
Ballet_view2	139.88	139.95	0.07	37.65	37.22	−0.43	3	4

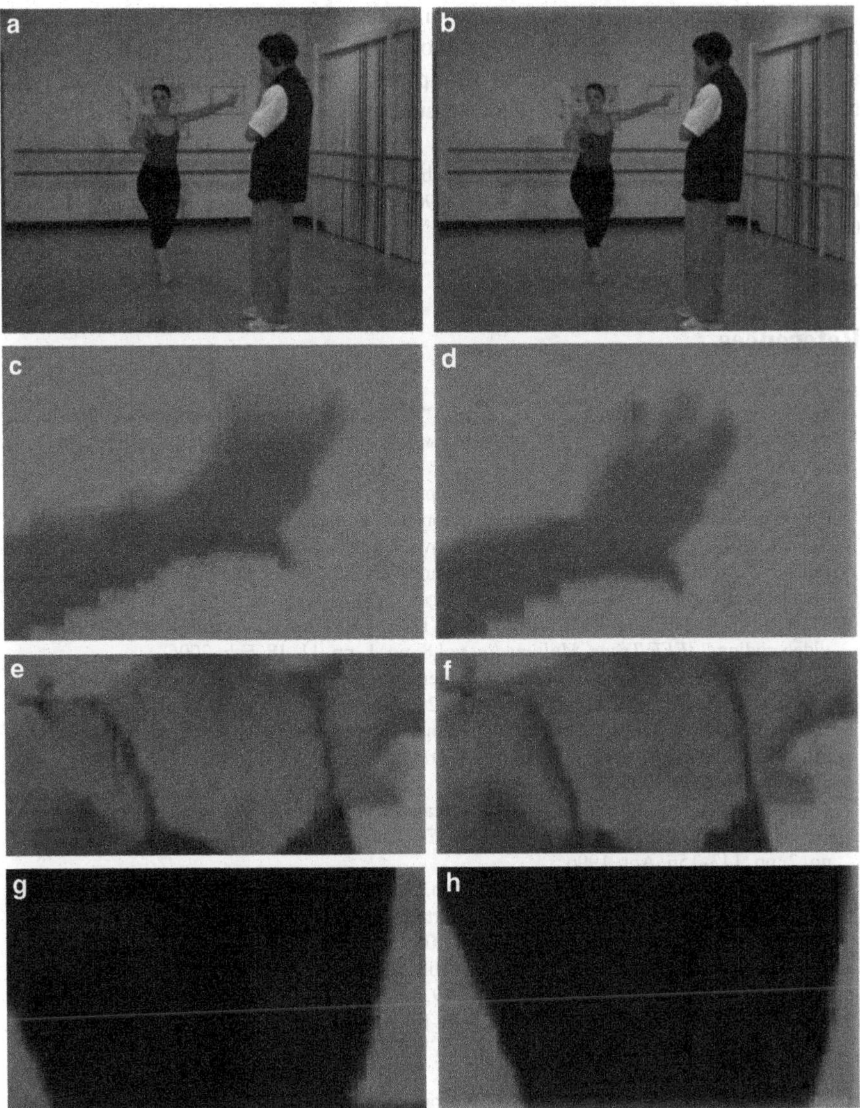

Fig. 4 Comparisons of regions of the reconstructed frame of the *ballet-view0*. *Left* is based on JMVM, *right* is based on JMVM with MJND. (**a**) Reconstructed frame from the JMVM-based method. (**b**) Reconstructed frame from the MJND-based method. (**c,e,g**) Corresponding regions in (**a**). (**d,f,h**) Corresponding regions in (**b**)

5 Conclusion

In this paper, based on the traditional JND models a new JND model named MJND is proposed, which combines the spatial, temporal and depth or stereo masking effect. In order to validate the performance of MJND, comparisons with STJND and FJND are conducted. And the results reveal that our model matched the perception redundancy much better. Moreover, the proposed MJND model is applied in multi-view video coding. Compared to the result of standard MVC, the better perceptual quality of the reconstructed video can be achieved.

Acknowledgements This work is supported by Major State Basic Research Development Program of China (973 Program) (2009CB320905), the Natural Science Foundation of China (60803147, 60736043)

References

1. K. N. Ngan, K. S. Leong, and H. Singh, "Adaptive cosine transform coding of images in perceptual domain," *IEEE Trans. Acoust., Speech, Signal Process.*, vol. 37, no. 11, pp. 1743–1749, Nov. 1989.
2. R. J. Safranek and J. D. Johnston, "A perceptually tuned sub-band image coder with image dependent quantization and post-quantization data compression," in *Proc. IEEE Int. Conf. Acoust., Speech, Signal Process.*, Pacific Grove, CA, May 1989, pp. 1945–1948.
3. A. B. Watson, G. Y. Yang, J. A. Solomon, and J. Villasenor, "Visibility of wavelet quantization noise," *IEEE Trans. Image Process.*, vol. 6, no.8, pp. 1164–1175, Aug. 1997.
4. C.-W. Tang, C.-H. Chen, Y.-H. Yu, and C.-J. Tsai, "Visual sensitivity guided bit allocation for video coding," *IEEE Trans. Multimedia*, vol.8, no. 1, pp. 11–18, Feb. 2006.
5. C.-W. Tang, "Spatial temporal visual considerations for efficient video coding," *IEEE Trans. Multimedia*, vol. 9, no. 2, pp. 231–238, Jan. 2007.
6. C.-H. Chou and Y.-C. Li, "A perceptually tuned sub-band image coder based on the measure of just-noticeable-distortion profile," *IEEE Trans. Circuits Syst. Video Technol.*, vol. 5, no. 6, pp. 467–476, Dec. 1995.
7. C.-H. Chou and C.-W. Chen, "A perceptually optimized 3-D sub-band codec for video communication over wireless channels," *IEEE Trans. Circuits Syst. Video Technol.*, vol. 6, no. 2, pp. 143–156, Apr. 1996.
8. X. Yang, W. Lin, Z. Lu, E. P. Ong, and S. Yao, "Motion-compensated residue preprocessing in video coding based on just-noticeable-distortion profile," *IEEE Trans. Circuits Syst. Video Technol.*, vol. 15, no. 6, pp.742–752, Jun. 2005.
9. X. Zhang, W. Lin, and P. Xue, "Just-noticeable difference estimation with pixels in images," *J. Visual Commun. Image Represent.*, vol. 19, pp. 30–41, Jan. 2008.
10. Z.Z. Chen and C. Guillemot, "Perceptually-Friendly H.264/AVC Video Coding Based on Foveated Just-Noticeable-Distortion Model," *IEEE Trans. Circuits Syst. Video Technol.*, vol. 20, no. 6, pp. 806–819, Jun. 2010.
11. D.V. De Silva, W.A. Fernando and S.T. Worrall, "3D Video Assessment With Just Noticeable Difference in Depth Evaluation," in *IEEE Int. Conf. Image Process.*, Hong Kong, Sep.2010, pp.4013–4016.
12. A. B. Watson, "DCTune: A technique for visual optimization of DCT quantization matrices for individual images," *Soc. for Info. Display Dig. Tech. Papers*, vol. XXIV, pp. 946–949, 1993.
13. J. Lubin, "A visual system discrimination model for imaging system design and evaluation," in *Vision Models for Target Detection and Recognition*, E. Peli, Ed. River Edge, NJ: World Scientific, 1995, pp.245–283.
14. J. Ribas-Corbera and S. Lei, "Rate control in DCT video coding for low-delay communications," *IEEE Trans. Circuits Syst. Video Technol.*, vol. 9, no. 1, pp. 172–185, Feb. 1999.
15. Methodology for the Subjective Assessment of the Quality of Television Pictures, ITU-R BT.500–11, 2002.

Audio, Image and Video Quality Assessment

Multi-camera Skype: Enhancing the Quality of Experience of Video Conferencing

(Florence) Ying Wang, Prabhu Natarajan, and Mohan Kankanhalli

Abstract We propose a novel approach towards real-time control, selection and transmission of the best view of human faces in Skype video conferencing. Our goal is to improve the Quality-of-Experience (QoE) of current video conferencing services by incorporating real-time multi-camera control and selection mechanism. Traditional 3D viewpoint selection algorithms rely on complex 3D-model computation and are not applicable for real-time applications. We define a new image-based metric, Viewpoint Saliency (VS), for evaluating the quality of views of human subject and a centralized multi-camera control mechanism to track and select the best view of human.

Keywords Viewpoint saliency (VS) • Multi-camera control

1 Introduction

An estimated quarter of the world's population uses the internet-supported services through online instant messaging and video-conferencing [11]. The number of users of video-conferencing applications such as Skype has been growing rapidly due to their interactivity in distant communication via voice and video. QoE (Quality of Experience) is a multi-dimensional construct of perceptions and behaviors of a user, which presents his/her emotional, cognitive and behavioral responses, both subjectively and objectively while using a system [22]. Current video conferencing systems such as Skype system support only one camera which does passive capture and transmission. Even if the camera is active, there is no adaptive feedback mechanism in Skype to capture the user properly. Instead, the user has to constantly constrain his motions and reactions in order to be seen by the remote user.

(Florence) Y. Wang • P. Natarajan (✉) • M. Kankanhalli
National University of Singapore, Singapore
e-mail: prabhu@comp.nus.edu.sg

J.S. Jin et al., *The Era of Interactive Media*,
DOI 10.1007/978-1-4614-3501-3_20,

This conflicts with natural communication and interaction. The usage of multiple cameras is becoming popular due to inexpensive price and versatile functionality. Our ultimate goal of this work is to propose a framework towards enhancing the QoE of current video conferencing applications by taking advantage of inexpensive cameras and the use of multi-camera sensing, tracking and computing technologies for selecting the best view of the human subject. Furthermore, our proposed system architecture can be easily incorporated into popular video conferencing applications such as Skype and Yahoo messenger.

Traditional single camera video conferencing applications (such as Skype) restrict the user's movement to be only within the single camera's field of view (FOV) and the notion of getting the best-view of the human face has not been addressed. We benefit the user by providing enhanced natural communication unconstrained by the single camera limitation and also benefit the remote user who can now enjoy the best view of the user all times. In our proposed framework, one of the issues would be the definition of the "best" view. Previously, there has never been a standard definition of "the best view" of objects (or humans). Given the 3D model of an object, traditional 3D viewpoint selection algorithms shed some light on best view selection in computer-graphics based synthetic environment. However, the assumption of 3D model's availability and the computational complexity make them impractical and extremely time consuming, and hence cannot help solve our problem in common video conferencing applications like Skype. To make best view acquisition feasible for video conferencing applications, we propose a novel image-based metric, Viewpoint Saliency (VS), for evaluating the quality of different viewpoints for a given human subject. This measure eliminates 3D model reconstruction, hence is computationally inexpensive. Using the VS measure, one camera that can potentially obtain the best view of the human subject can be automatically adjusted and selected among multiple cameras based on the human subject's movement and is streamed to the network via the Skype interface. However, this camera control process is transparent to the end users while the conferencing is in progress, i.e., the other party of the conferencing, without knowing this process, will always see the best view of the person he is talking to.

This paper is organized as follows: Sect. 2 discusses related works; Sect. 3 illustrates our proposed framework; Sect. 4 discusses experimental results and user study results. Conclusion and future works are given in Sect. 5.

2 Related Works

On system level, previous works are mainly in the areas of internet robotics, camera control and video conferencing. The work [12] have demonstrated a complex two arm tele-operator with video camera and [6] was the first system to permit Internet users to remotely view and manipulate a camera over the WWW. Controlling networked robotic cameras [16,18] were also studied for remote observation applications. In [7], the authors have presented a multi-modal camera selection mechanism using semantic features. In [10] the authors have combined fixed and active cameras for collaborative video conferencing. In [15], a 3D immersive video conferencing system has been presented that includes sophisticated display and multi-view camera setups. The works, Ranjan et al. [14] and Zotkin et al. [23] have presented a prototype to automate the manual camera control for remote repair tasks like piece selection and placement. Although previous studies have addressed the problem of camera control in multi-camera environments, none of them have been adopted for commonly used video conferencing applications such as Skype. Therefore, this work is the first one that attempts to apply multi-camera control to a common end-user application.

On computation level, related works are mainly in the areas of face tracking, 3D viewpoint selection and evaluation as well as visual attention analysis. Doubek et al. [4] presented a face tracking system in a multi-camera environment using static cameras. In [19], a system that tracks faces in meeting room scenarios using omni-directional views was presented. In 3D viewpoint selection and evaluation, various viewpoint quality evaluation metrics have been used in applications such as scene exploration [3], molecular visualization [18] and image based modeling. Some metrics such as viewpoint entropy [17] and viewpoint mutual information [5] are defined based on information theory. In [17], information theory was used to define viewpoint entropy, based on the relative area of the projected faces of an object over the sphere of directions centered at viewpoint. A major drawback of viewpoint entropy is that it depends on the polygonal discretization of object's faces. A heavily discretized region will boost the value of viewpoint entropy, and hence it favors small polygons more than large ones. For visual attention analysis, many computational models of attention models have been proposed: Ahmad's model [1], Niebur's model [13] and Itti-Koch's model [8]. Although these visual attention models reveal the relationship between human attention and image sub-regions, they do not study human attention in images of similar content captured from different viewpoints.

From the literature survey, it is clear that there is no video conferencing system which uses multiple cameras to provide an enhanced user experience to both parties of conferencing in a real time. Traditional 3D model based viewpoint selection algorithms cannot be applied because 3D model reconstruction is complex and time-consuming and may affect the response time of Skype and consequently influences its QoE [22]. It is necessary to develop an efficient viewpoint evaluation framework and camera coordination and selection mechanism to enable real-time best view selection of human faces.

3 System Architecture

We propose a multi-camera framework that selects the best-view of the human subject in video conferencing system based on Viewpoint Saliency (VS) measure (Sect. 3.2). Our proposed framework not only maximizes the user's activity area to be among multiple cameras' FOV, but also selects the camera with the best-view of the face

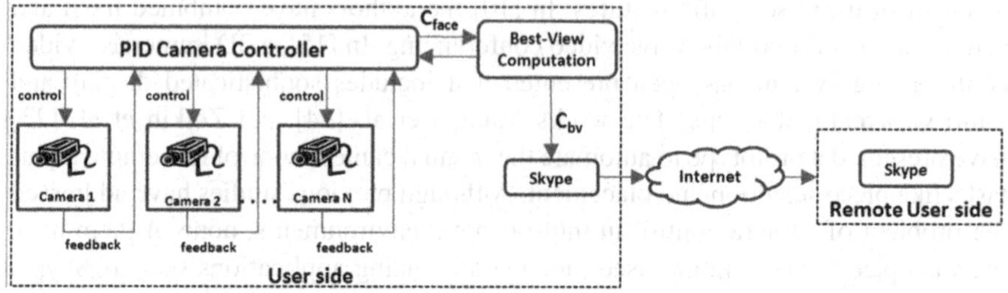

Fig. 1 System architecture

on-the-fly. We assume that the system is designed for one to one video conferencing, because traditional internet-based video conferencing applications are usually carried out by a single user and remote-user pair. The human behavior is assumed to be non-adversarial, i.e. he/she is not trying to actively avoid being captured by the cameras.

The proposed framework is shown in Fig. 1 with multiple (active or static) cameras that are controlled by a camera controller. The face is detected in each camera and its viewpoint saliency is computed. The camera with its detected face having high viewpoint saliency measure is considered to have the best-view and corresponding camera source is selected for the Skype during the conversation. The cameras are actively steered continuously to obtain the best possible views. When the human face is detected in only one camera, then the corresponding camera source is selected in the Skype. When human face is detected in many cameras, then the viewpoint saliency is computed for the face sub-images of those cameras. The camera with high viewpoint saliency measure is considered as the best-view and its corresponding camera source is selected in the Skype.

3.1 Camera Control

We have designed a light weight camera control algorithm for selecting the "best-view" camera that is ideal for video conferencing applications such as Skype, which is pre-installed on a standard desktop computer with multiple cameras connected. Each camera in the system will be in any of the three states: Initialization, viewpoint saliency computation and Tracking Best-View. The camera controller schedules each camera to any of the above states and interacts with the camera in each of the phases. In the Initialization phase, the camera scans for the human face in the image by performing auto-panning to search for the human face. When the human face is detected, the camera tries to center the face in the video frame using a PID controller. Once the face is brought to center of the image frame, the controller zooms the face to an optimal size (40% of the image) and the corresponding camera is added to a list C_{face} for best view computation. C_{face} is a set of cameras where the face is detected and centered.

The viewpoint saliency of the face sub-image is calculated as explained in the Sect. 3.2. Once the viewpoint saliency is computed, the camera controller ranks each camera in C_{face} based on the viewpoint saliency measure, such that camera with high viewpoint saliency is considered as best-view camera and has rank 1, and the next highest viewpoint saliency camera is ranked 2 and so on. The ranked cameras are stored in an ordered list, C_{bv}. The best view camera source is then selected in the Skype for video transmission. Periodically, the C_{face} and the C_{bv} lists are updated based on the viewpoint saliency measure computed for every 3 s. Apart from this, whenever the track is lost or face is not detected in a camera, the corresponding camera is removed from the C_{face} and C_{bv} list. Thus a re-ranking of cameras in C_{bv} is done based on the VS measure. Similarly when a face is detected in a new camera, the corresponding camera is added to C_{face} and hence the C_{bv} list is updated.

Once a camera is selected as the best-view camera, then the face is tracked within the camera by using a face detection based tracker until the track quality is low. Track quality is measured based on the following factors: viewpoint saliency measure and position of face in the video frame. The camera controller updates the C_{face} and C_{bv} lists periodically. When the camera loses its face or the viewpoint saliency is lesser than the neighboring camera or the face is far from the frame center, then the controller switches the best view source to another camera that has the highest viewpoint saliency with the face positioned at the image center.

In [21], the authors have used proportional feedback controller to control the camera to center the human face. Since a proportional controller has a slow response time and is sensitive to noise, we have therefore adopted the PID (Proportional Integral Derivative) Feedback control mechanism for centering and tracking the human face which has better stability than using only proportional feedback control. This is because PID controller uses present, past and future errors. The basic equation deriving the output of a PID controller is given by [2],

$$O_{(t+1)} = K^{p} * e_t + K^{i} * \sum_{j=0}^{t} e_j + K^{d} * \frac{de_t}{dt}. \tag{1}$$

where e_t is the error at time t; K^D, K^i and K^d are proportional, integral and derivative gains and $O_{(t+1)}$ is the desired output at time $(t + 1)$. In our framework, we had three PID controllers for pan, tilt and zoom operations. For video conversation, human face is always desired to be at the center of the video frame and with a close-up view. The PID controller steers the camera to center the face based on the current face location in the image. The PID gain values for pan, tilt and zoom are chosen empirically by the process of controller tuning [2]. Due to space limitation, we limit our discussion on PID camera controller.

3.2 Viewpoint Saliency

Traditional 3D viewpoint selection algorithm relies on the 3D models of the object. The computation is generally complex and time consuming. However, in applications such as video conferencing, the concept of objects (i.e. the remote person) is important to users. Therefore, we would like to develop a metric to evaluate the viewpoint quality of specific human subject in a conferencing scenario. This viewpoint evaluation metric should be computable in real time without requiring the 3D model of the human subject. Previous research in visual attention analysis and image quality assessment provides ideas of 2D feature assessment of images. We have combined it with ideas from 3D viewpoint selection to develop a new 2D based viewpoint evaluation metric. This reduces the computation cost since it works entirely in the 2D space. Our proposed viewpoint saliency (VS) metric computes a score for the quality of various viewpoints of objects captured in images. The definition of VS is as follows:

Let F = {F1, F2, F3, F4…} be the set of features extracted from an image (a view) of an object, let P = {p1, p2, p3, p4…} be the set of descriptors that describe the features included in F, where pi $\in R$ and $p_i \in [0,1]$. Each feature in F has one (or more) descriptor in P whose relative importance is given in a set of weights W = {w1, w2, w3, w4…}, where $\sum_i w_i = 1$. Let VS be the score for the quality of this view, i.e. viewpoint saliency (VS)

$$\mathrm{VS} = \sum\nolimits_{\mathrm{i}} \mathrm{w_i p_i}. \tag{2}$$

Two features are found to be important to the quality of a viewpoint: one is the contrast level within object region, denoted as pc; the other is the projected area of the object, denoted as pa; in the future, more important features may be recognized and added into the formulation of VS. Initially, we assume they are of same importance, hence, w1 = w2 = 0.5. Viewpoint saliency (VS) is computed as:

$$\mathrm{VS} = \mathrm{w1} \times \mathrm{pc} + \mathrm{w2} \times \mathrm{pa}. \tag{3}$$

In the following paragraphs, we provide details of the two descriptors, and possible extensions of the above definition.

3.3 Contrast Level Descriptor Pc

2D based viewpoint measure comes from observing pencil sketching techniques used by artists. They make use of contrast between a set of gray levels to depict the 3D world on 2D paper. Their drawings are information captured by their eyes without measured by any 3D geometry metrics. Additionally, the main function of the primate retina, in doing spatial analysis, is to extract contrast information from the luminance distribution [9]. Given an image I, the contrast level descriptor pc of the object region (which contains the object of interest) is computed as:

$$\mathrm{pc} = \frac{1}{\mathrm{N_p}} \sum\nolimits_{\mathrm{p_{i,j}} \subset \mathrm{O}} \mathrm{C_{p_{ij}}} \tag{4}$$

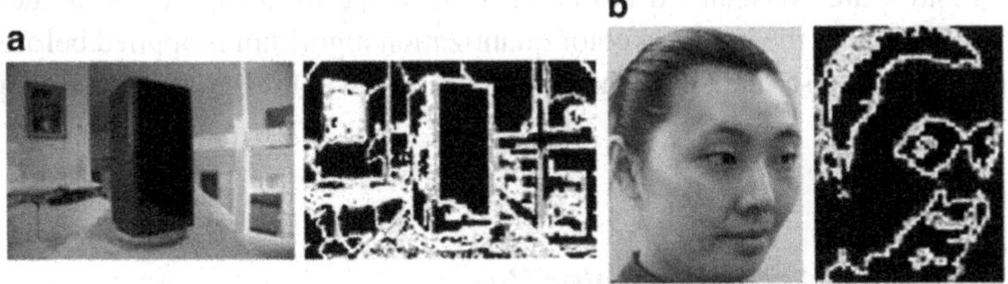

Contrast map of general object   Contrast map of human face

Fig. 2 Original images and their contrast maps

where O indicates a bounded object region, pi,j indicates one perception unit within the object region. A perception unit can either be a single pixel or a sub-region of O, which decides the granularity of pc. Np is the total number of perception units within the object region O. $C_{p_{ij}}$ is the contrast level value of the perception unit pi,j obtained from the contrast map of I.

The contrast map of an image is a map in which each perception unit is encoded with a contrast level value compared with its neighborhood. Examples of a contrast map of a general object and human face are shown in Fig. 2. These contrast maps are computed under the stimulus of color and can be visualized as the brightness of the region. The brighter the area, higher is the perceived contrast. An image of size M × N pixels, is construed as a perceived field with M × N perception units (each perception unit contains one pixel). The contrast value $C_{p_{ij}}$ on a perceived pixel at location (i, j) of the image is defined as follows:

$$C_{p_{ij}} = \sum\nolimits_{qm,n\subset O} d\left(p_{i,j}, q_{m,n}, \text{ stimulus}\right). \tag{5}$$

where $p_{i,j}(i \in [0, M], j \in [0, N])$ denotes a single perception unit, and $q_{m,n}$ denotes one neighborhood perception unit surround $p_{i,j}$. Θ is the set of all neighborhood perception units of $p_{i,j}$. Notice that the size of Θ controls the sensitivity of perception field: the smaller the size of Θ is, the more sensitive the perceived field is. For instance, Θ can be a 3 × 3 square window around $p_{i,j}$ which yields 8 neighbors. *stimulus* denotes the stimulus of the contrast among perception units, for instance, it can be color, texture, or orientation, etc. $d(p_{i,j}, q_{m,n}, stimulus)$ measures the difference between $p_{i,j}$ and $q_{m,n}$ under a certain stimulus such as color, which may employ any suitable distance measure such as Euclidean or Gaussian distance. By normalizing to [0, 1], all contrast values $C_{p_{ij}}$of the perception units in the perceived field (i.e., the image) form a "contrast map" that stores the contrast value for each perception unit, (i.e. each pixel). We find color to be a good stimulus for computing the contrast map. For Fig. 2, U and V components in LUV space are used to compute the distance between one perception unit and its neighbors, using the following distance measure:

$$\text{distance} = a\left(1 - e^{-\frac{d}{2q^2}}\right). \tag{6}$$

where a and q are constants, d is Euclidean distance in 2D space. To reduce the number of colors in the image, a color quantization algorithm is applied before calculating the contrast map. For the neighborhood window, 3 × 3 pixels square window is used.

3.4 Projected Area Descriptor Pa

Projected area is used as important information in the theory of viewpoint entropy [17]. Without any prior knowledge of the 3D structure of the object of interest, the projected area can be a good descriptor for interpreting the quality of viewpoint in 2D space. Given an image of an object with a rectangular object region, the projected area descriptor is computed as:

$$\mathrm{pa} = \frac{\mathrm{aWH}}{\mathrm{MN}} \tag{7}$$

where W and H are width and height of the object region, M and N are height and width of the image and a is the scaling factor. As mentioned earlier, both pc and pa range between 0 and 1, and describe the amount of information conveyed by contrast level and projected area in the objects' images. Then, by substituting pc and pa in Eq. (3), we obtain

$$\mathrm{VS} = \frac{\mathrm{W}_1}{\mathrm{N}_\mathrm{p}} \sum\nolimits_{\mathrm{p}_{\mathrm{i,j}} \subset \mathrm{O}} \sum\nolimits_{\mathrm{q}_{\mathrm{m,n}} \subset \Theta} d\left(\mathrm{p}_{\mathrm{i,j}}, \mathrm{q}_{\mathrm{m,n}}\right) + \mathrm{w}_2 \frac{\mathrm{aWH}}{\mathrm{MN}} \tag{8}$$

where w1 and w2 are the weights of pc and pa, indicating their relative importance. We use w1 = w2 = 0.5 as the default values.

From the experiments, we found that two factors greatly affect the result of VS: (a) texture of objects; (b) lighting condition. However, in our current work, we assume that the lighting condition remains the same for one cycle of the best view selection. When compared to the existing measure, i.e., viewpoint entropy, our proposed metric, viewpoint saliency can eliminate the segmentation of "faces" of objects and provide reasonably good viewpoint evaluation results for human subjects within milliseconds. Its simplicity in computation facilitates best view acquisition for video conferencing applications in real time.

4 Experimentation Results and User Study

We implemented our algorithm with three Canon VCC cameras on the C# platform integrated with Skype API. All cameras are connected to a single standard desktop computer where the video conferencing application, i.e., Skype, is installed.

Table 1 Users' average ratings of four scenarios

Scenarios	Ease of use	Enjoyment	Interactivity	Subjective-performance	Subjective-consistence
Scenario 1 (Conventional Skype)	3.00	3.00	2.33	2.67	2.33
Scenario 2 (1 PTZ camera Skype)	3.33	3.00	2.50	3.50	2.83
Scenario 3 (2 PTZ camera Skype)	4.00	4.00	3.33	3.50	3.50
Scenario 4 (3 PTZ camera Skype)	4.67	4.67	4.00	4.17	4.17

We have tested our multi-camera Skype system with three PTZ cameras and compared it against conventional Skype setting with one PTZ camera. Interested readers can watch the video demonstration of our implemented multi-camera Skype system here[1]. Due to its subjectivity, there are very few standard quantitative metrics for evaluating the QoE of a multimedia system. The QoE construct, and their correlations in user experience modeling has addressed in [20]. In order to evaluate the QoE of our system, based on the correlations between QoS construct and QoE construct [22], we adopted two important criterion in QoS construct: "interactivity" and "subjective consistency", and interpret them as the "the degree of interactivity to satisfy users' needs" and "the level of consistency to user desired results" and all the representative dimensions in QoE construct to evaluate the QoE of our system. Five representative dimensions in QoE construct [22], namely, concentration, enjoyment, telepresence, perceived usefulness and perceived ease of use are summarized and interpreted as another three criteria in our evaluation: "Ease of use: the level of ease to operate and use the system to achieve user desired results.", "Enjoyment: the level of enjoyment involved in using the system", "subjective performance: the level of perceived performance of the system in response time, cameras switching and video quality in remote video conferencing".

To compare conventional Skype with our multi-camera Skype system, Skype with one, two and three PTZ cameras are tested against conventional Skype with one PTZ camera (and no feedback camera control mechanism). We invited six users to use our system and give their five-scale rating (i.e. 1: bad, 2: poor, 3: fair, 4: good, 5: excellent) on five criteria (ease of use, enjoyment, interactivity, subjective-performance, and subjective-consistence). We first group them into three pairs and then let each person of the pair first act as the speaker (sender), and then act as the audience (receiver) to evaluate our system from two different roles. The average rating result given by users for our system against conventional Skype is shown in Table 1. As shown, our multi-camera Skype system has improved rating results in all dimensions of QoE construct compared with

[1] http://www.youtube.com/watch?v=xHM4PDfFTLE

conventional Skype. Also the user experience improves with the growing number of cameras. Conventional Skype has an average rating of 2.67 for the listed dimensions whereas our multi-camera Skype has an average rating of 4.28.

Under the dimensions of "interactivity", "subjective performance" and "subjective consistence", the average rating results are improved by nearly 50%, which we consider are due to the increase in speaker's activity region (speaker can move around in the office at the sender side) and the quality of video conversation is constantly preserved by always streaming the best view to the audience at the receiver side. The speaker can therefore, act more comfortably without worrying whether his remote audience can see him or not, which greatly eases the process of the video conferencing and enhances the interactivity among two parties of the conference.

5 Conclusion

We have proposed a framework towards enhancing the quality of experience of video conferencing applications. Within this framework, we have presented a novel approach towards real-time control, selection and transmission of the best view of human faces in Skype video conferencing. The best view selection is based on our 2D based measure: viewpoint saliency, which can greatly reduce the computational complexity and acquire the best view of human subject in real time in the video conferencing environment. Our experimental results show that our proposed framework is feasible and effective for enhancing the Quality of Experience (QoE) of the popular free video-conferencing application: Skype. In the future, the definition of viewpoint saliency can be further extended. For example, additional cues like pose estimation, gaze tracking can be included to enhance best view selection.

References

1. Ahmad, S., VISIT: A Neural Model of Covert Attention. In Advances in Neural Information Processing Systems, 4, 420–427, 1991.
2. Ang, K.H., Chong, G.C.Y., and Li, Y., PID Control System Analysis, Design, and Technology. In IEEE Trans. on Control Systems Technology, 13(4), 559–576, 2005.
3. Barral, P., Dorme, G., and Plemenos, D., Scene Understanding Techniques using a Virtual Camera. In Proc. of Eurographics, 2000.
4. Doubek, P., Nummiaro, K., Koller-Meier, E. and Gool, L. V., Face Tracking in a Multi-Camera Environment. 266, 2003.
5. Feixas, M., Sbert, M., and Gonzalez, F., A Unified Information-Theoretic Framework for Viewpoint Selection and Mesh Saliency. In ACM Trans. on Applied Perception, 6, 1–23, 2008.
6. Goldberg, K., Gentner, S., Sutter, C., and Wiegley, J., The Mercury Project: A feasibility study for internet robots. In IEEE Int. Conf. on Robotics and Automation, 1995.
7. Hornler, B., Arsic, D., Schuller, B., and Rigoll, G., Boosting multi-modal camera selection with semantic features. In Proc. of ICME, 1298–1301, 2009.

8. Itti, L., Koch, C., and Niebur, E., A model of saliency based visual attention for rapid scene analysis. In IEEE Trans. on PAMI., 1254–1259, 1998.
9. Khwaja, A. A., Goecke, and R., Image reconstruction from contrast information. In Digital Image Computing: Techniques and Applications, 226–233, 2008.
10. Liu, Q., Kimber, D., Wilcox, L., Cooper, M., Foote, J., and Boreczky, J., Managing a camera system to serve different video requests. In Proc. of ICME, 13–16, 2002.
11. Miniwatts Marketing Group., World Internet Users and Population Stats, 2010. Retrieved August 4, 2010, from Internet World Stats. http://www.internetworldstats.com/stats.htm.
12. Mosher, R. S., Industrial Manipulators. Scientific American, 211(4), 88–96, 1964.
13. Niebur, E., Koch, C., and Parasuraman, R., Computational architectures for attention. The attentive brain, Cambridge, MA: MIT Press, 163–186, 1998.
14. Ranjan, A., Birnholtz, J. P., and Balakrishnan, R., Dynamic shared visual spaces: experimenting with automatic camera control in a remote repair task. In Proc. of SIGCHI Conf. on Human Factors in Computing Systems., 1177–1186, 2007.
15. Schreer, O., Feldmann, I., Atzpadin, N., Eisert, P. Kauff, P., and Belt, H., 3D Presence -A System Concept for Multi-User and Multi-Party Immersive 3D Videoconferencing. In Proc. of European Conference on Visual Media Production, 1–8, 2008.
16. Song, D., Qin, N., and Goldberg, K., Systems, Control Models, and Codec for Collaborative Observation of Remote Environments with an Autonomous Networked Robotic Camera. In Autonomous Robots, 24(4), 435–449, 2008.
17. Vazquez, P. P., Feixas, M., Sbert, M., and Heidrich, W., Viewpoint selection using viewpoint entropy. In Proc. of Vision, Modeling and Visualization, 273–280, 2001.
18. Vazquez, P. P., Feixas, M., Sbert, M., and Llobet, A., Viewpoint Entropy: A new tool for obtaining good views for molecules. Data Visualization 2002 (Eurographics /IEEE TCVG Symposium Proceedings), 27–29, 2002.
19. Wallhoff, F., Zobl, M., Rigoll, G.,and Potucek, I., Face tracking in meeting room scenarios using omnidirectional views. In Int. Conf. on Pattern Recognition, 933–936, 2004.
20. Wang, Z., Bovik, A. C., Sheikh, H. R., and Simoncelli, E. P., Image quality assessment: From error measurement to structural similarity. In IEEE Trans. on Image Processing, 13(4), 600–612, 2004.
21. Wang, J., Kankanhalli, M.S., Yan, W.Q., and Jain, R., Experiential Sampling for Video Surveillance. In Proc. of First ACM Int. Workshop on Video Surveillance, 77–86, 2003.
22. Wu, W., Arefin, A., Rivas, R., Nahrstedt, K., Sheppard, R. M. and Yang, Z., Quality of Experience in distributed interactive multimedia environments: toward a theoretical framework. In ACM Int. Conf. on Multimedia, 481–490, 2009.
23. Zotkin, D., Duraiswami, R., Philomin, V., and Davis, L., Smart Videoconferencing. In Proc. of ICME, 1597–1600, 2000.

Content Aware Metric for Image Resizing Assessment

Lifang Wu, Lianchao Cao, Jinqiao Wang, and Shuqin Liu

Abstract Development of mobile multimedia techniques requires image resizing. An image quality assessment (IQA) metric is needed for objectively assessing image resizing approaches. Most of existing IQA approaches are designed for images of the same size, and are not suitable for image resizing application. In this paper, we propose a Content Aware Metric (CAM) to evaluate the similarity between resized image and the original one. By introducing the Structure Similarity (SSIM) metric for retargeting assessment, we firstly analyze how image resizing influences the different components of SSIM. Then we divide the important regions into lots of important sub images, which are represented by the coordinates of centers. We track the location of all the sub images and compute the similarity of corresponding sub images. The CAM is obtained by averaging the distance of all sub images. The CAM is effective for assessing the quality of Seam Carving, and the experimental results show that our metrics is consistent with human observation.

Keywords Image quality assessment • Content aware metric • Image resizing

L. Wu (✉) • L. Cao • S. Liu
School of Electronic Information and Control Engineering,
Beijing University of Technology, Beijing 100124, China
e-mail: lfwu@bjut.edu.cn

J. Wang
National Laboratory of Pattern Recognition (NLPR), Institute of Automation,
Chinese Academy of Sciences (CASIA), Beijing 100190, P.R. China
e-mail: jqwang@nlpr.ia.ac.cn

J.S. Jin et al., *The Era of Interactive Media*,
DOI 10.1007/978-1-4614-3501-3_21,

1 Introduction

The development of mobile multimedia techniques makes it possible for users to browse images/videos on mobile devices (such as iPad, PDAs and cellular phones). The resolution and aspect ratio of mobile devices and traditional TV and HDTV are much different from each other. How to optimally display a source image to the target screen is essential for image browsing. Content aware image retargeting adapts the images of various aspect ratios to the target screen and maximizes the viewer experience. In order to assess the performance of image resizing approaches, we need to assess image quality of resized images.

Image quality assessment generally includes subjective and objective assessment. The subjective assessment is implemented by statistics of human's evaluation. A typical approach is mean opinion scores (MOSs), this metric can represent a human's observation but it is time-consuming and expensive. The assessment results are usually affected by the environment and subject's status. In comparison, the objective assessment is simpler and easier to implement. Because humans are users of the image/video, the current research focuses on the objective assessment consistent with subjective assessment [1].

The objective assessment has been broadly studied. The assessment approaches can be generally classed into full reference (FR), reduced reference (RR) and non-reference (NR) approaches. The full reference approaches require the full access to the original image. The reduced reference approaches require the features of the original images. Non-reference approaches do not require the reference image. They assess the image quality using image statistics [2].

In our application, an image of the original size can be used as the reference image, therefore the NR approach is not suitable for our application. By now, some typical FR approaches have been proposed for image compression application. Peak signal-to-noise ratio (PSNR) and mean squared errors (MSE) compute the difference between the reference image and distorted image [3]. These approaches are simple for computation but the assessment results are not well matched to the perceived visual quality [4]. Just noticeable difference (JND) [5] is proposed based on property of Human Visual System (HVS). Based on the assumption that HVS is highly adapted for extracting statistical structural information, structural similarity (SSIM) [6] was proposed. Experimental results show that SSIM complies with the subjective mean opinion score (MOS) by Logarithm function, and the SSIM data of different JPEG images are more clustered around the MOS curve. SSIM is one of the successful metrics of image quality assessment. These above FR approaches require that the original images and distorted images have the same size, we thus believe that these approaches are also not suitable for image resizing assessment. It is necessary to develop a new objective assessment method for image resizing.

Liu et al. [7] proposed a top-down framework for image resizing assessment. In their framework, image features are organized from global to local viewpoints. They used Scale Invariant Feature Transformation (SIFT) [8] to find the correspondence between the original image and the resized image. For each matched pair of pixels, LLID and SSIM are used for matching respectively. Their experimental results show the efficiency of the proposed approach. In their framework, the image quality is represented using the quality of some feature points and the extraction of SIFT is time consuming.

In this paper we propose a Content Aware Metric to evaluate the similarity between the resized image and the original image. In our scheme, the sub images in the important regions are evaluated and the average evaluation represents the evaluation of the resized image. We firstly compute the importance of each pixel and determine important regions in the image. We divide the important regions into a lot of important sub images which are represented by the center pixel. And the correspondence of center pixel is found by the scheme of image resizing, which needs much less computations. SSIM is originally designed for image compression and it composes of three components: luminance, contrast and structure. We then analyze which components are influenced by image resizing (which component is affected by image resizing the most). By the analyzed results, we compute the Distance of corresponding sub images. The CAM is obtained by averaging the Distance of all sub images. The experimental results show that our metrics comply with human observation.

2 Structural Similarity in Image Resizing

SSIM is proposed by Wang [6], it is believed to be one of successful metrics of image quality assessment. In this section, we first introduce Wang's scheme, then we analyze how the image resizing influences three components respectively.

2.1 Structural Similarity Measure (SSIM)

By Wang's proposal, for image quality assessment, it is useful to apply the SSIM index locally rather than globally [6]. The local statistics within a local 8*8 square window is computed. Assume there are two nonnegative sub image signals f and g. Firstly, their mean (μ_f and μ_g) and standard variation (σ_f and σ_g) are computed respectively. And the correlation variation σ_{fg} of these two images is also computed. Furthermore, they define the luminance comparison function $l(f,g)$, the contrast comparison function $c(f,g)$ and the structural comparison function [6] $s(f,g)$ respectively. SSIM is the product of these three comparison functions.

$$SSIM = l(f,g)c(f,g)s(f,g) \tag{1}$$

Fig. 1 Six example images

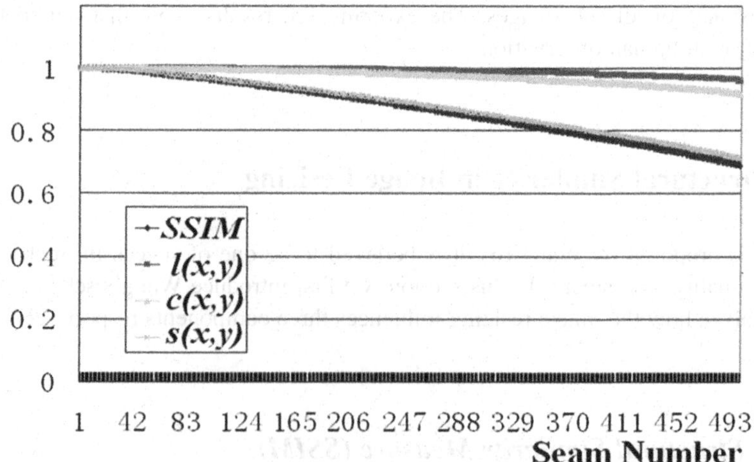

Fig. 2 Influence of seam carving on different components of SSIM

2.2 How Image Resizing Influences Different Components of SSIM

In fact, in the image resizing application, the luminance and contrast of the resized image are generally same as that of the original image. The variation of aspect ratio usually causes variation of the structure. In this paper, we resize the image using seam carving. Then we analyze variation of three components as the seam number increases.

We resize six images in Fig. 1 into the size of half width and height. Then we compute the averaged $l(f,g), c(f,g)$ *and* $s(f,g)$ and SSIM respectively as the seam number increase, as shown in Fig. 2.

From Fig. 2, we can see that increase of seam number causes less variation to *l(f,g)* and *c(f,g)*. And variation of *s(f,g)* and SSIM are almost similar to each other. In our application scenario, the removed seams cause less variation of luminance and contrast. But it possibly brings large intensity discontinuity, and it will cause more structural variation. By the above observation and analysis, structural component *s(f,g)* will be used in our work.

3 The Content Aware Metric (CAM)

The CAM gives an objective assessment. Through analysis of the importance of every pixel from the image content, we partition the image into important and unimportant regions. The CAM is used to measure the quality loss of the important regions.

3.1 Region Importance Determination

Generally, some pixels are important while others are comparatively unimportant in an image. By Itta's idea [10], saliency map can represent the visually important regions. Lots of saliency maps are used for importance determination in image retargeting since it could be used to model the visually importance of different regions [11]. Furthermore, the weight function *w(x,y)* is obtained by normalizing the importance of each pixel.

We segment the important regions by thresholding of the weight function *g(x,y)*, and the threshold r_0 is the average of *g(x,y)*.

Figure 3 show the original image and the corresponding weight function and important regions respectively. In Fig. 3c, the important pixels are marked as 0.

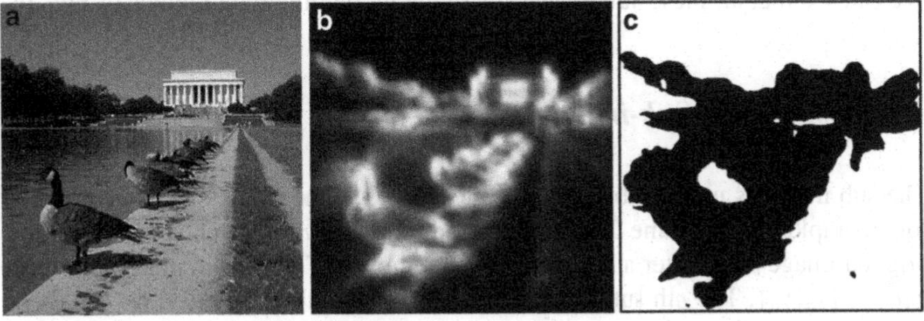

Fig. 3 the original image and its weight function. (**a**) The original image (**b**) the Weight function (**c**) the important regions

Fig. 4 the important sub-images of Fig. 3a

3.2 Important Sub-images

Following Wang's proposal [6], we segment the important regions into a lot of sub important images. In order to keep the symmetry of the sub-image, we define the size of the sub image as 9*9.

Let us assume that the number of sub-images we obtain is Num_{sub_image}. Each sub-image is represented by its center pixel.

$$sub\_image_n = \{x_n, y_n\}, n = 1, 2, \cdots, Num_{sub\_image}$$

In Fig. 4, the pixels marked as magenta are the center of sub important images. We can see that all these sub images distribute in the important regions of Fig. 3c.

3.3 Update the Sub-image

The sub image is updated by the image resizing scheme. Let's take seam carving for example. We assume that the resized image *g(u,v)* is obtained from the original image *f(x,y)* after a vertical seam is removed. The *n*th sub image is $sub\_image_n = \{x_n, y_n\}$. The *n*th sub-image in *g(u,v)* varies in three cases.

Case 1: The seam passes through the left region of the pixel $f(x_n, y_n)$. In this case, the center of the *n*th sub-image in the resized image *g(u,v)* moves leftward a pixel.

$$\begin{cases} u_n = x_n - 1 \\ v_n \doteq y_n \end{cases} \tag{2}$$

Case 2: The seam passes through the right region of the pixel $f(x_n, y_n)$. In this case, the center of the nth sub-image in the resized image *g(u,v)* keep invariant.

Case 3: The seam passes through the pixel $f(x_n, y_n)$. In this case we should find a new center of the corresponding sub image. Let's assume that the nearest left/right pixel of $f(x_n, y_n)$ are p(x_{n_left},y_{n_left}) and p(x_{n_right},y_{n_right}) respectively. And the nearest left/right center pixel of the corresponding sub-images are p($x_{n\_left\_cent}$, $y_{n\_left\_cent}$) and p($x_{n\_right\_cent}$,$y_{n\_right\_cent}$) respectively. There are also three sub-cases.

Case 3.1: If both the left and right neighboring pixels of the pixel $f(x_n, y_n)$ are the centers of other important sub-images, we think there is not corresponding sub image of sub_image_n in the image *g(u,v)*. The center of corresponding sub-image is set to zero.

Case 3.2: If the left (right) neighboring pixel is the center of another sub-image, the right (left) neighboring pixel is set as the center for the *n*th important sub-image.

Case 3.3: If neither the left nor right neighboring pixel is the center for some other important sub-images, the distances of the left and right neighboring pixels to the center of the left and right sub-images are computed respectively.

$$\begin{cases} Dis\_Ave_{n\_left} = (x_{n\_left} - x_{n\_left\_cent}) \\ Dis\_Ave_{n\_right} = (x_{n\_right\_cent} - x_{n\_right}) \end{cases} \tag{3}$$

The one with the larger distance is set as the corresponding center of the *n*th sub-image.

By now, we can get the corresponding sub images in *g(u,v)* for each sub images in the original image *f(x,y)*.

3.4 Definition of CAM

After pairing the center of the important sub images in the original and resized image, we compute the corresponding structural similarity. Let's analyze the definition of *s(f,g)* in Eq. (4) [6].

$$s(f,g) = \frac{\sigma_{fg} + C_3}{\sigma_f \sigma_g + C_3} \tag{4}$$

Where, C_3 is a small constant that prevents denominator very close to zero. In Eq. (4), if two sub-images *f* and *g* are identical, the *s(f,g)* will be 1.0. Otherwise, the more different two images are, the farther from 1.0 the *s(f,g)* is. Therefore, we define the Distance $Dis_{sub\_n}(f,g)$ as follows.

$$Dis_{sub\_n}(f,g) = \begin{cases} 1 & u_n = 0 \text{ and } v_n = 0 \\ 1 - s(f,g) & others \end{cases} \tag{5}$$

In the Eq. (5), if $u_n = 0$ *and* $v_n = 0$,it means there is not correspondence of sub_image_n in *g(u,v)*. We say the distance between the sub_image_n and its correspondence is the maximum 1.0. The CAM can be obtained by Eq. (6).

$$CAM(f,g) = \frac{1}{Num_{sub\_image}} \sum_{n=1}^{Num_{sub\_image}} Dis_{sub\_n}(f,g) \tag{6}$$

4 Experimental Results

4.1 Comparison of IQA

In order to assess the consistency of proposed CAM with human observation. We resize the images in Fig. 5 using seam carving to the width of reducing 100, 200, 300, 400, 500, 600, 700 and 800 pixels, the results are shown in Fig. 6. Each resized image is assessed using Liu's [7] and our approaches respectively. In order to compare Liu's and our results, we show one minus Liu's IQA in Fig. 7a. The difference of IQA of under a width and that of the former width is also computed to show the variation of IQA in Fig. 7b. Furthermore the IQA and variation of IQA of the two approaches are averaged and shown in Fig. 7c and d. To better show the trend of both algorithms, we plot the smoothed curve for average IQA with respect to image width. The smoothing functions for both algorithms are as bellows:

$$\begin{aligned} Liu's: \quad & y = 0.0672x - 0.0185 \\ Ours: \quad & y = 0.0107x^{1.8836} \end{aligned} \tag{7}$$

From Figs. 6 and 7 we can see that both our CAMs and Liu's results increase as the width of resized image reduces. It is consistent with the subjective observation. It means that the distance between resized image and the original image increase. The images at the third row have less visual distortion, and the corresponding CAMs and Liu's results are also smaller than other images under the same reduced width.

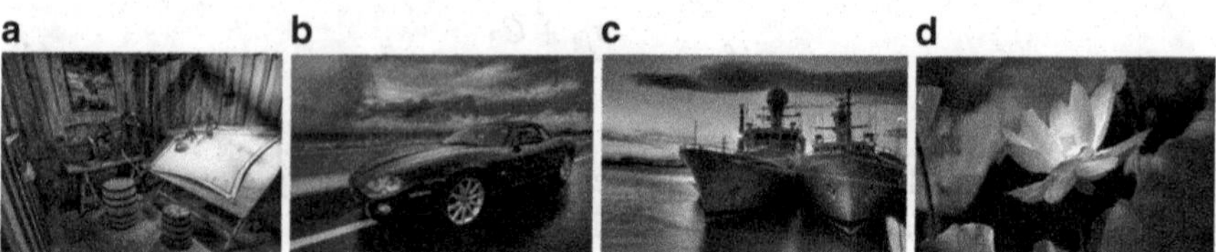

Fig. 5 Four original images

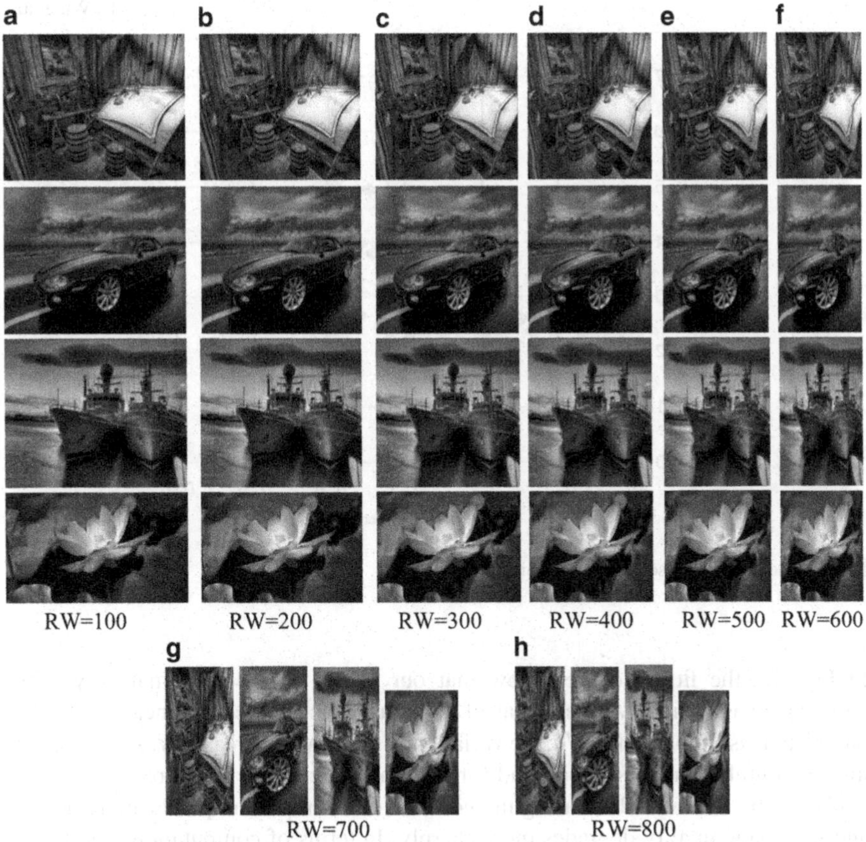

a b c d e f

RW=100 RW=200 RW=300 RW=400 RW=500 RW=600

g h

RW=700 RW=800

Fig. 6 Resized images of Fig. 5 with reduced width (RW)

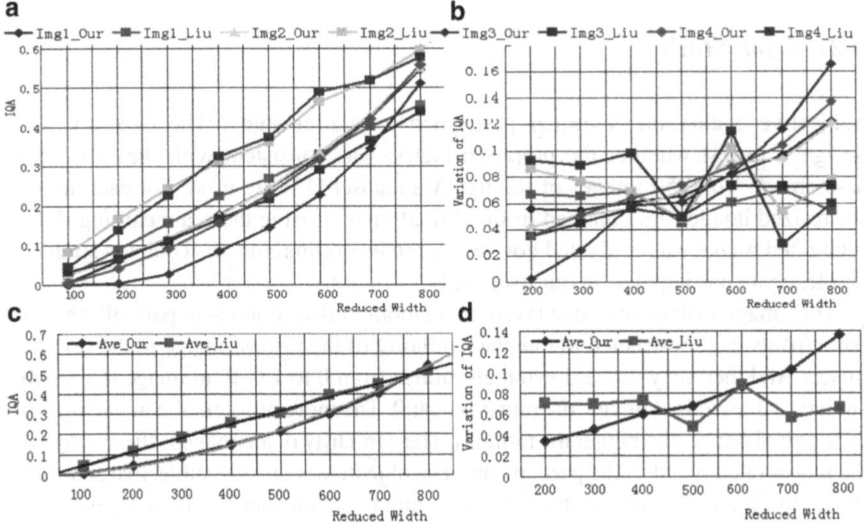

Fig. 7 IQAs of Fig. 6 using Liu's and our CAM

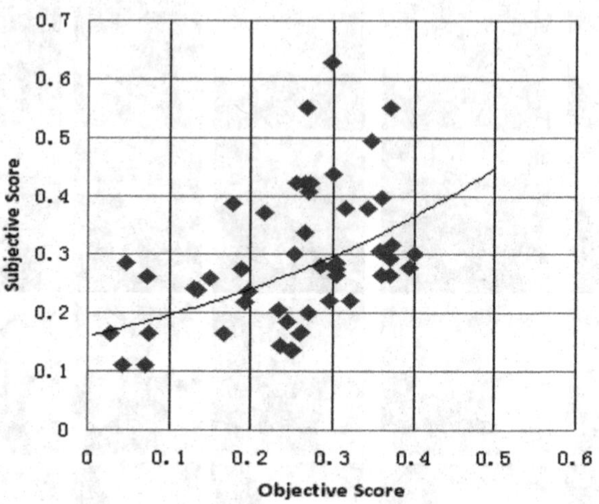

Fig. 8 The subjective score vs. the objective score

In Fig. 7c, the fitting curves show that our CAM increases dramatically with reducing image width whereas that of Liu's approach increases linearly. On the other hand, as shown in Fig. 7d, the variation of our CAM increases with decreasing image width but there is not a trend for Liu's approach. The above results may be explained by that with decreasing image width more important pixels are removed and the image quality degrades more sharply. In terms of computation efficiency, Liu's approach takes 5 ~ 10 times more computation time than our approach.

4.2 User Study

Subjective evaluation is further performed by a user study. The experiment is designed to test whether the proposed metric was consistent with the subjective assessment. Total 50 images of RetargetMe dataset [12] are used. For each image the resized images are obtained from original images using the seam carving. Each retargeted image was evaluated how similar to its original image. Total ten students and teachers participated in our user study.

The image pairs were displayed in random order. For each pair of images, participants were instructed to rate the similarity of the resized image to the original image. And then they wrote down their ratings from 0 to 1.0, if an image is visually similar to the original image, the rating is near 0. The more different the image is from the original image, the bigger the rating is. The similarity of an image is the average of the scores rated by all of the participants. The objective score and subjective score are shown in Fig. 8. We can see that the data is fitted with an exponential function.

5 Conclusions and Future Work

In this paper we have proposed an image quality assessment approach to resized image. SSIM is one of the successful metrics of image quality assessment. We firstly analyze how image resizing influences different components of SSIM by experiment. And we find the structure similarity is most important in image resizing. Furthermore, we extract important sub images and define CAM based on structural component of SSIM to measure the distance between the resized image and the original image. The experimental results show that CAM increases sharply with decreasing image width, which is consistent with human perception of images. Our approach can be used to assess performance of seam carving.

Acknowledgments This work was supported by the National Natural Science Foundation of China (Grant No. 60833006 and 60905008 and 61040052),and 973 Program (Project No. 2010CB327905).

References

1. Hae Jong Seo,Peyman Milanfar. Visual saliency for automatic target detection, boundary detection, and image quality assessment. Proc of SPIE vol. 7744, 77440 C-1–6.
2. Fei Gao,Xinbo Gao,Wen Lu,et. An Image Quality Assessment Metric with No Reference Using Hidden Markov Tree Model, Proc of SPIE. Vol. 7744,77440 C-1–8.
3. MARMOLIN H. Subjective MSE measures. IEEE Trans. on Systems, Man, and Cybernetics 16, 3 (1986), 486–489.
4. ESKICIOGLU A., FISHRE P. Image quality measures and their performance. IEEE Trans. on Communications 43, 12 (1995), 2959–2965.
5. WATSON A., SOLOMON J. Model of visual contrast gain control and pattern masking. Journal of the Optical Society of America A 14, 9 (1997), 2379–2391.
6. Z. Wang, A. C. Bovik, H. R. Sheikh, and E. P. Simoncelli. Image quality assessment: From error visibility to structural similarity. IEEE Transaction on Image Processing, 2004, 13 (4):600–612
7. Yong-Jin Liu, Xi Luo, Yu-Ming Xuan, Wen-Feng Chen, Xiao-Lan Fu, “Image Retargeting Quality Assessment,” In Eurographics 2011.
8. LOWE D.: Distinctive image features from scaleinvariant keypoints. International Journal of Computer Vision 60, 2 (2004), 91–110.
9. M. Rubinstein, A. Shamir, and S. Avidan, “Improved Seam Carving for Video Retargeting”. ACM Transactions on Graphics (TOG), 27, 3, Los Angeles, California: 1–9, 2008.
10. L Itti A saliency-based search mechanism for overt and covert shifts of visual attention. Vision Research, Vol 40, Issues 10–12, June 2000, Pages 1489–1506
11. Goferman, S., Zelnik-Manor, L., AND TAL, A. 2010. Context-aware saliency detection. IEEE Computer Vision and Pattern Recognition (CVPR) 2010 (ORAL), 2376–2383.
12. Rubstein, M., Gutierrez, D., Sorkine, O., AND Shamir, A. 2010. A comparative study of image retargeting. ACM Transaction Graphics 29, 6 (Dec.).

A Comprehensive Approach to Automatic Image Browsing for Small Display Devices

Muhammad Abul Hasan, Min Xu, and Xiangjian He

Abstract Recently, small displays are widely used to browse digital images. While using a small display device, the content of the image appears very small. Users have to use manual zooming and panning in order to see the detail of the image on a small display. Hence, an automatic image browsing solution is desired for user convenience. In this chapter, a novel comprehensive and efficient system is proposed to browse high resolution images using small display devices by automatically panning and zooming on Region-of-Interests (ROIs). The challenge is to provide a better user experience on heterogeneous small display sizes. First of all, an input image is classified into one of the three different classes: close-up, landscape and other. Then the ROIs of image are extracted. Finally, ROIs are browsed based on different intuitive and study based strategies. Our proposed system is evaluated by subjective test. Experimental results indicate that the proposed system is an effective large image displaying technique on small display devices.

Key words Visual attention • Image adaptation • Image browsing • Small display

M.A. Hasan • X. He
Centre for Innovation in IT Services and Applications (iNEXT),
University of Technology, Sydney, Australia
e-mail: Muhammad.Hasan@uts.edu.au; Xiangjian.He@uts.edu.au

M. Xu (✉)
Centre for Innovation in IT Services and Applications (iNEXT),
University of Technology, Sydney, Australia

Institute of Automation, Chinese Academy of Sciences National Laboratory of Pattern Recognition, China
e-mail: Min.Xu@uts.edu.au

J.S. Jin et al., *The Era of Interactive Media*,
DOI 10.1007/978-1-4614-3501-3_22,

1 Introduction

Advancements in small display technologies in recent years make it possible to develop many interactive multifunctional small electronic devices, such as mobile phones, iPod, PDAs, etc. The progress of development of these devices continues at a tremendous rate. Displaying a high resolution image on small display devices do not usually gives a detailed idea about the view content. People often put a lot of efforts by zooming and panning manually to view high resolution images. Manual effort is not convenient, so an automatic browsing solution is desired. A method described in [3] provides a detailed explanation of optimum browsing path generation based on information foraging theory. However, it does not provide technical details about extracting ROIs form images. In [4], Liu et al. propose another work based on attention analysis to browse large image on small display. The technique works fine with well focused objects. However, it fails to address wide variety of images. Moreover, the browsing technique has limitation to provide a smooth viewing effect. In our previous work [5], we propose a generic automatic image browsing technique for small display users. Although the proposed method works fine with images containing faces or images with medium depth, it does not provide good browsing effect for close-up and landscape images.

The amount of viewing content of a particular scene depends on the viewing distance. In a close up image, view plane contains small amount of information. On the other hand, total amount of information on landscape image is huge. Figure 1 shows the relationship between distance from eye position and size of field of view. When the view plane is far from the eye position, then the amount of visual

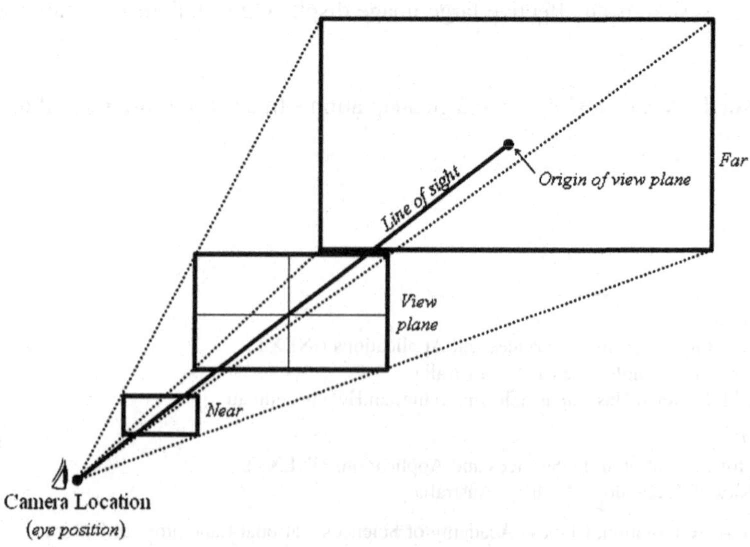

Fig. 1 Relationship between distance from camera location and field of view

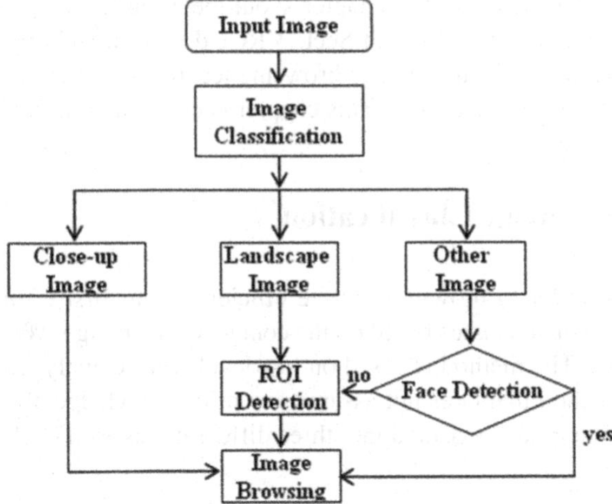

Fig. 2 Flow diagram of the proposed method

information is much greater than the near view plane. Information content of view plane increases proportionally with the increasing distance from the eyes position. The human eye movement behavior changes with the increasing contents of view planes. In case of looking at a scene carefully, human usually looks at a salient locations. The attention directs from one location to another location [1]. This behaviour is called fixation behaviour. Fixations are the brief pauses during the eye browsing process over multiple ROIs [2]. There are two attributes involved in measuring fixation: the fixation duration, and number of fixations. Fixation duration is the time that is used to observe the local region of the visual field and number of fixations is number of local regions to be observed. Longer fixation means more time used to observe a region to interpret its spatial representation. Higher number of fixations implies more number of attention regions present in the visual field and more information required to process a given task efficiently. Thus, an attention object is represented by four parameters: Region-of-Interest (ROI), attention value (AV), minimal perceptible size (MPS) and minimal perceptible time (MPT).

Based on the above discussion, we propose a comprehensive automatic method to browse images on heterogeneous size small displays as shown in Fig. 2. Since there are different categories of photography, one single browsing technique may not be sufficient to address browsing efficiently. Thus, we introduce a set of browsing techniques suitable for different types of images. The main contribution of this work is described as follows. The number of ROIs varies significantly with the increasing distance from camera. Human viewing behaviour also varies a lot with the increasing amount of viewing contents. Therefore, a generic viewing scheme may not be applicable for image browsing. Considering this issue, images are classified into *close-up*, *landscape* and *others* class. We propose a different ROI detection scheme and a browsing scheme for each of the image classes. Compared to our previous work [5], this method is more effective to handle any types of images.

The rest of this chapter's outline is as follows. Section 2 describes image classification. Then, in Sect. 3 ROI detection techniques are described. Section 4 describes the new image browsing techniques. Finally in Sect. 5, system evaluation results are discussed. This chapter is concluded in Sect. 6.

2 Image Classification

In order to browse a picture efficiently, our first effort is to classify images into pertinent classes based on the content of the image. We adapt a method described in [6]. The method is based on low level feature analysis. They propose an automatic method that does not assume any prior knowledge about the image. Primarily, the images are classified into three different classes, i.e. close-up, landscape and other.

2.1 Close-Up Image

Close-up is a type of photography technique which tightly frames an object or a person. It usually displays most detail of the object and does not include broader scene. This type of photography is usually taken by going close to the objects or by zooming in the objects with the help of photographic lenses. Object may consist of several integrated segments. However, all of the segments are coherent to each other. Separation of one section from rest of the parts does not convey the real meaning most of the time. In that sense, total image is considered as one single ROI to preserve the integrity of the image. Thus, this class of images does not need to be browsed on a given input image. Instead of that, full image is displayed on the screen adapted to the viewing screen.

2.2 Landscape Image

Landscape photos are a type of photography and represent different locations of the world representing the vastness and containing huge amount of natural/artificial elements. Each landscape photo usually does not focus on a specific object. It shows wide panorama and contains huge amount of information. Our ROI detection and browsing strategy for landscape images is based on saliency map calculation as described in Sect. 3.1.

2.3 Other Image

Images which fall neither in landscape images nor in close-up images are considered as other images. Significant ratios of pictures which are taken everyday belong to this class. In this type of images, the depth is not as high as landscape images. Contained objects are needed to be closely observed on small screen for better understanding. To do so, objects are extracted efficiently. According to our observation, human face dominates other class images. For a given other image, first step is to check human face occurrence on the image. If any face is found, then the face is considered as an ROI of the image. Otherwise, objects/salient regions in the image are extracted based on saliency measure. The ROI extraction procedure is described in Sect. 3.2. Finally, ROIs are browsed based on saliency values.

3 ROI Detection

As mentioned, close-up images consist of objects which are tightly fit in the frame. Thus, this kind of images is considered to have one ROI, which is the whole image. Therefore, the input image does not need to be browsed. Instead of that, the whole image is displayed on the viewing screen. For the other two classes of images, ROIs are detected. In the following sub-sections, *landscape* and *other image* ROI detection techniques are described.

3.1 ROI Detection in a Landscape Image

Landscape images provide detail scenic beauty of a natural scene and most of the contents of the images appear sharply focused. As the distance of the view plane is far from camera, the amount of visual information is much higher than the other images. For landscape images, we propose a ROI detection and browsing strategy using saliency map. To model biologically-plausible saliency architecture, Itti and Koch [7] propose a method to explain human visual search strategies. The framework provides an extremely parallel method to select a small number of interesting image locations from the total image. In our system, we adopt this method to calculate saliency maps of the landscape images. The computed saliency value of each pixel $S(x, y)$ represents the eye catching property belong to that pixel. The most eye-catching locations on the image are identified by higher salient values. Therefore, using saliency maps, it is possible to identify the locations of the salient objects effectively. However, it is not easy to segment objects precisely from landscape images. Landscape images present a huge amount of information on the view plane. In a landscape image, it is more important to identify the salient object locations rather than precisely segmenting the objects. To detect a salient regions from saliency map, all the local maximum are identified using a 7×7 pixel grid. Each local maximum is defined as SR_i of the corresponding image. SR_i with low saliencies should not be included in browsing steps. Thus, regions with low saliencies are eliminated using $S(SR_i^x, SR_i^y) > t$. Here, SR_i^x, SR_i^y represent x and y coordinates respectively, and t is the threshold value. In our system, we use $t = 0.5$.

Each location which satisfies this condition is considered as ROI. The size of ROI is determined by subjective evaluation. It is found that, to understand the region contents preserving the semantics, one third of the total image is desired to establish ROIs centering at (SR_i^x, SR_i^y). Landscape images contain larger number of fixations. Thus, the fixation duration for each location is low.

3.2 ROI Detection in an Other Image

In our daily life, most amateur photographers capture photo of their near and dear ones. These photos mostly contain human faces. It is a general interest to have a close look to the faces of the images rather than background objects. Thus, in our system, the faces of the images are considered as ROIs. Apart from that, images, which do not contain any face, usually contain some objects, animals, activities etc. In that case, only the focused objects are considered as ROIs. To detect ROIs, we adopt a method from our previous work which is proposed in [5]. In this method, a general ROI detection technique is proposed. The proposed method is suitable for detecting ROIs from medium depth image. In this method, first step is to check if there is any face occurred in the image. If any face is found then face browsing scheme is activated. For rest of the image, a graph based image segmentation technique is applied to measure saliency of a specific region $SS(i)$. Here i is location index. Based on the computed saliency, regions are browsed based on image browsing strategies.

4 Image Browsing

We propose class dependent image browsing techniques for different image classes. Using the identified ROIs, a well defined path is set for the purpose of smooth browsing. A browsing path p is defined as a set of successive n path segments. Figure 3 shows an example of a path segment and associated properties. We adopt path browsing technique described in our previous work [5].

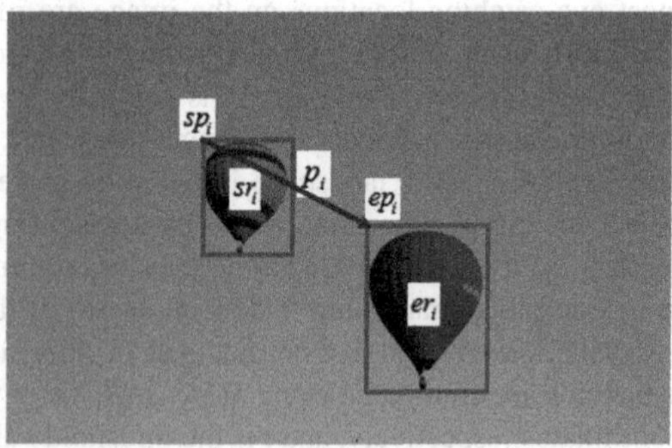

Fig. 3 Example of image browsing path segment p_i. Here sp_i is starting point of path segment i. ep_i is ending point of path segment i. sr_i is starting resolution of path segment i. er_i is ending resolution of path segment i

The transition from one ROI to another ROI has to be smooth. In order to do so, we apply panning, zooming or combination of both at the same time. Moreover, starting and ending resolutions are adjusted by gradually changing in the course of the browsing path segment. For more detail, readers are advised to go through the paper mentioned above.

Image browsing strategy is very important for efficiency reason. For landscape images, images with faces and images without faces, we propose different browsing strategies for comfortable viewing. For landscape image, the browsing starts using on saliency value. In order to avoid random effect, our system adapts the following strategy.

- Step 1. Display the most salient region.
- Step 2. Find the nearest salient region to browse.
- Step 3. Go to step 2 until all the ROIs are browsed.

For face detection scheme on other image, we take the following browsing strategy.

- Step 1. Display the most left and bottom face.
- Step 2. Find the nearest face to browse.
- Step 3. Go to step 2 until all the faces are browsed.

For an Other Image without faces, ROIs are browsed based on the saliency value. As we consider size, contrast and saliency for each region, highest visually important regions are visited first. Thus, the strategy is as follows.

- Step 1. Display the most salient region.
- Step 2. Browse rest of the regions according to saliency values.

Figure 4 shows examples of salient region extraction and image browsing path generation. Minimum perceptible time depends on image class. In our system, we assign 100 ms to landscape images and 500 ms to other images.

5 System Evaluation

We develop a prototype system to evaluate our proposed method. The system takes an image as input and produce a video as output. The output video contains the ROIs in a sequence. To evaluate the performance of our system, a subjective evaluation session has been arrange. As close up images contains only one ROI, the whole image is displayed in the output. Therefore, close up images are not included in the subjective evaluation. There are nine output videos presented in front of ten non-professional image evaluators (three videos from each category) to reflect their viewing experience. Three evaluating questions are as follows. (1) How do you evaluate the content regions of the output? (2) How is the generated browsing path? (3) How do you define your viewing experience? To mark viewer's

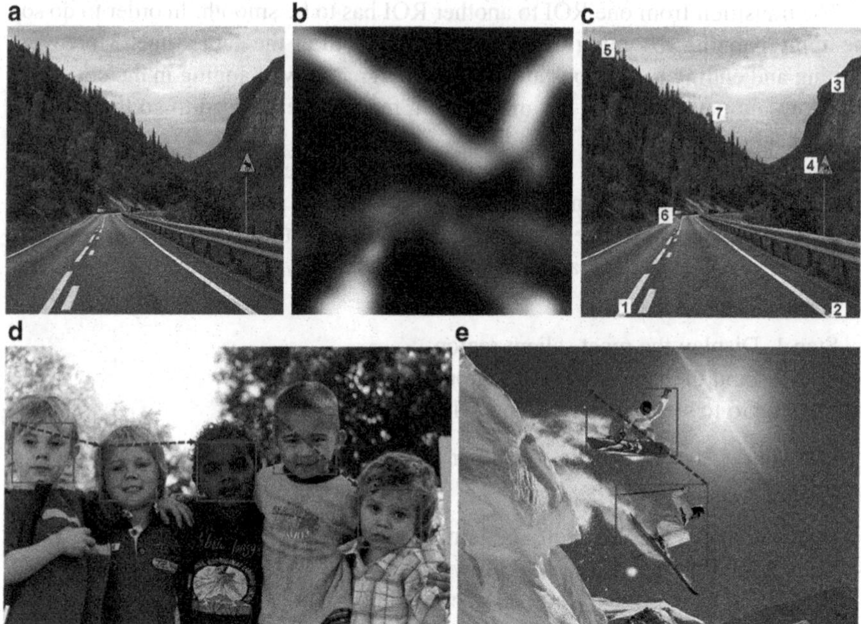

Fig. 4 Image browsing. (**a**) a landscape image (**b**) saliency map of the image (**c**) most salient location in order (**d**) face image browsing path (**e**) non face other image browsing path

Table 1 Subjective evaluation results of question 1

Image class	Average (%)	Good (%)	Excellent (%)
Landscape	6.67	13.33	80.00
Other (with face)	3.33	10.00	86.67
Other (without face)	13.33	13.33	73.33
Average	7.77	12.22	80.00

Table 2 Subjective evaluation results of question 2

Image class	Average (%)	Good (%)	Excellent (%)
Landscape	0.0	6.67	93.33
Other (with face)	0.0	3.33	96.67
Other (without face)	0.0	16.67	83.33
Average	0.0	8.89	91.11

responses there are three levels given in the response sheet: average, good and excellent. Tables 1–3 show summary of subjective evaluation results.

To summarize the subjective evaluation results, we find that 80.00% of the subjects supports that the ROIs of landscape images are true representatives of the given images, while only around 8% subjects think that more representative RIOs should be included in the output. For images which contain faces, subjects are

Table 3 Subjective evaluation results of question 3

Image class	Average (%)	Good (%)	Excellent (%)
Landscape	0.0	13.33	86.66
Other (with face)	0.0	10.00	90.00
Other (without face)	0.0	13.33	86.67
Average	0.0	13.33	86.67

more satisfied. Approximately 87% responses reflect that the displayed ROIs best describe the given images. Approximately 27% subjects expect more representative RIOs should be included along the automated browsing paths. For the second and third questions, it is found that the viewer's reaction to the presented outputs is encouraging. None of the subjective reaction goes bellow good scale. While 91% and 87% have voted "excellent" for question 2 and question 3 respectively.

6 Conclusion

A comprehensive image browsing technique is proposed to facilitate small display users. At the beginning, an image is classified into one of the three pre-defined classes based on the distance of the focused object from the camera. Then, ROIs are extracted and efficient browsing schemes are applied. According to subjective evaluation, it can be concluded that the automatic image browsing technique is a desired tool for users. As manual browsing requires significant amount of human intervention and automatic method for image browsing can be a promising aid to observe the detail of the image captured by small display devices.

Acknowledgements This research is supported by UTS Early Career Research Grant and National Natural Science Foundation of China No. 61003161.

References

1. M.I. Posner: Orientation of attention, Quarterly Journal of Experimental Psychology, vol. 32 (1), pp. 3–25, 1980.
2. J.H. Goldberg, X.P. Kotval: Eye movement-based evaluation of the computer interface, In S. K. Kumar (Ed.), advances in occupational ergonomics and safety, pp. 529–532, ISO press, 1998.
3. H. Liu, X. Xie, W.Y. Ma, H.J. Zhang: Automatic browsing of large pictures on mobile devices, in ACM International Conference on Multimedia, Barkeley, 2003.
4. H. Liu, S. Jiang, Q. Huang, C. Xu, W. Gao: Regionbased visual attention analysis with its application in image browsing on small displays, In proceedings of the 15th international conference on Multimedia, pp. 305–308, 2007.
5. M. A. Hasan, C. Kim: An automatic image browsing technique for small display users, In proceedings of the 11th International Conference on Advanced Communication Technology, pp 2044–2049, vol. 3, 2009.

6. R. Schettini, C. Brambilla, C. Cusano, G. Ciocca: Automatic classification of digital photographs based on decision forests, IJPRAI vol. 18(5), pp. 819–846, 2004.
7. L. Itti, C. Koch: A model of saliency based visual attention of rapid scene analysis, IEEE Trans. on PAMI, vol. 20, pp.1254–1259, 1998.
8. R. Lienhart, J. Maydt: An extended set of haar-like features for rapid object detection, In proceedings of IEEE ICIP 2002, vol. 1, pp. 900–903, Sep. 2002.
9. P. F. Felzenszwalb, D. P. Huttenlocher: Efficient graph based image segmentation, International Journal of Computer Vision, vol. 59(2), pp. 167–181, 2004.
10. J.V. Weijer, T. Gevers, A. Bagdanov: Boosting color saliency in image feature detection, IEEE Transaction on PAMI, vol. 28(1), pp. 150–156, 2006.
11. C. Harris, M. Stephens: A combined corner and edge detector, In proceedings of 4th Alvey Visual Conference, UK, 1988.

Coarse-to-Fine Dissolve Detection Based on Image Quality Assessment

Weigang Zhang, Chunxi Liu, Qingming Huang, Shuqiang Jiang, and Wen Gao

Abstract Although many approaches have been proposed for video shot boundary detection, dissolve detection remains an open issue. For a dissolve, we could find that the video frames reveal a "clarity–blur–clarity" visual pattern. Accordingly, the image quality in the dissolve also reveals a "high–low–high" pattern. Based on the above observation, in this paper a novel coarse-to-fine dissolve detection approach based on image quality assessment is presented. Firstly, the normalized variance autofocus function is employed to calculate the image quality value for its

W. Zhang (✉)
School of Computer Science and Technology, Harbin Institute of Technology, Harbin 150001, China

School of Computer Science and Technology, Harbin Institute of Technology at Weihai, Weihai 264209, China
e-mail: wgzhang@jdl.ac.cn

C. Liu
Graduate University of Chinese Academy of Sciences, Beijing 100190, China
e-mail: cxliu@jdl.ac.cn

Q. Huang
Graduate University of Chinese Academy of Sciences, Beijing 100190, China

Institute of Computing Technology, Chinese Academy of Sciences, Beijing 100190, China
e-mail: qmhuang@jdl.ac.cn

S. Jiang
Institute of Computing Technology, Chinese Academy of Sciences, Beijing 100190, China
e-mail: sqjiang@jdl.ac.cn

W. Gao
School of Computer Science and Technology, Harbin Institute of Technology, Harbin 150001, China

Institute of Digital Media, Peking University, Beijing 100871, China
e-mail: wgao@jdl.ac.cn

J.S. Jin et al., *The Era of Interactive Media*,
DOI 10.1007/978-1-4614-3501-3_23,

good performance and the image quality feature curve is obtained. The grooves on the curve, which are monotone decreasing to a local minimum and then are monotone increasing to a normal value, are detected by using a simple threshold-based method and deemed as dissolve candidates. After obtaining the coarse results, some refined features are extracted from these dissolve candidates and the final dissolve detection is accomplished with the help of the support vector machine based on a new dissolve length normalization method. The experimental results show that the proposed method is effective.

Keywords Dissolve detection • Coarse-to-fine • Image quality assessment • Dissolve length normalization • Shot boundary detection

1 Introduction

The last decade has witnessed the great advance of multimedia technology, the fast increase of the computer performance, and the significant improvement of the Internet, which led to the mass production and easily accessible of digital videos all over the world. However, when facing this huge amount of video information it is not easy for users to find their interested content. Therefore, there is a high demand for video content management techniques, including efficient video indexing, browsing and retrieving, etc. In the past few years, video content analysis attracted extensive attention of the researchers and many technical papers have been published. Among these video processing technologies, partitioning a video sequence into shots is deemed as the first step toward video-content analysis and content-based video browsing and retrieval [1]. A shot is a series of interrelated consecutive pictures taken contiguously by a single camera and representing a continuous action in time and space. Usually, a video consists of a series of shots.

Generally speaking, there are two kinds of transition from one shot to another, which are hard cut and gradual transition. A hard cut is an instantaneous transition from one shot to the next. There are no transitional frames between the two consecutive shots. For the gradual transition, a video transition effect is added between the two consecutive shots to improve the visual experience. There are many gradual transition types including dissolve, wipe, fade out/in, etc. Among them, dissolve is the most popular gradual transition type. Dissolve is the video effect that the content of the first shot gradually disappears while the content of the second one becomes more and more visible, just like the video frames shown in Fig. 1. Compared with the gradual transition detection, cut detection is relatively easy. Most of the presented techniques for cut detection could perform well and have a good precision [2]. However, for gradual shot transition, the more complex representations of the video content in the transitions bring the more trouble.

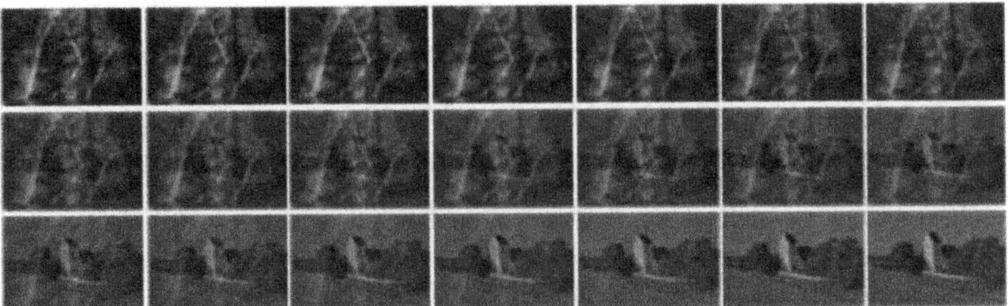

Fig. 1 A dissolve transition example

We mainly focus on detecting the most popular gradual transition type—dissolve. During the past few years, some algorithms have been proposed for dissolve detection. R. Lienhart [3] adopted several features, including edge change ratio (ECR) and edge-based contrast (EC), and applied some threshold selection strategies to detect dissolves. Su et al. [4] considered that object motion and camera motion are the main causes for error detection of dissolves. They built a nonlinear dissolve model and adopted the sliding window technology to improve the dissolve detection performance. Huang et al. [5] presented a dissolve detection approach based on contrast context histogram and local keypoint matching of video frames. B. Ionescu et al. [6] proposed a straightforward intensity-based dissolve method based on the amount of fading-out and fading-in pixels. Yuan et al. [7] conducted a formal study of the shot detection problem with a general formal framework, a comprehensive review of the existing approaches and a unified system based on graph partition model. Although many approaches have been proposed for dissolve detection, the reported results are not satisfactory. Until now, video dissolve transition is still an open issue.

In this paper, we attempt to detect the dissolve transition from the viewpoint of image quality assessment, and propose a coarse-to-fine approach for dissolve detection. In the coarse step, the image quality assessment based method is employed to detect the dissolve candidates. While in the fine step, the final dissolve detection is accomplished with the help of the Support Vector Machine (SVM). From Fig. 1 we can easily find which frame belongs to the dissolve. We carefully checked many dissolves and found that all the video frames in the dissolve are mixed with the same two clear frames. One is the last frame of the previous shot, the other the first frame of the subsequent shot. The frames between the transitions are fused and blurred, and according to the human vision system, the quality of these images is relative low. The middle frame of a dissolve is usually the most blurred and its quality is the lowest. The starting and ending frames of a dissolve are relative clear and have high visual quality. In summary, the video frames in a dissolve transition reveal a "clarity–blur–clarity" pattern. Correspondingly, the image quality of the dissolve reveals a "high–low–high" pattern. If a shot transition shows the similar pattern, it could be considered as a dissolve candidate. In order to adopt the image quality assessment to detect the dissolve candidates, the first step is to select an appropriate evaluating function for image quality. Based on the image quality values, we could adopt a simple threshold based method to detect the dissolve candidates. Then, some new refined features are extracted from the dissolve candidates based on a dissolve length normalization method, and the support vector machine (SVM) is implemented to get the final dissolve detection results. The main contribution of the paper can be summarized as follows:

(1) We propose to detect dissolve transition from the viewpoint of the image quality analysis.
(2) We propose a novel coarse-to-fine approach for dissolve detection.
(3) We propose a novel dissolve length normalization approach to deal with the variable length problem of the dissolve transition.

The rest of this paper is organized as follows. Section 2 presents the selection of the evaluating functions for image quality assessment; Sect. 3 provides the coarse-to-fine dissolve detection approach with SVM in detail; Sect. 4 discuses the experimental results; Sect. 5 concludes this paper.

2 Image Quality Assessment

The dissolve transition reveals a very clear visual pattern. If we can find a criterion by which could be indicated whether a frame belong to the dissolve or not, then the dissolve detection will become relatively easy. However, finding this criterion is as hard as dissolve detection. In this paper, instead of finding the ideal criterion, we try to measure the image quality of the video frames with the assumption that the image quality of the frames in a dissolve will be relatively low.

Actually, image quality assessment has been a hot research topic for a long time [8]. The situation we encounter is a typical no-reference image quality assessment problem. The dissolve reveals a "clarity–blur–clarity" pattern. In order to evaluate the image quality of the video frames, we adopt an autofocus function, which is used frequently for digital image blur measure. Autofocus functions are usually used to measure the focusing performance of micro-imaging systems. If the obtained images from these systems are blurred, they will output low values, which indicate that the quality of these images is low. Conversely, high autofocus function value indicates that the image is clear and the quality is high. As we known the frames in a dissolve transition show a "clarity–blur–clarity" pattern. Therefore, the autofocus function values should reveal a corresponding "high–low–high" quality pattern.

There are many autofocus functions available [9, 10], such as Brenner gradient, Tenenbaum gradient (Tenengrad), energy Laplace and normalized variance, etc. A. Santos et al. [9] made a lot of comparative experiments on 13 autofocus functions. According to their qualitative evaluation, relative (semiquantitative) evaluation and quantitative absolute evaluation, they draw the conclusion that among these autofocus functions the normalized variance could achieve good

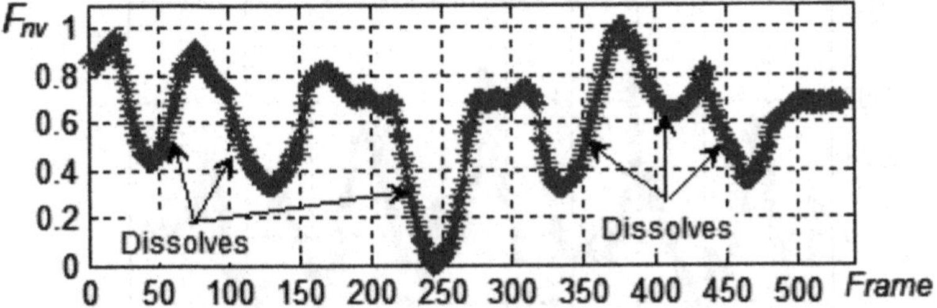

Fig. 2 The groove patterns on the normalized image quality curve of a short video clip which has six dissolves by using the normalized variance autofocus function

performance. Sun et al. [10] also made a comprehensive comparison study of 18 focus algorithms in which a total of 139,000 microscope images were analyzed. The experimental results show that the normalized variance function performs the best and is the optimal function to evaluate the blur of images. Therefore, we adopt it to calculate the quality value for each frame. The calculation of the normalized variance function is as below:

$$f(i) = \frac{1}{H \times W \times \mu_i} \sum_{x=1}^{W} \sum_{y=1}^{H} (I_i(x, y) - \mu_i)^2 \tag{1}$$

Where H and W are the height and width of the video frame respectively. $I_i(x, y)$ is the gray value of the pixel (x, y) in the grayscale of the original color video frame i. μ_i is the average gray value of the frame and is calculated as below:

$$\mu_i = \frac{1}{H \times W} \sum_{x=1}^{W} \sum_{y=1}^{H} I_i(x, y) \tag{2}$$

By using Eq. (1), a normalized image quality curve of a short video clip is shown in Fig. 2. This clip consists of six dissolves. From the figure, we could see that the groove patterns of these dissolves are rather clear.

3 Coarse-to-Fine Dissolve Detection

In this section, we describe the proposed coarse-to-fine approach for dissolve detection. In the coarse step, a threshold method based on image quality assessment is employed to detect the dissolve candidates. In the fine step, the final dissolve detection is accomplished with SVM.

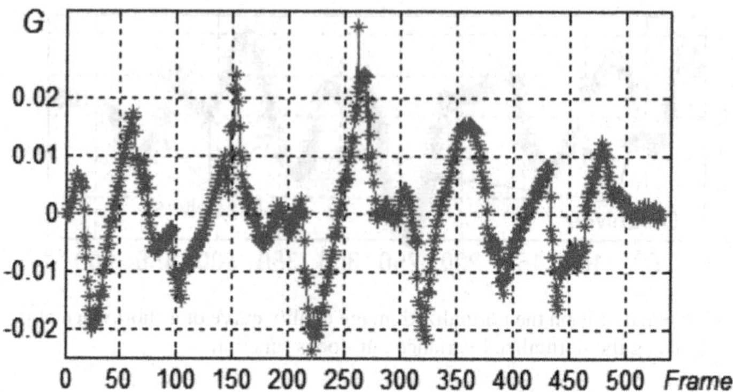

Fig. 3 The gradient curve based on the original image quality values

3.1 Dissolve Candidate Detection

Based on the normalized variance function we can obtain the image quality curve. In this section, we will detect the dissolve candidates based on the quality curve. As can be seen from Fig. 2, the image quality of different shot frames is not at the same level. Therefore, directly using a threshold to detect the dissolve is not feasible. In this section, we try to use the gradient of the normalized variance to normalize the image quality value. There are many way for gradient calculation. In the proposed method, the gradient calculation of the normalized variance is as follow:

$$\partial f(i)/\partial i = f(i+\beta) - f(i-\beta) \tag{3}$$

where $f(i)$ is calculated by Eq. (1). β is a parameter to amplify the gradient value and in this paper β is set as four according to experiments. Figure 3 shows the gradient curve of the image quality values in Fig. 2.

After gradient calculation, the dissolve groove pattern changes into another interesting pattern. The gradient value of the images in the same shot will become very small and near zero. However, for a dissolve the gradient value will first be smaller than zero. When the original normalized variance value reaches the minimum, the gradient value should be zero. After that, the gradient value increases and is bigger than zero. Thus, we use a heuristic method to detect the dissolve candidate patterns. First, two thresholds $\delta_1 > 0$ and $\delta_2 > 0$ are used to detect the gradient parts of dissolves. δ_1 and δ_2 are set small enough to catch all the dissolve patterns. Then, we label the curve into a step curve with -1, 0 and 1. The labeling rule is defined as below:

$$\begin{cases} D(i) = 1, & \partial f(i)/\partial i >= \delta_1; \\ D(i) = -1, & \partial f(i)/\partial i <= -\delta_2; \\ D(i) = 0, & \textit{otherwise}. \end{cases} \tag{4}$$

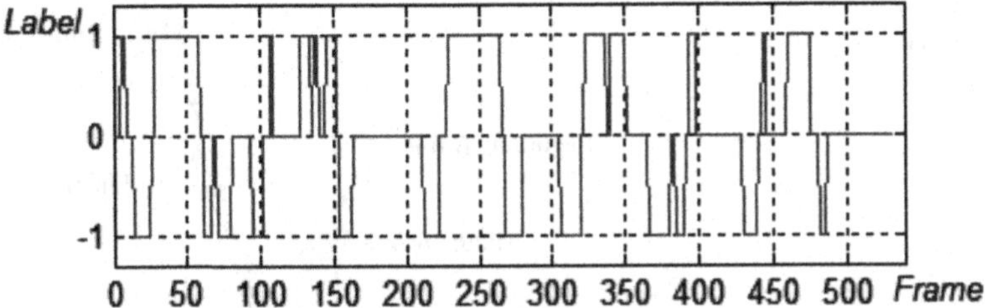

Fig. 4 The label step curve based on the gradient curve of the original image quality values

The label results of the curve in Fig. 3 are shown in Fig. 4. After labeling, we search through the curve along the original video timeline and merge the part whose value is below zero with another part whose value is above zero according to their distance in the timeline. By comparing Figs. 2 and 4 we could know that almost all the dissolve patterns will be detected by the above method. The obtained dissolve candidates will be further analyzed to achieve the final detection results.

3.2 *Dissolve Length Normalization*

In our view, one difficulty for dissolve detection is that the dissolve length is variable. On the other hand, many exiting machine-learning algorithms, such as the SVM, require the inputted features have the same length. Therefore, many methods utilize the multi-resolution approach [7], and build different models in different length scales to detect the dissolves. Another reason why they build so many models in different length scales is that there are no dissolve candidates in their approach and they have to slide different length windows along the timeline to detect the dissolves. Different from the existing dissolve detection approaches, we could obtain the dissolve candidates firstly. Then, a novel length normalization approach for dissolves could be employed to avoid the trouble of multi-scale modeling.

After obtaining the dissolve candidates, we can get the beginning and ending frame for each candidate. As described on above, the image quality in the dissolve reveals a “high–low–high” groove pattern, and there is a minimal image quality value in each dissolve. We propose to use the beginning, ending and minimal frame of the dissolve candidate to help normalizing the lengths of dissolve candidates. After obtaining these three frames, we extract two other frames. One is the middle frame of the beginning and the minimal frame; another is the middle frame of the minimal and ending frames of the dissolve. The length normalization rule is shown in Fig. 5. In all we use the extracted five frames to represent each dissolve and extract the refined features from these frames for further processing.

Fig. 5 The length normalization rule of dissolves

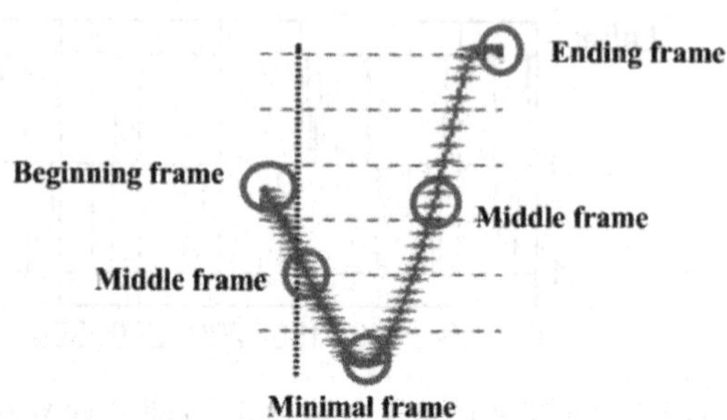

3.3 Dissolve Detection Based on SVM

After normalizing the dissolve candidates, we extract some new refined features from each candidate, including the HSV histogram distance (10 features) and the mutual information (10 features) among the five frames, the original image quality of the five frames (5 features), and the first order difference of the quality value (4 features). Totally 29 features are extracted. These features are extracted for the reason that they can reveal the special pattern of the dissolve and are useful for dissolve detection. The calculation of the histogram distance is as bellow:

$$D(X,Y) = \left(\sum_{b=1}^{B} |H_X(b) - H_Y(b)|^p \right)^{1/p} \tag{5}$$

where $H_X(b)$ and $H_Y(b)$ denote the bth bin value of the normalized HSV histograms of the X and Y frame in the selected five frames. B is the total bin number of the histograms. The calculation of the mutual information is as in Eq. (6). $Entropy(X)$ and $Entropy(Y)$ represent the entropy of frame X and Y respectively. $Entropy(X,Y)$ represents the joint entropy of frame X and Y.

$$\begin{aligned} MI(X,Y) &= Entropy(X) + Entropy(Y) - Entropy(X,Y) \\ Entropy(X) &= -\sum_{x \in A_X} P_X(x) \log P_X(x) \\ Entropy(Y) &= -\sum_{y \in A_Y} P_Y(y) \log P_Y(y) \\ Entropy(X,Y) &= -\sum_{x \in A_X, y \in A_Y} P_{XY}(x,y) \log P_{XY}(x,y) \end{aligned} \tag{6}$$

After obtaining these refined features, we fed them into the pre-trained SVM models to get the final dissolve detection results. SVM algorithm tries to classify different classes with the help of the support vector by maximizing the margin between these classes. It is a very effective method for classification. For more details about the SVM, refer to [11].

4 Experiments

Some videos in the TRECVID 2005 dataset are used to test the performance of the proposed method. Totally, there are eight news videos from different channels. The resolution of the videos is 352 × 240. Dissolve takes up 30.5% of the all transitions and 77.8% of the gradual transitions.

In order to show the normalized variance function is really better than other functions for image quality assessment, a qualitative experiment is designed. We presents the normalized image quality curves in Fig. 6, which are obtained by using other three autofocus functions such as Brenner gradient, Tenengrad and energy Laplace. From the figure, we could see that the Tenengrad curve does not reflect the groove pattern of the first dissolve and the Brenner gradient curve and energy Laplace curve both have a wrong groove pattern at the beginning. They may incur miss detection or wrong detection of dissolve. Furthermore, these curves have several glitches that will bring trouble to dissolve detection. In contrast, the normalized variance function is really a good choice for the image quality evaluation.

In the experiment, in order to not miss any dissolve transition, δ_1 and δ_2 in Eq. (4) are both set as 0.005 according to experience. The distance that controls the merging of two labeled parts in Fig. 4 is set as 20 frames. For SVM, the RBF kernel is selected for its good generality. We divide the video set into two sets. Four videos are for SVM model training and the other four for testing. We adopt the precision and recall to show the dissolve detection result.

After the threshold based dissolve candidate detection, nearly all of the right dissolves are detected. The reason is that the thresholds δ_1 and δ_2 are set small enough. In SVM model training, the percentage of the support vector is 30.7%, which means the extracted features are effective for dissolve detection. The final test precision is 73.3% and recall is 88.6%. The detection result for each test video is shown in Fig. 7.

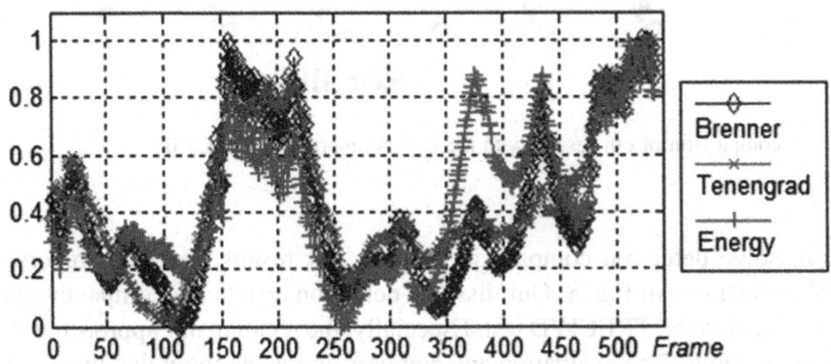

Fig. 6 The normalized image quality curves of Brenner gradient, Tenengrad and energy Laplace functions

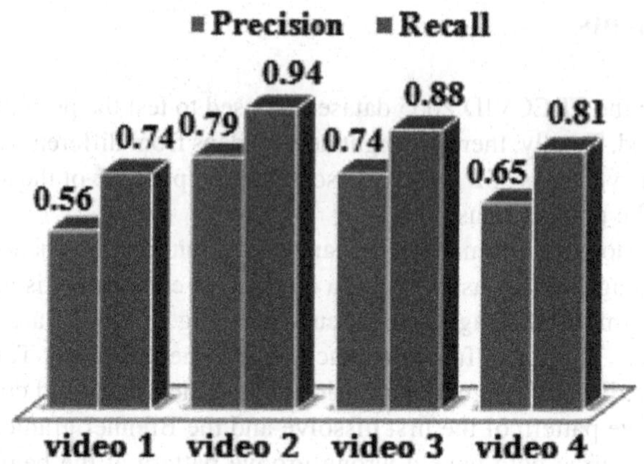

Fig. 7 The dissolve detection results of four videos

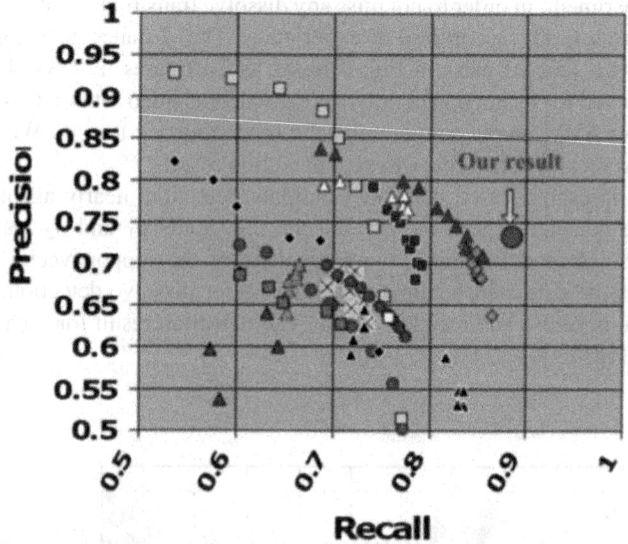

Fig. 8 The comparison of our results with the results reported in TRECVID

The dissolve detection comparison between our results and those reported in TRECVID is shown in Fig. 8. Our dissolve detection results are comparable to the results reported in the TRECIVD test. Especially, the recall in our approach is better than other methods. The evaluation and comparison results show that the proposed dissolve detection approach is effective.

5 Conclusions

In this paper, we try to detect dissolves from the viewpoint of image quality analysis and propose a novel coarse-to-fine framework for dissolve detection. In the coarse step, the dissolve candidates are detected with a simple threshold based method. In the fine step, the SVM is used to make the final detection decision. Because we detect dissolve candidates in advance, we can normalize the length of the dissolves easily. The experimental and comparison results show that the proposed method is effective and is comparable to the results reported in the TRECVID. In the future, we will further improve the proposed framework to get better results.

Acknowledgements This work was supported in part by National Natural Science Foundation of China: 61025011, 60833006 and 61070108, and in part by Beijing Natural Science Foundation: 4092042.

References

1. A. Hanjalic: Shot-Boundary Detection: Unraveled and Resolved?. IEEE Transactions on Circuits and Systems for Video Technology, vol. 12, no. 2. (2002)
2. http://www-nlpir.nist.gov
3. Rainer Lienhart: Reliable Transition Detection in Videos: A Survey and Practitioner's Guide. International Journal of Image and Graphics, 1(3):469–486 (2001)
4. Chih-Wen Su, Hong-Yuan Mark Liao, Hsiao-Rong Tyan, Kuo-Chin Fan, Liang-Hua Chen: A Motion-Tolerant Dissolve Detection Algorithm. IEEE Transactions on Multimedia, 7 (6):1106–1113 (2005)
5. Chun-Rong Huang, Huai-Ping Lee, Chu-Song Chen: Shot Change Detection via Local Keypoint Matching. IEEE Transactions on Multimedia, 10(6):1097–1108 (2008)
6. Bogdan Ionescu, Constantin Vertan, Patrick Lambert: Dissolve Detection in Abstract Video Contents. ICASSP 2011: 917- 920 (2011)
7. Jinhui Yuan, Huiyi Wang, Lan Xiao, Wujie Zheng, Jianmin Li, Fuzong Lin, Bo Zhang: A Formal Study of Shot Boundary Detection. IEEE Transactions on Circuits and Systems for Video Technology, 17(2): 168–186 (2007)
8. Zhou Wang, Bovik, A.C., Sheikh, H.R., Simoncelli, E.P.: Image Quality Assessment: from Error Visibility to Structural Similarity. IEEE Transactions on Image Processing, vol.13, no.4 (2004)
9. Santos A, Ortiz de Solórzano C, Vaquero JJ, Peña JM, Malpica N, del Pozo F: Evaluation of Autofocus Functions in Molecular Cytogenetic Analysis. Journal of Microscopy, 188, 264–72 (1997)
10. Sun Y, Duthaler S, Nelson BJ: Autofocusing in Computer Microscopy: Selecting the Optimal Focus Algorithm. Microscopy Research and Technique, 65(3), 139–149 (2004)
11. V. Vapnik: Statistical Learning Theory, Wiley. (1998)

Audio and Image Classification

Better Than MFCC Audio Classification Features

Ruben Gonzalez

Abstract Mel-Frequency Ceptral Coeffienents (MFCCs) are generally the features of choice for both audio classification and content-based retrieval due to their proven performance. This paper presents alternate feature sets that not only consistently outperform MFCC features but are simpler to calculate.

Keywords Audio classification • Content-based retrieval • Indexing • Spectral features • MFCC • Machine learning • k-NN classification • Musical instruments • Frog calls • Insect sounds • Speech and music discrimination • Acoustic event recognition

1 Introduction

Content-based retrieval is fundamentally a two-step task; salient features are first extracted from the data, which can be then used for class recognition via machine learning approaches. Effective audio content-based retrieval requires a robust feature set that can capture salient information in audio signals across a wide variety of audio classes. It also requires a robust method for classifying the audio based on the selected feature set. The most common classification methods used for this audio class recognition include Gaussian Mixture Models (GMM), K-Nearest Neighbour (k-NN), Neural Networks (NN), support vector machines (SVM), and Hidden Markov Models (HMM).

The choice of classification method has been shown to be largely insignificant. Arias [1] compared GMM and SVM to classify four audio classes (speech, music, applause, laughter) using features consisting of 8 MFCC features plus energy and their derivatives and found that performance was relatively comparable. Chu et al. [2]

R. Gonzalez (✉)
Institute for Intelligent Integrated Systems, Griffith University, School of Information and Communication Technology, Gold Coast, Australia

J.S. Jin et al., *The Era of Interactive Media*,
DOI 10.1007/978-1-4614-3501-3_24,

investigated the problem of correctly determining between one of five different classes of environmental sounds; Hallway, Café, Lobby, Elevator and Sidewalk using k-NN, GMM and SVN classifiers. While all three classifiers performed within 3 % of each other it was observed that, "the KNN classifier works well overall, outperforming GMM and is roughly 1,000 times faster than SVM." Peltonen [6] also found that overall k-NN performed better than GMM. Liu and Wan [7] found k-NN to outperform GMM in all cases. Lefèvre [3] also observed, "that the k-NN estimator outperforms the GMM estimator in identification tasks."

For reasons of efficiency and effectiveness, rather than operating directly on raw audio data, classification methods operate on an abstraction of the audio data expressed as a small feature set. The size of this feature set is known as its dimensionality. The objective in selecting these features is to capture properties of the underlying audio data that have statistical or psychological saliency. Sometimes as in the case of the MFCC, they also attempt to mimic psychological processes. The disadvantage of selecting any particular set of features is that any information that is not represented by them is automatically discarded.

Hence, while choice of classification method is relatively unimportant this is not the case with the choice of features for audio classification. A wide variety of features have been presented in the literature, being extracted from audio signals in either the temporal or frequency domains. Of these, the Mel-Frequency Cepstral features (MFCC), which are frequency transformed and logarithmically scaled, appear to be universally recognised as the most generally effective. The MFCC has been shown to outperform the MPEG7 features [4]. McKinney and Breebaart [5] evaluated four different feature sets comprising of the nine highest ranked individual features obtained from one of four methods including; (1) spectral and temporal features; (2) MFCC, (3) psychoacoustic features (roughness, loudness, sharpness, etc) and (4) features derived from the temporal envelopes from an auditory filterbank. This iterative ranking process ensured that each feature set was evaluated for its possible performance. While they found that for music genre recognition the temporal envelope features performed the best, for other classes of audio MFCC and spectral features performed better.

Peltonen [6] individually evaluated eleven types of time domain and frequency domain features including MFCC, band-energy ratios, LP-cepstra and LPC for a total of 26 different acoustic scenes using both kNN and GMM classifiers. He found that overall MFCC features outperformed the other features. Liu and Wan [7] evaluated a total of 58 different temporal and spectral features to classify 23 different musical instruments into five different classes (brass, keyboard, percussions, string and woodwind) using both k-NN and GMM. They found that temporal features alone gave the lowest performance, followed by spectral features alone and then MFCC features alone. The best performance was achieved when temporal, spectral and MFCC features were combined, followed closely by a combination of spectral and MFCC features.

This paper presents three alternate feature sets to the MFCC that are less computationally complex and superior in performance across a range of diverse datasets.

2 Audio Feature Extraction

This paper evaluates the performance of five different feature sets. The baseline feature set is comprised on only MFCC features. An enhanced MFCC (MFCC+) feature set adds spectral and temporal features to the MFCC. The three proposed feature sets include the Principle Spectral Coefficients (PSC), the Principle Cepstral Coefficients (PCC) and the Principle Spectral-Temporal Coefficients (PSTC).

Mel-frequency cepstral coefficients are calculated from the short-term Fourier Transform as the cepstrum of the mel-warped spectrum. The frequencies of the Fourier coefficients are remapped onto the mel scale using relationship (1) and octave-wide, triangular overlapping windows. Finally the cepstrum (2) is obtained using the remapped coefficients m(n).

$$Mel(f) = 2595 \log_{10}(1 + f/100) \tag{1}$$

$$c(k) = DCT\{\log|DFT\{m(n)\}|\} \tag{2}$$

The enhanced MFCC + dataset includes four common temporal features and six spectral features. The four c temporal features are the Zero Crossing Rate (ZCR), the root-mean-square (RMS) value, short-term energy (E), and energy flux (F). These are defined as follows:

$$ZCR = \sum_{k=2}^{K} |\text{sgn}(x(k)) - \text{sgn}(x(k-1))| \; \text{sgn}(n) = \begin{cases} 1, & n > 0 \\ 0, & n = 0 \\ -1, & n < 0 \end{cases} \tag{3}$$

$$E = \frac{1}{K}\left(\sum_{k=1}^{K} |X(k)|^2\right) \tag{4}$$

$$\text{F} = \text{E(n)} - \text{E(n} - 1) \tag{5}$$

The six spectral features used are the signal bandwidth (BW), spectral centroid (SC), and pitch (P) by means of subharmonic summation [8], pitch and harmonicity via Bregman's method [9] and the skew, which is the percentage of energy in the pitch relative to the harmonic partials.

$$BW = \sqrt{\left(\sum_{k=1}^{K} (k - SC)^2 |X(k)|^2\right) \Big/ \left(\sum_{k=1}^{K} |X(k)|^2\right)} \tag{6}$$

$$SC = \left(\sum_{k=1}^{K} k \times |X(k)|^2\right) \Big/ \left(\sum_{k=1}^{K} |X(k)|^2\right) \tag{7}$$

$$P = f : f >= 0 \wedge \forall g >= 0, H(f) >= H(g);$$

$$H(f) = \sum_{k=1}^{K} h_k X(k \cdot f) \tag{8}$$

Rather than just arbitrarily selecting features based on a subjective notion of saliency, it is possible from a statistical perspective to identify the principle components in any given data set. These principle components are guaranteed to optimally represent the underlying data for any number of components. Commonly either principle component analysis (PCA) or its equivalent Karhunen-Loeve (KL) transform can be used to obtain these components. In practice the KL transform is often approximated by means of the Discrete Cosine Transform (DCT). A statistically optimum feature set of the Principle Spectral Components (PSCs) can accordingly be obtained by taking the first few DCT coefficients of the spectrum obtained via a short-time Fourier transform (where || represents the complex magnitude):

$$PSC(k) = DCT\{|DFT\{x(n)\}|\} \tag{9}$$

A variation on the PSC that provides more even scaling of the feature set by whitening the spectrum is to use the Principle Cepstral Components (PCCs):

$$PCC(k) = DCT\{\log|DFT\{x(n)\}|\} \tag{10}$$

As the PSC and PCC methods are formed from a one-dimensional spectrum they are unable to capture the evolution of the spectrum over time. The temporal characteristics of sounds are known to be important for identifying some classes of audio. Accordingly the PSTC feature set captures the principle information contained in the time-frequency distribution of energy in the audio signals. This feature set is obtained by taking a two-dimensional Discrete Cosine Transform (DCT) of the audio signal's spectrogram.

3 Data Sets

To evaluate the performance of the proposed audio classification features five widely differing datasets were used.

The 'Four Audio' dataset consisted of 415 separate recordings of speech (71), music (197), applause (85) and laughter (62). These were obtained from various sources including recordings, live performances, and broadcast media. These were all of 2.5 s in duration and sampled at 44.1 kHz and 16 bits.

The 'Frog Calls' dataset consisted of 1,629 recordings of 74 different species of native Australian frog calls [10]. They were sampled at 22.05 kHz and 16 bits and were each of 250 ms in duration.

The "Insect" dataset consisted of recordings of the sounds made by 381 different species of insects and were categorised according to the four following families: Katydid, Cricket, Cicada, and others. These were all 5 s in duration and sampled at 44.1 kHz and 16 bits.

The "Musical Instruments" dataset consisted of 1,345 recordings of 97 different musical instruments [11]. These were categories into one of twelve different classes: piano, harpsichord, plucked string, bowed string, woodwind, brass, organ, tympani, metallic tuned percussive, wooden tuned percussive, non-tuned percussive, and others. These were all sampled at 44.1 kHz and 16 bits and were each of 500 ms in duration

The "Environmental" sounds dataset consisted of 205 recordings of a 20 classes of environmental sounds including: sirens, chimes, music, insect noises, ambient outdoor (wind, rain etc), storm, thunder, ambient office sounds, animal sounds, screams, laughter, car engines, traffic, power tools, explosions and gunshots. These were sampled at 11 kHz and 16 bits and were each of 500 ms in duration.

4 Experiments

For each given dataset, feature vectors of varying size ranging from 8 to 96 dimensions were formed as the first N features from each of the five feature sets. These vectors were then evaluated using a k-NN classifier (k = 1) using ten-fold cross validation.

Since most of the features used in the experiments were obtained via the short-time Fourier transform it was necessary to first determine the optimal window size. To do this the classifier was trained with features extracted from Fourier spectra at various window sizes. This was performed for all data sets and all feature sets. For the Four Audio, Frog Call, and Insect datasets the best results for all feature sets were obtained using the largest window size, being 1,024 samples. With the exception of the PSTC features, the best performance for all feature sets using the Instruments and Environmental datasets was achieved using a 512-sample window.

In the case of the PSTC features, the analysis window size was 256 samples for the Instruments dataset and 128 samples for the Environmental sounds dataset. The reason for this is that the number of vectors required for training puts downward pressure on the number of samples available from which to form each training vector. This results in a tradeoff between forming features that provide better spectral or temporal resolution. In the case of the Instruments and Environmental datasets, increased temporal resolution provided better performance.

To ensure that the classifier was equally trained in all cases, for any given dataset exactly the same number of samples were used in forming the training vectors for all of the feature sets. To ensure that performance of the feature sets was

Table 1 Feature set normalised error rate for the four audio dataset

	Dimensions (Feature set size)								
Features	8	16	18	26	32	42	64	74	96
PSC	0.297	0.219			0.183		0.129		0.121
PCC	0.245	0.170			0.144		0.119		0.116
MFCC	0.307	0.223	0.220		0.205		0.164		
MFCC+			0.215	0.168		0.161		0.145	
PSTC	0.135	0.121			0.100		0.094		0. 094

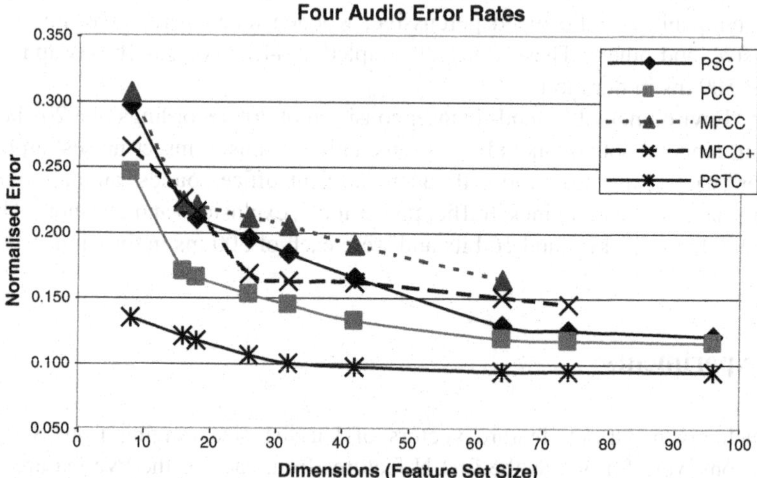

Fig. 1 Feature set normalised error rate for the four audio dataset

independent of the number of training vectors, the optimal number of training vectors for each feature set and data set was first determined. This was undertaken by extracting multiple vectors sequentially with no overlap from each recording. In all cases the best performance was obtained when the classifier was trained with the maximum amount of training vectors that could be extracted from the datasets, which was the same for all feature sets with the exception of the PSTC features.

For the "Four Audio" dataset the best performance was obtained using 100 training vectors for each recording for all feature sets except the PSTC feature set where 20 training vectors were used. The results shown in Table 1 and in Fig. 1 show the normalized classification error rate for each of the feature sets for each size of vector evaluated. For this dataset the PSTC features clearly outperformed all the others with the PCC features providing the second best performance. At lot dimensions the PSC features performed only marginally better than the MFCC but approached the PCC features at higher dimensions when enough coefficients were used. The MFCC features alone had the worst overall performance. The MFCC + enhanced features provided moderate performance at low dimensions that did not improve much at higher dimensions.

Table 2 Feature set normalised error rate for the frog call dataset

	Dimensions (Feature set size)								
Features	8	16	18	26	32	42	64	74	96
PSC	0.296	0.191			0.142		0.131		0.145
PCC	0.192	0.114			0.095		0.107		0.130
MFCC	0.283	0.226			0.195		0.214		
MFCC+			0.322	0.258		0.214		0.214	
PSTC	0.281	0.228			0.181		0.161		0.168

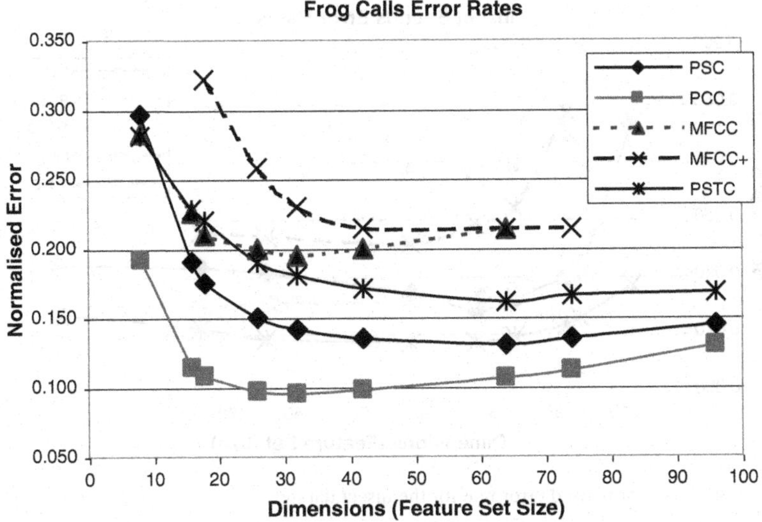

Fig. 2 Feature set normalised error rate for the frog call dataset

Due to the small amount of data available for analysis in the Frog Call dataset only five training vectors could be extracted from each recording while using a window size of 1,024 samples. In the case of the PSTC features only a single train vector could be extracted from the data and this seriously impeded the performance of the PSTC feature set. The results are shown in Table 2 and Fig. 2. While PSTC features outperformed the MFCC and MFCC + features, it fell behind the PSC and PCC features. The PCC features again outperformed the PSC features at all dimensions. Notably, the MFCC features outperformed the enhanced MFCC + features at all but the highest dimensions.

The best performance for the Insect sounds dataset was obtained using 50 training vectors (20 in the case of PSTC features) and a window size of 1,024 samples. This dataset provided similar results to the Frog Call dataset as demonstrated by the results shown in Table 3 and in Fig. 3. The PTFC features again provided the best overall performance at all dimensions. As is to be expected the MFCC + performed better than MFCC except at low dimensions, but both of these again demonstrated the worst performance. The PSC and PCC features

Table 3 Feature set normalised error rate for the insect dataset

	Dimensions (Feature set size)								
Features	8	16	18	26	32	42	64	74	96
PSC	0.046	0.021			0.014		0.021		0.022
PCC	0.049	0.022			0.016		0.015		0.015
MFCC	0.084	0.051			0.039		0.040		
MFCC+			0.049	0.032		0.026		0.028	
PSTC	0.018	0.013			0.008		0.009		0.014

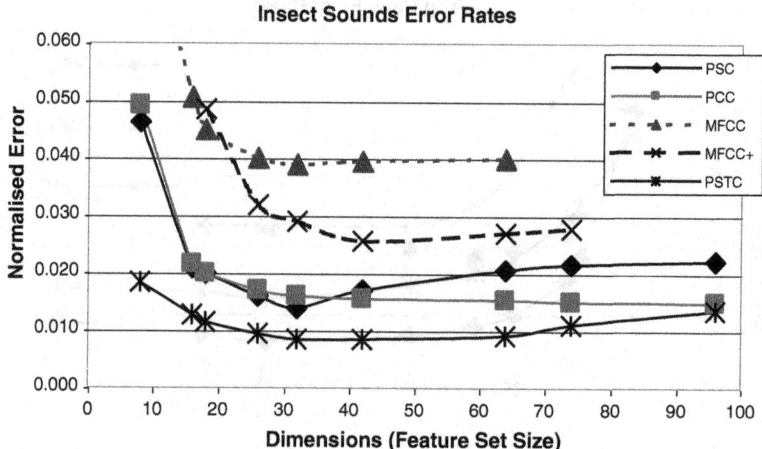

Fig. 3 Feature set normalised error rate for the insect dataset

Table 4 Feature set normalised error rate for the musical instrument dataset

	Dimensions (Feature set size)								
Features	8	16	18	26	32	42	64	74	96
PSC	0.599	0.491			0.379		0.281		0.233
PCC	0.646	0.581			0.507		0.439		0.407
MFCC	0.642	0.531			0.423		0.325		
MFCC+	0.451		0.373	0.326		0.286		0.250	
PSTC	0.480	0.402			0.327		0.293		0.308
PSC+			0.400	0.354		0.303		0.254	

provided very similar results except that the PSC features became less competitive at higher dimensions.

The Instrument dataset results departed markedly from those of the other datasets. The best performance in all cases was obtained using 50 training vectors and a 512 sample window for all feature sets except the PSTC features which made use of 5 training vectors and a 256 sample window. The enhanced MFCC + narrowly outperformed the PSTC features as shown in Table 4 and in Fig. 4. Notably the PCC features performed even worse than the standard MFCC features. Yet the

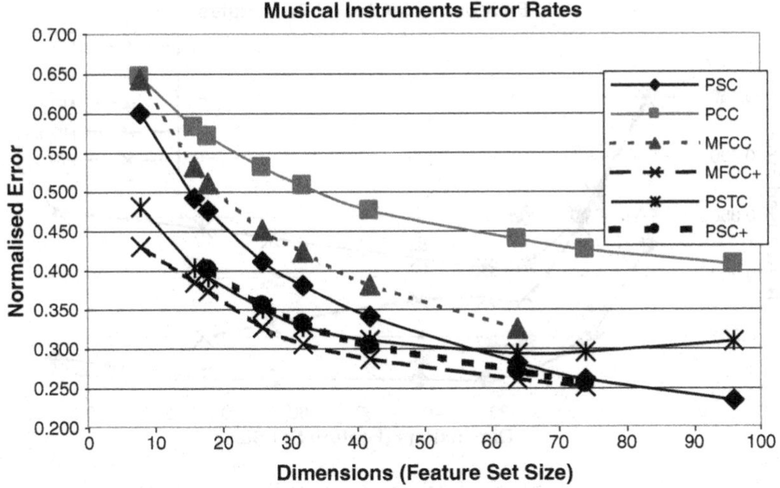

Fig. 4 Feature set normalised error rate for the musical instrument dataset

Table 5 Feature set normalised error rate for the environmental sounds dataset

	Dimensions (Feature set size)								
Features	8	16	18	26	32	42	64	74	96
PSC	0.326	0.252			0.213		0.214		0.232
PCC	0.348	0.274			0.240		0.211		0.219
MFCC	0.412	0.363			0.349		0.300		
MFCC+	0.453		0.342	0.282		0.280		0.249	
PSTC	0.446	0.369			0.307		0.332		0.355

PSC features managed to provide better performance than MFCC for all dimensions. To evaluate the contribution of the spectral and temporal features in the MFCC + dataset to the performance, these were added to the PSC data set to form an enhanced PSC + dataset. These enhanced PSC + features were able to approach but not exceed the performance of the MFCC + features.

The best performance with the Environmental sounds dataset was obtained using 10 vectors and a 512 sample window in all cases except the PSTC features which used 5 training vectors and as 128 sample window. The PSC features in this case provided the best performance as is shown in Table 5 and in Fig. 5. The PCC features only managed to surpass the performance of PSC at high dimensions. Notably the PTFC features provided moderate performance better than MFCC but worse than MFCC + at low to mid dimensions but deteriorating at higher dimensions. It is unclear if this was due to having insufficient samples to obtain enough training vectors at a high enough frequency resolution, or some other intrinsic characteristic of the dataset.

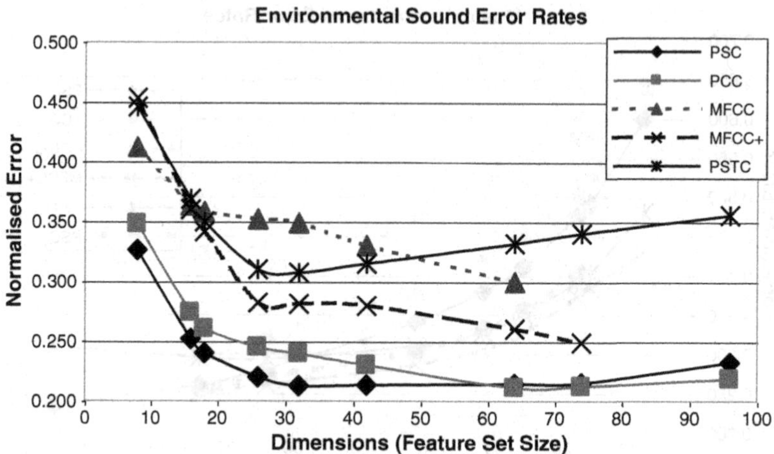

Fig. 5 Feature set normalised error rate for the environmental sounds dataset

5 Conclusions

This paper has presented three new feature sets for audio classification based on principle spectral components for audio indexing, content based retrieval and acoustic recognition that provide improved performance over feature sets comprised of only MFCC and MFCC plus spectral and temporal features in most cases. When sufficient data is available the PSTC features provide the best overall performance by a factor of 50–100 %. When insufficient data is available either the PSC or PCC feature sets generally provide better performance than MFCC and MFCC enhanced feature sets. These have the added benefit of requiring less processing to obtain than MFCC based feature sets.

References

1. José Anibal Arias, Julien Pinquier and Régine André-Obrecht, "Evaluation Of Classification Techniques For Audio Indexing," Proceedings of 13th European Signal Processing Conference, September 4–8, 2005. EUSIPCO'2005, Antalya, Turkey.
2. S. Chu, S. Narayanan, C.-C. Jay Kuo, and Maja J. Mataric. "Where am i? scene recognition for mobile robots using audio features". In Proc. of ICME, Toronto, Canada, July 2006
3. Lefèvre F., "A Confidence Measure based on the K-nn Probability Estimator", International Conference on Spoken Language Processing, Beijing, 2000
4. Kim, H-G., Moreau, N., Sikora., "Audio Classification Based on MPEG-7 Spectral Basis Representations" IEEE Trans. On Circuits And Systems For Video Technology, Vol. 14, No. 5, May 2004.

5. M.F. McKinney, J. Breebaart. "Features for audio and music classification." In Proc. of the Intern. Conf. on Music Information Retrieval (ISMIR 2004), pp. 151–158, Plymouth MA, 2004.
6. Peltonen, V., Tuomi, J., Klapuri, A., Huopaniemi, J., Sorsa, T., "Computational auditory scene recognition", Proceeding of. International Conference on Acoustics, Speech, and Signal Processing, 2002. (ICASSP '02). May 13–17, 2002, Orlando, FL, USA, vol.2, pp:1941–1944.
7. Mingchun Liu and Chunru Wan. 2001. "Feature selection for automatic classification of musical instrument sounds." In Proceedings of the 1st ACM/IEEE-CS joint conference on Digital libraries (JCDL '01). ACM, New York, NY, USA, 247–248.
8. D. J. Hermes, "Measurement of pitch by subharmonic summation" J. Acoust. Soc. Am. Volume 83, Issue 1, pp. 257–264 (January 1988)
9. Bregman, Albert S., Auditory Scene Analysis: The Perceptual Organization of Sound. Cambridge, Massachusetts: The MIT Press, 1990 (hardcover)/1994 (paperback).
10. D. Stewart, "Australian Frog Calls - Subtropical East", [Audio Recording]
11. McGill University Master Samples, 1993 "Vol 1: Classical Sounds" [Audio Recording]

A Novel 2D Wavelet Level Energy for Breast Lesion Classification on Ultrasound Images

Yueh-Ching Liao, King-Chu Hung, Shu-Mei Guo, Po-Chin Wang, and Tsung-Lung Yang

Abstract Infiltrative nature is a unique characteristic of breast cancer. Cross-sectional view of infiltrative nature can find a rough lesion contour on ultrasound image. Roughness description is crucial for clinical diagnosis of breast lesions. Based on boundary tracking, traditional roughness descriptors usually suffer from information loss due to dimension reduction. In this paper, a novel 2-D wavelet-based energy feature is proposed for breast lesion classification on ultrasound images. This approach characterizes the roughness of breast lesion contour with normalized spatial frequency components. Feature efficacies are evaluated by using two breast sonogram datasets with lesion contour delineated by an experienced physician and the ImageJ, respectively. Experimental results show that the new feature can obtain excellent performance and robust contour variation resistance.

Keywords Description • DPWT • Breast lesion classification • ImageJ • LECI

Y.-C. Liao (✉) • S.-M. Guo
Department of Computer Science and Information Engineering,
National Cheng Kung University, Tainan 701, Taiwan, Republic of China
e-mail: mhcy@ms2.hinet.net

K.-C. Hung
Department of Computer and Communication Engineering,
National Kaohsiung First University of Science and Technology,
Kaohsiung 811, Taiwan, Republic of China

P.-C. Wang • T.-L. Yang
Department of Radiology, Kaohsiung Veterans General Hospital,
Kaohsiung 813, Taiwan, R.O.C

J.S. Jin et al., *The Era of Interactive Media*,
DOI 10.1007/978-1-4614-3501-3_25,

1 Introduction

Breast cancer is one of the top ten cancer causes of death in Taiwan. Ultrasound (US) imaging with low cost and no ionizing has been widely used for breast cancer diagnosis [1]. One benefit of breast US image-reading is the effectiveness of reducing unnecessary biopsies [1,–2]. Due to extreme noise, physicians with different levels of experience often come up with different results for the same sonograms. Therefore, many computerization algorithms were proposed for minimizing the operator-dependent effects [3]. These approaches effectively assist differential diagnoses between benign and malignant breast lesions, especially for those lacking enough clinical experience or in overlooking status.

Computer-generated features can be categorized into texture [4] and contour [3, 5–9] groups. Textures are regional intensity distribution features characterizing the scattering properties of ultrasonic radio frequency echoes in B-mode images of breast tissues. The echo envelope can be described with statistical models where the normalized parameters are defined as texture features. Contour approaches characterize the infiltrative nature of malignant breast lesions (i.e., the spicularity and irregularity) based on the evidence [1] that infiltrative nature will induce a rough lesion surface and contour pattern on breast US image. The main merit of contour approach is the capability of high classification performance with very low computational cost as compared with texture.

Most contour features are developed for efficiently describing the roughness of pattern, e.g., morphometric parameters [3, 5–7] and 1-D wavelet-based channel energy [8, 9]. The extraction of contour features requires a contour tracking program that converts shape into a sequence of edge points. The mapping from 2-D to 1-D usually cause shape wrench especially for concave contour shape due to the dimension reduction. Shape wrench effect may lower the capability of roughness descriptor and reduce the distance between classes. For high classification performance, it is desirable for contour features to be inherent with shape information.

In this paper, a novel contour feature referred to as level energy of contour image (LECI) is presented for breast lesion classification on US image. LECI is defined as the level energy of detailed signals in the 2-D discrete periodized wavelet transform (DPWT) of a normalized binary contour image. The LECI is a 2-D feature based on the hypothesis that rough shape is always abundant in more spatial frequency components than smooth shapes (i.e., circle or ellipse) in any orientation. An optimized probabilistic neural network (PNN) [10, 11] is used for classification performance analyses. These evaluations are based on two breast sonogram datasets with the lesion contour delineated by an experienced physician and the image processing program ImageJ, respectively.

2 Materials and Methods

For feature efficacy evaluation, a dataset with 184 breast US images was built. The sonograms, randomly selected from the database of a medical center in Taiwan, were from May 17, 2002, to November 28, 2007. Patient ages ranged from 21 to 77 years with a mean age of 46.81 years. These sonograms including 2 adenosis, 48 cysts, 2 epidermal cysts, 65 fibroadenomas, 2 intramammonary LN, 60 ductal carcinomas, 1 lobular carcinoma, 3 metaplastic carcinomas, and 1 medullary carcinoma were pathologically proven. They were derived in a baseline gray-scale US examination that was performed by a sonographer (D.A.M., with 20 years of experience) with a scanner (Logiq 9; GE Healthcare, Milwaukee, Wis) and a broad-bandwidth linear array transducer (Model 7L; bandwidth, 3–7 MHz) to identify the largest section of the mass or abnormality seen with mammography. All sonograms and related clinical information went through procedures of anonymity.

The evaluation system composed of four functional processes is shown in Fig. 1. Contour marking of breast lesion on sonograms is performed by two approaches for variation simulation. One was a hand-painted set that was delineated by P. C. Wang, who is a physician with nine years of experience in breast sonography.

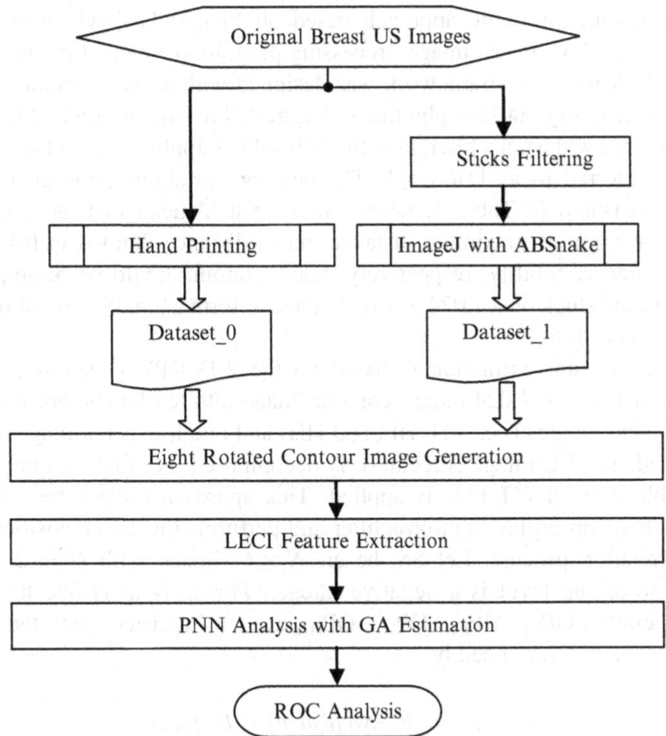

Fig. 1 The LECI feature efficacy evaluation system

Table 1 Breast lesion contour variation between dataset_0 and dataset_1

	Initial parameters (ABsnake)			Boundary differences		
Test dataset name	GT	IT	Initial pattern	Amax_dist	Amean_dist	Aarea_var
dataset_0	hand-painted			–	–	–
dataset_1	15	300	ellipse	B: 152.67 M: 119.18	B: 54.498 M: 44.994	B: 0.2132 M:0.2155

GT: Gradient threshold required for ABsnake
IT: Iteration times

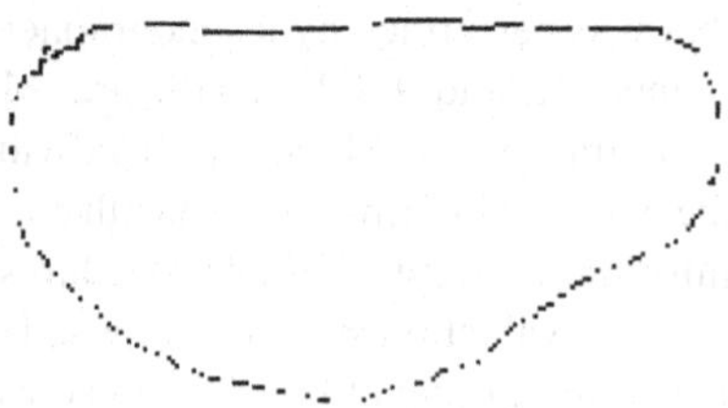

Fig. 2 A original binary contour image

This set, referred as Dataset_0, is consistent with the physician's cognition. The other was a semi-automatic approach based on ImageJ [12] which is a public framework for a Java-based image processing program developed by the National Institutes of Health. This framework was designed with an open architecture that provides extensibility via Java plugins. As suggested in [9], the original image will be firstly filtered with sticks filter, then the ABsnake is applied for contour marking. This set is referred to as Dataset_1. The contour variations between Dataset_0 and _1 is measured in Table 1. where Amax_dist, Amean_dist, and Aarea_var denote the average of maximum distance, mean distance defined in [8], and the average of area variability, respectively. Each contour should be resampling for 2,048 points and stuck on a 1,024 × 1,024 image to form a binary contour image, as the illustration of Fig. 2.

The LECI feature extraction is based on the 2-D DPWT that is applied to decompose a 1,024 × 1,024 binary contour image into ten levels. For each level, three high band images (i.e., LH, HL, and HH) and one low band image (i.e., LL) are produced. The LL image is recursively decomposed. For fast computation, the nonseparable 2-D DPWT [13] is applied. This approach creates four operators based on a homeomorphic high-pass filter and performs the decomposition with a 2-shift correlation process. Let SS_j be an $N \times N$ image with $N = 2^{-J}$ where J referred to as the level is a negative integer. For an l-tap Daubechies' filter, the four operators $\mathrm{OP_{LL}}$, $\mathrm{OP_{LH}}$, $\mathrm{OP_{HL}}$, $\mathrm{OP_{HH}}$ are $l \times l$ matrices with the element $\mathrm{w}(m,n), 0 \le m,n \le l$, defined by

$$\begin{aligned} \mathrm{w_{LL}}(m,n) &= h_m h_n, .\mathrm{w_{LH}}(m,n) = h_m g_n, \\ \mathrm{w_{HL}}(m,n) &= g_m h_n, \cdot\text{and} \cdot \mathrm{w_{HH}}(m,n) = G_m g_n, \end{aligned} \tag{1}$$

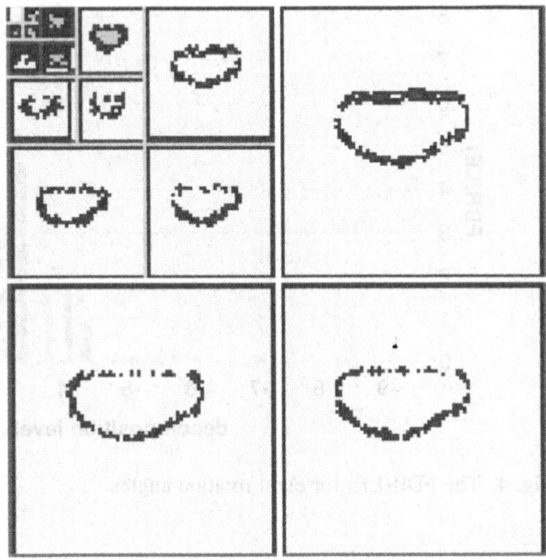

Fig. 3 2-D DPWT process for the example of Fig. 2

where h_m and g_n denote the low-pass and high-pass discrete filter coefficients of the 1-D DPWT, respectively. By using the 2-shift correlation process, the four sub-band images SS_j, SD_j, DS_j, and DD_j for $J < j \leq 0$ can be obtained with

$$\begin{aligned} ss_j(x,y) &= \sum_{m}^{l-1}\sum_{n=0}^{l-1} ss_{j-1}\left((2x+m)_l,(2y+n)_l\right)\cdot w_{LL}(m,n), \\ sd_j(x,y) &= \sum_{m}^{l-1}\sum_{n=0}^{l-1} ss_{j-1}\left((2x+m)_l,(2y+n)_l\right)\cdot w_{LH}(m,n), \end{aligned} \quad (2)$$

etc., where $(x)_l$ denotes the residual of x mod l. A 2-D DPWT processing result for the example of Fig. 2 is shown in Fig. 3. The level energy (LE) defined as the sub-band energies of each level is given by

$$\begin{aligned} [(LE)]_{\downarrow j} = &\sum\nolimits_{\downarrow}(X=0)^{\uparrow}(2^{\uparrow}(-j)) \sum\nolimits_{\downarrow}(y=0)^{\uparrow}(2^{\uparrow}(-j))\, [[([sd]_{\downarrow j}(x,y))^{\uparrow 2}/ss_{\downarrow}0 \\ &+ ([ds]_{\downarrow j}(x,y)\left([dd]_{\downarrow j}(x,y)\right)^{\uparrow 2}/ss_{\downarrow}0],\ j = J+1, J+2, \cdots, -1, 0, \end{aligned} \quad (3)$$

Since LE is composed of spatial frequency energies, it can be variant to pattern rotation. Figure 4 shows the rotation's influence of Dataset_1 on parameters LE_j in terms of the Fisher's discriminant ratio (FDR) [14], which is a feature efficacy index commonly used for feature selection. The FDR_j for $J < j \leq 0$ are defined by

$$\mathrm{FDR}(LE_j) = \frac{\left(\mu(LE_j(\mathrm{M})) - \mu(LE_j(\mathrm{B}))\right)^2}{\rho^2(LE_j(\mathrm{M})) + \rho^2(LE_j(\mathrm{B}))}, \quad (4)$$

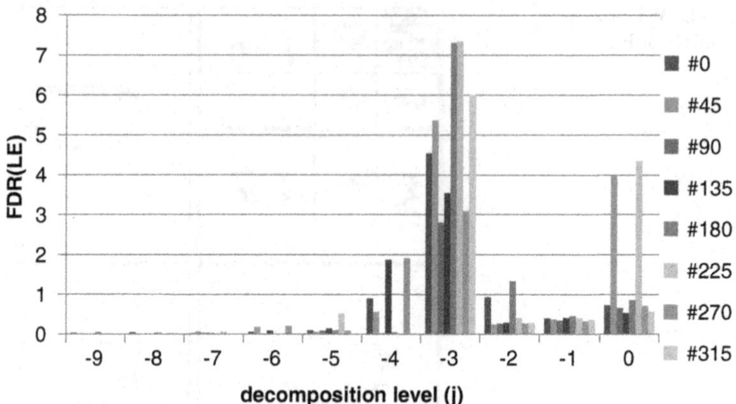

Fig. 4 The FDR(LE) for eight rotation angles

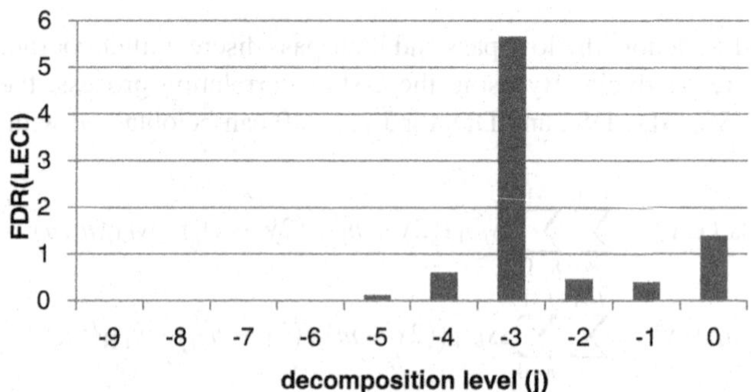

Fig. 5 The FDR of LECI feature

where $\mu(LE_j(\mathrm{M}))$ and $\rho(LE_j(\mathrm{M}))$ denote the mean and variance of malignant lesions LE_j, respectively, and $\mu(LE_j(\mathrm{M}))$ denotes the mean of benign lesions LE_j. Figure 4 shows the FDRs of eight rotation angles $\theta = 0°$, 45°, 90°, 135°, 180°, 225°, 270°, 315° where variation can be great. For resisting the rotation influence, we define the LECI feature with the average energy of the eight rotations, namely,

$$LECI_j = \left(\sum_{\theta} LE_j(\theta)\right) \Big/ 8 \tag{5}$$

The FDR for LECI feature is shown in Fig. 5 where the three LECI features of $j = -3$, and 0 can obtain excellent feature efficacy, especially for the first.

Classification performance is evaluated with the association of a probabilistic neural network (PNN) [10] and a genetic algorithm. The function of PNN can be specified by parameter *SPREAD* used for estimating the probability density function of training data. If *SPREAD* closes to zero, the network acts as a nearest neighbor classifier, otherwise the network will take into account several nearby design vectors. Since PNN performance can be influenced by the parameter *SPREAD*, a binary genetic algorithm (BGA) [15] is applied for an optimal value determination where initial population is randomly generated and elitism is used for reproduction selection processes. Finally, the k-fold cross-validation with k = 8 is applied in the PNN for the measurement of five receiver operating characteristic (ROC) [16] parameters involving the false alarm rate (FAR), sensitivity (Se), accuracy (Ac), positive predictive value (PPV), and specificity (Sp).

3 Experimental Results and Discussions

The classification performance evaluation system of Fig. 1 was performed on Microsoft windows XP professional version 2002 with service pack 3, Intel(R) core(TM)2 Duo CPU T8300 2.40GHz, 2.99GB RAM platform. Most programs including pre-processing and classification were implemented with the MATLAB software package version 7. All the features studied in the experiments are summarized in Table 2. where E_k are the 1-D wavelet-based channel energy feature [8, 9] and MP denotes morphometric parameters [3, 5–7].

By using the two lesion contour sets Dataset_0 and Dataset_1, the individual classification performances of features with $\mathrm{LECI_j}$ and some high efficient features are shown in Table 3. For the six features, $\mathrm{LECI}_{-9} \sim \mathrm{LECI}_{-4}$, two of the individual classification performances of ROC parameters, Ac and Se, whose values are less than 70% and 20% for all datasets, respectively. As a result, we have no choice but

Table 2 Notations of roughness descriptors tested in this study

Features	Parameters
$\mathrm{LECI_j}$	Proposed features for $j = -9, \ldots, -1, 0$.
$\mathrm{E_k}$	Wavelet channel energy features for $k = -11, \ldots, -2, -1$. [9]
MP01	Normalized residual mean square value (nrv): $nrv = \frac{\Psi_r^2}{\Psi_0^2}$ [3, 9]
MP02	Circularity (C): $C = \frac{P^2}{A}$ [3, 9]
MP03	Overlap ratio (RS): $RS = \frac{Area(S_0 \cap S_m)}{Area(S_0 \cup S_m)}$ [3, 9]
MP04	Roughness index(R): $R = \frac{1}{N} \sum_{i=1}^{N} \lvert d(i) - d(i+1) \rvert$ [3, 9]
MP05	Standard deviation of normalized radial length($\mathrm{D_{NRL}}$): $D_{NRL} = \sqrt{\frac{1}{N-1} \sum_{i=1}^{N} (d(i) - \bar{d})^2}$ [3, 9]
MP06	Area ratio(RA): $RA = \frac{1}{\bar{d} \cdot N} \sum_{i=1}^{N} (d(i) - \bar{d})$ [3, 9]
MP07	Elongation [5, 9]
MP08	Shape-moment-1 [5, 9]
MP09	Shape-moment-2 [5, 9]
MP10	Shape-moment-3 [5, 9]
MP11	Zero-crossings [6, 9]
MP12	Standard deviation of the shortest distance [7]

Table 3 Individual classification performance of **LECI**$_j$ and some high efficient features

Dataset_0 Dataset_1	ROC Parameters FAR	Se	AC	PPV	Sp	Spread
LECI$_{-9}$	0.025287	0.16912	0.69022	0.79167	0.97471	0.35
	0.033621	0.18474	0.69022	0.7625	0.96638	0.6
LECI$_{-8}$	0.058621	0.16912	0.66848	0.6125	0.94138	0.225
	0.033333	0.13787	0.67391	0.70833	0.96667	0.475
LECI$_{-7}$	0.041954	0.12408	0.66304	0.60417	0.95805	0.35
	0.008333	0.12316	0.68478	0.91667	0.99167	0.35
LECI$_{-6}$	0.016667	0.046875	0.65217	NaN	0.98333	0.225
	0.033621	0.18474	0.69022	0.74167	0.96638	0.225
LECI$_{-5}$	0.10029	0.29412	0.68478	0.63194	0.89971	0.35
	0.050287	0.35386	0.73913	0.81845	0.94971	0.35
LECI$_{-4}$	0.13534	0.36857	0.69022	0.6125	0.86466	0.35
	0.21839	0.78401	0.78261	0.66386	0.78161	0.35
LECI$_{-3}$	0	0.5239	0.83152	1	1	4.725
	0.008333	0.92279	0.96739	0.98333	0.99167	0.475
LECI$_{-2}$	0.2523	0.95313	0.82065	0.67395	0.7477	3.475
	0.21839	0.89154	0.82065	0.69091	0.78161	3.35
LECI$_{-1}$	0.016667	0.66176	0.86957	0.96154	0.98333	1.35
	0.058621	0.7068	0.8587	0.86676	0.94138	0.85
LECI$_0$	0.27701	0.76838	0.73913	0.60189	0.72299	1.35
	0.083621	0.87684	0.90217	0.85417	0.91638	0.35
MP02	0.016954	0.87776	0.94565	0.96863	0.98305	1.225
	0.025287	0.96875	0.97283	0.95578	0.97471	0.85
E$_{-7}$	0.016954	0.83088	0.92935	0.96548	0.98305	1.85
	0.075575	0.89246	0.91304	0.87092	0.92443	4.475
E$_{-6}$	0.016954	0.92371	0.96196	0.96875	0.98305	0.975
	0.083908	0.87592	0.90217	0.85643	0.91609	2.85

to reject the six features. LECI$_0$ has poor differentiation capability for Dataset_0, but it is suitable for Dataset_1 with (FAR, Se, Ac, PPV, Sp) equal to (0.083621, 0.87684, 0.90217, 0.85417, 0.91638). LECI$_{-3}$ has the best classification performance, especially for Dataset_1, this feature can obtain (FAR, Se, Ac, PPV, Sp) = (0.008333, 0.92279, 0.96739, 0.98333, 0.99167). For morphometric parameters, only MP02 can be competitive to the LECI$_{-3}$. This feature based on the hypothesis that of all plane figures with the same enclosed area, smoother pattern that has less perimeter can be a good roughness descriptor.

In order to improve the performance, it is desirable to combine some features with different characteristics to obtain the benefit of mutual compensation. Considering the combination of LECI$_{-3}$ or LECI$_0$ with other features, the classification performances of combined features are measured in Table 4. The individual classification performances of LECI$_{-3}$ for Dataset_0 is not satisfied with Se = 0.5239. However, Table 4. shows that the combination of LECI$_{-3}$ and other features can obtain better performance than the individual of LECI$_{-3}$ for Dataset_0, especially in Se parameter value. Se parameter means sensitivity which is very

Table 4 Classification performance of combined features with LECI

D6 Dataset_0 Dataset_1	ROC Parameters FAR	Se	AC	PPV	Sp
($LECI_{-3}$,MP02)	0.058908	0.8943	0.92391	0.8949	0.94109
	0	0.92371	0.97283	1	1
($LECI_{-3}$,E_{-7})	0.050287	0.87592	0.92391	0.9035	0.94971
	0.016667	0.92371	0.96196	0.96875	0.98333
($LECI_{-3}$,E_6)	0.033621	0.93842	0.95652	0.93842	0.96638
	0.008333	0.89246	0.95652	0.98333	0.99167
($LECI_0$,MP02)	0.067529	0.7693	0.875	0.86894	0.93247
	0.016667	0.82996	0.92935	0.96354	0.98333
($LECI_0$,E_{-7})	0.050862	0.86029	0.91848	0.90815	0.94914
	0.025287	0.89154	0.94565	0.95136	0.97471
($LECI_0$,E_6)	0.050575	0.86029	0.91848	0.90612	0.94943
	0.033621	0.78401	0.90217	0.9266	0.96638
($LECI_{-3}$,$LECI_0$)	0.033621	0.93934	0.95652	0.94026	0.96638
	0	0.96967	0.98913	1	1

important for prediction of malignant lesions. For dataset_0, these three combined features [($LECI_{-3}$,MP02), ($LECI_{-3}$, E_{-7}), ($LECI_{-3}$, E_{-6})] with Se parameter equal to [0.8943, 0.87592, 0.93842], respectively, are improved not only the individual of $LECI_{-3}$ with Se $= 0.5239$ but also these three individual of features (MP02, E_{-7}, E_{-6}) with Se parameter equal to (0.87776, 0.83088, 0.92371). The feature $LECI_{-3}$ is specifically suitable for Dataset_0 in combined $LECI_{-3}$ with other features. For both datasets, ($LECI_{-3}$,$LECI_0$) has the best classification performance which is a rather surprising result. Furthermore, ($LECI_{-3}$,MP02), ($LECI_{-3}$,E_{-7}), ($LECI_{-3}$, E_{-6}), and ($LECI_{-3}$,$LECI_0$) have confidence in classification performance of combined features, especially for Dataset_1.

4 Conclusions

Based on normalized binary contour image, a novel 2-D wavelet-based level energy feature has been presented for breast lesion classification on US images. This new approach tries to preserve shape information for feature and uses 2-D spatial frequency components for infiltrative nature description. Experiments are based on Taiwan women's sonograms and two contour delineation methods. Evaluated with an optimized PNN, the experimental results shows that high level energy features can robustly resist contour variation and obtain excellent classification performance. This study enables a high accuracy breast lesion computer-aid-diagnosis system to be fulfilled with a low cost contour approach.

References

1. A. T. Stavros, D. Thickman, C. L. Rapp, M. A. Dennis, S. H. Parker, and G. A. Sisney: Solid breast nodules: Use of sonography to distinguish between benign andmalignant lesions, *Radiology*, vol. 196, pp. 123–134, Jul. (1995).
2. T. M. Kolb, J. Lichy, and J.H. Newhouse: Comparison of the performance of screening mammography, physical examination, and breast US and evaluation of factors that influence them: An analysis of 27825 patient evaluations, *Radiology*, vol. 225, pp. 165–175, Oct. (2002).
3. A. V. Alvarenga, W. C. A. Pereira, A. F. C. Infantosi, and C. M. de Azevedo: Classification of breast tumours on ultrasound images using morphometric parameters, in *Proc. IEEE Int. Symp. on Intell. Signal Processing*, Sept., pp. 206–210(2005).
4. Qiuxia Chen and Qi Liu: Textural Feature Analysis for Ultrasound Breast Tumor Images, in *Proc. International Conference on Bioinformatics and Biomedical Engineering*, Apr., pp. 1–4 (2010).
5. Songyang Yu; Ling Guan: A CAD system for the automatic detection of clustered microcalcifications in digitized mammogram films, *IEEE Trans. Med. Imag.*, Vol. 19, pp. 115 – 126, (2000).
6. Shah, V.P.; Bruce, L.M.; Younan, N.H.: Applying modular classifiers to mammographic mass classification, IEMBS '04. 26th Annual International Conference of the IEEE, Engineering in Medicine and Biology Society, Vol. 1, pp. 1585 – 1588, Sept. (2004).
7. P. H. Tsui, Y.-Y. Liao, C. C. Chang, W. H. Kuo, K. J. Chang, and C. K. Yeh: Classification of benign and malignant breast tumors by 2-D analysis based on contour description and scatterer Characterization, *IEEE Trans. Med. Imag.*, vol. 29, pp. 513–522, Feb. (2010).
8. H. W. Lee, B. D. Liu, K. C. Hung, S. F. Lei, P. C. Wang, and T. L. Yang: Breast tumor classification of ultrasound images using wavelet-based channel energy and ImageJ, *IEEE Journal of Selected Topics in Signal Processing*, vol. 3, pp. 81–93, Feb. (2009).
9. Y. C. Liao, S. M. Guo, K. C. Hung, P. C. Wang, and T. L. Yang: Noise Resistance Analysis of Wavelet-Based Channel Energy Feature for Breast Lesion Classification on Ultrasound Images. PCM'10 Proceedings of the Advances in multimedia information processing, and 11th Pacific Rim conference on Multimedia: Part II pp. 549–558, Sept. (2010).
10. Farrokhrooz, M.; Karimi, M.; Rafiei, A.: A new method for spread value estimation in multi-spread PNN and its application in ship noise classification, ISSPA 9th International Symposium on Signal Processing and Its Applications, pp. 1 – 4, Apr. (2007).
11. Donald F. Specht: Probabilistic neural networks, In: Neural Networks, Volume 3, Issue 1, ISSN:0893–6080, (1990)
12. P. Andrey, T. Boudier: Adaptive active contours (snakes) for the segmentation of complex structures in biological images, ImageJ Conference (2006).
13. K. C. Hung, Y. S. Hung, and Y. J. Huang: A nonseparable VLSI architecture for two-dimensional discrete periodized wavelet transform, *IEEE Trans. VLSI Systems*, vol.9, pp.565–576, Oct. (2001).
14. C. M. Bishop: *Pattern Recognition and Machine Learning*, Springer, (2006).
15. Holland, J. H.," Genetic Algorithms," Scientific American, pp.66–72, July (1992).
16. T. Fawcett: An introduction to roc analysis,: *Pattern Recognition Letters*, vol. 27, pp. 861–874, June (2006).

Learning-to-Share Based on Finding Groups for Large Scale Image Classification

Li Shen, Shuqiang Jiang, Shuhui Wang, and Qingming Huang

Abstract With the large scale image classification attracting more attention in recent years, a lot of new challenges spring up. To tackle the problems of distribution imbalance and divergent visual correlation of multiple classes, this paper proposes a method to learn a group-based sharing model such that the visually similar classes are assigned to a discriminative group. This model enables the class draw support from other classes in the same group, thus the poor discrimination ability with limited available samples can be relieved. To generate effective groups, the intra-class coherence and the inter-class similarity are computed. Then a hierarchical model is learned based on these groups that the classes within the group can inherit the power from the discriminative model of the group. We evaluate our method across 200 categories extracted from *ImageNet*. Experimental results show our model has better performance in large scale image classification.

Keywords Group sharing • Large scale classification • Hierarchical model

L. Shen (✉)
Graduate University, Chinese Academy of Sciences, Beijing 100049, China
e-mail: lshen@jdl.ac.cn

S. Jiang • S. Wang
Key Laboratory of Intelligent Information Processing, Institute of Computing Technology, CAS, Beijing 100190, China
e-mail: sqjiang@jdl.ac.cn; shwang@jdl.ac.cn

Q. Huang
Graduate University, Chinese Academy of Sciences, Beijing 100049, China

Key Laboratory of Intelligent Information Processing, Institute of Computing Technology, CAS, Beijing 100190, China
e-mail: qmhuang@jdl.ac.cn

J.S. Jin et al., *The Era of Interactive Media*,
DOI 10.1007/978-1-4614-3501-3_26,

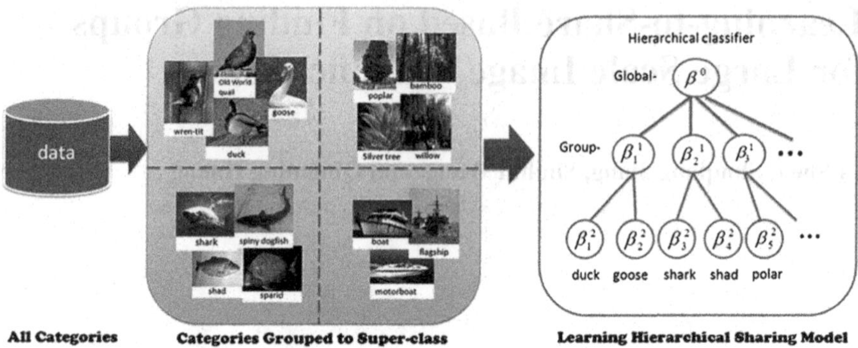

Fig. 1 Framework in the paper. The categories firstly are grouped based on visual similarity. Then use the hierarchical sharing model to train the classifiers, and the categories in a group will share a group vector

1 Introduction

Visual classification is an important issue in the area of multimedia and computer vision. In recent years, a general trend is towards large scale datasets with many categories [1, 2]. A lot of traditional image classification algorithms have been proposed in the literature. These methods have worked well on small databases. However, they may underperform when the number of categories significantly increases. Some new challenges spring up under the large scale scenario. Firstly, the distribution of multiple classes is usually imbalanced. Many categories have relatively larger available training samples than others, so their classifier may have better performance than the categories with fewer samples. Moreover, visual correlation among the categories is divergent. Some categories are visually similar, meanwhile some categories can be easily discriminated due to the large variance between them. For example, the diversity between the categories of "*duck*" and "*goose*" is slight. They may be confused with each other, however they can easily apart from others such as "*car*" or "*buildings*".

To deal with above challenges, some solutions have been proposed such as multi-task learning [3, 4] or adding exterior information, i.e. attribute and tags. Many researches are developed based on multi-task to relieve the imbalance problem by sharing information among tasks. Inspired by the above observations, the similar classes always have some common properties that the irrelative classes do not have. This phenomenon is helpful for modeling the sharing structure.

In this paper, we propose to learn to transfer effective information across related classes by a group-based sharing model. Resembling to the cascade classification [5], the model is hierarchical based on the coarse-to-fine rule. As shown in Fig. 1, Hierarchical Divisive Clustering [6] is firstly introduced in to effectively analyze intra-class coherence. Based on these analyses, the similarity of classes in pairs is measured to generate the group. Then a hierarchical structure is used to learn the layer-classifiers. The classes in a group are viewed as integral one that can be discriminated from other groups, and they will share the group properties to enhance their own strength. By this method, a hierarchical sharing structure will be learned that can be extended by further research for classification. In Sect. 2, we give a brief review about related work. In Sects. 3 and 4, we will describe the whole system in detail. Experiments are then discussed in Sect. 5.

2 Related Works

Considering that each class is a task, the multi-class image classification can be viewed as a mission consisting of multiple related tasks. There have mainly been two strategies to train the classifiers: learning the classifiers for each class separately [7, 8] or learning the classifiers for all categories simultaneously [3, 4]. Many researchers have shown that learning multiple tasks simultaneously can improve performances by virtually sharing information across correlated tasks, whereas it is a critical problem to model the sharing structure among multiple classes. Various attempts have been devised, for example, hierarchical Bayesian modeling assumes that a common hyper prior is shared by all categories [3, 4]. The model ignores the relationship among the categories, i.e. to decide which classes should share and what they will share.

How to effectively organize the concepts and data by representing the dependencies among object categories is a critical issue. *WordNet* is often applied to guide the classification as prior [9, 10], while the primitive structure is not completely consistent with visual similarity. Dirichlet Process is also used to identify groups of similar tasks, while the model is so complex [11]. Ruslan et al. [12] constructs a hierarchical model by depth-first search strategy to decide which classes a new class should share information with. The method is data-driven, but time-consuming. While adding one more class, all the parameters in structure should be re-trained. Besides, the structure is not coherent because it is influenced by the adding order.

3 Group Model Construction

The target of this step is to find the group which the categories within it are visually similar and can be apart from other ones as larger as possible. Firstly, we need to measure the similarity between classes. Since each class usually has hundred of samples, it is time-consuming to compute the distance between each element in one class and each one in the other. Meanwhile the samples are slightly different in a class, an average vector cannot represent the diversity of the whole class. An effective strategy is conducted to partition one class to a set of sub-clusters with each cluster being compact. There are several typical clustering methods, e.g. k-means [13]. But the specified numbers of clusters are unable to deal with various categories. In this study, we introduce Hierarchical Divisive Clustering [6] method to achieve the goal.

3.1 Partitioning to Sub-clusters

The basic idea of Hierarchical Divisive Clustering [6] algorithm is that, all samples are initialized as a singleton cluster. If the diversity of the cluster is large, the largest margin will split to two smaller clusters with decreased diversity. The partition will stop while the diversity is rather slight. Given a class samples $X_c = \{x_{c,1}, x_{c,2}, \ldots x_{c,Nc}\}, X_c \in R^d$ denote the feature vector of length d for the data belonged to class c and the total number is N_c. For the class c, we aim to get the clusters $S_c^k, k = 1 \ldots c_k$. c_k is the number of clusters in class c:

$$S_c^k = \left\{x_{c,1}^k, x_{c,2}^k \ldots x_{c,n_k}^k\right\}, \sum_{k=1}^{K} n_k = N_c, \tag{1}$$

We firstly compute the Euclidean distance matrix D_{Eu} and Geodesic distance matrix D_{Ge} base on K-nearest Neighbor Graph in pairs, and define a rate $R(x_{c,i}, x_{c,j}) = D_{Ge}(x_{c,i}, x_{c,j}) / D_{Eu}(x_{c,i}, x_{c,j})$ to measure the correlation between $x_{c,i}$ and $x_{c,j}$. We can use average rate to measure the compactness of the cluster:

$$\bar{R} = \frac{1}{n_k \cdot n_k} \sum_{i=1}^{n_k} \sum_{j=1}^{n_k} R(x_{c,i}, x_{c,j}) \tag{2}$$

With these definitions, HDC [6] algorithm is summarized in Algorithm 1. We use the average vector to represent each sub-cluster.

Algorithm 1 Hierarchical Divisive Clustering algorithm

Input: *thresholdr and* $X_c = \{x_{c,1}, x_{c,2}, \ldots x_{c,N_c}\}, X_c \in R^d$

Initialize: $S_c^1 = \{x_{c,1}, x_{c,2}, \ldots x_{c,Nc}\}$

While

Choose S_c^k with the largest $\bar{R}$, If $\bar{R} \leq$ *threshold* break. Otherwise, according to D_{Ge} select two furthest seed points x_L, x_R from S_c^k, $S_c^k(L) = \{x_L\}$,$S_c^k(R) = \{x_R\}$, $S_c^k = S_c^k \backslash \{x_L, x_R\}$

While $S_c^k \neq \varnothing$

$Ne_L = \{kNN(S_c^k(L)) \cap S_c^k\}$, $Ne_R = \{kNN(S_c^k(R)) \cap S_c^k\}$

If (inter $= Ne_L \cap Ne_R) \neq \varnothing$

inter$_L = \{dist(\text{inter}, S_c^k(L)) < dist(\text{inter}, S_c^k(R))\}$, others are inter$_R$

$S_c^k(L) = S_c^k(L) \cup \{Ne_L \backslash \text{inter}_R\}$, $S_c^k(R) = S_c^k(R) \cup \{Ne_R \backslash \text{inter}_L\}$,

Else

$S_c^k(L) = S_c^k(L) \cup Ne_L$, $S_c^k(R) = S_c^k(R) \cup Ne_R$,

End

$S_c^k = S_c^k \backslash \{Ne_L \cup Ne_R\}$

The cluster S_c^k splits into $S_c^k(L)$ and $S_c^k(R)$, $k = k+1$,compute the $\bar{R}_c^k(L)$ and $\bar{R}_c^k(R)$ according to Eq. (2)

Output: $S_c^k = \left\{x_{c,1}^k, x_{c,2}^k \ldots x_{c,n_k}^k\right\}$

3.2 Constructing Class Group

There are some traditional methods to calculate the distance between classes with several sub-clusters, i.e. single-linkage, complete-linkage and average-linkage. We adopt average-linkage to represent the pair-wise similarity.

After computing the distance among classes, we use Affinity Propagation [14]. The method aims to find the exemplar to represent the cluster, so the class dissimilar with others can be separated rather assigning to a group. Moreover, AP can find uniform clusters.

4 Learning the Group-Based Sharing Model

4.1 Traditional Classification Model

Suppose we are given a set of N training samples belonging to K categories, $X_k = \{(x_i, y_i)|i = 1 \ldots N\}$, where x_i denotes the training samples' feature and y_i denotes the corresponding class label. Considering the multi-class classification problem, it will be equivalent to several two-class ones. For class k, the label y_i of sample x_i can be transferred to a binary value indicating whether the sample belongs to it. It assumes the following probability model:

$$P\left(y_i = 1|x_i, \beta^k\right) = \frac{1}{1 + \exp\left(-\beta^k x_i\right)} \tag{3}$$

where $\beta^k = \left[\beta_0^k, \beta_1^k, \ldots \beta_D^k\right]$ is the regression coefficients for class K, and the β_0^k is the bias term. We append each instance with an additional dimension $x_i \leftarrow [x_i, 1]$ to adapt to β. Moreover, L_2 penalized term is added to obtain good generalization ability. The regularized logistic regression is in the following form:

$$\min_{\beta} \sum_{k=1}^{K} l^k\left(\beta^k\right) + \frac{\lambda}{2}\|\beta^k\|_2^2 \tag{4}$$

and the loss function is

$$l^k(\beta) = \sum_{x_i \in X_k} \log\left(1 + e^{-\beta^T x_i}\right) \tag{5}$$

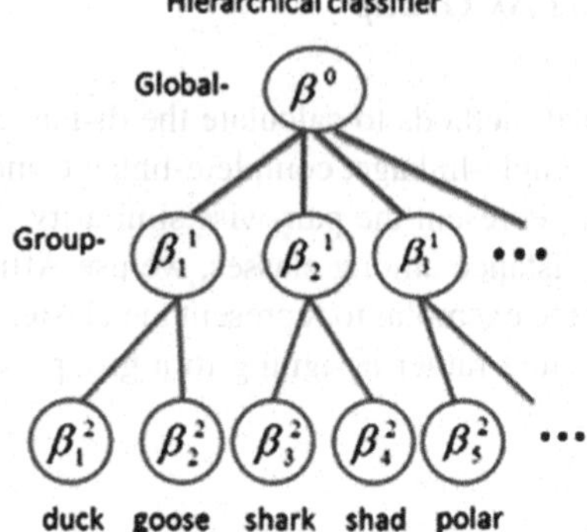

Fig. 2 Group Sharing Model

4.2 Group Sharing Model

The original C categories have been partitioned to Z groups, and each group has at least one category. z_c represents the group category c belongs to. The categories in a group can be viewed as a generalized category divided from other groups. The classes in lower level will inherit its parents' information. As shown in Fig. 2, the classifier of each class is the sum of classifiers along the tree [12].

For example, the classifier of "*duck*" is given by (6) β^0 is the global classifier shared cross all categories, β^1 is the group classifier shared by its child classes, *e.g.* β_1^1 is shared by "*duck*", "*goose*". β^2 is the specific classifier used by the special class.

$$\beta_{duck} = \beta^0 + \beta_1^1 + \beta_1^2 \tag{6}$$

According to the traditional logistic regression, the Group Sharing Model can be formulated as (7). $l^c(\beta^c)$ is computed by (5).

$$\min_{\beta} \frac{\lambda_0}{2}\|\beta^0\|_2^2 + \frac{\lambda_1}{2Z}\sum_{z=1}^{Z}\|\beta_z^1\|_2^2 + \frac{\lambda_2}{2C}\sum_{c=1}^{C}\|\beta_c^2\|_2^2 + \sum_{c=1}^{C} l^c(\beta^c) \tag{7}$$

where $\beta^c = \beta^0 + \beta_{z_c}^1 + \beta_c^2$.

4.3 Learning the Model

The hierarchical model have established after constructing the group. Given the tree structure, the model can be optimized efficiently using iterative procedure [12], as shown in Algorithm 2. The object function can be decomposed into several separated problem. For example, when $\beta^0$and β^2 are given, β_z^1 can be optimized efficiently based on Trust Region Newton method [15] as traditional single class model.

Algorithm 2 Group Sharing Model optimization

Input: *the group Z and basic-level classes C*
Initialize: $\beta^0 = 0, \beta^1 = 0, \beta^2 = 0$
While (not Converged)
  (1) Given β^0 and β^2, optimize global-level β^0 using Eq. (7)
  (2) for $i = 1{:}Z$
    Given β^0 and β^2, optimize parent-level β^1_z using Eq. (7)
    end
  (3) for $j = 1{:}C$
    Given β^0 and β^1, optimize basic-level β^2_c using Eq. (7)
    end
end
Output: Hierarchical classifiers β^0, β^1, β^2

5 Experimental Results

In this section, we systematically evaluate our proposed framework on a subset of the *ImageNet* dataset [2].We randomly select about 200 concepts covering sub-categories from *Animal*, *Plant*, *Instrument*, *Scene*, and *Food* which distribute different levels across wide domain. The set contain the simple concepts with coherent visual appearance such as "*apple*" and "*goldfish*", also has the concepts with large visual variance i.e. "*book*" and "*cup*". And the number of samples is quite different, from several to thousands.

We divide the samples of each class into two equal sets: one is for training, the other is for testing. The feature we used is Color Moment and PHOG-180 [16] to represent the color distribution and local shape of the image.

5.1 Constructing Group

In this step, we firstly use HDC [6] to describe the diversity within class. The number of subsets and the variance among them is determined by the property of class. As shown in Fig. 3 (left), the top two rows are extracted from two subsets of class "*duck*". The partition highlights the color's variance. The below two rows are extracted from two subsets of class "*dump truck*" that represent the multiple views of the truck. We measure the inter-class similarity by computing average distance among their subsets.

We compare the method with average vector. Figure 3 (right) shows the K-Nearest Neighbor concepts based on HDC method and average vector. It is shown that HDC method always has stable performance. When the class has a common appearance and the diversity within class is small, better result can be got in terms of average vector, such as "*tower*" is more similar to "*skyscraper*" than

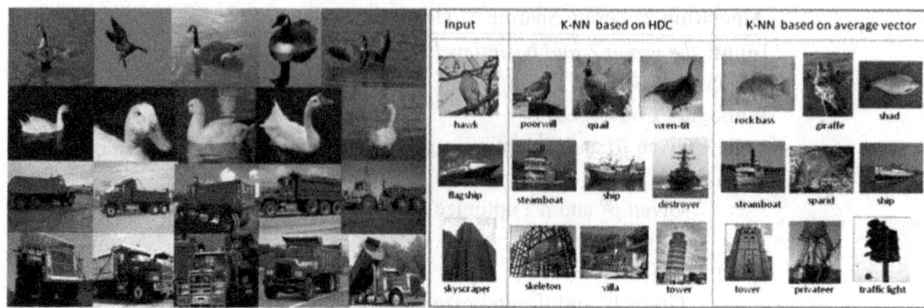

Fig. 3 (*Left*) Partition example: the subsets from class "*duck*" and "*dump truck*". (*Right*) Similarity measure compared with HDC and Average Vector

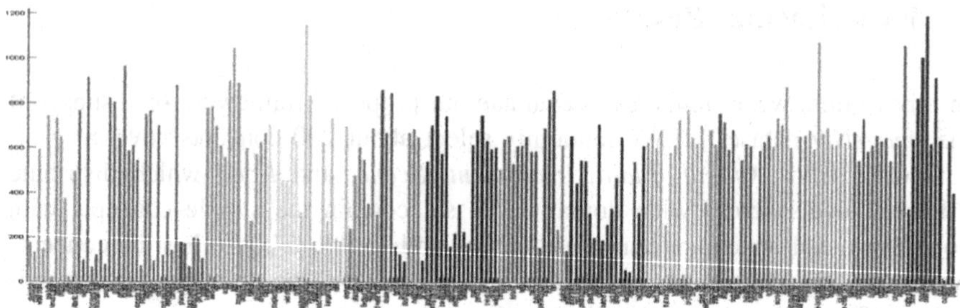

Fig. 4 The distribution of the training samples for 207 concepts

"*skeleton*". However, it may be inaccurate when the class has large intra-diversity and varied background.

Figure 4 shows the distribution of the training samples for 207 concepts. The concepts are arranged in groups represented by different colors. Observe that the union of many concepts is consistent with semantic similarity, i.e. {"*car*", "*rail-car*", "*truck*", "*tractor*", "*pantechnicon*", "*van*"}; {"*hawk*", "*duck*", "*quail*", "*wren-tit*", "*poorwill*", "*goose*"}; {"*squirrel*", "*kangaroo*", "*wolf*", "*fox*", "*lion*", "*tiger*"}; {"*boat*", "*destroyer*", "*flagship*", "*steamboat*", "*privateer*", "*ship*"}; {"*bed*", "*double bed*", "*sofa*"}. Moreover, the classes with visual concurrence such as {"*aircraft*", "*airplane*"}, {"*ship*", "*ocean*"} and {"*sky*", "*mountain*"} are also in the same groups. However, some unions are different from semantic similar. For example, "*mouse*" is related with "*keyboard*" and "*computer*" though they are not visually similar; a lot of instruments are not similar with each other, such as "*surgical knife*", "*scoop*" and "*reamer*". "*apple*" looks like "*tomato*" rather than "*grape*", and the "*ice bear*" is more similar to "*goose*" with the same color and similar background.

Table 1 Time cost and MAP compared among the methods

Model	Single class	Global sharing	Ruslan et al.	Group sharing
Time cost(/h)	21.5	6.5	170	12
MAP(%)	1.51	2.95	3.23	3.44

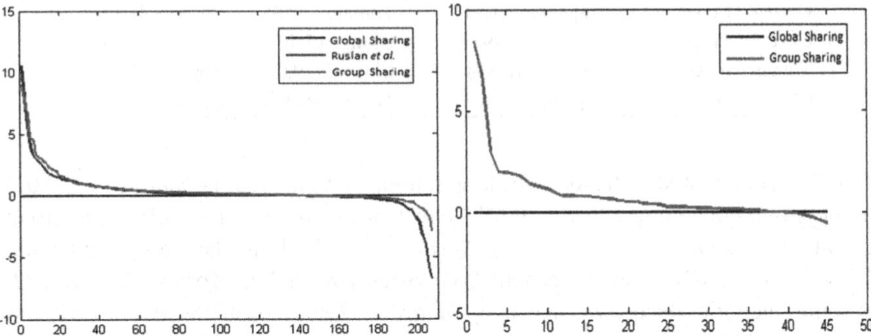

Fig. 5 (*Left*) *AP* improvements of Group Sharing and Ruslan et al. Model over Global Sharing Model. (*Right*) average *AP* improvements of the groups in Group Sharing Model over Global Sharing Model

5.2 Performance of the Model

In order to investigate the performance of Group Sharing Model, we compare it with the following three models: Single Class Model, is trained based on "1 against all" rule. The SGD-QN method [17] is introduced to train the model fast and effectively. Global Sharing Model, use a single global classifier for sharing [18]. Ruslan et al. [12] uses depth-first search strategy to decide which classes a new class should share information with.

Table 1 show the results of time cost and mean average precision(*MAP*). Due to the categories variance and the influence of complex background, the *MAP* of all categories is not so well. However, Group Sharing Model also have comparatively good performance. In term of the time cost, Global Sharing Model has the lowest the time cost (about 5.5 h). Due to the process of finding group and three level hierarchical modal, the complex of our Group Sharing Model is increasing (about 12 h). While it is still lower than the other two methods. The cost is of Single Class Model (about 21.5 h) is high despite using a fast optimization method. Ruslan et al. model is time-costing because of the dynamic structure and duplicate training (more than a week). It can use parallel method to decrease the tremendous complexity.

Figure 5 (left) displays the improvements in *AP*(%) of Group Sharing and Ruslan et al. [12] for all the categories over the Global Sharing Model. It shows the mid-level groups contribute to learning the data with large scale. Observe that the decrease in Ruslan et al. model is obvious. The category order and amount distribution of related classes may lead to the negative transfer. Figure 5 (right) shows the average improvements of groups (the number is 45) over Global Sharing Model.

Table 2 Most confused categories based on group sharing model

Categories	Top three of confused categories		
Whale shark (39.08)	Dolphin (8.34)	Sea turtle (5.97)	Cow shark (2.75)
Dolphin (8.89)	Whale shark (27.03)	Sea turtle (5.66)	Cow shark (2.56)
Sea turtle (7.25)	Whale shark (20.30)	Dolphin (6.36)	Cow shark (3.40)
Cow shark (2.94)	Whale shark (18.17)	Dolphin (7.95)	Sea turtle (5.30)
Orange (14.41)	Cayenne (11.71)	Tomato (7.58)	Cherry (3.39)
Cayenne (15.77)	Tomato (7.49)	Orange (7.40)	Cherry (5.17)
Tomato (6.70)	Orange (16.89)	Cayenne (9.01)	Apple (3.16)
Cherry (5.83)	Cayenne (14.03)	Tomato (6.20)	Orange (4.12)

In term of our model, the top three largest improvement in *AP* is "*mailbox*" (+9.01) in the group containing {"*pencil box*", "*envelope*"}, "*lettuce*" (+8.42) in the group containing {"*spinach*", "*olive*"}, and "*peacock*" (+7.24) in the group containing {"*cock*", "*macaw*"}. They are benefit from visually related categories. However, *AP* in some categories decreases, such as "*poniard*" (−2.86), "*slash pocket*" (−1.81) and "*tachina fly*" (−1.60). These concepts can be easily discriminated from the others, and the group may bring in extra noise.

In order to describe the group performance, we use a singleton classifier to classify all the test data. Table 2 displays the classifiers' performance and their most confused categories. It is shown that the model always confuses the visually similar samples in the same group. And these confusion may be acceptable.

6 Conclusion

In this paper, we propose to learn a hierarchical group-based sharing model by exploring the visual relatedness among categories. The categories with similar visual appearance are partitioned in a group and can improve the own strength with the aid of their groups. The fixed tree model can be effectively extended to further research, such as kernel learning, multi-feature integration and feature selection.

Acknowledgments This work was supported in part by National Natural Science Foundation of China: 61025011, 60833006 and 61070108, and in part by Beijing Natural Science Foundation: 4092042.

References

1. Russell, B., Torralba, A., Murphy, K., and Freeman, W. T. Labelme: a database and web-based tool for image annotation. IJCV, 2008, 77, 157–173.
2. L. Fei-Fei, ImageNet: crowdsourcing, benchmarking & other cool things, CMU VASC Seminar, 2010

3. Torralba, A., Murphy, K. P., and Freeman, W. T. Sharing visual features for multiclass and multiview object detection. PAMI, 2007, 29, 854–869.
4. Yu, K., Tresp, V., and Schwaighofer, A. Learning Gaussian processes from multiple tasks. ICML, 2005,1012–1019.
5. Paul A. Viola, Michael J. Jones. Fast and Robust Classification using Asymmetric AdaBoost and a Detector Cascade. Advances in Neural Information Processing Systems
6. L. Kaufman, P. J. Rousseeuw. Finding Groups in Data: An Introduction to Cluster Analysis. Wiley, New York. 1990.
7. K. Crammer and Y. Singer. On the learnability and design of output codes for multiclass problems, Comput. Learing Theory, 2000,pp. 35–46.
8. J. Weston and C. Watkins. Multi-class support vector machines, Proc. ESANN99, M. Verleysen, Ed., Brussels, Belgium,1999.
9. M. Marszalek and C. Schmid. Semantic hierarchies for visual object recognition. CVPR, 2007
10. Rob Fergus, Hector Bernal, YairWeiss, and Antonio Torralba. Semantic Label Sharing for Learning with Many categories. ECCV, 2010
11. Ya Xue, Xuejun Liao, Lawrence Carin. Multi-Task Learining for Classification with Dirichlet Process Priors. JMLR 8,2007, 35–63
12. Ruslan Salakhutdinov, Antonio Torralba, Josh Tenenbaum. Learning to Share Visual Appearance for Multiclass Object Detection. CVPR, 2011
13. MacQueen, J. B. Some methods for classification and Analysis of Multivariate Observations. Proceedings of 5th Berkeley Symposium on Mathematical Statistics and Probability,1967.
14. J. Frey and Delbert Dueck. Clustering by Passing Messages Between Data Points. University of Toronto Science 315, 972–976, February 2007
15. Chih-Jen Lin, Ruby C. Weng, S. Sathiya Keerthi. Trust Region Newton Method for Large-Scale Logistic Regression. JMLR 9,2008, 627—650
16. Bosch, A., Zisserman, A. and Munoz, X. Representing shape with a spatial pyramid kernel. CIVR,2007
17. Antoine Bordes, Léon Bottou, Patrick Gallinari. SGD-QN: Careful Quasi-Newton Stochastic Gradient Descent. JMLR 10,2009,1737–1754
18. T. Evegniou and M. Pontil. Regularized multi–task learning. KDD 2004.

Vehicle Type Classification Using Data Mining Techniques

Yu Peng, Jesse S. Jin, Suhuai Luo, Min Xu, Sherlock Au, Zhigang Zhang, and Yue Cui

Abstract In this paper, we proposed a novel and accurate visual-based vehicle type classification system. The system builts up a classifier through applying Support Vector Machine with various features of vehicle image. We made three contributions here: first, we originally incorporated color of license plate in the classification system. Moreover, the vehicle front was measured accurately based on license plate localization and background-subtraction technique. Finally, type probabilities for every vehicle image were derived from eigenvectors rather than deciding vehicle type directly. Instead of calculating eigenvectors from the whole body images of vehicle in existing methods, our eigenvectors are calculated from vehicle front images. These improvements make our system more applicable and accurate. The experiments demonstrated our system performed well with very promising classification rate under different weather or lighting conditions.

Keywords Vehicle type classification • License plate color recognition • Vehicle front extraction • Eigenvector • Type possibility • SVM

This work is supported by CSC-Newcastle joint scholarship.

Y. Peng (✉) • J.S. Jin • S. Luo • Y. Cui
The School of DCIT, University of Newcastle, Asutralia
e-mail: Yu.Peng@uon.edu.au

M. Xu
Faculty of Eng. & IT, University of Technology, Sydney, Australia

S. Au
Global Advanced Vison Ltd, China

Z. Zhang
School of Info., Xi'an University of Finance and Economics, China

J.S. Jin et al., *The Era of Interactive Media*,
DOI 10.1007/978-1-4614-3501-3_27,

1 Introduction

Nowadays, Intelligent Transport Systems (ITSs) have significant impacts on people' lives. ITSs are the applications that incorporate electronic, computer, and communication technologies into vehicles and roadways for monitoring traffic conditions, reducing congestion, enhancing mobility, and so on. Recently, vehicles based access control systems for highway, outdoor sites, buildings and even housing estates have become commonplace [1]. These systems rely on classifying vehicles into different types, such as car, van, bus, truck and etc. Besides vehicle authentication access, vehicle type classification is also used to compute the percentages of vehicle classes on a particular road and provides these data for traffic management. Vehicle types were classified by human operator before. This post-process method is time consuming and cannot be used in real-time applications, which are important components in ITSs. Comparing with a large amount of literature on automatic vehicle detection and tracking [2–4] which lead to the prototyping and initial development of ITSs, little work has been done in the field of vehicle classification. More research on the topic is desired for the industries' demands.

Existing methods for vehicle type classification generally fall into categories: sensor based and visual based. Sensor based methods employ buried inductive loops or radar to measure the size and length of vehicles. Vehicle types are identified basing on these measured features. Authors in [5] fed a back-propagation neural network the variation rate of frequency and frequency waveform, which were features of the time-variable signal generated when vehicles pass over buried inductive-loop coils. The output is five classified vehicles. The solution proposed in [6] used vehicle height and length profiles, which were obtained by a microwave radar sensor. The main drawback of such systems is its poor maintainability and high maintenance cost. On the other hand, large-scale deployment of traffic surveillance cameras and rapid development of image processing hardware and software have drawn the attention of using visual-based methods of vehicle type classification. Besides easier maintenance and higher flexibility, visual-based methods provide us more useful data such as license plate information, events such as crash or un-allowed stop, and road environment measurement. The information can hardly be obtained by sensor based methods. More information we obtain lead more accurate vehicle type classification. Moreover, the visual information could also be integrated into other ITSs application. It can maximize the benefits of traffic surveillance cameras.

Generally, there are three stages in visual based vehicle classification system: vehicle segmentation, feature extraction and vehicle classification. What makes existing methods different is what features are used and how to extract them. As stereo cameras are rarely used in ITSs, 2D features from vehicle images become intuitive choices. Methods in [1,7] extracted a number of features, such as Sobel edges, direct normalized gradients, locally normalized gradients, Harris corner response and etc., from car front images regions. However, many limitations were brought out since this kind method ignored vehicle body information such as length and width, which is a very crucial discernible feature. Moreover, ROI on car front image is defined in terms of license plate width relative to its center. However, this extracted ROI maybe very inaccurate car front information; because cars fronts' widths are very different but license plate in a same country or region have a same size. Authors in [8,9] were inspired by the facial expressional recognition. Their methods depend on eigenvectors and Gabor filter bank extracted from vehicle side images, respectively. However, the drawback of these two methods cannot be avoided as the underlying difference between vehicle type classification and facial expressional recognition. In the latter case, people's faces could be considered as planar. In vehicle type classification, the vehicle body information is 3D. What make the case worse is that camera perspective projection effect vehicles' 3D geometry features such as length, width, and height. Therefore, some researchers paid their attention on recovery of these vehicle parameters from the single camera view.

Parameterized 3D deformable models of vehicle structure became a popular method used in vehicle type classification [10–12]. In order to recover a vehicle' 3D geometric parameters from planar image, both of vehicle's side and front images are needed; moreover the whole body of vehicle should be contained. However, many traffic surveillance cameras such as the cameras in the entry of a building or the ones embedded on the traffic light cannot do this job.

Besides the limitations we have analyzed above, a drawback shared by all existing methods that the license plate information is ignored. Actually, in a same country or region, the authority regulates that different type vehicles should be with license plate of discriminated colors. For example, in China, large vehicle such as truck and bus is set up with yellow license plate; small vehicle such as passenger car, minivan, and sedan is allocated with blue or yellow license plate.

In this paper, we propose a more robust and more practical vehicle type classification system with high accuracy rate. In this system, only one camera, still mounted on a pole, facing the vehicle front and looking down on the observed highway, is used to monitor various vehicles. Our system incorporates various features extracted from every vehicle image such as with license plate color, width of vehicle front, and type probabilities. These utilized features can be easily obtained by existing camera arrangements on roads. This makes our system applicable in reality.

The rest of this paper is organized as follows. The next section describes the procedures of the whole proposed system. In Sect. 3, the novel method for localizing license plate and color recognition are presented. Section 4 details the procedure of extracting vehicle front image. Then, methods of defining vehicle front image and generating eigenvectors are presented in Sect. 5. The classification algorithm is described in Sect. 6. Section 7 demonstrates our experimental result. Finally, this paper is finished in Sect. 8 by a conclusion.

2 Overview of the Proposed System

Our proposed system consists of two parts: training and classify. As shown in Fig. 1a, we obtain a prediction model based on the features extracted from training images. These features consist of license plate color, width of vehicle front, and type probabilities. We first apply a novel method based on line segments features inside license plate image region to localize license plate quickly and accurately. In terms of RGB model, a simple decision tree training method to generate color classifier for license plate. We employ the background subtraction technique to obtain vehicle. The width of vehicle front is then learned. According to obtained license plate location and vehicle front width, we can correctly define various vehicle front images. From all vehicle front images, a set of eigenvectors is generated. Based on these eigenvectors, type probabilities of every vehicle images are calculated. Finally, we feed the obtained features into support vector machine (SVM) to generate classifiers for different vehicle types to obtain a type prediction model. In our experiment, we classified vehicles into five most popular types: truck, minivan, bus, passenger car, sedan (including sport-utility vehicle (SUV)). As shown in Fig. 1b, the same features extraction procedure in Fig. 1a is applied on every incoming image. According to these features, the trained prediction model classifies the vehicle image into a specific type. The following sections describe each of these four stages in more detail.

3 License Plate Localization and Color Recognition

Based on line segment features (LSFs) in our previous work [13], we localize quickly and accurately license plate of vehicle in image. Constructions of these three features and license plate localization based on these features are described in detail in our previous paper [13].

In a country or region, authority allocates different type vehicle license plate of various color. The license plate color is an important feature for vehicle type classification. Because all of our experimental images are captured in China and 98% vehicles in China are allocated with yellow, blue, or black. We cannot indicate a standard yellow, blue or black because color is very brightness sensitivity and also effected by the dust covering on LP. We apply decision tree method to generate

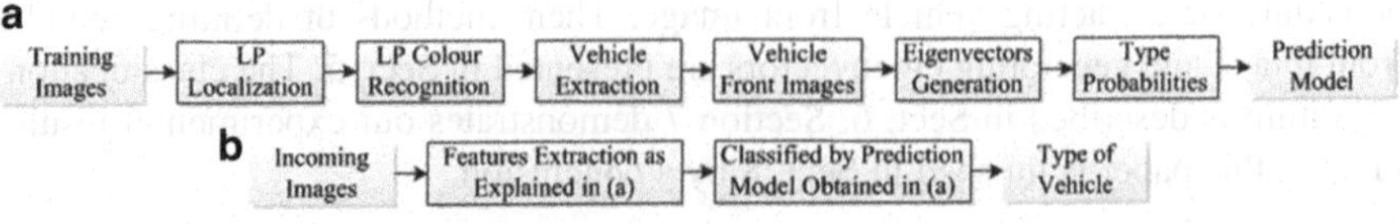

Fig. 1 Flowchart of the proposed type classification system

classifier for these three colors. According to RGB model, three features are obtained, as indicated in Eq. (1):

$$\{V_b, G_b = V_g/(V_b + 1), R_b = V_g/(V_b + 1)\} \quad (1)$$

Where V_b is intensity value in blue channel, G_b indicates the relationship between green channel and blue channel, and R_b presents the relationship between red channel and blue channel. All RGB values here are the mean intensity values over the license plate region in the correspondent channel. We then feed these three features into C4.5 decision tree [15] to generate classifiers for three final classes: yellow, blue, and black.

4 Vehicle Extraction

For classification, each vehicle should be detected and extracted from images. Because all images in our experiment are captured by a static camera, vehicle can be extracted through background subtraction. To make our subtraction algorithm robust, we capture several road images containing no vehicle under different lighting and weather conditions and then average them together as background. The subtraction operation is presented as follow:

$$D_k(x,y) = \begin{cases} 0, & if|I_k(x,y) - B_k(x,y)| \le T_d \\ 1, & otherwise \end{cases} \quad (2)$$

where D_k is the difference image, I_k is original image containing vehicle, B_k is the averaged background image, and T_d is a predefined threshold and chosen as the average of D_k. After subtraction, simple morphological operation is applied for noise removal. Figure 2c shows the result of the image subtraction based on Fig. 2a, b. Figure 2d is the result after noise removal using some morphological operations. Using this technique, each vehicle can be extracted from images. Because location of license plate has been calculated, we consider length of the line crossing the middle of license plate and vehicle's binary mask as vehicle front width.

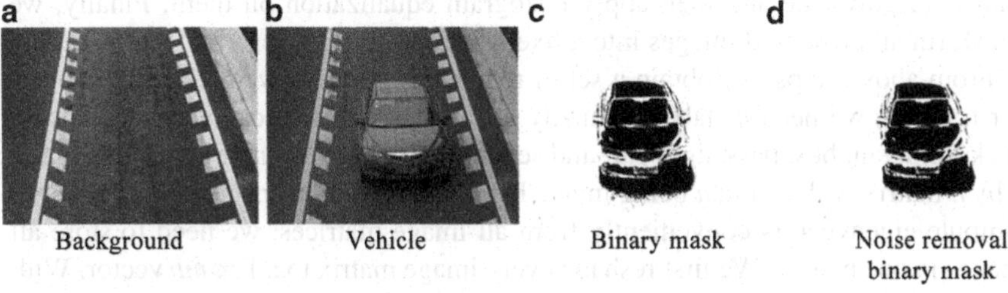

Fig. 2 Vehicle extraction from background

5 Eigenvector Generated from Vehicle Front Images

5.1 Defining Vehicle Front Image

We define vehicle front image based on location of license plate and width of the extracted vehicle's binary mask. Vehicle front image is defined relative to localized license plate and the width of vehicle front. The definition is thus independent on scale of the vehicle on the image.

5.2 Eigenvector Generated

Eigenvectors are derived from the covariance matrix of the probability distribution of the high-dimensional vector space of images. In our paper, eigenvectors extracted from vehicle front images are used for vehicle type classification. The eigenvector describe invariant characteristics of a vehicle front image. The mechanism behind eigenvector is Principal Component Analysis (PCA). In image classification, it is impossible to computing distance between two images pixel by pixel when comparing these two images, because the total noise contributed from every pixel will be very high. The noise could be anything that affects pixel's intensity value. Therefore, we usually compare two images in a subspace with much lower dimensionality than the total pixels' number. PCA is a popular method to find the subspace, namely eigenvectors. The eigenvector can separated all vectors maximally, which are images projected on the subspace, is called the first principle component of this image dataset. Theoretically, total number of eigenvectors we can find is the number of all images minus one. However, in practice, we only keep the ones with good separation capacity. Before generating eigenvector, vehicle front images should be processed.

It is extremely important to apply image pre-processing techniques to standardize the images. Most visual based classification algorithms are extremely sensitive to many factors such as camera angle, lighting condition, and image size. In our experiment, all vehicle images were captured by a static camera. In order to reduce the adverse effect of various lighting conditions, we first convert all vehicle front images to grayscale and then apply histogram equalization on them. Finally, we transform all processed images into a fixed size.

From above steps, we obtain a set of regularized training vehicle front images. For training, we need to label manually all images into five categories as above: truck, minivan, bus, passenger car, and sedan. Every image can be represented as a m by n matrix with m and n being image height and width, respectively. In order to compute eigenvectors conveniently from all image matrices, we need to store all images in one matrix. We first reshape every image matrix to a $1 \times mn$ vector. With k being the number of training images, we store all these images into a matrix of k

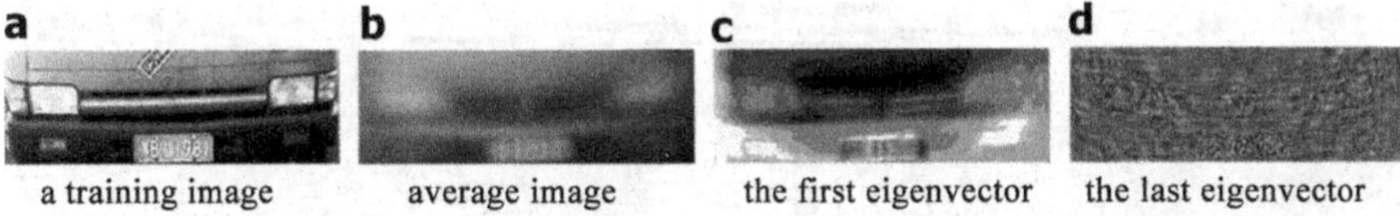

Fig. 3 Eigenvector generation from training images

columns $I = [I_1 I_2 \cdots I_k]$. The length of I_i is $m \times n$. Then we can compute the average image of all training images and the difference images:

$$a = \frac{1}{k}\sum_{i=1}^{k} I_i,\ \sigma_i = I_i - a \tag{3}$$

where a is the average image represented by a $1 \times mn$ vector, σ_i is a different image, and σ is a matrix storing all difference images. The covariance matrix of I is:

$$C = \frac{1}{k}\sum_{i=1}^{k} \sigma_i \sigma_i^T = \sigma\sigma^T \tag{4}$$

The principal components are the eigenvectors of C. Those eigenvectors that have the biggest associated eigenvalues contribute most to classify the training images. However, it is infeasible in eigenvector computation since $\sigma\sigma^T$ is a too huge matrix. In our experiment, the used vehicle front image is the size of 450 × 150. This makes the size of $\sigma\sigma^T$ 67,500 × 67,500. This computation burden was avoided by the method in [16]. Suppose u_i is an eigenvector of $\sigma^T\sigma$ and λ_i is the associated eigenvalue, then:

$$\sigma\sigma^T u_i = \lambda_i u_i \Rightarrow \sigma\sigma^T \sigma u_i = \lambda_i \sigma u_i \tag{5}$$

where we can deduce σu_i is an eigenvector of $\sigma\sigma^T$. This method greatly reduced the computation complexity since the size of $\sigma\sigma^T$ is only $k * k$.

As explained above, $(k-1)$ numbers of eigenvectors would be generated from k training images. As shown in Fig. 3c, d, they are the first eigenvector and last eigenvector in our experiment, respectively. These eigenvectors figured out main differences between all the training images. Moreover, every training image can be represented by a combination of the average image and eigenvectors. As shown in Fig. 3a, the training image is made up of:

$$a + 35.6\%v_0 - 13.5\%v_1 + 23.3\%v_2 + \cdots + 0\%v_{1320} + 0\%v_{1321} \tag{6}$$

where a is the average image of all training images, as shown in Fig. 3b; v_i is the ith eigenvector. The first eigenvector describes dominant features of vehicle, can discriminate different type vehicle maximally. However, there are mainly image noises in the last eigenvector, which make nearly no contribution to vehicle type

Fig. 4 Top 32 eigenvectors

classification. Rather than using all generated eigenvectors, we only pick up the eigenvectors with biggest eigenvalues. In our experiment, we choose the top 32 eigenvectors for classifying vehicles, as shown in Fig. 4.

Therefore, every training image is represented by 32 ratios, like $\{35.6, -13.5, 23.3, \cdots, -1.2\}$. In traditional eigenvector based classification system, to classify a new input object, the system first represents the new object by a set of ratios using the generated eigenvectors. The system then search through the list of ratios for all training images, find the one that is most similar to the ratios of the new input, then label the input same class. We make improvement in our system. Our system will find out the top ten training images those are most similar to the input image, calculate the type distributions of these ten training samples. We then obtain the type probabilities for the incoming image.

6 Classification

In our proposed method, license plate color is an important feature for vehicle type classification. Rather than taking the three values in red, green, and blue channel as three isolated features for SVM training, we train a decision model for license plate color recognition using these three features. There are two advantages of our method: first, as ocular information, license plate color is high-level feature that can be incorporated into other applications of ITSs; second, the type of vehicle is related with license plate color not the RGB values, accurate color recognition promises the performance of vehicle type classification. In our experiment, the two category color {yellow, blue, black} can be represented as (0,0,1), (0,1,0), and (1,0,0).

The second feature is the width of vehicle front. After extracting binary representative of vehicle from background, we consider the width of binary mask as width of vehicle front. In order to avoid camera perspective effects, we normalize the width via dividing it by the width of license plate in the same image. This is because license plates in the same country or region have a same size. Width of license plate is obtained in license plate localization step. For convenient computation in SVM, width features is scaled into the range [0, 1] before be inputted into SVM. We utilize tools provided by LIBSVM [17] in our system.

7 Experimental Results

In order to demonstrate the performance of our proposed vehicle type classification system, we analyzed the efficiency of license plate localization, license plate recognition, and vehicle type classification, respectively. There are total 1,377 images including 1,377 vehicles were used in our experiment. All images were captured from China's highways with a fixed camera. All captured vehicles falls into five classes: truck, minivan, bus, passenger car, sedan (including sport-utility vehicle (SUV)), as shown in Fig. 5.

For the first set of experiments, the performance of our proposed license plate localization is examined. In this set of experiments, we consider the localization correct when the overlay region of localized license plate with ground truth over 90%. Our system localized 1,336 license plate correctly from 1,377 vehicle images. Though the system can obtain this pretty high localization rate (97%) for our effective algorithm, we must also thanks to the simple background on highways.

In the second set of experiment, the performance of our color recognition algorithm was examined. There are three colors of license plate in our experiment: yellow, blue, and black. Moreover, over 95% of license plates in our image database are yellow or blue. For training by C4.5 decision tree method, we chose 200 yellow LPs, 200 blue LPs, and 20 black LPs.

We applied the obtained color prediction model from decision tree on all left 1,336 localized license plates image. Only 25 test images were misclassified. The high effectiveness of license plate localization and color recognition promise the performance of final vehicle type classification.

After eliminating 41 images of LP miss-localization and 25 images of color miss-recognition, there are total 1,311 images used in vehicle type classification. As shown in Table 1, we chose 80 images from every type vehicle images, respectively, and took the rest images as testing data.

All training images were transformed to the data format of SVM, as shown in Table 2. Each image instance is represented as a vector of real numbers. Moreover, all numbers were normalized in [0, 1].

Truck Bus Minivan Passenger car Sedan

Fig. 5 Five vehicle types

Table 1 Training images and testing images used in our experiment

	Truck	Minivan	Bus	Passenger Car	Sedan	Total
Training	80	80	80	80	80	400
Testing	76	122	43	250	420	911
Total	156	202	123	330	500	1,311

Table 2 Data format inputted into SVM

Image	Type	Feature1	Feature2	Feature3	Feature4	Feature5	Feature6	Feature7
X	Y	Color	Front Width	Truck Probability	Minivan Probability	Bus iProbability	Passenger car Probability	Sedan Probability

Table 3 Classification rate with the trained prediction model

	Truck	Minivan	Bus	Passenger Car	Sedan	Total
Testing	76	122	43	250	420	911
Correct classification	67	110	40	227	410	854
Classification rate	88.1%	90.1%	93.0%	90.8%	97.6%	93.7%

After training, we applied the prediction model on the rest images, which were also represented as SVM format. We obtain correct classification rates for the five categories: 88.1%, 90.1%, 93.0%, 90.8%, and 97.6%, respectively. The total correct classification rate is 93.7%. The experimental result is shown in Table 3. Our testing images were captured in various weather and lighting conditions. Obviously, our proposed vehicle classification system performed accurately and robustly. In the near future, more comparison experiment will be conducted to verify the superiority of our system over current methods.

8 Conclusion

In this paper, we have proposed a novel and effective vehicle type classification system based on vehicle front images. In our approach, vehicle image is represented by license plate color, vehicle front width, and five types (truck, bus, minivan, passenger car and sedan) probabilities. A prediction model obtained after training by SVM method. In our experiment, this prediction model classified the incoming vehicle image into a type accurately. The contributions of this paper can be summarized as follows: first, we originally incorporated license plate color as a discriminated feature into classification system; second, vehicle front is measured accurately based on license plate's location and background subtraction technique; third, the system learns type probabilities of a vehicle image rather than deciding type directly. Experimental results have shown the effectiveness of our vehicle type classification system.

References

1. Petrovic, V.S., Cootes, T.F.: Analysis of Features for Rigid Structure Vehicle Type Recognition in Proc. Brit. Mach. Vis. Conf., vol. 2,pp. 587–596.(2004)
2. Yang, W.: Joint Random Field Model for All-Weather Moving Vehicle Detection. Image Processing, IEEE Transactions on 19(9): 2491–2501(2010)

3. Leitloff, J., S. Hinz, et al.: Vehicle Detection in Very High Resolution Satellite Images of City Areas. Geoscience and Remote Sensing, IEEE Transactions on 48(7): 2795–2806(2010)
4. Chen, L.Y., Wu, B.F., Huang, H.Y., Fan, C.J.: A Real-Time Vision System for Nighttime Vehicle Detection and Traffic Surveillance, Industrial Electronics, IEEE Transactions on, vol.58, no.5, pp.2030–2044(2011)
5. Ki, Y.K., Baik, D.K.:Vehicle-Classification Algorithm for Single-Loop Detectors Using Neural Networks, Vehicular Technology, IEEE Transactions on, vol.55, no.6, pp.1704–1711 (2006)
6. Urazghildiiev, I., Ragnarsson, R., Ridderstrom, P., Rydberg, A., Ojefors, E., Wallin, K., Enochsson, P., Ericson, M., Lofqvist, G.: Vehicle Classification Based on the Radar Measurement of Height Profiles. Intelligent Transportation Systems, IEEE Transactions on, vol.8, no.2, pp.245–253(2007)
7. Negri, P., Clady, X., Milgram, M., Poulenard, R.: An Oriented-Contour Point Based Voting Algorithm for Vehicle Type Classification, Pattern Recognition, ICPR 2006. 18th International Conference on, vol.1, no., pp.574–577, 0–0 0(2006)
8. Zhang, C.C., Chen, X.; Chen, W.B: A PCA-Based Vehicle Classification Framework, Data Engineering Workshops, 2006. Proceedings. 22nd International Conference on, vol., no., pp.17(2006)
9. Ji, P.J., Jin, L.W., Li, X.T.: Vision-based Vehicle Type Classification Using Partial Gabor Filter Bank. Automation and Logistics, 2007 I.E. International Conference on, vol., no., pp.1037–1040, 18–21(2007)
10. Lai, A.H.S., Fung, G.S.K., Yung, N.H.C.: Vehicle type classification from visual-based dimension estimation. Intelligent Transportation Systems, 2001. Proceedings. 2001 IEEE, vol., no., pp.201–206(2001)
11. Gupte, S., Masoud, O., Martin, R.F.K., Papanikolopoulos, N.P.:Detection and classification of vehicles. Intelligent Transportation Systems, IEEE Transactions on, vol.3, no.1, pp.37–47 (2002)
12. Hsieh. J.W, Yu, S.H., Chen, Y.S., Hu, W.F.: Automatic traffic surveillance system for vehicle tracking and classification. Intelligent Transportation Systems, IEEE Transactions on, vol.7, no.2, pp. 175- 187(2006)
13. Peng, Y., Jin, J.S., Xu, M., Luo, S., Zhao, G.: Cascade-based License Plate Localization with Line Segment Features and Haar-Like Features. Accepted by the 6th International Conference on Image and Graphics, ICIG(2011)
14. Zhang, J., Yan,Y., Lades, M.: Face recognition: Eigenface, elastic matching, and neural nets," Proceedings of the IEEE, vol.85, no.9, pp.1423–1435(1997)
15. 15.Quinlan, J.R.: C4.5: Programs for Machine Learning. San Mateo, Calif.: Morgan Kaufmann (1993)
16. Turk, M.A., Pentland, A.P.: Face recognition using eigenfaces, Computer Vision and Pattern Recognition, 1991. Proceedings CVPR '91., IEEE Computer Society Conference on, vol., no., pp.586–591, 3–6(1991)
17. Chang, C.C., Lin, C.J.: LIBSVM: A library for support vector machines. ACM Trans. Intell. Syst. Technol. 2, 3, Article 27 (2011)

Stereo Image and Video Analysis

Stereo Perception's Salience Assessment of Stereoscopic Images

Qi Feng, Fan Xiaopeng, and Zhao Debin

Abstract 3D quality assessment (QA) has been widely studied in recent years, however, the depth perception and its influence to stereoscopic image's quality is still not mentioned. To the best of our knowledge the proposed approach is the first attempt in stereo perception's salience assessment of stereoscopic image. We research how depth perception's salience influences the quality of stereoscopic image. Under the assumptions that humans acquire different depth perception to the stereoscopic images with different discrepancy, four groups of multiview's images with parallel camera structure are chosen to test. By comparing the results of the proposed model and the subjective experiment, it shows that the proposed model has good consistency with the subjective experiment.

Keywords 3D quality assessment • Stereo perception • Discrepancy

1 Introduction

In the recent years, thanks to Hollywood's current fascination with three-dimensional (3D) movie, 3D visual technology is gaining a strong momentum such as 3D displays and 3D handheld devices. However, one of the major concerns for the wide adoption of 3D technology is the ability to provide sufficient visual quality. An added dimension of perceptual quality is the quality of 3D experience termed as "quality of experience assessment (QoE)" [1]. Different from traditional 2D images and videos, 3D QoE include such as the perception of depth, naturalness

Q. Feng (✉) • F. Xiaopeng • Z. Debin
School of Computer Science and Technology, Harbin Institute of Technology,
150001 Harbin, China
e-mail: fqi@jdl.ac.cn; xpfan@jdl.ac.cn; dbzhao@jdl.ac.cn

J.S. Jin et al., *The Era of Interactive Media*,
DOI 10.1007/978-1-4614-3501-3_28,

of visual stimulus, visual comfort, ability to fuse the stereoscopic pairs and so on. Among them, the perception of depth directly responds to the quality of people viewing a stereoscopic image which relate to human immersed realism feeling. The perception of depth can be represented as 3D's depth salience. Therefore, measuring depth's salience and its quantificational level are significantly for 3D QoE, especially for human's subjective experience.

Similar to 3D QA, both subjective and objective assessment methods can be used in gauging 3D QoE. Subjective testing requires human observers to view videos and provide their opinion of quality. Quality measurement using objective models (computational algorithms) can provide a more practical solution. Although many subjective test of 3D images and videos [2–4] is the most reliable way to obtain correct quality evaluation, it is time consuming, expensive, and unsuitable in real-time applications. Therefore, it is more practical to have objective metrics to predict the perceived quality reliably. However, up to now, only a few objective metrics [5,6] have been proposed for stereoscopic images. Previous works [5] propose a no-reference (NR) perceptual quality assessment for JPEG coded stereoscopic images based on segmented local features of artifacts and disparity. In addition, other perceptual quality metrics have been proposed, which a Just Noticeable Difference in Depth (JNDD) model [6] is used to assess stereoscopic quality by measuring asymmetric noises. By 2D objective image quality metrics, in [7], the structural similarity index (SSIM) is used as a measure for a monoscopic quality component to combine with stereoscopic quality component. An objective metric that considers stereoscopic crosstalk perception has also been proposed in [8].

However, few metrics take into account measuring the salience and intensity of stereo perception when people look at stereoscopic images. Actually, based on the visual attention (VA) theory of human visual system (HVS), our perception of the visual scene is only directed to a limited area at any given time. Saliency-based method has arguably been one of the most efficient trends in detecting the representative points or areas of one scene in 2D QA. Similar in 3D QA, if a stereoscopic scene is given, in addition to the content can affect our attentive points or regions, depth perception also attract our more attention. The saliency and intensity of depth have higher correlation with human perception of stereoscopic image quality. Therefore, it is necessary to research the relations of stereo perception's saliency and stereoscopic image quality which objective model should combine the content of the scene to assess the quality.

In this paper, we propose a method to locate the stereo perception region and exploit discrepancy between the left image and right image to measure stereo perception. Finally, subjective experiment is conducted to verify that the proposed metric maintains good consistency with the observer's perception. The rest of the paper is organized as follows: Sect. 2 presents the proposed stereo perception metric in details. In Sect. 3, the experimental results of the subjective test and the proposed metric are compared. Finally, we conclude the paper in Sect. 4.

2 Stereo Perception Metric

In general, 3D perception is based on various depth cues such as illumination, relative size, motion, occlusion, texture gradient, geometric perspective, disparity, and many others. In the context of binocular stereoscopic analysis, the disparity is used to represent shifted amount between two corresponding points in left and right images, which is regarded as the main factor of stereo perception. However, from a physiological point of view, stereo perception comes from slightly different scenes projected on the retina of each eye [9]. This slightly difference is represented as discrepancy which our brains are capable of measuring it and of using it to estimate depth. To mimic this physiology action, as is shown in Fig. 1, the metric is proposed based on three main processes, stereo view warping, locating stereo perceivable region and stereo perception calculation.

2.1 Stereo View Warping

Stereo images contain occluded regions that are spatially coherent groups of pixels. The occlusion pixels can be seen in one image of a stereo pair but not in the other. Their distribution and magnitude determine the intensity of depth [10]. This subsection describes stereo view warping method which is exploited to searching occlusion pixels and generate discrepancy map.

2.1.1 Discrepancy Compensated View Prediction (DCVP)

In the following we describe discrepancy compensated view prediction method that is used to calculate one view's discrepancy from the other view of stereo pairs. In virtual view synthesis, $I[l,x,y]$ is defined as the intensity of the pixel in real left view at pixel coordinates (x,y). View warping predicts to synthesize virtual view r' from

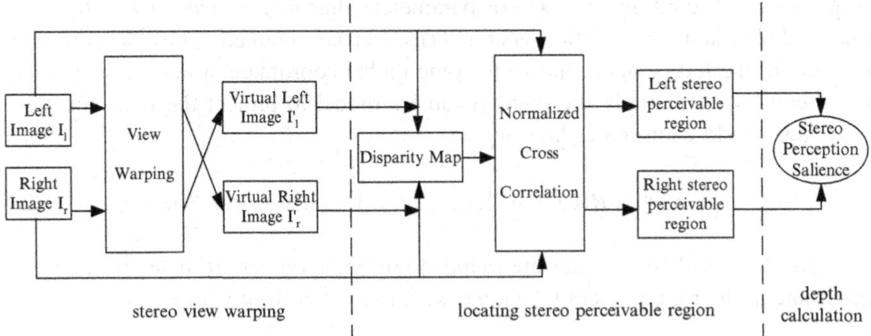

Fig. 1 The proposed stereo perception's salience metric

real left view. The value of $I[r', x - mx, y - my]$ is predicted from $I[l, x, y]$ where (mx, my) is a discrepancy vector computed in a block wise manner.

2.1.2 View Warping Transform

However, DCVP does not take advantage of some essential features of stereo pairs. Firstly, the differences between both views of a stereo scene usually cannot be accurately predicted. For example, in moving from one camera to the other the discrepancy in the screen pixel coordinates of an object between cameras will depend on the depth of the object. Objects closer to the camera will move much more than objects that are far from the camera. Secondly, effects such as rotations, zooms, or different intrinsic camera properties are often difficult to DCVP. Finally, since many applications of stereo video such as 3D video compression and 3D displays require accurate camera parameters, DCVP is also unavailable at calculating views discrepancy.

Considering the features of stereoscopic image, a virtual view is warped from previous real view and then subtract from its real view to calculate this view's discrepancy. Specifically, a virtual frame pair is generated based on the H.264/AVC for multi-view video compression view synthesis technique [11] and then exchange the virtual frame pair and real frame pair to calculate view point discrepancy respectively.

To synthesize virtual right view $I[r', x, y]$, we require the transformed distance of the pixel $I[l, x, y]$ from the real right camera, this distance denote by normalizing $d(x, y)$ which can be calculated from the left view depth map $D_l(x, y)$.

$$d(x,y) = \frac{1}{\left(\frac{D_l(x,y)}{255} \times \left(\frac{1}{S_{\min}} - \frac{1}{S_{\max}}\right) + \frac{1}{S_{\max}}\right)}, \tag{1}$$

where $D_l(x, y)$ is the depth value at (x, y) of left image. $S_{\min}$, $S_{\max}$ are the nearest and farthest depth value of left image from camera or the origin of 3D space respectively. According the camera parameters, intrinsic matrix $A(L)$, rotation matrix $R(L)$, and a translation vector $T(L)$ can be obtained. They describe the location of the left camera relative to some global coordinate system. Using these parameters, we can apply the pinhole camera model to project the pixel location (x, y) into world coordinates $[u, v, w]$ via

$$[u, v, w] = R(L) \times A^{-1}(L) \times [x, y, 1] \times d[x, y] + T(L). \tag{2}$$

Next, the world coordinates are mapped into the target coordinates $[x', y', z']$ of the frame in the right camera which we wish to predict from via

$$[x', y', z'] = A(R') \times R^{-1}(L) \times \{[u, v, w] - T(R)\}. \tag{3}$$

Finally, to obtain a pixel location, the target coordinates are converted to homogenous form $[x'/z', y'/z', 1]$ and the intensity for pixel location (x, y) in the virtual frame is $I'[x, y] = I[x'/z', y'/z']$.

An important issue in view synthesis is the accurate camera parameters and depth maps. For our tests, we choose some sequences (the test sequences are downloaded from Heinrich-Hertz-Institute and Tanimoto Lab at Nagoya University) according with these requirements.

2.2 Locating Stereo Perceivable Region

In order to avoiding vertical discrepancy, the stereoscopic images in our experiments are captured by two cameras with parallel optical axes. However, this parallel structure makes the outside boundaries in both left and right images cannot project on the retina of each eye simultaneously. In addition, from early physiological and psychological test [9], stereo perception mainly emerges into the region of occlusion pixels which are generated by the change of depth. We represent these regions as discrepancy map. This subsection calculates the discrepancy map and searches stereo perceivable region.

2.2.1 Calculating Discrepancy Map

Given a stereoscopic images with a left image (reference image) I_l and a right image (target image) I_r, stereo view warping convert each pixel to transform $I_{l'}$ and $I_{r'}$ respectively. The difference $\Delta I_{l,l'}(x, y)$ between pixel at (x, y) in left image and corresponding pixel in the warped left image (at the same location) is expressed as

$$\Delta I_{l,l'}(x, y) = \frac{1}{3} \sum\nolimits_{c \in \{R,G,B\}} \left| I_{l_c}(x, y) - I_{l'_c}(x, y) \right|, \tag{4}$$

where $I_{l_c}(x, y)$, $I_{l'_c}(x, y)$ are the intensity of color channel c at (x, y) in the real left image and the warped left image respectively. Similarly,

$$\Delta I_{r,r'}(x, y) = \frac{1}{3} \sum\nolimits_{c \in \{R,G,B\}} \left| I_{r_c}(x, y) - I_{r'_c}(x, y) \right|. \tag{5}$$

Hence, the discrepancy map is expressed as DM:

$$DM(x, y) = \Delta I_{l,l'}(x, y) + \Delta I_{r,r'}(x, y). \tag{6}$$

Through view warping transform, the pixels in the foreground and background transfer different distance at same time. The occlusion pixels can be obtained.

Due to the occlusion pixels only at the object's edge with different depth, $DM(x, y)$ is also non-zero at these positions. Thus, discrepancy map DM could represent the position of depth change, i.e. the position of stereo perception.

2.2.2 Searching Stereo Perceivable Region

Stereo view warping transform could calculate not only accurate location of unknown pixels due to the occlusions, but also some pixels at the image bound are filled by null. On account of stereo perception only be acquired within the binocular fusion region, the mutual scene region of both left and right can be combined by our eyes. Therefore, the number of horizontal pixels in the mutual scene region denotes the width of stereo perceivable region accurately. Here, Normalized Cross Correlation (NCC) [12] method is used to compute the mutual number of horizontal pixels between the stereoscopic images I_l and I_r, as following,

$$C(I_l, I_r) = \frac{(I_l - \bar{I}_l)(I_r - \bar{I}_r)}{\sqrt{(I_l - \bar{I}_l)^2 (I_r - \bar{I}_r)^2}}, \tag{7}$$

where $\bar{I}_l$ and $\bar{I}_r$ are the mean value of the elements from I_l and I_r.

In the process of matching, NCC measures the max similarity $C_{\max}(I_l, I_r)$ between mutual regions of anchor pixels. As a direct theoretical conclusion from the formulation, NCC is invariant to global bias and gain changes. So this method can acquire the robust stereo perceivable region, even for slightly distorted images.

2.3 *Calculating Stereo Perception's Salience*

This subsection calculates the stereo perception's salience of stereoscopic images in stereo perceivable region.

The stereo perception's salience is defined based on the distribution and intensity of the discrepancy map in stereoscopic images. From our subjective experimental, more discrepancy area and larger discrepancy could enhance the stronger experience of stereo perception respectively. We convert the assessment of stereo perception's salience into the calculation of discrepancy. Due to the parallel structure of the stereo cameras, only horizontal discrepancy should be taken into consider. The discrepancy from left view can be measured as:

Table 1 Subjective test conditions and parameters

Method	ITU-T BT.500-11: SS (Single stimulus)
Evaluation scales	5 grades
Stereo images	24bits/pixelcolor(1024 × 768, 1280 × 960)
Test participants	15 students (12 males, 3 females; age range: 22–31 years old)
Display	ViewSonic VX2268wm (22' Active Shutter 3D LCD)
DisplayResolution	1680 × 1050
Displayrefresh rate	120 Hz
Glasses	nVIDIA GeForce 3D Vision wireless stereoscpic glasses
Glassesrefresh rate	60 Hz
Viewingdistance	1 m
Roomillumination	Dark

$$\mathrm{D}_l(u) = 1 - \frac{\sum_{x=u}^{u+U-1}\sum_{y=v}^{v+V-1}(l(x,y-\bar{l}_{u,v})(r(x-u,y)-\bar{r}_{u,v})}{\sqrt{\sum_{x=u}^{u+U-1}\sum_{y=v}^{v+V-1}(l(x,y-\bar{l}_{u,v})^2\sum_{x=u}^{u+U-1}\sum_{y=v}^{v+V-1}(r(x-u,y)-\bar{r}_{u,v})^2}}, \tag{8}$$

where $\bar{I}_{u,v}$ and $\bar{I}'_{u,v}$ are the mean value of the template $U \times V$ from the left image and the warped left image. For right view's $D_r(u,v)$ is similar to $D_l(u,v)$. Therefore, $\frac{1}{2}(D_l(u,v) + D_r(u,v))$ is used to represent stereo perception's salience of stereoscopic images through an value at [0,1].

3 Subjective Experimental

To our best knowledge, only one public stereoscopic image databases are available in the stereoscopic image quality assessment community. However, this database does not focus on the stereo perception and not provide camera parameters. We collect four groups of natural stereoscopic images with different disparity and conduct subjective experiments to evaluate the stereo perception's salience based on this database. These sequences are downloaded from (ftp://ftp.hhi.de/HHIMPEG3DV/HHI/; http://www.tanimoto.nuee.nagoya-u.ac.jp/) under the permission of Heinrich-Hertz-Institut and Tanimoto Lab at Nagoya University, respectively. The sequences provide 16 grades ("Alt_Moabit" and "Book_Arrival") and 80 grades ("Champagne_tower" and "Pantomime") horizontal disparity. Only four adjacent views' sequence frames are chosen in our experiments which avoid over more than 50 pixels to exceed the range of binocular fusion. The four quality scales (QP: 27, 37, 42 and reference) are selected for H.264/AVC encoder. All levels of compression are applied to both the left and right images, resulting in a 4 × 4 matrix of symmetric coding combinations for each reference image. The subjective test conditions and parameters are summarized in Table 1.

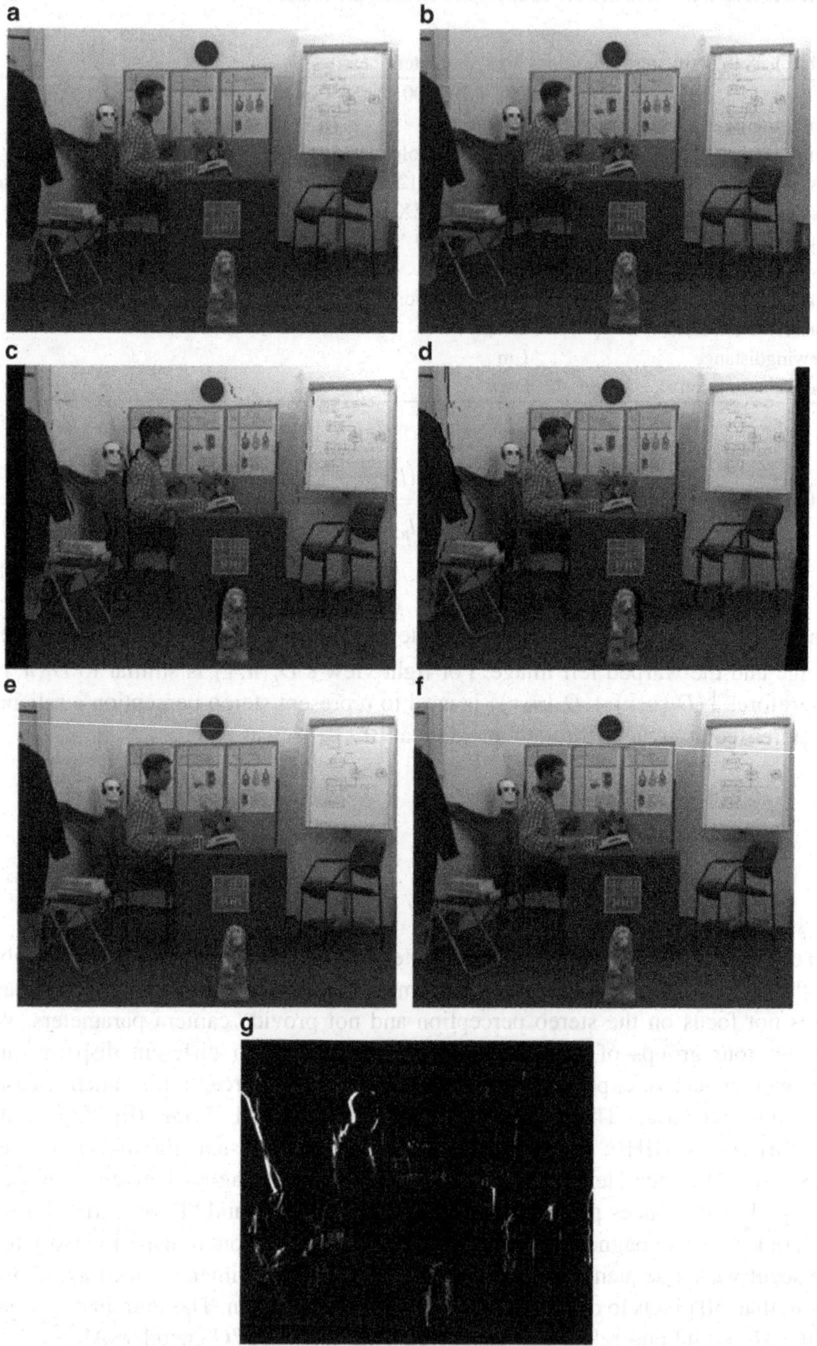

Fig. 2 The intermediate results of 'bookarrival' from our method. (**a**) The first frame of bookarrival sequence at view10. (**b**) The first frame of bookarrival sequence at view12. (**c**) Warped image from view10 to view12. (**d**) Warped image from view12 to view10. (**e**) and (**f**) Stereo perceivable region of view10 and view12. (**g**) The discrepancy map adopt by contrast enhancement of view10 and view12

4 Experimental Results

In order to verify the performance of our proposed model, we follow the standard performance evaluation procedures employed in the video quality experts group (VQEG) FR-TV Phase II test, where Pearson linear correlation coefficient (CC), between objective (MOSp) and subjective (MOS) scores is calculated at 0.934 (Fig. 2).

From the Scatter plots as shown in Fig. 3, our method results maintain good consistency with the subjective test results when MOS is bigger than 3. While at low MOS score, the proposed metric has poor performance. It's mainly because the observers cannot distinguish the slight change of depth within little discrepancy, especially by the influence of distortion. From Table 2 we can draw two conclusions. Firstly, for reference stereo frame pairs, the values of neighbor views are less than the values of interval views. It indicates that increasing discrepancy can enhance stereo perception's salience. However, there is a threshold on the discrepancy because excess disparities exceed the stereo experience of human perception. Through the subjective experiments, we get the threshold is 0.2. Secondly, for compressed stereo frame pairs, the values of high QP compressed frames decrease slowly. It denotes that high compressions influence the perception of stereo experience slightly.

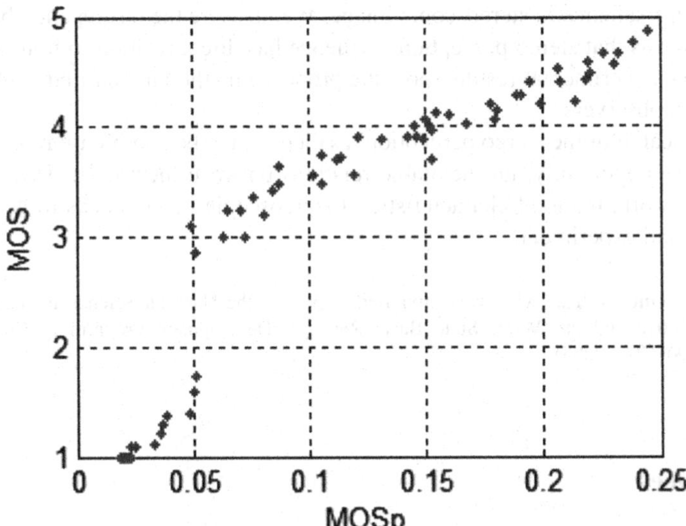

Fig. 3 Scatter plots of MOS versus MOSp

Table 2 Results of the proposed subjective test conditions and parameters

		Reference	QP = 27	QP = 37	QP = 42
Bookarrival	View10&11	0.1491	0.1425	0.1363	0.1310
	View10&12	0.1981	0.1917	0.1854	0.1799
	View10&13	0.2194	0.2130	0.2062	0.2004
	View10&14	0.2452	0.2386	0.2320	0.2259
Alt_Moabit	View1&2	0.0533	0.0513	0.0499	0.0483
	View1&3	0.0891	0.0873	0.0859	0.0840
	View1&4	0.1186	0.1159	0.1143	0.1121
	View1&5	0.1497	0.1476	0.1452	0.1429
Champagne_tower	View25&26	0.0665	0.0608	0.0547	0.0504
	View25&27	0.1178	0.1124	0.1071	0.1016
	View25&28	0.1601	0.1549	0.1499	0.1452
	View25&29	0.1945	0.1886	0.1833	0.1777
Pantomime	View20&21	0.0228	0.0216	0.0194	0.0183
	View20&22	0.0240	0.0222	0.0208	0.0189
	View20&23	0.0384	0.0367	0.0351	0.0329
	View20&24	0.0552	0.0541	0.0527	0.0514

5 Conclusion

This paper presents an objective assessment model that target on calculating stereo perception's salience in stereoscopic image. We measure the discrepancy based on the hypothesis that stereo perception's salience has direct relation to it at different scales. The experimental results show the proposed method has similar assessment result with observers.

The research of the stereo perception's salience may be combination of QA and QoE. More importantly, no inevitable relations between them exist. However, in the future work, the total characteristic of stereoscopic image needs to be proved in theory and experiment.

Acknowledgements This work was supported in part by the National Science Foundations of China:60736043 and the Major State Basic Research Development Program of China (973 Program 2009CB320905)

References

1. L. Goldmann, F. De Simone, and T. Ebrahimi. A comprehensive database and subjective evaluation methodology for quality of experience in stereoscopic video. Electronic Imaging (EI), 3D Image Processing (3DIP) and Applications (2010).
2. ITU-T, "Subjective video quality assessment methods multimedia applications", Rec. P.910 (2008).

3. Payman Aflaki, Miska M. Hannuksela, Jukka Häkkinen, Paul Lindroos and Moncef Gabbouj, "Subjective study on compressed asymmetric stereoscopic video", in ICIP 2010, pp.4021–4024, Sep (2010).
4. Alexandre Benoit, Patrick Le Callet, Patrizio Campisi and Romain Cousseau, "Quality assessment of stereoscopic images". EURASIP Journal on Image and Video Processing, Volume (2008).
5. Z.M.P. Sazzad, S. Yamanaka, et al., "Stereoscopic Image Quality Prediction", International Workshop on Quality of Multimedia Experience, San Diego, CA, U.S.A. (2009).
6. Y. Zhao, Z.Z. Chen, C. Zhu, Y.P. Tan, and L. Yu, "Binocular just-noticeable-difference model for stereoscopic images," IEEE Trans. Signal Processing, vol. 18, no. 1, pp.19–22, January (2011).
7. A. Boev, A. Gotchev, K. Egiazarian, A. Aksay and G. Akar, "Towards compound stereo-video quality metric: aspecific encoder-based framework," Proc. of the 17th Southwest Symposium on Image Analysis and Interpretation(SSIAI 2006), Denver, CO, USA, pp. 218–222, March (2006).
8. Liyuan Xing, Junyong You, Touradj Ebrahimi, Andrew Perkis, "A perceptual quality metric for stereoscopic crosstalk perception", in ICIP 2010, pp.4033–7, Sep (2010).
9. I. P. Howard and B. J. Rogers, "Binocular Vision and Stereopsis," Oxford University Press, Oxford ISBN 0-19-508476-4 (1995).
10. S. S. Intille and A. F. Bobick. Disparity-space images and large occlusion stereo. In Proc. of the 3rd Euro- pean Conf. on Comp. Vision, pages 179–186 (1994)
11. Y. Mori, N. Fukushima, T. Yendo, T. Fujii, M. Tanimoto, View generation with 3D warping using depth information for FTV, Image Communication, vol. 24, issue 1–2, 2009, pp. 65–72
12. J. P. Lewis, "Fast normalized cross-correlation," Vision Interface, 1995.

Confidence-Based Hierarchical Support Window for Fast Local Stereo Matching

Jae-Il Jung and Yo-Sung Ho

Abstract Various cost aggregation methods have been developed for finding correspondences between stereo pairs, but their high complexity is still a problem for practical use. In this paper, we propose a confidence-based hierarchical structure to reduce the complexity of the cost aggregation algorithms. Aggregating matching costs for each pixel with the smallest support window, we estimate confidence levels. The confidence values are used to decide which pixel needs additional cost aggregations. For the pixels of small confidence, we iteratively supplement their matching costs by using larger support windows. Our experiments show that our approach reduces computational time and improves the quality of output disparity images.

Keywords Cost aggregation • Hierarchical structure • Confidence • Low complexity • Stereo matching

1 Introduction

It is an old, but steady research topic to find dense correspondences from two or more images captured at different positions. It is called dense stereo matching, and its output is a disparity image, a set of the displacement vectors between correspondences. The dense disparity images have a number of applications such as robot vision, image-based rendering, and surveillance system, and their applicability is drastically increasing.

Although the principle of stereo matching seems to be straightforward, the ambiguity of images in practice makes stereo matching difficult. The ambiguity comes from homogeneous regions and periodic textures, and it is a main problem of

J.-I. Jung • Y.-S. Ho (✉)
Gwangju Institute of Science and Technology (GIST), 123 Cheomdan-gwagiro, Buk-gu, Gwangju 500-712, South Korea
e-mail: jijung@gist.ac.kr; hoyo@gist.ac.kr

J.S. Jin et al., *The Era of Interactive Media*,
DOI 10.1007/978-1-4614-3501-3_29,

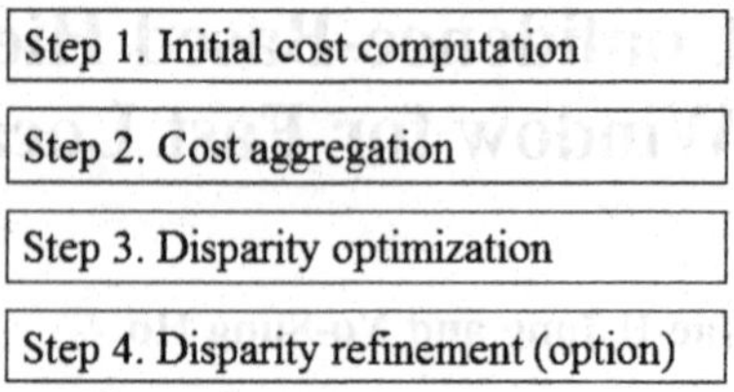

Fig. 1 General flow of stereo matching

Step 1. Initial cost computation

Step 2. Cost aggregation

Step 3. Disparity optimization

Step 4. Disparity refinement (option)

stereo matching. Various stereo matching algorithms have been proposed to overcome this problem, and they generally have four steps [1] as shown in Fig. 1. Initial cost computation calculates matching costs for assigning different disparity hypotheses to different pixels, and cost aggregation spatially aggregate initial costs over support regions. Disparity optimization minimizes a predefined energy function locally or globally, and disparity refinement refines output disparity images.

Step 1 to Step 3 are mandatory, and Step 4 is optional. In general, stereo matching algorithms are categorized to two approaches: local and global algorithms. While the local methods use a local optimization method, the winner-takes-all (WTA), in Step 3, the global algorithms adopt global optimization methods such as graph-cut, belief propagation, and dynamic programming [2,3]. The global methods use additional prior knowledge such as smoothness and occlusion constraints. The global algorithms tend to show better results than the local algorithms, and they hold high ranks in the evaluating chart of Middle bury.

In both the local and global algorithms, the core part currently be watched is cost aggregation of Step 2. The performance of the local algorithms completely depends on cost aggregation, and it also plays an important role in the global algorithms. Therefore various cost aggregation algorithms have been proposed [9,10].

2 Cost Aggregation

Different cost aggregation algorithms use their own methods to select the support region and function for calculating new costs. Each method helps costs be robust to ambiguous regions in stereo images.

The easiest and oldest aggregation approach is to aggregate the cost of assigning disparity *d* to given pixel *p* with the average cost of all pixels in a square window, but it has the critical disadvantage that it is not able to handle disparity discontinuity boundaries. To overcome this property, the shiftable-window approach was proposed, which calculate matching cost with multiple square windows centered at different locations and selects the one having the smallest cost [5].

Other approaches use color segmentation based on the property that the depth discontinuity boundaries tend to co-locate the color discontinuity boundaries. The segmentation-based approaches select the sizes and shapes for support windows according to the segmentation results [6]. However it requires color segmentation as a prior, which is an ill-posed problem and has high computational complexity. To remove these constraints, the edge detection-based approach was proposed [7].

Instead of searching for an optimal support window with arbitrary shape and size, the recently proposed adaptive-weight algorithm adjusts the support-weight of each pixel in a fix-sized square window [8]. However, the computation cost is high.

The recent cost aggregation algorithms show sufficiently good results without any global optimization, but its computational complexity is quite high. It is a crucial problem in practical use. Some algorithms are proposed for fast cost aggregation. Rhemann et al. smooth the cost volume with a weighted box filter, and the weights are based on the edge preservation [9,10]. Some researchers proposed its solution using graphics hardware [11], but it is not a root solution.

In this paper, we propose a confidence-based hierarchical structure to reduce a complexity of the cost aggregation algorithms. At first, we calculate data costs for each pixel with the smallest support window, and conduct confidence estimation. The confidence values are used to decide which pixels need additional cost aggregations.

3 Proposed Algorithm

The proposed algorithm uses the hierarchical structure and the confidence concept to reduce the computational complexity.

3.1 Hierarchical Structure

We can consider two types of hierarchical structure: pyramids of support window and image plane. Figure 2 shows these two methods. Type I and type II represent the pyramid of support window and pyramid of image plane, respectively.

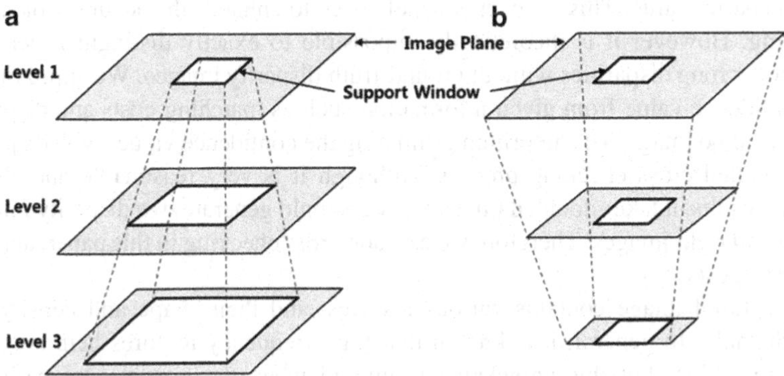

Fig. 2 Two types of hierarchical structure: (**a**) pyramid of support windows and (**b**) pyramid of image planes

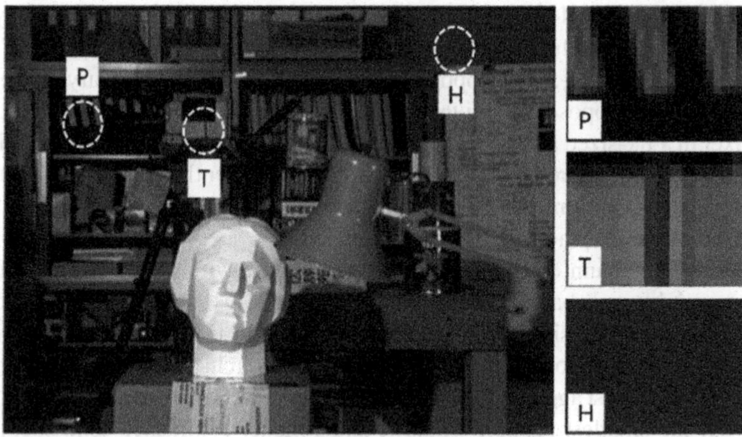

Fig. 3 Three texture types in *tsukuba* image: periodic (P), textured (T), and Homogeneous (H). The three images on the *right column* show the enlarged textures of the three parts

They have different advantages and disadvantages. While type II loses texture information and decrease the total disparity range in high levels, type I can keep them. However, type I induces higher computational complexity than type II.

The problems of type II are very critical, because the texture information plays a core role in stereo matching and the reduced disparity range is very ambiguous to be directly used in lower levels. Therefore, we adopt type I in our algorithm and introduce the confidence-based structure to reduce computational complexity.

3.2 Confidence Measurement

The confidence in stereo matching means the probability that a certain pixel has a right disparity value. This concept is widely used to enhance the accuracy of stereo matching. However it is theoretically impossible to exactly distinguish between right and wrong disparities without ground-truth disparity images. We approximate the confidence value from given information such as matching costs and disparity pairs of stereo image. The algorithm estimating the confidence values with disparity pair is called cross checking process. Although it is very reasonable and shows reliable results, it takes doubled time since we should generate two disparity images for left and right images. Therefore we exclude cross checking in this paper, and use matching costs.

A captured image contains various textures, and their shape and density are unpredictable. In general, it is known that high frequency textures help accurate stereo matching, but this knowledge is invalid when the textures are periodic. Figure 3 shows *tsukuba* image from middle bury, which has various textures. We marked three parts on the image, which have special textures. The three images

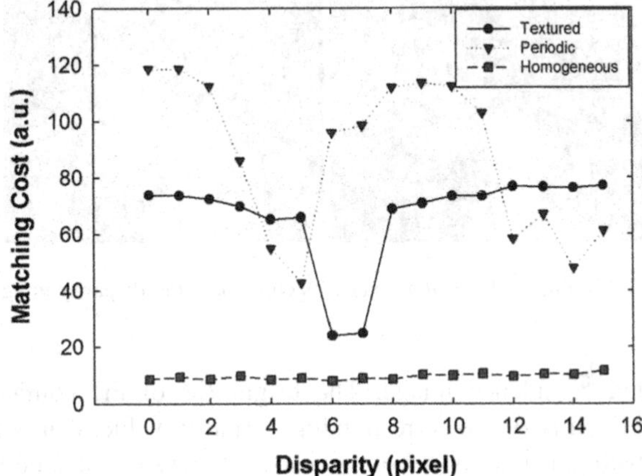

Fig. 4 Matching costs of the three texture types: textured, periodic, and homogeneous

on the right column show the enlarged textures of each part. The part P and part T have high frequency textures, but the texture of the part P is periodic. The "P" and "T" are initial letters of "periodic" and "textured", respectively. The part H has low frequency textures, and the "H" is an initial letter of "Homogeneous". It is known that homogeneous regions and periodic-textured regions induce inaccurate stereo matching.

We extract each matching costs according to disparity candidates so as to analysis the relationship between texture types and matching costs. Figure 4 shows the matching cost, calculated by the adaptive support weight, according to disparities. The textured region has an exact minimum, but the minimums of others are ambiguous. The homogeneous region shows low matching costs on the whole, but notable minimum does not exist. Although there are notable local minimums in the periodic textures, it is not clear which minimum is correct.

The WTA algorithm, of course, can find the disparity having the smallest matching cost, but we cannot conclude this disparity is correct because these are various unexpected textures disturbing cost aggregation.

In our proposed algorithm, we use the confidence value to distinguish the pixels with reliable matching costs in whole pixels and stop aggregating costs in next level of the pyramid of support window. It helps to reduce the computational time. Therefore, it is very important to extract reliable pixel with an accurate measure. Some confidence measurements were proposed such as the first minimum cost value, and the ratio of the first minimum cost to the second minimum cost. Since our main goal is to extract very accurate pixels, we define the confidence measure as (1).

$$Confidence(i) = 255 \cdot \exp \lambda(1^{st}C(i) - 2^{nd}LC(i)) \tag{1}$$

where $1^{st}C(i)$ is the smallest matching cost of pixel i, and $2^{nd}LC(i)$ is the second local minimum matching cost of pixel i. λ and constant value 255 are scaling and normalizing factors. Figure 5 shows the original *tsukuba* image, its disparity image,

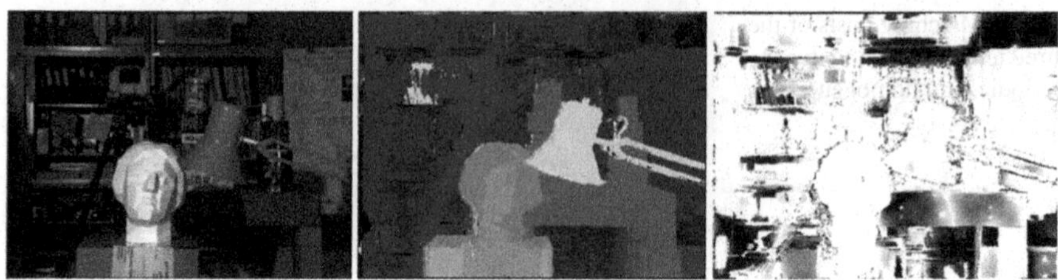

Fig. 5 Original *tsukuba* image, its corresponding disparity image, and confidence image

and confidence image. The brightness of the confidence image represents the reliability of the corresponding disparity value. Our confidence measure is able to distinguish not only homogeneous regions but also periodic regions.

3.3 Confidence-Based Hierarchical Cost Aggregation

With the confidence image and hierarchical support window, we can reduce the computational complexity of cost aggregation. The following code is the pseudo code for our algorithm.

```
For each Support_Window_Size, from small size,
  For each pixel i,
    if(Flg(i) == FALSE)
      Calculate Cost_new(i) using Cost_Aggregation
      Calculate Confidence(i) from Data(i)
  Refine Confidence(i)
  For each pixel i,
    if(Confidence(i) > Th)
      set Flg(i) = TRUE
    if else
      Cost_old(i) + = Cost_new(i)
Disparity with WTA
```

At first, we select the number of level and initiate the matching cost. We aggregate the matching cost with the smallest support window, and calculate the confidence values of whole pixels. The confidence image is refined by using Gaussian smooth filter to consider neighbor confidence values. If the confidence value is greater than a certain threshold value, we set the flag for the current pixel with "TRUE". This flag is used to decide whether the current pixel needs additional aggregation process or not. In the next level, we only aggregate costs for pixel whose flag is "FALSE". These processes are repeated until cost aggregation process with the largest support window is done. The final disparity image is obtained by using WTA.

Figure 6 shows the disparity and flag images according to each level. As the level increases, the "TRUE" flag, which means the current pixel does not need

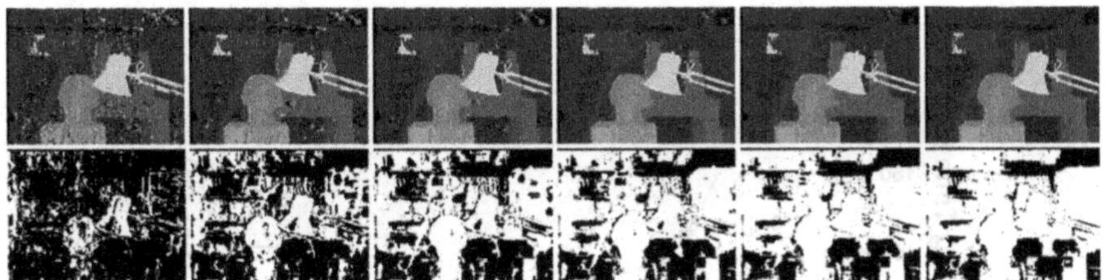

Fig. 6 Change of disparity and flag images according to increased hierarchical level

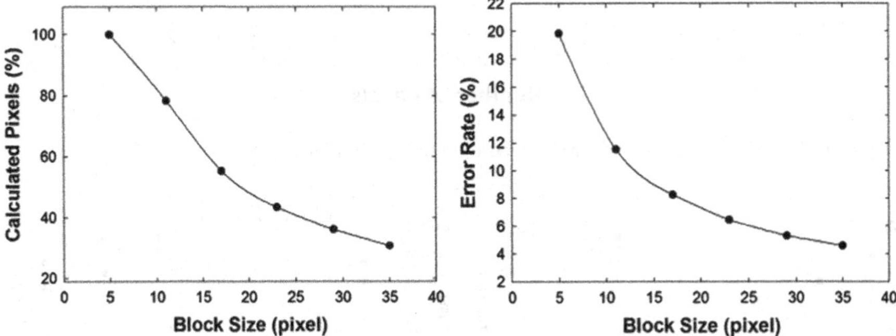

Fig. 7 Calculated pixels and error rates according to support window size

additional aggregation, also increase. The quality of the final disparity image is also improved.

We measure the number of calculated pixel and error rates at each level, and demonstrate them in Fig. 7. As the size of support window increases, the number of calculated pixels decreases. It means we can skip many pixels in the higher level which needs more time than lower level. The accuracy of stereo matching is also improved as the level increases.

Figure 8 shows the relationship between the number of levels and computational complexity. While a number of levels induces time-saving, the error rates are also incresed. In this paper, we set the number of levels with three to five according to the maximum support window size.

4 Experimental Results

In order to evaluate the performance of our proposed algorithm, we used the Middlebury stereo benchmark [12]. In our test run, the algorithm's parameters are set to constant values. The window size is chosen to be 19, 35, and 71. We did not handle occlusion regions.

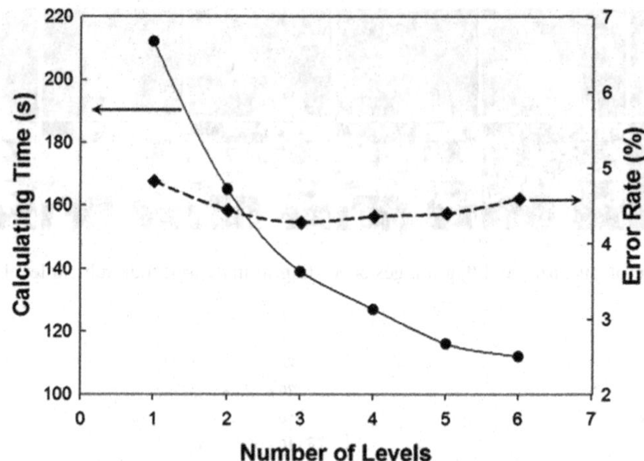

Fig. 8 Calculating time and error rates according to the number of levels

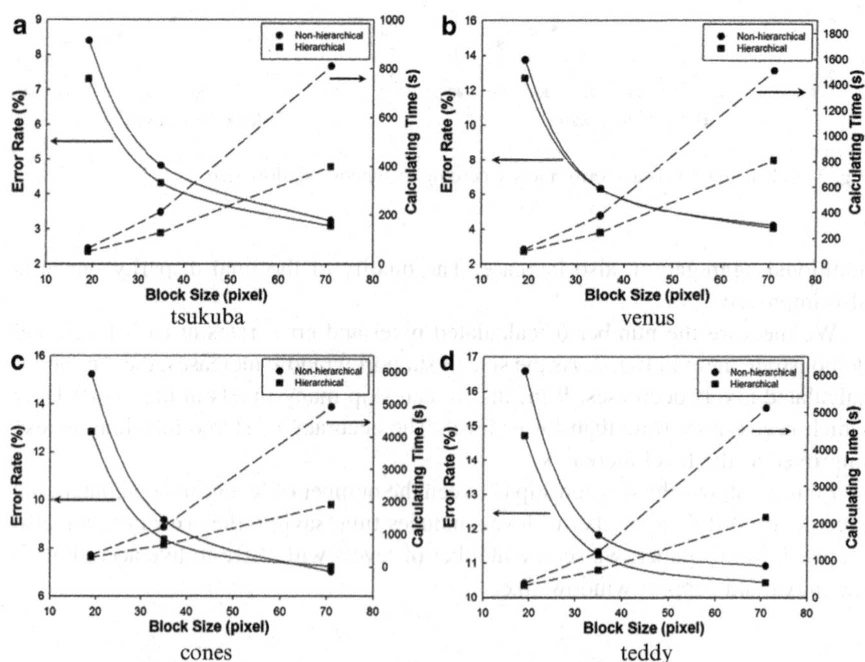

Fig. 9 Comparison between non-hierarchical and hierarchical cost aggregation

Figure 9 shows the comparison between non-hierarchical and hierarchical cost aggregation. The calculating times of the proposed algorithm are shorter than those of the non-hierarchical approaches. Especially the gaps increase when the maximum size of support window is large. In most test images, the error rates of

Table 1 Objective evaluation for the proposed algorithm with Middlebury test bed

	Non-hierarchical				Hierarchical			
Test image	Non-occ	All	Disc	Time (s)	Non-occ	All	Disc	Time (s)
Tsukuba	4.81	6.78	8.82	212	4.35	6.22	8.41	127
Venus	6.32	7.47	11.69	377	6.31	7.54	10.31	245
Cones	9.17	17.81	17.53	1,230	8.36	17.88	16.81	677
Teddy	11.81	18.31	22.27	1,226	11.24	19.22	21.52	739

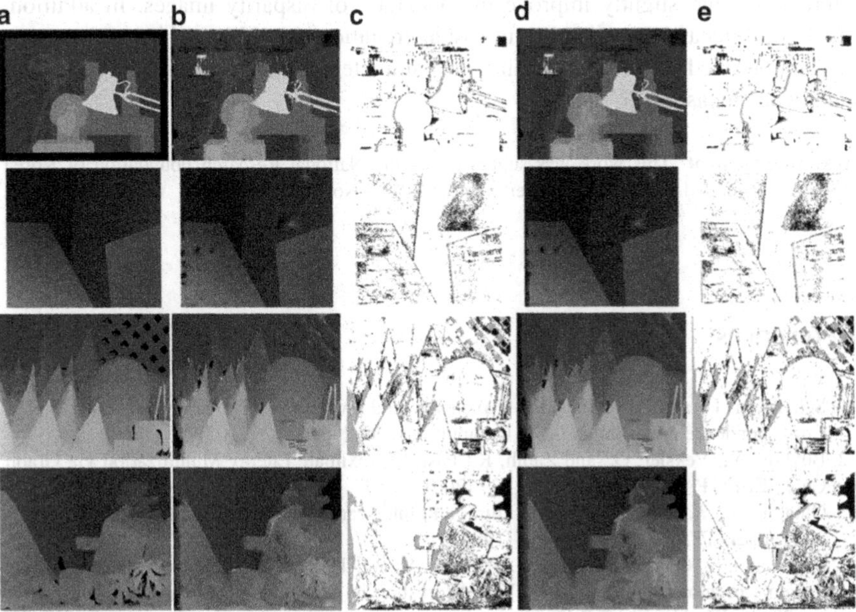

Fig. 10 Final disparity and error images obtained by non-hierarchical and hierarchical cost aggregation: (**a**) ground-truth, (**b**) and (**c**) disparity and error images of non-hierarchical cost aggregation, (**d**) and (**e**) disparity and error images of hierarchical cost aggregation

non-occluded regions of the proposed method are smaller than those of the conventional approaches. It is a basic assumption that the pixels in the support window have similar disparity value. Sometimes large support window opposes this assumption. However our algorithm prevents this problem.

Table 1 shows the detail bad pixel ratios and operation times of both approaches when the support size is 34. Our algorithm reduces the computational complexity and improves accuracy in non-occluded regions and near discontinuities. Figure 10 demonstrates our results along with corresponding error images. One can see that our algorithm performs well in the reconstruction of disparity borders, while it also finds correct disparities for regions of low texture.

5 Conclusions

The recently proposed cost aggregation algorithms are very effective, but they have high computational complexity. In this paper, we proposed the confidence-based hierarchical structure to reduce the complexity of cost aggregation. The proposed method adopts the pyramid of support window, and confidence values based on matching costs. It aggregates the matching cost with the small support, the size of support increases according to confidence values. A variety of experiments show that our proposed algorithm can reduce the computational complexity of cost aggregation and slightly improve the accuracy of disparity images. In addition, our algorithm can be applied to any cost aggregation algorithm and its performance can be improved by further adjusting the parameters such as pyramid structures and confidence measure.

Acknowledgement This work was supported by the National Research Foundation of Korea (NRF) grant funded by the Korea government (MEST) (No. 2011–0030822).

References

1. Scharstein, D. and Szeliski, R.: A Taxonomy and Evaluation of Dense Two-frame Stereo Correspondence Algorithms. Int. J. Comput. Vis., 47(1–3):7–42 (2002)
2. Boykov, Y., Veksler, O., and Zabih, R.: Fast Approximate Energy Minimization via Graph Cuts. IEEE TPAMI, 23(11):1222–1239 (2001)
3. Ohta, Y. and Kanade, T.: Stereo by Intra- and Interscanline Search Using Dynamic Programming. IEEE TPAMI, 7(2):139–154 (1985)
4. Forstmann, S., Ohya, J., Kanou, Y., Schmitt, A., and Thuering S.: Real-time stereo by using dynamic programming.. In Proc. CVPR Workshop on Real-time 3D Sensors and Their Use, pp. 29–36. Washington, DC (2004)
5. Veksler, O.: Fast variable window for stereo correspondence using integral images. In Proc. IEEE Conference on Computer Vision and Pattern Recognition, pp. 556–561 (2003)
6. Gong, M. and Yang, R.: Image-gradient-guided Real-time Stereo on Graphics Hardware. In Proc. International Conference on 3-D Digital Imaging and Modeling, pp. 548-555. Ottawa (2005)
7. Wang, L., Kang, S. B., Shum H.-Y., and Xu, G.: Cooperative Segmentation and Stereo Using Perspective Space Search. In Proc. Asian Conference on Computer Vision, pp. 366-371. Jeju Island (2004)
8. Yoon, K.-J. and Kweon, I.-S.: Locally Adaptive Support-weight Approach for Visual Correspondence Search. In Proc. IEEE Conference on Computer Vision and Pattern Recognition, pp. 924-931 (2005)
9. Rhemann1 C., Hosni1 A., Bleyer M., Rother C., Gelautz M.: Fast Cost-Volume Filtering for Visual Correspondence and Beyond. in Proc. The IEEE Conference on Computer Vision and Pattern Recognition, pp. 3017-3024 (2011)
10. Gong, M., Yang, R., Wang, L., and Gong, M.: A Performance Study on Different Cost Aggregation Approaches Used in Real-Time Stereo Matching. Int. J. Comput. Vis. 75(2), 283–296 (2007)

11. Yang, R., Pollefeys, M., and Li, S.: Improved Real-time Stereo on Commodity Graphics hardware. In Proc. IEEE Conference on Computer Vision and Pattern Recognition Workshop on Realtime 3D Sensors and Their Use, Washington, DC (2004)
12. Middlebury, http://vision.middlebury.edu/stereo

Occlusion Detection Using Warping and Cross-Checking Constraints for Stereo Matching

Yo-Sung Ho and Woo-Seok Jang

Abstract In this paper, we propose an occlusion detection algorithm which estimates occluded pixels automatically. In order to detect the occlusion, we obtain an initial disparity map with an optimization algorithm based on the modified constant-space belief propagation (CSBP) which has low complexity. The initial disparity map gives us clues for occlusion detection. These clues are the warping constraint and the cross check constraint. From both constraints, we define a potential energy function for occlusion detection and optimize it using an energy minimization framework. Experimental results show that the result of the occlusion detection from the proposed algorithm is very close to the ground truth.

Keywords Disparity map • Cross-checking • Occlusion handling • Stereo matching

1 Introduction

Stereo matching, widely researched topic in computer vision, is one of the most useful ways for acquiring depth information from two images. Stereo matching acquires 3D data by finding the corresponding points in other images for pixels in one image. The correspondence problem is to compute the disparity map that is a set of the displacement vectors between the corresponding pixels. For this problem, two images of the same scene taken from different viewpoints are given and it is assumed that these images are rectified for simplicity and accuracy of the problem. From this assumption, corresponding points are found in same horizontal line of two images.

Y.-S. Ho (✉) • W.-S. Jang
Gwangju Institute of Science and Technology (GIST), 123 Cheomdan-gwagiro, Buk-guGwangju 500-712, Republic of Korea
e-mail: hoyo@gist.ac.kr

J.S. Jin et al., *The Era of Interactive Media*,
DOI 10.1007/978-1-4614-3501-3_30, © Springer Science+Business Media, LLC 2013

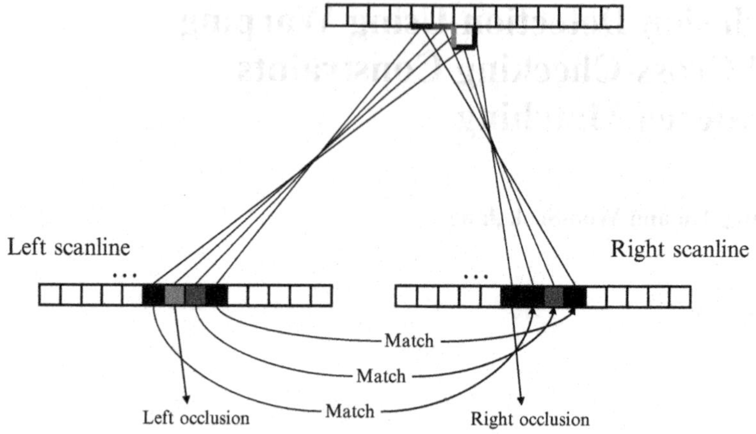

Fig. 1 Matching between two scanlines

Since two images are captured from different positions, occluded pixels exist in stereo images. The occluded pixels are only visible in one image, so accurate estimation of disparity value in these pixels is difficult. Figure 1 illustrates the case of occlusion. Occlusion is an important and challenging in stereo matching. Works that detects occluded pixels and assigns reasonable disparity values to the occlusion pixels is needed for reliable disparity map. The simplest method that detects occluded pixels and estimates disparities of occluded pixels is to use cross-checking [1] and extrapolation. Cross-checking tests that disparity value from the left and right disparity maps are consistent for each pixel. This determines occluded pixels. The disparities of visible pixels are extended into occluded pixels by extrapolation.

Two kinds of constraints have been typically used for occlusion detection in stereo matching. These are the uniqueness constraint and the ordering constraint. The uniqueness constraint [2] uses the fact that the corresponding points between two input images are one-to-one mapping. Several stereo matching methods using uniqueness constraint alternate between occlusion estimation using the estimated disparity map and disparity estimation using the estimated occlusion map [3]. The ordering constraint preserves the order of matching along the scanline in two input images [4]. The ordering constraint has limitation. It is violated in image that contains thin objects or narrow holes.

In this paper, we propose a more accurate occlusion detection method. The proposed method tries to improve conventional methods using above constraints. We do not consider the ordering constraint, because of its ambiguity presented above.

The remainder of this paper is organized as follows. In Sect. 2, we present the proposed occlusion detection method. Section 3 analyzes experimental results. Finally, Sect. 4 concludes this paper.

2 Proposed Method

The proposed method tries to improve conventional methods using the discussed constraints. We do not consider the ordering constraint, because of its ambiguity. We also do not apply occlusion estimation and disparity estimation alternately.

Figure 2 represents the overall framework of the proposed algorithm. First, initial disparity maps are obtained for the left and right images. CSBP is used for optimization of the initial disparity map. Afterward, occlusion is detected using both disparity maps and then, disparity estimation for occluded pixel is performed. Finally, the final disparity map with occlusion handling is generated.

2.1 Initial Disparity Based on Modified CSBP

Many stereo matching algorithms define energy functions and solve it through several optimization techniques such as graph cut and belief propagation. The energy function of Markov Random Field (MRF) is defined as

$$E(f) = \sum_{s} D_s(f_s) + \sum_{s,t \in N(s)} S_s, t(f_s, f_t) \tag{1}$$

where $D_s(\cdot)$ is the data term of node s. $S_s, t(\cdot)$ is the smoothness term between node s and t. f_s represents the state of each node s. $N(s)$ is the neighbors of the node s. In stereo matching, a node represents a pixel in an image and data term is generally defined by intensity consistency of pixel correspondences for hypothesized disparity. We use the luminance difference between two pixels as the matching cost. Matching cost as the data term of MRF is defined as

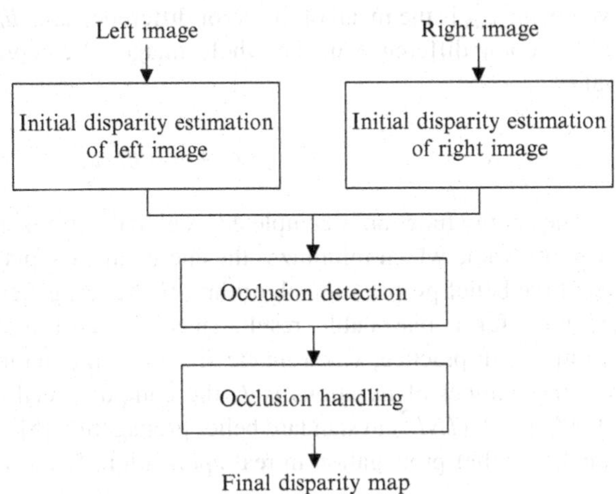

Fig. 2 Overall framework of our proposed method

$$D_s(d_s) = \min(|I_l(x_s, y_s) - I_r(x_s + d_s, y_s)|, T_d) \quad (2)$$

where I_l and I_r are left image and right image, respectively. xs and ys are horizontal and vertical coordinates of the pixel s in the image. d_s is disparity of pixel s. T_d controls the limit of the data cost. The smoothness term in stereo matching is based on the degree of difference between disparities of neighboring pixels. In our method, smoothness term is defined as

$$S_s, t(d_s, d_t) = \min(\lambda|d_s - d_t|, T_s) \quad (3)$$

where T_s is the constant controlling to stop increasing of the cost. λ represents the smoothness strength and is generally represented by a scalar constant. However, this smoothness strength is very sensitive. Thus, we adaptively refine a smooth strength to make our method more practical. First, color differences between pixel s and its neighboring pixels are calculated. High color difference means color edges in the color image. We assume that the color edge is remarkably consistent with the depth edge. The smoothness strength should be small in the depth edge. On the other hand, the smoothness strength can be high in non-edge. The color difference is defined as

$$diff_{s,t} = \sum_{c \in \{R,G,B\}} |I_c(s) - I_c(t)| \quad (4)$$

The sum absolute difference (SAD) is used as a difference measure and each color channel of R, G, B components is used for color difference. After obtaining the color difference, the scale of the color difference is controlled to set the average of the color difference to "1". New color difference scale is as follows.

$$diff_{scale} = 1 - (diff_{s,t} - diff_{mean}) / diff_{\max} \quad (5)$$

where $diff_{mean}$ is the mean of the color difference and $diff_{\max}$ is the maximum value of the color difference in the whole image. We replace λ value in (3) with λ' value.

$$\lambda' = \lambda \cdot diff_{scale} \quad (6)$$

The energy function is completed. A global optimization method is used to find a disparity value which minimizes the energy at each pixel. We obtain a good result using the belief propagation algorithm. However, general belief propagation is too complex for a reasonable result, since the cost is converged after numerous iterations. In practice, when image size is N, the number of disparity levels is L, and the number of iterations is T, the computational complexity is originally O $(4TNL^2) = O(TNL^2)$ in standard belief propagation [5]. Thus, it is not good to apply standard belief propagation in real application. Even if quality is a little low, low

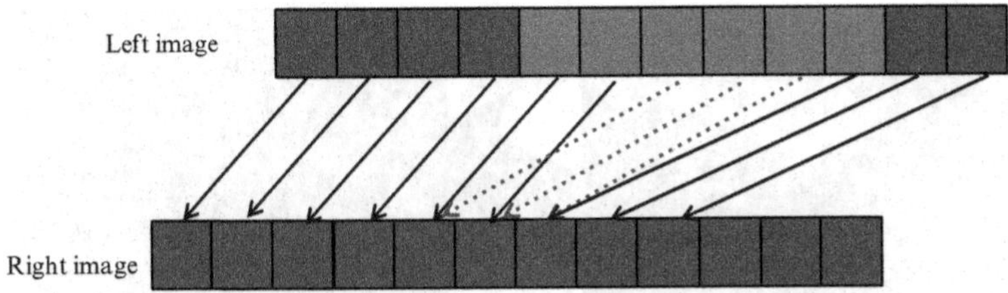

Fig. 3 Warping constraint

complexity algorithm is needed. One of the fast belief propagation reduce the complexity to O(*TNL*) by using hierarchical coarse-to-fine manner [6]. This algorithm facilitates real-time computation if it uses GPU implementation. However, we want a lower complexity algorithm. CSBP [7] is the fastest and takes the smallest memory among fast belief propagation algorithms. Its complexity depends on only constant space, that is O(1). However, CSBP cannot make enough quality for result. Since we sufficiently refine the result of CSBP, we select the CSBP algorithm as our optimization algorithm.

2.2 Occlusion Detection

We present two different kinds of constraints for occlusion detection. These are the warping constraint and the cross check constraint. In the warping constraint, all pixels in the left image are projected to the right images using the left disparity map for the left occlusion map. If the multiple pixels in the left image are projected on only one pixel in the right image, all but one pixel are occluded pixels. In this case, if the disparity map is reliable, the pixel which has the largest disparity value among the multiple matching pixels is the visible pixel and the rest of the pixels are the occluded pixels. However, our initial disparity map based on the modified CSBP is not perfect. Thus, we consider all multiple matching pixels as the candidates of the occluded pixels. Figure 3 illustrates the warping constraint. Red pixels can be regard as the candidates of the occluded pixels.

In order to find the accurate occlusion map with inaccurate disparity map, we define the energy function for warping constraint. The energy function is based on possibility.

$$E_g(D_l) = \sum_s w_b |o_s - G_l(s, D_l)| \tag{7}$$

where $G_l(s, D_l)$ is a binary map by the warping constraint. Multiple matching pixels in the left image are set to "1". 0_s is the occlusion value by assumption. When pixel s is supposed to the occluded pixel, the occlusion value $0s$ is set to "1". w_b is the

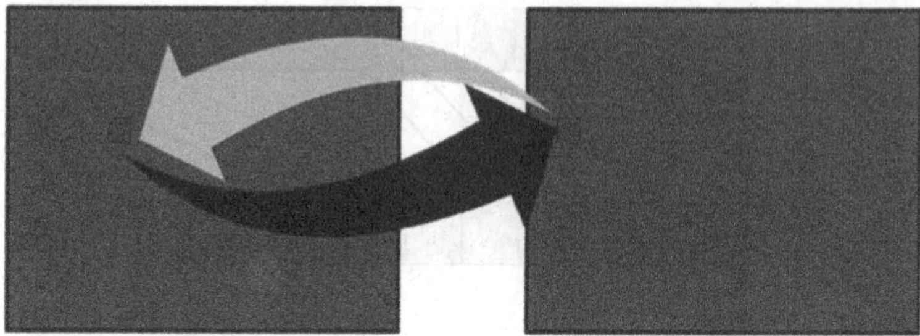

Fig. 4 Cross check constraint

weighting factor which is applied to the pixel of the largest disparity value and the other pixels differently.

The cross check constraint evaluates the mutual consistency from both disparity maps. If a particular pixel in the left image is not occluded pixel, the disparity values from the left and the right disparity maps should be consistent. Figure 4 illustrates the cross check constraint. Corresponding points have the same disparity value in both images.

The energy function for cross check constraint is defined as

$$E_c(D_l, D_r) = \sum_s |o_s - C_l(s; D_l, D_r)| \tag{8}$$

$$\left\{ \begin{array}{l} C_l = 0, \; if \; D_l(x_s) = D_r(x_s - D_l(x_s)) \\ C_l = 1, \; otherwise \end{array} \right\} \tag{9}$$

where D_l and D_r are the left disparity map and right disparity map respectively. x_s is a pixel in left image. When C_l is "0", it means that the disparity value of the current pixel is reliable.

The final energy function for occlusion detection is defined as

$$\begin{aligned} E_o = & \sum_s (1 - o_s) D_s(d_s) + \lambda_o o_s \\ & + \lambda_g E_g(D_l) + \lambda_c E_c(D_l, D_r) + \sum_{s,t \in N(s)} \lambda_s |o_s - o_t| \end{aligned} \tag{10}$$

The final function includes the difference of luminance component for data term in addition to the warping constraint and the cross check constraint. This comes from the assumption that the large difference of luminance makes wrong matching, even if a particular pixel is regarded as a visible pixel by two constraints. The last term represents the smooth term for the occlusion detection function and it uses the relation among the neighboring pixels of pixel s. This final function is optimized by belief propagation.

3 Experimental Results and Analysis

Table 1 lists the values for the parameters used in the proposed method. These parameters are acquired by experiments to balance energy terms. As I presented before, the smoothness strength (λ) is adaptively set.

In order to evaluate the performance of our proposed method, we follow the methodology which measures the percentages of bad matching pixels [8]. First, we evaluate the occlusion map. The occlusion map in Fig. 5 illustrates the visual comparison of our occlusion maps with ground truth. In order to show the superiority of the proposed method, we also presented the other method using uniqueness constraint [9]. Since its algorithm was adapted to fit our framework, it does not produce exactly the same result as in their method. Table 2 shows the percentage of

Table 1 Parameters for experiment

T_d	T_s	λ_o	λ_G	λ_C	λ_s
30	105	7.5	3	12	4.2

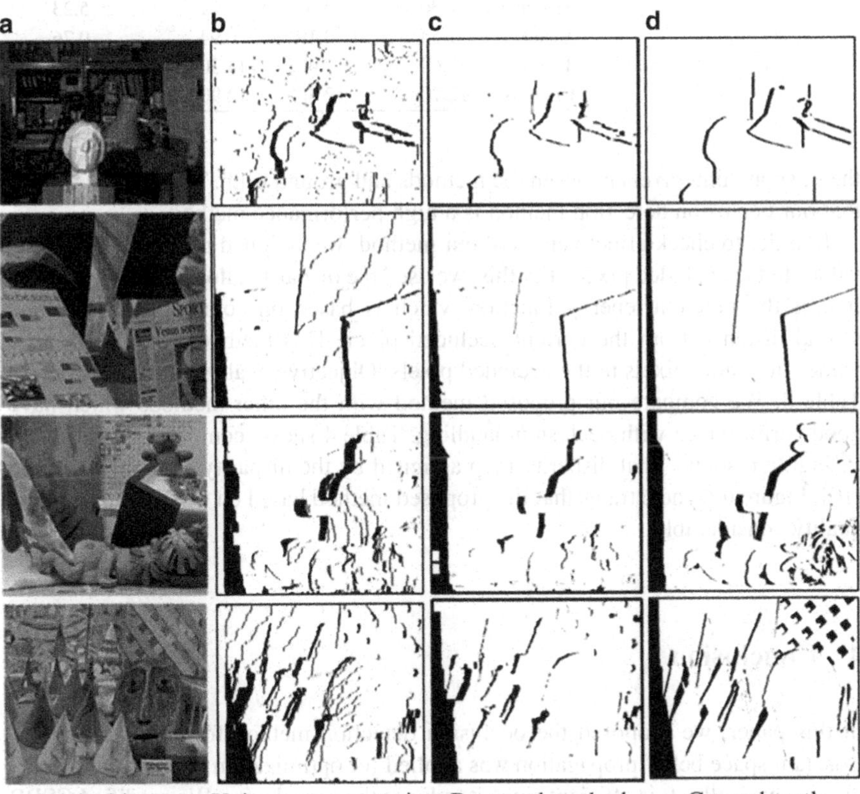

Fig. 5 Result of occlusion detection

Table 2 Evaluation for occlusion map (Error rate, %)

Image	Uniqueness constraint	Proposed method
Tsukuba	5.80	**1.74**
Venus	4.14	**1.16**
Teddy	11.32	**4.75**
Cone	14.09	**6.78**

Table 3 Performance comparison of disparity map (Error rate, %)

Image	CSSP	Uniqueness constraint	Proposed method
Tsukuba	4.17	3.10	2.30
Venus	3.11	2.79	1.54
Teddy	20.20	18.02	13.62
Cone	16.50	15.49	12.70

Table 4 Comparison with the other methods (Error rate, %)

Image	Proposed method	GC + occ [3]	CCH + SegAggr [11]	VarMSOH [12]
Tsukuba	2.30	2.01	2.11	5.23
Venus	1.54	2.19	0.94	0.76
Teddy	13.62	17.40	14.30	14.30
Cone	12.70	12.40	12.90	9.91

the mismatching pixels between the methods and ground truth. These results verify that our occlusion detection method is a high performance method.

In order to check effectiveness of our method, we assigned reasonable disparity values to the occluded pixels. For this, we used the disparity allocation method [10]. It uses the potential energy function which is based on color dissimilarity and spatial distance from the current occluded pixel. This method extends disparity values of visible pixels to the occluded pixels. Objective evaluation is presented in Table 3. We compare our proposed method with the other methods which have good performance with occlusion handling. Table 4 shows comparison results.

Figure 6 shows final disparity map assigned by the disparity allocation method [10]. Figure 6 demonstrates that the proposed method based on CSBP improves the quality considerably.

4 Conclusion

In this paper, we proposed the occlusion detection method for stereo matching. Constant space belief propagation was applied for optimization of an initial disparity map basically. It is efficient since it reduces the complexity. We modified CSBP for better result. Occlusion detection was performed by the warping constraint and the cross check constraint. The experimental results show that the proposed method

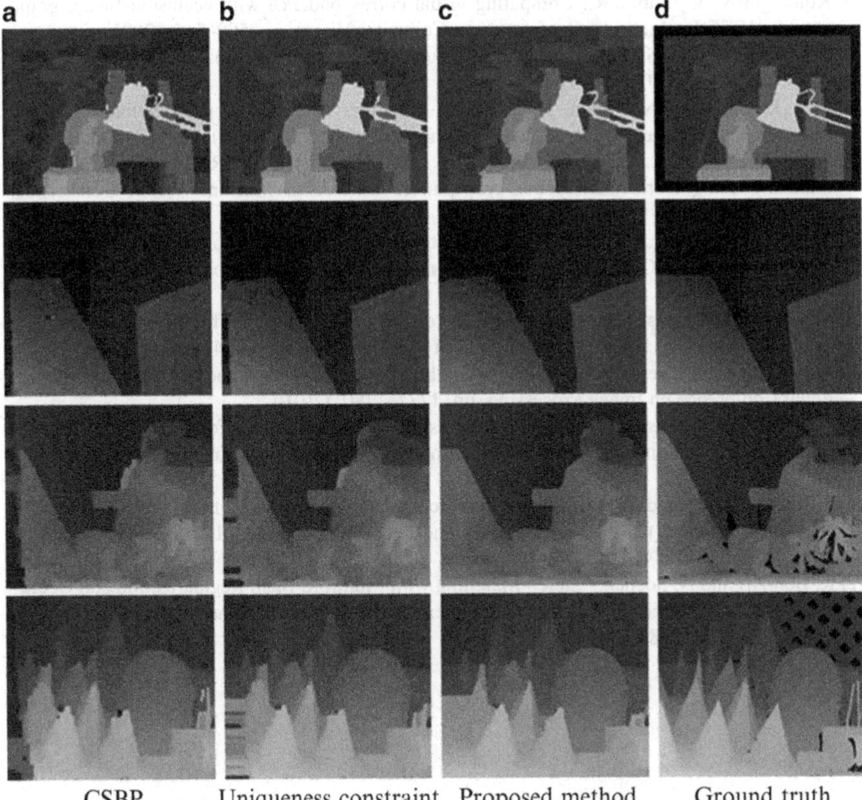

Fig. 6 Result of final disparity map

works very well for stereo images. If we perform stereo matching again using the obtained occlusion from proposed method, a more accurate disparity map can be obtained.

Acknowledgement This work was supported by the National Research Foundation of Korea (NRF) grant funded by the Korea government (MEST) (No. 2011-0030822).

References

1. Hirschmuller, H., Innocent, P.R., Garibaldi, J.M.: Real-time correlation-based stereo vision with reduced border errors. In: International Journal of Computer Vision, vol. 47(1/2/3), pp. 229–246. (2002)
2. Marr, D., Poggio, T.A.: Cooperative computation of stereo disparity. In: Science, vol. 194 (4262), pp. 283–287. (1976)

3. Kolmogorov, V., Zabih, R.: Computing visual correspondence with occlusions using graph cuts. In: IEEE International Conference on Computer Vision, pp. 508–515. (2001)
4. Bobick, A., Intille, S.: Large occlusion stereo. In: International Journal of Computer Vision, vol.33(3), pp. 181–200. (1999)
5. Sun, J., Zheng, N.N., Shum, H.Y.: Stereo matching using belief propagation. In: IEEE Transactions on Pattern Analysis and Machine Intelligence, vol. 25(7), pp. 787–800. (2003)
6. Yang, Q., Wang, L., Yang, R., Wang, S., Liao, M., Nister, D.: Real-time global stereo matching using hierarchical belief propagation. In: British Machine Vision Conference, pp. 989–998. (2006)
7. Yang, Q., Wang, L., Ahuja, N.: A constant-space belief propagation algorithm for stereo matching. In: IEEE Computer Society Conference on Computer Vision and Pattern Recognition, pp. 1458–1465. (2010)
8. Scharstein, D., Szeliski, R.: A taxonomy and evaluation of dense two-frame stereo correspondence algorithms. In: International Journal of Computer Vision, vol. 47(1), pp. 7–42. (2002)
9. Min, D., Yea, S., Vetro, A.: Occlusion handling based on support and decision. In: International Conference on Image Processing, pp. 1777–1780. (2010)
10. Jang, W., Ho, Y.: Disparity map refinement using occlusion handling for 3D scene reconstruction. In: International Conference on Embedded System and Intelligent Technology, pp. 213–216. (2011)
11. T. Liu, P. Zhang, and L. Luo, “Dense stereo correspondence with contrast context histogram, segmentation-based two-pass aggregation and occlusion handling,” Lecture Notes in Computer Science, vol. 5414, pp. 449–461, 2009.
12. R. Ben-Ari and N. Sochen, “Stereo Matching with Mumford-Shah Regularization and Occlusion Handling,” IEEE Transactions on Pattern Analysis and Machine Intelligence, vol. 32, no. 11, pp. 2071–2084, Nov. 2010.

Joint Multilateral Filtering for Stereo Image Generation Using Depth Camera

Yo-Sung Ho and Sang-Beom Lee

Abstract In this paper, we propose a stereo view generation algorithm using the Kinect depth camera that utilizes the infrared structured light. After we capture the color image and the corresponding depth map, we first preprocess the depth map and apply joint multilateral filtering to improve depth quality and temporal consistency. The preprocessed depth map is warped to the virtual viewpoint and filtered by median filtering to reduce truncation errors. Then, the color image is back-projected to the virtual viewpoint. In order to fill out remaining holes caused by disocclusion areas, we apply a background-based image in-painting process. Finally, we obtain a synthesized image without any visual distortion. From our experimental results, we realize that we obtain synthesized images without noticeable errors.

Keywords Depth image-based rendering • Kinect depth camera • Multilateral filtering • Three-dimensional television

1 Introduction

Three-dimensional television (3DTV) is the next-generation broadcasting system. Owing to advances in display devices, such as stereoscopic or multi-view displays, 3DTV provides users with a feeling of "being there", or presence, from the simulation of reality [1]. In this decade, we expect that the technology will be progressed enough to realize the 3DTV including content generation, coding, transmission, and display.

Y.-S. Ho (✉) • S.-B. Lee
Gwangju Institute of Science and Technology (GIST), 261 Cheomdan-gwagiro, Buk-gu, Gwangju 500-712, Republic of Korea
e-mail: hoyo@gist.ac.kr

J.S. Jin et al., *The Era of Interactive Media*,
DOI 10.1007/978-1-4614-3501-3_31,

In 2002, the advanced three-dimensional television system technologies (ATTEST) project began the research for 3DTV [2]. ATTEST introduced a novel 3D broadcasting system including four main stages: 3D contents generation, coding, transmission, and rendering/display. While the previous approach dealt with two stereoscopic video streams—one for the left view and one for the right view—on the broadcasting system, ATTEST adopted two streams for monoscopic video and the corresponding depth map that is composed of per-pixel depth information.

The virtual image can be synthesized by a depth image-based rendering (DIBR) technique using the color video and the corresponding depth video [3]. We can deal with the depth map as 3D information of the real scene. The virtual image can be generated by following procedure. First, whole pixels of the color image of the original viewpoint are back-projected to the world coordinate using the camera geometry and the depth map. Then, the points in the world coordinate are reprojected on the image plane of the virtual viewpoint. This procedure is called "3D warping" in the computer graphics literature [4].

Although the DIBR technique is suitable for 3DTV, it has some problems. The most significant problem of the DIBR technique is that when we synthesize the virtual image, we can see newly exposed areas, which are occluded in the original view but become visible in the virtual images. These areas are called disocclusion. This disocclusion area is an annoying problem since the color image and the depth map cannot provide any information. Therefore, the disocclusion areas should be filled out so that the virtual image seems more natural.

In order to remove the disocclusion, several solutions were introduced. Those methods are mainly categorized by two approaches: filling out the disocclusion by using near color information such as interpolation, extrapolation, mirroring of background color, and preprocessing using a Gaussian smoothing filtering [3]. Recently, an asymmetric smoothing filtering is proposed for preprocessing [5]. This method reduces not only the disocclusion areas but also the geometric distortion that is caused by a symmetric smoothing filter.

While the disocclusion and the geometric distortion are mostly removed by the asymmetric depth map filtering, the synthesized view is deformed due to the distorted depth map. Recently, many solutions based on depth map filtering have been tried to solve the problem of the low depth quality. One of the solutions is the depth map filtering near the object boundary [6]. Although we can reduce the deformation of the depth map by restricting the filtered areas, the depth quality is still unsatisfactory.

In this paper, we propose a stereo view generation algorithm. The main contribution of this paper is that we synthesize the virtual image using the original color image and the preprocessed depth map and also we implement the entire process by aiming at the depth camera which utilizes the infrared structured light. The virtual image can be obtained by preprocessed depth map in virtual viewpoint and background-based image in-painting process.

2 Depth Image-Based Rendering (DIBR) Techniques

Color video and depth video can be used for synthesizing the virtual images in DIBR technique. The block diagram of DIBR technique is depicted in Fig. 1. Each process is explained in detail in this section.

2.1 Depth Map Preprocessing

When synthesizing the virtual image, we can find the disocclusion area. Since there is no information of the disocclusion area, we need to fill out it. One of the solutions is preprocessing of depth map using smoothing filter [3]. The main advantage of smoothing is that the sharpness of depth discontinuity is weakened and most disocclusion areas are filled with neighboring pixels.

Figure 2 shows various smoothing results for "Interview". As shown in Fig. 2b, the simple smoothing filter can fills out the disocclusion areas. However, it causes a geometric distortion that the vertical edges of the synthesized image are bent. This problem gives the discomfort to viewers. In order to reduce the geometric distortion, asymmetric smoothing method is proposed [5]. In this approach, the strength of filtering of a depth map in the horizontal direction is less than that in the vertical direction. Figure 2c shows the asymmetric smoothing result.

The synthesized image after asymmetric smoothing of the depth map has good subjective quality. However, the filtered depth map has many errors. It is desirable that the filter is applied so that the filtered areas are reduced through the prediction of the disocclusion areas. By aiming at this assumption, discontinuity-adaptive depth map filtering is proposed [6]. This approach assumes that the disocclusion area is detected nearby object boundaries and the depth map is filtered only near those regions. Therefore, the filtered region of the depth map is reduced. As shown in Fig. 2d, the deformation of the object is reduced.

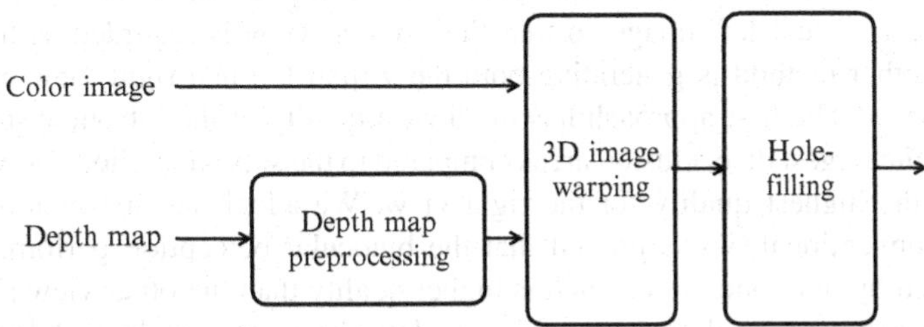

Fig. 1 Block diagram of depth image-based rendering technique

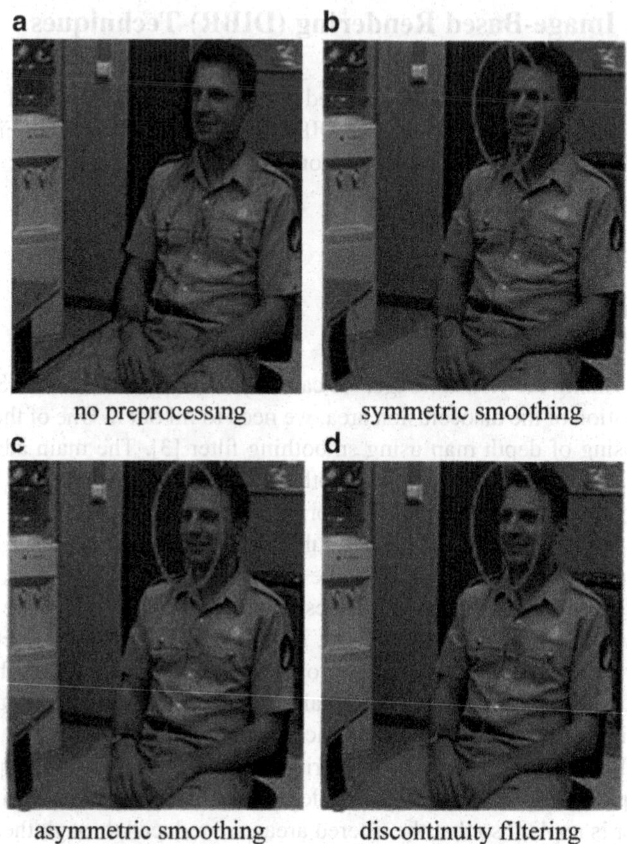

Fig. 2 Smoothing results for "Interview"

2.2 3D Image Warping

We assume that the camera configuration is parallel for simplicity. There are two approaches of stereoscopic image generation using DIBR technique. One is generating a virtual left image so that the original view is regarded as the right view. Another method is generating both the virtual left and right view by using original view. The first approach has the lowest quality of the left view since this view has the largest disocclusion areas compared to the second method. However, it gives us the highest quality for the right view. We adopt the first method since several conventional works proved that the binocular perception performance is determined by only one view which is higher quality than the other view [7].

Figure 3 shows the relationship of the pixel displacement and the real depth. The new coordinates (x_l,y) of the virtual viewpoint from the original coordinates (x_r,y) according to the depth value Z is determined by

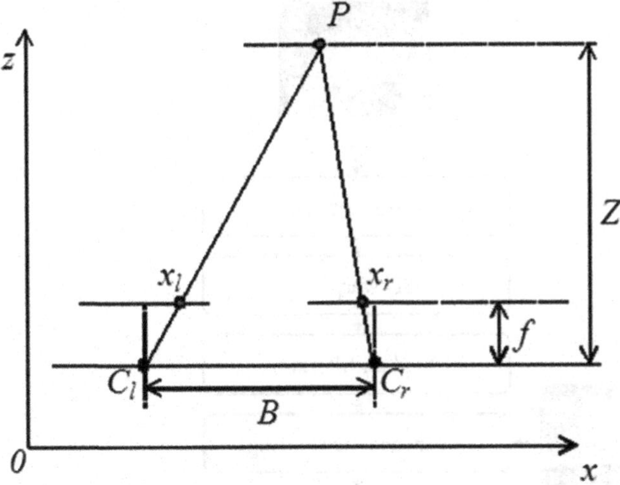

Fig. 3 Relationship between disparity and depth

$$x_l = x_r + \frac{fB}{Z} \tag{1}$$

where f represents the focal length of the camera and B represents the distance between cameras.

2.3 *Hole-Filling*

After depth map preprocessing and 3D warping, most unknown regions of the virtual image are filled out. Due to the truncation error in the 3D warping process, the small-sized holes are remained. Therefore, we need to fill those holes. The common method in this step is linear interpolation using neighbor pixels.

3 Proposed Stereo View Generation Algorithm

The proposed method exploits a depth camera, which interprets 3D scene information from a continuously-projected infrared structured light [8]. Figure 4 shows the overall block diagram of our algorithm. The first three steps are categorized by depth map preprocessing and remaining parts are included in the view synthesis operation.

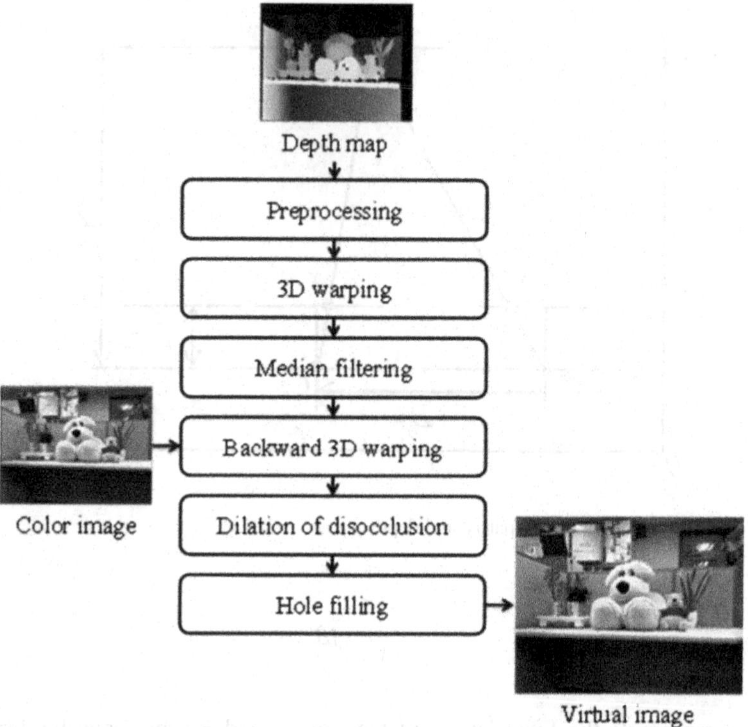

Fig. 4 Overall block diagram of the proposed method

3.1 Depth Map Preprocessing Using Image Inpainting

Since the position of the transmitter of infrared structured light and the receiver is different and there exist errors of the sensor itself, we obtain the depth map with some areas where the infrared sensor cannot retrieve the depths. Therefore, in the preprocess step, these areas are filled out by original image in-painting algorithm [9]. Figure 5 shows the depth preprocessing result using image in-painting algorithm.

After the image inpainting, the depth map is filtered by a temporal filtering using joint multilateral filter. We expand the conventional algorithm that exploits the joint bilateral filter to temporal domain [10]. The filter is designed by

$$D(x,y) = \arg\min_{d \in d_p} \frac{\sum_{u \in u_p} \sum_{v \in v_p} \sum_{w \in w_p} W(u,v,w) \cdot C(u,v,w,d)}{\sum_{u \in u_p} \sum_{v \in v_p} \sum_{w \in w_p} W(u,v,w)} \tag{2}$$

Fig. 5 Result of depth map inpainting

where $p=(x,y)$, $d_p=\{D(x\text{-}1,y,t), D(x+1,y,t), D(x,y\text{-}1,t), D(x,y+1,t), D(x,y,t\text{-}1), D(x,y,t+1)\}$, $u_p=\{x\text{-}r,\ldots,x+r\}$, $v_p=\{y\text{-}r,\ldots,y+r\}$, $w_p=\{t\text{-}r,\ldots,t+r\}$. Here, $W(u,v,w)$ and $C(u,v,w,d)$ is computed by

$$W(u,v,w)=\exp\left\{-\frac{\|I(x,y,t),I(u,v,w)\|^2}{2\sigma_R{}^2}\right\}\cdot \exp\left\{-\frac{(x-u)^2+(y-v)^2+(t-w)^2}{2r^2}\right\} \quad (3)$$

$$C(u,v,w,d)=\min(\lambda\Gamma,|D(u,v,w)-d|) \quad (4)$$

where λ is a constant to reject outliers.

We apply an outlier reduction operation in the temporal domain to avoid a motion estimation or optical flow technique for moving objects. Therefore, the temporal position w_p is selected by

$$w_{ourlier\_reduction}=\{w_p \mid |I(x,y,t)-I(x,y,w_p)|<2\lambda L \quad |D(x,y,t)-D(x,y,w_p)|<\lambda L\} \quad (5)$$

After the preprocessing, the 3D warping operation is performed using the depth map. During this step, the warped depth is truncated in integer value and as a result, the depth map includes truncation errors. These errors are easily removed by median filtering. Figure 6a shows the warped depth map and Fig. 6b shows the result of median filtering.

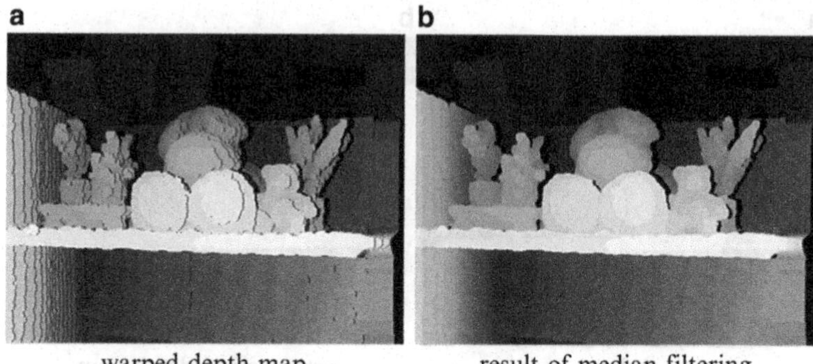

Fig. 6 Result of 3D warping

Fig. 7 Back-projected color image

3.2 *Virtual View Synthesis*

Using the warped depth map, the color image can be back-projected. It is computed by

$$I_{virtual}(x,y) = I_{original}\ \{x + D(x,y), y\} \tag{6}$$

where $D(x,y)$ represents the depth value at pixel position (x,y). The back-projected color image is shown in Fig. 7. As shown in Fig. 7, most of pixels are filled but remaining holes near the object are found.

In order to fill out those holes, we exploit the background in-painting operation. The in-painting algorithm first defines the region to be in-painted Ω and its boundary $\partial\Omega$ and the pixel p, the element of Ω is in-painted by its neighboring region $B_\varepsilon(p)$. In the proposed algorithm, we replace the boundaries facing the foreground with the corresponding background region located on the opposite side. This can be calculated by

$$p_{fg} \in \partial\Omega_{fg} \rightarrow p_{bg} \in \partial\Omega_{bg} \tag{7}$$

$$B_\varepsilon(p_{fg}) \rightarrow B_\varepsilon(p_{bg}) \tag{8}$$

where fg and bg represent the foreground and the background, respectively.

4 Experimental Results

We have evaluated the proposed algorithm with two aspects: visual quality and computational time. The resolution of the color image and the depth map is 640×480. The parameters for stereo view generation are set as follows: $B = 48$ mm for the distance between cameras and $f = 200$ mm for the focal length of the camera.

Figure 8 shows the view synthesis result. Figure 8a shows the original color image and Fig. 8b–d represents the synthesis results of asymmetric filter, discontinuity-adaptive filter, and the proposed algorithm, respectively. As shown in Fig. 8d, remaining holes are naturally removed compared to other methods since the proposed algorithm conducted the background-based image in-painting operation.

Figure 9 shows the enlarged figures of Fig. 8. As shown in Fig. 9a, b, there still remains the geometric errors in background. However, even though the proposed algorithm performed relatively unnatural hole-filling, it never deformed the depth map at all and caused geometric errors.

Table 1 shows the computational time of each process. From those results, the proposed system enabled the entire processing up to 18.87 fps. Without any techniques for real-time processing, such as GPU programming or fast algorithms, stereo video was easily generated in nearly real-time.

5 Conclusions

In this paper, we have proposed a stereo view generation algorithm using depth camera. The proposed scheme focused on the natural view synthesis. Therefore, we performed the depth preprocessing and view synthesis. The depth map is

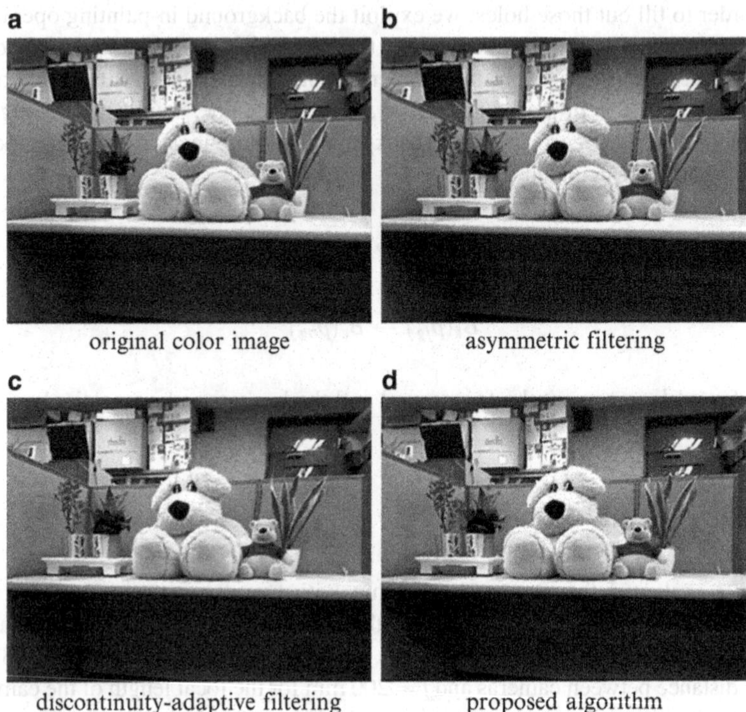

Fig. 8 Results of view synthesis

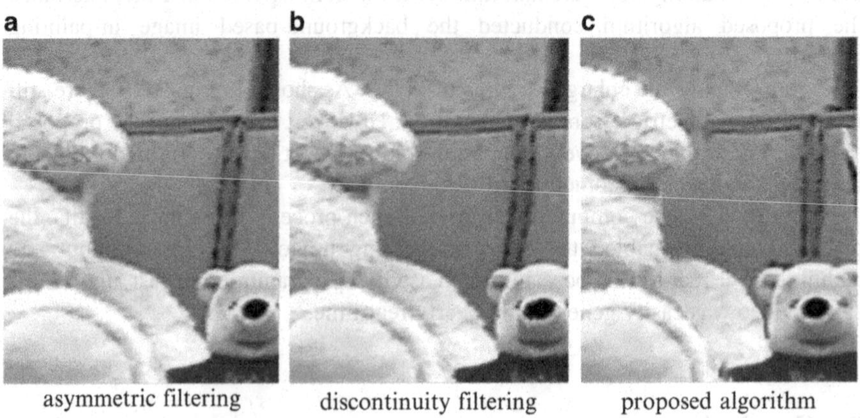

Fig. 9 Results of view synthesis

preprocessed by several image processing techniques and the synthesized image is obtained by background-based image in-painting operation. From experimental results, we noticed that we obtained the natural synthesized image.

Table 1 Computational time

Process	Computational time (ms)
Depth preprocessing	12.00
3D warping	11.00
View synthesis	5.00
Background in-painting	25.00
Total	53.00 (18.87 fps)

Acknowledgement This work was supported by the National Research Foundation of Korea (NRF) grant funded by the Korea government (MEST) (No. 2011-0030822).

References

1. Riva, G., Davide, F., Ijsselsteijn, W.A.: Being There: Concepts, Effects and Measurement of User Presence in Synthetic Environments. Amsterdam, The Netherlands: Ios Press, (2003)
2. Redert, A., Op de Beeck, M., Fehn, C., IJsselsteijn, W., Pollefeys, M., Van Gool, L., Ofek, E., Sexton, I., Surman, P.: ATTEST-Advanced Three-Dimensional Television System Technologies. Proc. of International Symposium on 3D Data Processing, 313–319 (2002)
3. Fehn, C.: Depth-image-based Rendering (DIBR), Compression and Transmission for a New Approach on 3D TV. Proc. of SPIE Conf. Stereoscopic Displays and Virtual Reality Systems XI, Vol. 5291, 93–104 (2004)
4. Mark, W.R.: Post-Rendering 3D Image Warping: Visibility, Reconstruction, and Performance for Depth-Image Warping. PhD thesis, University of North Carolina at Chapel Hill, Chapel Hill, NC, USA, (1999)
5. Zhang, L., Tam, W. J.: Stereoscopic Image Generation Based on Depth Images for 3D TV. IEEE Trans. on Broadcasting, Vol. 51, 191–199 (2005)
6. Lee, S., Ho, Y.: Discontinuity-adaptive Depth Map Filtering for 3D View Generation. Proc. of Immersive Telecommunications, T8(1–6) (2009)
7. Stelmach, L., Tam, W., Meegan, D., Vincent, A., Corriveau, P.: Human Perception of Mismatched Stereoscopic 3D Inputs. Proc. of International Conference on Image Processing, Vol. 1, 5–8 (2000)
8. PrimeSense, http://www.primesense.com/?p=487
9. Telea, A.: An Image Inpainting Technique based on The Fast Marching Method. Journal Graphics Tools, Vol. 9, 25–36 (2004)
10. Yang, Q., Wang, L., Ahuja, N.: A Constant-Space Belief Propagation Algorithm for Stereo Matching. Proc. of Computer Vision and Pattern Recognition, 1458–1465 (2010)

Object Detection

Justifying the Importance of Color Cues in Object Detection: A Case Study on Pedestrian

Qingyuan Wang, Junbiao Pang, Lei Qin, Shuqiang Jiang, and Qingming Huang

Abstract Considerable progress has been made on hand-crafted features in object detection, while little effort has been devoted to make use of the color cues. In this paper, we study the role of color cues in detection via a representative object, i.e., pedestrian, as its variaility of pose or appearance is very common for "general" objects. The efficiency of color space is first ranked by empirical comparisons among typical ones. Furthermore, a color descriptor, called MDST (Max DisSimilarity of different Templates), is built on those selected color spaces to explore invariant ability and discriminative power of color cues. The extensive experiments reveal two facts: one is that the choice of color spaces has a great influence on performance; another is that MDST achieves better results than the state-of-the-art color feature for pedestrian detection in terms of both accuracy and speed.

Keywords Pedestrian detection • Color space analysis • Color descriptor • Invariant descriptor

---

Q. Wang (✉) • Q. Huang
Graduate University of Chinese Academy of Sciences, Beijing 100049, China

Key Lab of Intell.Info.Process, Institute of Computing Technology, CAS,
Beijing 100190, China
e-mail: qywang@jdl.ac.cn; qmhuang@jdl.ac.cn

J. Pang
Beijing Municipal Key Laboratory of Multimedia and Intelligent Software Technology,
College of Computer Science and Technology, Beijing University of Technology,
Beijing 100124, China
e-mail: jbpang@jdl.ac.cn

L. Qin • S. Jiang,

Key Lab of Intell.Info.ProcessInstitute of Computing Technology, CAS,
Beijing 100190, China
e-mail: lqin@jdl.ac.cn; sqjiang@jdl.ac.cn

J.S. Jin et al., *The Era of Interactive Media*,
DOI 10.1007/978-1-4614-3501-3_32,

1 Introduction

In recent years, detecting the predefined objects in images has been an attracting problem in computer vision, e.g., face [1–3], pedestrian [4–9]. Accurate detection would have immediate impacts on many real applications, such as intelligence surveillance [10] and driver assistance systems [11, 12]. Detecting non-rigid objects in images is still a challenging task, due to the variable appearance and the wide range of poses. In this paper, pedestrian is used as a typical case, because its variable poses and diversity of clothing are representative and challenging for "general" objects, e.g., animals, car, et [13].

Recently shape information [4–6], mainly described by gradients, has been exhaustively explored and successfully used in detection, and yet color cues do not attract enough attention. Moreover, color cues have been facilely considered to be useless, due to the variability in the color of clothing. In our best knowledge, we first try our best to systematically evaluate the role of color cues, and show that color cues can achieve competitive results in pedestrian detection. Our study is based on the following methodology: (1) There are a variety of color spaces, yet which one is better for detection is still a controversy problem [8, 9]; therefore, typical color spaces are naturally compared (see Fig. 1.). (2) A simple yet efficient color descriptor is proposed to be evaluated on the selected color spaces.

Although the INRIA pedestrian dataset [4], as our primary testbed, may be relatively simple [9], our experiments about color cues still reap a huge harvest. First, we show that there are significant differences of performance among color spaces, thus, the choice of color spaces is very important in detection. Second, different coding schemes lead to diverse accuracies, and thus the selection of coding method is a key to boost performance. Third, the combination of color descriptors with the shape-based feature [4] shows the complementary yet important role of color cues in object detection.

The remainder of this paper is organized as follows. In Sect. 2, we give an overview of the related works. In Sect. 3, we introduce different color spaces and

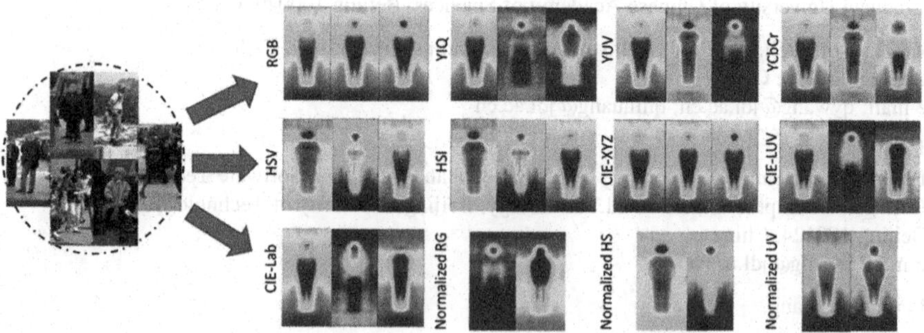

Fig. 1 The average positive examples of INRIA dataset are visualized in the different color spaces and the corresponding channels. Some images show clear silhouette-like boundary, while other just enhances parts of the pedestrians, e.g., head in YIQ space

describe the details on evaluating color spaces. Then our proposed color descriptor will be presented in Sect. 4. In Sect. 5 we perform the detailed experimental evaluations. Finally, we conclude this paper in Sect. 6.

2 Related Work

Color information is very popular in image classification [14, 15], but it does not attract enough attention in object detection, and most people still doubt the efficiency of color for detection. On the other side, a few literatures use color cues in naïve approaches, and set a minor role for color in detection.

In HOG [4], the orientation of the gradient for a pixel is selected from the R, G and B channels according to the highest gradient magnitude. Thus some color information can be captured by the number of a channel is chosen in HOG [4]. Comparing with HOG, Schwartz et al. [7], further, construct a three bin histogram that tabulates the number of times each color channel is chosen. So they call this color descriptor as color frequency. This color feature mainly captures the color information of faces, due to the possible homologous skin color in faces. However, the information of whole body tends to be ignored as illustrated in Fig. 1.

Walk et al. [8] observe that the colors of pedestrians may be globally similar, e.g., the color of faces is similar to the one of hands. Therefore, color self-similarity (CSS) is introduced to capture the similarities among whole body. This feature captures pair-wise spatially statistics of color distribution, e.g., color of clothes ignored by the color frequency descriptor [7]. On the other hand, the computational cost of CSS is intensive, because CSS calculates the global self-similarity within the detection window. For instance, the dimension of CSS for a 128×64 window is 8,128.

Both of the above works are integrated with Support Vector Machine (SVM) classification framework, while Dollar et al. [9] use color cues in boosting via an integral channel features approach. The color features are firstly generated by summing the pixel values in the pre-designed templates. The discriminative feature is chosen by boosting classifiers. It is a type of first-order feature, and the disadvantages of the color frequency descriptor [7] still exist in this coding method. On the other interesting side, Dollar et al. [9] and Walk et al. [8] give totally different conclusion on using color spaces for object detection. In this paper, the efficiency of color spaces will be first systematically ranked by empirical comparisons.

3 Analysis of Color Space

In this section, the typical color spaces are introduced, and then evaluated to rank the performance of color spaces for pedestrian detection.

3.1 Color Spaces

Color is usually described by the combined effect of three independent attributes / channels. For example, R, G and B are the widely used color channels. There are many other color spaces in computer vision or related communities, because different color spaces can describe the same object from different perspectives. In this paper, we divide the color spaces into three categories according to the application purposes.

Color spaces for Computer Graphics. These color spaces are mainly used in display system, for example, RGB, HSV and HSI. And RGB, HSV and HSI are chosen to be evaluated in our experiment.

Color Spaces for TV System. YIQ and YUV are analogue spaces for NTSC (National Television System Committee) [16] and PAL (Phase Alternating Line) [17] systems respectively, while YCbCr is a digital standard. And YIQ, YUV and YCbCr are all picked in our experiment.

CIE Color Spaces. The CIE (International Commission on Illumination) [18] system characterizes colors by a luminance parameter Y, and two color coordinates x and y. Some typical CIE spaces, i.e., XYZ, LUV and Lab, will be evaluated.

In addition, in many applications in order to keep the luminance invariance, the intensity attribute is discarded and only the chrominance is kept. So, in our experiment we will also evaluate this kind of color spaces, including normalized RG, normalized HS and normalized UV [8].

3.2 Evaluation of Color Spaces

One of our goals is to find and explain that which color space would be the best one for pedestrian detection. On the other side, the color feature may have great influence on the accuracy, and thus feature should be simple and unbiased to reflect the ability of color spaces. As illustrated in Fig. 1, color histogram may be a good choice to describe the distribution of colors. A localized color histograms, termed HLC (Histogram of Local Color), is advocated as our evaluation feature.

HLC. It firstly converts an image into different channels, and then divides each color channel image into small spatial non-overlapped regions ("block"). In each block, a local 1-D histogram of color values is accumulated[1]. Next, the channel-level HLC is constructed by concatenating the histograms in all blocks. The image-level HLC is finally obtained by concatenating the channel-level HLCs (see Fig. 2). In our experiments, we compute histograms on 16×16 pixels blocks.

[1]During histogram calculation, trilinear interpolation is applied to avoid quantization effects.

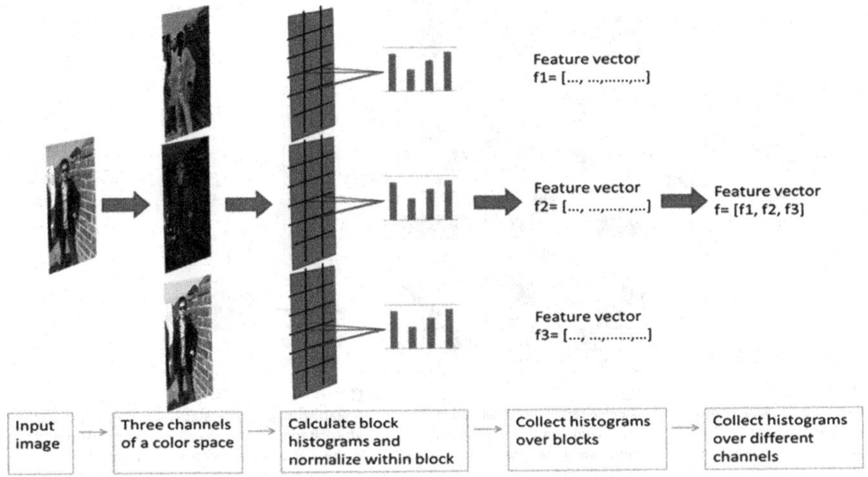

Fig. 2 The HLC extract procedure. A three-channel color space is used as an example

4 Max Dissimilarity of Different Templates

As shown in Fig. 1, the boundary of the whole or parts of pedestrian can be clearly illustrated. Our work is to explore a descriptor that can capture the boundary effectively regardless of variability of clothing or its color. Max DisSimilarity of different Templates (MDST), based on the max-coding, is designed to capture the local boundary and to increase the translation invariance of feature.

MDST. Firstly, the image is divided into non-overlapped regions (we call it as "cells"). The feature/"attribute" of a cell is calculated in the enlarged local area/ "calculation unit"[2] which centers on the cell, as shown in Fig. 3a. In the calculation unit, 12 templates, shown in Fig. 3b, are designed to capture the local boundary information. The number 0, 1 and 2 indicate three different cells in a template. For the j-th cell in the i-th template, an n-dimension color histogram, $cell_{ij}$, is extracted to calculate the dissimilarity values.

$$ds_{ij} = dissim(cell_{i0}, cell_{ij}) \quad i = 1, 2, 3, 12; j = \{1, 2\} \tag{1}$$

Where "*dissim*" is a function to measure the dissimilarity between two cells. There are many possibilities to define dissimilarity for histogram comparison. In our experiments, a number of well-known distance functions, L1-norm, L2-norm, chi-square-distance, and histogram intersection, are all evaluated, and histogram intersection works best.

[2]In our experiment, we use a 3x3-cell to be the calculation unit as the oblique line indicates.

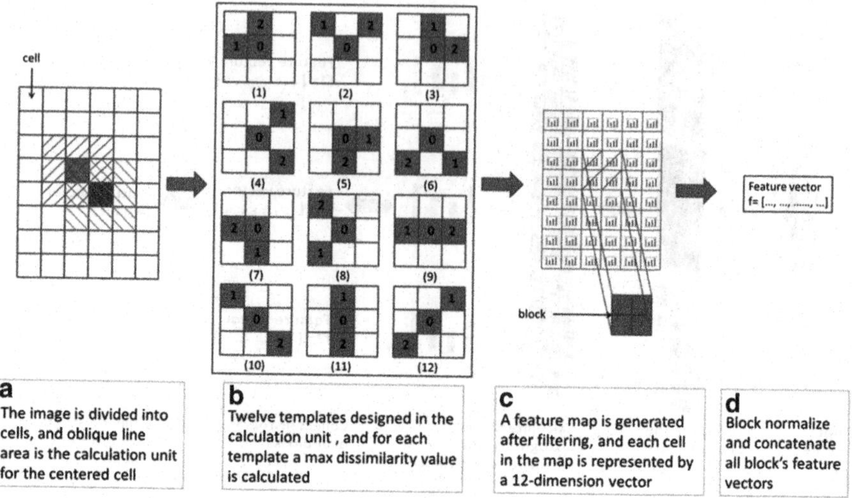

Fig. 3 The method of calculating the MDST for an example

The dissimilarity scores, mds_i, in the i-th template is calculated by max-pooling between 0–1and 0–2 dissimilarity pairs,

$$mds_i = \max(ds_{i1}, ds_{i2}) \;\; i = 1, 2, 3, 12 \tag{2}$$

So, the feature for a cell is extracted by assembling the score mds_i in all 12 templates as

$$f = [mds_1, mds_2, mds_3, mds_{12}]. \tag{3}$$

The feature vectors further are normalized in a 2 × 2 cell (termed as "block"), as illustrated in Fig. 3c. We get a 48-dimension feature over one block after the block-wise normalization, and the MDST can concatenate features in all blocks. In our experiments, the cell size is 8 × 8 pixels for a 128 × 64 window, which would have 1,536-dimension MDST.

5 Experimental Results and Discussions

In our experiment, we utilize two evaluation protocols that are the per-window and per-image evaluation. The per-window evaluation methodology is to classify manually normalized examples against windows sampled at a fixed density from images without pedestrians, corresponding to the miss rate against False Positive Per Window (FPPW). While in the per-image evaluation, a detector is densely scanned across an image with or without pedestrians and nearby detections merged using non maximal suppression (NMS), corresponding to the miss rate against False Positive Per Image (FPPI).

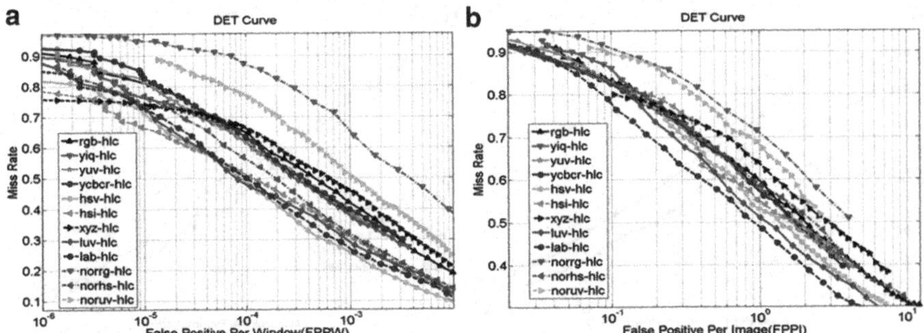

Fig. 4 Evaluation of diverse color spaces on HLC. (**a**) The per-window evaluation result. (**b**) The per-image evaluation result

The per-window evaluation can avoid NMS, however, it does not measure errors caused by detecting at incorrect scales, positions or false detections arising from body parts [19]. While the per-image evaluation method takes into consideration of all the impact factors. In addition, our experiment comparisons are mainly under 10^{-4} FPPW and 10^0 FPPI, which is adopted by most evaluation schemes in pedestrian detection.

For all subsequent experiments, we use the stochastic optimization based linear SVM [20], i.e., Pegasos, to train the detectors, due to the large number of training examples. During the training procedure, one round of retraining (bootstrapping) protocol is utilized as Dalal et al. suggested in [4].

5.1 Evaluation of Color Space

In Fig. 4a, b, we plot the performance of HLC on various color spaces according to the per-window and per-image evaluations. This figure clearly shows that the perspective of describing colors has great influences on the performance.

Firstly, the performance of normalized RG, normalized HS and normalized UV [8] are all worse than the corresponding RGB, HSV and YUV. According to the fact that the human eyes have three different types of color sensitive cones [21], the response of the eyes is best described in terms of three "tristimulus values". Therefore, the intensity attribute of a color space, ignored by normalized color space, may be critical to describe pedestrian.

Secondly, the four best performed spaces are ranked in a descendent order, CIE-Lab, CIE-LUV, HSV and HSI. The color spaces in TV system are not as discriminative as any one of the four ones. On the contrary, CIE-based color spaces (CIE-Lab and CIE-LUV) are designed to approximate human vision [18]; HSV and HSI are relevant to the perception of human eyes [22]. Therefore, the color spaces CIE-Lab, CIE-LUV, HSV and HSI, associate with the human perception, and achieve better performance for detection.

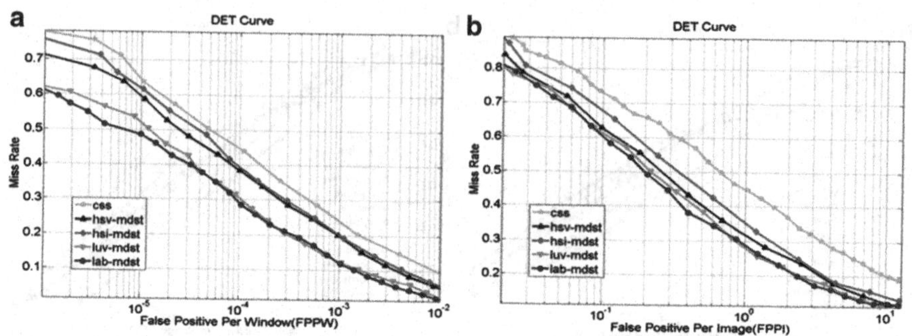

Fig. 5 Comparisons between MDST and CSS. (**a**) The per-window evaluation result. (**b**) The per-image evaluation result

5.2 *The Performance of MDST*

To consider the influence of the color spaces on descriptors, we plot the per-window and per-image evaluation curves of the MDST in Fig. 5. Not surprisingly, the performances of the MDST on four color spaces are consistent with the results of our color space evaluation experiment. Therefore, CIE-Lab/CIE-LUV color spaces could be the best ones for pedestrian detection.

In these two Fig. 5a, b, the performances of MDST are better than CSS (HSV as suggested in [8]), which is the current state-of-the-art color descriptor. In terms of computational cost, the dimension of MDST is 1,536, while the dimension of CSS is 8,128 for a 128 × 64 window. Thus, the MDST is a better color descriptor for its lower computational cost and better performance.

We will evaluate the augmented HOG-MDST feature to study whether the two descriptors can complement with each other or not, because Histogram of Oriented Gradients (HOG) [4] is the most successful shape descriptor in pedestrian detection. In Fig. 6a, b, it can be seen that MDST raises detection rate 4% at 10^{-4} FPPW and 6% at 10^{0} FPPI, comparing with HOG. On the other side, the performances of different color spaces are also consistent with the results of color space evaluation under 10^{-4} FPPW and 10^{0} FPPI.

In the comparison between MDST and CSS, the MDST combined with HOG has better performance than CSS. In our experiment, the HOG-MDST (CIE-Lab) can achieve 86% detection rate at 10^{0} FPPI; while the HOG-CSS (HSV) feature can only achieve 83.5% detection, raising 4.5%. For a more intuitive comparison, we show the detection results of HOG, HOG-CSS and HOG-MDST (CIE-Lab) in Fig. 7. Figure 7(1) indicates that MDST has no negative effect on detection; while from Fig. 7(2) and (3), we can get that MDST has a superior accuracy than CSS in complex scenes.

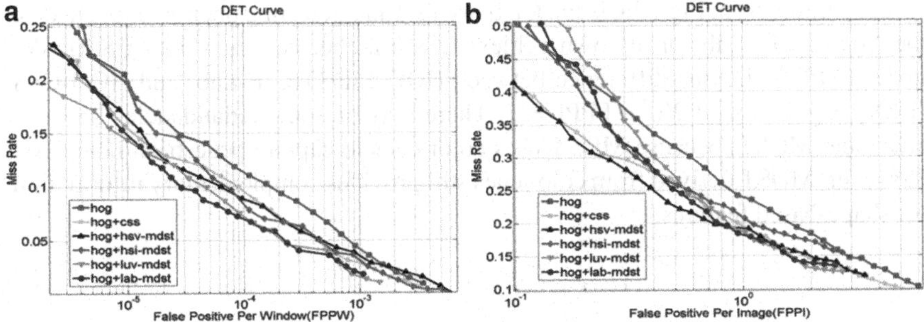

Fig. 6 Comparisons between MDST+HOG and CSS+HOG. (**a**) The per-window evaluation result. (**b**) The per-image evaluation result

Fig. 7 The *first row* is the detection results of HOG. The *second row* is the detection results of HOG-CSS (HSV) and the *third row* corresponds to HOG-MDST (CIE-Lab) at FPPI = 10^0

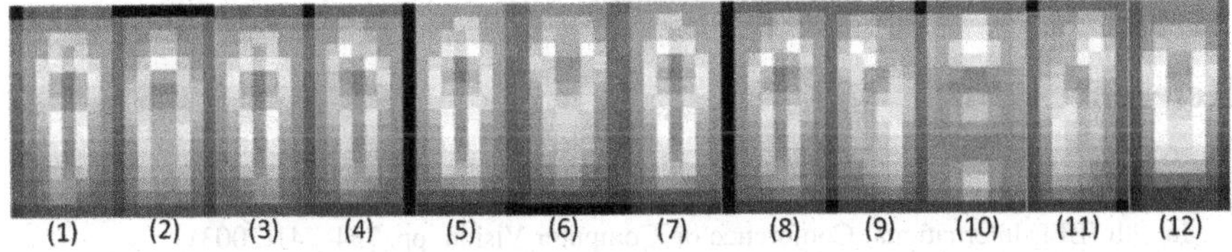

Fig. 8 The average feature map of the 12 templates for INRIA dataset

5.3 Further Discussions on MDST

The average feature maps of INRIA dataset are illustrated in Fig. 8. These average feature maps (1) $\sim$ (12) correspond to the result of templates (1) $\sim$ (12) in Fig. 3c, respectively. These figures capture the coarse boundary around pedestrians. The color cues achieve translation invariance locally, because of the max-pooling used in these templates.

In addition, from Figs. 5a, b and 6a, b, we find an interesting phenomenon, that is, the MDST(CIE-Lab) on its own achieves 18% higher accuracy than CSS(HSV) under FPPI; while, the difference between HOG-MDST(CIE-Lab) and HOG-CSS (HSV) is just around 2% at FPPI = 1. There may be some redundancies between HOG and MDST, because MDST uses color cues to capture pedestrian boundary. However, MDST derived from color cues still provides complementary information for shape-based features.

6 Conclusions

In this paper, our experiment justifies the role of color in object detection, and shows color cues play an important role. First, the typical color spaces are systematically evaluated for pedestrian detection. The results of our evaluation experiments indicate that the choice of color spaces has a great influence on performance. CIE-Lab/CIE-LUV spaces, for pedestrian, are the most suitable color spaces. Secondly, the performance of the MDST shows that max-coding scheme can effectively capture the local boundary information and outperform the state-of-the-art.

In future work, we plan to evaluate MDST on more different objects, e.g., car, cat, house [13], and explain more insights why max-coding scheme is efficient for color cues.

Acknowledgements This work was supported in part by National Basic Research Program of China (973 Program): 2009CB320906, in part by National Natural Science Foundation of China: 61025011, 61035001 and 61003165, and in part by Beijing Natural Science Foundation: 4111003.

References

1. Viola, P., Jones, M., Snow, D.: Detecting pedestrians using patterns of motion and appearance. In: 9th IEEE International Conference on Computer Vision, pp. 734–741(2003)
2. Wojek, C., Walk, S., Schiele, B.: Multi-Cue Onboard Pedestrian Detection. In: 23rd IEEE Conf. Computer Vision and Pattern Recognition, vol. 1, pp.794–801(2010)
3. Geronimo, D., Lopez, A., Sappa, A.: Survey of Pedestrian Detection for Advanced Driver Assistance Systems. In: IEEE Transactions on Pattern Analysis and Machine Intelligence (2010)
4. Dalal, N., Triggs, B.: Histogram of oriented gradients for human detection. In: 18th IEEE Conf. Computer Vision and Pattern Recognition, vol.1, pp. 886–893(2005)
5. Schwartz, W., Kembhavi, A., Harwood, D., Davis, L.: Human detection using partial least squares analysis. In12th IEEE International Conference on Computer Vision, pp. 24–31(2009)
6. Van de Sande, K. E. A., Gevers, T., Snoek, C. G. M.: Evaluation of color descriptors for object and scene recognition. In: 21th IEEE Conf. Computer Vision and Pattern Recognition(2008)
7. Shalev-Shwartz, S., Singer, Y., Srebro, N.: Pegasos: Primal Estimated sub-GrAdientSOlver for SVM. In: International conference on Machine learning (2007)

8. Rowley, H., Baluja, S., Kanade, T.: Neural network-based face detection. In: IEEE Transactions on Pattern Analysis and Machine Intelligence (1998)
9. Viola, P., Jones, M.: Rapid object detection using a boosted cascadeof simple features. In14th IEEE Conf. Computer Vision and PatternRecognition, volume 1, pp. 511–518 (2001)
10. Huang, C., Ai, H., Li, Y., Lao, S.: Vector boosting for rotation invariantmulti-view face detection. In: 10th IEEE International Conference on Computer Vision, pages 446–453 (2005)
11. Everingham, M., Van~Gool, L., Williams, C. K. I., Winn, J., Zisserman, A.: The Pascal Visual Object Classes (VOC) Challenge. In: International Journal of Computer Vision, jun (2010)
12. Wikipedia for NTSC information, http://en.wikipedia.org/wiki/NTSC
13. Wikipedia for PAL information, http://en.wikipedia.org/wiki/PAL
14. Ng, J., Bharach, A., Zhaoping, L.: A survey of architecture and function of the primary visual cortex. In: Eurasip Journal on Advances in Signal Processing (2007)
15. Maji, S., Berg, A. C., Malik, J.: Classification Using Intersection Kernel Support Vector Machines is efficient. In: 21th IEEE Conf. Computer Vision and Pattern Recognition(2008)
16. Felzenszwalb, P., McAllester, D., Ramanan, D.: A Discriminatively Trained, Multi-scale, Deformable Part Model. In: 21th IEEE Conf. Computer Vision and Pattern Recognition(2008)
17. Walk, S., Majer, N., Schindler, K., Schiele, B.: New features and Insights for Pedestrian detection. In: 23rd IEEE Conf. Computer Vision and Pattern Recognition, pp.1030–1037 (2010)
18. Dollar, P., Tu, Z., Pernoa, P., Belongie, S.: Integral channel features. In: 20th British Machine Vision Conference(2009)
19. Gevers, T., Smeulders, A.: Color Based Object Recognition. In:Pattern Recognition, Volume 32, Pages 453–464 (1997)
20. Wikipedia for CIE, http://en.wikipedia.org/wiki/International_Commission_on_Illumination
21. Dollar, P., Wojek, C., Schiele, B., Perona, P.: Pedestrian Detection: A Benchmark. In22nd IEEE Conf. Computer Vision and Pattern Recognition (2009)
22. Wikipedia for HSL and HSV information, http://en.wikipedia.org/wiki/HSL_and_HSV

Adaptive Moving Cast Shadow Detection

Guizhi Li, Lei Qin, and Qingming Huang

Abstract Moving object detection is an important task in real-time video surveillance. However, in real scenario, moving cast shadows associated with moving objects may also be detected, making moving cast shadow detection a challenge for video surveillance. In this paper, we propose an adaptive shadow detection method based on the cast shadow model. The method combines ratio edge and ratio brightness, and reduces computation complexity by the cascading algorithm. It calculates the difference of ratio edge between the shadow region and the background according to the invariability of the ratio edge of object in different light. Experimental results show that our approach outperforms existing methods.

Keywords Shadow detection • Ratio edge • Ratio brightness • Video surveillance

G. Li (✉)
Graduate University of Chinese Academy of Sciences, Beijing 100049, China
e-mail: gzli@jdl.ac.cn

L. Qin
Key Lab of Intell. Info. Process., Chinese Academy of Sciences, Beijing 100190, China

Institute of Computing Technology, Chinese Academy of Sciences, Beijing 100190, China
e-mail: lqin@jdl.ac.cn

Q. Huang
Graduate University of Chinese Academy of Sciences, Beijing 100049, China

Key Lab of Intell. Info. Process., Chinese Academy of Sciences, Beijing 100190, China

Institute of Computing Technology, Chinese Academy of Sciences, Beijing 100190, China
e-mail: qmhuang@jdl.ac.cn

J.S. Jin et al., *The Era of Interactive Media*,
DOI 10.1007/978-1-4614-3501-3_33,

1 Introduction

In recent years, moving objects detection is a hot topic in computer vision, with a lot of applications such as surveillance system, vehicle tracking and video conferences. However, when detecting moving objects in real world scenes, the cast shadow associated with the moving object is also detected. For instance, cars may cause the sun to cast shadows on the road. Labeling the cast shadow is favorable to detect the accurate shape of object, thus shadow detection is a key issue unavoidable.

There are many approaches for shadow detection. Usually, they can be divided into three categories: color-based, statistic-based, and texture-based.

The color-based methods attempt to describe the color feature change of shadow pixels. Cucchiara et al. [1] operate brightness, saturation, and hue properties in the HSV color space. For avoiding using the time consuming HSV color space transformation, Schreer et al. [2] adopt the YUV color space, and distinguish the shadow regions from the foreground regions according to the observation that the YUV pixel value of shadows is lower than the linear pixels. According to the shadow model, Salvador et al. [3] identify an initial set of shadow pixels basing on RGB color space, according to the fact that shadow region darkens the surface; they combined color invariance with geometric properties of shadow. Though color-based methods have shown its power in shadow detection, they may not be reliable to detect moving shadows when the moving objects have similar color with moving shadows,

The principle of statistic-based methods is to build pixel-based statistical models detecting cast shadows. In [4], Zivkovic et al. using Gaussian Mixture Model (GMM) to detect moving cast shadows. The method consists of building a GMM for moving objects, identifying the distribution of moving objects and shadows, and modifying the learning rates of the distributions. In [5], Nicolas et al. propose Gaussian Mixture Shadow Model (GMSM). The algorithm models moving cast shadows of non-uniform and varying intensity, and builds statistical models to segment moving cast shadows by using the GMM learning ability. Claudio et al. [6] also use a statistical approach combined with geometrical constraints for detecting and removing shadows, but it is only for gray-scale video sequences. The statistic-based methods identify distribution of shadow pixel value and are robust in different scenes. Though the methods reduce false hits of property descriptions (i.e. color or intensity) of shadow, they cannot eliminate them. Generally, they need to be initialized by property descriptions.

The texture-based methods are based on the fact that the texture of shadow region remains same as that of the background, while the texture of moving object is different with that of the background. Zhang et al. [7] explore ratio edges for shadow detection. They prove that the ratio edge is illumination invariant. The local ratios are modeled as a chi-squared distribution in shadow districts. In addition to using scene brightness distortion and chromaticity distortion, Choi et al. [8] proposes three estimators which use the properties of chromaticity, brightness, and local intensity ratio. The chromaticity difference obeys a standard normalize distribution between the shadow region and the background. The texture-based methods may be the most promising technique for shadow detection, the textual information of different scenes can be captured by the above methods. However, the above methods have complex progress about computation.

In this paper, we propose an adaptive shadow detection method based on the cast shadow model. The method is made up of ratio edge and ratio brightness, and reduces complexity by the cascading algorithm. Though this paper uses ratio edge that has been defined in [7], it is different from calculating the chi-square distribution of ratio edge in [7]. In this paper, we calculate the difference of ratio edge between the shadow region and the background according to the invariability of the ratio edge of object in different lighting condition. Experimental results show that our approach outperforms existing methods.

The paper is organized as follows. Section 2 describes the cast shadow model. Section 3 presents the overall process, which includes the ratio edge, ratio brightness, and spatial adjustment. Section 4 shows the experimental results, and the conclusion is presented in Sect. 5.

2 Cast Shadow Model

In the real world, shadows can be generally divided into static shadow and dynamic shadow. Static shadows are cast by static object such as buildings, trees, parked cars etc. Dynamic shadows in video are cast by moving objects such as moving vehicles, pedestrians, etc. Generally speaking, the illumination can be divided into two kinds: a light source (i.e. Sun) and an ambient light (i.e. Sky), as shown in Fig. 1. Shadow is deprived the direct light source by the foreground object. Each pixel of shadow

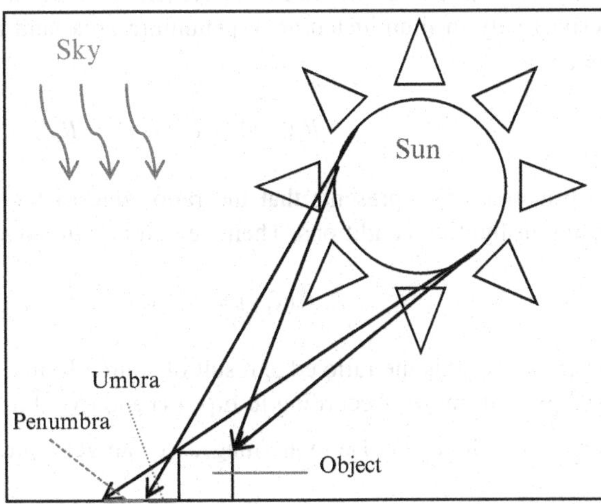

Fig. 1 Cast shadow model

has the same ambient light; the pixels which do not belong to the shadow not only have the ambient light, but also have the same light source.

The color intensity of a pixel can be given by

$$f(x,y) = r(x,y) * p(x,y) \tag{1}$$

where $f(x,y)$ is the color intensity, $r(x,y)$ is the illumination function and $p(x,y)$ is the reflectance factor. The illumination function $r(x,y)$ is expressed as a function of the intensity of the light source c_i, the intensity of the ambient light c_a, the direction L of the light, and the object surface normal [9]:

$$r(x,y) = \begin{cases} c_a + c_i * \cos(L, n(X,Y)) & \textit{illuminated area} \\ c_a + i(x,y) * c_i * \cos(L, n(x,y)) & \textit{penumbra area} \\ c_a & \textit{umbra area.} \end{cases} \tag{2}$$

where $i(x,y)$ represents the transition inside the penumbra between shaded and illuminated regions and $i(x,y) \in [0,1]$.

We define the neighboring region of a pixel as follows:

$$\Omega(x,y) = \{f(x+i, y+i) | 0 < i^2 + j^2 \leq r^2\} \tag{3}$$

where r represents the radius of the neighboring region. In this paper, the ratio edge of pixel $f(x,y)$ is then defined as follows [7]:

$$R(x,y) = \sum_{(i,j)\in\Omega(x,y)} \frac{f(x,y)}{f(i,j)} \tag{4}$$

We consider $i(x,y)$, $L, n(x,y)$ and c_a to be constant in one neighboring region. Let R_i, R_p, and R_u be the ratio edge results of the same object when the region is respectively in illuminated area, penumbra area, and umbra area. By [7], we can get:

$$R_i(x,y) = R_p(x,y) = R_u(x,y). \tag{5}$$

Equation (5) represents that the ratio edge of the object keeps unchanged in different lighting conditions. Then we define ratio edge difference as follows:

$$C(x,y) = R_F(x,y) - R_B(x,y) \tag{6}$$

where $R_F(x,y)$ is the ratio edge result of source frame, $R_B(x,y)$ is the ratio edge of background image. According to Eqs. (4) and (5), if a pixel belongs to the shadow region and there is noise in an image, we can get $C_s(x,y) \sim N\left(0, \varepsilon(x,y)^2\right)$.

We assume that the shadow pixels are corrupted with the illuminated pixels and Gaussian white noise, according to Eqs. (1) and (2):

$$f_S(x,y) = \alpha(x,y)f_B(x,y) + \lambda(x,y), \lambda(x,y) \sim N\left(0, \sigma(x,y)^2\right) \tag{7}$$

where $f_B(x,y)$ is the intensity of a pixel in the background image, $f_S(x,y)$ is the intensity of a pixel in the shadow region of the source frame, $0 \le \alpha(x,y) \le 1$ relates to the intensity of shadow pixels, $\lambda(x,y)$ is Gaussian noise. Then we can define ratio brightness as follows:

$$B(x,y) = \frac{f_F(x,y)}{f_B(x,y)} \tag{8}$$

where $f_F(x,y)$ is pixel of the source frame, $f_B(x,y)$ is pixel of the background image. If we consider that $\alpha(x,y) \approx \alpha$ is constant within a neighboring region, the ratio brightness of shadow pixel becomes

$$B_S(x,y) = \frac{f_S(x,y)}{f_B(x,y)} = \theta(x,y) \tag{9}$$

where $\theta(x,y) = \alpha + \lambda(x,y)/f_B(x,y) \sim N\left(\alpha, (\sigma(x,y)/f_B(x,y))^2\right)$.

3 The Procedure of Shadow Detection

In this section, we present the detailed procedures of shadow detection. The proposed method is a multi-stage approach and the flow chart is shown in Fig. 2.

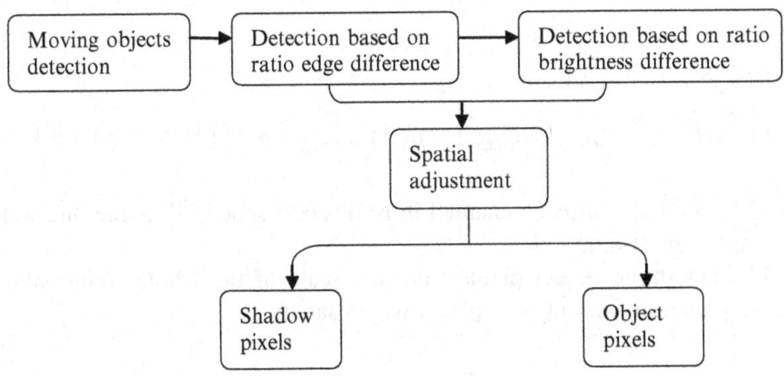

Fig. 2 Flow chart of the algorithm

3.1 Moving Object Detection

In this step, GMM [10] is used to estimate background image. We detect the foreground by subtracting the estimated background image from the current frame. In the set of foreground pixels, there are moving objects pixels as well as the shadow pixels. In this paper, we use the following notations: in frame n, F_n is the binary mask of foreground pixels to be detected, S_n is the binary mask of moving shadows to be detected, and O_n is the binary mask of moving objects.

At first, we assume all the foreground pixels are shadows pixels, and will discriminate the shadow pixels and object pixels in following steps:

$$S_n = F_n = 1,\ 0_n = 0 \tag{10}$$

3.2 Moving Shadow Detection Based on Ratio Edge Difference

We use the Eq. (6) for determining whether a pixel is a moving object pixel or shadow pixel. Generally, if a pixel belongs to the shadow, the probability that the neighboring pixels of the pixel belong to shadow region is higher, and the ratio edge differences are near zero. We can define $\mu_{C(x,y)}$ as follows:

$$\mu_{C(x,y)} = \frac{1}{N_S} \sum_{(i,j)\in\Omega_S(x,y)} C(i,j) \tag{11}$$

where N_S is the number of pixels in Ω_S. According to the Eq. (4), $\mu_{C(x,y)}$ of the shadow pixel has a normalized Gaussian distribution. However, we cannot confirm the distribution of moving object pixel.

We can initially determine shadow pixels by $\mu_{C(x,y)}$, because $\mu_{C(x,y)}$ of shadow pixel is nearby zero. Therefore, a pixel can be identified as an object pixel as follows:

$$\begin{aligned} &0_n(x,y) = 1; S_n(x,y) = 0 \\ &if\left(\left(\left(\left|\mu^R_{C(x,y)}\right| > \mu^R_S\right)\left(\left|\mu^G_{C(x,y)}\right| > \mu^G_S\right)\left(\left|\mu^B_{C(x,y)}\right| > \mu^B_S\right)\right)\&S_n(x,y) = 1\right) \end{aligned} \tag{12}$$

where $\mu^K_{C(x,y)}$ is $\mu_{C(x,y)}$ of each channel in RGB color space; μ^K_S is the threshold of each channel, and $0 < \mu^K_S < 1$.

We can determine object pixels from the scale of the whole foreground. To reduce computation, we only use pixels which satisfy

$$\left|\mu^K_{C(x,y)}\right| \le \mu^K_S \tag{13}$$

Then, we estimate $m^K_{\mu_C}$ and $\sigma^K_{\mu_C}$ using max likelihood estimation (MLE) [11] as follows:

$$m^K_{\mu_C} = \frac{1}{N_C} \sum_{(x,y)\in C} \mu^K_C(x,y); \left(\sigma^K_{\mu_C}\right)^2 = \frac{1}{N_C} \sum_{(x,y)\in C} \left(\mu^K_C(x,y) - m^K_{\mu_C}\right)^2 \quad (14)$$

where C is the set pixels that satisfy Eq. (13) in the set of $(S_n(x,y) = 1)$, and N_C is the number of pixel in C.

We compute the threshold α^K_h and α^K_i using the estimated $m^K_{\mu_C}$ and $\sigma^K_{\mu_C}$ as follows:

$$\alpha^K_h = m^K_{\mu_C} + 1.96 * \sigma^K_{\mu_C}; \alpha^K_i = m^K_{\mu_C} - 1.96 * \sigma^K_{\mu_C} \quad (15)$$

with reliability of 95%; then the pixel is determined as an object pixel as follows:

$$\begin{aligned} &0_n(x,y) = 1; S_n(x,y) = 0 \\ &if \left(\left(\begin{array}{c} \left(\mu^R_{C(x,y)} > \alpha^R_h\right) \Big| \left(\mu^R_{C(x,y)} > \alpha^R_i\right) \Big| \left(\mu^G_{C(x,y)} > \alpha^G_h\right) \Big| \\ \left(\mu^G_{C(x,y)} > \alpha^G_i\right) \Big| \left(\mu^B_{C(x,y)} > \alpha^B_h\right) \Big| \left(\mu^B_{C(x,y)} > \alpha^B_i\right) \Big| \end{array} \right) \& S_n(x,y) = 1 \right) \end{aligned} \quad (16)$$

3.3 *Moving Shadow Detection Based on Ratio Brightness Difference*

In this part, we use the Eq. (9) for determining whether a pixel is a moving object pixel or shadow pixel. An analogous process about ratio edge difference can be applied on ratio brightness difference. We define $\mu_{B(x,y)}$ as follows:

$$\mu_{B(x,y)} = \frac{1}{N_S} \sum_{(i,j)\in\Omega_S(x,y)} B(i,j), \quad (17)$$

According to the Eq. (9), $\mu_{B(x,y)}$ of a pixel in shadow region is Gaussian distribution. We can find that $\mu_{B(x,y)}$ generally should be less than 1.0 by Eq. (7), thus a pixel is estimated as an object pixel as follows:

$$\begin{aligned} &0_n(x,y) = 1; S_n(x,y) = 0 \\ &if \left(\left(\begin{array}{c} \left(I_{low} < \mu^R_{B(x,y)} < I_{high}\right) \Big| \left(I_{low} < \mu^G_{B(x,y)} < I_{high}\right) \Big| \\ \left(I_{low} < \mu^B_{C(x,y)} < I_{high}\right) \end{array} \right) \& S_n(x,y) = 1 \right) \end{aligned} \quad (18)$$

where $\mu_{B(x,y)}^{K}$ represent $\mu_{B(x,y)}$ in R, G or B; I_{low} and I_{high} represent the threshold, and $0 < I_{low} < 1, < I_{high}$.

Just like ratio edge difference process, we determine whether a pixel is a shadow pixel or moving object pixel by the whole mean and variation. To reduce computation complexity, we just use pixels satisfy

$$0 < \mu_{B(x,y)}^{K} < I_{low} \tag{19}$$

Then we estimate $m_{\mu_B}^{K}$ and $\sigma_{\mu_B}^{K}$ by MLE as follows:

$$m_{\mu_B}^{K} = \frac{1}{N_B} \sum_{(x,y)\in B} \mu_B^K(x,y); \left(\sigma_{\mu_B}^{K}\right)^2 = \frac{1}{N_B} \sum_{(x,y)\in B} \left(\mu_B^K(x,y) - m_{\mu_B}^{K}\right)^2 \tag{20}$$

where B is the set pixels that satisfying Eq. (19) in the set of ($S_n\,(x,y) = 1$), and N_B is the number of pixel in B.

We compute the threshold β_h^K and β_i^K using the estimated $m_{\mu_B}^{K}$ and $\sigma_{\mu_B}^{K}$ as follows:

$$\beta_h^K = m_{\mu_B}^{K} + 1.96 * \sigma_{\mu_B}^{K};\ \beta_i^K = m_{\mu_B}^{K} - 1.96 * \sigma_{\mu_B}^{K} \tag{21}$$

within the reliability of 95%; then the pixel is determined as an object pixel as follows:

$$0_n(x,y) = 1;\ \ S_n(x,y) = 0$$
$$if\left(\left(\begin{array}{l}\left(\mu_{B(x,y)}^{R} > \beta_h^R\right)\middle|\left(\mu_{B(x,y)}^{R} > \beta_i^R\right)\middle|\left(\mu_{B(x,y)}^{G} > \beta_h^G\right)\middle|\\ \left(\mu_{B(x,y)}^{G} > \beta_i^G\right)\middle|\left(\mu_{B(x,y)}^{B} > \beta_h^B\right)\middle|\left(\mu_{B(x,y)}^{B} > \beta_i^B\right)\middle|\end{array}\right) \& S_n(x,y) = 1\right) \tag{22}$$

3.4 *Spatial Adjustment*

We will adjust the property of some small isolated regions. For example a moving object pixel that is surrounded by shadow pixels will be determined to be a shadow pixel and the adjustment will be carried out to the shadow pixels in a similar way.

4 Experimental Results

In this section, we present some experimental results obtained by the proposed approach. And we compare the results with other algorithm. For the proposed approach, the choices of parameters (i.e. r, μ_S^K, I_{low}, I_{high}) influence the accuracy rate

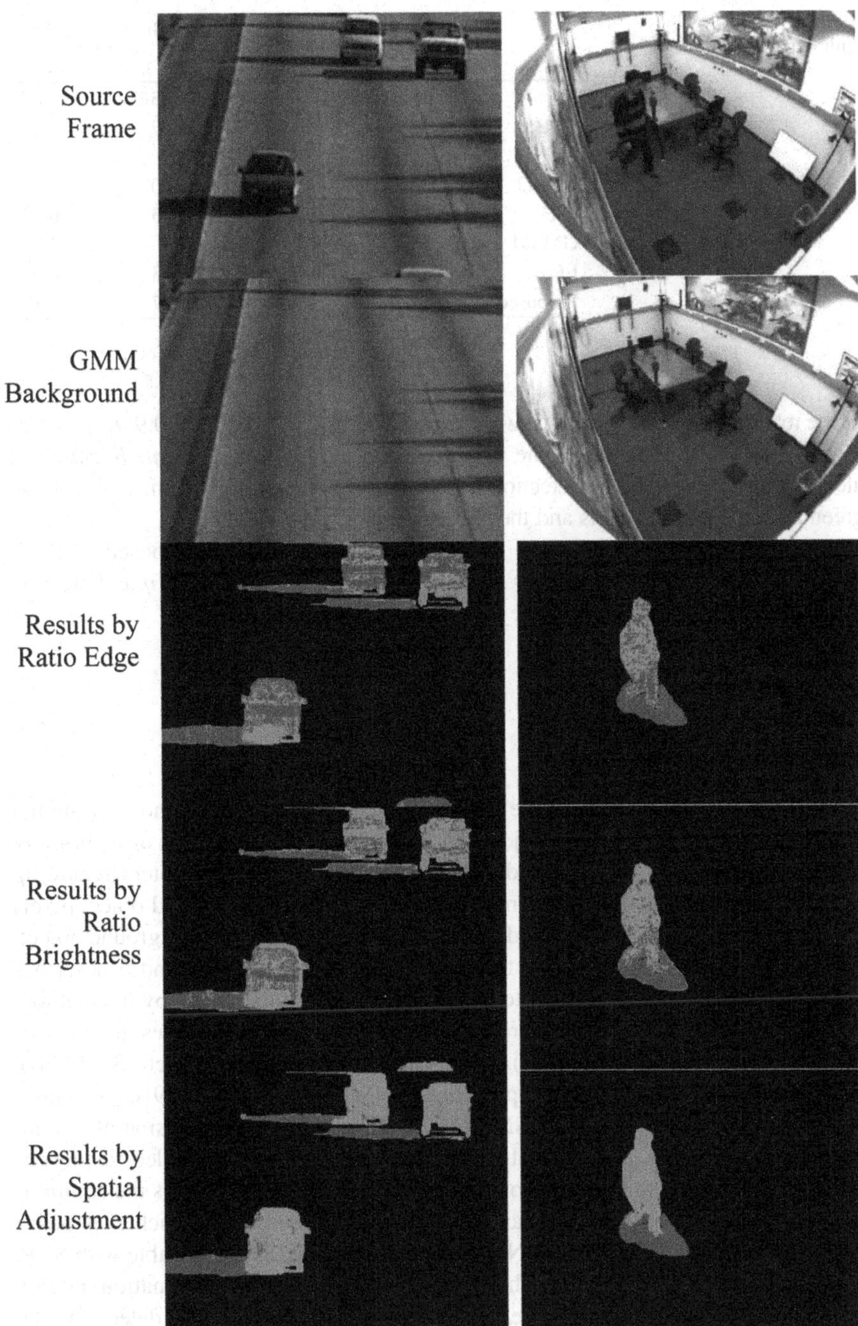

Fig. 3 Shadow detection results

Table 1 Comparison with other algorithms

	Highway		Intelligent room	
	η (%)	ξ (%)	η (%)	ξ (%)
SP	58.55	87.13	79.85	87.82
SNP	76.71	66.60	85.07	76.60
DNM1	60.23	86.63	82.2	88.2
DNM2	72.17	77.86	78.60	86.8
ICF	71.82	79.29	73.45	86.52
GMSM	75.43	74.67	73.6	79.1
ER	67.17	90.19	88.63	88.91
Proposed	74.76	91.75	86.27	89.17

of the results. In our experiments, we choose $r = 3$, $\mu_S^K = 2.0, I_{low} = 0.9, I_{high} = 1.5$. Figure 3 shows two frames of the video sequences (*HighwayI* and *Intelligentroom*) along with the final shadow detection results by the proposed algorithm. In Fig. 3, the green region is object pixels and the red region is shadow pixels.

We also give the quantitative evaluation results about the proposed method. The performance is expressed by using the shadow detection rate η and shadow discrimination rate ξ [12], and they are defined as follows:

$$\eta = \frac{TP_S}{TP_S + FN_S} \times 100\%; \xi = \frac{\overline{TP_F}}{TP_F + FN_F} \times 100\% \tag{23}$$

where subscript S and F respectively represent shadow and foreground; TP_F are the number of correctly identified object pixels, and FN_F is the number of incorrectly identified object pixels; TP_S and FN_S denote analogous parameters regarding shadow identification; $\overline{TP_F}$ is the number of ground-truth foreground object pixels minus the number of pixels marked as shadows, but belonging to foreground object. Therefore, η indicates how well the algorithm detects shadows, and ξ describes how well shadows are discriminated from actual foreground pixels by the method.

We compare our proposed approach with the following approaches: the statistical parametric approach (SP [13]), statistical nonparametric approach (SNP [14]), deterministic non-model based approaches (DNM1 [1] and DNM2 [9]), the Gaussian mixture shadow model (GMSM [11]), and the shadow suppression algorithm based on edge ratio (ER [7]). In our analysis, we use two video sequences (*HighwayI* and *Intelligentroom*) for shadow detection. Table 1 shows the comparison results. From the table, we can see that our proposed method achieves better performances than SP, DNM1, DNM2, ICF, GMSM, and is comparable with SNP, ER. The proposed method reaches the highest shadow discrimination rate in *HighwayI* and *Intelligentroom* sequences, a little lower shadow detection rate than SNP in *HighwayI* sequence, and a little lower shadow detection rate than ER in *Intelligentroom* sequence.

5 Conclusion

In this paper, we propose an approach to automatically detect shadow using ratio edge and ratio brightness. The approach can be operated very simply because it determines the shadow threshold automatically without an additional training step. Experimental results show the proposed approach is effective. The performance of our approach is better or comparable with other methods.

Acknowledgements This work was supported in part by National Basic Research Program of China (973 Program): 2009CB320906, in part by National Natural Science Foundation of China: 61025011, 61035001 and 61003165, and in part by Beijing Natural Science Foundation: 4111003.

References

1. R. Cucchiara, C. Grana, M. Piccardi, A. Prati, and S. Sirotti, "Improving Shadow Suppression in Moving Object Detection with HSV Color Information," Proc. Intelligent Transportation Systems Conf., pp. 334–339, 2001.
2. O. Schreer, I. Feldmann, U. Goelz, and P. Kauff.: Fast and Robust Shadow Detection in Videoconference Applications, Proc. Fourth IEEE Int'l Symp. Video Processing and Multimedia Comm., pp. 371–375, 2002.
3. E. Salvador, A. Cavallaro, and T. Ebrahimi.: Cast Shadow Segmentation Using Invariant Color Features," Computer Vision and Image Understanding, pp.238–259, 2004.
4. Zoran Zivkovic, Ferdinand van der Heijden.: Efficient adaptive density estimation per image pixel for the Task of Background Subtraction, Pattern Recognition Letters, 2006.
5. N. Martel-Brisson, and A. Zaccarin.: Learning and Removing Cast Shadows through a Multidistribution Approach, IEEE Trans.Pattern Analysis and Machine Intelligence, vol. 29, no. 7, pp. 1133–1146, July 2007.
6. Claudio Rosito Jung.: Efficient Background Subtraction and Shadow Removal for Monochromatic Video Sequences, IEEE Transactions on Multimedia, vol. 11, no. 3, pp. 571–577, April 2009.
7. W. Zhang, X. Z. Fang, and X. K. Yang.: Moving cast shadows detection using ratio edge, IEEE Trans. Multimedia, vol. 9, no. 6, pp.1202–1214, Oct. 2007.
8. JinMin Choi, YungJun Yoo, and JinYoung Choi.: Adaptive Shadow Estimator for Removing Shadow of Moving Object, Computer Vision and Image Understanding, pp. 1017–1029, 2010.
9. J. Stauder and R. M. Ostermann.: Detection of moving cast shadows for object segmentation, IEEE Trans. Multimedia, vol. 1, no. 1, pp.65–76, Mar. 1999.
10. C. Stauffer and W. E. L. Grimson.: Learning patterns of activity using real-time tracking, IEEE Trans. Pattern Anal. Machine Intell., vol. 22, pp. 747–757, 2000.
11. Richard O. Duda, Peter E. Hart, David G. Stork.: Pattern Classification, 2nd ed.,Wiley-Interscience, 2000.
12. A. Prati, I. Mikic, M.M. Trivedi, and R. Cucchiara.: Detecting Moving Shadows: Algorithms and Evaluation, IEEE Trans.Pattern Analysis and Machine Intelligence, vol. 25, no. 7, pp. 918–923, July 2003.
13. I. Mikic, P. C. Cosman, G. T. Kogut, and M. M. Trivedi.: Moving shadow and object detection in traffic scenes, Proc. Int. Conf. Pattern Recognition, pp. 321–324, Washington, DC, 2000.
14. Thanarat Horprasert, David Harwood, Larry S. Davis.: A statistical approach for real-time robust background subtraction and shadow detection, in: Proceedings of the IEEE International Conference on Computer Vision, 1999.
15. Kunfeng Wang, Qingming Yao, Xin Qiao, Shuming Tang, Fei-Yue Wang.: Moving object refining in traffic monitoring applications, in: Proceedings of the 2007, IEEE Conference on Intelligent Transportation Systems, pp. 540–545, October 2007.

A Framework for Surveillance Video Fast Browsing Based on Object Flags

Shizheng Wang, Wanxin Xu, Chao Wang, and Baoju Wang

Abstract Conventional surveillance video coding frameworks are designed to maximize the coding efficiency or to improve the adaptability. However, the problem that how to construct a flexible framework for browsing surveillance video has become another important issue as well as improving the efficiency of coding and adaptability of video bitstream. This paper proposes a framework for efficient storing and synopsis browsing of surveillance video based on object flags. The main contributions of our work are that: (1) the framework provides an applicable video coding approach for video surveillance by combining with the video synopsis method; (2) our method can improve the storage efficiency and provide users a fast browsing scheme for surveillance video. The experiments of implementing the framework based on the H.264/AVC video codec are shown.

Keywords Surveillance • Video synopsis • Fast browsing • Object flags

S. Wang (✉)
CBSR & NLPR, Institute of Automation, Chinese Academy of Sciences,
Beijing 100190, P.R. China

Chinese Academy of Sciences Research and Development Center for Internet of Things,
Wuxi 214135, P.R. China
e-mail: szwang@cbsr.ia.ac.cn

W. Xu • C. Wang • B. Wang
CBSR and NLPR, Institute of Automation, Chinese Academy of Sciences,
Beijing 100190, P.R. China
e-mail: wxxu@cbsr.ia.ac.cn; cwang@cbsr.ia.ac.cn; wsz316@cbsr.ia.ac.cn

J.S. Jin et al., *The Era of Interactive Media*,
DOI 10.1007/978-1-4614-3501-3_34,

1 Introduction

Digital video surveillance has become an important application over the past years. Techniques involved, including video coding and browsing, which are essential in the application of video surveillance, have gained more and more attention.

In recent years, there are mainly two kinds of surveillance video coding schemes: One is block-based hybrid video coding scheme which is based on macroblock in common video coding standards. In [1], Kunter et al. designed a background sprite image containing all the background information of a certain sequence, and proposed a coding module by introducing the background frame as reference in the coding process to the current H.264/AVC coding framework. And Zhang et al. [2] put forward an efficient coding scheme by coding difference frames selectively to further improve the coding efficiency of surveillance video. The other coding scheme introduces the object-based video compression technique. For instance, in Hakeem's paper [3], the proposed system used background modeling, object detecting and tracking to extract objects in the videos, and then data redundancy can be further removed in video coding by applying different compression strategies to different objects. Meanwhile, Scalable Video Coding [4] and Distributed Video Coding [5] also have some promising applications in video surveillance. However, the problem that how to browse and retrieve surveillance video more conveniently stays unresolved to some extend.

In the field of video browsing, video abstraction has attracted considerable attention and various methods have been proposed [6]. As a summary of a long video, video abstraction can provide access to large volumes of video content in a relatively short time. Therefore, it is a very useful approach for video browsing associated with some others, such as fast-forward browsing [7], advanced widgets [8], direct manipulation [9] and the video object annotation [10]. Unlike the conventional method of video abstraction, a dynamic video synopsis for video abstraction is proposed in [11]. Consequently, video synopsis is expected to have many promising applications in the field of video surveillance.

In this paper, we propose a surveillance video coding scheme combined with the video synopsis, which is expected as a comprehensive solution to code, store and browse surveillance video. The paper is organized as follows: a brief introduction of our framework is referred in the Sect. 2. Section 3 describes the design and coding of object flags in detail. In Sect. 4, we present our process of synopsis reconstruction based on object flags. Section 5 shows experimental results and analysis. Finally, our conclusions are given in Sect. 6.

2 Framework Overview

In this paper, a novel video coding framework for surveillance video fast browsing is proposed. As shown in Fig. 1, it not only codes the original video, but also records the materials for synopsis video reconstruction. And then the original video and

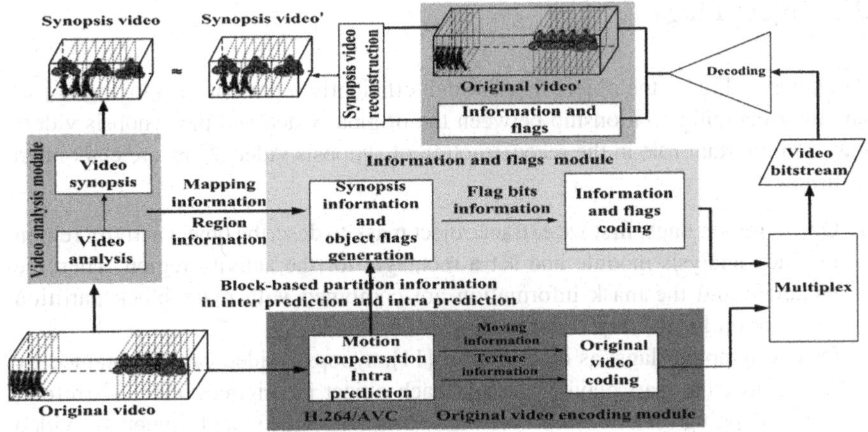

Fig. 1 Framework for Surveillance video synopsis browsing

such information can be derived from bitstream at decoder. As a result, our framework facilitates users to switch between original video and synopsis video conveniently.

Different from the conventional hybrid coding framework in H.264/AVC, the novel coding framework introduces video analysis module, and introduces information and flags module to the traditional video coding framework.

Video analysis module consists of video analysis and video synopsis. Video analysis includes background modeling, moving object extraction, object tracking in the surveillance video under the fixed scene, and outputs the region information. Video synopsis focuses on reassigning the spatial-temporal relationship among objects extracted by video analysis via energy function, and outputs the mapping information of objects.

Information and flags module is responsible for the generation of synopsis information and object flags as well as their coding. In this module, synopsis video information is derived from the mapping information obtained from video analysis module. As shown in Fig. 3, the mapping relationship of objects from original video to synopsis video helps to get synopsis information, which includes the total number of frames in synopsis video and the number of moving objects in each frame. Object flags are obtained from the combination of macroblock partition information derived from original video coding module and region information with mapping information derived from video analysis module. We write the coding bits into the extension of original video bitstream. This framework is equivalent to the traditional one if video analysis module and information and flag module are not used.

We use lossless method to code synopsis information and object flags, and all data are coded via fixed-length coding except for the quadtree flags of region information.

3 Object Flags

As shown in Fig. 1, the object flags, which efficiently represent the moving object and their mapping relationship between the original video and the synopsis video, play an important role in the reconstruction of synopsis video. They are elaborated as follows:

1. Object region flags: first we extract object mask to describe object activity region in video analysis module and set a rectangle for the activity region. Then the rectangle and the mask information are combined with macroblock partition information for the object flag coding.
2. Object mapping flags: as described in [11], synopsis video can be obtained by reassigning the start playing time of each object in original video. Therefore, such mapping relationship between original video and synopsis video determines the display order of objects in synopsis video.

3.1 Object Region Flags

Region flags are used to reduce the storage cost of object region information at encoder, and to describe the region of moving object in the original video accurately. In this paper, a classical method for region of interest (ROI) marking and coding based on region quadtree is utilized.

Quadtree [12], which is introduced in the early 1970s and is acquired based on the principle of recursive space decomposition, has become a major method for representing spatial data. In the spirit of conventional region quadtree representation, each ROI is represented by a sequence of nodes which is a series from the root node of the tree to the leaf node. So the traditional way requires a large number of flags to mark the non-leaf node.

Based on the above analysis, it is possible to reduce the storage cost by omitting the non-leaf nodes to represent the ROI. Specifically, we combine the mask of moving object generated by video analysis module with the information of the macroblock partition obtained from the traditional coding module. As shown in Fig. 2, we first mark the ROI with a rectangle derived from video analysis module, and then divide the rectangle into subblocks referring to macroblock partitions from video coding module and finally mark upon the divided subblocks according to the masks from video analysis module. As shown in Fig. 2c, there are eight macroblocks intersected with rectangle, which are the regions we need to mark with eight quadtrees to describe the silhouette of a pedestrian. Figure 2e presents the eight quadtrees corresponding to eight macroblocks from top row (left to right) to bottom row. As for H.264/AVC coding standard, we select the precision of 16×16, 8×8 and 4×4 to obtain quadtree data structure. Here we suppose the subblock with precision of 16×8 or 8×16 is consisted of two 8×8 subblocks with the same marker, and then we use one node to represent the subblock in the quadtree. Similarly, we use one node to represent the subblock with precision of 8×4 or 4×8 in the quadtree.

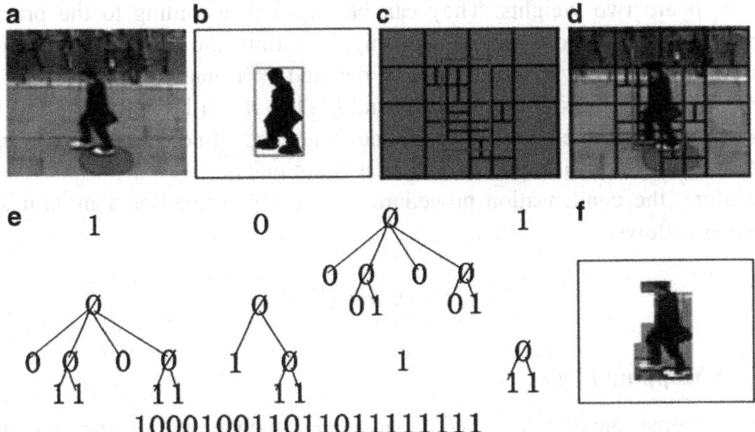

Fig. 2 Flag bits based on masks of object and macroblock partition information: (**a**) Original video, (**b**) Mask information, (**c**) Macroblock partition information with rectangle, (**d**) ROI to be extracted, (**e**) Marking based on quadtree, (**f**) Obtained ROI

Finally, eight quadtrees are generated to represent all the macroblocks overlapped with ROI. Using the adaptive precision based on the macroblock partition, we regard all subblocks in the rectangle as leaf nodes labeled with '0' or '1', Here subblocks labeled with '0' are non-ROI or minor ROI with an area smaller than the predetermined threshold, otherwise it is a ROI.

3.2 *Object Mapping Flags*

a. Video Synopsis

Video synopsis is a novel abstraction method for fast browsing of surveillance video by putting objects extracted from different frames together, thus efficiently reducing the spatial-temporal redundancies when browsing the original video. The first step of video synopsis is object tube extraction. After getting the set of object tubes, namely object queue B, temporal shifting should be implemented to reassign the displaying time of object tubes in synopsis video according to energy function. In [11], the authors present the generation of synopsis video as a minimization of energy function they formulated. The energy function is composed of activity cost function E_α, collision cost function E_c and temporal consistency cost function E_t, and they are used to penalize discarding the active pixels, pixel-level occlusion and relative timing alteration of object tubes respectively. The energy function is shown as follow:

$$E(M) = \sum_{b \in B} E_\alpha(\hat{b}) + \sum_{b,b' \in B} (\alpha E_t(\hat{b}, \hat{b}')) + \beta E_c(\hat{b}, \hat{b}') \tag{1}$$

Where α, β are two weights. They can be adjusted according to the practical application. M is the mapping relationship indicating the start playing time of object tubes in B for synopsis. M can be denoted as a mapping function $f(i, k)$, where i is the frame ID of original video and k is the object ID in frame $i. f(i, k)$ is the corresponding frame ID of synopsis video when the k-th object in the i-th frame is mapped. And $f(i, k)$ is equal to 0 when it is not mapped.

Therefore, the condensation procedure can be represented as a minimization problem as follows:

$$M_{best} = \underset{M}{arg\ min}\,(E(M)) \tag{2}$$

b. Object Mapping Flags

By using synopsis method described in part a, we can obtain the synopsis video and its corresponding mapping information automatically. In our work, we assume that: there are N frames in original video; the number of objects in frame i of original video is denoted as $R(i) = O_i, i = 1, 2 \ldots, N$. Assuming there are M frames in synopsis video, the number of objects in frame j of synopsis video is denoted as $P(j) = S_j, j = 1, 2, \ldots, M$. And assume the total number of objects extracted from original video is K. $T_k = \left[t_k^s, t_k^e\right]$ denotes the time interval of k-th object in original video, while $\hat{T}_k = \left[\hat{t}_{k,}^s, \hat{t}_k^e\right]$ denotes the time interval of object k in synopsis video, $k \in \{1, 2, \ldots K\}$; object k in frame i is denoted as $Object_i(k)$, $k \in \{1, 2, \ldots, R(i)\}$.

Based on the assumptions above, the mapping function obtained in part a can be expressed as below:

$$f(i,k) = \begin{cases} m & if\ object\ is\ mapped \\ 0 & otherwise \end{cases} i \in [t_k^s, t_k^e],\ m \in \{1,2,\ldots,M\} \tag{3}$$

3.3 *Writing Bitstream*

After designing and formatting the synopsis information and object flags, we write them all to the extension of picture parameter set and slice header of H.264/AVC [13] video bitstream. Meanwhile, we set each frame as a slice. The synopsis information records the frame number and the number of objects in each frame of synopsis video. Object flags explain the location and silhouette of an object. Table 1 shows the format of the object flags in detail. Object flags are consisted of seven components to describe the attributes of an object. The scheme uses fixed-length to code all the components data except for the quadtree flags. For an input video with the resolution of $W \times H$, and the synopsis video with M frames, we estimate the possible value for the components: region_top_left_x, region_top_left_y, region_width, region_hight, synopsis_map_num. In the Table 1,

Table 1 Formation of object flag in the extension data of slice header

Component	Variable	Definition	Illustration
region_top_left_x	x	The coordinate of left corner of rectangle	$min\,(x)>0,\ max\,(x)<W$
region_top_left_y	y	The coordinate of top corner of rectangle	$min\,(y)>0,\ max\,(y)<H$
Region_width	w	The width of rectangle	$min\,(w)>1,\ max\,(w)<\alpha * W$
Region_hight	h	The height of rectangle	$min\,(h)>1,\ max\,(h)<\beta * H$
flag_tree_on	f	A switch upon quadtree coding	'0': turn off, '1': turn on
quadtree flags chain	p	The length of bits coding the run lengths	Coded with fixed length q at encoder
	$R[n]$	A sequence of binary bits generated by RLC	$n = k * (1 + p),\ k>0$
synopsis_map_num	m	the map numbering to synopsis video	$m \in \{1,2,\ldots,M\}$

$\alpha,\ \beta$ are two parameters selected empirically to adapt to the size of objects in test sequence, and their values satisfy the constraints: $\alpha,\ \beta \in (0,\ 1]$. In general, we set α, β bigger in the case of indoor surveillance videos, whereas setting them smaller for outdoor surveillance videos.

As for the quadtree flags, we use the Run-length Coding (RLC) [14] to write them into bitstream to make further lossless compression. The sequence of flags generated by RLC is consisted of binary bits which record k pairs of quadtree flag's value and its run length. Since the quadtree flags are a chain of flags with the value of 0 or 1, we assign every flag value with one bit in RLC. A fixed length of bits is predetermined empirically to code the variable p, which is the length of bits coding the run lengths. As for the length of the flag chain generated by RLC, we do not need to code it at encoder actually for it can be counted based on the macroblock partition and the rectangle of ROI at decoder.

To improve the flexibility of our coding scheme, we make use of the reserved bits of the sequence parameter set to design a switch to decide whether to adopt synopsis video coding based on object flags. When such switch is on, the flags for the reconstruction of synopsis video are coded, otherwise, there is no supernumerary cost for the coding of original video.

4 Synopsis Video Reconstruction

Once the decoder receives the binary bitstream, it can easily obtain the synopsis information and object flags. In our experiment, we generate and update the backgrounds by using the Principal Background Selection (PBS) method [15]. Specifically, we use PBS algorithm to generate backgrounds from input original video at encoder, and we achieve the backgrounds from the reconstructed original video using the same principles at decoder. Afterwards, the synopsis video can be reconstructed based on the object flags, synopsis information and the decoded original video.

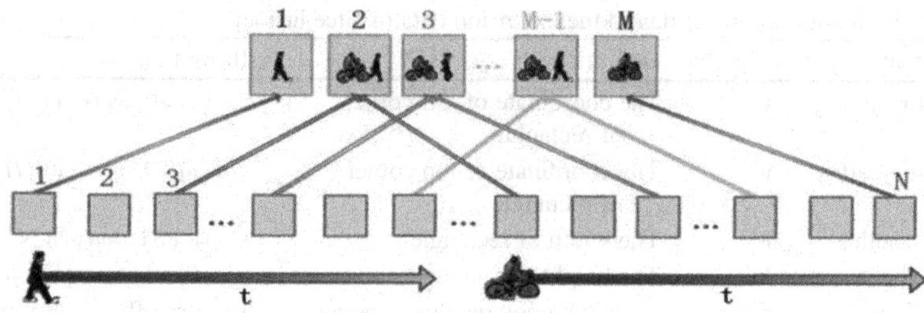

Fig. 3 The mapping diagram of the decoded videos

We take the structure shown in Fig. 3 as an example for the reconstruction process. And the assumptions in Section 3.2 are used again to state our implementation. As shown in Fig. 3, after the original video and object flags are obtained at decoder, what needs to be done is the extraction of all subblocks of the k-th object in the i-th frame of original video according to its quadtree $Qtree_i\,(k, b),\ b \in MB\,(i, k)$ where b is a subblock, and its transition to the location of its mapping frame in synopsis video. By implementing the transition function $Copy\,(Object_i(k, b), m)$, the corresponding synopsis video can be reconstructed shortly. Moreover, we can also provide a random playing of synopsis video according to the requirement of users. The process of random playing is to find out all of the ROI in the determined frame j of the synopsis video. We can know that the number of moving objects in the j-th frame of the synopsis video can be expressed by the equation:

$$P(j) = sum(f(i, k), j) \tag{4}$$

5 Experiments

We develop a synopsis browsing framework for surveillance video by integrating the video synopsis module as well as information and flags module into the JM12.4 platform [16]. We call the new codec of the framework JM12.4-S in the following part. These two sequences are MPEG-4 test sequence "Hall Monitor" [17] and the sequence "Daytime" [18] from AVS work group. Four different quantitative parameters (QP) are selected for each sequence to test the performance of our framework.

5.1 The Performance of Synopsis Video Reconstruction

Firstly, the synopsis method introduced in the Sect. 3.2 is applied to generate the synopsis video of two test sequences. Along with the video analysis and video synopsis, the region information and mapping information are achieved and saved. Meanwhile, the information of synopsis video is also obtained. Afterwards, the

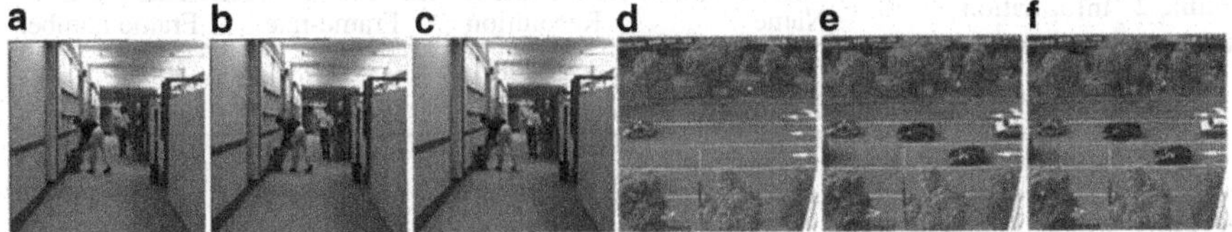

Fig. 4 Comparison on appearance. (**a**) frame 117 in "Hall_monitor" sequence; (**b**) frame 56 in its synopsis at encoder and (c) frame 56 in its reconstructed synopsis at decoder (QP=32); (**d**) frame 490 in "Daytime" sequence; (**e**) frame 75 in its synopsis at encoder and (**f**) frame 75 in its reconstructed synopsis at decoder (QP=32)

method mentioned in Sect. 3.3 is implemented to code the synopsis information and object flags into video bitstream. At decoder, the object flags, synopsis information and original video are decoded from video bitstream, so the synopsis can be reconstructed arbitrarily. The durations of two synopsis videos are both set to 125 frames. Frames selected from the original videos, synopsis videos at encoder and reconstructed synopsis videos at decoder are shown in Fig. 4.

As shown in Fig. 4, both the sequences "Hall Monitor" and "Daytime" are compressed into a shorter synopsis reserving the most informative activities. Furthermore, our framework not only generates the synopsis video of an input video at encoder, but it also provides a convenient object-based video synopsis browsing method for users at decoder only using a sequence of flags.

5.2 *The Performance of New Framework*

We make comparisons on the storage space and objective quality between videos coded by original JM12.4 platform and those coded by JM12.4-S to evaluate our system's performance. The conditions of our experiment are that: (a) IPPP coding scheme and CABAC coding mode in H.264/AVC main-profile are applied to the two test sequences, (b) one slice per frame with FMO turned-off is occupied and (c) only the first frame is coded using intra-coded way, (d) synopsis information is written into the bitstream and (e) all the region information of objects are encoded only with intra lossless coding. In such coding conditions, Original video and its corresponding synopsis video are coded with JM12.4 directly, while only the object flags and the synopsis information along with the original video are coded with JM12.4-S. The duration of videos to be coded are presented in Table 2.

From the results of the experiment in Table 3, the same change trends on size and PSNR towards different QPs could be observed. When original video is coded with JM12.4-S, object flags are not coded into the extension data of H.264/AVC [13] bitstreams, which leads to the same storage space and objective quality with those of JM12.4. When synopsis video is coded, a complete video needs to be coded with JM12.4. Compared with the average 38.68% and 22.73% increase respectively in

Table 2 Information of testing sequences

Name	Resolution	Frame-rate	Frame number
Hall monitor	352*288	25 fps	300
Daytime	320*240	25 fps	1000

Table 3 Experimental results on storing surveillance video (PSNR: db, Size: bits)

		JM12.4(-S)		JM12.4		JM12.4-S	
		Original video		Synopsis video		Synopsis video	
Seqs	QP	Size	PSNR	Size (Increase rate)	PSNR	Flag size (Increase rate)	PSNR
Hall	24	6590024	40.37	1621136 (24.60%)	40.61	51510 (0.78%)	39.88
	28	2361912	38.13	846432 (35.84%)	38.25	44664 (1.89%)	37.36
	32	1049080	35.67	468856 (44.69%)	35.61	42491 (4.05%)	35.11
	36	560096	33.00	277616 (49.57%)	33.01	41377 (7.39%)	32.43
Daytime	24	9565696	38.66	1207256 (12.62%)	39.73	64357 (0.67%)	36.92
	28	4396376	35.5	814632 (18.53%)	36.27	61725 (1.4%)	34.33
	32	2157928	32.08	515888 (23.91%)	32.81	58808 (2.73%)	31.44
	36	1133128	29.32	315992 (35.84%)	29.87	55818 (4.93%)	28.56

storage space toward two test sequences in JM12.4, only an increase of 3.53% and 2.43% is observed in JM12.4-S. Therefore, the system can realize high efficient storage of synopsis video based on object flags by adding them into bitstreams. Meanwhile, the decrease of number of smaller sub-blocks (8×8 and below) with the increase of QP leads to the decrease of the number of leaf nodes needed to label ROI. In other words, the size of object flags would decrease with the increase of QP.

6 Conclusion

In this paper, a novel framework for efficient storing and fast browsing of surveillance video is presented and discussed. We utilize video synopsis method to obtain synopsis video information and object flags for reconstruction of synopsis video. Meanwhile, we put forward a scheme for efficiently storing and synopsis browsing of surveillance video based on object flags, which can display original video and synopsis video in a flexible way. This scheme enjoys a promising surveillance-oriented application especially in the field of video browsing and retrieval. In the future work, we plan to refer to inter-frame prediction in video coding to further eliminate redundancy in the temporal domain when encoding flags, and combine the scalable video coding with online video synopsis, and develop a surveillance video scalable coding framework based on video synopsis.

References

1. M. Kunter, P. Krey, A. Krutz, and T. Sikora, "Extending H.264/AVC with a background sprite prediction mode," Proc. IEEE ICIP, pages 2128 – 2131, (2008)
2. X.G. Zhang, L.H. Liang, Q. Huang, Y.Z. Liu, T.J. Huang, and W. Gao, "An efficient coding scheme for surveillance videos captured by stationary cameras," Proc. VCIP, pages 77442A-1–10, (2010)
3. A. Hakeem, K. Shafique, and M. Shah, "An object-based video coding framework for video sequences obtained from static cameras," Proc. ACM MM, pages 608–617, (2005)
4. R. Schafer, H. Schwarz, D. Marpe, T. Schierl, and T. Wiegand, "MCTF and scalability extension of H.264/AVC and its application to video transmission, storage and surveillance," Proc. VCIP, page 596 011–1–596 011–12, (2005)
5. J. Ascenso, C. Brites and F. Pereira, "Improving Frame Interpolation with Spatial Motion Smoothing for Pixel Domain Distributed Video Coding," 5th EURASIP Conf. on Speech, Image Processing, Multimedia Communications and Services, Smolenice, Slovak Republic, (July. 2005)
6. Truong, B. T. and Venkatesh, S. Video abstraction: A systematic review and classification. ACM Trans. Multimedia Comput.Commun. Appl. 3, 1, Article 3, 37 pages, (Feb. 2007)
7. N. Petrovic, N. Jojic, and T. Huang. Adaptive video fast forward. Multimedia Tools and Applications, 26(3):327–344, (August. 2005)
8. HURST, W., GOTZ, G., AND JARVERS, P. 2004. Advanced user interfaces for dynamic video browsing. In Proceedings of the 12th Annual ACM International Conference on Multimedia, New York, 742–743, (October. 2004)
9. Dragicevic, P., Ramos, G., Bibliowitcz, J., Nowrouze-zahrai, D., Balakrishnan, R., and Singh, K. Video browsing by direct manipulation. In Proc. ACM CHI 2008, 237–246, (2008)
10. D. B. Goldman, C. Gonterman, B. Curless, D. Salesin, andvS. M. Seitz. Video object annotation, navigation, and composition. In UIST, pages 3–12, (2008)
11. A. Rav-Acha, Y. Pritch, and S. Peleg, Making a Long Video Short: Dynamic Video Synopsis. Proc. IEEE Conf. Computer Vision and Pattern Recognition, pages 435–441, (June. 2006)
12. R. Finkel and J.L. Bentley. Quad Trees: A Data Structure for Retrieval on Composite Keys. Acta Informatica 4(1), pages 1–9, (1974)
13. "Advanced Video Coding for Generic Audiovisual Services," ITU-T Recommendation H.264 (2005)
14. H. Samet. Data structures for quadtree approximation and compression. Image Processing and Computer Vision, 28(9), (1985)
15. Shikun Feng, Shengcai Liao, Zhiyong Yuan and Stan Z. Li. "Online Principal Background Selection for Video Synopsis", Proc. 20th International Conference on Pattern Recognition (ICPR), pp.17–20, (2010)
16. http://iphome.hhi.de/uehring/tml/download/old_jm/jm12.4.zip
17. http://trace.eas.asu.edu/yuv/hall_monitor/hall_cif.7z
18. ftp://159.226.42.57/AVS_FTP/incoming/dropbox/Video_Test_Sequences/surveillance/yuv420_ w320_h240_1.rar

Pole Tip Corrosion Detection Using Various Image Processing Techniques

Suchart Yammen, Somjate Bunchuen, Ussadang Boonsri, and Paisarn Muneesawang

Abstract In this paper, three features are proposed for detecting the pole tip corrosion in the hard disk drives by using various techniques of image processing. The proposed method is divided into three parts. The first part involves with preparing the template image of the pole tip. The second part involves with selecting a region of interest. The third part involves with constructing the three features. The first feature is the area around the top shield of the pole tip. The second and third features are the row coordinate and the length along the lower edge around the top shield, respectively. Finally, the last part involves with measuring the detection efficiency. From experimental results with the 647 tested pole tip images, this shows that the method using the combination of the first feature and the second feature gives the better detection efficiency than that using the combination of the others in term of specification, precision and accuracy, respectively.

Keywords Corrosion detection • Feature extraction • Pole tip • Image processing

1 Introduction

In Thailand, the hard drive industry makes a profit be one of the top ten of the revenue every year. In fact, Thailand has been manufacturing base for the largest hard drive in the world since 1987. In the hard disk drive process, manufacturers have to check the quality of the hard drives in every step before the products are sent out to distributors. The checking process of the quality of the hard disk drives is a very important step. If the produced hard drives do not meet the specification requirements, this will lead to reduce customer confidence. Thus, if there are any

S. Yammen (✉) • S. Bunchuen • U. Boonsri • P. Muneesawang
Department of Electrical and Computer Engineering, Faculty of Engineering,
Naresuan University, Phitsanulok, Thailand
e-mail: sucharty@nu.ac.th; somjate_b@mail.nu.ac.th

J.S. Jin et al., *The Era of Interactive Media*,
DOI 10.1007/978-1-4614-3501-3_35,

problems in the process, manufacturers will provide priority to resolve suddenly such problems. One in the checking system of the hard drive quality is to detect corrosion of the Pole Tip, which is an alloy used as material for making reading and writing heads. This corrosion is caused by chemicals and the environment in the hard drive manufacturing process. The corrosion is now detected by human eyes via a computer monitor in the format of two-dimensional Pole Tip images. Human error often tends to occur in this step due to his fatigued eyes while the inspector is continuously working long hours. This error results in the quality of the hard drive products such as reduced lifespan, and makes customers lack of product confidence. To solve or reduce this human error, many researchers currently focus on automatic system development for corrosion detection.

Recently, researchers have developed an automatic system for detection in various fields. For examples, Cui et al. [4] proposes an image segmentation technique including with auto-correlation and fisher classification techniques to detect defects on the fabric. Kumar [7] proposes three methods to detect defects on the pattern of the fabric. The first method involves with collecting statistics of the fabric on pattern using the morphological technique. The second method involves with investigating spectrum using various transforms. The last method involves with modeling. Lin et al. [9] proposes statistical techniques obtained from the histogram with an adaptive threshold value to check defects on the railway.

In this paper, an automatic system for corrosion detection based on the three proposed features is developed by using various techniques in image processing. The used techniques are the correlation method [8], the Otsu method [10, 1], the connected component labeling method [2], the canny operator [3, 6], and the chain code method [11, 12].

This paper is organized as follows. The proposed method for corrosion detection is given in Sect. 2. Section 3 gives experimental results, and provides thoroughly discussions. Finally, conclusion is presented in Sect. 4.

2 Proposed Method for Corrosion Detection

In this work, techniques of image processing are applied for constructing three features. The combination of the three features is used for corrosion detection of the Pole Tip in the hard drive. The overall proposed algorithm can be concluded as the block diagram shown in Fig. 1.

In Fig. 1, the procedure of the proposed method for corrosion detection of the Pole Tip is divided into three main parts.

The first part involves with creating the template of the Pole Tip image, which is produced by the expertise. To begin creating the template, the hard drive experts select the best 2,048 × 2,048 image from the 647 Pole Tip images, which consist of 358 images of the Pole Tip corrosion as shown in Fig. 2a and 289 images of the Pole Tip non-corrosion as shown in Fig. 2b.

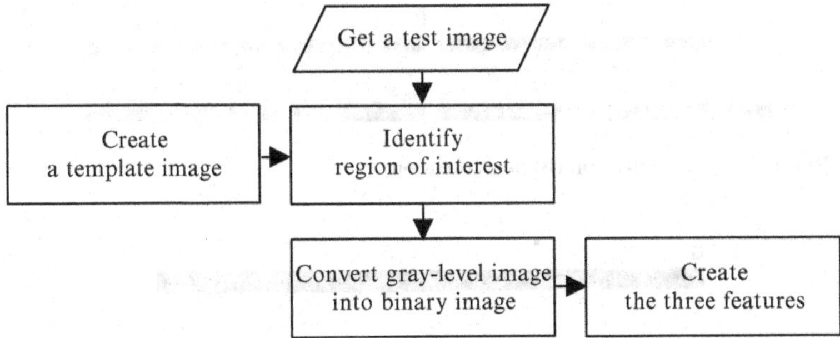

Fig. 1 Block diagram for the proposed method

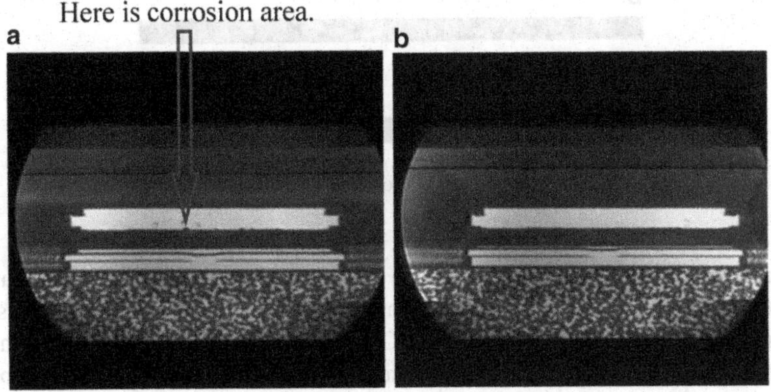

Fig. 2 Two Pole Tip images: (**a**) corrosion (**b**) non-corrosion

Fig. 3 200 × 1,200 template image of the top shield

Since corrosion occurs only at the top shield, experts have selected the top shield region of the Pole Tip. Thus, the best Pole Tip image is selected to crop into a 200 × 1200 image as a gray-scale template image shown in Fig. 3.

The second part involves with selecting a region of interest (ROI); that is, a Top Shield image from the testing Pole Tip image by using the correlation method between the 200 × 1200 template and the 2,048 × 2,048 testing Pole Tip image. In this step, a two-dimensional cross-correlation method is generally applied to identify the area of top shield in the testing Pole Tip image. For example, the 200 × 1,200 Top Shield of the Pole Tip corrosion image is the ROI image as shown in Fig. 4a and the 200 × 1,200 Top Shield of the Pole Tip non-corrosion image is the ROI image as shown in Fig. 4b.

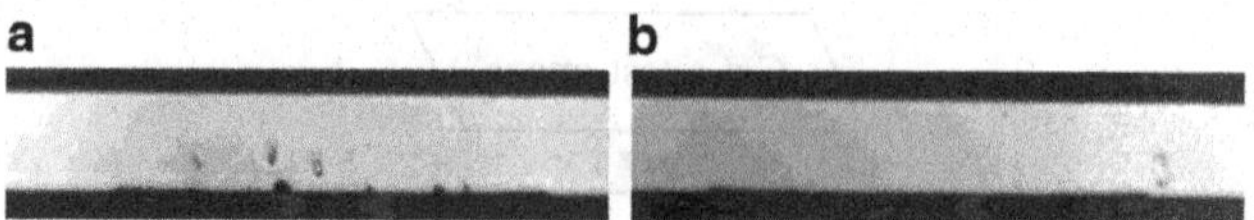

Fig. 4 ROI images: (**a**) corrosion (**b**) non-corrosion

Fig. 5 Binary images: (**a**) corrosion (**b**) non-corrosion

Furthermore, the ROI gray-scale image is converted into a binary image by using the Otsu method to set automatically optimum threshold value. Figure 5a shows the resulting binary image obtained from the ROI corrosion image in Figs. 4a and 5b shows the resulting binary image obtained from the ROI non-corrosion image in Fig. 4b.

The third part involves with extracting three features. The output binary image obtained from the second part is filled up missing pixels by using the connected component labeling method to create the first feature, which is the corrosion area around the Top Shield image.

In this research work, the connected component labeling method is used to detect the corrosion area around the Top Shield binary image. The proposed labeling method has two following steps.

The first step passes over each pixel of the binary image to check whether the value of pixels that are North-East, North, North-West and West of the current pixel has the same value of the current pixel; that is, one. If all pixels are in the same area, we record and assign the same temporary label to the current pixel and 8-connectivity pixels that have only one. This algorithm continues this way, and we create new area temporary labels whenever the current pixel has a different value to eight-connectivity pixels.

The second step replaces each temporary label by the label of its equivalence class. Therefore, the first feature is developed as an either corrosion or non-corrosion area of the top shield. If the area is greater than zero, the Pole Tip will have corrosion.

For example, Fig. 6a shows the resulting corrosion area of the top shield (white region) obtained from labeling the corrosion binary image in Figs. 5a and 6b shows

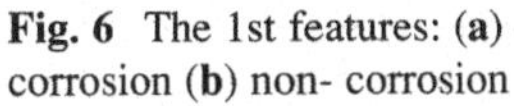

Fig. 6 The 1st features: (**a**) corrosion (**b**) non- corrosion

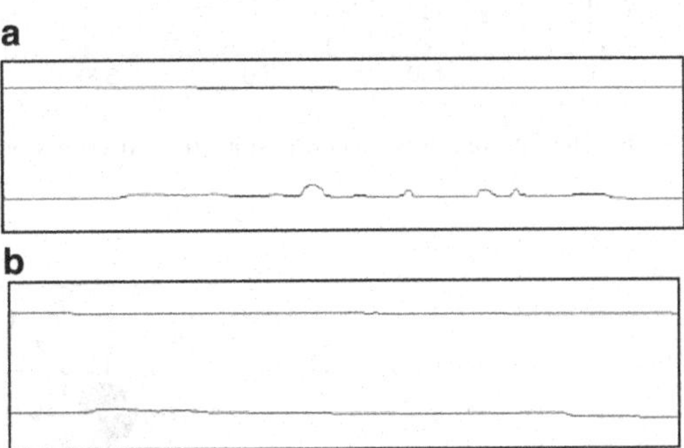

Fig. 7 Edges: (**a**) corrosion (**b**) non-corrosion

the resulting non-corrosion area image obtained from labeling the non-corrosion binary image in Fig. 5b.

Next, the edge of the ROI image is done by using the canny operator is to make the second feature, which is the coordinate along the lower edge around the Top Shield image. To create the second feature, the top shield binary image in Fig. 5 is first converted into the edge by using the canny operator.

Figure 7a, b show the resulting corrosion and non-corrosion edges, respectively. Then, the row coordinates along the lower edge around top shield of the Pole Tip image are recorded into a data sequence $\{x[n]\}$ for $n = 0, 1, 2, \ldots, 1199$.

Thus, the second feature is a difference sequence by two, which is given as $\{d[n]\}$ for $n = 0, 2, \ldots, 598$. If the value of the $d[n]$ element for some n integer is greater than one, it will have corrosion along the lower edge around top shield of the Pole Tip as shown in Fig. 8a while if not, the pole tip will have non-corrosion as shown in Fig. 8b.

Then, converting the ROI edge into the chain code by using the eight-connected chain code as shown in Fig. 9 is to construct the third feature, which is the length along the lower edge around the Top Shield image.

To determine the length along the lower edge around the top shield, let us pass over each pixel of the lower edge in Fig. 7. Each pixel on the edge called the current pixel has the value of one. All eight-connected pixels around the current pixel are checked whether the value is one. The labels in Fig. 9 are assigned where the value

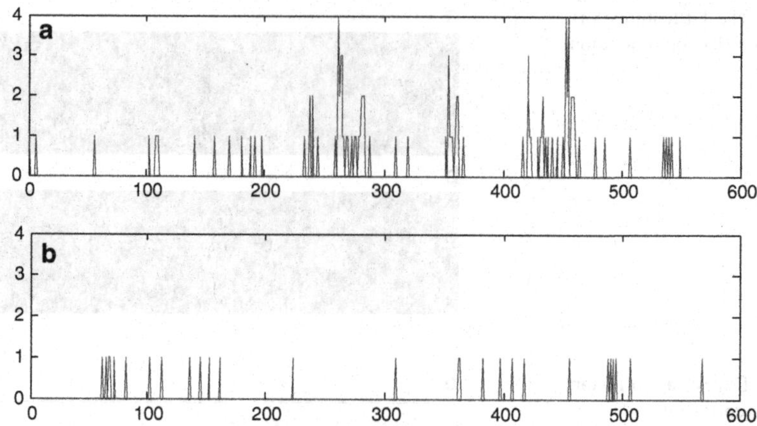

Fig. 8 The 2nd features: (**a**) corrosion (**b**) non-corrosion

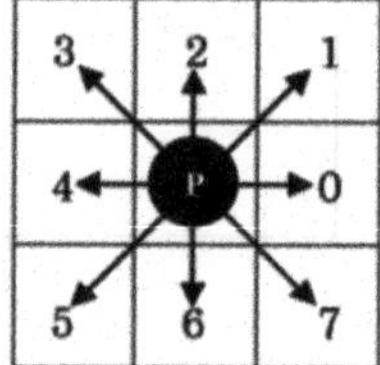

Fig. 9 Eight-connected chain code

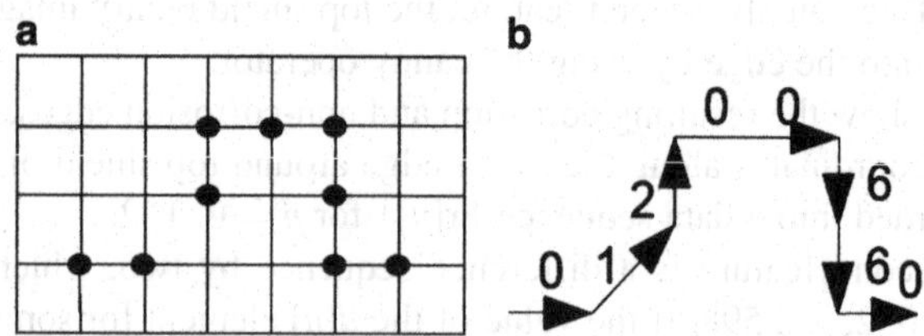

Fig. 10 The 3rd feature: (**a**) edge (**b**) chain code of the edge

is one. After that the (0, 2, 4, 6) labels are replaced with number 1 and the (1, 3, 5, 7) labels are replaced with number$\sqrt{2}$. Finally, the length of the lower edge is the sum of all numbers obtained from the chin code. For example, the edge in Fig. 10a is converted into the label; that is, "01200660" as shown in Fig. 10b, and each label is replaced with numbers; that is, "$1\sqrt{2}111111$". The length is given as $1 + \sqrt{2} + 1 + 1 + 1 + 1 + 1 + 1$ or it is equal to 8.414.

3 Results and Discussions

In this section involving the evaluation of the detection efficiency, how well the proposed method does. The three features are applied to detect the corrosion, and are compared in term of four measures [6] of the detection efficiency: sensitivity, specification, precision and accuracy.

The first measure of the detection efficiency is given by the ratio between the number of non-corrosion pole tip images, which have been validated and the total number of non-corrosion pole tip images; that is,

$$\text{Sensitivity} = \text{TT}/(\text{TT} + \text{TF}) \tag{1}$$

"TT" in Eq. (1) is the number of correctly detected non-corrosion pole tip images, and "TF" is the number of incorrectly detected non-corrosion pole tip images.

The second measure of the detection efficiency is given by the ratio between the number of corrosion pole tip images, which have been validated and the total number of corrosion pole tip images; that is,

$$\text{Specification} = \text{FF}/(\text{FF} + \text{FT}) \tag{2}$$

where "FF" is the number of correctly detected corrosion pole tip images, and "FT" is the number of incorrectly detected corrosion pole tip images.

The third measure of the detection efficiency is given by the ratio between the number of non-corrosion pole tip images, which have been validated and the total number of detected non-corrosion pole tip images; that is,

$$\text{Precision} = \text{TT}/(\text{TT} + \text{FT}) \tag{3}$$

The last measure is given by the ratio between the total number of correctly detected pole tip images and the total number of pole tip images; that is,

$$\text{Accuracy} = (\text{TT} + \text{FF})/(\text{TT} + \text{FF} + \text{TF} + \text{FT}) \tag{4}$$

In the experimental results, the 647 tested pole tip images consist of 289 non-corrosion images and 358 corrosion images, which are acquired on the DUV Optical Microscope. After the proposed method described in Sect. 2 is applied for corrosion detection to 647 tested pole tip images, non-corrosion or corrosion classification results obtained from each of the three features and the combination of the two features are given in Table 1.

As seen in Table 1, the proposed method using the 1st feature and the 3rd feature provides evidence that is an extremely poor detection result in case of corrosion and non-corrosion, respectively. However, the 2nd feature provides the best detection result in case of non-corrosion, and the combination of the 1st feature and the 2nd feature also provides the best detection result in case of corrosion.

Table 1 The classification results

		The number of detected images			
		Non-corrosion		Corrosion	
Methods	Used features	True	False	True	False
1	1st	283	6	169	189
2	2nd	285	4	320	38
3	3rd	279	10	317	41
4	1st and 2nd	281	8	345	13
5	1st and 3rd	281	8	338	20
6	2nd and 3rd	283	6	323	35

Table 2 Performance evaluation of the proposed method

Methods	Used Features	Sensitivity	Specification	Precision	Accuracy
1	1st	0.9792	0.4720	0.5995	0.6986
2	2nd	0.9861	0.8938	0.8823	0.9350
3	3rd	0.9654	0.8854	0.8718	0.9211
4	1st, 2nd	0.9723	0.9636	0.9557	0.9675
5	1st, 3rd	0.9723	0.9441	0.9335	0.9567
6	2nd, 3rd	0.9792	0.9050	0.8927	0.9381

To illustrate four efficiency measures of the proposed method, the data set in Table 1 substituted into Eqs. (1)–(4) yields the four measures in Table 2.

From Table 2, the combination of the two features used for non-corrosion and corrosion detection yield the best values of specification, precision and accuracy while the 2nd feature gives the best value of sensitivity. The method using the 1st feature and the 2nd feature provides highest accuracy, which is equal to 0.9675. This method yields better results than the others. Although some of the 647 tested pole tip images are incorrectly detected by using the proposed method, the experts can be accepted for this small error.

4 Conclusions

In this paper, researchers have proposed the image processing techniques to detect corrosion of the pole tip in the format of the three features: the area of the top shield, the coordinate along the lower edge around the top shield, and the length along the lower edge around the top shield. From the experimental results, it has been found that the best detection result can be met in term of specification, precision and accuracy if the combination of the two features is used at the same time as a 2×1 feature vector formulated as a set of the two features for identifying non-corrosion or corrosion detection. The 2nd feature also provides the best either non-corrosion or corrosion detection in term of sensitivity. The study shows that the 647 tested pole tip images detected by using only two of the three proposed features can be measured and identified effectively either non-corrosion or corrosion cases in term of specification, precision and accuracy.

Acknowledgments This project is financially supported by the Industry/University Cooperative Research Center (I/UCRC) in HDD Component, the Faculty of Engineering, Khon Kaen University and National Electronics and Computer Technology Center, National Science and Technology Development Agency, Thailand. In addition, the researchers would like to thank the Western Digital (Thailand) company for providing the research data supports.

References

1. Alasdair Mcanddrew. (2004). Introduction to digital image processing with matlab. USA: Thomson.
2. Baraghimian, G. A. (1989, 20–22 Sep 1989). Connected component labeling using self-organizing feature maps. Paper presented at the Computer Software and Applications Conference, 1989. COMPSAC 89., Proceedings of the 13th Annual International.
3. Bing, W., & ShaoSheng, F. (2009, 28–30 Oct. 2009). An Improved CANNY Edge Detection Algorithm. Paper presented at the Computer Science and Engineering, 2009. WCSE '09. Second International Workshop on.
4. Cui, B., Liu, H., & Xue, T. (2008). Application of a New Image Recognition Technology in Fabric Defect Detection. Paper presented at the Proceedings of the 2008 International Seminar on Future BioMedical Information Engineering.
5. Gonzalez, R. C., & Woods, R. E. (2002). Digital image processing. Upper Saddle River, N.J.: Prentice Hall.
6. Han, J., & Kamber, M. (2006). Data mining: concepts and techniques. Amsterdam; Boston; San Francisco, CA: Elsevier; Morgan Kaufmann.
7. Kumar, A. (2008). Computer-Vision-Based Fabric Defect Detection: A Survey. Industrial Electronics, IEEE Transactions on, 55(1), 348–363.
8. Liang, P., Zhiwei, X., & Jiguang, D. (22–24 Oct. 2010). Fast normalized cross-correlation image matching based on multiscale edge information. Paper presented at the Computer Application and System Modeling (ICCASM), 2010 International Conference on.
9. Lin, J., Luo, S., Li, Q., Zhang, H., & Ren, S. (2009, 5–8 July 2009). Real-time rail head surface defect detection: A geometrical approach. Paper presented at the Industrial Electronics, 2009. ISIE 2009. IEEE International Symposium on.
10. Otsu, N., (1979). A Threshold Selection Method from Gray-Level Histograms. Systems, Man and Cybernetics, IEEE Transactions on, 9(1), 62–66.
11. Shafeek, H. I., Gadelmawla, E. S., Abdel-Shafy, A. A., & Elewa, I. M. (2004). Assessment of welding defects for gas pipeline radiographs using computer vision. NDT & E International, 37(4), 291–299.
12. Sonka, M., Hlavac, V., & Boyle, R. (2008). Image processing, analysis, and machine vision. Toronto: Thompson Learning

Real-Time Cascade Template Matching for Object Instance Detection

Chengli Xie, Jianguo Li, Tao Wang, Jinqiao Wang, and Hanqing Lu

Abstract Object instance detection finds where a specific object instance is in an image or a video frame. It is a variation of object detection, but distinguished on two points. First, object detection focused on a category of object, while object instance detection focused on a specific object. For instance, object detection may work to find where toothpaste is in an image, while object instance detection will work on finding and locating a specific brand of toothpaste, such as Colgate toothpaste. Second, object instance detection tasks usually have much fewer (positive) samples in training compared to that of object detection. Therefore, traditional object instance detection methods are mostly based on template matching.

This paper presents a cascade template matching framework for object instance detection. Specially, we propose a three-stage heterogeneous cascade template matching method. The first stage employs dominate orientation template (DOT) for scale and rotation invariant filtering. The second stage is based on local ternary patterns (LTP) to further filter with texture information. The third stage trained a classifier on appearance feature (PCA) to further reduce false-alarms. The cascade template matching (CTM) can provide very low false-alarm-rate comparing to traditional template matching based methods and SIFT matching based methods. We demonstrate the effectiveness of the proposed method on several instance detection tasks on YouTube videos.

Keywords Cascade • Template matching • Object instance • Detection

C. Xie (✉) • J. Wang • H. Lu
National Laboratory of Pattern Recognition, Institute of Automation,
Chinese Academy of Sciences, 100190 Beijing, China
e-mail: clxie@nlpr.ia.ac.cn; jqwang@nlpr.ia.ac.cn; luhq@nlpr.ia.ac.cn

J. Li • T. Wang
Intel Labs, China
e-mail: jianguo.li@intel.com; tao.wang@intel.com

J.S. Jin et al., *The Era of Interactive Media*,
DOI 10.1007/978-1-4614-3501-3_36,

1 Introduction

Object detection is a hot-topic in the field of computer vision. There are a lot of researches, such as [1–5]. However, with the advance in camera phone and mobile computing, people want to not only detect objects in images anywhere they took, but also go beyond to the identity of the object. That is to say, they want to know what it is specifically of the detected objects. For instance, when we walk on street and find one beautiful handbag, but we do not know what brand and type is it and where to buy it. This case does not belong to object detection. Thus, a new research topic arises, namely object instance detection, which becomes more and more important in nowadays mobile computing scenario. There are some typical applications in smart phones, such as Google's goggle.

Concretely, object instance detection aims at finding and locating specific instances of objects, such as Colgate toothpaste boxes, Coca-cola cans, or Canon DLSR camera, in an image and video frames. It is quite different to existing techniques such as object detection, object category recognition, image retrieval.

Given an example of handbag recognition, these four techniques have different goals. Object detection tries to find and locate general handbags in images. Object instance detection attempts to find and locate a specific handbag (for instance a specific type of Louis Vuitton handbag) in images. Object category recognition just wants to know whether the image contains a handbag or not. And in image retrieval, people just find images in a large database which has similar global appearance to the given query handbag image.

In this paper, we propose a three-stage cascade template matching framework to object instance detection as shown in Fig. 1. Specially, the first stage employs DOT [1] for fast, scale and rotation invariant non-target filtering. The second stage is based

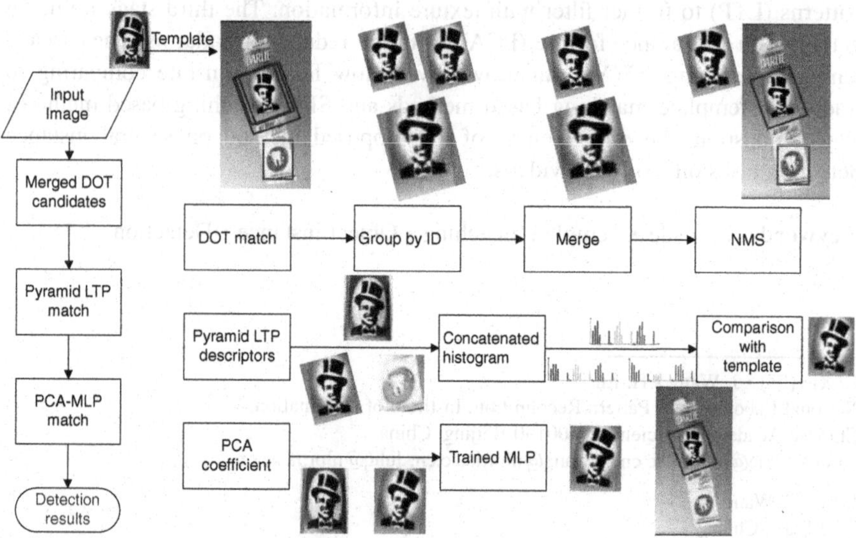

Fig. 1 Framework overview

on local ternary patterns (LTP) to further filter non-target with texture information. The third stage trained a neural-network (MLP) classifier on appearance feature (PCA) to further reduce false-alarms. The three-stage cascade is heterogeneous.

The contributions of this work could be summarized as follows:

(1) We present a cascade template matching framework for object instance detection.
(2) Through effective combination the DOT, LTP and PCA-MLP matches, the cascade-template-matching not only provides high hit-rate and low false alarms, but also yields real-time processing speed.
(3) The approach is scale and rotation invariant to the object instance.

In the reminder of this paper, we first discuss some related works on instances detection. And then our approach is represented in details. Following that, comparisons between ours and the state-of-art ones are shown with some discussion and analysis. And finally, the whole work is concluded.

2 Related Works

There exist two typical types of works in object instance detection: first is template matching based methods; second is the learning based methods.

In template matching, SIFT [6] features were widely used. SIFT describes scale and rotation invariant local features in image, and has been applied to object instance recognition. However, SIFT cannot locate more than two instances in one query image. Besides, SIFT is a bit slowly in computing. SURF [7] is proposed to replace SIFT features with fast processing speed.

Triplet of feature descriptors [8] is proposed for detection and recognition. These triplets are labeled via modified K-means clustering algorithm, which is followed by inverse lookup matching and triplet votes.

DOT (dominant orientation templates) [1] is proposed for texture less instances detection or tracking, which assumes a simple and slow motion environment. While in object instance detection, scale and lighting may change greatly, scenes in adjacent frames may transit quickly or suddenly. And occlusion is not the major limitation. In the case of general videos, to take advertisement clip as an example, the scene and content change largely and sometimes quickly. Thus, one can't assume continuity of object or near constant of background.

Mustafa Ozuysal [9] proposed FERNS, which belong to the learning based method. It formulates feature point recognition in object instance detection in a Naïve Bayesian classification framework through non-hierarchical point-pair feature groups (these groups are called ferns). This yields simple, scalability and efficient results in terms of number of classes. From the point of feature selection, ferns can be regards as some kind of variety of random forest.

In some old works, object instance detection can be divided into two steps. First is detecting object class in test images or frames. Second is recognizing instances of object for the detection results.

Nevertheless, the proposed solution attempts to deal with the problem in a whole, with the cascade template matching framework.

3 Cascade Template Matching

This section we will describe the cascade template matching framework (CTM) in details. And explain how they are built and trained at real-time speed.

The CTM approach consists of the DOT stage, the pyramid LTP stage and the PCA-MLP stage. It takes gradient information, texture information and appearance features into consideration, separately.

3.1 Framework Overview

For the purpose of robust and rapidly discovering specified instances of object class, coarse to fine framework is adopted (Fig. 1). First stage makes use of multi-angle multi-scale gradient template to extract candidates based on a variation of DOT [1]. Then a local texture descriptor, histogram of pyramid LTP, is calculated to further filter false positive samples from first stage. Finally, machine learning method (currently used multi-layer perception neuron network) is employed to pick positive from negatives in the results of stage 2. Therefore, accurate detection results (category instances) are found effectively.

Given an input image or a video frame, CTM proceeds in three steps:

(1) A merged version of the DOT detector [1] was applied: For all candidate windows C_i (not using tracking information), we use three-step merge algorithms to preliminary reduce some overlap ones.
(2) Pyramid LTP template matching is utilized to quickly filter false alarms.
(3) PCA-MLP layer as the last stage tells the most difficult negative samples from positives, with the combination of MLP classifiers and PCA features.

Note that the proposed method is not restricted to specific descriptors or classifiers in each layer. Taking the third stage as an example, MLP can be replaced with SVM or other classifiers.

3.2 Merged DOT Based Template Matching

In the original, only maximum response for each template is accepted, or ESM tracking lib to filter, which is rather slow. In this paper, we apply a three-step merge algorithm to DOT candidates.

(1) Grouping candidates from the same template by overlap ratio and filter out noise (groups with candidates less than a group threshold T_g). Here, N_c stands for

number of candidates. C_{ic} means the ic^{th} candidate. And function Group(C_{ic}, C_{jc}) puts the ic^{th} and jc^{th} candidates into one merge pool. Similarly, N_g stands for number of groups. While function Filter_out_group(G_{ig}) deletes the ig^{th} group.

Step 1: group

```
For ic = 0:Nc-1
      For jc = i+1:Nc
      If not_in_one_group(Cic,Cjc)
        If is_overlap_enough(Cic,Cjc)
        Group(Cic, Cjc);
    For ig = 0:Ng-1
    If num_of_group(Gig) < Tg
      Filter_out_group(Gig);
    Update(Ng);
```

(2) Merging rectangles in each group G_i by average with Laplace estimation, if the number is more than the merge threshold T_m. In this section, function num_of (G_{ig}) computes the number of candidates in ig^{th} group. And MC_{ig} stands for the ig^{th} merged candidate.

Step 2: merge

```
For ig = 0:Ng-1
      num_ig = num_of(Gig);
      Gig.confidence /= num_ig;
      If num_ig > Tm
    MCig.coor=(sum(Gig.cand.coor)*2+num_ig)/
(2*num_ig);
```

(3) Suppressing non-maximum rectangles of different templates at same location of current video frame. Function is_overlap_enough(MC_{im}, MC_{in}) computes the overlap area of the im^{th} and the in^{th} merged candidates. While function Amensalism(a,b) means we mark a and b as exclusion, and discard one by some criterion.

Step 3: non-max suppress

```
Nc = num_of(MC);
    For im = 0:Nc;
      For in = 0:Nc
      If is_overlap (MCim, MCin) > Thresholdoverlap
        Amensalism(MCim, MCin);pt?>
```

Note that, the original DOT suppresses the non-maximum responses of the same template in order to reduce false alarm. (Or it use ESM lib to track these candidates,

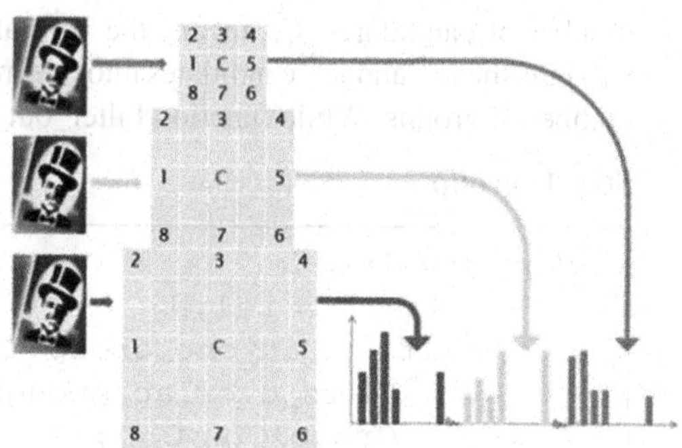

Fig. 2 Pyramid LTP descriptor

which slows down the process). While in the three-step merging algorithm, non-maximum responses belonging to different templates at same location are suppressed, so that missing rate can be cut down at this stage and false positive rate can be maintained at a low level by following stages.

3.3 *Pyramid LTP Histogram Match*

LBP [10] is a general used texture descriptor, while sensitive to light changes. LTP [11] is a generalization of LBP, which split local ternary pattern into positive and negative LBP parts. LTP is much robust to illumination by adding a threshold to comparison center pixel with its neighbors.

To reflect differences in different resolution, we propose pyramid LTP. Given a normalized candidate, we calculate LTP at three different resolutions, and then concatenate them into a histogram (Fig. 2) after a normalization operation to each histogram separately.

After histogram calculation and normalization, the distance D(H1, H2) between histograms of candidate and template is compared with corresponding threshold T_h. Candidates passed the T_h pass the second stage.

Though there are several methods to calculate distance between two histograms, such as correlation, chi-square (CHISQR) and histogram intersection. It seems that CHISQR performs similar with histogram intersection, while better than correlation. Please refer to Sect. 4.2 for details. D(H1, H2) with CHISQR is adopted in this work.

3.4 *PCA-MLP Match*

After processed by the first two stages, the left false positives are hard to distinguish from true positives. Therefore, non-linear classifier and appearance features are adopted to further remove false from truth.

Fig. 3 Scale and orientation normalization of merged-candidates with respect to template

In this paper, we adopted PCA features to reduce the dimension of appearance feature, and adopted multiple layer perception (MLP) as the non-linear classifier.

Before extracting the PCA (principal component analysis) feature, candidates reach this stage are first scale-rotation normalized with respect to template, according to match index within previous stage. As computing appearance descriptor is a bit time cost, it is hoped that the number of input is as small as possible (Fig. 3).

4 Experiment Validation

4.1 Experiment Dataset

We crawled the YouTube web site and gather two types of videos, containing toothpaste category with several different instances, and Canon DLSR camera EOS D7. Please refer to below table for details. Each video clip contains around 750 frames (about 30 s at 25 fps). The training and testing number of video clips varies as some of the classes have more frames and some are less. We just split them equally into training and testing sets.

There are two Darlie instances, since we would like to see whether the cascade template matching framework can discriminate different instances in the same object class (Table 1). (In this experiment, we would see the differentiation of instance Darlie-2 and other toothpaste instances, including Darlie-1).

Figure 4 below are overall detection results. Thin red and green windows are first and second stages outputs. And bold blue boxes denote the final results. It is clear that, the cascade template matching framework can filter false alarms while maintaining true positives.

Table 1 Training and test data amount (in number of video clips)

Category	Toothpaste					Canon EOS camera
Subclass	Colgate	Darlie-1	Darlie-2	Aquafresh	Crest	
Train	10	8	9	8	10	6
Test	10	7	8	8	10	5
Template image	Colgate			Aquafresh	Crest	

Fig. 4 Some detection results, where *thin red window* indicates first stage candidate, *green window* stands for the pyramid stage output, and *bold blue* denotes the final result. Each line is for an object instance. Specifically, they are, from *top* to *bottom*, Colgate toothpaste, Darlie-1 toothpaste, Darlie-2 toothpaste, Aquafresh toothpaste, Crest toothpaste and Cannon EOS camera

Our approach can also deal with slight occlusion; see the middle two of Crest at row 5. And due to pyramid LTP, influences by illuminate changes are minimized (last example of Crest at row 5).

In Figure 4, Darlie-2 at row 3 could find other instances of Darlie class at the cost of accuracy down by decreasing the threshold (last two at row 3), or just can't find other kinds of instances (e.g. Darlie-1 at the third column of this row). In other

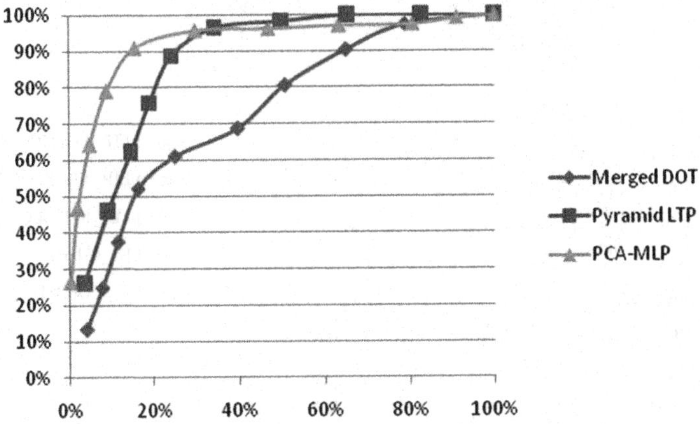

Fig. 5 Single stage performances comparison

words, our approach has the ability to distinguish between different instances of same object category.

For Canon camera, it shows that cascade template matching is suitable to not only flat object, but also to 3D instances.

Besides, our approach takes 29 ms on the average for each frame on Core2Duo 2.8G, 4G RAM, which satisfy the real-time application.

4.2 Performance at Each Single Stage

Figure 5 shows performances of each single stage: merged DOT stage, the pyramid LTP stage, and the PCA-MLP stage. Merged DOT can be considered as original DOT though the performance improves. From the ROC curves, we can see that every stage is useful since different information is used: gradient information, texture information and color appearance information.

Theoretically, the product of these three stages reflects the capability of the whole cascade. The experimental results of the whole CTM cascade will be shown at Sect. 4.3.

4.3 Different LTP Schemes

In this experiment, we compare performance of pyramid LTP (pLTP) and LTP with different histogram compute methods mentioned in Sect. 3.3. Figure 6 shows the results of comparison.

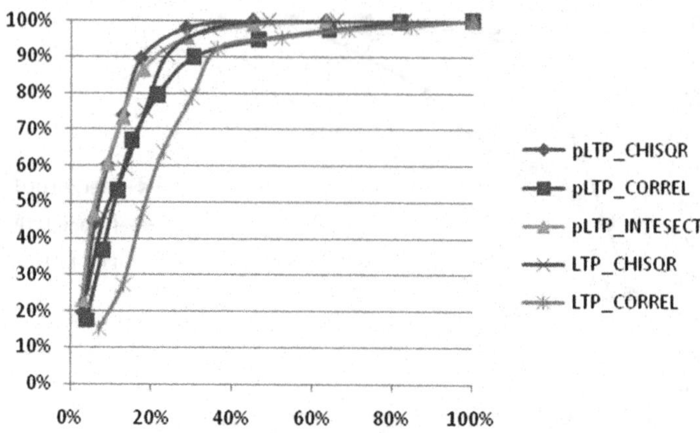

Fig. 6 Pyramid LTP versus LTP with different histogram comparison schemes

Table 2 Cascade templates matching versus SIFT & DOT

Methods	True responses	False alarms
SIFT	2,627	631
CTM	2,698	66
DOT	2,013	2,105

It is obvious that for both pyramid LTP and LTP, CHISQR works better than correlation. And pyramid LTP (pLTP) with CHISQR outperforms other schemes.

4.4 Cascade Template Matching Versus SIFT and DOT

In this part, we compared CTM with original DOT and SIFT. Table 2 shows the total true responses and false alarms on the whole test set (48 video clips).

As the first stage in CTM, our merged DOT is with a lower threshold than original to avoid filtering true responses. Another benefit is that, lower threshold results in more candidates, while more candidates means both more positive and negative training examples for following LTP and PCA-MLP stages.

As the videos are crawled from YouTube, there is no label information of object instance at all. Therefore, we just record the total true responses and false alarms of each method for comparison. True response means the output window just covers most of the right object instance. Others are considered as false alarms. Responses to partial instances (occluded more than 25% by others, or truncated more than 25% by image boundary, etc.) are not counted.

It is obviously, our approach can reduce false positives significantly; meanwhile keep a relative high detection rate.

Moreover, CTM and DOT have the ability to detect two or more instances in one image (e.g. the last but one at row 5 in Fig. 4).

On another side, SIFT takes more than 1 s for a frame on average, much slower than ours' 29 ms.

5 Conclusions

In this paper, we raise the problem of object instance detection, and propose a cascade template matching framework (CTM) for object instance detection. The framework consists of three heterogeneous stages: merged DOT, pyramid LTP and PCA-MLP, which utilize gradient information, pyramid texture histogram and color appearance information separately. Experiments show that CTM yields fast and accurate instance detection on some sets of YouTube videos.

Acknowledgement This work was partly supported by the National Natural Science Foundation of China (Grant No. 60833006 and 60905008), and 973 Program (Project No. 2010CB327905).

References

1. Stefan Hinterstoisser, Vincent Lepetit, Slobodan Ilic, Pascal Fua and Nassir Navab: Dominant Orientation Templates for Real-Time Detection of Texture-Less Objects. CVPR, 2010.
2. Juergen Gall and Victor Lempitsky: Class-specific Hough Forests for Object Detection. CVPR 2009.
3. Christoph H. Lampert, Matthew B. Blaschko and Thomas Hofmann: Beyond Sliding Windows: Object Localization by Efficient Subwindow Search. CVPR 2008.
4. Subhransu Maji, Alexander C. Berg: Max-Margin Additive Classifiers for Detection. ICCV 2009.
5. P. Felzenszwalb, R. Girshick, D. McAllester and D. Ramanan: Object Detection with Discriminatively Trained Part Based Models. PAMI Vol.32, No.9, September 2010.
6. Lowe, D.G.: Distinctive Image Features from Scale-Invariant Keypoints. Int'l J. of Computer Vision 60 (2004) 91–110.
7. Herbert Bay, Tinne Tuytelaars and Luc Van Gool: Surf: Speeded up Robust Features. In Proceedings of the ninth European Conference on Computer Vision, 2006.
8. C. Lawrence Zitnick, Jie Sun, Richard Szeliski and Simon Winder: Object Instance Recognition using Triplets of Feature Symbols. Microsoft Research, Technical Report, 2007–53.
9. Mustafa Ozuysal, Pascal Fua and Vincent Lepetit: Fast Keypoint Recognition in Ten Lines of Code. CVPR 2007.
10. Heikkila M., Pietikainen M and Schmid C: Description of Interest Regions with Local Binary Patterns. Pattern Recognition, 42(3): 425–436, 2009.
11. Xiaoyang Tan and Bill Triggs: Enhanced Local Texture Feature Sets for Face Recognition under Difficult Lighting Conditions. IEEE Transactions on Image Processing, 2010

Action Recognition and Surveillance

An Unsupervised Real-Time Tracking and Recognition Framework in Videos

Huafeng Wang, Yunhong Wang, Jin Huang, Fan Wang, and Zhaoxiang Zhang

Abstract A novel framework for unsupervised face tracking and recognition is built on Detection-Tracking-Refinement-Recognition (DTRR) approach. This framework proposed a hybrid face detector for real-time face tracking which is robust to occlusions, facial expression and posture changes. After a posture correction and face alignment, the tracked face is featured by the Local Ternary Pattern (LTP) operator. Then these faces are clustered into several groups according to the distance between feature vectors. During the next step, those groups which each contains a series of faces can be further merged by the Scale-invariant feature transform (SIFT) operator. Due to extreme computing time consumption by SIFT, a multithreaded refinement process was given. After the refinement process, the relevant faces are put together which is of much importance for face recognition in videos. The framework is validated both on several videos collected in unconstrained condition (8 min each.) and on Honda/UCSD database. These experiments demonstrated that the framework is capable of tracking the face and automatically grouping a serial faces for a single human-being object in an unlabeled video robustly.

Keywords Real-time • Video • Unsupervised • Tracking • Refinement • Face recognition

---

H. Wang (✉)
School of Computer Science and Engineering, Beihang University, Beijing, China

School of Software Engineering, Beihang University, Beijing, China
e-mail: wanghuafeng@buaa.edu.cn

Y. Wang • Z. Zhang
School of Computer Science and Engineering, Beihang University, Beijing, China
e-mail: yhwang@buaa.edu.cn; zxzhang@buaa.edu.cn

J. Huang • F. Wang
School of Software Engineering, Beihang University, Beijing, China

J.S. Jin et al., *The Era of Interactive Media*,
DOI 10.1007/978-1-4614-3501-3_37,

1 Introduction

Many video-based surveillance applications require faces to be detected, tracked and recognized in a special scene in order to extract semantic information about scene content and human behavior. In particular, most video surveillance applications rely on the detection of human activities captured by static cameras. However, human faces tracking under unconstrained environment by using view-based representation requires establishing image contexts in successive frames of a moving face which may undergo affine, illuminant or partial occlusion transformations. For example, the task of faces' acquisition under outdoor conditions may be confronted with varying lighting conditions (e.g. sunny/cloudy illumination, foreground shadows), or temporary disappearance and so on. Hence, detecting and tracking faces under such complex environment remains a delicate task to achieve.

In this paper, we mainly focus on building a framework which is able to detect and track faces in videos. It should be emphasized that the whole face detecting and tracking procedure is much different from TLD [1] which was system tracks, learns and detects a specific face in real-time in unconstrained videos because our framework works in a completely unsupervised way. Rather than trying to get better performances than state of the art face detection algorithms presented in Sect. 2, the framework is designed to combine face detection with a tracking and recognition process as illustrated in Fig. 1.

The rest of this paper is organized as follows. Previous work is reviewed in Sect. 2. The unsupervised tracking and recognition model is presented in Sect. 3 (the algorithm for constructing efficient framework is described in subsections. We evaluate our framework on an open environment with pose, facial expression and illuminant problems. The details of the task and our experiments are described in Sect. 4. Conclusion can be seen in Sect. 5.

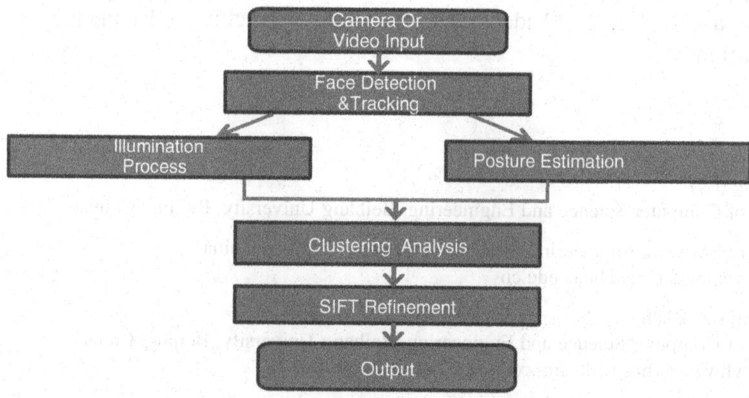

Fig. 1 An overview of the work-flow of framework

2 Related Work

Real-time and multi-view face detection is significantly important in the video-based face detection. There approximately exists two kinds of real-time face detection method: one is Cascade AdaBoost approach proposed by Viola and Jones [2], the other is method using color information to detect and validate human face [3]. By the way, Schneiderman and Kanade [4] claimed their system to be the first one in the world for multi-view face detection.

Generally speaking, there are three main categories for face detection based on video. Firstly, frame based detection. As far as this category to be concerned, there are lots of traditional methods such as statistical modeling methods, neural network-based methods, SVM-based methods, HMM methods, Boost methods and color-based face detection [5]. However, ignoring the temporal information provided by the video sequence is the main drawback of those approaches. Secondly, integrating detection and tracking, this says that detecting face in the first frame and then tracking it through the whole sequence. Since detection and tracking are independent and information from one source is just in use at one time, loss of information is unavoidable. Finally, instead of detecting each frame, temporal approach uses temporal relationships between the frames to detect multiple human faces in a video sequence. In general, the related methods consist of two phases, namely detection and prediction and then update-tracking. This helps to stabilize detection and to make it less sensitive to thresholds compared to the other two kinds of detection approaches.

Recently, there has been a significant interest in semi-supervised learning, i.e. exploiting both labeled and unlabeled data in classifier training [6]. Especially, Zdenek Kalal [1] proposed the TLD method which was designed for long-term tracking of arbitrary objects in unconstrained environments. The object was tracked and simultaneously learned in order to build a detector that supports the tracker once it fails and the detector was build upon the information from the first frame as well as the information provided by the tracker.

However, in terms of those methods mentioned above, a serious problem occurs because in-class variability of multi-view faces dataset is larger than that of front-view faces dataset. Though Detector-Pyramid Architecture AdaBoost (DPAA) [6] can handle this problem, the complexity increased leads to high computational load and over-fitting in training. Over-fitting has been addressed in [7], however, robust approaches are still being awaited. In this paper, a nearly real-time but multi-view face recognition approach in videos will be proposed.

3 Unsupervised Tracking and Recognition Model

In this section, we focus on presenting a novel unsupervised tracking and recognition model. Firstly, to address the complicated problems brought by the traditional object tracking under significant changes in both object itself and environmental conditions, the framework combines LK tracking approach [8] with face detection. Secondly, the continuous tracking results are used to incrementally adapt the specific face models to individuals. The collaborative tracking method can handle large face pose changes, and can efficiently support specific face models online. Thirdly, after applying illuminant model and pose estimation, the faces acquired will be labeled according to distance between faces and pushed into an online face database for further selection process. Finally, an effective sift [9] operator is exploited to refine the labeled result. Each step is detailed as bellow.

3.1 Detection and Tracking

Detection and tracking task in the framework were achieved by combining Viola–Jones face detection approach with an optical flow tracker which is able to calculate the motion between two image frames which are taken at times t and t + δ_t at every voxel position. For frames, a voxel at location (x,y,t) with intensity I(x,y,t) will have movement by δ_x, δ_y and δ_t between the two image frames, and the following image constraint equation can be given:

$$I(x,y,t) = I(x + \delta_{x,y} + \delta_{y,t} + \delta_t) \tag{1}$$

In order to achieve good result, we experimentally made a comparison between optical flow algorithm and other tracking approaches (for example, camshift etc.) and drew the conclusion that optical flow is much better robust one. Given a sample S, the determination formula looks like (2).

$$\begin{cases} if\ \exists\forall_i Adaboost_i(S) > 0,\ then\ S \in Pos \\ \qquad\qquad else\ S \in Neg \end{cases} \tag{2}$$

The real-time tracked faces were stored in a track-node structure. A track-node includes two parts: one is for describing tracked face; another is indexing of valid status. And all the track-nodes form a circular list. Such kind of list works in a real-time way to produce complex and diverse faces belonging to certain individuals. Hence, face detection and tracking by using both motion and optical cues was used to bring about the required consistency in face tracking.

3.2 Illumination Model

To solve illuminant problem, there are lots of researches. But the most important and effective one should be LTP [10] (local ternary pattern) which is an extend of LBP(local binary pattern). LTP exploits a 3-valued coding that includes a threshold around zero for improved resistance to noise. LTP inherits most of the other key advantages of LBP such as computational efficiency.

In [10], it incorporates a series of steps chosen to counter the effects of illumination variations, local shadowing and highlights, while still preserving the essential elements of visual appearance for use in recognition. In detail, the steps are: first, Gamma Correction. This is a nonlinear gray-level transformation; second, Difference of Gaussian (DoG) Filtering. Because Gamma correction does not remove the influence of overall intensity gradients such as shading effects. DoG filtering is a convenient way to obtain the resulting band-pass behavior; third, masking. it will avoid that either strong artificial gray-level edges are introduced into the convolution, or invisible regions are taken into account during contrast equalization; fourth, Contrast Equalization (CE). The final step of the preprocessing chain globally rescales the image intensities to standardize a robust measure of overall contrast or intensity variation. The CE calculation is as described in formula (3):

$$I(x,y) = \frac{I(x,y)}{\left(\mathrm{mean}(\min(\tau, |\mathrm{I(x,y)}|^{\mathrm{a}}))\right)^{1/a}} \tag{3}$$

where $a = 0.1$ *and* $\tau = 10$.

After above steps, LTP feature is determined as follows (formula (4)). Where v means value and t stands for threshold. While v(x,i) stands for the value of pixel point of (x,i).

$$f(i) = \begin{cases} 1, v(x) - v(i) > t \\ -1, v(x) - v(i) > t \\ 0, else \end{cases} \tag{4}$$

Though the illumination variation process seems a little bit complex, it works perfectly well in our experiment.

3.3 Pose Estimation and Face Alignment

Face posture status is sure to be a dynamic one in videos. To make face alignment, we should first solve the problem of estimating the posture. In [11], Piotr Dollar proposed a fast and accurate algorithm for computing the 2D pose of objects in images called cascaded pose regression (CPR). CPR progressively refines a loosely specified initial guess, where each refinement is carried out by a different regressor. The entire system is automatically learned from human annotated training examples.

CPR is implemented as a sequence of regressors progressively refining the estimate of the pose θ. At each step t = 1….T in the cascade, a regressor Rt computes a new pose estimate θ_t from the image and from the previous regressor's estimate θ_{t-1}. However, the key point of pose estimation is how the feature is selected (see the formula (5)).

$$h(\theta_1, G(o, \theta_2)) = h(\theta_\delta o \theta_1, G(o, \theta_\delta o \theta_2)) \tag{5}$$

Where θ is pose, h means feature, o stands for object, G is appearance under pose θ, and $\theta_\square o \theta_{1or2}$ means a combination of pose.

After cascaded pose regression process, the face feature is described by uniform local binary pattern which will be further handled in clustering and refinement process.

3.4 Clustering Analysis

As an unsupervised face tracking and recognition framework or model, there are two key issues to deal with. The first one should be clustering the samples into several groups in which each group consists of the same faces with multi-view. Suppose that Clust stands for clustering, N is the total number of clustering, Dist (f_i,f_j) stands for the distance between feature f_i and feather f_j, and Dist(f_i,$Clust_j$) as minimum distance between feature f_i and $Clust_j$. The distance between feature and Clust will be calculated as formula (6):

$$Dist(f_i, Clust_j) = \min(Dist(f_i, f_j)), f_j \in Clust_j \tag{6}$$

For calculating the clustering distance each other, we define Dist($Clust_i$,$Clust_j$) as formula (7):

$$Dist(Clust_i, Clust_j) = \min(Dist(f_i, f_j)), \\ f_i \in Clust_i, f_j \in Clust_j \tag{7}$$

After the clustering process, the tracked faces can be clustered into several groups for further refinement process.

3.5 Refinement Process

However the clustering algorithm can't ensure that every single face falls into the exact subspace where it actually belongs to. So group refinement will be necessary. It aims at merging faces which belong to the same class, but were assigned to different groups. Since the single face may more or less experience a little bit of affine transformation, SIFT [9], which can robustly identify objects even among

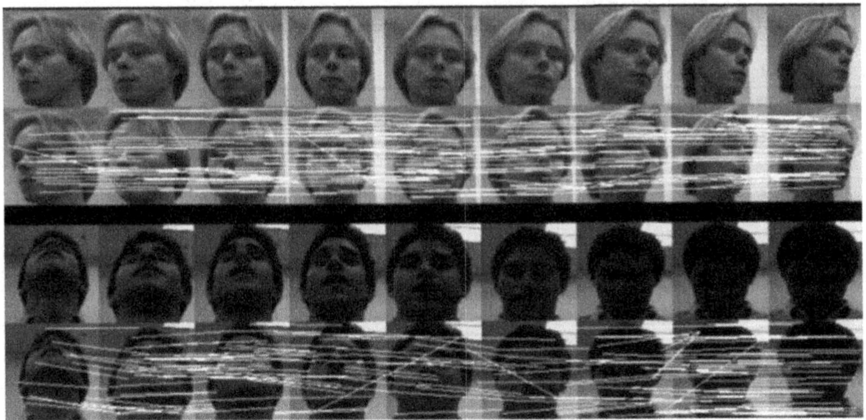

Fig. 2 Faces in different folders are grouped

clutter and under partial occlusion, because the SIFT feature descriptor is invariant to scale, orientation, and affine distortion, and partially invariant to illumination changes, will be a good choice for refinement process to achieve better clustering result. And in practice, SIFT detects and exploits a much larger number of features from the images, which reduces the contribution of the errors caused by these local variations in the average error of all feature matching errors. Hence the detailed second key issue will be applying SIFT selection to each group which has been stored in file folder format and the folder has already been labeled with a certain name. As we all know that SIFT usually needs a large of computational time consumption. To deal with this problem, the framework exploits a multithreaded Mechanism. In comparison with tracking and detection process, the refinement process is slightly lagged. It is just the refinement process, and will not affect the overall framework performance. This refined effect can be demonstrated in Fig. 2.

As can be seen from the above process, the related faces have been stored together in a uniform folder. This means that each face in video sequence has been established relationships with other faces. Based on these grouped faces, you may select one group to compare the one that stored in existing database for further human recognition.

4 Experimental Result

4.1 Experiment on Real-Time Camera Datasets

We have implemented above algorithms on a laptop computer with attached video camera, and have tested them extensively over a wide range of conditions. In the experiment, all the tracked faces are aligned to grayscale images 64*64 pixels

Table 1 Face tracking results in three videos

No	Total	Tracked	Untracked	Tracked/total (%)	Untracked/total (%)	Non-faces
1	76	73	3	96	4	2
2	57	57	0	100	0	3
3	82	80	2	97	3	1

Table 2 Comparison of before and after SIFT refinement

No	Human objects	Tracked non-face	Folder number without SIFT	After SIFT refinement
1	Four persons	2	15	6
2	Three persons	3	11	4
3	Three persons	1	14	4

per individual. Tracking of face detectors were tested on three video sequences illustrated in Fig. 7. The sequences contain human objects in challenging conditions that include sudden motion, motion partial occlusions, head posture change. Tracking result was listed in Table 1.

As indicated in Table 1, the framework 's tracking accuracy is near 97%. The non-faces being tracked is mainly as a result of swift motion of the face. We also make a comparative research on TLD which got much focus in CVPR 2010. TLD really achieved good performance in object tracking, but for face tracking we do need a special one. There are two leading points in our presented framework: one is that our framework is capable of multi-faces tracking simultaneous but TLD can only track one face at one time (this conclusion is drawn based on open-TLD); another is that it needn't real-time training at the tracking stage.

Since the framework is the unsupervised one, all the tracked faces will be labeled by using just Arabic number. And then the labeled result will be stored in the correspondent local file folders which have the same name with the previous face label. Dealt with by a daemon process, faces belong to one person should be to full extent merged according to their SIFT feature. In order to clearly know about how well our framework works, we made a comparison among purely using SIFT, combination of tracking and SIFT, and only tracking. Table 2 illustrates the comparison between before and after SIFT refinement process.

4.2 Experiments on the Honda/UCSD Data Set

More experiments were carried out to check the performance of the proposed framework. For comparison, we used Honda/UCSD database [12]. The Honda/UCSD video dataset was collected for video-based face recognition. It consists of 59 video sequences involving 20 individuals. Each sequence contains

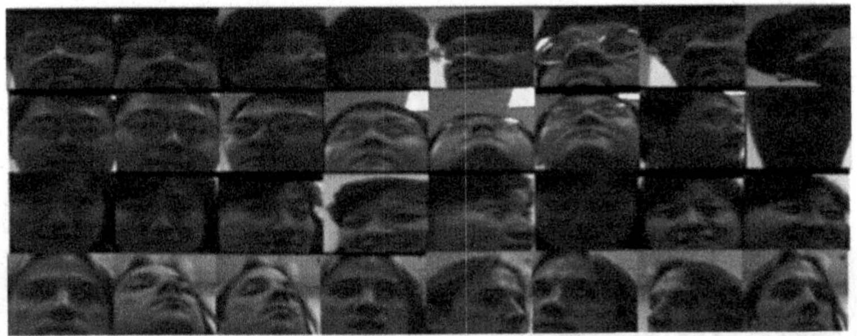

Fig. 3 Sample from Honda/UCSD database (all the images were detected in real time)

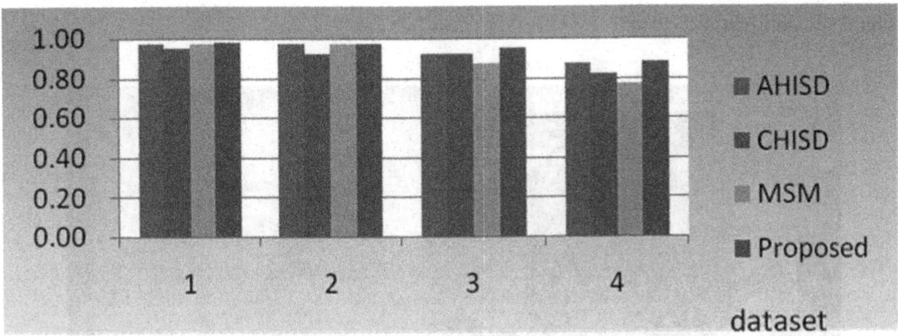

Fig. 4 Comparison between our proposed approach and other algorithms, X-axel stands for the sequence number of dataset and Y-axel stands for the recognition rate. The recognition rate of proposed method is the ratio clustered faces and total faces

approximately 300–500 frames. Because the approach is an unsupervised one, we just made a comparison between the traditional algorithms which include AHISD [13] (affine hull based image set distance), CHISD [13] (convex hull based image set distance),MSM(mutual subspace method) [14] and our proposed approach which based on faces selected and stored in folders by our framework. To illustrate clearly the comparison, we define our proposed method as LTP(illumination invariant) plus cascaded pose regression (CPR) (pose invariant) plus Clustering analysis, and finally add SIFT refinement. The detected faces were resized to 64*64 grayscale images. Some sample faces from Honda/UCSD database were shown in Fig. 3. And Fig. 4 illustrates a comparison among them.

Actually, the proposed framework has two recognition phases: one is to determine which group the tracked face belongs to; another is to merge faces which belong to the same person but fell into different groups by applying SIFT operator. Therefore it should theoretically achieve the high recognition accuracy. But under the very prompt movement or very bad light conditions, some negative samples can be found in Fig. 5. That is why our framework could not ensure 100% recognition rate unless that light conditions are relatively stable and the target moving speed is not very fast.

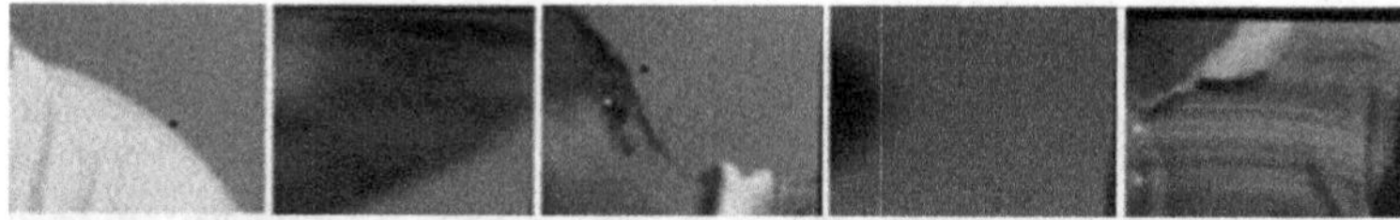

Fig. 5 Several wrong tracking objects

Fig. 6 Testing sample videos

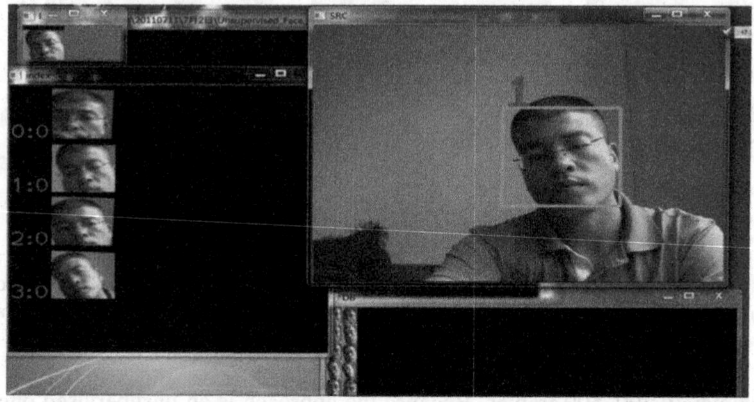

Fig. 7 The running framework it is divided four windows: main window (SRC) shows the original image from video, detection and tracking window indicates the real-time detected face (above the index window), SIFT window demonstrates the refinement result (index, the first column number means the index of DB group and the behind colon number means these two DB group belong to the same person), DB window indicates the face DB groups

5 Conclusion

We have developed a reliable face tracking and recognition framework. The performance of the framework is analyzed by videos. From the test results, we can conclude that the framework is able to detect and track faces, even if a feature has been partial occluded (Fig. 6). However, the tracking framework may fail if there is a sudden, large, movement within a single frame sequence (That's the main reason why the negative sample happened). However, by using a combination of tracking, clustering and SIFT refinement, our proposed framework works very well. The snapshot of framework can be found in Fig. 7.

Acknowledgment This work is funded by the National Basic Research Program of China (No. 2010CB327902), the National Natural Science Foundation of China (No. 60873158, No. 61005016, No. 61061130560) and the Fundamental Research Funds for the Central Universities.

References

1. Z. Kalal, K. Mikolajczyk, and J. Matas. Face-TLD: Tracking-Learning-Detection Applied to Faces. International Conference on Image Processing 1(1):3789–3792 (2010)
2. Paul Viola and Michael Jones.: Rapid Object Detection using a Boosted Cascade of Simple Features. Conference on Computer Vision and Pattern Recognition, 1(1):511 (2001)
3. J. Yang and A. Waibel A real-time face tracker. In Proceedings of the Third IEEE Workshop on Applications of Computer Vision, 1(1): 142–147 (1996)
4. H. Schneiderman and T. Kanade.: A statistical method for 3d object detection applied to faces and cars. In Proceedings of IEEE Computer Society Conference on Computer Vision and Pattern Recognition, 1(1):1746 (2000)
5. R.L. Hsu, M. Abdel-Mottaleb, and A.K. Jain.: Face Detection in Color Images. Pattern Analysis and Machine Intelligence,24(5):696–706 (2002)
6. Yan Wang, Yanghua Liu, Linmi Tao, Guangyou Xu.: Real-time multi-view face detection and pose estimation in video stream. 18th International Conference on Pattern Recognition, 4(1):354–357 (2006)
7. M. Nakamura, H. Nomiya and K. Uehara.: Improvement of boosting algorithm by modifying the weighting rule. Annals of Mathematics and Artificial Intelligence, 41(1):95–109 (2004)
8. T. Camus.: Real-Time Quantized Optical Flow. Journal of Real-Time Imaging, 3(1): 71–86 (1997)
9. David G. Lowe.: Distinctive image features from scale-invariant key points. International Journal of Computer Vision, 60(2): 91–110 (2004)
10. Xiao yang Tan and Bill Triggs.: Enhanced Local Texture Feature Sets for Face Recognition under Difficult Lighting Conditions. Proceedings of the 3rd international conference on Analysis and modeling of faces and gestures,1(1):168–182 (2009)
11. Piotr Dollár, Peter Welinder, Pietro Perona.: Cascaded Pose Regression. In Proceedings of CVPR. 1(1): 1078–1085 (2010)
12. K. C. Lee, J. Mo, M. H. Yang, and D. Kriegman.: Video based face recognition using probabilistic appearance manifolds. Computer Society Conference on Computer Vision and Pattern Recognition, 1(1):313 (2003)
13. Cevikalp H., Triggs B.: Face recognition based on image sets. Computer Vision and Pattern Recognition, 1(1): 2567–2573 (2010)
14. K. Fukui and O. Yamaguchi.: Face recognition using multiview point patterns for robot vision. In International Symposium of Robotics Research, pp.192–201 (2003)

Recognizing Realistic Action Using Contextual Feature Group

Yituo Ye, Lei Qin, Zhongwei Cheng, and Qingming Huang

Abstract Although the spatial–temporal local features and the bag of visual words model (BoW) have achieved a great success and a wide adoption in action classification, there still remain some problems. First, the local features extracted are not stable enough, which may be aroused by the background action or camera shake. Second, using local features alone ignores the spatial–temporal relationships of these features, which may decrease the classification accuracy. Finally, the distance mainly used in the clustering algorithm of the BoW model did not take the semantic context into consideration. Based on these problems, we proposed a systematic framework for recognizing realistic actions, with considering the spatial–temporal relationship between the pruned local features and utilizing a new discriminate group distance to incorporate the semantic context information. The Support Vector Machine (SVM) with multiple kernels is employed to make use of both the local feature and feature group information. The proposed method is evaluated on KTH dataset and a relatively realistic dataset YouTube. Experimental results validate our approach and the recognition performance is promising.

Y. Ye • Z. Cheng
Graduate University of Chinese Academy of Sciences, Beijing 100049, China
e-mail: ytye@jdl.ac.cn; zwcheng@jdl.ac.cn

L. Qin
Key lab of Intelligent Information Processing, Institute of Computing Technology, CAS, Beijing 100190, China
e-mail: lqin@jdl.ac.cn

Q. Huang (✉)
Graduate University of Chinese Academy of Sciences, Beijing 100049, China

Key lab of Intelligent Information Processing, Institute of Computing Technology, CAS, Beijing 100190, China
e-mail: qmhuang@jdl.ac.cn

J.S. Jin et al., *The Era of Interactive Media*,
DOI 10.1007/978-1-4614-3501-3_38,

Keywords Action recognition • Spatial–temporal local feature • Local feature group • Discriminate group distance • Mahalanobis distance

1 Introduction

Recognizing human activities is one of the most promising fields of computer vision. It is receiving increasing attention due to its wide range application such as smart surveillance, human-computer interface, virtual reality, content based video retrieval and video compression.

Although a large amount of research has been reported on human actions recognition, there still remain some open issues, and one of the most important issues is action representation. Among the traditional approaches, holistic information is always used to model human actions. Bobick and Davis [1] proposed the MEI and MHI method, which is capable of encoding the dynamics of a sequence of moving human silhouettes. Ke et al. [2] used segmented spatial–temporal volumes to model human activities. Although their methods are efficient, most of the holistic approaches have either the requirement of pre-processing or an expensive computational cost. Due to the limitation of holistic approaches, part-based approaches which only use several "interesting" parts received more attention. And one of the most popular presentations is the Bag of Visual Words model (BoW) [3, 5]. The procedure of BoW is clustering a large number of local features to make visual words vocabulary and then quantizing different features to their corresponding nearest visual words.

Notwithstanding its great success and wide adoption in BoW, this method still has some issues. First, single visual word discards rich spatial information among local features, which is of great importance in human activities recognition. Some previous works [8–10] have verified that modeling these visual contexts can improve the performance. The common approach is trying to identify the combination of visual words with statistically stable spatial configurations. Liu et al. [8] utilized feature pursuit algorithms such as AdaBoosting to model the relationship of visual words. Ryoo and Aggarwal [9] introduced the spatial–temporal relationship match (STR match), which considers spatial and temporal relationship among detected features to recognize activities. Hu et al. [10] proposed the spatial–temporal descriptive video-phrases (ST-DVPs) and descriptive video-clips (ST-DVCs) to model the spatial and temporal information of visual words. Generally, model the relationship of visual words can benefit the recognition. However, the quantization error introduced during visual vocabulary generation may degrade the accuracy, which can be seen in Fig. 1. The method proposed in this paper models the spatial and temporal information of local features rather than the visual words to avoid the influence of the quantization error.

Second, the distance metric, such as Euclidean distance and L1-norm, commonly used for generating visual vocabulary, does not take the semantic context into consideration. This may render them to prone to noise, for that the local features with similar semantic could be clustered in different visual words. Inspired by the metric learning framework of Zhang et al. [11], we present a new spatial

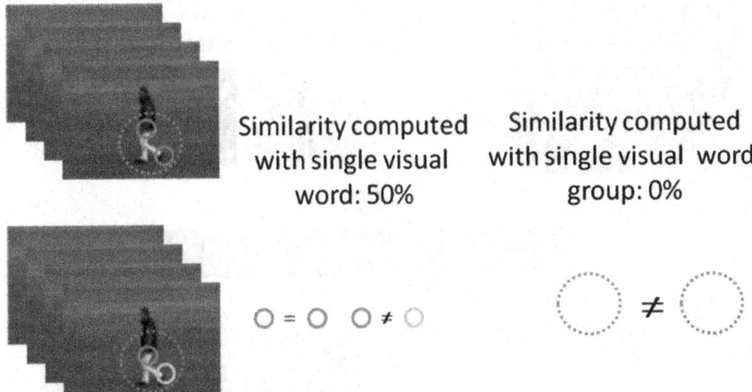

Fig. 1 The quantization error are magnified when combining visual words together, resulting in the accuracy reduction

context weighted Mahalanobis distance metric to measure the similarity between different features, and furthermore, the group distance can also be computed based on it, which is named as discriminate group distance.

Based on these problems, we propose an action recognition framework, which utilizes the group of local features to construct visual vocabulary, and then quantizes the new group to its corresponding nearest word, using the proposed new discriminate group distance. Combining with the histogram of single features, different actions can be recognized using the SVM classifier. The whole process is illustrated in Fig. 2.

The remainder of this paper is organized as follows. Section 2 introduces our proposed local feature group detector. Section 3 illustrates the discriminate group distance and the corresponding classifier. Section 4 presents and discusses our experimental results on KTH and YouTube dataset. We conclude the paper in Sect. 5.

2 Local Feature Group Detection and Representation

To extract the local feature group, we first utilize the 3D-Harris [3] detector to detect the interest points, and use the HOF and HOG as in [3] to represent interest points. For each interest point, two kinds of information can be acquired, the local feature descriptor D and the scale information S. Then each local feature can be denoted as $F(S, D)$, and a local feature group can be represented as $G\{F_1, F_2, F_3 \ldots F_n\}$, where n is the number of features in a group.

To make local feature group representative and robust, group extraction algorithm should be accord with some rules: (1) feature group should be robust to noise, such as background action and camera shake; (2) feature group should be scale invariant; (3) the number of local features in a feature group should be small.

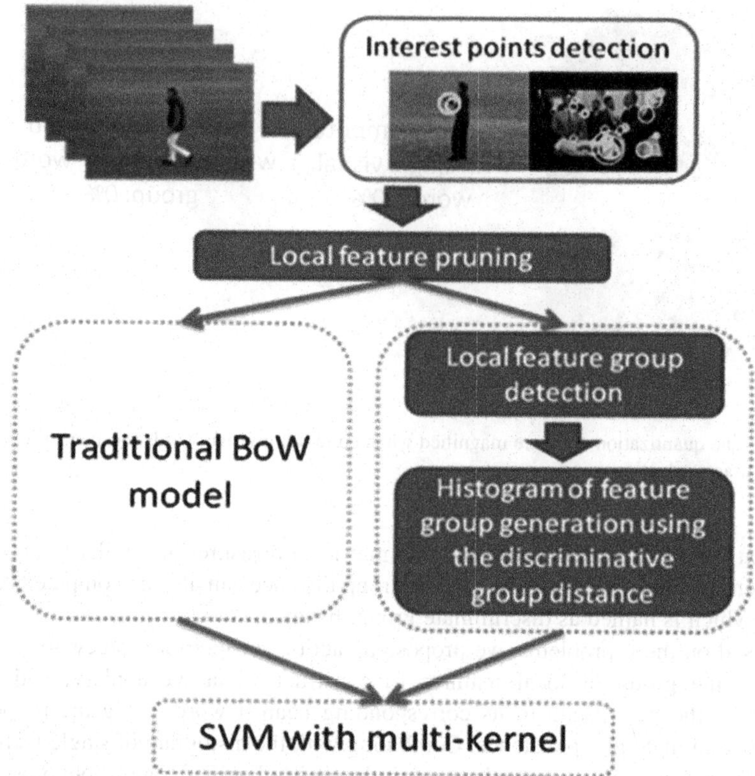

Fig. 2 The proposed framework

Feature pruning algorithm proposed in [8] is adopted to make the extracted features satisfy the rule 1. The group extraction method will be discussed in Sect. 2.1, which has taken into account of the rule 2 and rule 3.

2.1 Local Feature Group Extraction

Different algorithms have been proposed to detect local feature groups [8–10]. In this paper, we define the co-occurred local features, which satisfy certain spatial–temporal restriction, as a feature group. In order to satisfy the second rule shown above, we use the scale information as the basis to compute the spatial–temporal distance between local features. As for the third rule, if too many local features are combined, the repeatability of the local feature group will decrease. Furthermore, if more local features are contained in a local feature group, there would be more possible feature-to-feature matches between two groups, which would make the computation of group distance time consuming. As a tradeoff, we fix the number of local features in each local feature group as 2 in this paper.

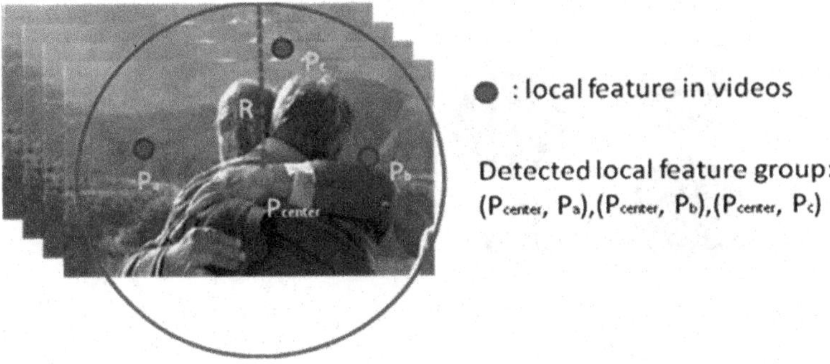

Fig. 3 The feature group detector. It extracts the local features positioned in the radius R, and constructs the feature groups

To detect local feature group, we use the detector illustrated in Fig. 3. In this figure, a sphere with radius R is centered at a local feature. A local feature group is formed by the centered local feature and other local features within the sphere. To make the feature group invariant to scale, the radius is set as

$$R = S_{center} \times \lambda \tag{1}$$

where S_{center} is the scale of centered local feature and λ is a parameter that controls the spatial–temporal span of local feature group. A large λ will overcome the sparseness of local feature group and indentify stable spatial–temporal relationship between local features. However, a larger λ also requires more computational cost.

By scanning every local feature with the detector, the local feature groups, each of which contains two local features, are generated. It should be noted that, the new group contains different features rather than different quantized visual words, which makes it robust to quantization error.

By extracting local features and feature groups, two kinds of information can be acquired. They are further passed to the BoW model with a new discriminate group distance. Then we can get two histograms, corresponding to the local features and feature groups. Finally, different actions can be classified by SVM with multiple kernels.

Section 3.1 will introduce the discriminate group distance, which is a combination of context weighted Mahalanobis distance metric. Section 3.2 will present the related SVM classifier. With two kinds of information, multi-kernel learning strategy is employed to improve the recognition accuracy.

2.2 *Discriminate Group Distance and Metric Learning*

The discriminate group distance is defined as a combination of spatial–temporal context weighted Mahalanobis distance between two feature groups. Note that

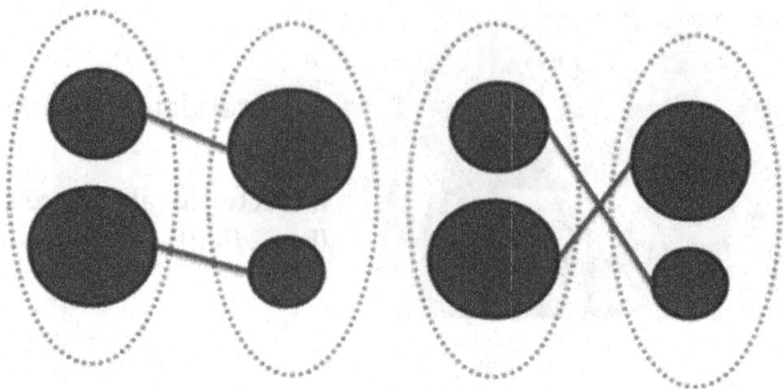

Fig. 4 The possible match orders when each local group contains two local features

discriminate group distance is computed between groups containing identical number of local features, so there are *n!* feature to feature matches when each group contains *n* local features. As illustrated in Fig. 4, when $n = 2$, there are two possible matches.

In [11], a best match order is defined as the one that maximize the spatial similarity based on the scale and orientation information. As for this paper, we take every match into consideration and select the one with the minimal distance. And as in Fig. 4, the second match order should be chosen. When $n = 2$, the discriminate group distance can be represented as

$$GD(G_I, G_J) = \min\left(\sum_{k=1}^{2} d(D_I^k, D_J^k), \sum_{k=1}^{2} d(D_I^k, D_J^{3-k})\right) \tag{2}$$

In the formula above, $GD(G_I, G_J)$ denotes the discriminate group distance between G_I and G_J, $D^k{}_I$ is the k*th* local feature in group *I* and $d(D^k{}_I, D^k{}_J)$ represents the Mahalanobis distance between feature $D^k{}_I$ and $D^k{}_J$.

As for the $d(D^k{}_I, D^k{}_J)$ shown above, a Mahalanobis distance is utilized which could incorporate the semantic context between local feature groups. Thus, it can be represented as

$$d(D_I^k, D_J^k) = (D_I^k - D_J^k)^T A (D_I^k - D_J^k) \tag{3}$$

For we use HOF and HOG to present the local feature as [3], *A* is a 144×144 matrix to be learned from the semantic labels of the local feature groups.

Intuitively, we try to find a good distance metric which makes the feature groups with similar semantic contexts close to each other and those with different semantic appearing far away. To achieve this, metric learning algorithm proposed in [11] is applied, whose result is acquired through iterative calculation when given a set of local features and their corresponding labels.

2.3 Multi-Kernel SVM Classifier

For classification, we use a non-linear SVM with the histogram intersection kernel, which can be presented as

$$K(H_I, H_J) = \sum_{k=1}^{N} \min(h_I^k, h_J^k) \tag{4}$$

where $H_I = \{h_I^n\}$ and $H_J = \{h_J^n\}$ are the histograms either for the local features or the feature groups.

Note that, there are two kinds of histograms. To combine the information effectively, two methods are utilized: *multi-kernel1* (MK_1) and *multi-kernel2* (MK_2), which can be represented respectively as

$$MK_1 = \frac{(K_1(H_I, H_J) + K_2(H_I, H_J))}{2} \tag{5}$$

$$MK_2 = \sqrt{K_1(H_I, H_J) \times K_2(H_I, H_J)} \tag{6}$$

$K_1(H_I, H_J)$ and $K_2(H_I, H_J)$ are the kernel matrices for local features and feature groups respectively.

3 Experiments

We have tested the proposed methods on the dataset KTH and YouTube, and the results prove that the methods can enhance the action recognition performance. Section 4.1 will briefly introduce the dataset KTH and YouTube, Sects. 4.2 and 4.3 would present and discuss the experiment on KTH and YouTube respectively.

3.1 KTH and YouTube Dataset

KTH is a relatively simple dataset which contains about 600 videos performed by 25 actors. "walking", "jogging", "running", "boxing", "hand waving" and "hand clapping" are the six actions in the dataset. Videos are taken at slightly different scales with various backgrounds, indoor and outdoor environments. Each video contains repeated executions of a single action in a resolution of 160×120, 25 fps.

YouTube is a dataset "in the wild", its source is YouTube videos and the videos are collected by Liu et al. [8]. It contains about 1,160 videos and includes 11 categories: "basketball shooting", "volleyball spiking", "trampoline jumping",

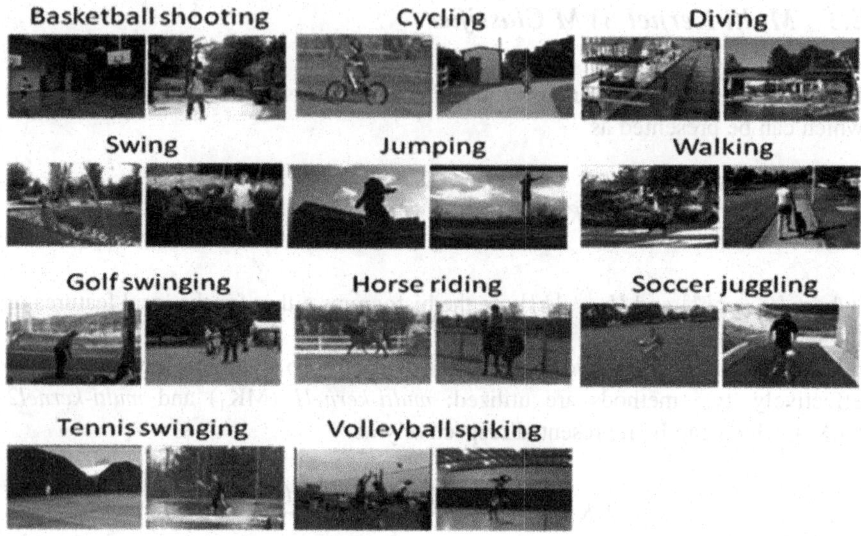

Fig. 5 Examples of the YouTube dataset

"soccer juggling", "horseback riding", "cycling", "diving", "swing", "golf swinging", "tennis swinging" and "walking with a dog". Figure 5 gives a brief impression, from which we can drive some visualized properties such as the cluttered background, variations in object scale, varied viewpoints and varied illuminations. Besides, the videos also mix steady cameras and shaky cameras, which make the noise pruning even more necessary.

3.2 Experiments on KTH Dataset

Since the KTH datasets is relatively "clean", feature pruning is not necessary. We performed two groups of experiments. The first one is to test the selection of the parameter λ in feature group extraction, and the second one is to test the selection of the parameter K in the clustering algorithm k-means of vocabulary construction. As for the training set and testing set, we apply the leave-one-out-cross-validation (LOOCV) scheme and use the mean value as the accuracy.

Traversing every possible value of the pair (λ, K) in the procedure will be time consuming. So in our experiment, the selection of λ will be tested with a constant value of K, and the selection of K will be tested with a stable λ. The results are illustrated on Fig. 6, from which *group* stands for the accuracy using only local feature group information, and *multi-kernel1* and *mutli-kernel2* represent the accuracy acquired by the mutli-kernel SVM classifier as illustrated in Sect. 3.2. It can be seen that combining local feature and feature group information will get a better accuracy. Meanwhile, with the growth of λ, the tendency of the accuracy is rising

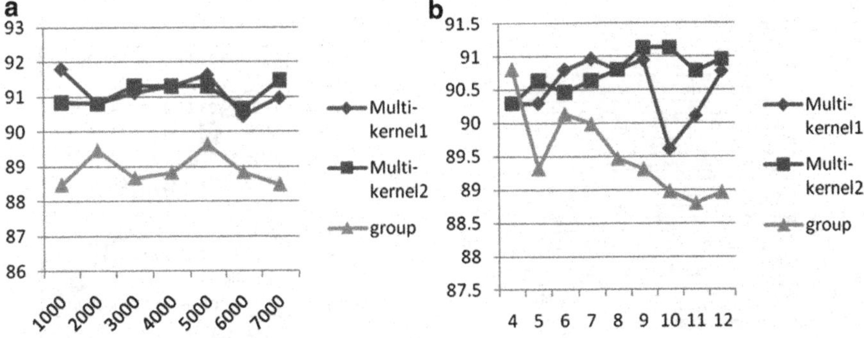

Fig. 6 Influence of parameters, (**a**) denotes the relationship between average accuracy and parameter K when $\lambda = 8$, (**b**) implies the influence of parameter λ, when $K = 2{,}000$

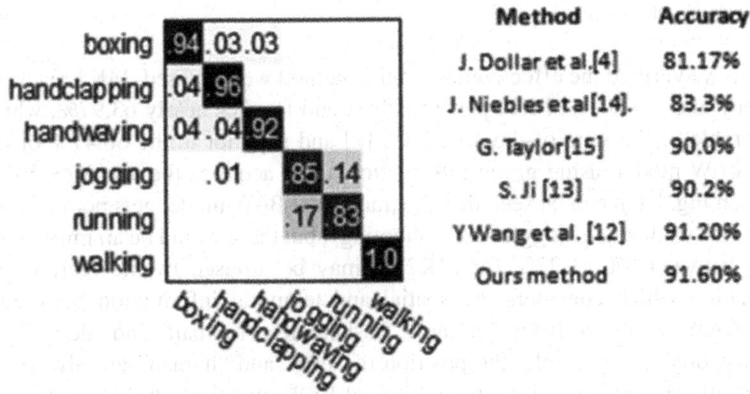

	boxing	handclapping	handwaving	jogging	running	walking
boxing	.94	.03	.03			
handclapping	.04	.96				
handwaving	.04	.04	.92			
jogging		.01		.85	.14	
running				.17	.83	
walking						1.0

Method	Accuracy
J. Dollar et al.[4]	81.17%
J. Niebles et al[14].	83.3%
G. Taylor[15]	90.0%
S. Ji [13]	90.2%
Y Wang et al. [12]	91.20%
Ours method	91.60%

Fig. 7 Confusion table for the method we proposed and the comparison with other literature about the result on KTH using LOOCV scheme

while computational time is also increasing (Fig. 7). On the KTH dataset, 9 and 5,000 are assigned to λ and K respectively and the performance of the proposed method is comparable with the state-of-the-art result on KTH which is 91.2% [12].

3.3 *Experiments on YouTube Dataset*

For the YouTube dataset, the recognition is also carried out through the LOOCV scheme. Feature points of YouTube videos are processed by the pruning method, which leads to a nearly 2% improvement of recognition accuracy, i.e. from 58.1% to 60.5%. We use the parameter $\lambda = 4$ and $K = 2{,}000$ in these experiments.

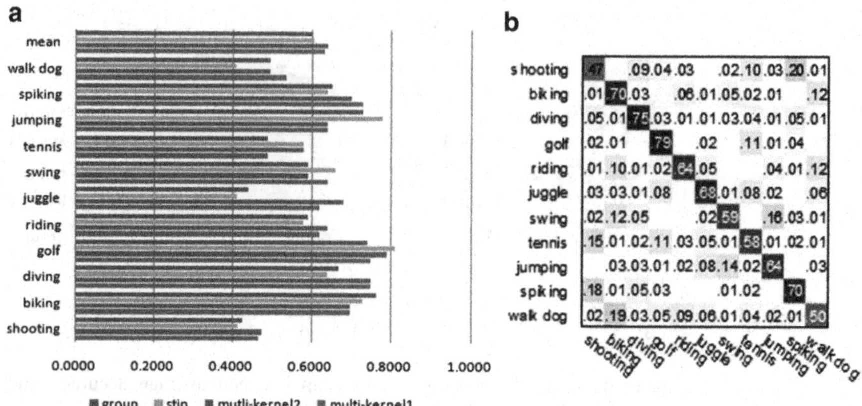

Fig. 8 Results on YouTube dataset. (**a**)The average accuracy for multi-kernel1, multi-kernel2, BoW and group methods are 63.07%, 63.97%, 60.47% and 59.87% respectively, and (**b**) denotes the confusion table of multi-kernel2

Then we verified the effectiveness of the method we proposed. MK1 reaches the accuracy about 63.07%, MK2 performs best and reaches nearly 63.97%, which is comparable of the state-of-the-art 65.4% [8] and superior to the 60.47% of traditional BoW model, using group information alone acquires the accuracy 59.87%. Based on Fig. 8a, it can be seen that the traditional BoW model gets poor results on the action "walk dog", "juggle" and "shooting", but there would be an improvement varied between 6% to 27% for MK2. It may be aroused by the feature group information which considers the spatial and temporal information between the local features extracted from "human", "basketball", "football" and "dog". Taking "walking dog" for example, the position of "dog" and "human" are always obey some spatial restriction, while the traditional BoW model which only presents the distribution of the local features discards this spatial information. However, it also should be noted that the feature group information may bring some kinds of spatial temporal restriction and may decrease the accuracy on some action with large intra-class variation such as "swing". On the whole, features group would be the complement for the local features rather than a replacement, combing these two kinds of information may acquire promising result. Figure 8b shows the confusion matrix, we can see that "biking" and "riding horse" which share the similar motion are often misclassified as "walking dog", "shooting" and "volleyball spiking" are often confused due to their common action jumping with a ball.

4 Conclusions

We propose a systematic framework for recognizing realistic actions, which considers the spatial–temporal relationship between the local features and utilizes a new discriminate group distance using a combination of the Mahalanobis distance for the clustering algorithm in the BoW model. The effectiveness has been tested on the datasets KTH and YouTube. Experimental results verify that our framework is effective, and combing the spatial temporal information between local features improves the recognition accuracy.

Acknowledgements This work was supported in part by National Basic Research Program of China (973 Program): 2009CB320906, in part by National Natural Science Foundation of China: 61025011, 61035001 and 61003165, and in part by Beijing Natural Science Foundation: 4111003.

References

1. A. Bobick and J. Davis. The representation and recognition of action using temporal templates. IEEE Transactions on Pattern Analysis and Machine Intelligence, 23(3):257–267, 2001.
2. Ke Y, Sukthankar R and Hebert. Spatial–temporal shape and flow correlation for action recognition. In IEEE Conference on Computer Vision and Pattern Recognition, 2007.
3. I. Laptev and T. Lindeberg. Space-time interest points. In *ICCV*, 2003.
4. P. Dollar, V. Rabaud, G. Cottrell, and S. Belongie. Behavior recognition via sparse spatio-temporal features. In *VS-PETS*, 2005.
5. L. Fei-Fei and P. Perona. A Bayesian hierarchical model for learning natural scene categories. In *CVPR*, 2005.
6. P. Scovanner, S. Ali, and M. Shah. A 3-dimensional SIFT descriptor and its application to action recognition. In ACM International Conference on Multimedia, 2007.
7. H. Jhuang, T. Serre, L. Wolf, and T. Poggio. A biologically inspired system for action recognition. In IEEE International Conference on Computer Vision, 2007.
8. Jinen Liu, Jiebo luo, Mubarak Shah. Rcognizing realisitic actions from videos “in the wild”. In IEEE Conference on Computer Vision and Pattern Recognition, 2009
9. RYoo, M.S and AGGARWAL, J.K. Spatio-temporal relationship match: Video structure comparison for recognition of complex human activities. In IEEE International Conference on Computer Vision, 2009.
10. Qiong Hu, Lei Qin, Qingming Huang, Shuqiang Jiang, and Qi Tian. Action Recognition Using Spatial–Temporal Context,” Analysis and Search. 20th International Conference on Pattern Recognition, August 23–26, 2010, Istanbul, Turkey.
11. Shiliang Zhang, Qingming Huang, Gang Hua, Shuqiang Jiang, Wen Gao, and Qi Tian, Building Contextual Visual Vocabulary for Large-scale Image Applications, in Proceedings of ACM Multimedia Conference, *ACM MM* (Full Paper), Florence, Italy, pp.501–510, Oct.25–29, 2010.
12. Y Wang, G Mori, “Human Action Recognition by Semi-Latent Topic Models,” PAMI, 2009.
13. S. Ji, W. Xu, M. Yang, and K. Yu. 3D convolutional neural networks for human action recognition. In *ICML*, 2010. 3362, 3366
14. J. Niebles, H. Wang, and L. Fei-Fei. Unsupervised learning of human action categpries using spatial-temporal words. IJCV, 2008. 3366.
15. G. Taylor, R. Fergus, Y. Lecun, and C. Bregler. Convolutional learning of spatio-temporal features. In ECCV, 2010. 3361, 3362, 3366, 3367.

Mutual Information-Based Emotion Recognition

Yue Cui, Suhuai Luo, Qi Tian, Shiliang Zhang, Yu Peng, Lei Jiang, and Jesse S. Jin

Abstract Emotions that arise in viewers in response to videos play an essential role in content-based indexing and retrieval. However, the emotional gap between low-level features and high-level semantic meanings is not well understood. This paper proposes a general scheme for video emotion identification using mutual information-based feature selection followed by regression. Continuous arousal and valence values are used to measure video affective content in dimensional arousal-valence space. Firstly, rich audio-visual features are extracted from video clips. The minimum redundancy and maximum relevance feature selection is then used to select most representative feature subsets for arousal and valence modelling. Finally support vector regression is employed to model arousal and valence estimation functions. As evaluated via tenfold cross-validation, the estimation results achieved by our scheme for arousal and valence are: mean absolute error, 0.1358 and 0.1479, variance of absolute error, 0.1074 and 0.1175, respectively. Encouraging results demonstrate the effectiveness of our proposed method.

Key words Affective content analysis • Mutual information-based feature selection • Support vector regression

---

Y. Cui (✉) • S. Luo • Y. Peng •
L. Jiang • J.S. Jin
School of Design, Communication and Information Technology,
University of Newcastle, Australia
e-mail: yue.cui@uon.edu.au; suhuai.luo@newcastle.edu.au; yu.peng@uon.edu.au;
ljiang@uon.edu.au; jesse.jin@newcastle.edu.au

Q. Tian
Department of Computer Science, University of Texas at San Antonio, San Antonio, TX, USA
e-mail: qitian@cs.utsa.edu

S. Zhang
Key Laboratory of Intelligent Information Processing, Institute of Computing Technology,
Chinese Academy of Sciences, China
e-mail: slzhang@jdl.ac.cn

J.S. Jin et al., *The Era of Interactive Media*,
DOI 10.1007/978-1-4614-3501-3_39,

1 Introduction

With the exploration of multimedia contents, there has been an increasing emphasis on identifying the rich semantics in video data. A large body of research confirms that videos can be emotionally expressive [1–8], and emotional references of viewers play an essential role in the intelligent content-based multimedia retrieval and selection. This entails video affective analysis and emotion detection for video understanding, indexing, filtering and some video-related applications.

However, bridging the emotional gap between low-level features and high-level semantic meanings is likely to be particularly challenging, and the relationship between them is still not entirely understood. So as to explain human emotions, scientists and psychologists have investigated a variety of models including categorical [2, 3] and dimensional types [1, 5, 7, 8]. From the categorical point of view, affective contents consist of a set of basic emotions, such as "fear","sadness",and "happiness" [2], or "anger","sad","fear","happy",and "neutral" [3]. In order to identify movies into the pre-specified classes, Kang trained Hidden Markov Models (HMM) [2] and Xu et al. used fuzzy clustering and HMM techniques [3]. In a dimensional model, emotion is represented by points in a continuous dimensional affective space which reflects more accurate and extensive emotional types. Three-dimensional and two-dimensional spaces have been developed and investigated in representation of affective contents, such as pleasure–arousal–dominance (P–A–D) [7, 8] and arousal–valence (A–V) models [1, 5]. In P–A–D models, pleasure is also described as valence, which reflects the type of emotion. Arousal is used to characterize the intensity of emotion. Dominance describes the level of attention or rejection of the emotion. In addition to P–A–D models, A–V models have been used to characterize emotional space by the dimensions of arousal and valence. Hanjalic and Xu [1] used linear combinations for arousal and valence modelling. Support vector regression (SVR) models were used to map the affective features into affective states [5]. While great success has been made in affective representation and analysis, affective estimation still needs to be improved to bridge the emotional gap.

In the present study, we employ mutual information-based method to examine audio-visual features which are most representative for affective representation, and use SVR to model affective functions in A–V feature space. The rest of paper is organized as follows. Section 2 presents the overview of video emotion recognition system. Affective feature extraction and mutual information-based feature selection will be introduced in Sects. 3 and 4. In Sect. 5, SVR is performed to build affective modelling to represent emotions. The experimental results are discussed in Sect. 6. Finally, Sect. 7 concludes this paper and draws our future work.

2 System Overview

An overview of video emotion recognition system is shown in Fig. 1. Initially, videos were segmented into clips due to the diversity of affective contents. A variety of audio-visual features (*X*) were extracted from video clips. Mutual information-based

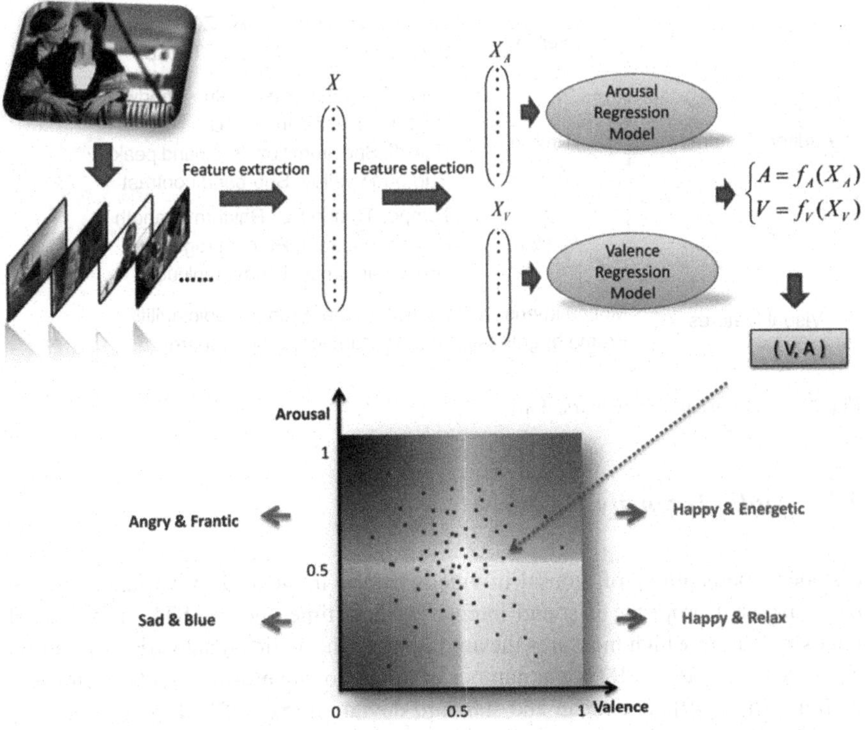

Fig. 1 Overview of video emotion recognition system

feature selection was subsequently performed to generate arousal (X_A) and valence (X_V) feature subsets , respectively, allowing for a more effective characterization of multivariate relationships among low-level features and more accurate estimation of affects in A–V space. Arousal and valence regression models were learned using the optimal feature subsets, and arousal and valence scores were finally obtained, corresponding to a point in affective space.

3 Audio–Visual Feature Extraction

Rich affective information is conveyed through audio and visual channels. Auditory and visual features extracted directly from video stream play an essential role for understanding the semantic meanings. In the present study, 49 low-level features have been extracted from each video clip including 43 auditory features covering audio intensity, audio timbre and audio rhythm, and 6 visual features as shown in Fig. 2. The detailed implementations can be found in [6].

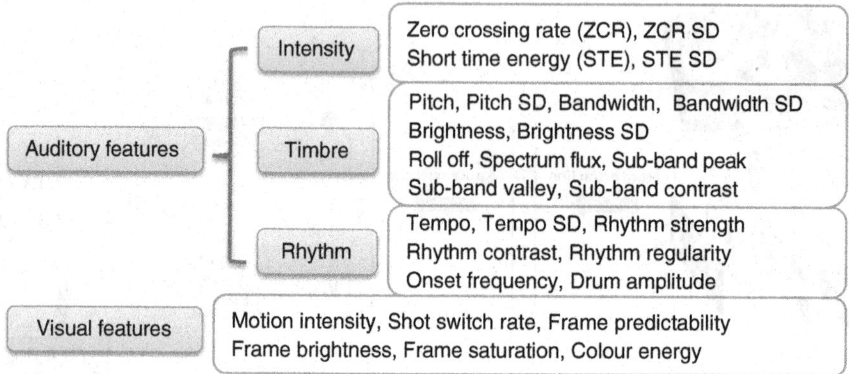

Fig. 2 Audio-visual feature extraction

3.1 Audio Intensity Features

Listeners' perceptions of arousal in videos can be influenced by variations in the basic acoustic property of sound intensity. Short time energy (STE) is a typical intensity feature which measures the amplitude of the audio signal varies with time. Zero crossing rate (ZCR) is the number of an audio waveform cross the zero axes within a frame [9]. The mean and standard deviation (SD) of STE and ZCR were calculated.

3.2 Audio Timbre Features

Pitch is an audio feature which describes an estimate of pitch percept. Bandwidth represents the amplitude weighted average of the differences between the spectral components and the centroid [10]. Brightness of sound is the gravity centre of the spectrum. Sub-band peak, Sub-band valley and Sub-band contrast of 8 channels were also extracted. Spectrum flux shows the variation of spectrum between the adjacent two frames [11].

3.3 Audio Rhythm Features

Rhythmic information influences on perceived emotional expression in music and videos. Tempo estimates listeners' perception of the speed of the rhythm. The mean and SD of tempo were computed. Rhythm strength, Rhythm contrast and Rhythm regularity have also been used previously [6]. Onset frequency and Drum amplitude were extracted on the basis of onset detection and drum detection.

3.4 Visual Features

Visual information provides abundant contents and impacts our emotions. Six visual features including Motion intensity, Shot switch rate, Frame predictability, Colour energy, Frame brightness and Frame saturation were extracted. Motion as a visual feature has been believed to have an impact on individual affective response [1]. Motion intensity represents the degree of change in motion and estimates from the difference of two frames. Similarly, shot patterns are tools for directors to create desired pace of action, and shorter shot lengths are used to create stressed, accented moments [1]. We extracted Shot switch rate which represents the shot switching frequency. Feelings could also be related with frame predictability. If frames are predictable, viewers could infer them from context. In contrast, unpredictable frames could produce a sudden response. Emotion is evoked unconsciously by the colours of scenes, so colours can be linked with certain dimensions of emotion. For example, colourful scenes are used to evoke joyous feelings in videos. By contrast, fear or sad emotion is romanced by dim scenes. A basic colour space that relates both to how humans perceive colour and how computers display it is hue, saturation and value (HSV). We extracted Frame saturation and Frame brightness (i.e. value), which have been investigated in previous affective analyses [12, 13], and reported to be linked with physiological arousal in the body. Additionally, Colour energy [13] measuring colour contrast was also extracted.

4 Mutual Information-Based Feature Ranking and Selection

Optimal arousal and valence feature subsets can be achieved by selecting the most relevant features and eliminating redundant features. Feature ranking followed by a wrapper method is accepted as a recommended part of a feature selection procedure [14]. Feature ranking evaluates all of the features by looking at the intrinsic characteristics of the data with respect to ground truth labels. Wrapper methods evaluate the effectiveness of a subset by the mean absolute error (MAE) of regression. During the feature ranking stage, we first linearly normalized all the features to the range between 0 and 1, since features have different scales. We then employed the minimum redundancy and maximum relevance (mRMR) filter method introduced by Peng et al. [15, 16]. The mRMR feature ranking is obtained by optimizing two criteria, i.e., maximum relevance and minimum redundancy, simultaneously. This method computes the mutual information I of two variables, x and y, by their probabilistic density function $p(x)$, $p(y)$ and $p(x,y)$:

$$I(x;y) = \iint p(x,y) \log \frac{p(x,y)}{p(x)p(y)} dxdy \tag{1}$$

The maximum relevance criteria are used to search for features satisfying Eq. (2), which maximizes *D(S,c)* with the mean value of mutual information values between an individual feature x_i and class *c*:

$$\max D(S,c), D = \frac{1}{|S|}\sum_{x_i \in S} I(x_i;c) \tag{2}$$

The minimum redundancy criteria are used to minimise *R(S)* in order to eliminate rich redundancy between the two features x_i and x_j:

$$\min R(S), R = \frac{1}{|S|^2}\sum_{x_i,x_j \in S} I(x_i,x_j) \tag{3}$$

The mRMR feature set is obtained by optimizing the criteria in Eqs. (2) and (3) simultaneously. The detailed implementation algorithm is described in [15, 16].

In the wrapper stage, the initial candidate feature subset consisted solely of the top ranked feature. Then a regression function was trained and the MAE was computed. Sequential inclusion of ranked features into the feature subset led to further MAEs being obtained via regression loops. The optimal feature subset was chosen when the lowest MAE with the smallest number of features was attained. The procedure was verified via tenfold cross-validation on the training set in order to ensure that ranking and selection were unbiased. Optimal feature set was determined by selecting features with the highest selection frequency (i.e. 10). These steps were repeated 10 times in the regression procedure, meaning the maximum possible selection frequency was 100.

5 Arousal and Valence Estimation

SVR uses kernels to satisfy Mercer's condition in order that original input space can be mapped into a high-dimensional dot product space. In our method, a non-linear regression function is required to sufficiently model the data. SVR was implemented using the LIBSVM toolbox [17], with the Gaussian radial basis function (RBF) kernel, i.e., $K(x_i,x_j) = \exp(-\gamma\|x_i - x_j\|^2), \gamma{>}0$. Unlike linear kernels, RBF kernels can handle cases where the relationship between ground truth labels and features are nonlinear [18]. The parameters *C* (a constant determining the tradeoff between training error and model flatness) and γ (Gaussian kernel width) were optimized via cross-validation on the training data. Note that, as different features had different scales, we linearly scaled training data to conform to a range between 0 and 1, the same scaling method was then applied to the test data. In order to ensure generalization and reduce variability, we evaluated our method using tenfold cross-validation. The final regression results represented the average of these ten independent experiments.

6 Experimental Results

6.1 Video Data and Ground Truth Labels

One hundred and thirty minutes videos randomly selected from *Titanic* and *Forrest Gump*, which consist of abundant affective information were used to validate the proposed approach. Initially, videos were segmented into clips with a length of 14 s and each with 2 s overlap between the last and following clips. This yielded a total of 655 segments. Ground truth labels were collected from a user study. Several university students were invited and required to carefully label each segment with an arousal and a valence value. As shown in Fig. 3, arousal and valence values were continuous with a range between 0 and 1 in order to describe users' feelings as accurately as possible. Arousal values from 0 to 1 indicate a continuum from calm to exciting, and valence values from 0 to 1 indicate emotions from depressed to pleasant.

6.2 Experimental Results

Different cross-validation experiments may identify different features. For this reason, we assessed the arousal and valence features by the frequency with which they were selected. We listed the characteristics of the most frequently selected features in Table 1. We observe Shot switch rate and Spectrum flux contribute to both arousal and valence, and they rank top within all the features. Frame predictability is also correlated with both arousal and valence very much. Other arousal features include STE and STE SD, Tempo SD, Sub-band contrast, Motion intensity and Drum amplitude. Other valence features include Frame brightness, Frame saturation, Sub-band valley and Brightness of sound (see Table 1).

Arousal and valence estimation results in terms of MAE and variance of absolute error (VAE) are shown in Table 2. Our method achieved MAEs of 0.1358 and 0.1479, and VAEs of 0.1074 and 0.1175 for arousal and valence, respectively.

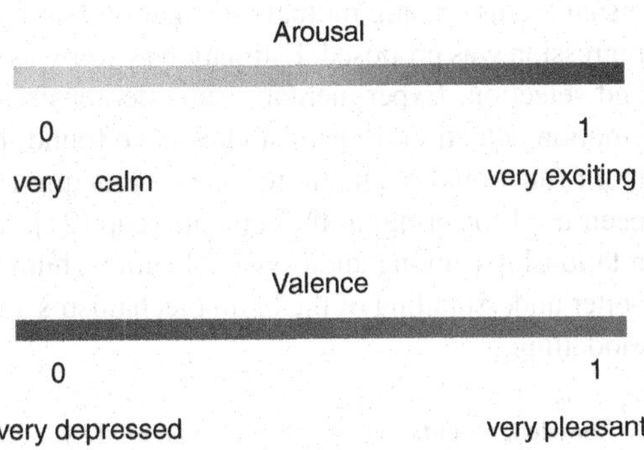

Fig. 3 Continuous arousal and valence values

Table 1 Arousal and valence frequently selected features

Arousal		Valence	
Feature	Selection frequency	Feature	Selection frequency
Shot switch rate	100	Shot switch rate	100
Spectrum flux	100	Spectrum flux	100
Short time energy SD[a]	100	Frame brightness	100
Short time energy	90	Frame predictability	80
Tempo SD[a]	90	Frame saturation	70
Frame predictability	90	Sub-band valley channel 6	70
Sub-band contrast channel 6	70	Brightness	60
Motion intensity	70		
Drum amplitude	60		
Sub-band contrast channel 3	60		

[a] Standard deviation

Table 2 Arousal and valence estimation results

	Arousal		Valence	
Method	MAE[a]	VAE[b]	MAE[a]	VAE[b]
Previous method in [19]	0.3569	0.1209	0.2864	**0.0703**
Present method	**0.1358**	**0.1074**	**0.1479**	0.1175

[a] Mean absolute error
[b] Variance of absolute error

We compare the performance of arousal and valence estimation results with our previous method for music video affective analysis reported in [19]. As shown in Table 2, the present method improves arousal and valence modelling.

7 Conclusion and Future Work

In this paper, a framework for video emotion recognition based on abundant audio-visual features using mutual information-based feature selection and support vector regression was proposed. Estimation power was enhanced by mRMR feature ranking and selection. Experimental results demonstrate our method is effective for video emotion detection. Recent studies have found that semantics can be represented by brain functional magnetic resonance imaging (fMRI) response [20], and fMRI has been used for bridging the semantic gap [21]. In the future, we will investigate the relationships among audio-visual features, human emotions and brain fMRI data for better understanding of the brain mechanisms and video affective representation and modelling.

Acknowledgements This work was supported by a CSC-Newcastle scholarship.

References

1. Hanjalic, A., Xu, L.Q.: Affective video content representation and modeling. IEEE Transactions on Multimedia, vol. 7, pp. 143–154 (2005)
2. Kang, H.B.: Affective content detection using HMMs. Proceedings of the 11th ACM International Conference on Multimedia (MM), Berkeley, California, USA, pp. 259–262 (2003)
3. Xu, M., Jin, J.S., Luo, S., Duan, L.: Hierarchical movie affective content analysis based on arousal and valence features. Proceeding of the 16th ACM International Conference on Multimedia (MM), Vancouver, Canada, pp. 677–680 (2008)
4. Xu, M., Chia, L.T., Jin, J.: Affective content analysis in comedy and horror videos by audio emotional event detection. In: IEEE International Conference on Multimedia and Expo (ICME), pp. 621–625. IEEE Press, New York (2005)
5. Zhang, S., Huang, Q., Jiang, S., Gao, W., Tian, Q.: Affective visualization and retrieval for music video. IEEE Transactions on Multimedia, vol. 12, pp. 510–522 (2010)
6. Zhang, S.L., Tian, Q., Huang, Q.M., Gao, W., Li, S.P.: Utilizing Affective Analysis for Efficient Movie Browsing. 16th IEEE International Conference on Image Processing, Vols 1-6, pp. 1833–1836 (2009)
7. Arifin, S., Cheung, P.Y.K.: Affective level video segmentation by utilizing the pleasure-arousal-dominance information. IEEE Transactions on Multimedia, vol. 10, pp. 1325–1341 (2008)
8. Zhang, S., Xu, Y.J., Jia, J., Cai, L.H.: Analysis and Modeling of Affective Audio Visual Speech Based on PAD Emotion Space. 6th International Symposium on Chinese Spoken Language Processing, pp. 281–284 (2008)
9. Li, D.G., Sethi, I.K., Dimitrova, N., McGee, T.: Classification of general audio data for content-based retrieval. Pattern Recognition Letters 22, pp. 533–544 (2001)
10. Lu, L., Liu, D., Zhang, H.J.: Automatic mood detection and tracking of music audio signals. IEEE Transactions on Audio Speech and Language Processing 14, pp. 5–18 (2006)
11. Lu, L., Zhang, H.J., Li, S.Z.: Content-based audio classification and segmentation by using support vector machines. Multimedia Systems 8, pp. 482–491 (2003)
12. Valdez, P., Mehrabian, A.: Effects of Color on Emotions. Journal of Experimental Psychology-General 123, pp. 394–409 (1994)
13. Wang, H.L., Cheong, L.F.: Affective understanding in film. IEEE Transactions on Circuits and Systems for Video Technology 16, pp. 689–704 (2006)
14. Guyon, I., Elisseeff, A.: An introduction to variable and feature selection. Journal of Machine Learning Research 3, pp. 1157–1182 (2003)
15. Ding, C., Peng, H.: Minimum redundancy feature selection from microarray gene expression data. Journal of Bioinformatics and Computational Biology 3, pp. 185–205 (2005)
16. Peng, H., Long, F., Ding, C.: Feature selection based on mutual information: criteria of max-dependency, max-relevance, and min-redundancy. IEEE Transactions on Pattern Analysis and Machine Intelligence 27, pp. 1226–1238 (2005)
17. Chang, C.-C., Lin, C.-J.: LIBSVM: a library for support vector machines. ACM Transactions on Intelligent Systems and Technology 2, 27:21–27:27 (2011)
18. Hsu, C.-W., Chang, C.-C., Lin, C.-J.: A Practical Guide to Support Vector Classification. Department of Computer Science and Information Engineering, National Taiwan University, Taipei (2003)
19. Cui, Y., Lin, J.S., Zhang, S.L., Luo, S.H., Tian, Q.: Correlation-Based Feature Selection and Regression. Advances in Multimedia Information Processing-PCM, Pt I 6297, pp. 25–35 (2010)
20. Mitchell, T.M., Shinkareva, S.V., Carlson, A., Chang, K.M., Malave, V.L., Mason, R.A., Just, M.A.: Predicting human brain activity associated with the meanings of nouns. Science 320, pp. 1191–1195 (2008)
21. Hu, X., Deng, F., Li, K., Zhang, T., Chen, H., Jiang, X., Lv, J., Zhu, D., Faraco, C., Zhang, D., Mesbah, A., Han, J., Hua, X., Xie, L., Miller, S., Lei, G., Liu, T.: Bridging low-level features and high-level semantics via fMRI brain imaging for video classification. Proceedings of the International Conference on Multimedia (MM), Firenze, Italy, pp. 451–460 (2010)

Visual Analysis and Retrieval

Partitioned K-Means Clustering for Fast Construction of Unbiased Visual Vocabulary

Shikui Wei, Xinxiao Wu, and Dong Xu

Abstract Bag-of-Words (BoW) model has been widely used for feature representation in multimedia search area, in which a key step is to vector-quantize local image descriptors and generate a visual vocabulary. Popular visual vocabulary construction schemes generally perform a flat or hierarchical clustering operation using a very large training set in their original description space. However, these methods usually suffer from two issues: (1) A large training set is required to construct a large visual vocabulary, making the construction computationally inefficient; (2) The generated visual vocabularies are heavily biased towards the training samples. In this work, we introduce a partitioned k-means clustering (PKM) scheme to efficiently generate a large and unbiased vocabulary using only a small training set. Instead of directly clustering training descriptors in their original space, we first split the original space into a set of subspaces and then perform a separate k-means clustering process in each subspace. Sequentially, we can build a complete visual vocabulary by combining different cluster centroids from multiple subspaces. Comprehensive experiments demonstrate that the proposed method indeed generates unbiased vocabularies and provides good scalability for building large vocabularies.

Key words BoW • Image retrieval • Partitioned K-means clustering

S. Wei (✉)
Institute of Information Science, Beijing Jiaotong University, Beijing 100044, China

School of Computer Engineering, Nanyang Technological University, Singapore
e-mail: shkwei@gmail.com

X. Wu • D. Xu
School of Computer Engineering, Nanyang Technological University, Singapore
e-mail: xinxiaowu@ntu.edu.sg; dongxu@ntu.edu.sg

J.S. Jin et al., *The Era of Interactive Media*,
DOI 10.1007/978-1-4614-3501-3_40,

1 Introduction

Recently, Bag-of-Words model has become popular in multimedia search area due to its simplicity and effectiveness [10]. One key step of BoW model is to vector-quantize local image descriptors and generate a visual vocabulary [11]. Traditionally, a visual vocabulary is generated by directly clustering a large training set of local descriptors in their original description space and treating each cluster centroid as a visual word. Examples include flat k-means clustering (FKM) based vocabulary schemes [4, 12, 6]. Although these methods are quite effective, their time and space complexity are extremely high, making them unpractical for handling a large quantity of data [8]. To alleviate this problem, several improved clustering algorithms, such as approximate k-means clustering (AKM) [11] and hierarchical k-means clustering (HKM) [9, 13], are proposed for efficiently constructing visual vocabularies. Compared with the flat k-means clustering, these two schemes are more efficient in both vocabulary construction and visual word assignment, while they lead to a bigger quantization error.

However, a common characteristic of all abovementioned methods is that each visual word is generated by averaging over the description vectors falling in a certain cluster. In order to cover a large scope of varied image scenes, we need to build a very large visual vocabulary with hundreds of thousands or even millions of visual words. To do this, these methods require a very large training set for clustering, which lead to highly computational time and huge memory usage, especially for the high-dimensional image local descriptors. More importantly, since a cluster centroid (or visual word) is a feature vector obtained by averaging over the training descriptors within a certain cluster, it is similar to the training samples, leading to a biased visual vocabulary. While the biased visual vocabulary works well for some specific image datasets, it cannot meet the requirement in rapidly growing image database with diverse image content.

To address the above problems, we introduce a partitioned k-means clustering (PKM) scheme, which can build a large and unbiased visual vocabulary using a quite small training set. Instead of clustering the training samples in their original description space, we first split the full space into a set of subspaces and then cluster the training samples separately in each subspace. In this way, a visual subvocabulary is built in each subspace, where a visual subword is represented by a feature subvector. Sequentially combining different visual subwords in different visual subvocabularies by Cartesian product, we can construct a complete visual vocabulary. Since a large number of visual words that are very different from the training samples are generated by the combination operation, the vocabularies have the advantage of being readily applicable in arbitrary type of image datasets. That is, the newly coming image datasets with various scenes can be effectively represented by an existing visual vocabulary, which will avoid re-building a new index structure for new datasets. In addition, since the final vocabulary is generated from a small subvocabulary set, the memory usage is trivial even for storing a very large vocabulary.

2 Formulation of Partition Quantization

The basic idea of PKM is to decompose an unmanageably large task into some smaller sub-tasks [3]. Instead of directly quantizing the input vector in its entire space, PKM first partitions the entire vector into a number of subvectors with lower dimensionality, and then separately quantizes each subvector with its own vocabulary. That is, we need to construct the subvocabularies individually in subspaces [7].

Formally, we assume that the input vectors belong to a D-dimensional vector space $\mathbb{R}^D$, which can be the original feature space or its transformed space (e.g, PCA projection). $\mathbb{R}^D$ is divided into a set of subspaces, which is formulated as follows:

$$\mathbb{R}^D = (R_{b_0+1}^{b_1}, R_{b_1+1}^{b_2}, \cdots, R_{b_{N-1}+1}^{b_N}) \tag{1}$$

where $b_{i-1}+1$ and b_i determine the component boundaries of subspace $R_{b_{i-1}+1}^{b_i}$ in the original space $\mathbb{R}^D$. Note that all the subspaces are obtained by uniformly partitioning the space components into several groups. For example, a 128-dimensional space can be divided into two non-overlapped 64-dimensional subspaces.

For each input subspace $R_{b_{i-1}+1}^{b_i}$, a separate vector quantizer Q_i is constructed, which can be denoted as a 3-tuple:

$$Q_i = (V_i, R_{b_{i-1}+1}^{b_i}, F_i), \tag{2}$$

where,

$$V_i = \{v_i^1, v_i^2, \cdots, v_i^L\} \tag{3}$$

is a finite indexed subset of $R_{b_{i-1}+1}^{b_i}$, i.e. visual subvocabulary. v_i^j are the visual words in V_i, and L is the number of visual words. $R_{b_{i-1}+1}^{b_i}$ indicates the subspace in which the quantizer Q_i is built,

$$F_i : R_{b_{i-1}+1}^{b_i} \rightarrow V_i \tag{4}$$

is a mapping function which maps the input subvector $X_{b_{i-1}+1}^{b_i} \in R_{b_{i-1}+1}^{b_i}$ to a visual word in V_i according to the following rule:

$$F_i(X_{b_{i-1}+1}^{b_i}) = \arg\min_{v_i^j \in V_i} d(X_{b_{i-1}+1}^{b_i}, v_i^j) \tag{5}$$

where $d(X_{b_{i-1}+1}^{b_i}, v_i^j)$ is the Euclidian distance between the input subvector $X_{b_{i-1}+1}^{b_i}$ and visual word v_i^j.

After constructing individual quantizers in all subspaces, we can form a final quantizer by concatenating these subquantizers sequentially as follows:

$$Q = (Q_1, Q_2, \cdots, Q_N). \tag{6}$$

Now, given an input vector $X^D \in \mathbb{R}^D$, X^D is first partitioned into

$$X^D = (X_1^{b_1}, X_{b_1+1}^{b_2}, \cdots, X_{b_{N-1}+1}^{b_N}). \tag{7}$$

Then subvectors $X_{b_{i-1}+1}^{b_i}$ are individually quantized. Finally, the quantization results are combined to form final vector description. This process can be formulated as follows:

$$\begin{aligned} Q(X^D) &= (Q_1(X_1^{b_1}), Q_2(X_{b_1+1}^{b_2}), \cdots, Q_N(X_{b_{N-1}+1}^{b_N})) \\ &\to (F_1(X_1^{b_1}), F_2(X_{b_1+1}^{b_2}), \cdots, F_N(X_{b_{N-1}+1}^{b_N})) \end{aligned} \tag{8}$$

Since $F_i(X_{b_{i-1}+1}^{b_i}) \in V_i$, the final quantization result $Q(X^D)$ is in the Cartesian product V of the N subvocabularies, which is defined by

$$Q(X^D) \in V = V_1 \times V_2 \times \cdots \times V_N \tag{9}$$

As shown in (9), the final vocabulary is the Cartesian product of all N subvocabularies, which contains a large number of visual words different from training samples and thus effectively copes with the varied image datasets.

3 Image Search Framework with Visual Vocabulary from PKM

By mapping local descriptors to visual words, we can then describe the image with an collection of orderless visual words, i.e. Bag-of-Words. In this way, visual information search can be converted to the keyword-like search, and some indexing and searching methods in text retrieval area can be employed directly. In this section, we will present the details on the construction of visual vocabulary, indexing of image database, and searching using index structure.

3.1 Visual Vocabulary Construction

Using the squared error measure (SEM), we define

$$\|X^D - Q(X^D)\| = \sum\nolimits_{i=1}^{N} \|X_{b_i-1}^{b_i} - F_i(X_{b_i-1}^{b_i})\| \tag{10}$$

which indicates that we can minimize the global squared error by independently minimizing the squared error in each subquantizer. In fact, minimizing the squared error is an optimal problem. In our scheme, we use the k-means clustering method to perform this process, i.e, partitioned k-means clustering. Given the training set of images, the visual vocabulary construction process are detailed as follows:

1. Extract local descriptors (D-dimensional) from all the training images
2. Divide the description space into N subspaces $\{R_{b_{i-1}+1}^{b_i} | i = 1, 2, \cdots, N\}$
3. Perform independently k-means clustering on all descriptors in each subspace and form subvocabulary V_i with L visual words
4. Build the final vocabulary V by using Cartesian Product, i.e., $V = V_1 \times V_2 \times \cdots \times V_N$.

3.2 Image Database Indexing

In this section, we will detail the process of visual word assignment and image indexing. In this paper, we use the inverted table to index database images, which stores a mapping from visual words to the database images. Given a set of descriptor vectors $\{X^D\}$ extracted from all database images, the detailed mapping and indexing steps are given as follows:

1. Divide X^D into N subvectors $\{X_{b_{i-1}+1}^{b_i} | i = 1, 2, \cdots, N\}$
2. Quantize independently $X_{b_{i-1}+1}^{b_i}$ using quantizer Q_i
3. Form the final visual word by concatenating all the subwords.
4. If an inverted list has existed for this visual word, the image identifier of the descriptor is inserted as an entry to the list. Otherwise, build an inverted list first and then insert the entry.
5. Repeat the above steps until the descriptors in all database images are indexed.

3.3 Image Database Searching

Given one query image, we introduce how to quickly search similar images from the database. Since we have indexed all the database images using their visual words, the searching process is according to the inverted lists. Given the descriptor vectors $\{q^i\}$ extracted from the query image q, we describe the searching process as follows:

1. Quantize q^i and obtain a visual word $v_i \in V$ with steps 1–3 in indexing stage
2. Calculate the score $S(q^i, d_j)$ by voting ids of image d_j within inverted list of the visual word v_i
3. Repeat the above steps until all the descriptors in the query image are handled

4. Accumulate the scores of the same database image d_j by $S(q, d_j) = \sum_{i=1}^{Z} S(q^i, d_j)$, where Z is the total number of descriptors in the query image q
5. Sort database images according to their scores and return the top-ranked ones

For score calculation in steps 3 and 5, we employ a variant of tf-idf scheme in [5], which is generally used in the BoW-based image search systems.

4 Experiments

4.1 *Experimental Setup*

In our experiments, three classical visual vocabulary construction schemes, i.e. FKM, AKM (eight trees), and HKM (two layers), are implemented for comparison with the proposed PKM scheme. All the methods are evaluated on three public image datasets, i.e, Holiday photo dataset [1], Oxford building dataset [2], and Flickr1M dataset [1], which are all available online.

Performance evaluation is based on the mean average precision (MAP), which corresponds to an average area under the recall and precision curves over all queries. Note that for fair comparison, additional information such as multi-assignment and hamming embedding is not used in all the experiments.

4.2 *Impact of Training Data*

In this subsection, we will test the impact of training data type on different methods. To avoid overfitting problem, Holiday and Oxford datasets are crossly treated as database and training data. Figure 1 shows the experimental results, in which each column shows the sensitivity of one method on different training data and databases. As shown in Fig. 1a, e, the image search performance is very different when employing the vocabularies constructed from diverse training types. If the database is Holiday dataset, using the vocabularies from Holiday training data is clearly better than using Oxford training data as shown in Fig. 1(a), and vice versus. This means that the FKM scheme is remarkably affected by the training type and heavily biased towards the training samples. This observation also holds for the HKM and AKM schemes as shown in Fig. 1b, c, f, g.

In contrast, the performance curves from different training types in both Fig. 1d and h are relatively consistent with each other. For example, when the database is Holiday dataset, image search performance for two training types is nearly the same. This means that the PKM scheme is not heavily dependent on the type of training samples, leading to more stable performance for diverse databases.

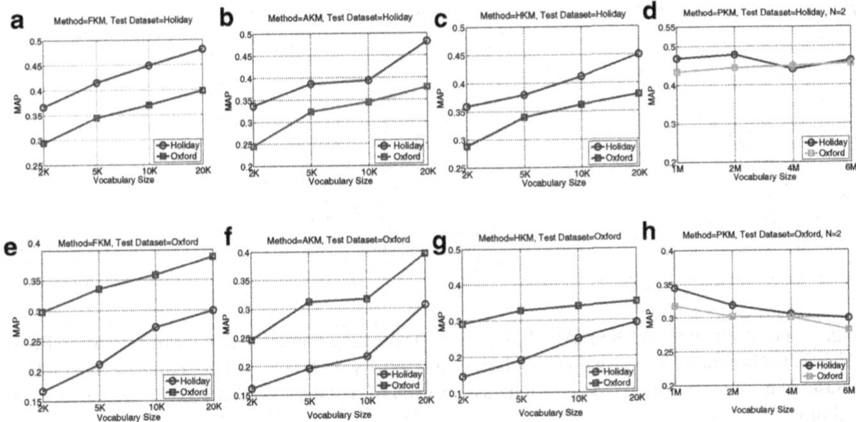

Fig. 1 The effect of training data type on image search performance for different datasets. The sensitivity of FKM, AKM (8 trees, 500 checking points), HKM (two layers) and PKM on different training data and databases is shown in subfigures (**a**,**e**), (**b**,**f**), (**c**,**g**) and (**d**,**h**), respectively

4.3 Scalability

One key advantage of PKM scheme is that it can easily generate a large and unbiased visual vocabulary using only a small training set. In this subsection, we will show the capability of various methods for building large-scale vocabularies given a fixed number of training samples. Here, the number of training descriptors is fixed to 1 M.

For FKM, AKM,and HKM schemes, it's impossible to build a visual vocabulary larger than 1 M visual words due to their intrinsic properties. In contrast, the proposed PKM scheme can easily generate a huge vocabulary that can be much larger than the size of training set. However, a large vocabulary can provide more discriminative capability and thus remarkably improve the image search performance, as shown in Fig. 2. Therefore, this property of PKM is crucial for boosting image search effectiveness and efficiency, since a small size of training set means less computational cost for vocabulary construction and a large vocabulary means more discriminative capability for distinguishing more images. That is, the proposed PKM scheme can easily handle large-scale image database.

Note that PKM scheme cannot perform better than other three schemes with the same size of vocabulary. The possible explanation is that a large number of visual words in PKM vocabulary may never occur in image database. This means that only a small part of vocabulary is actually employed during the image indexing procedure. This problem can be readily solved in the PKM scheme by increasing the size of visual vocabulary.

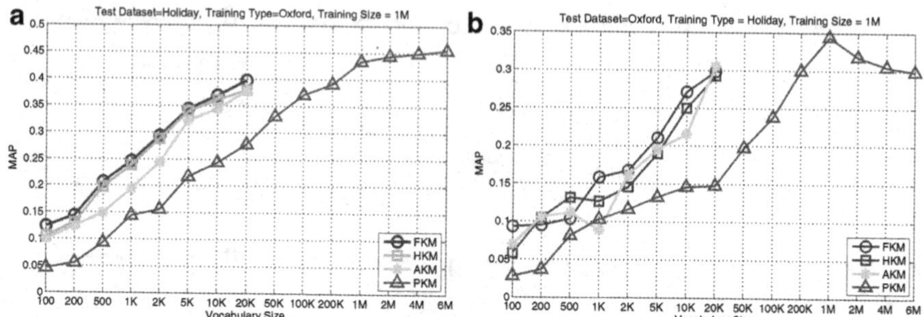

Fig. 2 The scalability of FKM, AKM (8 trees, 500 checking points), HKM (two layers) and PKM (N = 2) for building large visual vocabularies. (**a**) Holiday dataset is used for database and Oxford dataset is used for training; (**b**) Oxford dataset is used for database and Holiday dataset is used for training

4.4 Complexity Evaluation

In this subsection, we analyze the space and time complexity of different visual vocabulary construction schemes. Since the on-line query stage is more important for users, we only discuss the complexity in the searching process.

For space complexity, we consider the main memory usage during index structure (here, the inverted table) loading and query preprocessing. In fact, the size of the classical inverted table is proportioned to the number of local image descriptors in all database images. Since we use the same index structure for all the methods, the memory usage is the same for all the methods. Therefore, the main difference lies in the query preprocessing step. For FKM and HKM schemes, the memory usage is only related to the size of visual vocabulary and descriptor dimension, i.e, $O(K * D)$. However, the HKM scheme requires more space, as the intermediate nodes need to be stored to accelerate the assignment process. For the AKM scheme, more memory is needed for constructing random forests, which is generally much larger than the vocabulary itself. In contrast, the space complexity of PKM scheme is only $O(K^{1/m} * D)$. Clearly, the space complexity of PKM scheme is much lower than three commonly used schemes.

For time complexity, the main computational cost in the searching process lies in the word assignment and score voting processes. In the word assignment, the main cost lies in searching nearest visual words. For FKM-based image search system, the computational cost is linearly increased with respect to the vocabulary size K, leading to a complexity of $O(K)$. In addition to the vocabulary size, the computational cost of the HKM- and PKM-based image search systems is also related to the number of layers l and the number of subspaces N, respectively. For a fixed K, the time complexity of HKM and PKM is $O(K^{1/l})$ and $O(K^{1/N}/N)$, respectively. Therefore, if l and N are the same, the PKM clearly outperforms HKM in terms of efficiency. The AKM-based image search system has been reported in [11] to have the same computational complexity with the HKM method. However,

Table 1 Time costs (seconds) on word assignment for different image search schemes. Two layers for HKM, eight trees for AKM with 5 and 500 checking points, two subspaces for PKM

	Vocabulary size						
Method	1 K	2 K	5 K	10 K	20 K	1 M	4 M
FKM	195.09	384.58	987.94	1989.72	4,023.03	N/A	N/A
HKM	66.45	74.11	94.91	97.38	120	638.41	N/A
AKM-5	344.69	382.06	385.88	390.72	446	1,011.27	N/A
AKM-500	14,852.16	13,421.75	11,772.44	12,203.39	12,482.13	11,838.53	N/A
PKM	**37.45**	**39.34**	**49.08**	**53.50**	**63.95**	**280.44**	**560.02**

Table 2 Time costs (seconds) on score voting for different image search schemes. Two layers for HKM, eight trees for AKM, two subspaces for PKM

	Vocabulary size						
Method	1 K	2 K	5 K	10 K	20 K	1 M	4 M
FKM	320.670	210.34	153.83	115.52	109.20	N/A	N/A
HKM	331.39	207.48	138.28	115.83	99.70	82.13	N/A
AKM	337.11	233.84	154.56	113.13	102	84.77	N/A
PKM	**622.63**	**467.38**	**298.34**	**197.84**	**148.02**	**86.47**	**83.95**

it becomes less efficient when increasing the number of random trees and the number of points to be checked, especially for a large visual vocabulary. The experimental results in Table 1 also validate these observations.

The second time-consuming process is from the score voting process. In essential, the voting process is to accumulate the scores between query descriptors and matched database descriptors. Therefore, its cost is related to the number of query descriptors and their matched descriptors, i.e., $O(N_q * N_{ave})$. Here, $N_{ave} = N_{total}/K$ is the average number of entries in a cell, and N_{total} is the number of all descriptors in the database. these factors are the same for all the methods. However, the proposed PKM scheme is slower than other schemes with the same vocabulary size, as shown in Table 2. The possible explanation is it is more unbalanced for the PKM scheme to map local image descriptors into cells, which will decrease the voting efficiency [4]. In fact, voting efficiency can be dramatically improved by employing large visual vocabularies, this problem can be easily solved by the PKM scheme as it can efficiently generate very large visual vocabularies. Note that all the results are obtained by using a computer with 2.80 GHZ Intel Xeon X5660 CPU, 32 GB RAM and matlab implementation.

In brief, when we employ large visual vocabularies, the proposed PKM scheme outperforms other schemes in terms of total computational cost from word assignment and score voting.

4.5 Evaluation on Large-Scale Image Search

In this subsection, we evaluate the image search effectiveness of the proposed method on the large-scale image database. We evaluate all systems on two

Table 3 Evaluation on large-scale image search

Method	*TrainingSet − TestSet*	
	Holiday-Oxford	Oxford-Holiday
FKM-1M	N/A	N/A
AKM-1M	0.152862	0.232586
HKM-1M	0.171809	0.229290
PKM-1M	**0.186245**	**0.225464**
PKM-4M	**0.180939**	**0.253320**

large-scale databases, i.e. Flickr1M + Holiday and Flickr1M + Oxford datasets, which contain over 1M images. The SIFT descriptors are extracted and also available online [1, 2]. Table 3 lists the experimental results. After removing the effect of overfitting, the proposed PKM scheme achieves comparable or better performance to the existing methods even when the vocabulary size is the same. For example, using Holiday dataset as training data and Oxford dataset as test data, the MAP of PKM is 0.186245, which is better than the AKM and HKM schemes with the same vocabulary size of 1 M. Increasing the vocabulary size, which is easy and fast for the PKM scheme, can further improve the image search performance. If we increase the vocabulary size to 4 M, the PKM can significantly improve the image search performance from 0.225464 to 0.253320 for Holiday dataset. The experimental results validate again the advantages of proposed scheme for handling the biased vocabulary problem. Note that the performance slightly degrades for the Oxford dataset when increasing the visual vocabulary size to 4 M. The explanation is that only a small set of local descriptors in the query image takes part in the query process. When K is extreme huge, there are a large number of null cells in the inverted table. Therefore, the probability of mapping all query descriptors to null cells is high for the Oxford test dataset. The experimental results in Fig. 2(a) also indicates this observation.

5 Conclusions

To effectively handle different image datasets, this paper introduces the PKM scheme to build the large and unbiased visual vocabularies. In contrast to the existing methods that directly build visual vocabularies in the original description space, the proposed method splits the original space into a set of subspaces and constructs sub-vocabularies separately in these subspaces. By combining all the sub-vocabularies via Cartesian product, a complete visual vocabulary can be formed. Comprehensive experiments demonstrate that the proposed method indeed generates unbiased visual vocabularies and achieves promising performance in terms of image search effectiveness and efficiency. Our future work will focus on analysis for the distribution of visual words with non-null cells in a quantitative fashion.

Acknowledgements This paper is partially supported by the Singapore National Research Foundation & Interactive Digital Media R & D Program Office, MDA under research grant NRF2008IDM-IDM004-018 and also partially supported by Singapore A*STAR SERC Grant (082 101 0018).

References

1. http://lear.inrialpes.fr/people/jegou/data.php\#holidays.
2. http://www.robots.ox.ac.uk/~vgg/data/oxbuildings/index.html.
3. A. Gersho and R. Gray. *Vector quantization and signal compression*. Kulwer Academic Publishers, 1992.
4. H. Jegou, M. Douze, and C. Schmid. Improving bag-of-features for large scale image search. *IJCV*, pages 1–21.
5. H. Jegou, M. Douze, and C. Schmid. Hamming embedding and weak geometric consistency for large scale image search. In *ECCV*, pages 304–317, 2008.
6. H. Jégou, M. Douze, and C. Schmid. Product quantization for nearest neighbor search. *T-PAMI*, pages 117–128, 2010.
7. G. Motta, F. Rizzo, and J. Storer. Partitioned vector quantization: application to lossless compression of hyperspectral images. In *ICASSP*, pages 241–244.
8. Y. Mu, J. Sun, T. Han, L. Cheong, and S. Yan. Randomized locality sensitive vocabularies for bag-of-features model. *ECCV*, pages 748–761, 2010.
9. D. Nister and H. Stewenius. Scalable recognition with a vocabulary tree. In *CVPR*, volume 5, 2006.
10. E. Nowak, F. Jurie, and B. Triggs. Sampling strategies for bag-of-features image classification. In *LNCS*, volume 3954, pages 490–503, 2006.
11. J. Philbin, O. Chum, M. Isard, J. Sivic, and A. Zisserman. Object retrieval with large vocabularies and fast spatial matching. In *CVPR*, pages 1575–1589, 2007.
12. J. Sivic and A. Zisserman. Video Google: A text retrieval approach to object matching in videos. In *ICCV*, volume 2, pages 1470–1477, 2003.
13. S. Zhang, Q. Huang, G. Hua, S. Jiang, W. Gao, and Q. Tian. Building contextual visual vocabulary for large-scale image applications. In *Proc. ACM Multimedia*.

Component-Normalized Generalized Gradient Vector Flow for Snakes

Yao Zhao, Ce Zhu, Lunming Qin, Huihui Bai, and Huawei Tian

Abstract The abstract should summarize the contents of the paper and should contain at least 70 and at most 150 words. It should be written using the *abstract* environment. Snakes, or active contours, have been widely used for image segmentation. An external force for snakes called gradient vector flow (GVF) largely addresses traditional snake problems of initialization sensitivity and poor convergence to concavities, and generalized GVF (GGVF) aims to improve GVF snake convergence to long and thin indentations. In this paper, we find and show that in the case of long and thin even-width indentations, GGVF generally fails to work. We identify the crux of the convergence problem, and accordingly propose a new external force termed as component-normalized GGVF (CN-GGVF) to eliminate the problem. CN-GGVF is obtained by normalizing each component of initial GGVF vectors with respect to its own magnitude. Comparisons against GGVF snakes show that the proposed CN-GGVF snakes can capture long and thin indentations regardless of odd or even widths with remarkably faster convergence speeds, and achieve lower computational complexity in vector normalization.

Keywords Active contour models • Snakes • Convergence • External force • Gradient vector flow (GVF)

Y. Zhao (✉) • L. Qin • H. Bai • H. Tian
Institute of Information Science Beijing Key Laboratory of Advanced Information Science and Network Technology, Beijing Jiaotong University, Beijing 100044, China
e-mail: yzhao@bjtu.edu.cn.; lunming.qin@hotmail.com

C. Zhu
School of Electrical and Electronic Engineering, Nanyang Technological University, Singapore 639798, Singapore
e-mail: eczhu@ntu.edu.sg

J.S. Jin et al., *The Era of Interactive Media*,
DOI 10.1007/978-1-4614-3501-3_41, © Springer Science+Business Media, LLC 2013

1 Introduction

Since snakes, or active contours, were first proposed by Kass et al. in 1987 [1], they have become one of the most active and successful research areas in image processing applications [2]. Snakes are curves defined within an image domain that deform under the influence of internal and external forces to conform to desired features (like edges). Internal forces defined within the curve itself are determined by the geometric properties of the curve, while external forces are derived from the image data, which have been the most discussed issue in snakes.

An energy function associated with the curve is defined, so that the problem of finding desired features is converted into an energy minimization process. Due to its high efficiency, snake model has found many applications, including edge detection [1], shape recovery [3], object tracking [4, 5], and image segmentation [6, 7]. However, there are two key shortcomings with the traditional snake. First, the initial contour must be close enough to the desired features, otherwise the snake will likely converge to a wrong result. Second, it is difficult for the snake to move into boundary concavities [8].

An external force for snakes, called gradient vector flow (GVF) [9], was introduced to largely overcome both the limitations of the traditional snake. GVF is computed as a diffusion of the gradient vectors of a gray-level or binary edge map derived from an image. Although GVF has been widely used and improved in various models [4, 5, 10], it still exhibits some defects, such as the difficulty in forcing a snake into long and thin indentations as well as noise sensitivity. In [11], Xu and Prince proposed a generalized version of GVF (GGVF) by introducing two spatially varying weighting functions, which has been reported to improve GVF snake convergence to long and thin indentations as well as robustness to noise.

In this work, we find that when the width of the long and thin indentation is an even number of pixels, whatever parameter values are selected, the GGVF snake generally fails to move into the indentation. Since external forces are defined to move the contour toward the desired features, we reasonably conjecture that in order to drive the GVF or GGVF snake into a long and thin indentation, (at least) a concatenated and interruption-free pixel line from the top to the bottom within the indentation must be present, where each pixel has an external force component with a significant magnitude pointing to the bottom. We derive that such the directionally consistent external force components are very small at some points which are easily obliterated in the vector-based normalization in GGVF.

To completely eliminate the obliteration problem, we propose a new external force for snakes, termed component-normalized GGVF (CN-GGVF), which is obtained by normalizing each component of initial GGVF vectors with respect to its own magnitude. The component-based vector normalization method levels up the weights of the directionally consistent external force components so as to deal successfully with the obliteration problem. As an enhancement of the original vector-based normalization in GGVF, the proposed component-based one has lower computational complexity. Experimental results and comparisons against the GGVF snake demonstrate that the proposed CN-GGVF snake exhibits the capability of capturing long and thin indentations regardless of odd or even widths with remarkably fast convergence speed.

The remainder of the paper is organized as follows. Section 2 reviews the traditional snake, GVF and GGVF snakes, and gives some new observations on the GGVF model. Section 3 investigates the GGVF fields within the long and thin indentations to find the real crux of the convergence problem. Section 4 presents the proposed CN-GGVF snake. The performance of the CN-GGVF snake is examined in Sect. 5 and the conclusion is given in Sect. 6.

2 Background and New Observations

2.1 Traditional Snake Model

A traditional snake is represented by a parametric curve $\mathbf{c}(s) = [x(s), y(s)]$, $s \in [0, 1]$, that deforms through the spatial domain of an image to minimize the energy function [1]

$$E(\mathbf{c}(s)) = \int_0^1 \left[\frac{1}{2}(\alpha|\mathbf{c}'(s)|^2 + \beta|\mathbf{c}''(s)|^2) + E_{ext}(\mathbf{c}(s))\right] ds \tag{1}$$

where $\mathbf{c}'(s)$ and $\mathbf{c}''(s)$ are the first and second derivatives of $\mathbf{c}(s)$ with respect to s, and α and β are weighting parameters controlling the snake's tension and rigidity, respectively. The first two terms within the above integral stand for the internal energy. The external energy $E_{ext}(\mathbf{c}(s))$ derived from the image data takes on its smaller values at the desired features. Typical external energy functions for a gray-level image $I(x, y)$ for seeking step edges are given as [1]

$$E_{ext}^{(1)}(x, y) = -|\nabla I(x, y)|^2 \tag{2}$$

$$E_{ext}^{(2)}(x, y) = -|\nabla[G_\sigma(x, y) * I(x, y)]|^2 \tag{3}$$

where ∇ is the gradient operator, $G_\sigma(x, y)$ is a 2-D Gaussian function with standard deviation σ, and $*$ denotes linear convolution. Representative external energy functions for a line-drawing (black on white) [12] are

$$E_{ext}^{(3)}(x, y) = I(x, y) \tag{4}$$

$$E_{ext}^{(4)}(x, y) = G_\sigma(x, y) * I(x, y). \tag{5}$$

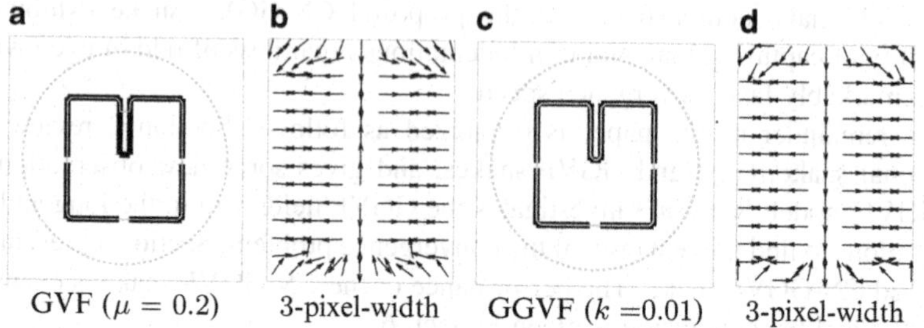

Fig. 1 Line-drawing of a square with a long and thin 3-pixel-width indentation and broken boundaries overlapped with an initial (*dashed line*) and the resulting (*solid line*) (**a**) GVF snake ($\mu = 0.2$ and $n = 160$) and (**c**) GGVF snake ($k = 0.01$ and $n = 160$). (**b**) GVF and (**d**) GGVF fields, sampled by a factor of 3 in y direction, within the indentation

To minimize $E(\mathbf{c}(s))$, the snake has to evolve dynamically as a function of time t, given by

$$\mathbf{c}_t(s,t) = \alpha\mathbf{c}''(s,t) - \beta\mathbf{c}''''(s,t) - \nabla E_{ext}(\mathbf{c}(s,t)). \tag{6}$$

A numerical solution of $\mathbf{c}(s, t)$ on a discrete grid can be obtained by discretizing (6) and solving the discrete equation iteratively from an initial contour $\mathbf{c}(s, 0)$[1, 13].

2.2 GVF Snake Model

Xu and Prince proposed gradient vector flow (GVF) [9] as an external force for snakes to largely overcome the two key shortcomings of the traditional snake. The GVF field $\mathbf{v}(x, y) = [u(x, y), v(x, y)]$ is defined as the equilibrium solution of the following partial differential equation:

$$\mathbf{v}_t(x,y,t) = \mu\nabla^2\mathbf{v}(x,y,t) - |\nabla f|^2[\mathbf{v}(x,y,t) - \nabla f] \tag{7}$$

where $\mathbf{v}_t(x, y, t)$ is the partial derivative of $\mathbf{v}(x, y, t)$ with respect to t, and $\nabla^2 = \partial^2/\partial x^2 + \partial^2/\partial y^2$ denotes the Laplacian operator. f is an edge map derived from the image and defined to have larger values at the desired features, which is typically the additive inverse of an external energy function as given in (2)–(5). μ controls the smoothness degree of the GVF field and should be set according to the noise level in the image (larger μ for higher noise levels).

Figure 1a, b illustrates the performance of a GVF snake in capturing a long and thin indentation. Figure 1a shows a 160 $\times$160-pixel line-drawing of a square-shaped object (shown in black) with a long and thin 3-pixel-width indentation and broken boundaries. It also displays both the initial and resulting GVF snakes ($\alpha = 0.1$ and $\beta = 0$) marked by dashed and solid lines, respectively. Figure 1b shows the GVF field within the 3-pixel-width indentation, which is sampled by a factor of 3 in y direction.

For the GVF snake, there is an iterative process used to diffuse the external force vectors. In computation of the GVF field, the iteration number (denoted as n) required to solve the partial differential equation (7) for an $n_1 \times n_2$-pixel image is $\sqrt{n_1 \times n_2}$ [9]. As shown in Fig. 1a, the GVF snake ($\mu = 0.2$ and $n = 160$) converges after $w = 200$ iterations, where w denotes the number of iterations for contour convergence in this and the following experiments. Clearly, the snake cannot converge completely to the true boundary within the indentation.

2.3 GGVF Snake Model and New Observations

By introducing two spatially varying weighting functions in the GVF formulation, Xu and Prince proposed an external force referred to as generalized gradient vector flow (GGVF) [11]. GGVF was reported to improve GVF snake convergence to long and thin indentations and robustness to noise. The GGVF field is defined as the equilibrium solution of the following vector partial differential equation:

$$\mathbf{v}_t(x, y, t) = g(|\nabla f|)\nabla^2 \mathbf{v}(x, y, t) - h(|\nabla f|)[\mathbf{v}(x, y, t) - \nabla f] \quad (8)$$

where

$$g(|\nabla f|) = \exp(-|\nabla f|/k) \quad (9)$$

$$h(|\nabla f|) = 1 - \exp(-|\nabla f|/k). \quad (10)$$

The parameter k regulates to some extent the tradeoff between the first term (known as smoothing term) and the second term (known as data term) in the right hand of (8) and it should be set according to the amount of noise in the image (larger k for more noise).

The GGVF field computed using (9) and (10) as its weighting functions tends to conform to the edge map gradients at strong edges, but to vary smoothly away from the boundaries. The partial differential equation (8) can be implemented using an explicit finite difference scheme [9]. The scheme is stable if the time step Δt and the spatial sample intervals Δx and Δy satisfy $\Delta t \leq \Delta x \Delta y / 4 g_{\max}$, where $g_{\max}$ is the maximum value of $g(|\nabla f|)$. There is also an implicit scheme for the numerical implementation of (8), which is unconditionally stable but slower than the explicit one [11].

Figure 1c, d illustrates the performance of a GGVF snake on the above line-drawing. The initialization and the selection of the parameters α, β, and n of the GGVF snake are the same as the GVF snake in Fig. 1a. Superposed on the original image, the initial and stabilized GGVF snakes are marked by a dashed line and a solid line, respectively, as shown in Fig. 1c. Figure 1d shows the GGVF field within the 3-pixel-width indentation, which is also sampled by a factor of 3 in y direction. After $w = 200$ iterations, the GGVF snake ($k = 0.01$ and $n = 160$) succeeds in converging completely to the 3-pixel-width indentation from the far-off initialization.

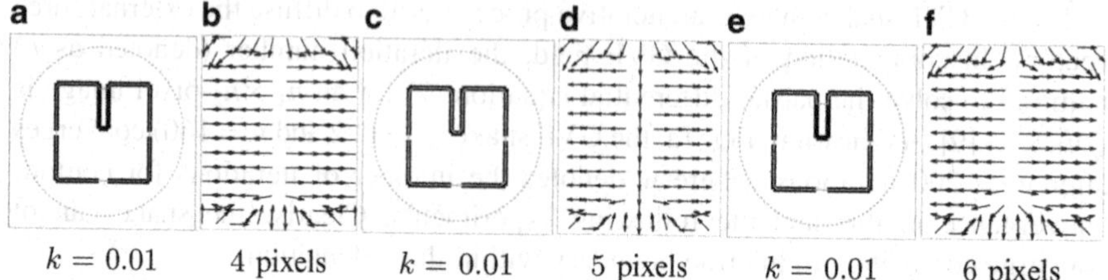

Fig. 2 Initial (*dashed line*) and stabilized (*solid line*) GGVF snake ($k = 0.01$ and $n = 160$) on a line-drawing with a long and thin (**a**) 4-, (**c**) 5-, and (**e**) 6-pixel-width indentation. The corresponding vector fields within the (**b**) 4-, (**d**) 5-, and (**f**) 6-pixel-width indentations

However, we find that when the width of the long and thin indentation is an even number of pixels, the GGVF snake generally fails to converge to the indentation. Figure 2 shows the performance of the GGVF snake ($k = 0.01$ and $n = 160$) in capturing the long and thin 4-, 5-, and 6-pixel-width indentations. The initialization and the parameters of the GGVF snake are the same as those in Fig. 1. As shown in Fig. 2, the GGVF snakes converge after $w = 200$ iterations. The GGVF snake in Fig. 2c can converge completely to the 5-pixel-width indentation. However, it fails to move into the long and thin 4- and 6-pixel-width indentations, as shown in Fig. 2a and e, respectively. Note that whatever the relevant parameters are selected, the GGVF snake generally cannot detect the even-width indentation. The corresponding GGVF fields, sampled by a factor of 3 in y direction, within the 4-, 5-, and 6-pixel-width indentations, are shown in Fig. 2b, d, and f, respectively.

3 Problem Identification and Analysis

3.1 *Desired External Force Field for Capturing Long and Thin Indentations*

Since external forces generally play a decisive role in driving snakes to the desired features, we conjecture that in order to move the GVF or GGVF snake into a long and thin indentation, (at least) a concatenated and interruption-free pixel line from the top to the bottom within the indentation must be present, where each pixel has an external force component with a significant magnitude pointing to the bottom.

As displayed in Fig. 1b, since there are some upward external forces within the 3-pixel-width indentation, the GVF field fails to move the snake into the indentation. As shown in Figs. 1d and 2d, due to the consistent downward and significant external forces within the odd-width indentation, the GGVF snake can successfully converge to the odd-width indentation. On the other hand, because there are no consistent downward external forces within the even-width indentation, as shown in Fig. 2b, f, the GGVF snake is unable to detect the even-width indentation.

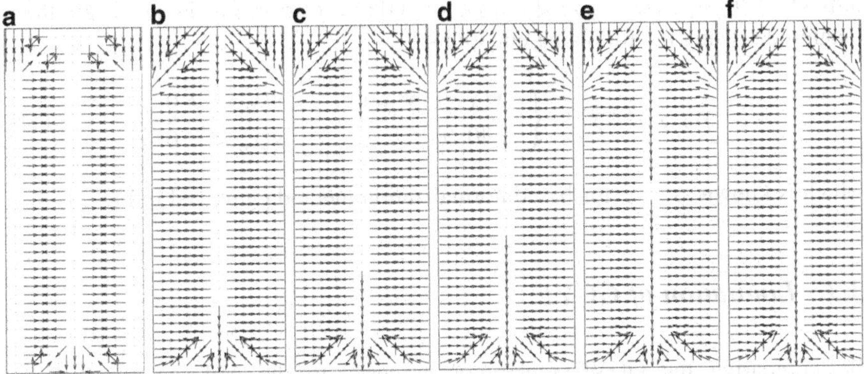

Fig. 3 Normalized GGVF fields ($k = 0.\ 01$) within the 3-pixel-width indentation with (**a**) $n = 0$, (**b**) $n = 4$, (**c**) $n = 8$, (**d**) $n = 12$, (**e**) $n = 16$, and (**f**) $n = 20$

3.2 Generation of the Desired External Force Field

As described in [11], GGVF is computed as a diffusion of the gradient vectors of a gray-level or binary edge map derived from an image. The GGVF field calculated using (8) tends to conform to the edge map gradients at strong edges, but to vary smoothly away from the boundaries. Consequently, the GGVF external forces in each homogeneous region are mainly generated from the diffusion of the edge map gradients at its own boundary (those from other regions appear to be shielded by these edge map gradients). Specifically, the GGVF vectors in Fig. 1d within the long and thin 3-pixel-width indentation are primarily generated from the diffusion of the edge map gradients at the indentation boundary. Because there are no vertical components of the edge map gradients at both sides of the indentation, we conclude that the downward external force components are derived from the edge map gradients at the top or the bottom of the indentation, or both.

Using an edge map obtained from the original image shown in Fig. 1, an iterative process of computing GGVF field ($k = 0.\ 01$) within the 3-pixel-width indentation is illustrated in Fig. 3. The initial vector field, i.e., the gradient of the edge map, is shown zoomed in Fig. 3a. The GGVF fields after 4, 8, 12, 16, and 20 iterations are shown zoomed in Fig. 3b–f, respectively. The generation process demonstrates that the consistent downward external force components are derived from the edge map gradients at both the top and bottom of the indentation. The diffusion process of the GGVF field within the 5-pixel-width indentation can also be obtained, which is almost the same as in Fig. 3.

Note that after diffusion, external forces are normalized as unit vectors to make the snake evolve at a constant speed in actual implementations. In GGVF [11], the initial GGVF vectors $\mathbf{v}(x, y) = [u(x, y), v(x, y)]$ are normalized with respect to their magnitudes using the following equations:

$$\mathbf{v}_{vn-ggvf}(x,y) = \begin{cases} \mathbf{v}(x,y)/|\mathbf{v}(x,y)|, & |\mathbf{v}(x,y)| \neq 0 \\ [0,0], & |\mathbf{v}(x,y)| = 0 \end{cases} \tag{11}$$

which is known as a vector-based normalization method employed in Figs. 1–3.

3.3 *Limitation of GGVF*

By comparing the GGVF snake convergences to the odd- and even-width indentations in Figs. 1 and 2, we find that there is only one difference among all the initial conditions, that is the indentation width. As described above, the consistent downward external force components within the odd-width indentation are derived from the edge map gradients at both the top and bottom of the indentation. Due to the only change in the indentation width, it is concluded that the edge map gradients at both the top and bottom also generate the consistent downward external force components within the even-width indentation.

As shown in Figs. 1d and 2d, the edge map gradients at both sides of the indentation are symmetric about the middle column of pixels within the odd-width indentation. From (8) we can derive that at the points of the middle column, the external forces generated from these horizontal edge map gradients are counteracted with each other. Therefore, only the downward external force components are present at the points of the middle column. After performing the vector-based normalization (11), there are consistent downward external forces with magnitude 1 within the odd-width indentation.

However, when the indentation width is an even number of pixels, there does not exist such a middle column of pixels. The horizontal components are present at every point within the indentation. Since there are no consistent downward external force components within the even-width indentation in Fig. 2b, f, we reasonably conjecture that the downward components are very small at some points within the indentation. These components are readily obliterated by their orthogonal counterparts when calculated by the vector-based normalization (11). To solve the obliteration problem of our conjecture, we should increase the downward external force components to make them play a leading role in driving the snake into the long and thin even-width indentation.

4 CN-GGVF Snake: The Proposed Model

The above analysis suggests that the external force components pointing toward the bottoms of the even-width indentations should be powerful enough to overcome the conjectural obliteration problem. To achieve this purpose, a new class of external force called component-normalized generalized gradient vector flow (CN-GGVF) is introduced in this paper. CN-GGVF is calculated by separately normalizing each component of initial GGVF vectors with respect to its own magnitude.

The CN-GGVF field $\mathbf{v}_{cn-ggvf}(x,y) = [u_{cn-ggvf}(x,y), v_{cn-ggvf}(x,y)]$ is defined as

$$\mathbf{v}_{cn-ggvf}(x,y) = [sgn(u(x,y)), sgn(v(x,y))] \tag{12}$$

where $sgn(\cdot)$ is the sign function, and $u(x, y)$ and $v(x, y)$ are the x- and y-components, respectively, of the external force at (x, y) in the GGVF field. As mentioned in Sect. 2.3, the numerical implementation of the partial differential equation (8) specifying GGVF can use either an explicit finite difference method which must satisfy a stable condition, or an implicit scheme that is unconditionally stable [11].

Equation (12) is actually a vector normalization approach. Relative to (11), (12) is referred to as component-based normalization. Note that the magnitudes of the normalized GGVF vectors calculated by (11) are usually equal to 1, while those of the CN-GGVF vectors are $\sqrt{2}$ generally. To normalize an initial GGVF field derived from an image of $N \times N$ pixels, the vector-based normalization needs $2 \times N \times N$ multiplication operations, $2 \times N \times N$ division operations, and $N \times N$ square root operations. While the proposed component-based normalization only requires $2 \times N \times N$ comparison operations, comparing favorably to the computational complexity of the original one.

We call the active contour that uses the CN-GGVF field as its external force a CN-GGVF snake. By replacing the standard external force $-\nabla E_{ext}(\mathbf{c}(s))$ in (6) with a CN-GGVF field $\mathbf{v}_{cn-ggvf}(x, y)$, we obtain the corresponding dynamic CN-GGVF snake equation as

$$\mathbf{c}_t(s,t) = \alpha\mathbf{c}''(s,t) - \beta\mathbf{c}''''(s,t) + \mathbf{v}_{cn-ggvf}(\mathbf{c}(s,t)) \tag{13}$$

which can be solved numerically using the identical finite element approach of the traditional snake given in Sect. 2.1. The properties of the CN-GGVF snakes are shown below.

5 Experimental Results and Analysis

In this section, the performance of the CN-GGVF snake in capturing the long and thin indentations is tested. We also compare the performance of the GGVF and CN-GGVF snakes on a real photographic image. The snakes are dynamically reparameterized during deformation to maintain contour point separation to within 0. 5–1. 5 pixels. All edge maps used in active contours are normalized to the range [0, 1].

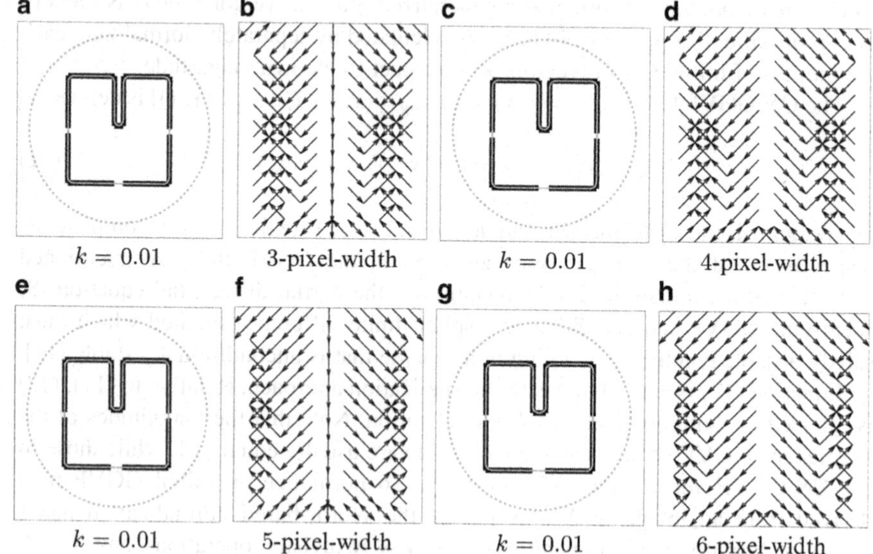

Fig. 4 Initial (*dashed line*) and stabilized (*solid line*) CN-GGVF snake ($k = 0.01$ and $n = 160$) on a line-drawing with a long and thin (**a**) 3-, (**c**) 4-, (**e**) 5-, and (**g**) 6-pixel-width indentation. The corresponding CN-GGVF field, sampled by a factor of 3 in the y direction, within the (**b**) 3-, (**d**) 4-, (**f**) 5-, and (**h**) 6-pixel-width indentation

5.1 Convergence to Long and Thin Indentations

Figure 4 shows the performance of the CN-GGVF snakes on the above line-drawings with long and thin 3-, 4-, 5-, and 6-pixel-width indentations. All initial conditions are the same as the GGVF snakes in Figs. 1 and 2. Specifically, the parameters for the CN-GGVF snakes are set as $\alpha = 0.1$, $\beta = 0$, $k = 0.01$, and $n = 160$. An edge map $-I(x, y)$ is used to compute all external force fields. All stabilized snakes indicated by solid lines are derived from the same initialization marked by a dashed line.

As shown in Fig. 4, after the initial GGVF vectors are normalized by (12), the consistent downward and significant external force components are present at every point within all long and thin indentations. The vector fields within the even-width indentations in Fig. 4d and h confirm our conjecture that the consistent downward external force components are certainly present, and considerably smaller than their orthogonal counterparts. All CN-GGVF snakes are able to converge completely to the long and thin indentations after only $w = 120$ iterations, comparing favorably to the required iterations for all the GGVF snake convergences.

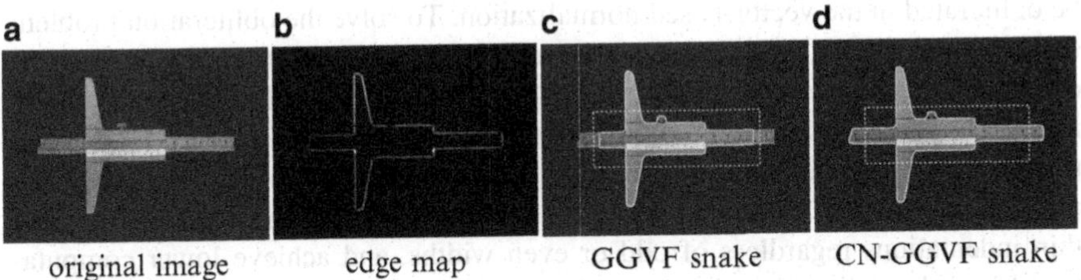

Fig. 5 (**a**) 423 ×600-pixel photographic image of a depth vernier caliper. (**b**) Edge map $|\nabla[G_\sigma(x,y) * I(x,y)]|^2$ with $\sigma = 3$. Results (*solid lines*) of the (**c**) GGVF and (**d**) CN-GGVF snakes ($\alpha = 1$, $\beta = 0$, $k = 2$, and $n = 200$) from the same initialization (*dashed line*)

5.2 *Real Photographic Image*

An experiment is performed on a photographic image to show an improved performance of the CN-GGVF snake over the GGVF snake. Figure 5a shows an original 423 × 600-pixel image of a vernier depth gauge. Figure 5b displays an edge map of the photographic image calculated by $|\nabla[G_\sigma(x,y) * I(x,y)]|^2$. The Gaussian filter with $\sigma = 3$ is employed to suppress the noise. Figure 5c and d shows the resulting GGVF and CN-GGVF snakes, respectively. Both the stabilized snakes (solid lines) with $\alpha = 1$ and $\beta = 0$ are derived from the same initialization (dashed line).

In this experiment, the goal is to segment the vernier depth gauge. As shown in Fig. 5c, the GGVF snake ($k = 2$ and $n = 200$) converges after $w = 800$ iterations, which is unable to move into the long and thin indentation at either side of the vernier depth gauge. The main reason for the failure is that the external force components pulling the snake to the desired boundary within the indentations are too small to prevail over the internal forces. In contrast, after only 150 iterations, the CN-GGVF snake ($k = 2$ and $n = 200$) in Fig. 5d converges to the true boundary precisely from the same initialization. Note that if the initialization is closer to the true boundary or more appropriate parameter values are selected, the GGVF snake may also perform well. From another point of view, this experiment also exemplifies the CN-GGVF snake robustness to initialization and parameter variations.

6 Conclusion

In this paper, we find and show that the GGVF snake is generally incapable of converging to long and thin even-width indentations regardless of the parameter value choices. We have identified the cause behind the convergence problem, that is, the directionally consistent external force components necessary to pull the snake toward the indentation bottoms are very small at some points which tend to be obliterated in the vector-based normalization. To solve the obliteration problem that plagues GGVF, we propose a novel external force for snakes, known as component-normalized GGVF (CN-GGVF). CN-GGVF is obtained by separately normalizing each component of initial GGVF vectors with respect to its own magnitude. Experiments demonstrate that compared with the GGVF snakes, the proposed CN-GGVF snakes are more effective and efficient in capturing long and thin indentations regardless of odd or even widths, and achieve lower computational complexity in vector normalization as well as better performance on the real photographic image testing.

Acknowledgements This work was supported in part by NSFC (No. 61025013, No. 60903066, and No. 60972085), Sino-Singapore JRP (No. 2010DFA11010), BNSF (No. 4112043, No. 4102049), SRFDPHE (No. 20090009120006), JPNSFC (No. BK2011455), and FRFCU (No. 2011JBM029, No. 2009JBZ006).

References

1. M. Kass, A. Witkin, and D. Terzopoulos, "Snakes: Active contour models," *Int. J. Comput. Vis.*, vol. 1, no. 4, pp. 321–331, 1988.
2. C. Xu, D. Pham, and J. Prince, "Image segmentation using deformable models," in *Handbook of Medical Imaging, Medical Image Processing and Analysis*, M. Sonka and J. M. Fitzpatrick, Eds. Bellingham, WA: SPIE, 2000, vol. 2, ch. 3, pp. 129–174.
3. X. Xie and M. Mirmehdi, "MAC: Magnetostatic Active Contour Model," *IEEE Trans. Pattern Anal. Mach. Intell.*, vol. 30, no. 4, pp. 632–646, 2008.
4. A. Mansouri, D. Mukherjee, and S. Acton, "Constraining active contour evolution via Lie Groups of transformation," *IEEE Trans. Image Process.*, vol. 13, no. 6, pp. 853–863, 2004.
5. N. Ray and S. Acton, "Motion gradient vector flow: An external force for tracking rolling leukocytes with shape and size constrained active contours," *IEEE Trans. Med. Imag.*, vol. 23, no. 12, pp. 1466–1478, 2004.
6. B. Li and S. Acton, "Active contour external force using vector field convolution for image segmentation," *IEEE Trans. Image Process.*, vol. 16, no. 8, pp. 2096–2106, 2007.
7. P. Ghosh, L. Bertelli, B. Sumengen, and B. Manjunath, "A nonconservative flow field for robust variational image segmentation," *IEEE Trans. Image Process.*, vol. 19, no. 2, pp. 478–490, 2010.
8. A. Abrantes and J. Marques, "A class of constrained clustering algorithms for object boundary extraction," *IEEE Trans. Image Process.*, vol. 5, no. 11, pp. 1507–1521, 1996.
9. C. Xu and J. Prince, "Snakes, shapes, and gradient vector flow," *IEEE Trans. Image Process.*, vol. 7, no. 3, pp. 359–369, 1998.
10. J. Cheng and S. Foo, "Dynamic directional gradient vector flow for snakes," *IEEE Trans. Image Process.*, vol. 15, no. 6, pp. 1563–1571, 2006.
11. C. Xu and J. Prince, "Generalized gradient vector flow external forces for active contours," *Signal Process.*, vol. 71, no. 2, pp. 131–139, 1998.
12. L. Cohen, "On active contour models and balloons," *CVGIP: Image Understand.*, vol. 53, no. 2, pp. 211–218, 1991.
13. L. Cohen and I. Cohen, "Finite-element methods for active contour models and balloons for 2-D and 3-D images," *IEEE Trans. Pattern Anal. Mach. Intell.*, vol. 15, no. 11, pp. 1131–1147, 1993.

An Adaptive and Link-Based Method for Video Scene Clustering and Visualization

Hong Lu, Kai Chen, Yingbin Zheng, Zhuohong Cai, and Xiangyang Xue

Abstract In this paper we propose to adaptively cluster video shots into scenes on page rank manner and visualize video content on clustered scenes. The clustering method has been compared with state-of-arts methods and experimental results demonstrate the effectiveness of the proposed method. In visualization, the importance of the shots in the scene can be obtained and incorporated into the visualization parameters. The visualization results of the test videos are shown in global and detail manner.

Keywords Video scene clustering • Page-rank • Visualization

1 Introduction

As video content are becoming more and more distributed, easily obtained, and edited, it is necessary to present the video content in a more compact and informative manner for browsing, navigation, retrieval, edition, etc. In [1], a radial tool is presented to hierarchically visualize structured video content. Specifically, a system which combines automatic video segmentation and a characteristic key-frame extraction is proposed. In the outer circular rings, the segmented video are shown. And in each segment, logos are detected and shown in the rings. The duration of the logo appearance is mapped to the circle segment size.

In [2], *Jesen–Shannon divergence (JSD)* is employed to measure the difference between neighboring video frames to segment a video into shots, and also choose key frames in each shot. Then an innovative 3D visualization approach is proposed. In the visualization, video key frames and the useful information related to the

H. Lu (✉) • K. Chen • Y. Zheng • Z. Cai • X. Xue
Shanghai Key Lab of Intelligent Information Processing, School of Computer Science, Fudan University, Shanghai, China
e-mail: honglu@fudan.edu.cn

J.S. Jin et al., *The Era of Interactive Media*,
DOI 10.1007/978-1-4614-3501-3_42,

process of key frame selection are displayed in different layers of detail. The visualization tool can help for a quick and clear understanding to the video content.

In [3], volume visualization techniques are used for summarizing video sequences and presenting the video content. Min Chen et al. [4] propose visual signature for symbolizing abstract visual features that depict individual objects and motion events.

Hangzai Luo et al. [5, 6] analyze the news web and propose to incorporate the knowledge of news video for video visualization. It can provide more informative information on the news videos and is useful for users to browse, navigate and understand the news video content. Shiliang Zhang et al. [7] focus on music videos and propose not only to perform the personalized MV affective analysis, but also novel affective visualization to convert the abstract affective states intuitively and friendly to users.

Thus, how to effectively analyze the video content and extract interesting, important information, and also with detail tuning to present video content to users is important for video analysis, browse, and retrieval.

The remainder of the paper is organized as follows. Section 2.1 reviews video scene clustering and pagerank based methods. And pagerank clustering method is presented in Sect. 2.2. The video visualization method is presented in Sect. 3. Scene clustering and visualization results are given in Sect. 4. And we conclude our work in Sect. 5.

2 Video Scene Clustering on PageRank

2.1 Video Scene Clustering and PageRank Method

In content based video analysis, the first step is shot boundary detection, which can be regarded as well solved problem. Then on the detected shots, how to group shots of a video into clusters of disparate scenes and extract compact information is a key step toward high-level video semantic understanding, event identification, indexing, and retrieval [8]. Much work has been proposed for video scene segmentation and summarization [9–15]. These methods can be grouped into that based on normal methods such as spectral method, Markov Chain Monto Carlo (MCMC) [13, 15], and that based on graph partitioning methods [10–12, 14].

Since graph connectivity can well represent that two shots are similar, much work has been proposed to model scene segmentation as a graph partitioning problem. Specifically, in [10], audio and visual features are extracted first for each shot. Then scene transition graph [11] is constructed by considering the visual and audio feature similarity and time constraint. The time constraint means that if two shots are far in temporal order, although the visual and audio similarities are high, the final similarity between two shots is low. In [12], a video coherence measure is proposed by adopting the normalized cuts criterion that emphasizes the homogeneity between shots in the same scene and inhomogeneity between those in different scenes. A graph partitioning method is proposed in [14] for video scene segmentation.

Based on the constructed graph, link based analysis can be performed. These years, link based analysis has been widely used in region-of-interest detection, image search, and event recognition [16–19]. In this paper, we present an efficient approach to cluster video shots into scenes based on link analysis.

It is well known that Google uses pagerank [20] to rate the webs in the Internet and makes great success. In these years, pagerank has been widely accepted and applied in other fields. For example, in [16], inter-image level and intra-image level link analysis is performed to find the highly ranked images as exemplars of objects and to localize object instances in each image. In [17], pagerank is used for large-scale image search. Yushi Jing and Shumeet Baluja [18] and Naveed Imran et al. [19] successfully use pagerank to rank the pictures and informative features in pictures that finish picture search and event recognition. The theme lies that the most informative pictures and features are those which have more links to other pictures and features.

Due to the success of using pagerank in computer vision tasks, we propose to use pagerank for video scene clustering and visualization. First, it can rank the node values in the set well and can be used for clustering. Second, the representative shots in the cluster can be obtained at the same time for video scene visualization and summarization. The detail description will be in Sect. 2.2.

2.2 *PageRank Clustering*

In this section, we present our proposed method for video scene clustering by using pagerank. First, the video is segmented into a sequence of shots $\mathcal{S} = \{S_1, S_2, \ldots, S_M\}$, say M of them, by using a popular shot-boundary detector [21, 22]. Each shot is considered as a basic unit for clustering. The *shot color histogram* (SCH)—the bin-wise median of all the frame color histograms within the shot [23]—is computed as the shot feature for scene clustering. The frame, and thus the shot, color histogram is obtained in HSV (Hue-Saturation-Value) color space with its color coordinates uniformly quantized into 12 (Hue), 4 (Saturation), and 4 (Value) bins, respectively, resulting in a total of 192 bins (or quantized colors). The color space is selected due to its good performance in other work of image and video analysis [24, 25]. Then, the similarity between two shots are measured by intersection on histograms of two shots, i.e. $\mathcal{S}(s_i, s_j) = \sum_{k=1}^{N} min(X_i(k), X_j(k))$.

Same to that in [14], the scene likeness is defined based on the shot similarity.

$$\mathcal{L}(s_i, s_j) = \begin{cases} 1, \mathcal{S}(s_i, s_j) \geq \tau \\ 0, otherwise \end{cases} \tag{1}$$

Since pagerank is fitted to digraph and the scene likeness can be reformed into digraph, we make the connection bidirectional. The pagerank value is computed as below.

$$PR(u) = \sum_{v \in B_u} \frac{PR(v)}{L(v)} \tag{2}$$

where the PR value for a node u is dependent on the PR values for each node v out of the set B_u (it contains all nodes linking to node u), divided by the number $L(v)$ of links from node v. And the algorithm is described in Algorithm 1.

In the algorithm, the parameters α is used to control the compactness of the clusters. If α is large, the formed clusters are more compact. Based on our empirical study, it works well when α lies in range of $\left[\frac{1}{5*|V_k|}, \frac{1}{|V_k|}\right]$.

Algorithm 1 PageRank clustering algorithm

Definitions:

V: Set of nodes;

C: Set of shots under consideration for inclusion in V;

R: Set of shots that have not been assigned to any scene clusters.

Algorithm:

```
k ← 0
R = V
While R ≠ ∅
    k ← k + 1
    s_1^k = arg max_{s_i ∈ R} L(s_i, R − {s_i})
    V_k ← s_1^k
    R ← R − {s_1^k}
    C_k ← {s_i | L(s_i, s_1^k) = 1, s_i ∈ R}
    R ← R − C_k
    j ← 1
    While C_k ≠ ∅
        for s_i ∈ C_k
            PR = PageRank(V_k ∪ s_i)
            if PR(s_i) ≥ α
                j ← j + 1
                s_j^k = s_i
                V_k ← V_k ∪ {s_j^k}
                C_k = C_k − {s_i}
                C_k ← C_k ∪ {s_i | L(s_i, s_j^k) = 1, s_i ∈ R}
                R ← R − {s_i | L(s_i, s_j^k) = 1, s_i ∈ R}
            else
                R = R ∪ {s_i}
                C_k = C_k − {s_i}
```

3 Video Content Visualization

During video scene clustering, we can also represent the video content in a graph using the clustering parameters. Specifically, for each shot, a key frame is extract from it. Then the clustered shots are represented with links between them in the graph. The size of the frame in each shot is proportional to the pagerank value as computed in Eq. (2) of the corresponding shot. In other words, the larger the pagerank value of the shot, it is shown larger in the visualized scene cluster graph. And the not clustered shots, i.e. each shot is a cluster, are shown separately in the graph.

Figure 1 shows the scene clustering result by using pagerank for Tennis1 video. In the figure, the formed clusters are the wide-angle views of the court, close-up views of the players, medium views of the players and the court, and other clusters containing only one or two shots of transition scenes or commercial breaks,

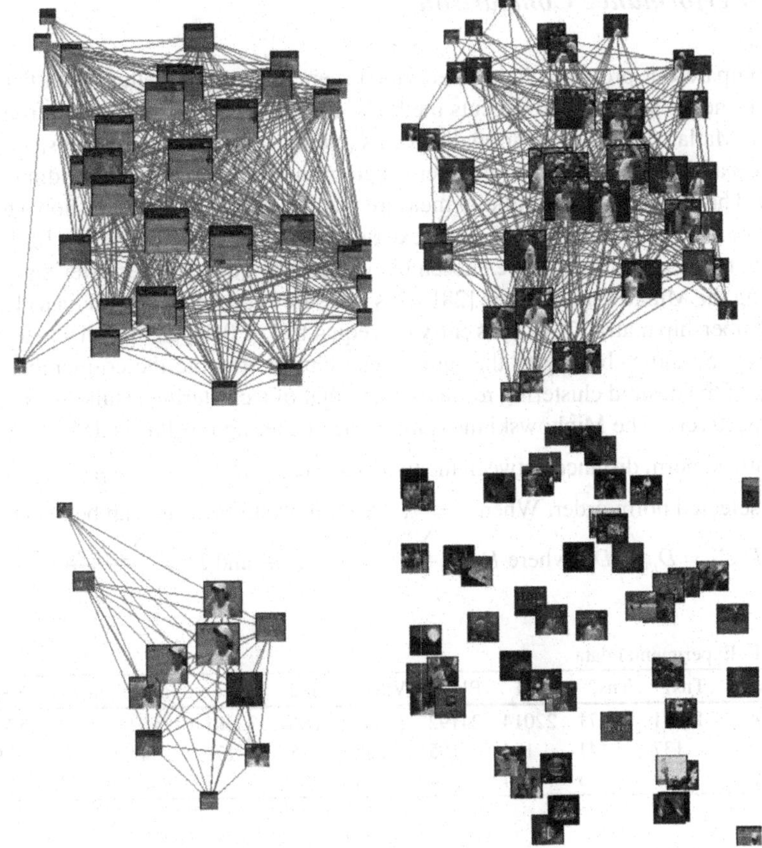

Fig. 1 Scene clustering result by using pagerank for Tennis1 video

respectively. From the figure, we can easily extract the informative, representative shots of the video, i.e., the clusters formed, and the bigger images in each scene can represent the representative content of the cluster.

4 Experiments

4.1 Experimental Data

The experimental data used is tabulated in Table 1. The video data include sports and news videos. And the videos are digitized at 25 frames/s and the durations range from 7 to 47 min. To measure the clustering performance, we manually label the scene type of each shot as the ground truth.

4.2 Performance Comparison

We compare our proposed link-based video scene clustering method with that by using k-means and normalized cuts methods. For the k-means method, we use the code in Matlab 7.1. And the normalized cuts (Ncuts) code is from the website.[1] For k-means and Ncuts, the cluster number is determined by the Davies–Bouldin index (DBI). The DBI is a cluster validity measure that has been widely used, shown to be effective [26], and employed in some existing studies of video clustering [27].

In our experiments, we have chosen to evaluate the quality of a clustering result by using the Minkowski measure [28]. This measure is computed based on a cluster co-membership matrix C, with its entry $C_{i,j}$ equal to 1 or 0 depending on whether or not shots S_i and S_j belong to the same scene cluster. Denote the co-membership matrix of the desired clustering result as T and that of a clustering result obtained as C, respectively. The Minkowski measure of the clustering result C is defined as the normalized norm distance between the two matrices, i.e. $D(T,C) = \frac{\|T-C\|_\gamma}{\|T\|_\gamma}$, where γ is the selected norm order. When $\gamma = 1$, the Minkowski measure can be expressed as $D(T,C) = D_m + D_f$, where $D_m = \frac{\sum_{i,j} \mathbf{1}(T_{i,j}=1 \& C_{i,j}=0)}{\sum_{i,j} |T_{i,j}|}$ and $D_f = \frac{\sum_{i,j} \mathbf{1}(T_{i,j}=0 \& C_{i,j}=1)}{\sum_{i,j} |T_{i,j}|}$.

Table 1 Experimental data

Video data	Tns1	Tns2	Bkt1	Bkt2	Vlb1	Vlb2	Soc1	Soc2	News1	News2
Frame #	17981	24171	22014	24192	31608	11664	32301	12562	71378	57462
Shot #	137	141	194	195	240	56	179	48	476	342
Scene #	4	3	4	4	4	3	3	2	5	5

[1] http://www.cis.upenn.edu/~jshi/software/.

Table 2 Performance comparison

	k-means				Normalized cuts				Pagerank			
Video	K_{KM}	D_{KM}	D_m	D_f	K_{NC}	D_{NC}	D_m	D_f	K_{PR}	D_{PR}	D_m	D_f
Tns1	7	1.26	0.44	0.82	54	0.66	0.62	0.04	56	0.58	0.49	0.09
Tns2	8	0.78	0.32	0.46	45	0.75	0.69	0.05	38	0.63	0.56	0.06
Bkt1	10	0.97	0.55	0.42	65	0.80	0.71	0.09	56	0.88	0.63	0.26
Bkt2	6	1.42	0.23	1.19	35	0.78	0.65	0.13	71	1.04	0.76	0.29
Vlb1	9	0.63	0.41	0.22	68	0.64	0.62	0.02	67	0.92	0.62	0.30
Vlb2	5	1.62	0.09	1.53	40	0.54	0.53	0.01	15	0.67	0.63	0.04
Soc1	8	0.98	0.63	0.35	50	0.83	0.79	0.04	17	1.03	0.42	0.61
Soc2	2	0.60	0	0.60	27	0.71	0.71	0.01	4	0.16	0.12	0.04
News1	20	4.21	0.25	3.96	18	0.92	0.90	0.02	209	0.87	0.86	0.01
News2	18	8.57	0.03	8.54	26	0.92	0.91	0.01	210	0.89	0.88	0.01
Mean		2.10	0.30	1.81		0.76	0.71	0.04		0.77	0.60	0.17

Table 3 Computational complexity of scene clustering methods

Method	Complexity
k-means	$O(KnMT) + O(nM^2)$
Normalized cuts	$O(nMT) + O(nM^2)$
Pagerank clustering	$O(nM^2)$

D_m and D_f denote the miss and false classification rates, respectively. Consequently, the lower the Minkowski measure, the smaller the miss and false classification rates, and the better the scene clustering result.

The experimental results on the performance comparison are shown in Table 2. In the table, K_{KM}, K_{NC}, and K_{PR} represent the cluster numbers determined by using the k-means, Ncuts, and pagerank methods. In pagerank based method, τ is 0.6 and α is $\frac{1}{3.5*|V_k|}$.

It can be observed from Table 2 that our method can obtain better clustering performance than k-means and comparable performance with normalized cuts method.Also, our method can obtain more small clusters.

4.3 Complexity Analysis of Video Scene Clustering Methods

In this section, we analyze the computational complexity of the methods and tabulated in Table 3. In k-means and normalized cuts methods, the maximum cluster number is set to $\sqrt{M}$, where M is the number of shots. And DBI measure is computed based on the clustering results to determined the optimal cluster number and to get the corresponding clustering result.

Let K be the number of the resulting scene clusters, M the total number of shots, n the feature dimension, and T the number of k-means iterations before convergence. The computational complexity of k-means clustering can be shown to be O

Table 4 Computing times (in seconds) taken by k-means clustering (T_{KM}), normalized cuts (T_{NC}), and the proposed pagerank (T_{PR}) clustering method

Video data	Tns1	Tns2	Bkt1	Bkt2	Vlb1	Vlb2	Soc1	Soc2	News1	News2
T_{KM}	109.99	114.88	361.20	347.52	733.25	8.93	261	5.42	6265.60	2330.83
T_{NC}	40.37	44.27	116.52	133.41	218.63	2.77	98.41	2.07	1980.01	678.79
T_{PR}	2.77	1.57	2.65	3.12	3.63	0.76	1.83	0.40	9.10	8.57

(*KnMT*) [29]. Considering to compute DBI for determining the optimal cluster number, an additional complexity of $O(nM^2)$ is required by k-means. Similar analysis is done to normalized cuts method.

In our experiment, we used a Intel Core 2 Duo 2.53GHz PC with 2G memory. The time comparison is shown in Table 4. It can be observed from Table 4, since our proposed pagerank based method process a binary scene likeness matrix and not on the original high dimensional shot features, our method performs much faster. The improvement is much more when the video has much larger number of shots or the resulted number of clusters.

4.4 Video Visualization

Based on the clustering results, we can visualize the video on the clusters, the representative shots in the scene, the link between the shots. Figure 2 shows the visualization results for News1 video. In the figure, we can observe the news story part to some talking show, some soccer match, etc., and the anchor person scene.

On the other hand, Fig. 3 gives the accumulated time coverage information of the first five formed clusters in the test videos. The time coverage is computed on the number of frames of the formed scenes to the total number of frames of the video. It can be observed from Fig. 3 that in sports videos, the first formed clusters can have large time coverage of the whole video and can be termed as *dominant scenes*. And in news videos, the first formed scenes are anchor person view and the news story scenes having high visual similarity. Since the news stories are normally diverse, the accumulated time coverage of the first formed scenes is not much high.

5 Conclusions

We propose in this paper of video shot clustering based on pagerank, which considers the similarity of video shots as link between shots. In the clustered scenes, the shots within that which have larger links with other shots are visualized larger. The parameters can be obtained during shot clustering. Experimental results demonstrate that the clustering method can obtain better performance and can also provides a compact and informative content.

a

b

c

d

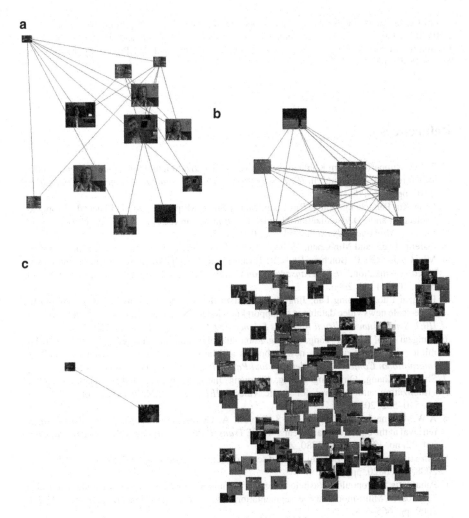

Fig. 2 Scene clustering result by using pagerank for News1 video

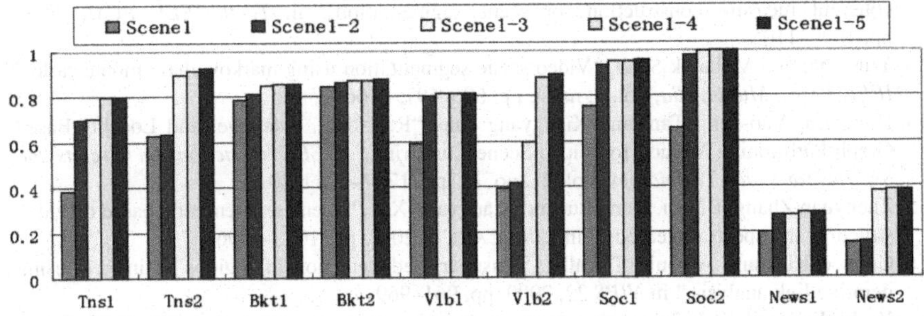

Fig. 3 Time coverage information of the first five formed scenes

Acknowledgements This work was supported in part by 973 Program (Project No. 2010CB327900), Natural Science Foundation of China (No. 60875003 and 60873178), Shanghai Committee of Science and Technology (No. 11ZR1403400), and 211-Project Sponsorship for Young Professors.

References

1. Tobias Ruppert and Jorn Kohlhammer, "A radial visualization tool for depicting hierarchically structured video content," in *IEEE Symposium on Visual Analytics Science and Technology*, 2010, pp. 409–416.
2. Qing Xu, Pengcheng Wang, Bin Long, Mateu Sbert, Miquel Feixas, and Riccado Scopigno, "Selection and 3D visualization of video key frames," in *IEEE International Conference on Systems, Man and Cybernetics (SMC)*, 2010, pp. 52–59.
3. Gareth Daniel and Min Chen, "Video visualization," *IEEE Visualization*, 2003, pp. 409–416.
4. Min Chen, Ralf P. Botchen, Rudy R. Hashim, and Daniel Weiskopf, "Visual signatures in video visualization," *IEEE Transactions on Visualization and Computer Graphics*, vol. 12, no. 5, pp. 1093–1100, 2006.
5. Hangzai Luo, Jianping Fan, Jing Yang, William Ribarsky, and Shinichi Satoh, "Analyzing large-scale news video databases to support knowledge visualization and intuitive retrieval," in *IEEE Symposium on Visual Analytics Science and Technology*, 2007, pp. 107–114.
6. Hangzai Luo, Jiahang Yang, Aoying Zhou, Jianping Fan, and Tianming Hu, "Knowledge mining and visualization on newswebpages and large-scale news video database," in *IFIP International Conference on Network and Parallel Computing*, 2008, pp. 452–459.
7. Shiliang Zhang, Qingming Huang, Shuqiang Jiang, Wen Gao, and Qi Tian, "Affective visualization and retrieval for music video," *IEEE Trans. Multimedia*, vol. 12, no. 6, pp. 510–522, 2010.
8. A.W.M. Smeulders, M. Worring, S. Santini, A. Gupta, and R.Jain, "Content-based image retrieval at the end of the early years," *IEEE Trans. Pattern Analysis and Machine Intelligence*, vol. 22, no. 12, pp. 1349–1380, 2000.
9. Christian Petersohn, "Logical unit and scene detection: a comparative survey," in *SPIE-IS&T*, 2008, vol. 6820, pp. 1–17.
10. Panagiotis Sidiropoulos, Vasileios Mezaris, Ioannis Kompatsiaris, Hugo Meinedo, and Isabel Trancoso, "Multi-modal scene segmentation using scene transition graphs," in *ACMMM*, 2009, pp. 665–668.
11. Minerva Yeung and Boon-Lock Yeo, "Time-constrained clustering for segmentation of video shots into story units," in *IEEE ICPR*, 1996, pp. 375–380.
12. Xiaoqin Zhang, Xianglin Zeng, Weiming Hu, and Wanqing Li, "Normalized cut based coherent measure construction for scene segmentation," in *Tenth IEEE PCM*, 2009, pp. 1099–1105.
13. Yun Zhai and Mubarak Shah, "Video scene segmentation using markov chain monte carlo," *IEEE Trans. Multimedia*, vol. 8, no. 4, pp. 686–697, 2006.
14. Hong Lu, Yap-Peng Tan, and Xiangyang Xue, "Real-time, Adaptive, and Locality-Based Graph Partitioning Method for Video Scene Clustering," *IEEE Transactions on Circuits and Systems for Video Technology*, vol. 21, no. 11, pp. 1747–1759, 2011.
15. Zhenyuan Zhang, Bin Li, Hong Lu, and Xiangyang Xue, "Scene segmentation based on video structure and spectral methods," in *10th ICARCV*, 2008, pp. 1093–1096.
16. Gunhee Kim and Antonio Torralba, "Unsupervised detection of regions of interest using iterative link analysis," in *NIPS 22*, 2009, pp. 961–969.
17. Yushi Jing and S. Baluja, "Visualrank: pagerank for google image search," *IEEE Trans. Pattern Analysis and Machine Intelligence*, vol. 30, no. 11, pp. 1877–1890, 2008.

18. Yushi Jing and Shumeet Baluja, "Pagerank for product image search," in *WWW*, 2008, pp. 307–315.
19. Naveed Imran, Jingen Liu, Jiebo Luo, and Mubarak Shah, "Event recognition from photo collections via pagerank," in *ACMMM*, 2009, pp. 621–624.
20. Lawrence Page, Sergey Brin, Rajeev Motwani, and Terry Winograd, "The pagerank citation ranking: Bringing order to the web," *Technical Report, Stanford InfoLab*, 1999.
21. H. J. Zhang, A. Kankanhalli, and S. W. Smoliar, "Automatic partitioning of full-motion video," *Multimedia Systems*, vol. 1, pp. 10–28, 1993.
22. H. Lu and Y.-P. Tan, "An Effective Post-Refinement Method for Shot Boundary Detection," *IEEE Transactions on Circuits and Systems for Video Technology*, vol. 15, no. 11, pp. 1407–1421, 2005.
23. A. M. Martinez and J. R. Serra, "A new approach to object-related image retrieval," *Journal of Visual Languages and Computing*, vol. 11, no. 3, pp. 345–363, 2000.
24. Xia Wan and C.-C. Jay Kuo, "Color distribution analysis and quantization for image retrieval," in *SPIE Proceeding Volume 2670, Storage and Retrieval for Still Image and Video Databases IV*, 1996, pp. 8–16.
25. A. M. Ferman, A. M. Tekalp, and R. Mehrotra, "Robust color histogram descriptors for video segment retrieval and identification," *IEEE Transactions on Image Processing*, vol. 11, no. 5, pp. 497–508, 2002.
26. J. C. Bezdek and N. R. Pal, "Some new indexes of cluster validity," *IEEE Transactions on Systems, Man and Cybernetics*, vol. 28, no. 3, pp. 301–315, 1998.
27. A. Hanjalic and H. J. Zhang, "An integrated scheme for automated video abstraction based on unsupervised cluster-validity analysis," *IEEE Transactions on Circuits and Systems for Video Technology*, vol. 9, no. 8, pp. 1280–1289, 1999.
28. R. R. Sokal, "Clustering and classification: background and current directions," *Classification and clustering, Edited by J. Van Ryzin*, pp. 1–15, 1977.
29. Richard O. Duda, Peter E. Hart, and David G. Stork, *Pattern classification*, Wiley-Interscience, New York, second edition, 2000.

An Unsupervised Approach to Multiple Speaker Tracking for Robust Multimedia Retrieval

M. Phanikumar, Lalan Kumar, and Rajesh M. Hegde

Abstract Tagging multi media data based on who is speaking at what time, is important especially in the intelligent retrieval of recordings of meetings and conferences. In this paper an unsupervised approach to tracking more than two speakers in multi media data recorded from multiple visual sensors and a single audio sensor is proposed. The multi-speaker detection and tracking problem is first formulated as a multiple hypothesis testing problem. From this formulation we proceed to derive the multi speaker detection and tracking problem as a condition in mutual information. The proposed method is then evaluated for multi media recordings consisting of four speakers recorded on a multi media recording test bed. Experimental results on the CUAVE multi modal corpus are also discussed. The proposed method exhibits reasonably good performance as demonstrated by the detection (ROC) curves. The results of analysis based on the condition in mutual information are also encouraging. A multiple speaker detection and tracking system implemented using this approach gives reasonable performance in actual meeting room scenarios.

Keywords Multi media retrieval • Multiple speaker detection • Unsupervised multi modal approach

1 Introduction

Searching and indexing through multi media data is a central problem in multi media information retrieval. Hence tagging multi media data based on who is speaking at what time assumes significance especially in recordings of meetings

M. Phanikumar • L. Kumar • R.M. Hegde (✉)
Department of Electrical Engineering, Indian Institute of Technology Kanpur, Kanpur, India
e-mail: rhegde@iitk.ac.in; lalank@iitk.ac.in

J.S. Jin et al., *The Era of Interactive Media*,
DOI 10.1007/978-1-4614-3501-3_43, © Springer Science+Business Media, LLC 2013

and conferences. Speaker detection and tracking refers to checking whether a target speaker is active in a given segment from a multi media file, and then finding all segments in a multi media file where that target speaker is active. In [1], two approaches based on internal and external segmentation of audio data has been described for speaker detection and tracking. This is a unimodal approach where the audio modality alone has been used. However the performance of speaker detection and tracking systems can be improved by using multi modal (media) data. In particular, visual information can be used, as it has significant correlation with audio. There are two different methods in exploiting the information contained in each modality, one approach is fusing of modalities at feature level and the other is fusing at the statistical model level. Authors in [2–4] have adopted the former approach by utilizing the causal relationship between audio and video signals. Majority of these methods use covariance or mutual information between audio and visual information either in an explicit or an implicit fashion. Authors in [5, 6], have addressed the problem of speaker detection with two speakers using mutual information present in the audio and visual modalities. In this paper we discuss a novel unsupervised approach to detect the active speaker when N speakers ($N \geq 2$) are present in a multi media recording. The multi-speaker detection and tracking problem is first formulated as a multiple hypothesis testing problem. From this formulation we proceed to derive the multi speaker detection and tracking problem as a condition in mutual information. The proposed method is then evaluated for multi media recordings consisting of four speakers recorded on a multi media recording test bed. Experimental results on the CUAVE multi modal corpus are also discussed. Analysis results highlighting the complementarity of the audio visual features are also discussed. Significance of the speaker tracking problem in multi media information retrieval is also briefly discussed prior to the conclusion. A two speaker detection problem [2], is also included in the Appendix for completeness.

2 An Unsupervised Approach to Multiple Speaker Detection and Tracking

In this section, an unsupervised approach to multiple speaker (more than two speakers) detection and tracking is proposed. A multiple speaker tracking problem is formulated herein, as a multiple hypothesis testing problem. From thereon, a relationship in mutual information between audio and video signals that comprise the multi media data is derived. In this approach, the audio observations from a particular segment of multi media data are represented by x_t^a and the video observations of the N speakers are denoted by $x_t^{v_1}, x_t^{v_2}, \ldots\ldots, x_t^{v_N}$. The multiple speaker tracking problem can then be formulated as a multiple hypothesis test [7], as follows

$$
\begin{aligned}
H_0 &: x_t^a, x_t^{v_1}, x_t^{v_2} ..., x_t^{v_N} \sim p(x_t^a, x_t^{v_1}) p(x_t^{v_2}) ... p(x_t^{v_N}) \\
H_1 &: x_t^a, x_t^{v_1}, x_t^{v_2} ..., x_t^{v_N} \sim p(x_t^a, x_t^{v_2}) p(x_t^{v_1}) ... p(x_t^{v_N}) \\
&\quad . \\
H_{N-1} &: x_t^a, x_t^{v_1}, x_t^{v_2} ..., x_t^{v_N} \sim p(x_t^a, x_t^{v_N}) p(x_t^{v_1}) ... p(x_t^{v_{N-1}})
\end{aligned}
\tag{1}
$$

where H_0 is the hypothesis corresponding to the case when *speaker1* is active and H_{N-1} is the case where *speaker N* is active. However the decision is based on minimizing the Bayes risk

$$
R = E(C) = \sum_{i=0}^{N-1} \sum_{j=0}^{N-1} p(H_i|H_j) p(H_j) \tag{2}
$$

where *E*(*C*) is the expected cost of making a decision. Note that the Bayes risk is formulated as a probability of error in this case. The decision rule that minimizes *R* is reduced to a hypothesis testing problem which minimizes

$$
C_i(x_t^a, x_t^{v_1}, x_t^{v_2} ..., x_t^{v_N}) = \sum_{j=0, j \neq i}^{N-1} p(H_j|x_t^a, x_t^{v_1}, x_t^{v_2} ..., x_t^{v_N}) \tag{3}
$$

$$
C_i(x_t^a, x_t^{v_1}, x_t^{v_2} ..., x_t^{v_N}) = \sum_{j=0}^{N-1} P(H_j|x_t^a, x_t^{v_1}, x_t^{v_2} ..., x_t^{v_N}) - p(H_i|x_t^a, x_t^{v_1}, x_t^{v_2} ..., x_t^{v_N}) \tag{4}
$$

where C_i is the average cost of deciding in favor of hypothesis H_i, when (x_t^a, x_t^{v1}, x_t^{v2}..., x_t^{vN}) is observed. Minimizing $C_i(.)$ is equivalent to maximizing $p(H_i|x_t^a, x_t^{v_1}, x_t^{v_2} ..., x_t^{v_N})$. Thus, the decision rule is formulated to decide in favor of hypothesis H_k if

$$
\begin{aligned}
p(H_k|x_t^a, x_t^{v_1}, x_t^{v_2} ..., x_t^{v_N}) > p\ (H_i|x_t^a, x_t^{v_1}, x_t^{v_2} ..., x_t^{v_N}); \\
i \neq k, i = 0, 1, ..., N-1
\end{aligned}
\tag{5}
$$

Considering equal priors, we have

$$
\begin{aligned}
p(x_t^a, x_t^{v_1}, x_t^{v_2} ..., x_t^{v_N}|H_k) > p(x_t^a, x_t^{v_1}, x_t^{v_2} ..., x_t^{v_N}|H_i); \\
i \neq k, i = 0, 1, ..., N-1
\end{aligned}
\tag{6}
$$

Expressing this inequality as a M-ary maximum likelihood (ML) decision rule, we have

$$
\frac{p(x_t^a, x_t^{v_1}, x_t^{v_2} ..., x_t^{v_N}|H_k)}{p(x_t^a, x_t^{v_1}, x_t^{v_2} ..., x_t^{v_N}|H_i)} > 1, i \neq k, i = 0, 1, ..., N-1 \tag{7}
$$

Taking the expectation the normalized likelihood ratio statistic with respect to the joint probability density of the random variables underlying the audio visual observations, we have

$$E\left\{\frac{1}{M}\sum_{t=0}^{M-1} log_2\left(\frac{p(x_t^a, x_t^{v_1}, x_t^{v_2} \ldots, x_t^{v_N}|H_k)}{p(x_t^a, x_t^{v_1}, x_t^{v_2} \ldots, x_t^{v_N}|H_i)}\right)\right\} > 0 \tag{8}$$

where $i \neq k, i = 0, 1, \ldots, N-1$ and M is the number of observations in each time slice of the multi media data. Simplifying further we can arrive at the inequality

$$E\left\{\sum_{t=0}^{M-1} log_2\left(\frac{p(x_t^a, x_t^{v_{k+1}})}{p(x_t^a)p(x_t^{v_{k+1}})}\right)\right\} > E\left\{\sum_{t=0}^{M-1} log_2\left(\frac{p(x_t^a, x_t^{v_{i+1}})}{p(x_t^a)p(x_t^{v_{i+1}})}\right)\right\} \tag{9}$$

However it can be shown that

$$E\left\{log_2\left(\frac{p(x,y)}{p(x)p(y)}\right)\right\} = I(X,Y) \tag{10}$$

where $I(X,Y)$ is the mutual information between random variables X and Y. From Eqs. (9) and (10), a condition in mutual information can be realized as

$$I(X^a, X^{v_{k+1}}) > I(X^a, X^{v_{i+1}}), i \neq k, i = 0, 1, \ldots, N-1. \tag{11}$$

The value of k which satisfies the condition in mutual information as in Eq. (11), is the identity of the active speaker among the N possible speakers.

3 Performance Evaluation

In this section we describe the multi media data used in our experiments and the performance evaluation results of the proposed unsupervised approach to multiple speaker detection and tracking.

3.1 *The CUAVE Database*

The Clemson University Audio–Visual Experiments (CUAVE) database [8], is a speaker-independent corpus of both connected and continuous digit strings of high quality video and audio of a representative group of speakers totaling over 7,000 utterances. The database consists of two parts: one of individual speakers and the other of speaker pairs. The first part, with individual speakers, consists

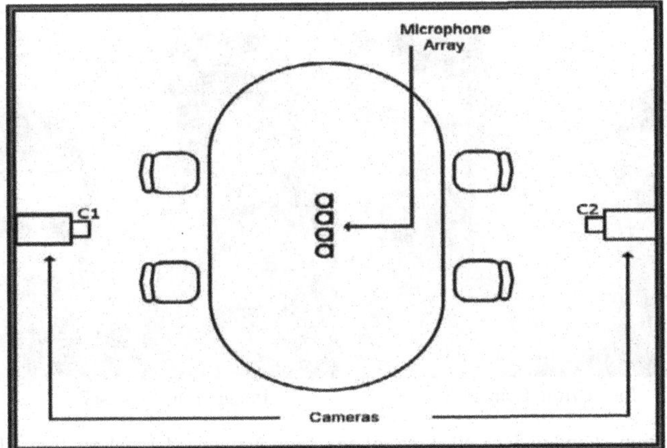

Fig. 1 Schematic diagram of the test bed used in acquiring multi media data

of 36 speakers. The selection of speakers is done such that there is an even representation of male and female speakers with different skin tones and accents as well as other visual features such as glasses, facial hair, and hats. The second part of the database includes 20 pairs of speakers. The database was recorded in an isolated sound booth at a resolution of 720 ×480 with the NTSC standard of 29.97 fps, using a 1-mega pixel-CCD, MiniDV camera. An on-camera microphone was used to record audio. The two speakers in the group section are labeled persons A and B. There are three sequences per person. Person A speaks a continuous-digit sequence, followed by speaker B and vice versa. For the third sequence, both speaker A and B overlap each other. The data is fully-labeled manually at the millisecond level.

3.2 Multi Modal Database Using the Lab Test Bed

The multi modal data is collected from the test bed illustrated in Fig. 1. The experimental test bed at MiPS lab, IIT Kanpur is a typical meeting room setup which can accommodate four participants around a table. The recording setup consists of two cameras and a microphone array to capture multi modal data. Each recording has four subjects with one subject active at any particular instant of time. The data has been recorded for a total of ten subjects, with four examples from each subject. Each example is of 30 s duration. The frame rate used is 30 fps and the stereo audio signal was sampled at 44 KHz.

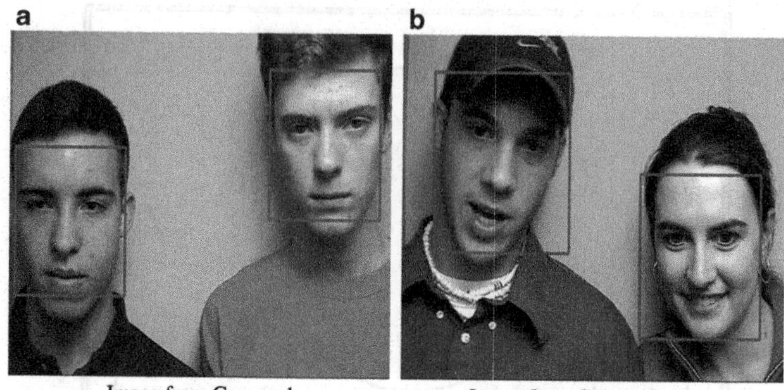

Fig. 2 Illustration showing face tracking of the four juxtaposed speakers from the CUAVE database

3.3 Experimental Results

In order to assess the performance of the proposed multi-modal approach to multiple speaker detection and tracking system, two sets of experiments are performed. The first set of experiments are conducted on the multi media data from the CUAVE database. The second set of experiments are performed on the Lab test bed data. Since the CUAVE database consists of only two speakers in each recording, we juxtapose another recording from the database, where both speakers remain silent. Experiments are now conducted on a subset of such four speaker multi media data i.e four video signals and one audio signal (since in second sample both speakers remain silent). It is reasonable to assume that this does not affect our performance evaluation, since all the recordings are done in same environment and setup. For each speaker, the face region is extracted and converted into a gray scale image. The results of face tracking on two sets of videos from the CUAVE database are shown in Fig. 2a, b respectively.

If we divide each face region into T segments, each comprising of $M \times N$ pixels, the visual features can then be computed for each segment as the norm of the normalized intensity values. This results in a $1 \times T$ dimensional video feature vector for each speaker. Thirteen dimensional Mel frequency cepstral coefficients (MFCC) are used as audio features. The resulting $13 \times T$ MFCC features are projected on to a maximally informative subspace using the technique described in [3]. This results in a $1 \times T$ dimensional feature vector for the audio and a $1 \times T$ dimensional feature vector for the video of the four speakers. Mutual information is now calculated using Parzen kernel density estimator. The system detection performance for the procedure enumerated above is shown in Fig. 3a. Similar ROC curves are also illustrated in Fig. 3b, for the data collected from the multi modal test bed described earlier. The ROC curves indicate that the detection performance of the proposed approach is good since it lies in the upper triangle of the ROC plane.

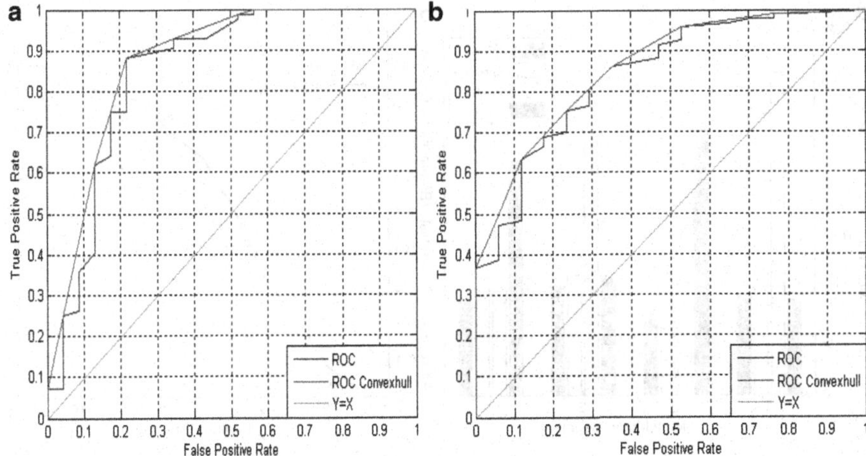

Fig. 3 (**a**) ROC curves for the four speaker detection task on the CUAVE multi modal corpus, (**b**) ROC curves for the four speaker detection task on the multi media data recorded in the Multi modal test bed

Table 1 Table listing the area under the curve and accuracy for multiple speaker detection on CUAVE and the test bed data

Dataset	Accuracy (%)	AUC (%)
CUAVE data base	84.11	0.85
Test bed data	84.55	0.84

The area under curve (AUC) is a measure of the discrimination capability of the classifier. The high value of AUC represents the good discrimination capability of true speaker from others. In Table 1, accuracy and AUC are listed for both the CUAVE data and the test bed data. The high AUC value indicates that the proposed method is a good discriminator.

3.3.1 Separability Analysis

In order to correlate the system performance with the condition in mutual information derived earlier we also illustrate mutual information scores for four segments of multimedia data from the CUAVE database as in Fig. 4a. Note that in each of these segments one speaker is active while the other speakers are inactive. It can be noted from Fig. 4a, that the mutual information score is maximum for the active speaker when computed against the inactive speakers. We also demonstrate the better separability of the audio visual features when compared to the audio only features using the Bhattacharya distance measure. The Bhattacharya distance (BD), is a special case of the Chernoff distance measure. The Bhattacharya distance

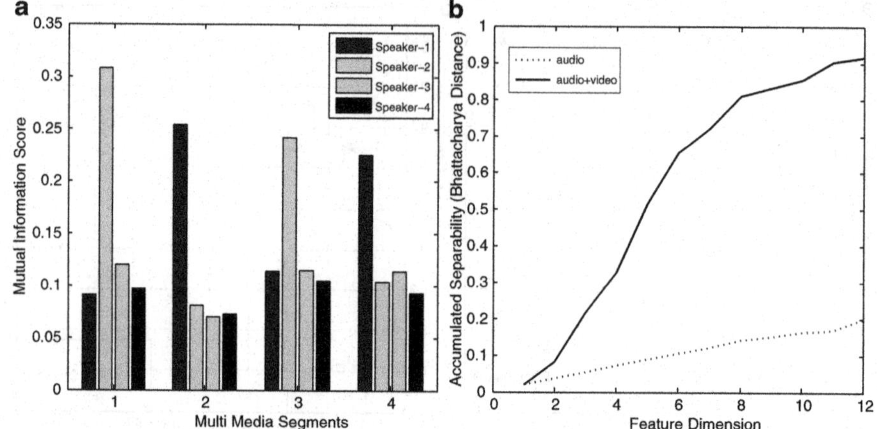

Fig. 4 (**a**) Mutual Information (MI) scores for four segments of multi media data with four speakers with one speaker active (**b**) Accumulated separability (Bhattacharya distance) versus feature dimension for audio only and audio–visual features

D between the two feature vectors f_k and f_l with n number of component pairs is given by

$$D(f_k,f_l) = \sum_{i=1}^{n} D_i(f_k,f_l) \tag{12}$$

Further the Bhattacharya distance for a two class and a multi (M) class case as in [9], is given by

$$B_{pair}(X) = \frac{1}{2}\int [p(X|\omega_1)p(X|\omega_2)]^{1/2}dX \tag{13}$$

$$B_M(X) = \frac{1}{2}\sum_{i>j}^{M}\sum_{j=1}^{M}\int [p(X|\omega_i)p(X|\omega_j)]^{1/2}dX \tag{14}$$

where Eq. (13) gives the Bhattacharya distance between two class and Eq. (14), gives the Bhattacharya distance between M classes. We therefore illustrate the separability analysis results as the BD versus the feature dimension for both unimodal (speech only) and multi modal (speech+video) in Fig. 4b. The accumulated separability of the multi modal features when compared to unimodal speech features can be noted from Fig. 4b. The purpose of these plots is to illustrate that information in multi media data can be effectively utilized when the multi modal observations are used jointly in some form or the other when compared to unimodal audio or video.

3.4 Multiple Speaker Face Tracking System Using the Proposed Approach

A multiple speaker face tracking system is also implemented and tested on the multimedia test bed data. For the purpose of tracking, five multimedia files of each nearly one and half minute length were recorded. The speaker face tracking requires the detection of speaker state along the whole sequences of multimedia file. So temporal window of 2 s (60 frames) is shifted by 1 s (30 frames) along the sequence. The results are compared to the ground truth at the center point of each temporal window. The estimates are therefore scored at 1 s intervals through each multimedia file. An accuracy of 78.50% for speaker tracking is obtained on the multimedia test bed data. Motivated by the tracking results, an active speaker face tracking system has also been implemented. The results of tracking speaker 2 and speaker 4 when they are active are shown in Fig. 5. An on line demonstration of this tracking system can be viewed at the URL: http://home.iitk.ac.in/~rhegde/tracking.html.

Fig. 5 Illustration showing active speaker tracking of the four speakers captured from the multi modal test bed, When speaker-2 is active (*top*) and When speaker-4 is active (*bottom*)

4 Conclusion

In this work we have described an unsupervised approach to multiple speaker detection and tracking. The problem is first addressed as a multiple hypothesis testing problem and a condition in mutual information derived for the same. The unsupervised nature of the proposed technique makes it feasible for real time implementation of multi modal video search based on tagging multi media data. The technique can also help in generating annotated multi media data bases for meetings, lectures, and conference recordings with minimal manual interference. Issues of normalizing the audio and visual feature vectors and effective ways of computing maximally informative projections to normalize the feature vector dimensions are currently being addressed. Work on developing a web based video retrieval system based on this technique for retrieving meeting data is also currently under progress.

Appendix: Information Theoretic Approach to Detection of Two Speakers

In this appendix, an information theoretic approach to the two speaker detection problem [2], is described. The detection problem herein is formulated as a hypothesis test. Assuming x^v_{lt} and x^v_{rt} denotes video features of the left and right speakers respectively and the features of the audio signal are x^a_t, then hypothesis test is stated as

$$\begin{aligned} H_0 &: x^v_{lt}, x^v_{rt}, x^a_t \sim p(x^v_l, x^a_t)p(x^v_r) \\ H_1 &: x^v_{lt}, x^v_{rt}, x^a_t \sim p(x^v_l)p(x^v_r, x^a_t) \end{aligned} \tag{15}$$

H_0 is the hypothesis indicating that the audio signal is associated with the speaker on the left, while H_1 indicates that the audio signal is associated with the speaker on the right. Using a consistent probability density estimator for $p(x^v_l)$, $p(x^v_r)$, $p(x^v_l, x^a_t)$, $p(x^v_r, x^a_t)$ and taking the expectation with respect to the joint probability density of X^v_l, X^a and X^v_r, X^a, gives

$$E\left\{\frac{1}{N}\sum_{t=0}^{N-1} log\left(\frac{p(x^v_{lt}, x^v_{rt}, x^a_t|H_1)}{p(x^v_{lt}, x^v_{rt}, x^a_t|H_0)}\right)\right\} = E\left\{\frac{1}{N}\sum_{t=0}^{N-1} log\left(\frac{p(x^v_{lt})p(x^v_{rt}, x^a_t)}{p(x^v_{lt}, x^a_t)p(x^v_{rt})}\right)\right\} \tag{16}$$

Consequently application of the chain rule yields

$$E\left\{\frac{1}{N}\sum_{t=0}^{N-1} log\left(\frac{p(x^v_{lt})p(x^v_{rt}, x^a_t)p(x^a_t)}{p(x^v_{lt}, x^a_t)p(x^v_{rt})p(x^a_t)}\right)\right\} = I(X^a; X^v_r) - I(X^a; X^v_l) \tag{17}$$

Hence the difference between the estimated mutual information (or their bounds) is equivalent to the log-likelihood ratio of the hypothesis test as discussed in [2].

Acknowledgements This work was supported by the BITCOE IIT Kanpur under project numbers 20080250, 20080252, and 20080253.

References

1. Robert B. Dunn., Douglas A. Reynolds., and Thomas F. Quatieri., Approaches to Speaker Detection and Tracking in Conversational Speech, Digital Signal Processing. Vol. 10, Elsevier Inc., (2000) 93–112.
2. John W. Fisher. and Trevor Darrell., Speaker association with signal-level audiovisual fusion, IEEE Transactions on Multimedia. Vol. 6, IEEE (2004) 406–413.
3. Patricia Besson., Vlad Popovici., Jean-Marc Vesin., Jean-Philippe Thiran., and Murat Kunt, Approaches to speaker detection and tracking in conversational speech, IEEE Transactions on Multimedia. Vol. 10, IEEE (2008) 63–73.
4. Nock H.J., Iyengar.G., and Neti.C., Speaker localisation using audio–visual synchrony: An empirical study, ACM International Conference on Multimedia. Vol. 10, ACM (2003).
5. Emanuel Parzen., On estimation of a probability density function and mode, In: The Annals of Mathematical Statistics. Vol. 33, Institute of Mathematical Statistics (1962) 1065–1076.
6. Patricia Besson. and Murat Kunt., Hypothesis testing for evaluating a multimodal pattern recognition framework applied to speaker detection, Journal of Neuro-Engineering and Rehabilitation. Vol. 5, BioMed Central (2008).
7. Steven M. Kay., Fundamentals of statistical signal processing, In: Detection Theory. Vol. 2, Prentice Hall (2002).
8. Eric K. Patterson., Sabri Gurbuz., Zekeriya Tufekci., and John N. Gowdy, Moving-talker, speaker-independent feature study and baseline results using the CUAVE multimodal speech corpus, Journal on Applied Signal Processing. Vol. 2002, EURASIP (2002) 1189–1201.
9. K. Fukunaga, Introduction to Statistical Pattern Recognition, Academic Press, Boston (1990).

On Effects of Visual Query Complexity

Jialie Shen and Zhiyong Cheng

Abstract As an effective technique to manage large scale image collections, content-based image retrieval (CBIR) has been received great attentions and became a very active research domain in recent years. While assessing system performance is one of the key factors for the related technological advancement, relatively little attention has been paid to model and analyze test queries. This paper documents a study on the problem of determining "visual query complexity" as a measure for predicting image retrieval performance. We propose a quantitative metric for measuring complexity of image queries for content-based image search engine. A set of experiments are carried out using IAPR TC-12 Benchmark. The results demonstrate the effectiveness of the measurement, and verify that the retrieval accuracy of a query is inversely associated with the complexity level of its visual content.

Keywords Image • Performance • Evaluation • CBIR

1 Introduction

The emergence of the Internet and advancements in information technology can provide an economical reproduction and distribution platform for digitized media. As a powerful technique to manage large image collections, content-based image retrieval (CBIR) has been recently received great attentions and became a very active research domain. As a result, many different approaches have been proposed [1–10]. While a large amount of efforts have been invested in the domain, the technologies are still in their infancy. One of the major reasons for this stagnation is

J. Shen (✉) • Z. Cheng
School of Information Systems, Singapore Management University, 80 Stamford Road, Singapore 178902, Singapore
e-mail: jlshen@smu.edu.sg; zy.cheng.2011@smu.edu.sg

J.S. Jin et al., *The Era of Interactive Media*,
DOI 10.1007/978-1-4614-3501-3_44, © Springer Science+Business Media, LLC 2013

due to unavailability of a standard evaluation methodology to make cross method comparison to identify the state-of-the-art. Its importance has been recognized in the information retrieval and multimedia system community. There are four basic steps in the procedure to evaluate performance of CBIR systems [11–14]. They are,

1. construct an image test collection TC;
2. generate a set of visual queries and ground truth information GT;
3. run each image query set IQ through a particular CBIR system; and
4. assess performance of the system via an empirical distribution of particular measurement metric.

As shown above, the testbeds and the query sets involved could greatly influence the robustness and reliability of CBIR system evaluation. And the whole procedure may be strongly biased by human subjectivity. For example, in Step 2, some researchers can select images in favor of their algorithms as test queries. This can directly lead to unreliable system performance assessment. When interacting with CBIR system, users describe their information needs and search intent with an image query example. The central goal of corresponding search process is to rank visual documents according to their relevance/irrelevance to the given query. Based on the view, retrieval problem can be naturally modeled as one of binary classifications (a relevant class vs an irrelevant class). It is not hard to find that for a given CBIR technique, the higher complex visual queries are utilized, the poorer search (or classification) performance can be expected. This suggests that developing a systematical scheme to measure visual query complexity is very useful to gain a deeper structural insight into the behavior of CBIR system. It can enable us to carry out a comprehensive performance evaluation using different test queries. Another direct application domain is to use the measure to refine visual query structure. Motivated by this concern, a novel framework is proposed for quantitatively measuring the image complexity, in which images are represented by a set of visual keyblocks. To validate our proposed scheme, a set of experiments have been carried out using ImageCLEF test collection. The results demonstrate the effectiveness of the measurement, and verify that the retrieval accuracy of a query is inversely associated with the complexity level of its visual content. Further, our empirical study also shows that relatively fine-grained partition and larger codebook size can lead to more effective complexity computation. To the best of our knowledge, this is the first work on modeling visual query complexity quantitatively.

2 Estimating Image Complexity

2.1 Complexity Definition

Design of our framework is motivated by text processing. Each image is evenly segmented into blocks with regular geometric configuration such as rectangles. Each of the blocks is replaced with the most similar *keyblock* in precomputed *codebook*. With the indexes of *keyblocks* in the *codebook*, the image can be viewed as a document comprised by a matrix of indexes. Transforming the matrix using certain order (e.g., the scan order or the zig-zag order) to a one-dimensional (1-D) list, the image is thus syntactically analogous to a text document, which is essentially a list of terms. Based on the concept of *perplexity* in information theory, the measurement of image complexity can be defined as

$$C(I) = 2^{\mathrm{H(I)}} \tag{1}$$

where $H(I)$ is the entropy of an image I, which is estimated by the Shannon theorem [15]. Suppose that $\{w_1, w_2, \ldots, w_n\}$ is a list of indexes for image I in a database D; then the entropy is calculated as

$$H(I) = -\frac{1}{n} \log P(w_1, w_2, \ldots, w_n) \tag{2}$$

where $P(w_1, w_2, \ldots, w_n)$ is the probability of $\{w_1, w_2, \ldots, w_n\}$ over D.

2.2 Codebook Generation and Image Encoding

Blocks in an image are similar to the words in a text document. A codebook, which is similar to the word dictionary, needs to be precomputed. To achieve this, the related computation includes three steps: (1) every image in database is evenly partitioned into multiple blocks. For example, 3 × 3 means cutting an image into nine regions in 3 rows and 3 columns; (2) low-lever features (e.g., color, texture and shape) are then extracted from each block; and (3) a clustering algorithm, such as K-means, is applied to generate the codebook from the blocks in database. The keyblocks in the codebook are defined as the centers of the obtained clusters. The number of the clusters is the codebook size. For each block in an image, find the best match in the codebook and replace the block by the index of the best match code. Each image is then a matrix of indexes, which can be treated as 1-D code vector in the codebook. This property is similar to a text document, which can be viewed as a linear list of keywords.

2.3 N-block Model

This study assumes that the blocks in each image are not independent and they correlate with all the other blocks in the image. However, when the size of the codebook is large, modeling so many relations becomes difficult. So we make a second assumption that the blocks are connected in the order from left to right, and top to bottom. Each block is conditionally dependent on its previous words. In fact, this constraint can be removed by assuming more general models in arbitrary order. We only take this assumption for simplicity.

Given an image *I* encoded with a codebook *C*, let $\{w_1, w_2, \ldots, w_n\}$ denotes the code string of *I*. Based on the chain rule, the probability is written as

$$P(w_1, w_2, \ldots, w_k) = \prod_{k=1}^{n} P(w_k | w_1, w_2, \ldots, w_{k-1}) \tag{3}$$

where $P(w_k | w_1, w_2, \ldots, w_{k-1})$ is the conditional probability of code w_k given previous code $\{w_1, w_2, \ldots, w_{k-1}\}$. In reality, it is a serious problem to accurately compute the conditional probabilities. However, approximation can be possible based on some assumptions. We suppose that each code depends only on its immediate vertical and horizontal neighbors (analogy to the assumptions of *n- gram language model*).

According to the degree of dependency on remote codes, we defined three kinds of N-blocks models, uni-block, bi-block and tri-block. In uni-block model, the codes are considered independent to each other. In bi-block model, the probability of a given code depends only on the previous code, and in tri-block model the codes are assumed to depend on the preceding two codes. The three models can be expressed in Eq. (4–6) respectively.

$$P(w_1, w_2, \ldots, w_n) = \prod_{k=1}^{n} P(w_k) \tag{4}$$

$$P(w_1, w_2, \ldots, w_n) = \prod_{k=1}^{n} P(w_k | w_{k-1}) \tag{5}$$

$$P(w_1, w_2, \ \ldots, w_n) = \prod_{k=1}^{n} P(w_k | w_{k-2k-1}) \tag{6}$$

Notice that the assumptions can be generalized to an arbitrary length *n*. However, for a large *n*, it is not easy to approximate the conditional probabilities.

Let C^+ be the set of all nonempty code string with symbols in *C*, and *N(s)* denotes the occurrences of a code string $s \in C^+$ in the image database D. Then the estimated conditional probability can be formulated as follows according to uni-block model, for $\forall w_k \in C$

$$P(w_k) = \frac{N(w_k)}{\sum_{w \in C} N(w)} \tag{7}$$

In this model, the appearing of zero probability is avoided spontaneously because of the nature of clustering method.

Bi-blocks and tri-blocks, however, are sparsely distributed in the image. Thus a prior probability is assigned for an unseen bi-block $w_{k-1}w_k$. Accordingly, the amount of this prior probability should be discounted from the appearing words to meet the condition that the sum of probability is 1. The conditional probability of bi-block model is, for $\forall w_k, w_{k-1} \in C$

$$P(w_k|w_{k-1}) = \begin{cases} \dfrac{N(w_{k-1}w_k)}{N(w_{k-1})}\left(1 - \dfrac{N(w_{k-1})}{\sum_{w\in C}N(w)} \cdot \dfrac{1}{|C|}\right) & \text{if } N(w_{k-1}w_k)>0 \\ \dfrac{N(w_{k-1})}{\sum_{w\in C}N(w)} \cdot \dfrac{1}{|C|} & \text{otherwise} \end{cases} \quad (8)$$

$|C|$ is the number of keyblock in codebook. With the tri-block model, the conditional probability is, for $\forall w_k, w_{k-1}, w_{k-2} \in C$

$$P(w_k|w_{k-2}w_{k-1}) = \begin{cases} \dfrac{N(w_{k-2}w_{k-1}w_k)}{N(w_{k-2}w_{k-1})}\left(1 - \dfrac{N(w_{k-2}w_{k-1})}{N(w_{k-2})|C|}\right) & \text{if } N(w_{k-2}w_{k-1}w_k)>0 \\ \dfrac{N(w_{k-2}w_{k-1})}{N(w_{k-2})} \cdot \dfrac{1}{|C|} & \text{if } N(w_{k-2}w_{k-1})>0 \\ \dfrac{N(w_{k-2})}{\sum_{w\in C}N_w} \cdot \dfrac{1}{|C|} \cdot \dfrac{1}{|C|} & \text{otherwise} \end{cases} \quad (9)$$

Note that other more sophisticate smoothing methods, such as the one used in [16] which combines back-off and discounting, can be also applied here, instead of just assigning a small constant prior probability to the unseen bi-block or tri-block.

3 Experimental Setup

In the empirical study, we first study the effectiveness of the proposed measurement of image complexity using different N-block models, and then verify the assumption that the query image with higher complexity can lead to lower retrieval accuracy. A reliable measurement should be consistent with human cognitive perspective that an image with multiple objects or heterogeneous visual content is more complex than the one with single object or homogeneous visual appearance.

The visual content of image is closely associated with its complexity. According to the proposed computational method, the complexity is also influenced by the number of partition blocks in an image. Combining both factors, we can have a strong assumption about the characteristics of complexity varying with partition methods for images with different complexity level. For an image with homogenous visual content, its complexity should keep stable with increasing block number partitioned. This is because an image coded by 4 same blocks should have the same complexity as the image consisting of 20 same blocks. While for an image with heterogeneous visual content, there will be more different blocks when partitioning it into more blocks. Thus, its complexity should increase with the increase of block number. However, when the block number increases to some level, the complexity will gradually become stable. The main reason is that when the block size is small enough (maybe in pixel level), the image will be represented by the same number of different blocks, and the distribution of these different blocks will be the same even continuing to increase the block number. So the increasing level and growth rate of complexity with the increase of partition block number should be different for images with different levels of complexity. Here the increasing level means the level of partition granularity when complexity stops increasing. In other words, the more complex image, its complexity will keep increasing till finer partition (more blocks).

To verify these hypothses, two experiments are conducted on a standard test collection. *Experiment 1* is to compute the complexities of images in different concepts, and their complexity variation characteristics with the increase of block number. *Experiment 2* is to confirm the relations between query complexity and retrieval precision.

3.1 Test Collection and Visual Feature Extraction

The IAPR TC-12 Benchmark,[1] is constructed as test collection in our experiments. The collection consists of 20,000 still natural images taken from locations around the world and comprising an assorted cross-section of still natural images. This includes pictures of different sports and actions, photographs of people, animal, cities, landscapes and many other aspects of contemporary life. The benchmark has been used as the evaluation resources in *ImageCLEF* retrieval task for three years. To reduce the influence of image size variation, images with size 480 × 360 are selected as test collection. There are totally 10,971 images in this collection. In our experiments, a 64-D global feature [17] is calculated as composite visual feature representation for each image. The feature vector consists of three different kinds of visual features: 44-D color correlogram, 14-D color texture moment and 6-D RGB color moment. Then the three features are separately normalized into unit length and concatenated into the final 64-D feature. Euclidean distance is used as a similarity measurement.

[1]http://www.imageclef.org/photodata

Table 1 The size of codebooks for different partition methods

Partition	Codebook size	Partition	Codebook size	Partition	Codebook size
2 × 2	100	3 × 3	100	4 × 4	175
5 × 5	274	6 × 6	395	7 × 7	537
8 × 8	702	9 × 9	888	10 × 10	1,097

3.2 Experimental Methodology

Experiment 1: This experiment is to verify the effectiveness of the proposed complexity measure, and demonstrate the variation of complexity with different levels of granular partitions. In order to achieve the goal, 27 topic concepts are carefully selected which are blue sky, night shot of cathedrals, desert, surfing, tennis match, animal swimming, motorcyclist racing, sunset over water, ship, scenes in Inka-Trail, football match, snowcapped building, cycling, beach, accommodation with swimming pool, statue, scenes with building, tourist group, mountain, waterfall, church, wild animal, bedroom, meat dishes, school building, family shot, crowd of people. The partition methods with corresponding codebooks sizes are in Table 1.

Experiment 2: The goal of this experiment is to empirically verify the hypothesis that lower complex query images lead to better retrieval results than the ones with higher complexity. To facilitate the experimental study, three CBIR systems are applied and we use the standard queries in *ImageCLEF* photo retrieval tasks as the test image queries.

CBIR Systems: In order to demonstrate that the relation of query complexity and search performance is independent of the retrieval system, three retrieval methods are applied:

1. Vector Space Model: Since images are represented by an list of keyblock indexes in codebook, VSM approach used in text retrieval can be directly transplanted. The classical TF-IDF weigh is used to denote the block weights.
2. Histogram Model: In this model, the feature vectors **I** and **q** are the keyblock histograms. And the similarity measure is defined as

$$S(\mathbf{q},\mathbf{I}) = \frac{1}{1 + dis(\mathbf{q},\mathbf{I})} \tag{10}$$

$$dis(\mathbf{q},\mathbf{I}) = \sum_{i=1}^{N} \frac{|w_{i,I} - w_{i,q}|}{1 + w_{i,I} + w_{i,q}} \tag{11}$$

where the q and I, which are the feature vectors of query and image I, are keyblock histograms. $w_{i,I}$ is the frequency of $c_i (c_i \in C)$ appearing in I. Similarly, $w_{i,q}$ is the frequency of c_i appearing in q.

3. SIMPLIcity: It is a region-based retrieval system proposed by Wang et al. [18]. In the system, an image is represented by a set of regions, roughly corresponding to objects, which are characterized by color, texture, shape, and location. The integrated region matching measure, which integrates properties of all the regions in the images, is used as similarity measurement. For more details, please refer to [18].

Query Topics: The standard query topics in *ImageCLEFphoto 2007* are used in this experiment. There are 60 query topics, and each contains three image examples. The query examples are not included in the test collection. Because the test collection only contains 480 × 360 images in *IAPR TC-12 Benchmark*, we remove some queries that may not have enough relevant images in the test collection. The assessment pool for each query topic are provided by *ImageCLEF*. If the number of relevant images for a query is less than 20 in the pool (after removing the ones whose size are not 480 × 360), then the query is excluded. Besides, the query examples with different size are also removed. There are 48 query topics with 104 query examples left after filtering.

Evaluation Criterion: Relevance assessment of results is based on the visual content of images. Typically a relevant image will have the subject of the topic in the foreground, and the image will not be too dark in contrast. We use *precision at K (P@K)* as performance evaluation measure. *P@K* is the proportion of relevant instances in the top *K* retrieved results, computed as $P@K = \frac{\text{No. of relevant results in top } K}{K}$. In the empirical study, only the top 20 results are evaluated and thus $K = 20$.

4 Experimental Results

The experimental results are presented and analyze in this section. We intended to apply three N-block models to compute the image complexity. Tri-blocks are sparse in the collection (many tri-blocks only appear once), however, which poses a significant effects on the results. Thus in the following discussion, we only consider the uni-block model and bi-block model.

4.1 Complexity Variation Characteristics

In *Experiment 1*, the complexities of images in different concepts are computed under different levels of partition granularity (namely different numbers of blocks in an image). We define that the complexity of a concept is the average complexity of all images in the concept. In uni-block model, the complexities of all concepts increase dramatically with the number of blocks increases. Besides, the relative complexity of different concepts is not consistent with our perspective either. For example, the obtained complexity of *blue sky* is higher than that of *touristgroup*

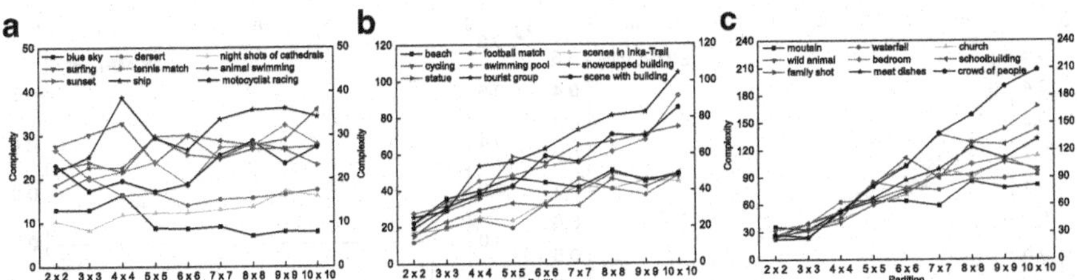

Fig. 1 When the number of partition blocks increases, the complexities of different concepts variation characteristics

in this model. These results are against our original intention described in Sect. 3. The reason for the results is that the blocks are assumed to be independent in uni-block model, and the spatial distribution information of blocks is ignored.

Figure 1 shows the results obtained by bi-block model. Concepts are divided into three groups according to the value of complexity (there are no strict bounds between groups). The concepts in (a) (we use (a) to denote Fig. 1a for simplicity, and it is the same to (b) and (c)) have the lowest complexity and those in (c) have the highest complexity. When the partition is relatively coarse (such as 2×2), the difference of complexity between some concepts are not very clear. As the partition become finer (more blocks), the complexities of some concepts increase faster while some grow relatively slower or even keep stable. The complexities of concepts in (a) roughly keep stable as the block number increases, because images in these concepts have simple or homogeneous visual content (e.g., ***bluesky*** and ***desert*).** The concept ***nightshotofcathedrals*** in this group is because the selected images show homogenous visual appearance especially the color. The complexities of concepts in (b) and (c) are increasing as the block number increases, and the complexity growth rates of concepts in (c) are generally larger than those of concepts in (b). Even only comparing the complexities of concepts in (b), the growth rates are different when the block number exceeds 25 (5×5). This phenomenon is exactly what we expect. As explained in Sect. 3, image with more complex visual content, the complexity increasing level and growth rate should be deeper and larger. However, the most fine-grained partition is limited to 10×10 in current experiment, the results have not shown different increasing levels. But we can anticipate that if the block number keeps increasing, the complexities of concepts in (b) will become stable before the complexities of concepts in (c). If we see the complexities of concepts in (a) in the way that the partition is already fine enough so that they keep stable, then the anticipation is also verified.

4.2 Relation Between Query Complexity and Query Performance

In ***Experiment 2***, query complexity is calculated based on 6 x 6 partition with codebook size 375. The VSM and Histogram Model (HM) adopt the same partition method and codebook. Figure 2a shows the trend of retrieval precision changes

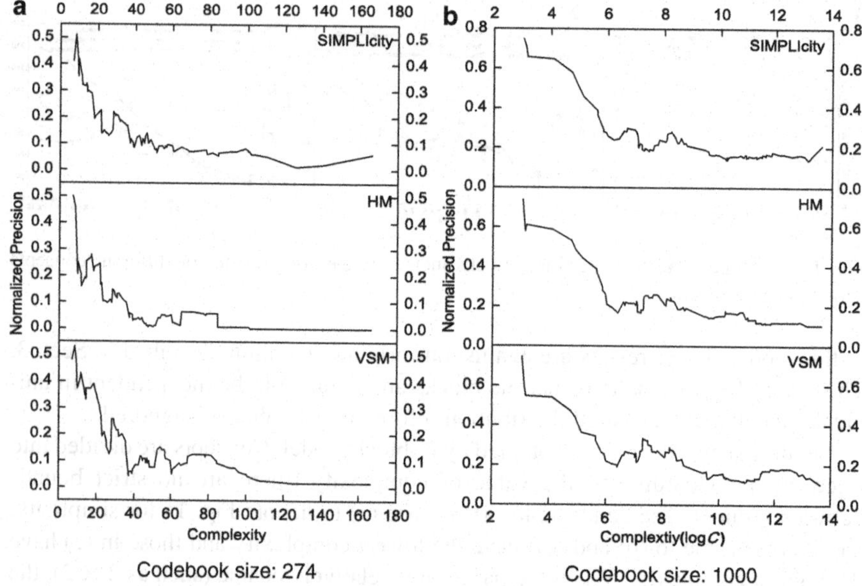

Fig. 2 The relationship between query complexity and query performance

when query complexity is increasing. The precisions in the figure are normalized results of three models, and the curves are processed by adjacent averaging smoothing method. Although there are some differences between results based on three models, the general trends are the same: the retrieval precision decreases as the query complexity increases. Because only the standard queries are used in the experiment, the number of queries is relatively small. It is unavoidable that there are some fluctuations in the statistical results. Besides, the relatively coarse partition and small codebook size which also have some impacts on the results. To demonstrate this point, we increase the codebook size to 1,000 to computer the query complexity, and the results are shown in Fig. 2b. The x axis here is the logarithm value of complexity, because the complexity varies in a very large range in this case. Comparing the two figures, we can see that with larger codebook, the change trends are smoother and more obvious.

5 Conclusion

In this study, a framework is developed to quantitatively measure the complexity of image. With this method, images used as query examples are partitioned into blocks and represented by indexes of keyblocks in the generated codebook. A set of experiments are carried out using a standard image collection. The results demonstrate the effectiveness of the measurement, and verify that the retrieval accuracy of a query is inversely related to the complexity level of its visual content. Besides, the results also show that it is better to use relatively fine-grained partition and larger codebook size to compute the complexity.

References

1. J. Laaksonen, M. Koskela, S. Laakso, and E. Oja. How to complete performance graphs in content-based image retrieval: Add generality and normalize scope. IEEE TPAMI, 2005.
2. J. Huang, S. R. Kumar, and M. Mitra. Combining supervised learning with color correlograms for content-based image retrieval. In ACM Multimedia, 1997.
3. N. Vasconcelos and M. Kunt. Content-based retrieval from image databases: current solutions and future directions. In ICIP (3), 2001.
4. AHH. Ngu, Q. Sheng, D. Huynh, and R. Lei. Combining multi-visual features for efficient indexing in a large image database. The VLDB Journal, 2001.
5. W. Ma and B. Manjunath. Netra: A toolbox for navigating large image database. In Proceedings of IEEE International Conference on Image Processing, 1997.
6. Y. Chen and J. Z. Wang. Image categorization by learning and reasoning with regions. Journal of Machine Learning Research, 2004.
7. M. S. Lew, N. Sebe, C. Djeraba, and R. Jain. Content-based multimedia information retrieval: State of the art and challenges. ACM TOMCCAP, 2006.
8. Z.-J. Zha, X.-S. Hua, T. Mei, J. Wang, G.-J. Qi, and Z. Wang. Joint multi-label multi-instance learning for image classification. In CVPR, 2008.
9. Z.-J. Zha, L. Yang, T. Mei, M. Wang, Z. Wang, T.-S. Chua, and Xian-S. Hua. Visual query suggestion: Towards capturing user intent in internet image search. ACM TOMCCAP, 2010.
10. Y. Gao, M. Wang, H.-B. Luan, J. Shen, S. Yan, and D. Tao. Tag-based social image search with visual-text joint hypergraph learning. In ACM Multimedia, 2011.
11. A. Narasimhalu, M. Kankanhalli, and J. Wu. Benchmarking multimedia databases. Multimedia Tools and Applications, 1997.
12. Proceedings of mira 99: Evaluating interactive information retrieval, glasgow, scotland, uk, april 14–16, 1999. In S. W. Draper, M. D. Dunlop, I. Ruthven, and C. J. van Rijsbergen, editors, MIRA, Workshops in Computing. BCS, 1999.
13. J. Shen and J. Shepherd. Efficient benchmarking of content-based image retrieval via resampling. In ACM Multimedia, 2006.
14. C. D. Manning, P. Raghavan, and H. Schutze. Introduction to Information Retrieval. Cambridge University Press, 2008.
15. C.Shannon. Prediction and entropy of printed english. Bell Syst. Tech. J., 1951.
16. L. Wu, M. J. Li, Z. W. Li, W. Y. Ma, and N. H. Yu. Visual language modeling for image classification. In MIR, 2007.
17. X. Li, C. G. M. Snoek, and M. Worring. Learning tag relevance by neighbor voting for social iimage retrieval. In MIR, 2008.
18. J. Z. Wang, J. Li, and G. Wiederhold. SIMPLIcity: Semantics-sensitive integrated matching for picture libraries. IEEE TPAMI, 2001.

Watermarking and Image Processing

Reversible Image Watermarking Using Hybrid Prediction

Xiang Wang, Qingqi Pei, Xinbo Gao, and Zongming Guo

Abstract In this paper, a hybrid prediction algorithm is designed to improve the histogram shifting based reversible watermarking method. This algorithm not only uses the local information near a pixel, but also utilizes the global information of the whole image. As a result, it produces a sharper histogram for watermark embedding. In addition, we enable the use of sorting idea by introducing an estimation function of the hybrid prediction. Experimental results illustrate that the proposed watermarking method outperforms many recently proposed methods.

Key words Reversible watermarking • Histogram shifting • Hybrid prediction

1 Introduction

Due to the reversible watermarking method can exactly recovers the host image in the decoder, it has been often used to protect the copyrights of some high-fidelity products, such as medical and military images. So far, there are huge reversible watermarking algorithms have been presented in the literature, e.g., the compression technique based methods [1, 2], integer transform based methods [3, 4] and histogram shifting based methods [5–7].

X. Wang • Q. Pei (✉)
State Key Laboratory of Integrated Service Networks, Xidian University,
Xi'an, Shaanxi 710071, China
e-mail: wangxiangnis@gmail.com; qqpei@mail.xidian.edu.cn

X. Gao
School of Electronic Engineering, Xidian University, Xi'an, Shaanxi 710071, China
e-mail: xbgao@mail.xidian.edu.cn

Z. Guo
Institute of Computer Science and Technology, Peking University, Beijing 100871, China
e-mail: guozongming@icst.pku.edu.cn

J.S. Jin et al., *The Era of Interactive Media*,
DOI 10.1007/978-1-4614-3501-3_45,

Among them, the histogram shifting based methods have attracted many interests owing to the better capacity control ability and smaller location map. Thodi et al. [5] proposed the classical histogram shifting model. In their model, the embedding process mainly includes two steps: the prediction and histogram shifting. The result of prediction highly determines the performance of the histogram shifting and the whole watermark embedding process. If the pixels of the host image are predicted by an efficient prediction algorithm, their prediction errors are mostly equal to (or nearly equal to) zero. The statistical histogram of the prediction errors has a sharp curve with the highest peak value at the origin. According to the histogram shifting strategy, the prediction errors around the origin are used to embed the watermark, and the others are shifted to make free space for embedding. Therefore, the sharper the histogram is, the less distortion the histogram shifting generates.

In [8], Sachnev et al. introduced the rhombus pattern prediction into histogram shifting. The rhombus pattern prediction is experimentally proved to be more efficient than JPEG-LS (used in [5]). So it is more suitable for histogram shifting. In addition, by exploiting Kamstra's sorting idea [9], small prediction errors in the embedding process are preferentially selected to embed the watermark. Experimental results show that this method achieves significant improvement over Thodi's method.

Inspired by Sachnev et al.'s work, it seems that we can employ more efficient prediction algorithms to improve the watermark embedding performance. However, although there are numerous of prediction algorithms perform better than JPEG-LS and rhombus pattern prediction, most of them cannot be directly brought into the reversible watermark embedding process. Two reasons account for this failure. First, the prediction value of each pixel should keep the same between the encoder and the decoder to guarantee the reversibility of the watermark, which is not necessary for the prediction algorithm. Secondly, the steps of the reversible watermark embedding are not independent to each other. The prediction algorithm needs to be well integrated with other steps (the histogram shifting, sorting, etc.). In fact, finding an appropriate prediction algorithm is an important task for reversible watermarking methods.

In this paper, we design a hybrid prediction algorithm for the histogram shifting based reversible watermarking method. The hybrid prediction algorithm robustly exploits the correlation within the whole image, and produces better results than the rhombus pattern prediction and JPEG-LS. In addition, the hybrid prediction algorithm also has the property required by the sorting idea. We will give a detailed description of how to incorporate the sorting idea and the hybrid prediction.

The rest of this paper is organized as follows. In Sect. 2, we present the hybrid algorithm. Section 3 describes the embedding and decoding process. The experiments comparing with some other methods are reported in Sect. 4. Finally, we conclude our work in the last section.

2 Hybrid Prediction

The hybrid prediction algorithm consists of two components: the local prediction and the global prediction.

2.1 Local Prediction

The local prediction is similar with Sachnev et al.'s rhombus pattern prediction. Considering a 512×512 sized image *I*, we first divide the pixels of the host image into two sets:

$$S1 = \{I(a,b) : a \in [1,512], b \in \{2k - a\%2\}\},$$
$$S2 = \{I(a,b) : a \in [1,512], b \in \{2k + a\%2 - 1\}\},$$

where $k \in [1, 256]$ and % represents the modulo operator. The white and block boxes in Fig. 1 denote the pixels in set $S1$ and $S2$, respectively. For a pixels $I(i, j)$ in set $S1$, we calculate the prediction value according to its four neighboring pixels. For simplicity, we define the vector $\mathbf{x}_{i,\,j}$ (Fig. 2) consisting of these four pixels:

$$\mathbf{x}_{ij} = \{I(i,j-1), I(i,j+1), I(i-1,j), I(i+1,j)\}. \tag{1}$$

Then, $I(i, j)$ is predicted as follows:

$$\dot{I}(i,j) = \lfloor E(\mathbf{x}_{ij}) \rfloor, \tag{2}$$

where $\lfloor \cdot \rfloor$ represents the floor operation. Notice that the pixels used to predict $I(i, j)$ belong to set $S2$, i.e., belong to a different set with the predicted one.

The efficiency of the local prediction relies on the texture complexity around the pixel. It can achieve an accurate predicted value for a pixel in smooth area. However,

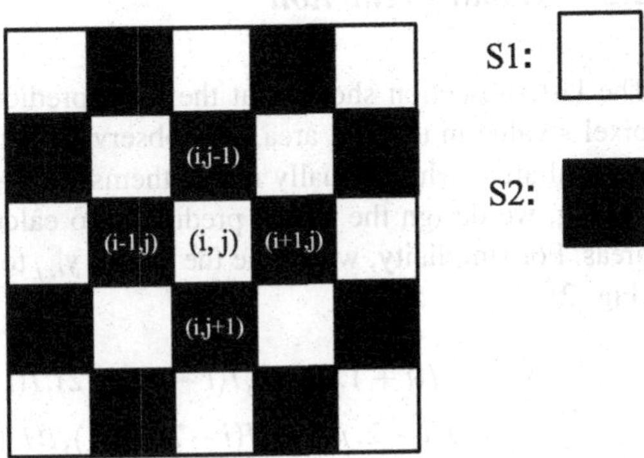

Fig. 1 Labeling of $S1$ and $S2$

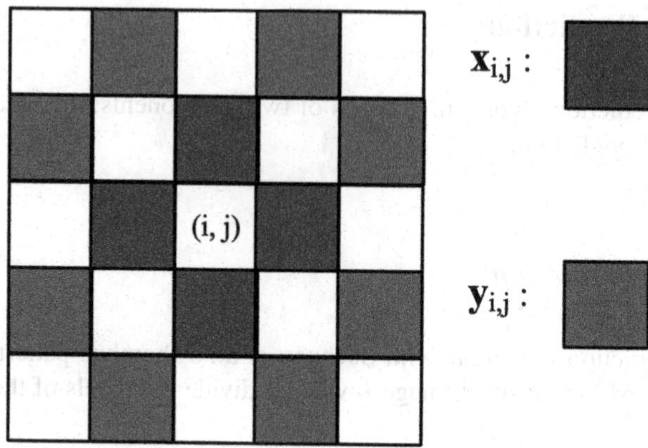

Fig. 2 Labeling of $\mathbf{x}_{i,j}$ and $\mathbf{y}_{i,j}$

the local prediction usually not work efficiently in textural area. Therefore, the local texture information can be exploited to indicate the efficiency of the local prediction. For pixel $I(i, j)$, the local texture information is computed as follows:

$$v_{loc}(i,j) = \frac{\sqrt{\sum_{k=1}^{4} (\mu(i,j,k) - \bar{\mu}(i,j))^2}}{4}, \tag{3}$$

where $\mu(i, j, 1) = | I(i, j-1) - I(i-1, j) |$, $\mu(i, j, 2) = | I(i-1, j) - I(i, j+1) |$, $\mu(i, j, 3) = | I(i, j+1) - I(i+1, j) |$, $\mu(i, j, 4) = | I(i+1, j) - I(i, j-1) |$ and $\bar{\mu}(i,j) = \sum_{k=1}^{4} \mu(i,j,k)/4$. A small $v_{loc}(i, j)$ indicates that the pixel $I(i, j)$ is in smooth area, and the predicted value might be quit close to its original value, and vice versa.

2.2 Global Prediction

The last subsection shows that the local prediction cannot efficiently predict the pixel's value in textural area. It is observed that the natural image includes many textural areas which usually repeat themselves at various locations. Based on this finding, we design the global prediction to calculate the prediction value in such areas. For simplicity, we define the vector $\mathbf{y}_{i,j}$ to include eight pixels around $I(i, j)$ (Fig. 2):

$$\begin{aligned}\mathbf{y}_{i,j} = \{&I(i+1,j-2), I(i-1,j-2), I(i+1,j+2), I(i-1,j+2),\\ &I(i-2,j-1), I(i-2,j+1), I(i+2,j-1), I(i+2,j+1)\}.\end{aligned} \tag{4}$$

Clearly, if two pixels have similar neighborhoods, the value of these pixels might be close to each other. So neighborhood sets **x** (1) and **y** (4) are exploited to estimate the similarity between two pixels, which is defined as follows:

$$Sim(I(i_1,j_1),I(i_2,j_2)) = \frac{1}{8}\|\mathbf{x}_{i_1j_1} - \mathbf{x}_{i_2j_2}\|_{l^2} + \frac{1}{16}\|\mathbf{y}_{i_1j_1} - \mathbf{y}_{i_2j_2}\|_{l^2}. \tag{5}$$

We then sort all the pixels in the set $S1$ in the ascending order in terms of the local variance v_{local}. Suppose the set $S1$ after sorting is:

$$\hat{S1} = \{I(i_1,j_1),I(i_2,j_2),I(i_3,j_3),...,I(i_n,j_n)\}.$$

If $k < l$, we have $v_{loc}(i_k, j_k) \leq v_{loc}(i_l, j_l)$. Then, for a pixel $I(i_k, j_k)$ in set $\hat{S1}$, its global prediction value is computed as follows:

$$\ddot{I}(i_k,j_k) = \left\lfloor \frac{\sum_{l=1}^{k-1} \omega(I(i_l,j_l),I(i_k,j_k))I(i_l,j_l)}{\sum_{l=1}^{k-1} \omega(I(i_l,j_l),I(i_k,j_k))} \right\rfloor, \tag{6}$$

where $\omega(I(i_l,j_l),I(i_k,j_k)) = e^{-Sim(I(i_l,j_l),I(i_k,j_k))/h}$, and h is the parameter to control the decay of the exponential function. The above equation indicates that when calculate the global prediction value of $I(i_k, j_k)$, only pixels before $I(i_k, j_k)$ in the set $\hat{S1}$ are used. This definition ensures that the global prediction value of each pixel keeps consistent between the encoder and the decoder.

Equation (6) also indicates that the efficiency of global prediction depends on how similar the predicted pixel is to the other pixels. So we define the following equation to estimate the global prediction efficiency:

$$v_{glob}(I(i_k,j_k)) = \frac{\sum_{l=1}^{k-1} \omega(I(i_l,j_l),I(i_k,j_k))Sim(I(i_l,j_l),I(i_k,j_k))}{\sum_{l=1}^{k-1} \omega(I(i_l,j_l),I(i_k,j_k))}.$$

The above equation first calculates the similarities between the current pixel and its previous pixels in set $\hat{S1}$. Then the similarities are normalized to indicate the efficiency of the global prediction.

2.3 *Hybrid Prediction*

In this subsection, we introduce how to use both the local and the global prediction to predict a pixel value, which is named as hybrid prediction. Specifically, the hybrid prediction value of the pixel $I(i, j)$ is calculated as:

- If $v_{loc}(i,j) < v_{glob}(i,j)$, we set $\hat{I}(i,j) = \dot{I}(i,j)$ and $v_{hyb}(i,j) = v_{loc}(i,j)$.
- If $v_{loc}(i,j) \geq v_{glob}(i,j)$, the hybrid prediction value and $v_{hyb}(i,j)$ is computed as:

$$\widehat{I}(i,j) = \frac{e^{-v_{loc}(i,j)}\dot{I}(i,j) + e^{-v_{glob}(i,j)}\ddot{I}(i,j)}{e^{-v_{loc}(i,j)} + e^{-v_{glob}(i,j)}},$$

and

$$v_{hyb}(i,j) = \frac{e^{-v_{loc}(i,j)}v_{loc}(i,j) + e^{-v_{glob}(i,j)}v_{glob}(i,j)}{e^{-v_{loc}(i,j)} + e^{-v_{glob}(i,j)}}. \quad (7)$$

We incorporate the global prediction into local prediction only when the global prediction performs better. Because this means that the pixel is probably in the textural area. In this case, the global prediction is used to refine the local prediction results. Furthermore, Eq. (7) indicates that if the global prediction performs remarkably better than the local prediction, it occupies a larger proportion in hybrid prediction, and vice versa. Because the weights ($e^{-v_{loc}(i,j)}$ and $e^{-v_{glob}(i,j)}$) are calculated based on $v_{loc}(i, j)$ and $v_{glob}(i, j)$, which are the estimations of the local and global prediction efficiency, respectively. Accordingly, an estimation value v_{hyb} used for sorting (introduced later) is computed to indicate the efficiency of the hybrid prediction.

3 Encoder and Decoder

3.1 Histogram Shifting

The classical histogram shifting technique in [5] is utilized in this work to embed the watermark efficiently. For a pixel $I(i, j)$, its prediction error is computed as follows:

$$d(i,j) = I(i,j) - \widehat{I}(i,j).$$

Then, the prediction error $d(i, j)$ of the pixel $I(i, j)$ is shifted or expanded according to two thresholds T_l and T_r as follows:

$$d^w(i,j) = \begin{cases} d(i,j) + T_l, & \text{if } d(i,j) < T_l, \\ 2d(i,j) + w, & \text{if } d(i,j) \in [T_l, T_r], \\ d(i,j) + T_r + 1, & \text{if } d(i,j) > T_r, \end{cases} \quad (8)$$

where $w \in \{0, 1\}$ is a watermark bit to be embedded and the superscript w means *watermarked*. The embedded pixel value is reconstructed as $I^w(i,j) = \widehat{I}(i,j) + d^w(i,j)$. In the decoder, the pixels are recovered as follows:

$$d(i,j) = \begin{cases} d^w(i,j) - T_l, & if\ d^w(i,j) < 2T_l, \\ \left\lfloor \frac{d^w(i,j)}{2} \right\rfloor, & if\ d^w(\mathbf{x}_k) \in [2T_l, 2T_r + 1], \\ d^w(i,j) - T_r - 1, & if\ d^w(i,j) > 2T_r, \end{cases} \tag{9}$$

Evidently, the watermark can be extracted by reading the LSBs of $d^w(i, j)$.

The overflow/underflow problem is inevitable in the reversible watermarking method. In this study, we use Thodi's *DS-HS-FB* technique to deal with this problem. Due to space limitation, this technique is not presented here. The details can be found in [5].

3.2 Sorting

The introduction of sorting significantly improves the embedding performance of histogram shifting. However, the sorting idea requires that embedding watermark into a pixel should not affect the embedding of other pixels, which leads to the failure of incorporating sorting into many prediction algorithms (e.g. JPEG-LS). The hybrid prediction, like the rhombus pattern prediction, divides the pixels of the host image into two parts: $S1$ and $S2$. When embedding the watermark into $S1$, we use the pixels in $S2$ to compute the prediction value. Therefore, changing a pixel in $S1$ will not affect the embedding process of other pixels. Based on this property, the sorting idea is introduced to the histogram shifting process.

The value v_{hyb} (7) is computed to estimate the efficiency of the hybrid prediction. The pixel with small v_{hyb} usually have small prediction error. Therefore, we should give high priority to such pixels during the embedding process. In order to achieve that, we first sort the pixels in terms of v_{hyb}. Then, according to the watermark capacity, a part of pixels are selected (in ascending order) to embed the watermark, and the others are left unchanged. Therefore, after sorting, the pixels introducing small distortion (with small prediction error) are first used for embedding. Whereas the classical histogram shifting processes the pixels one by one according to their positions in the image, which definitely generates more embedding distortion.

3.3 Encoder

A two-pass embedding scheme is designed to embed the watermark into the host image. In the first pass, half of the watermark is embedded into the pixels in the set $S1$. In the second pass, the rest watermark is embedded into $S2$. For simplicity, we only give the embedding process for the preselected parameters (T_l and T_r), but the embedding process can be easily extended to embed a desired amount of watermark that meets the requirement.

Step-1: Sort all the pixels in the set $S1$ in ascending order based on v_{hyb}. Define the sorted set as $S1'$.

Step-2: Establish a location map M, and assume its length is m. Divide the pixels in set $S1'$ into three parts: $S1'_1$, $S1'_2$ and $S1'_3$. $S1'_3$ includes the last m pixels in set $S1'$, and $S1'_1$ consists of the first m pixels with $d \in [T_l, T_r]$, and the rest pixels constitute $S1'_2$.

Step-3: Embed the location map M into $S1'_3$ by least significant bit (LSB) replacement, and record the original LSB sequence as L.

Step-4: Embed the sequence L into $S1'_1$ by Eq. (8). Then embed the watermark into $S1'_2$ according to Eq. (8).

Step-5: Repeat *Step 1-4*, and embed the rest watermark into set $S2$.

Finally, we obtain the image carrying the whole watermark, and the embedding process is finished.

3.4 Decoder

The encoder first embed the watermark into set $S1$, and then into $S2$. The decoder, in contrary, have to first recovery the pixels of $S2$ (also extract the watermark). Then, the watermark carried by $S1$ can be correctly extracted. Only in this way, we can ensure the consistency between the encoder and the decoder.The decoding process is summarized as follows.

Step-1: Sort all the pixels in the set $S2$ in ascending order based on v_{hyb}. Suppose the sorted set is $S2'$.

Step-2: Extract the location map M by reading the LSBs of the last m pixels. Based on the location map M, determine the pixels which are modified by encoder (named as *watermarkable*).

Step-3: Among all the *watermarkable* pixels, we can identify which pixels are carrying watermark by the condition $d^w \in [2T_l, 2T_r + 1]$. Then the sequence L (see *Step-3* of encoder) and the watermark are extracted by reading the LSBs of these pixels.

Step-4: Recover the *watermarkable* pixels according to Eq. (9), and the last m pixels of $S2'$ by replacing their LSBs with the corresponding values in sequence L.

Step-5: Repeat the same extracting and recovering process to set $S1$.

Finally, the watermark is extracted and the original image is restored.

4 Experimental Results

We first evaluate the hybrid prediction by comparing with the rhombus pattern prediction. Figure 3 shows that the proposed prediction method produces a sharper histogram than the rhombus pattern prediction. As aforementioned, the

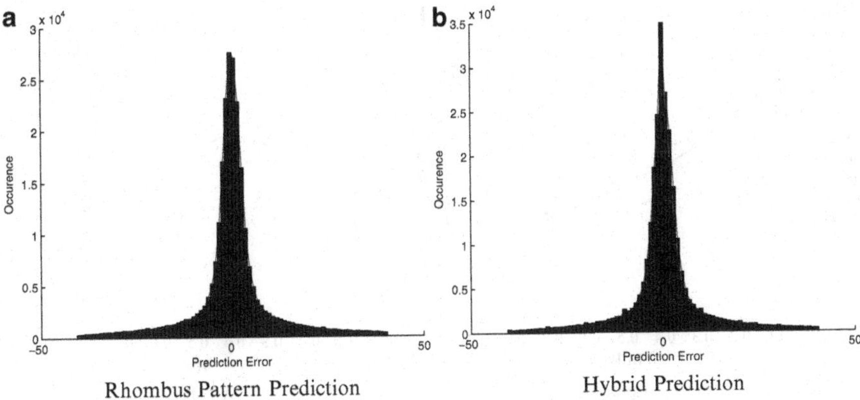

Fig. 3 Histograms of rhombus pattern prediction and hybrid prediction. The tested image is Barbara

performance of histogram shifting depends on the shape of the histogram. Therefore, the hybrid prediction is more suitable for the histogram shifting.

The proposed method is compared with three state-of-the-art algorithms (capacity versus distortion) to well demonstrate the performance of the proposed method: (1) Hu et al.'s method [10]; (2) Luo et al.'s method [11]; (3) Sachnev et al.'s method [8]. Four standard 512 ×512 sized gray-scale images are used in the experiments: "Lena," "Baboon," "Barbara" and "Airplane" (F-16). We implement the methods (1)–(3), and the arithmetic lossless compression coding is employed to compress the location map.

The comparison results in Fig. 4 indicate that the proposed method performs better than the methods (1)–(3) at almost all embedding rates. Notice that, "Barbara" has more repeated textures than the other three images. Therefore, the global prediction performs more efficiently. As a result, the advantage is more obvious on "Barbara." On the contrary, Fig. 4 also presents that the superiority is not clear on "Baboon." Because textures of "Baboon" are mostly irregular.

5 Conclusion

In this paper, we design a hybrid prediction algorithm for embedding watermark reversibly. This prediction algorithm achieves a shaper histogram than previous works. Therefore, it is more suitable for histogram shifting. In addition, by designing an estimation equation, the sorting idea is introduced to our embedding process, which significantly improves the performance of the histogram shifting. Finally, the superiority of the proposed method is experimentally verified by comparing with other existing schemes.

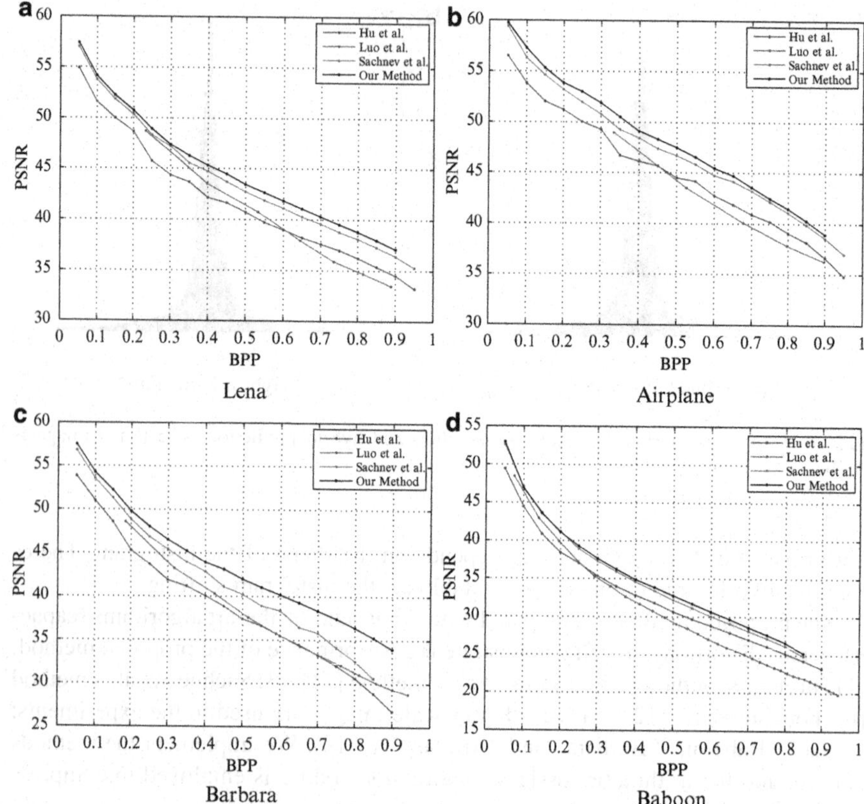

Fig. 4 Performance comparison of other four methods with the proposed method

Acknowledgements This work was supported by the National Grand Fundamental Research 973 Program of China under Grant No.A001200907, the Planned Science and Technology Project of Shaanxi Province 2009K08-38, the National Natural Science Foundation of China under contract No.61101250 and the Natural Science Basic Research Plan in Shaanxi Province of China (Program No.2010JQ8026).

References

1. Fridrich, J., Goljan, M., Du, R.: Invertible authentication watermark for jpeg images. In: Proc. Int. Conf. Inf. Technol.: Coding and Comput. (2001) 223–227
2. Celik, M.U., Sharma, G., Tekalp, A.M., Saber, E.: Lossless generalized-lsb data embedding. IEEE Trans. Image Process. **14**(2) (2005) 253–266
3. Tian, J.: Reversible data embedding using a difference expansion. IEEE Trans. Circuits Syst. Video Technol. **13**(8) (2003) 890–896

4. Wang, X., Li, X., Yang, B., Guo, Z.: Efficient generalized integer transform for reversible watermarking. IEEE Signal Process Lett. **17**(6) (2010) 567–570
5. Thodi, D.M., Rodriguez, J.J.: Expansion embedding techniques for reversible watermarking. IEEE Trans. Image Process. **16**(3) (2007) 721–730
6. Gao, X., An, L., Li, X., Tao, D.: Reversibility improved lossless data hiding. Signal Process. **89**(10) (2009) 2053–2065
7. Gao, X., An, L., Yuan, Y., Tao, D., Li, X.: Lossless data embedding using generalized statistical quantity histogram. IEEE Trans. Circuits Syst. Video Technol. (99) (2011) Early Access.
8. Sachnev, V., Kim, H.J., Nam, J., Suresh, S., Shi, Y.Q.: Reversible watermarking algorithm using sorting and prediction. IEEE Trans. Circuits Syst. Video Technol. **19**(7) (2009) 989–999
9. Kamstra, L., Heijmans, H.J.A.M.: Reversible data embedding into images using wavelet techniques and sorting. IEEE Trans. Image Process. **14**(12) (2005) 2082–2090
10. Hu, Y., Lee, H.K., Li, J.: De-based reversible data hiding with improved overflow location map. IEEE Trans. Circuits Syst. Video Technol. **19**(2) (2009) 250–260
11. Luo, L., Chen, Z., Chen, M., Zeng, X., Xiong, Z.: Reversible image watermarking using interpolation technique. IEEE Trans. Inf. Forensics Secur. **5**(1) (2010) 187–193

A Rotation Invariant Descriptor for Robust Video Copy Detection

Shuqiang Jiang, Li Su, Qingming Huang, Peng Cui, and Zhipeng Wu

Abstract A large amount of videos on the Internet are generated from authorized sources by various kinds of transformations. Many works are proposed for robust description of video, which lead to satisfying matching qualities on Content Based Copy Detection (CBCD) issue. However, the trade-off of efficiency and effectiveness is still a problem among the state-of-the-art CBCD approaches. In this paper, we propose a novel frame-level descriptor for video. Firstly, each selected frame is partitioned into certain rings. Then the Histogram of Oriented Gradient (HOG) and the Relative Mean Intensity (RMI) are calculated as the original features. We finally fuse these two features by summing HOGs with RMIs as the corresponding weights. The proposed descriptor is succinct in concept, compact in structure, robust for rotation like transformations and fast to compute. Experiments on the CIVR'07 Copy Detection Corpus and the Video Transformation Corpus show improved performances both on matching quality and executive time compared to the pervious approaches.

Keywords CBCD • Frame-level descriptor • Rotation invariant • HOG

S. Jiang (✉) • P. Cui
Key Lab of Intell. Info. Process., Chinese Academy of Sciences, Beijing 100190, China

Institute of Computing Technology, Chinese Academy of Sciences, Beijing 100190, China
e-mail: sqjiang@jdl.ac.cn; pcui@jdl.ac.cn

L. Su • Q. Huang • Z. Wu
Graduate School of Chinese Academy of Sciences, Beijing 100049, China
e-mail: lsu@jdl.ac.cn; qmhuang@jdl.ac.cn; zpwu@jdl.ac.cn

J.S. Jin et al., *The Era of Interactive Media*,
DOI 10.1007/978-1-4614-3501-3_46, © Springer Science+Business Media, LLC 2013

1 Introduction

Recently, online video websites such as YouTube, Yahoo!, Google, etc. have taken the fancy of the users for the convenience of browsing large amount of videos for free. Meanwhile, many illegal copies without authorities are uploaded. To protect intellectual properties, Content Based Copy Detection (CBCD) issue aroused researchers' great interest. As the TRECVID'08 CBCD evaluation plan [1] describes, a copy is not an exact duplicate but a segment derived from original document, with some transformations such as cropping, recoding, flipping, inserting pictures, etc. Therefore, a copy usually differs from its corresponding resource in both format and content, which makes CBCD a challenging task.

Many approaches towards CBCD have obtained satisfying results. It can be concluded that an effective descriptor is the key point in CBCD systems. As [2] pointed out, an effective descriptor must have the following two advantages: *robustness* and *discriminability*, which make the descriptor invariant to various transformations generated from the original source. Besides, facing to the exponential growth of digital video resources, CBCD approaches call for a *fast* and *compact* video descriptor, which is important in a user-oriented system.

Numerous descriptors have been proposed to meet these advantages mentioned above. Previous methods are mostly based on video keyframes. Researchers study physical global features, such as color moment and histogram [3, 4] in keyframes to deal with large corpus. These global features are compact and simple, but they suffer from serious problems like brightness changes and fail in more complex tasks. Recently, local features especially Local Interest Points (LIPs) are brought forth as effective methods to describe frames and images. In [5], Zhao et al. match LIPs with PCA-SIFT description and introduce fast filtering procedure. Wu et al. treat every keyframe as a Bag of visual Words (BoW), which are regarded as the clustering centers of LIPs [6]. Ngo et al. detect and localize partial near-duplicates based on LIPs matching between the frames rearranged by time stamps [7]. Local feature description of keyframes has shown its invariant property to many kinds of transformations, however, there are still some problems: (a) Extraction and matching process of LIPs is particularly time consuming; (b) There exist many mismatched LIPs which will greatly degrade the final performance; (c) All these approaches depend on a robust keyframe extraction scheme.

On noticing these problems that the keyframe based approaches faced with, researchers propose some non-keyframe approaches instead. Kim et al. extract ordinal signatures from the video clip and propose a spatio-temporal sequence matching solution [8]. Wu et al. introduce self-similarity matrix for robust copy detection [9]. In [2], Yeh et al. contribute a frame-level descriptor which encoded the internal structure of a video frame by computing the pair-wise correlations between pre-indexed blocks. These descriptors are compact in structure and retain the most relevant information of a frame/clip. Besides, they are suitable to be integrated into a fast copy detection scheme.

Motivated by the non-keyframe approaches, in this paper, we propose a novel frame-level descriptor which combines the Histogram of Oriented Gradient (HOG) [10] and the Relative Mean Intensity (RMI) together by means of a weighting scheme. A frame is partitioned into rings which are invariant for the transformations such as rotation and flipping. Besides, instead of treating each frame as a whole, using a series of rings can save the local patterns and further make the descriptor more discriminative. RMI of each ring represents the bottom physical feature of a frame, and HOG, which is well-known for counting occurrences of orientation in localized portions of an image, has been improved in this paper with RMI as the weight. Compared with existing representations of video, the proposed descriptor offers the following advantages:

- **Succinct** in concept: Combination of two naive features
- **Compact** in structure: Encodes each frame at a certain sample rate
- **Invariant** for common transformations: Lighting, flipping, rotation, etc.
- **Fast** in extraction and matching procedure

The remaining of the paper is organized as follows. In Sect. 2, we detail the extraction and matching process of the proposed descriptor. Section 3 shows the experimental results on CIVR'07 corpus and Video Transformation Corpus. Finally, we conclude the paper with future work in Sect. 4.

2 Descriptor Extraction

2.1 Preprocessing

2.1.1 Frame Border Removal

Border is a common trick made in a copy [11]. For each frame, we are interested in the significant content without borders. Besides, the intensities of the border are useless in frame analysis, as shown in Fig. 1. We adopt a simple method, which removes the first few lines of each direction (left, right, top, bottom) whose sum of intensity is less than a threshold (20% of the maximum in this paper). Figure 1c, d show the results of frames after border removal of (a) and (b).

Fig. 1 Frames border removal. (**a**) and (**b**) are frames from the source video and query video. (**c**) and (**d**) are results of boder removal for (**a**) and (**b**)

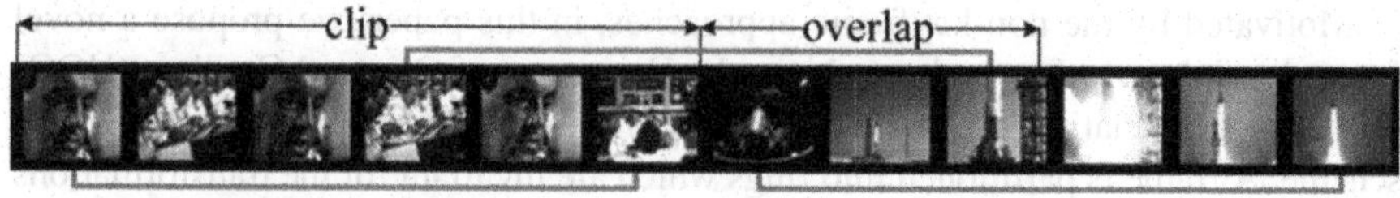

Fig. 2 Video clips and overlaps

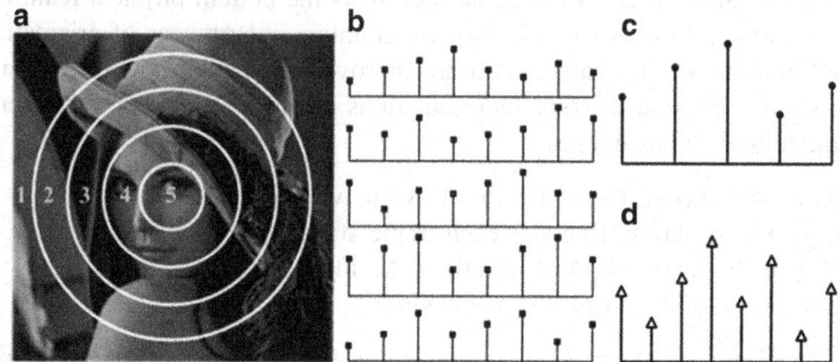

Fig. 3 Illustration of the extraction process, $n_L = 5$, $n_G = 12$.(**a**) is the original frame with five rings; (**b**) HOG of each ring; (**c**) is the relative mean intensity of each ring; (**d**) is the final descriptor

2.1.2 Frame Resizing

As [1] describes, copies may have different sizes with the original source. Here we employ a linear interpolation process to resize the query frames to the same size with its reference. This process is necessary because different sizes may cause different forms of the descriptors.

2.2 Frame Description

2.2.1 Extraction Process

The descriptor is extracted by encoding the pixel information of each frame. For a given video, with overlaps, we segment it into clips, which are the basic processing units in our approach. Figure 2 shows an example. For each frame *Fr* in a video clip, we divide it into n_L rings. In Fig. 3a, the area between two white circles is called a ring. A ring reserves the RGB intensities of symmetrical positions in a frame, which makes it invariant for rotation and flipping.

Next, for the *i*th ring of a frame, the relative mean intensity (RMI) is calculated:

$$RMI(i) = \sum_{p \in ring(i)} p(x, y) / \sum_{p \in Fr} p(x, y) \quad (1)$$

where *p(x,y)* stands for the intensity of point *(x,y)*.

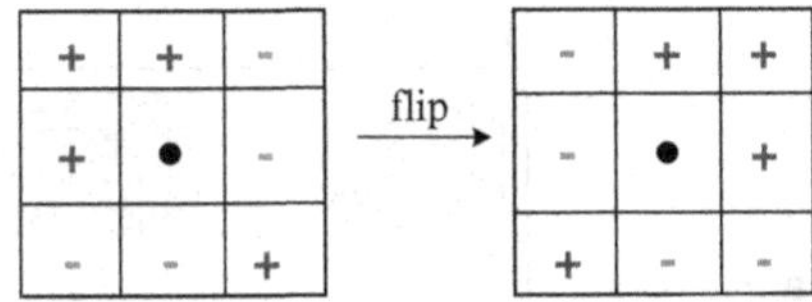

Fig. 4 Flipping frames with different gradients maps

From Eq. (1), it is easily concluded that RMI is a global feature of each ring. It represents the *intra*-ring information and can help maintain a similar *inter*-ring relationship between the query video and the reference. Besides, it is not sensitive to some complex brightness changes.

To describe the local distribution of a frame, we adopt HOG. HOG is a widely used feature for object detection, especially for human detection [12]. For each point of a ring, n_G (chosen as even number) gradient orientations are calculated. HOGs of each ring are illustrated in Fig. 3b. As can be seen from Fig. 4, if the query is flipped from the reference, the gradient orientations are opposite. To avoid this change, instead of directly using the gradient orientations, we divide their absolute values into certain number of bins. With the increasing of bin number n_G, the discriminative power of HOG increases. However, the computation complexity also rises, and it will enlarge the influence of noise. We need to combine HOG and RMI into the video description to promote the discriminability.

To combine these two features, we sum the n_L HOGs with each RMI of the same ring as the weight:

$$\mathbf{D}_{nG\times 1} = \mathbf{HOG}_{nG\times nL} \times \mathbf{RMI}_{nL\times 1}$$
$$= \begin{pmatrix} HOG_{11} & HOG_{12} & \cdots & HOG_{1,nL} \\ HOG_{21} & HOG_{22} & \cdots & HOG_{2,nL} \\ \vdots & \vdots & \ddots & \vdots \\ HOG_{nG,1} & HOG_{nG,2} & \cdots & HOG_{nG,nL} \end{pmatrix}_{nG\times nL} \times \begin{pmatrix} RMI_1 \\ RMI_2 \\ \vdots \\ RMI_{nL} \end{pmatrix}_{nL\times 1} \quad (2)$$

D is the final descriptor. Different from the traditional HOG, it involves the intensity and inner distribution of each frame. From the calculating process, we find that **D** is overall a global descriptor with the length of n_G. It encodes the inner relationship of a frame and the local changes of intensities. Figure 10 shows more examples.

2.2.2 Matching Process

To match two descriptors $\mathbf{D_1}$ and $\mathbf{D_2}$, we choose χ^2 distance as the similarity metric. In the matching process, a double-minimization process is employed in matching process [9]. In the first step, for an input query video, we find the clips with the minimal distance (maximal similarity) between descriptors in each source video. Then, we select the one with the lowest distance in the source. This process is illustrated in Fig. 5.

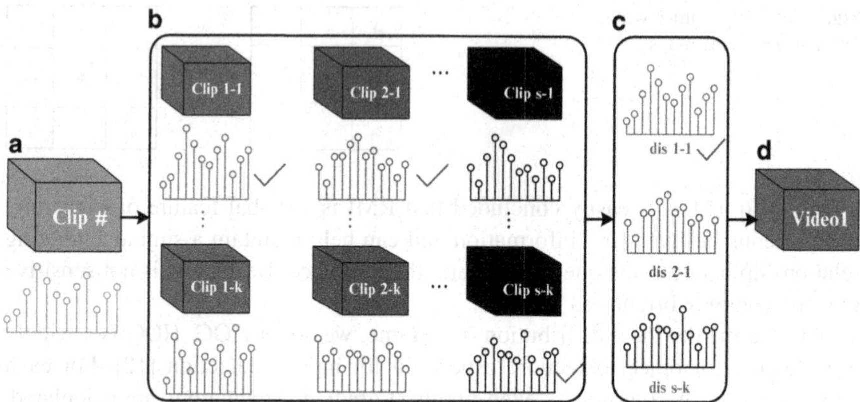

Fig. 5 A double-minimization process for matching. Each cube represents a video or a video clip, the diagram below each cube is the descriptor. (**a**) Query clip; (**b**) Finding the minimal distance in each source video; (**c**) Finding minimal distance among all the source videos; (**d**) Matching result

3 Experimental Results

3.1 Dataset

Experiments are conducted using the CIVR'07 Copy Detection Corpus (MUSCLE VCD) [13].The CIVR'07 corpus are based on two tasks: task 1 retrieves copies of whole long videos while task 2, a much harder task, detects and locates the partial-duplicate segments from all the videos. The source data contains about 100 h of 352 × 288 videos. These videos come from web, TV archives and movies, and cover documentaries, movies, sport events, TV shows and cartoons. Meanwhile, there are 15 queries for ST1 with different transformations like change of colors, blur, recording with an angle and inserting logos. There are also three queries for ST2 with transformations mentioned above.

The Video Transformation Corpus (VTC) [14] aims at recognizing transformations happened in video copies. It consists of ten types: Analog VCR Recording, Blur, Caption, Contrast, Picture in Picture, Crop, Ratio, Resolution Reduction, Adding Noise and Monochrome. There are 300 sources and 20 queries for each kind of transformation. Besides, we also add the CIVR'07 corpus into the mentioned transformations.

According to the evaluation plot [13], criterion of the detection scheme is defined as:

$$Matching\ Quality = \frac{Num\ Of\ Corrects}{Num\ Of\ Queries} \tag{3}$$

To implement fast copy detection, we down sample the frames in a fixed rate: we select one frame every ten frames. Noticing that the adjacent frames always conserve similar content information, our sample strategy is proved to be efficient and effective by the experiments (Fig. 6).

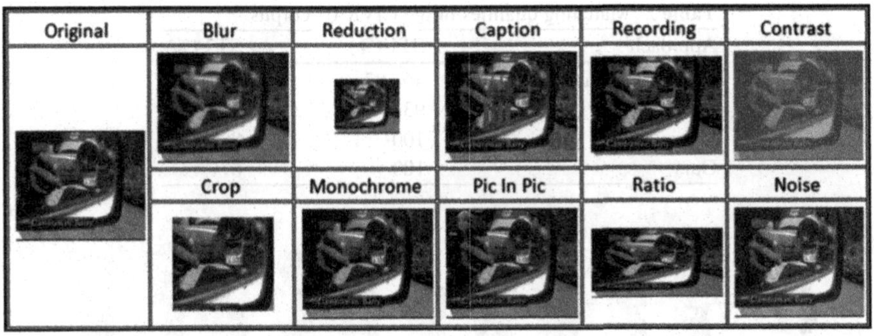

Fig. 6 Example of ten transformation types

Table 1 Matching qualities with different n_L and n_G for CIVR'07 ST1

n_L / n_G	4 (%)	8 (%)	12 (%)	16 (%)
4	93	93	100	100
8	93	100	100	100
12	93	100	100	100
16	93	100	100	100

3.2 Parameters

We choose ring number (n_L) and HOG bin number (n_G) as parameters in the experiments.

- n_L: As n_L gets larger, the descriptor will possess more discriminate power. However, while the dimension increases, the descriptor is more sensitive to the border removal technique which may lower down the overall performance.
- n_G: Theoretically, with more HOG bins, more information can be captured by the descriptor. However, for the existence of noise, the performance will be degraded if there are too many bins.

Table 1 shows the results of different parameters on CIVR'07 corpus.

3.3 Detection Results

3.3.1 Experiment-I: Matching Qualities

Without loss of generality, we set the parameters (n_L and n_G) to be 4/8/12/16. Table 1 lists the matching qualities with the corresponding value. Table 2 shows the results of the CIVR'07 corpus with the comparison to some existing approaches and Fig. 7 shows the performance on the Video Transformation Corpus (VTC).

Table 2 Matching qualities of the CIVR'07 corpus

Approach	ST1 (%)	ST2 (%)
CIVR'07 teams [13]	46~87	17%~87
Yeh et al. [2]	93	73
Previous work [15]	100	80
Ours	100	87

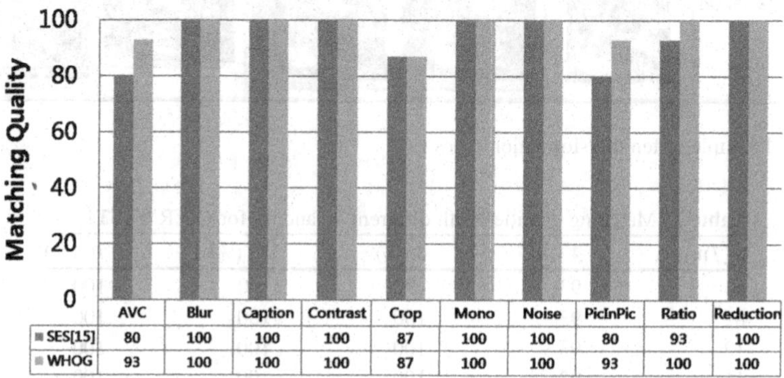

Fig. 7 Matching qualities of the VTC compared with our previous work [15]

Table 3 Executive time of different approaches (in seconds)

Approach	ST1	ST2
Yeh et al. [2]	1,394	570
Previous work [15]	849	368
Ours	69	44

3.3.2 Experiment-II: Comparison of the Proposed Descriptor, HOG and RMI

In this experiment, we test the RMI, traditional HOG and the proposed descriptor in CIVR'07 ST1. According to the result, it is clear that the proposed descriptor shows improved performance than the versions only using RMI and HOG.

3.3.3 Experiment-III: Executive Time

Table 3 shows the matching time of different approaches. According to the table, the proposed approach runs faster than (Fig. 8) previous works.

3.3.4 Experiment-IV: Similarity Metric

Besides χ^2 distance, we also try Euclidean distance, Cosine distance and Correlation Coefficient. The proposed descriptor is robust enough for different similarity

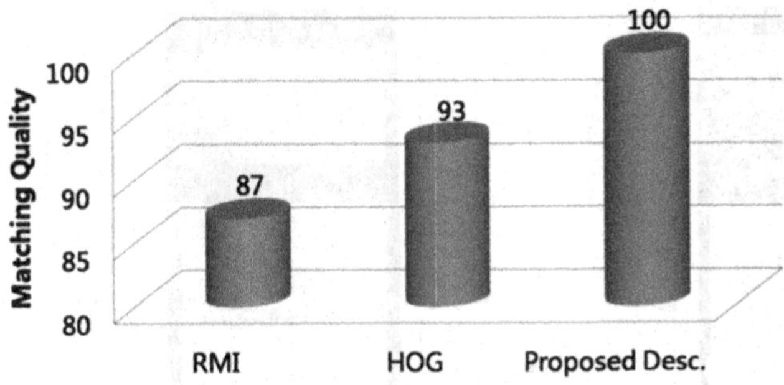

Fig. 8 Comparison of RMI, HOG and the proposed descriptor on ST1

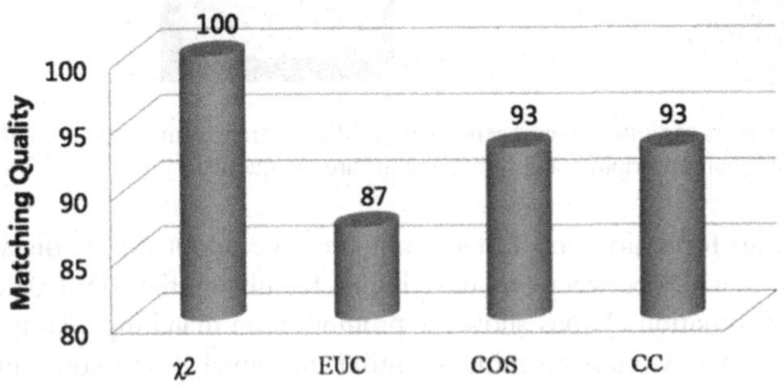

Fig. 9 Matching qualities under different measurement metrics

metrics, among them χ^2 distance performs better and we employ it as the metric in this paper. Figure 9 illustrates the different matching results using the above four metrics.

These experiments show that the descriptor is effective and efficient. But the length of the basic processing unit (see Sect. 2.2.1) is pre-fixed without further consideration. As long as we obtain a robust shot detection scheme, it can be easily extended to shot-based descriptor, which will help promote the segment accuracy of CIVR'07 ST2 and more (Fig. 10) complex partial near duplicated videos.

4 Conclusions

In this paper, we propose a novel descriptor by combining two common applied characteristics, relative mean intensity (RMI) and histogram of gradient (HOG). RMI represents the global intensity level while HOG describe the change of each pixel. As an effective descriptor, it is succinct in concept, compact in structure,

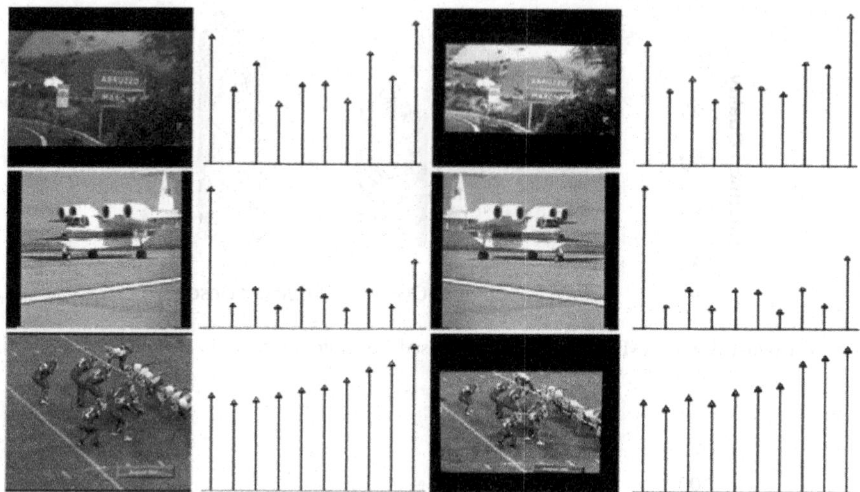

Fig. 10 Descriptors of similar frames generated by different transformations. The left columns are the sources and their descriptors, the right columns are the queries

robust for transformation and fast to compute. We adopt the χ^2 distance as the metric of similarities between two descriptors. Results on the CIVR'07 corpus and Video Transformation Corpus show the promotion on matching quality.

In future work, we aim to mine a similar clip-level descriptor, which can be treated as a cube of feature and it can draw correlations between adjacent frames. Another direction is to fuse this descriptor into keyframe based approach to further accelerate the CBCD framework.

Acknowledgements This work was supported in part by National Natural Science Foundation of China: 61025011, 60833006, 61070108 and 61001177, and in part by Beijing Natural Science Foundation: 4092042.

References

1. TRECVID, http://www-nlpir.nist.gov/projects/trecvid.
2. M. Yeh and K. Cheng, "Video copy detection by fast sequence matching," In Proc. Of ACM Int. Conf. on Multimedia, pp. 633–636, Oct. 2009.
3. A. Qamra, Y. Meng, and E. Y. Chang, "Enhanced perceptual distance functions and indexing for image replica recognition," In IEEE Trans. Pattern Anal. Mach. Intell.,vol. 27, no. 3, pp. 379–391, Mar. 2005.
4. M. Bertini, A. D. Bimbo, and W. Nunziati, "Video clip matching using MPEG-7 descriptors and edit distance," In Proc. of the ACM Int. Conf. on Image and Video Retrieval, pp. 133–142, 2006.
5. W. L. Zhao, C. W. Ngo, H. K. Tan, and X. Wu, "Near-duplicate keyframe identification with interest point matching and pattern learning," In IEEE Trans. On Multimedia, vol. 9, no. 5, pp. 1037–1048, Sep. 2007.

6. X. Wu, W. L. Zhao, and C. W. Ngo, "Near-duplicate keyframe retrieval with visual keywords and semantic context," In Proc. Of ACM Int. Conf. on Image and Video Retrieval, pp. 162–169, 2007.
7. H. Tan and C. W. Ngo, "Scalable detection of partial near-duplicate videos by visual-temporal consistency," In Proc. of ACM Int. Conf. on Multimedia, pp. 145–154, Oct. 2009.
8. C. Kim and B. Vasudev, "Spatio-temporal sequence matching for efficient video copy detection," In IEEE Trans. on Circuits and Systems for Video Technology, vol. 15, no. 1, pp.127–132, Jan. 2005.
9. Z. P. Wu, Q. M. Huang, and S. Q. Jiang, "Robust copy detection by mining temporal self-similarities," In IEEE Int. Conf. on Multimedia and Expo, 2009.
10. http://en.wikipedia.org/wiki/Histogram_of_oriented_gradients
11. J. Law-To, L. Chen, A. Joly, I. Laptev, O. Buisson, V. Gouet-Brunet, N. Boujemaa, and F. Stentiford, "Video copy detection: a comparative study," In Proc. of the ACM Int. Conf. on Image and Video Retrieval, pp. 371–378, 2007.
12. N. Dalal and B. Triggs, "Histograms of Oriented Gradients for Human Detection," In IEEE Int. Conf. on Computer Vision and Pattern Recognition, pp.886–893, 2005.
13. MUSCLE-VCD-2007, http://www-rocq.inria.fr/imedia/civrbe-nch/index.html.
14. Z. P. Wu, S. Q. Jiang, and Q. M. Huang, "Near-Duplicate Video Matching with Transformation Recognition," In proceedings of the ACM International Conference on Multimedia, pp. 549–552, 2009.
15. P. Cui, Z. P. Wu, S. Q. Jiang, and Q. M. Huang, "Fast Copy Detection Based on Slice Entropy Scattergraph," In IEEE Int. Conf. on Multimedia and Expo, Singapore, pp.149–154, Jul.19–23, 2010.

Depth-Wise Segmentation of 3D Images Using Dense Depth Maps

Seyedsaeid Mirkamali and P. Nagabhushan

Abstract Unlike the conventional image segmentation problems dealing with surface-wise decomposition, the depth-wise segmentation is a problem of slicing an image containing 3D objects in a depth-wise sequence. The proposed depth-wise segmentation technique uses depth map of a 3D image to slice it into multiple layers. This technique can be used to improve viewing comfort with 3D displays, to compress videos and to interpolate intermediate views. The technique initially finds the edges of the dense depth map using a graduate edge detection algorithm. Then, it uses the detected edges to divide rows of a depth map into line-segments based on their entropy values. Finally, it links the line—segments to make object-layers. The experiments done through depth-wise segmentation technique have shown promising results.

Keywords Depth-wise segmentation • 3D image • Depth map • Mean-shift • Entropy

1 Introduction

Image segmentation has long been a basic problem in computer vision. It is useful in many applications such as image/video compression, object tracking and object recognition. However, automatic segmentation is a nontrivial problem due to the variety of unknown factors and possible geometries in the computation.

The conventional segmentation algorithms used the advantages of color and texture information; the use of depth information also has some interesting advantages. Firstly, it is invariant to illumination and texture change. Secondly, it is invariant to camera pose and perspective variation [1]. Moreover, the steady growth in the production of

S. Mirkamali (✉) • P. Nagabhushan
Department of Studies in Computer Science, University of Mysore, Mysore, India
e-mail: s.s.mirkamali@hotmail.com; p.nagabhushan@hotmail.com

J.S. Jin et al., *The Era of Interactive Media*,
DOI 10.1007/978-1-4614-3501-3_47,

3D depth cameras (e.g. Time-of-Light and Kinect) implies that achieving high-quality depth images is becoming increasingly accessible and flexible. Therefore, it is not dificult to imagine that every captured image will have depth data in the future. Accordingly, taking advantage of the depth information for segmentation is becoming an important issue. To the best of our knowledge, it has not yet been thoroughly discussed in literatures, especially for depth-wise segmentation of a scene.

In this paper, we propose a novel depth-wise image segmentation method with the objective that the extracted layers not only preserve object boundaries but also maintain their depth order using information available in the depth map of the input . This method can be used to improve viewing comfort with 3D displays [2], to compress videos [3] and to interpolate intermediate views [4]. In this paper, we first find edges of objects using a graduate base edge detection algorithm [5]. We then use entropy measures to find the line segments in every line of the depth map between the computed edges. The line segments are linked to make object-layers using the proposed linking algorithm.

We assume that there is a depth map for each 3D image and objects are naturally and linearly separable (e.g. Fig. 4a–c). The depth data could be achieved by using a range map camera, depth camera or multi-view stereo techniques [6, 7]. Since no dataset is available to have depth images which satisfy our assumptions we considered to make use of computer generated scenes and their depth maps in our experiments. Our method contributes the following two aspects. First, we introduce a novel segmentation method which uses entropy to separate each row of the depth map into line-segments. Second, we introduce a link perception method to connect parts of the objects and make a complete object and later make an object-layer. The experiment results demonstrate that our segmentation method, which uses the depth map of a 3D image, can reliably extract objects and their corresponding layers.

1.1 Related Work

There are many robust image segmentation algorithms [8] such as thresholding [9], mean shift [10], normalized cut [11] and watershed algorithm [12]. Mean shift based segmentation algorithms are the most reliable segmentation approaches for the task of multi-object segmentation. However, for a depth image, directly using these intensity-based segmentation methods to decompose a depth image into object-layers will result in undesirable over-segmentation due to the lack of knowledge about the objects and their depth relation.

However, by incorporating the additional depth information and layer separation, robust segmentation can be achieved. For multi-object segmentation from the multi-view video of a dynamic scene, Xiping and Jie [13] proposed an algorithm that uses Maximum A Posterior (MAP) estimation to compute the parameters of a layered representation of the scene where each layer is modeled by its motion, appearance and occupancy. The MAP estimation of all layer parameters is equivalent to tracking multiple objects in a given number of views. Expectation-Maximization (EM) is employed to establish the layer occupancy and visibility posterior probabilities. Some other methods formulate the problem of multi-view object segmentation based on layer separation using Epipolar Plane Image (EPI) [14], a volume constructed by collecting multi-view images taken from equidistant locations along a line. This category of methods suffer from an important limitation: all of them classify moving objects as the first layer of a scene and other objects are left as the background layer.

Our work is closely related to depth-based segmentation proposed by Francois and Chupeau [3]. They used a Markovian statistical approach to segment the depth map into regions homogeneous in depth. In their approach two types of information are used to overcome the segmentation, which are depth map and stereoscopic prediction error. Another approach, proposed by Jin et al. [4], also worked on layered representation of scenes based on multiple image analysis. In their approach, the problem of segmentation is formulated to exploitation of the color and edge information. The color information is analyzed separately in YUV-channels and edge information is used in intermediate processes. The proposed method works fine in many cases. However, in case of periodic texture in the background both the disparity and color segmentation processes will fail.

In summary, many approaches have been proposed to segment a gray scale image into multiple levels based on objects gray levels and also few of them have worked on layered representation of a 3D image. However, the problem of how to properly extract the layers based on objects and their depth values is still a challenging problem. In this paper, we propose a depth-wise segmentation approach which uses depth map to decompose a scene into layers based on the depth of objects. The method incorporates a graduate based edge detection and entropy measures to segment the depth map into super pixels. The super pixels are further linked to make object-layers.

2 The Proposed Depth-Wise Segmentation Method

Suppose that a 3D image I having a depth map D with L gray levels $L = \{0,1,\ldots, L-1\}$, containing the Z value of an image I, is to be sliced into m object-layers $OL = \{ol_1, ol_2,\ldots,Ol_m\}$.

The proposed segmentation method is to first decompose the objects detected by edge detection into over-segmented lines (line-segments) using their entropy values and then to link the line-segments of an object to make compound objects and later object-layers. The major steps of this method are summarized in Fig. 1.

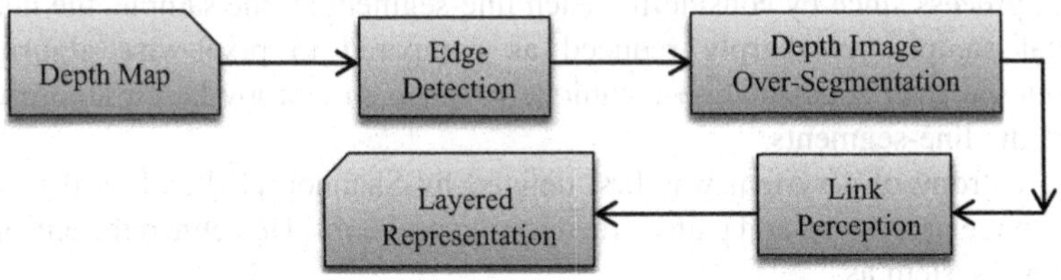

Fig. 1 Block diagram of the proposed depth-wise segmentation method

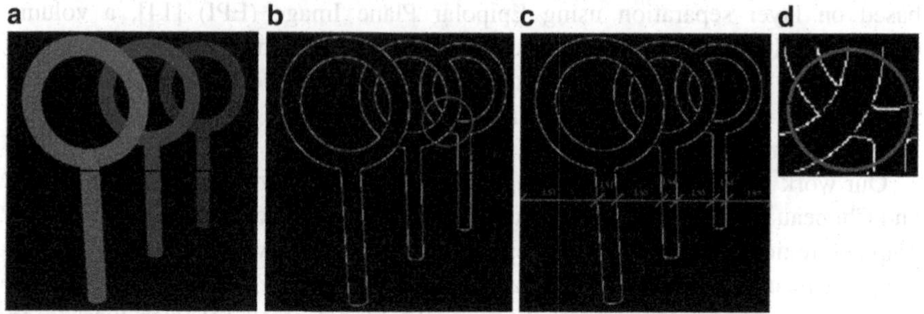

Fig. 2 (**a**) depth map of a 3D image (**b**) result of edge detection applied on depth map (**c**) showing a row with 7 line-segments (LS1. . .LS7) (**d**) zoomed area in Fig. 2b, showing the weakness of the edge detection method

2.1 Edge Detection

Edge detection is a method to identify points in a digital image at which the image brightness changes sharply or, more formally, has discontinuities. In a depth map, a sharp change shows a change between two objects in two different layers. We use this phenomenon to identify the objects in different layers of a 3D image.

A large number of techniques were proposed for edge detection. The most popular edge detectors are graduate based edge detectors. We choose to use a technique proposed by Shannon [5] because of the following advantages. Firstly, the technique can preserve pixels on sharp but weak edges. Secondly, the method is robust to noise compared to other edge detection techniques. Result of applying the edge detection on a depth image is shown in Fig. 2b.

2.2 Depth Image Over-Segmentation

Edges computed in edge detection stage are used in over-segmentation stage to find the start and ending points of line-segments. This stage characterizes the number of objects and the layers independently. We choose to use over-segmentation of a depth image due to the following reasons: first, each line-segment in depth images can be viewed as a patch with an object number and a layer number. Second, employing over-segmentation can decrease the computational complexity of the linking process since by considering each line-segment as one sample, the number of total samples is sharply reduced as compared to pixel-wise algorithms. In proposed over-segmentation technique, we use an entropy-based algorithm to extract the line-segments.

The entropy of a system was first defined by Shannon [15] and used to solve many image processing and pattern recognition problems. He defined the entropy of an n-state system as

$$H = -\sum_{i=1}^{n} p_i log(p_i) \tag{1}$$

where p_i is the probability of occurrence of the event i and

$$\sum_{i=1}^{n} p_i = 1,\ 0 \le p_i \le 1 \tag{2}$$

Conventional Quantifier measures the energy contribution of each row by considering the problem occurrence of $+ve$ and $-ve$ transitions among the total number of pixels in each row in horizontal direction and quantifies the entropy as

$$E(t) = p \log\left(\frac{1}{p}\right) + (1-p)\log\frac{1}{1-p}\cdots \tag{3}$$

where t is the 0–1 and 1–0 transitions, p represents number of times 0–1 and 1–0 transitions occur in each row and *1-p* represents the non-probable occurrence of transitions.

Depending upon the transition (0–1 or 1–0) as described above, *E(t)* could be $E^-(t)$ or $E^+(t)$ so that we could define a total entropy along a row *i* as

$$E(i) = E^-(t) + E^+(t) \tag{4}$$

where $E^-(t)$ is the entropy due to the transitions from 1 to 0 and $E^+(t)$ is the entropy due to the transitions from 0 to 1 [16].

A line-segment *LS* is defined as a gap between every *-ve* transition followed by a $+ve$ transition. In which, every $-ve$ transition is considered as the starting point of a line-segment and a $+ve$ transition is considered as the ending point of the line-segment *LS* (e.g. Fig. 2c).

We assigned two attributes to a line-segment. The first is object number. We define an object-number *(ON)* of a line-segment as

$$LS_{i,j}.ON = \begin{cases} LS_{i-1,k}.ON \\ \quad if\ LS_{i,j}.ON \cap LS_{i-1,k}.ON \neq \emptyset \\ \quad and\ \ \left|V_{i,j} - V_{i-1,k}\right| \le Tk = 1\ldots p \\ oc+1 \quad otherwise. \end{cases} \tag{5}$$

where *i* is the row number of the depth map *D* in which a line-segment belongs, *j* is a number of a line-segment in *i*th row, *k* is a number of a line-segment in (*i*–1)th row, *p* is the number of line-segments in (*i*–1)th row, *T* is object connectivity value which is calculated manually, *oc* is the number of available object values and

$$V_{i,j} = mode(D(i,q))q = s_{i,j}toe_{i,j} \tag{6}$$

where s and e are starting and ending points of a line-segment respectively. An example of extracted object numbers is shown in Fig. 3b in this image each color shows a different object number.

The second feature of a line-segment is its layer-number. A layer-number *(LN)* of a line-segment is defined as

$$LS_{i,j}.LN = \begin{cases} k & \text{if } V_{i,j} = V_k \text{ for } k = 1 \ldots lc \\ n+1 & \text{otherwise} \end{cases} \tag{7}$$

Where lc is denoting the number of available layers and V_k is the depth value of the kth layer (L_k). An example of extracted layer numbers is shown in Fig. 3c in this image each color shows a different layer number.

2.3 Link Perception

The idea behind the proposed link perception method is based on two assumptions. First, every object should appear only in one object-layer completely. Second, all the objects in a layer are in one object-layer.

The line segmentation algorithm may divide an object into a few parts. In the worst case, there is a possibility of associating an object with different layers. To overcome these problems and also to satisfy assumptions, we drive a straight-forward algorithm based on set theories.

The first step in this algorithm is to link all the parts of an object and all the layers to which the object belongs and make a compound object CO using conditions (8).

$$\begin{cases} CO_l.LN = CO_l.LN \cup LS_{i,j}.LN \\ \quad \text{if } LS_{i,j}.ON = CO_l.ON \\ \begin{cases} CO_{l+1}.LN = LS_{i,j}.LN \\ CO_{l+1}.ON = LS_{i,j}.ON \end{cases} \quad \text{otherwise} \end{cases} \tag{8}$$

where $CO.LN$ and $CO.ON$ denote the layer number and object number of a compound object CO respectively.

The second step is to link all the compound objects which are in the same layer to construct an object-layer using the following condition.

$$OL_m = OL_m \cup CO_l \text{ if } CO_l.LN \cap OL_m.LN \neq \emptyset \tag{9}$$

where l is the compound object number and m is an object-layer number.

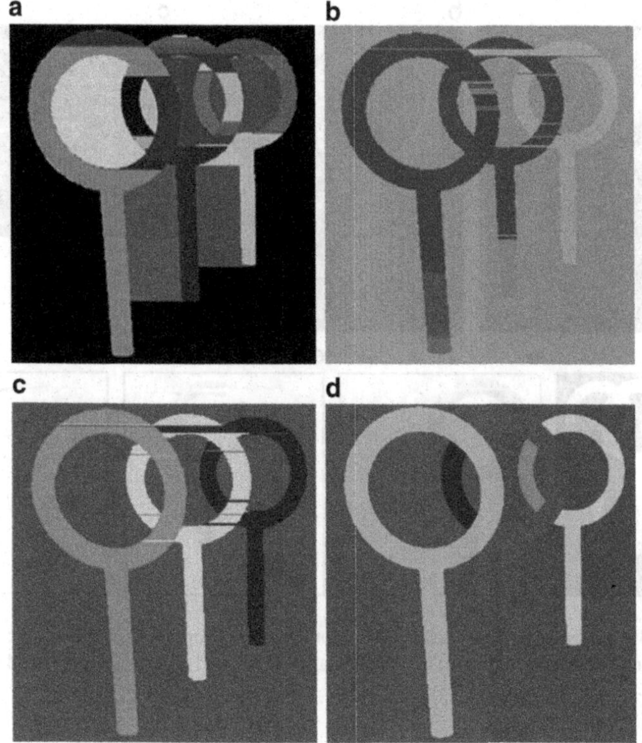

Fig. 3 Intermediate results of the: (**a**) over-segmentation based on object numbers; (**b**) over-segmentation based on layer numbers; (**c**) combined segmentation result after applying the link perception method; (**d**) segmentation result

3 Experimental Results

To verify the efficiency of the method, experiments have been carried on many 3D images along with their depth map. Since a dataset containing clutter of linearly separable objects of the captured static scenes, with their proper depth map yet does not exist in community, we chose to use computer generated 3D images and their depth map. In all experiments, the connectivity value was fixed as $T = 3$. Parameter T determines the distance between object-layers. The bigger value will result in connection of multiple object-layers.

One of the challenges of image segmentation techniques is over-segmentation of occluded objects. In these cases, an object will separate into some parts because of lack of knowledge about the parts of the objects. Figure 3 shows one of those challenging examples which three rings are positioned in a line toward the camera

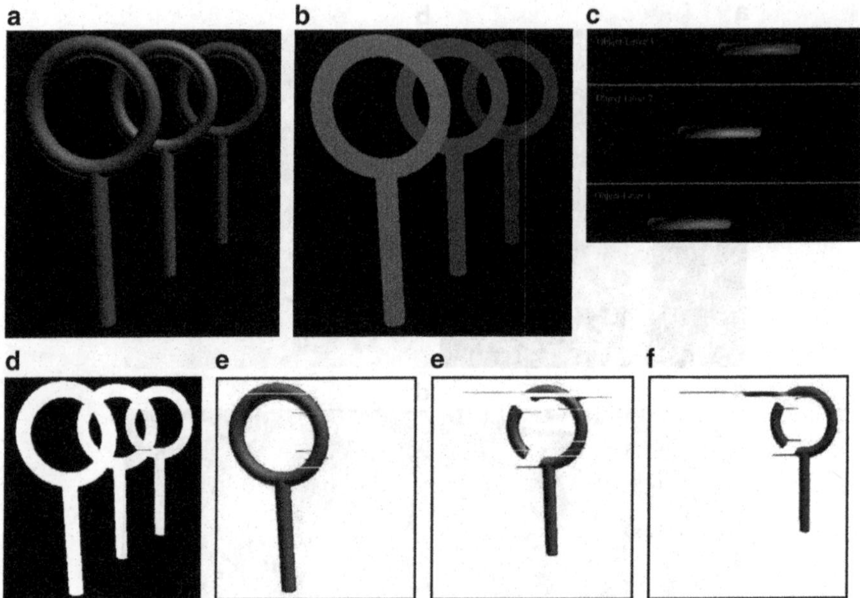

Fig. 4 (**a**) 3D image of a static scene; (**b**) depth map; (**c**) top view of the scene; (**d**) layered representation of the background; (**e**) first object-layer; (**f**) second object-layer; (**g**) third object-layer

and occluded by their neighboring objects. Figure 3c shows the result of our proposed segmentation algorithm which preserves all the parts of a ring in a class. On the other hand, Fig. 3d shows the result of the mean-shift segmentation applied on the same depth image that is Fig. 3a It is clearly visible that each ring in the second and third positions is separated into two different classes; each class is shown by a different color.

In this paper, we used two critical images to illustrate the efficiency of the proposed method. Figures 4 and 5 show the examples as well as the results with (a) showing the original 3D image, (b) showing depth image (darker colors representing larger z values), (c) showing the top down view of the 3D scene to compare the extracted layers visually.

Figure 4a shows a 3D image containing three rings. This image has been created to show how robust the proposed method is against the occlusion. The depth map and top view of the scene are given in Fig. 4b–c. The layered representation of image in Fig. 4a is shown in Fig. 4d–g. The four layers correspond to (a) background (e–g) three rings each in a different object-layer. It is clearly visible that the main features of all the three rings are well preserved and all of them are well classified into their corresponding layers using the proposed method. There are also some small parts of objects which are miss-classified in incorrect layers. It is just because of the incorrect detected edges (see Fig. 2b).

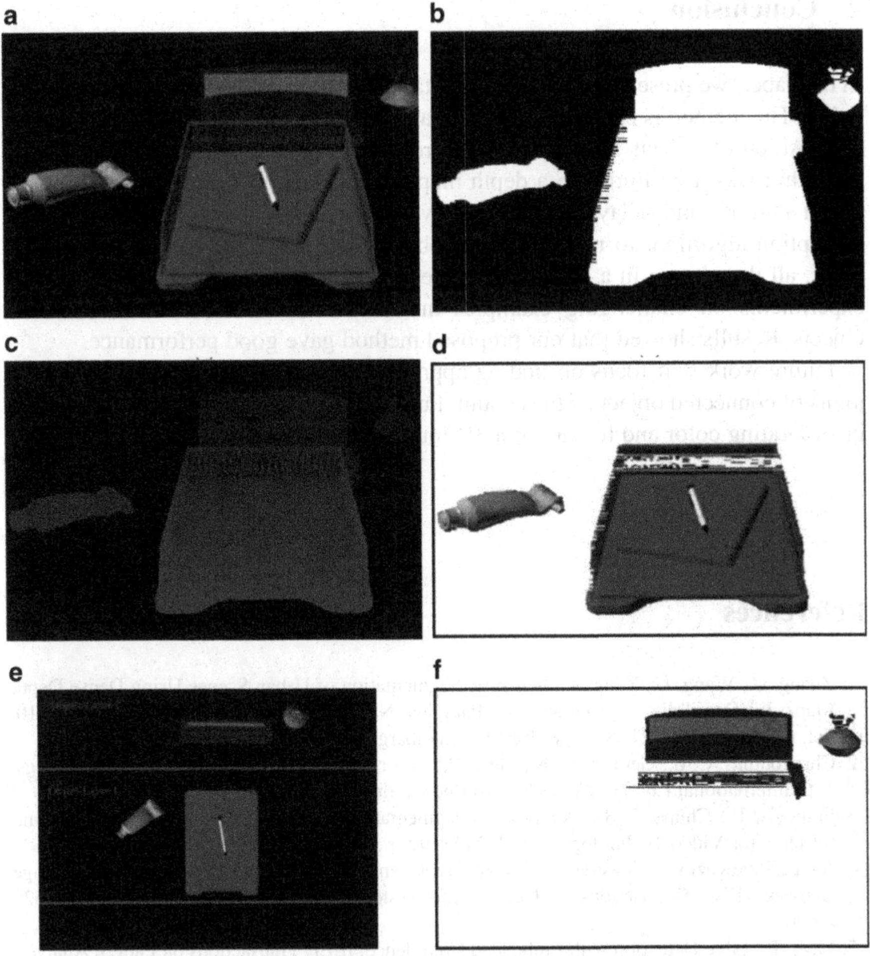

Fig. 5 (**a**) 3D image of a static scene; (**b**) depth map; (c) top down view of the scene; (**d**) layered representation of the background; (**e**) first object-layer; (**f**) second object-layer

Figure 5a is a 3D image of a clutter of office objects in which some of them are occluded and positioned in different layers. Figure 5b is the depth map of the given 3D image and Fig. 5c is the top view of the scene used to identify the exact number of layers. Figure 5d–f are extracted layers of the 3D image. It is shown in these images that the layers are correctly extracted and objects are almost complete with just small errors in boundaries of the inbox in the first layer using our method (Fig. 5e).

4 Conclusion

In the paper, we present an image segmentation method called depth-wise segmentation. The method is capable of layering a 3D image into multiple layers based on the position of objects in the scene with respect to the camera. An entropy based algorithm was used to divide a depth map into line-segments. After assigning an object number and a layer number to every line-segment, we employed a link perception algorithm to merge divided objects and make the completed objects. Later, all the objects in a layer were linked to make object-layers. We conducted experiments on challenging examples in which the scene contained occluded objects. Results showed that our proposed method gave good performance.

Future work will focus on finding appropriate methods detecting edges taking joints of connected objects into account. Furthermore, on-going work is focused on incorporating color and texture of a 3D image into the link perception stage.

References

1. Zhang, C., Wang, L., Yang, R.: Semantic Segmentation of Urban Scenes Using Dense Depth Maps. In: Daniilidis, K., Maragos, P., Paragios, N. (eds.) Computer Vision – ECCV 2010, vol. 6314, pp. 708–721. Springer Berlin/Heidelberg (2010)
2. Christoudias, C.M., Georgescu, B., Meer, P.: Synergism in low level vision. In: Proceedings. 16th International Conference on Pattern Recognition, pp. 150–155 vol.154. (Year)
3. Francois, E., Chupeau, B.: Depth-based segmentation. IEEE Transactions on Circuits and Systems for Video Technology 7, 237–240 (1997)
4. Jin, L., Przewozny, D., Pastoor, S.: Layered representation of scenes based on multiview image analysis. IEEE Transactions on Circuits and Systems for Video Technology 10, 518–529 (2000)
5. Meer, P.: Edge Detection with Embedded Confidence. IEEE Transactions on Pattern Analysis and Machine Intelligence 23, 1351–1365 (2001)
6. Zhang, G., Jia, J., Wong, T.-T., Bao, H.: Consistent Depth Maps Recovery from a Video Sequence. IEEE Transactions on pattern analysis and machine intelligence 31, 974–988 (2009)
7. Scharstein, D., Szeliski, R.: A taxonomy and evaluation of dense two-frame stereo correspondence algorithms. International Journal of Computer Vision 47, 7–42 (2002)
8. Pal, N.R., Pal, S.K.: A review on image segmentation techniques. Pattern recognition 26, 1277–1294 (1993)
9. Otsu, N.: A threshold selection method for grey level histograms. IEEE Trans. Syst. Man Cybern 9, 62–66 (1979)
10. Comaniciu, D., Meer, P.: Mean shift: A robust approach toward feature space analysis. IEEE Transactions on pattern analysis and machine intelligence 603–619 (2002)
11. Shi, J., Malik, J.: Normalized cuts and image segmentation. IEEE Transactions on Pattern Analysis and Machine Intelligence 22, 888–905 (2000)
12. Haris, K., Efstratiadis, S.N., Maglaveras, N., Katsaggelos, A.K.: Hybrid image segmentation using watersheds and fast region merging. IEEE Transactions on Image Processing 7, 1684–1699 (1998)

13. Xiping, L., Jie, T.: Multi-level thresholding: maximum entropy approach using ICM. Proceedings 15th International Conference on Pattern Recognition., vol. 3, pp. 778–781 vol.773 (2000)
14. Criminisi, A., Kang, S.B., Swaminathan, R., Szeliski, R., Anandan, P.: Extracting layers and analyzing their specular properties using epipolar-plane-image analysis. Computer vision and image understanding 97, 51–85 (2005)
15. Shannon, C.E.: A mathematical theory of communication. Bell Syst.Tech. J. 27, 370–423 (1948)
16. D.Gowda, S.: Equivalence Amongst Document Images at Multiple levels Through Hierarchial Structural Attributes. Department of Studies in Computer Science, vol. PhD. University of Mysore, Mysore (2009)

A Robust and Transparent Watermarking Method Against Block-Based Compression Attacks

Phi Bang Nguyen, Azeddine Beghdadi, and Marie Luong

Abstract In this paper, we present a new transparent and robust watermarking method against block-based compression attacks based on two perceptual models. In order to resist to block-based compression, the main idea is to embed the watermark into regions that are not or less affected by blocking effect. These auspicious regions are selected based on a spatial prediction model of blocking effect. Then, the embedding strength is optimally determined using a JND model. The combination of these two models provides more gain in robustness and transparency. Experimental results demonstrate that our proposed method achieves a good invisibility and robustness against common "signal processing" attacks, especially to JPEG compression.

Keywords Watermarking • Pyramid transform • Human visual system • Blocking effect prediction • JND

1 Introduction

One of the most challenging issues in watermarking is to solve the trade-off between robustness and transparency. Unfortunately, these criteria are conflicting. Indeed, to enhance robustness, we have to increase the watermark strength at the expense of loss in transparency and vice versa. Designing algorithms for such an optimizing problem is still a challenge for the watermarking community. We believe that one of the most promising solutions to this issue is to take into account HVS (Human Visual

P.B. Nguyen (✉) • A. Beghdadi • M. Luong
L2TI Laboratory, Galilee Institute, University Paris 13,
99 Ave. J. B. Clement, 93430 Villetaneuse, France
e-mail: nguyen@univ-paris13.fr; beghdadi@univ-paris13.fr; marie.luong@univ-paris13.fr

DOI 10.1007/978-1-4614-3501-3_48,

System)'s properties in the design of watermarking algorithms. By this way, we can maximize robustness by introducing a perceptual constraint on transparency.

In the literature, most of existing approaches that resist to Jpeg compression are based on the selection of the frequency bands, i.e. embedding in low or middle frequencies prevent the signal from the quantization artifacts. Koch and Zhao [1] are among the first researchers who propose a method in DCT domain which is based on a JPEG compression model and pulse position modulation technique. The copyright code is first encrypted and then embedded into random quantized DCT coefficients selected in the middle-frequency band. In [2], Cox et al. proposed another non-blind DCT based technique which allows a better robustness to JPEG compression by embedding the watermark into low frequency components. However, embedding in the low frequency band often causes visible distortions and hence, decreases the watermark transparency. To overcome this problem, some authors have considered HVS in the design of their watermarking algorithm. In [3], a watermark robust to a desired compression quality level is constructed using the difference between the original and the reconstructed image after compression. The used visual component is simply the local average brightness. In [4], Seo et al. proposed to embed in the DC component of the 8×8 DCT block due to the remark that this component contains most of image energy and is the least affected by the quantization process. However, this strategy risks a visible distortion. A (Just-Noticeable-Distortion) model is therefore employed to guarantee the watermark imperceptibility. Finally, an important research that should be considered is the study of Eggers and Girod [5] about the effects of quantization on digital watermark. They proved that the robustness of an additive watermarking scheme (via correlation based detector) after Jpeg compression can be predicted with sufficient accuracy. Indeed, they propose a close form of the detection output which is a function of the statistics of the host signal, the watermark and the quantization step size.

Here, we propose an approach very different from the literature. The Jpeg compression process is now regarded from an image quality point of view where its impact is "blocking effect" rather than quantization effect. Firstly, the onset of blocking effect (before compression) is predicted. The main idea is to predict how a block-based compression procedure affects the image at a given bit rate. Then, the watermark is selectively inserted into locations not or less affected by the blocking effect and hence can survive compression. We present two perceptual models to achieve gain in transparency and robustness (against Jpeg compression) at the same time, that are the Blocking Effect Prediction (BEP) and the Pyramidal JND (PJND) model. These models are proposed to control the imperceptibility of the watermark and to improve its robustness against Jpeg compression. The idea of the BEP model is to predict the onset of blocking effect (before compression) to selectively embed the watermark into regions less affected by Jpeg compression (indicated by the BEP map). The JND model is then used to control the watermark strength. This JND allows hiding the watermark just beneath the detection threshold and therefore guarantee the watermark transparency. An interesting remark is that although the BEP model is used to improve the robustness to Jpeg compression, we can still have gain in transparency. The same results are obtained with the JND model. A combination of these two models is finally proposed which offers more gain in robustness and transparency.

The paper is organized as follows: Sects. 2 and 3 present the PJND and the BEP models. Section 4 introduces three embedding schemes using these models. The performance evaluation is reported in Sect. 5 and finally, we give some conclusions and perspectives in Sect. 6.

2 JND Model

In this section, we describe briefly our proposed JND model which has been designed for the pyramid transform [6]. Such a model has been successfully exploited in watermarking [7, 8]. For each level of the pyramid, a JND map is computed by incorporating the most relevant HVS's properties such as contrast sensitivity function (CSF), luminance masking and contrast masking.

2.1 *Incorporating CSF and Luminance Adaptation*

The CSF describes the variation of HVS's sensitivity as a function of spatial frequency and therefore has to be applied in frequency domain. To adapt this phenomenon for spatial domain, we refer to the approach in [7]. For each level of the Laplacian pyramid, the contrast threshold (CT) at the pixel *(x,y)* could be expressed as the contrast threshold at the peak frequency of the channel $CT(f_k^{peak})$ weighted by the contribution of the level:

$$CT_k(x,y) = CT(f_k^{peak}) \frac{L_k(x,y)}{\sum_{k=1}^{K} L_k(x,y)} \tag{1}$$

where $L_k(x,y)$ is the kth level Laplacian coefficient at the pixel *(x,y)*, $CT(f_k^{peak})$ is the contrast threshold at the peak frequency of the level, computed as its inverse CSF. To this end, we use the Barten's model [9] thanks to its flexibility and relative simplicity:

$$CSF(f,L) = a.f.\exp(-b.f).\sqrt{1+c.\exp(b.f)} \tag{2}$$

where c is a constant, a and b are functions of the global luminance L (in cd/m2) which is computed as follows:

$$L(x,y) = L_0 + L_I(x,y) \tag{3}$$

where L_0 is the ambient luminance and L_I is the local luminance computed, for each pixel, from the corresponding Gaussian value in the (k+1)th level, $G_{k+1}(x,y)$, followed by a grayscale to luminance transformation:

$$L_I(x,y) = \max(L_{\max}(\frac{G_{k+1}(x,y)}{255})^{\gamma}, L_{\min}) \tag{4}$$

where L_{max} and L_{min} are respectively the maximum and minimum luminance of the display, whereas γ is the exponential factor used in the gamma correction of the display. The detection threshold $T_{0k}(x,y)$ which accounts for contrast sensitivity and luminance adaptation is then computed by:

$$T_{0k}(x,y) = CT_k(x,y).G_{k+1}(x,y) \tag{5}$$

2.2 Contrast Masking

The JND threshold is finally obtained by incorporating a contrast masking model inspired from [10]:

$$JND_k(x,y) = \begin{cases} T_{0k}(x,y) & \text{if } |L_k(x,y)| \leq T_{0k}(x,y) \\ T_{0k}(x,y).\left(\dfrac{|L_k(x,y)|}{T_{0k}(x,y)}\right)^{\varepsilon} & \text{otherwise} \end{cases} \tag{6}$$

where ε is a factor that describes the degree of masking, $0.6 \leq \varepsilon \leq 1$ [10].

3 BEP Model

Blocking effect is the consequence of partitioning image into blocks and processing each block independently (with assumption that information contained in the image are independent), as is generally the case with block-based compression methods. The impact of blocking effect on an image region depends strongly on its local activity (i.e. homogeneous, edge or texture). A number of local descriptors could be used to characterize the region's activity either in spatial domain or in frequency domain. In order to make our approach independent of compression method, we use a descriptor in the spatial domain, the local variance, thanks to its simplicity. Indeed, we assume that a pixel is affected by blocking effect if its gradient (in the compressed image) is null and its variance (in the original image) is not null. Based on this analysis, the BEP map can be computed via a learning process described as follows [11].

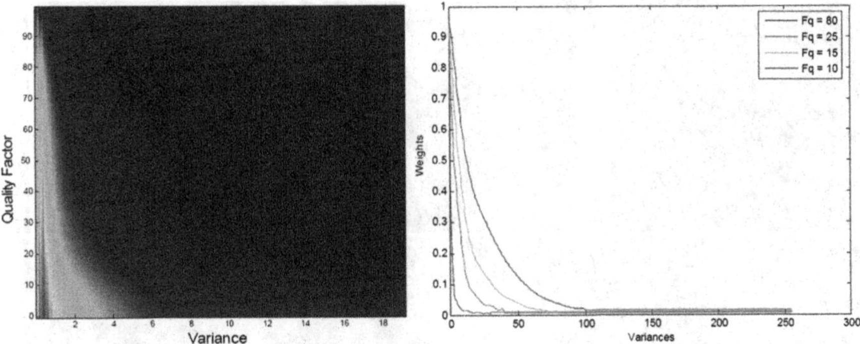

Fig. 1 The accumulation matrix (*left*) and the curve fitting (*right*) applied on the accumulation matrix at quality factors of 80, 25, 15 and 10

3.1 Learning Process

The learning process is performed off-line on an image database. For each pixel *(x,y)* of the *k*th image in the database, we associate an influence factor defined as:

$$\varphi(x,y,k,V,q) = \begin{cases} 1, & \textit{if } g(x,y,k,V,q) = 0 \wedge V(x,y,k) \neq 0 \\ 0, & \textit{otherwise} \end{cases} \tag{7}$$

where g is the pixel gradient computed in the compressed image, V is the local variance computed in the original image, on a 3×3 window centered at the pixel, and q is the quality factor of the compression process.

By compressing all images in the database at different quality factors, we can construct an accumulation matrix, denoted as H. Each element of H represents the influence factors accumulated over pixels and over images. For each pair of values (V, q):

$$H(V,q) = \sum_{x,y,k} \varphi(x,y,k,V,q) \tag{8}$$

After a normalization step, we have $H(V,q) \in [0, 1]$ which represents the probability represents the probability of being affected by blocking effect of a pixel which has the variance v and is compressed at a quality factor q. Figure 1 displays a part of the accumulation matrix. For the sake of visibility, only variance values lower than 18 are illustrated. Indeed, one can see that the probability of being affected by blocking effect is inversely proportional to the variance as well as the quality factor as expected. The precision of the accumulation matrix depends on the size and the content richness of the training database. Nevertheless, there is no guarantee that all possible values of the local variance are present in the tested

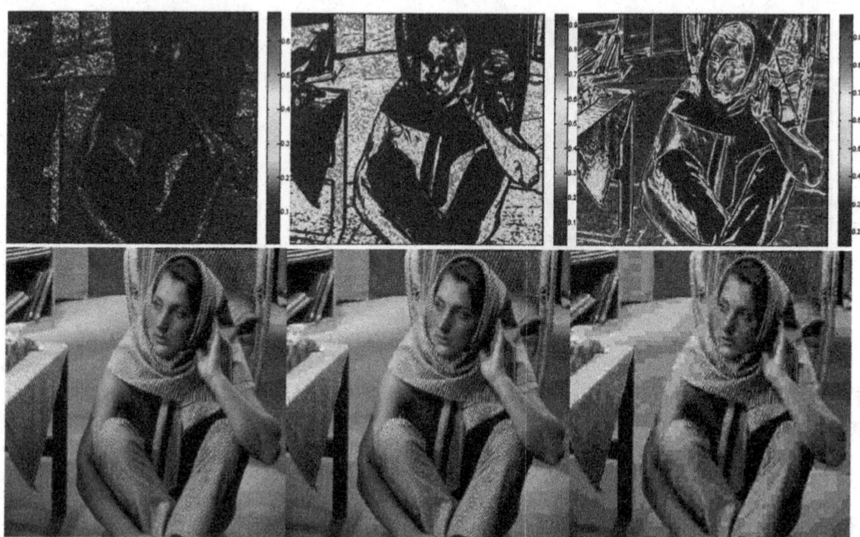

Fig. 2 The "Barbara" images compressed at q = 80, 20, 5 (*bottom*) and their corresponding BEP maps (*top*)

database, i.e. low variance values are more often encountered than high variances since homogeneous regions tend to be predominant in natural images. This leads to a lack of some variance values in the voting matrix. To cope with this problem, a curve fitting is applied on the experimental data to obtain an accumulation matrix for variance values in the interval [0 255]. This selected interval does not theoretically cover all possible variance values but practically sufficient since the variance values of 8×8 blocks typically do not exceed this limit. Figure 1 illustrates the data fitting. For the sake of visibility, only four quality factors (corresponding to four lines in the accumulation matrix) are shown. Each curve in the figure is a function of the variance and could be interpreted as the probability that a pixel with local variance v belongs to a blocking effect area at a given quality factor q.

3.2 Prediction Process

Once the accumulation matrix computed, the BEP map of an arbitrary image can be derived using a simple procedure. For a given quality factor q, the BEP map of an image is obtained following the two steps:

1. Compute the local variance image V
2. For each pixel (x,y), assign the value corresponding to the local variance $V(x,y)$ as given in H

For an intuitive evaluation of the proposed method, Fig. 2 displays an image compressed at different quality factors and its corresponding BEP map where red and blue regions correspond to high and low probabilities of being affected by blocking effect, respectively. It is clear that this probability increases with the decrease of quality factor. Moreover, homogeneous regions are affected more quickly by blocking effect than textured regions. As expected, there is a consistency between the prediction and the actual compression. The same observations are also obtained for different images.

4 Embedding Using JND and BEP Maps

For the sake of simplicity, we consider only the zero-bit additive scheme that embeds a bipolar pseudo-random sequence $W_k \in \{-1, 1\}$ into each level of the Laplacian pyramid. Three embedding strategies are proposed as below.

4.1 *Scheme 1*

A straightforward strategy is to hide the watermark just beneath the detection threshold using the following scheme:

$$L_{wk}(x,y) = L_k(x,y) + JND_k(x,y).W_k(x,y) \tag{9}$$

By this way, the embedding strength is determined in an optimal way and hence, achieves the trade-off between robustness and transparency.

4.2 *Scheme 2*

Two strategies can be considered. In the first strategy, the embedding strength is adapted according to the BEP map while in the second one, the binary BEP map is used to select "relevant regions" (image regions that are less vulnerable to blocking effect) for embedding.

$$\text{S1)}\ L_{wk}(x,y) = L_k(x,y) + \alpha(1 - PBEP_k(x,y))W_k(x,y) \tag{10}$$

$$\text{S2)}\ L_{wk} = L_k(x,y) + \alpha.BPBEP_k(x,y).W_k(x,y) \tag{11}$$

where α is a global factor for controlling the watermark strength, PBEP and BPBEP are the Pyramidal BEP map and its binary version, respectively.

The PBEP map is computed by applying a Gaussian pyramid transform on the BEP map. Then, its binary version is obtained by thresholding this PBEP map. It is worth to notice that a threshold of 0.5 means the selected regions are supposed affected by blocking effect with a probability of 50%. So, we set this threshold to 0.3 to ensure certainly that selected zones are the least affected.

Assuming that the BEP map works correctly, a linear correlation based detector is used as follows:

$$Cor_{lc} = \frac{1}{N}\sum_{i=1}^{N} f(i).w(i) \tag{12}$$

where w is the watermark, f is the watermarked coefficient (possibly attacked) and N is the number of watermarked coefficients.

We would like to know which scheme is better. In general, the product of f and w is approximately the same for the two strategies (since the watermark survives at regions unaffected by blocking effect and destroyed elsewhere) but the linear correlation obtained from S1 is always lower than in S2 since it is divided by a larger number of embedded coefficients N. Hence, S2 should be chosen.

4.3 Combined Scheme

In the second scheme, we demonstrated how the robustness against Jpeg compression of a watermarking system can be improved by using the BEP map. Nevertheless, the embedding strength is not optimally defined since it requires an additional global factor. On the other hand, the first scheme offers an explicit and more sophisticated manner to determine the visual detection threshold for the watermark strength. Hence, it is necessary to take advantages of these two schemes. Such a solution can be obtained by combining the BEP map and the JND map. The embedding rule is defined as follows:

$$L_{wk}(x,y) = L_k(x,y) + BPBEP_k(x,y).JND_k(x,y).W_k(i) \tag{13}$$

Figure 3 shows the BPBEP and the PJND map of the "Parrot" image for the first five levels of the pyramid.

5 Performance Evaluation

Performances of the three proposed schemes are evaluated in terms of robustness and transparency. For the first scheme, by using the BEP map, the watermark can survive Jpeg compression at very low quality (q=6) but considerably fragile to other attacks (see Table 1). Furthermore, the watermark transparency is also improved due to the fact that only a small portion of the image is chosen for embedding.

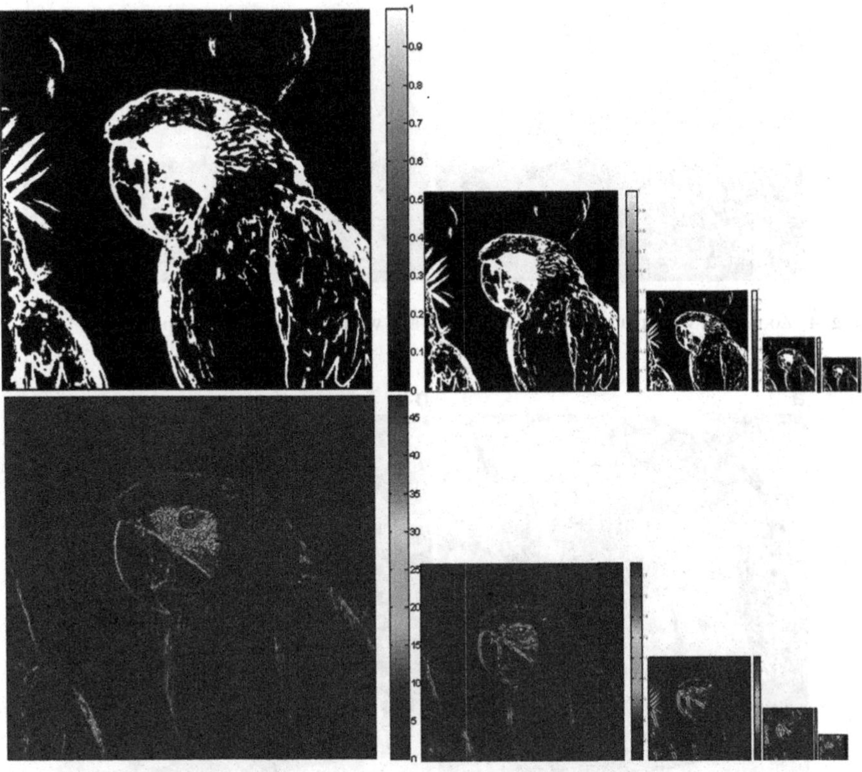

Fig. 3 The BPBEP (*top*) and the PJND maps (*bottom*)

Table 1 Robustness evaluation (tested on the "Parrot" image with some common "signal processing attacks" and Photoshop manipulations). The shown values represent the breakdown limit of the method (the strongest level of attacks to which the watermark still survives)

Attack type	BEP	JND	BEP+JND
Centered cropping	12%	0.5%	1%
Jpeg compression	q = 6	q = 9	q = 3
Jpeg 2000	0.8 bpp	0.1 bpp	0.08 bpp
Gaussian noise	$\sigma = 20\%$	$\sigma = 70\%$	$\sigma = 70\%$
Wiener filtering	Ok	Ok	Ok
Median filtering	*3 × 3*	5 × 5	5 × 5
Sharpening	Failed	Ok	Ok
Blurring	Failed	Ok	Ok
Bit plan reduction	Failed	Ok	Ok
Histogram equal	Ok	Ok	Ok
Rescale (50%)	Ok	Ok	Ok

Figure 4 illustrates watermarked images from schemes with and without using BEP map. For a fair comparison, the same embedding rule (i.e. the same parameter α) is applied.

Fig. 4 Zoom of a watermarked image with (*left*) and without (*right*) BEP map

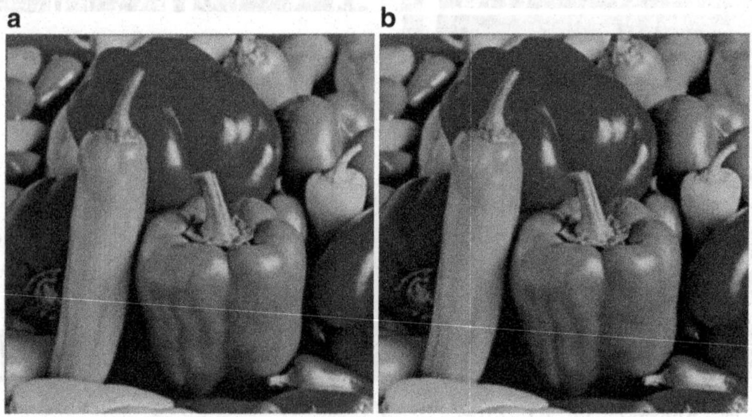

Fig. 5 (**a**) Original image and (**b**) Watermarked image

For the second scheme, the transparency is optimally achieved by using the JND map. As shown in Fig. 5, the original and the watermarked image are perceptually undistinguishable (see [7] for a complete visual quality evaluation of the watermark). The robustness is also significantly improved (see Table 1).

Now, the question is whether we have more gain in robustness and transparency when combining the BEP and JND maps. Figure 6 displays the detector output of the combined scheme and the JND based scheme against Jpeg compression. It can be seen that using both BEP and JND maps offers a significant gain in robustness to Jpeg compression.

It is also necessary to know if the overall robustness (against other attacks) decreases or increases with the combined schemes. Table 1 shows that for scheme 2 and the combined scheme, the watermark survives many severe attacks but there are no significant difference in robustness between these two schemes to attacks exclude Jpeg compression. Furthermore, robustness against some attacks "like Jpeg" (Jpeg2000) is even slightly improved. This can be explained by interesting remark on common characteristic of the two maps (see Fig. 3). The -

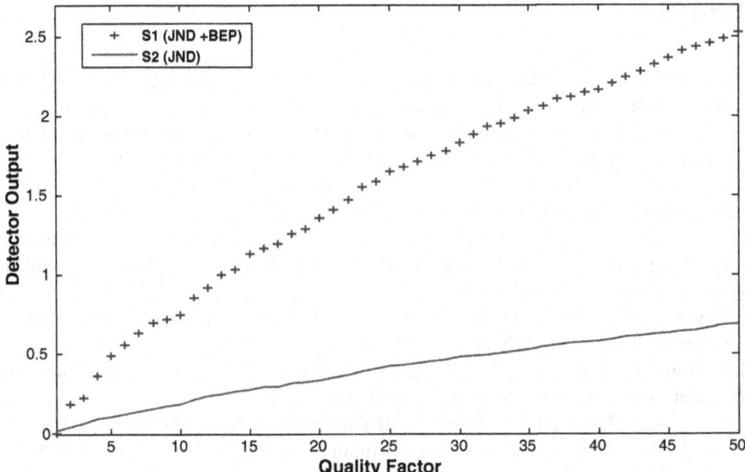

Fig. 6 Detector output of S1 and S2 schemes after Jpeg compression attacks at different quality factors

JND map also presents very high values at regions "selected" by the BEP map so that most of watermark energy concentrates at these common regions. This leads to the fact that embedding at other regions does not help to increase much in terms of watermark energy.

Finally, it is clear that the transparency of the combined scheme is even better than the second one (that uses only JND map) due to the fact that we embed in only a small portion of the image and the embedding strength is controlled by the JND map.

6 Conclusion and Perspectives

A novel approach that allows improving at the same time the robustness and transparency of a watermarking system has been proposed and evaluated. The obtained results are threefold. Firstly, using BEP map helps to significantly improve the performance of a watermarking system not only in terms of robustness to Jpeg compression but also in terms of transparency. Secondly, the use of the JND map in the embedding helps to control the watermark transparency. Finally, the combined scheme gives more gain in both robustness and transparency. It is worth to notice that the proposed algorithm is quite flexible and can be exploited for other block-based compression standards just by redoing the learning process when constructing the BEP map. It could be straightforward to extend the BEP map to color by applying the scheme to each color channel separately.

References

1. E. Koch and J. Zhao, “Toward robust and hidden image copyright labeling,” in IEEE Workshop on Nonlinear Signal and Image Processing, Greece, June 1995, pp. 452–455.
2. I. J. Cox, J. Kilian, T. Leighton, and T. Shamoon, “Secure spread spectrum watermarking for multimedia,” IEEE ICIP’97, vol. 6, no. 12, pp. 1673–1687, December 1997.
3. H. J. Lee, J. H. Park, and Y. Zheng, “Digital watermarking robust against jpeg compression,” in Information Security, LNCS. 1999, vol. 1729, pp. 167–177, Springer-Verlag.
4. H-U. Seo, J-S. Sohn, B-I. Kim, T-G. Lee, S-I. Lee, and D-G. Kim, “Robust image watermarking method using discrete cosine decompostion and just noticeable distortion,” Proc. of the 23rd ITC-CSCC’ 2008, pp. 765–768.
5. J. J. Eggers and B. Girod, “Quantization effects on digital watermarks,” Signal Processing, vol. 81, pp. 239–263, February 2001.
6. P. J. Burt and E. H. Adelson, “The Laplacian Pyramid as a Compact Image Code”, in IEEE Transactions on Communications, April 1983, pp. 532–540.
7. P. B. Nguyen, A. Beghdadi and M. Luong, "Robust Watermarking in DoG Scale Space Using a Multi-scale JND Model", Lecture Notes in Computer Science, vol. 5879, pp. 561–573, ISBN: 978-3-642-10466-4, Muneesawang, P.; Wu, F.; Kumazawa, I.; Roeksabutr, A.; Liao, M.; Tang, X. (Eds.), 2009
8. P. B. Nguyen, A. Beghdadi, and M. Luong, “Perceptual watermarking using pyramidal JND maps”, in Proc. of 10th IEEE ISM’08, pp. 418–423, Berkeley, CA, USA (2008).
9. P. G. J. Barten, “Evaluation of Subjective Image Quality with the Square-Root Integral Method”, in Jour. of the Opt. Society of America A: Vol. 7, Issue 10, Oct. 1990, pp. 2024–2031.
10. G. E. Legge and J. M. Foley, “Contrast Masking in Human Vision”, in Jour. of the Opt. Soc. of America, 1980, pp. 1458–1471.
11. A. Chetouani, G. Mostafaoui and A. Beghdadi, “Predicting blocking effects in the spatial domain using a learning approach”, in Proc. of SIGMAP 2008, pp. 197–201, Porto, Portugal, 2008.

A New Signal Processing Method for Video Image-Reproduce the Frequency Spectrum Exceeding the Nyquist Frequency Using a Single Frame of the Video Image

Seiichi Gohshi

Abstract A new non-linear signal processing method is proposed in this paper.

Enhancers are widely used in real time signal processing machines to improve the image quality. It does not actually increase the resolution but improves the degree of resolution as perceived by the human eye. It is almost impossible to create components exceeding the Nyquist frequency using conventional linear signal processing methods.

Super Resolution (SR) is a highly interesting research field and many ideas and methods have been proposed and some of which have the potential to enhance resolution. However, most of these ideas use several frames of video images and they have not been widely discussed in the frequency domain.

The new signal processing method in this paper uses just a single frame of the video image and creates components exceeding the Nyquist frequency. The simulation results are discussed with regard to the picture quality well as the frequency domain.

Keywords: Image • Video • Resolution • Super resolution • Nyqusit frequency • Single frame of video

1 Introduction

Enhancing the resolution of images is a traditional research field. This field is called Super Resolution (SR) and a variety of methods have been proposed in the last two decades [1][2][10][11]. Since their SR results are shown as images and are not shown the FFT result, we can tell their performance in the frequency domain.

S. Gohshi (✉)
Kogakuin University 1-24-2, Nishishinjuku, Shinjuku-ku, 160-0023 Tokyo, Japan
e-mail: gohshi@cc.kogakuin.ac.jp

J.S. Jin et al., *The Era of Interactive Media*,
DOI 10.1007/978-1-4614-3501-3_49,

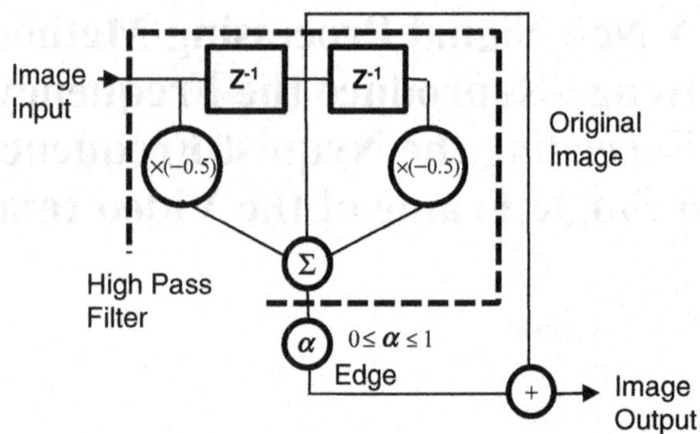

Fig. 1 An Example of a Conventional Enhancer

There are many more methods available for enhancement of still images than for moving images as video. It is possible to use complex and iterative methods for still images because we can spend several days for a single frame. However, it is very difficult to use these techniques for moving images. In television images move at a rate of 25 or 30 frames a second, and in cinema it is a 24 frames a second.

It is not easy to use a computer to improve the image quality for TV and cinema images because of the need to create more than 24 frames a second [2][10]. There are regulations regarding the methods used to improve and enhance the TV and cinema images, and this adds to the complexity and cost of the process even when real time hardware is needed.

Digital TV receivers use the conventional enhancers. However, conventional enhancers do not increase the resolution and only improves the degree of resolution as perceived by the human eye. It is almost impossible to create the spectrum exceeding the Nyquist frequency with enhancers. Recently various SR technologies were introduced into the video signal processing field. SR uses several frames of images during the processing but these technologies have not yet been thoroughly discussed in the frequency domain [8].

A new method that is able to create the components in the frequency spectrum exceeding the Nyquist frequency using only a single frame of image is proposed in this paper. The algorithm is simple enough to be embodied in a small hardware device and adapts well to real time use with TV and Cinema.

2 The Conventional Enhancer

Fig. 1 shows a conventional enhancer that consists of a high pass filter and an adder [3]. It detects edges in the input image with the high pass filter. The edges are multiplied by alpha and are added to the input image to enhance the high frequency. The commonly used coefficients of the high pass filter are [−0.5, 1, −0.5].

The maximum value of alpha is 1.0 and it maximizes the edges in the input image. The minimum value of alpha is 0, which gives the same image as the input one.

Fig. 2 HDTV Spectrum

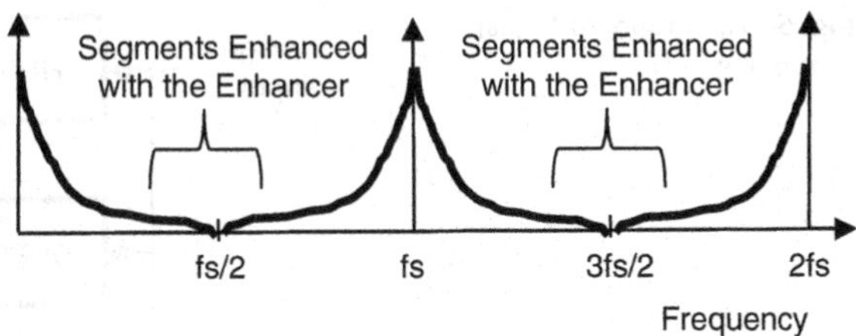

Fig. 3 The Enhanced HDTV Spectrum

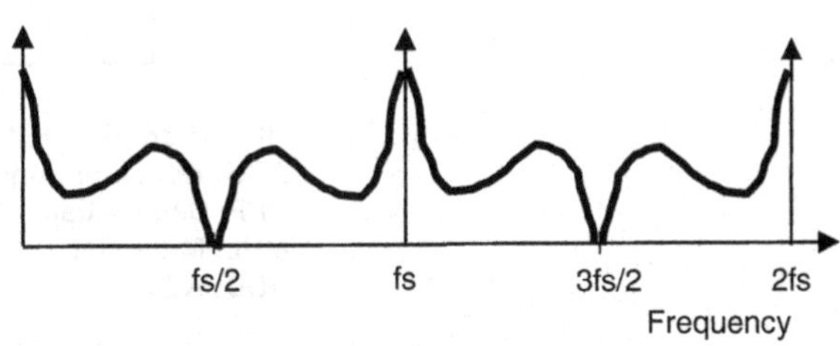

Fig. 4 The Up converted TV Spectrum from HDTV to 4k

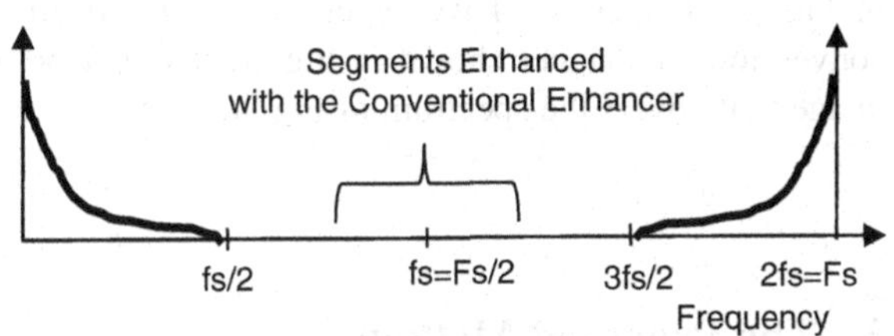

Fig. 2 and Fig. 3 explain the signal processing of Fig. 1 in the frequency domain. The high pass filter extracts the frequency component around the Nyquist frequency components and it is added to the original image to increase the sharpness of the image.

This type of enhancers is widely used in cameras, image processing software programs and digital TV receivers. However, it is almost impossible to improve the image quality if the original image does not have components near the Nyquist frequency. It is not possible to generate components exceeding the Nyquist frequency using this type of conventional enhancer. The up-converted images from Standard TV(SDTV) to HDTV do not have components around the Nyquist frequency. For this reason, it is not possible to produce the improved images using the conventional enhancer for up-converted images. 4K displays are available in the market and have attracted some potential buyers as an next generation TVs[4] [5][6]. Most of the important content for 4K is up-converting from HDTV. Up-converting from HDTV to 4K presents us with exactly the same problems as when up-converting from SDTV to HDTV.

Next, we discuss this issue in the frequency domain. Fig. 2 shows an example of the frequency spectrum of HDTV. "fs" is the sampling frequency and "fs/2" is the Nyquist frequency, which means the maximum frequency of the signal. "Segments Enhanced with the Enhancer" in Fig. 2 refers to the components that can be boosted by the conventional enhancer shown in Fig. 1. The enhanced spectrum is shown in Fig. 3. Fig. 4 shows an up-converted spectrum from HDTV to 4K. As can be seen

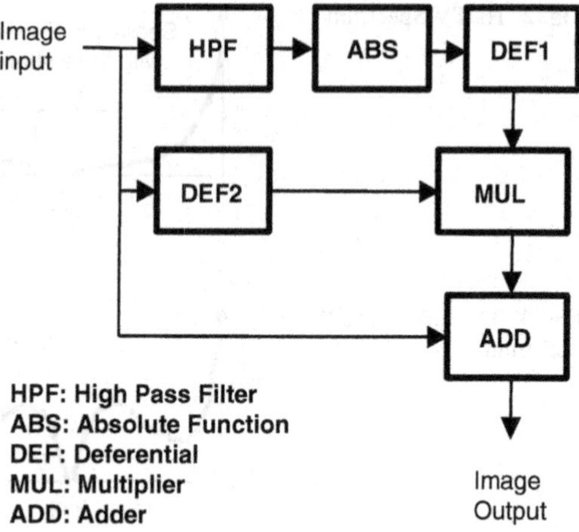

Fig. 5 The Proposed Signal Processing

in Fig. 4, it does not have spectrum around fs. It can be seen that using the conventional enhancer shown in Fig. 1, it is not possible to obtain an enhanced image that covers the spectrum of Fig. 4.

3 The Proposed Method

It is necessary to create the element exceeding the Nyquist frequency when we enhance the image quality of up-converted images. A non-linear signal processing method that creates harmonic distortion is a good candidate. Although there is a wide range of non-linear functions, we select an absolute function. The absolute funtion enables us to create harmonic waves with very simple hardware.

Appendix A shows the theoretical proof that the absolute function creates the harmonic waves. Fig. 5 shows the proposed signal processing block diagram and Fig. 6 shows the signal forms of each block of Fig. 5.

We assume the input signal is shown in Fig. 6(a). The input image is distributed to three blocks. The top row is the route to the high pass filter whose output is shown in Fig. 6(b). The scale of the vertical axis of Fig6(b), (c), (d), (e) and (f) is not the same as the ones of Fig. 6(a) and (g) because the level of the high pass filter output is small. The vertical axis of Fig. 6(b) is more expanded than the one of Fig. 6(a). The absolute value of Fig. 6(b) is given in Fig. 6(c). The DEF1 block processes it to Fig. 6(d). The function of DEF1 and DEF2 are shown in Fig. 7. The output of DEF1 (Fig. 6(d)) is given to MUL(Multiplier).

The input image is also provided to MUL via DEF2. The output of DEF2 is shown in Fig. 6(e) and is multiplied with the output of DEF1. The result of the product is shown in Fig. 6(f) and is added to the input image, which gives the sharpened edge shown in Fig. 6(g).

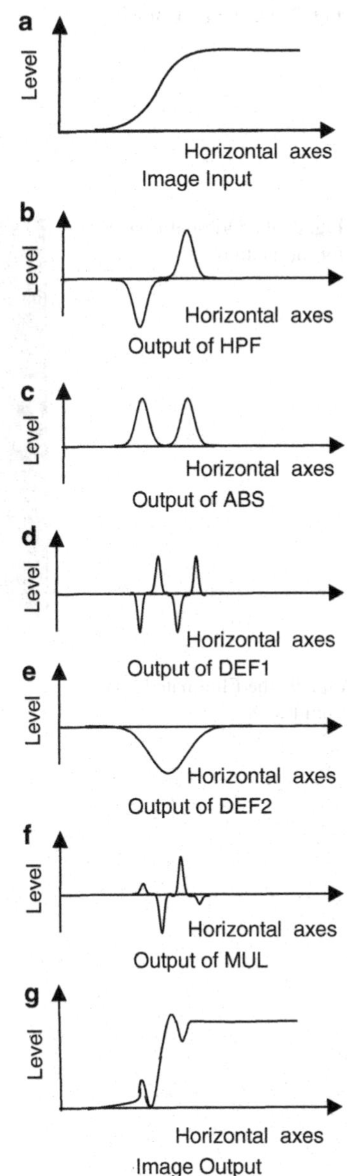

Fig. 6 The Wave Forms of from (a) to (g) in Fig. 5

4 The Simulation Result

We conducted simulations to prove that our method is effective. Since we need the evidence of creation of components exceeding the Nyquist frequency, we have to create an image with the spectrum shown in Fig. 4. Fig. 9 shows an image based on

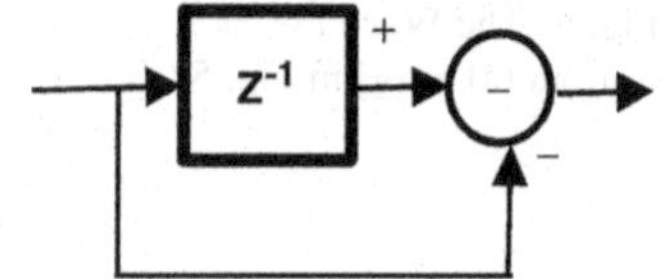

Fig. 7 Deferential Block

Fig. 8 the Original Image for Simulation

Fig. 9 the Eliminated Image from Fig. 8

Fig. 8 that has been enlarged to twice its original horizontal and vertical dimensions. The kernel of the digital filter is shown in equation (1)

$$\begin{pmatrix} 1/4 & 1/2 & 1/4 \\ 1/2 & 1 & 1/2 \\ 1/4 & 1/2 & 1/4 \end{pmatrix} \tag{1}$$

Fig. 10 Image Enhanced with a Conventional Enhancer (Fig. 1)

The size of the original image in Fig. 8 was enlarged and Fig. 9 shows upper right side of the enlarged image. Fig. 9 is not resized to check the image quality.

Fig. 10 shows the simulation result with the Fig. 1 method. The image is processed horizontally and vertically as a one dimensional signal. Visually, there seems to be no difference between Fig. 9 and Fig. 10. This is an expected result because Fig. 9. does not have the components near fs(the Nyquist frequency) in Fig. 3.

Fig. 11 shows the simulation result of the signal processing method shown in Fig. 5. The input image is Fig. 9.

The resolution of the scarf and the back of the chair is significantly enhanced compared with Fig. 10. This means that our method improves the resolution of the images that could be enhanced using a conventional enhancer.

We now discuss the improvement in frequency domain. Figs. 12,13 and 14 show the two dimensional FFT results of Figs. 9,10 and 11 respectively. The vertical axis means the vertical frequency and the horizontal axis means horizontal frequency from –pi to pi respectively. There is almost no difference between Figs. 12 and 13.

It is in accord with the previous discussion that there is no difference between Figs. 9 and 10. The frequency spectrum in Fig. 12 is limited between –pi/2 and pi/2. The linear signal processing method shown in Fig. 1 does not create components exceeding+-pi/2.

There is a big difference between Figs.12 and 14. The frequency spectrum is extended to exceed+-pi/2 in Fig. 14. These FFT results provide evidence that our method extends the components that the original image does not have.

We used an input image with the frequency spectrum shown in Fig. 4. It does not have the components exceeding lfs/2(pi/2). Fig. 14 shows that our method creates the components exceeding pi/2 that is the Nyquist frequency of the original image. Therefore, these results show that our method creates the components exceeding the Nyquist frequency.

Fig. 11 Image Processed with the Proposed Method

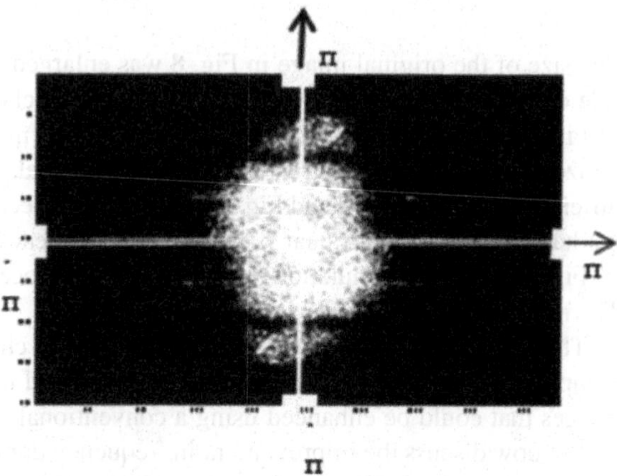

Fig. 12 Two Dimensional Result of Fig. 9

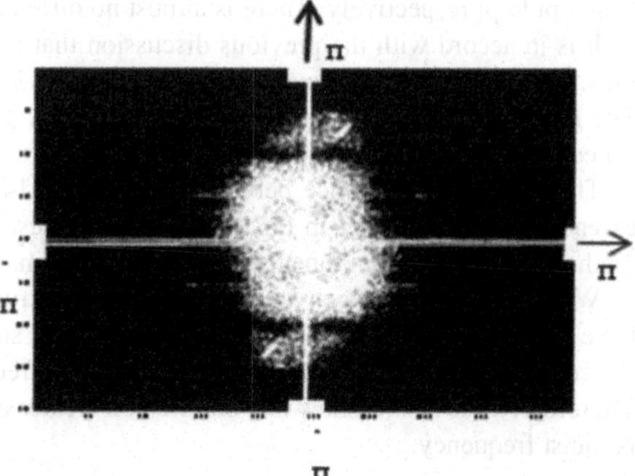

Fig. 13 Two Dimensional Result of Fig. 10

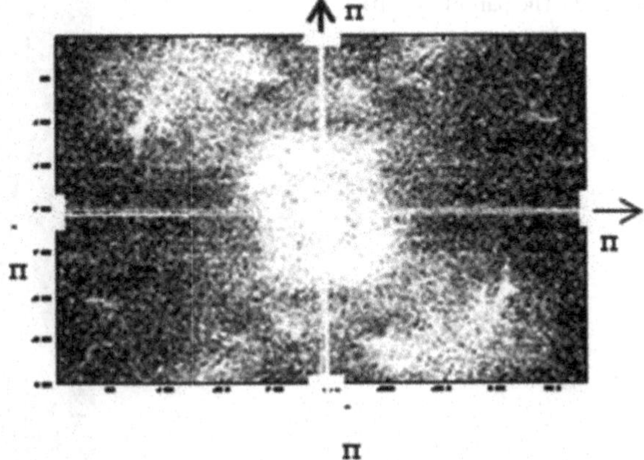

Fig. 14 Two Dimensional Result of Fig. 11

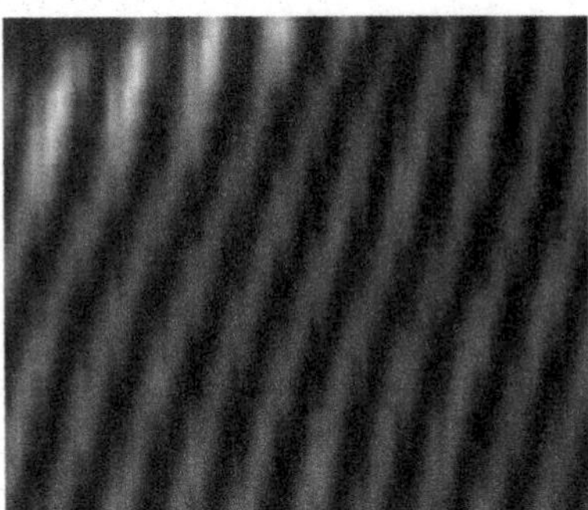

Fig. 15 The part of Fig. 10

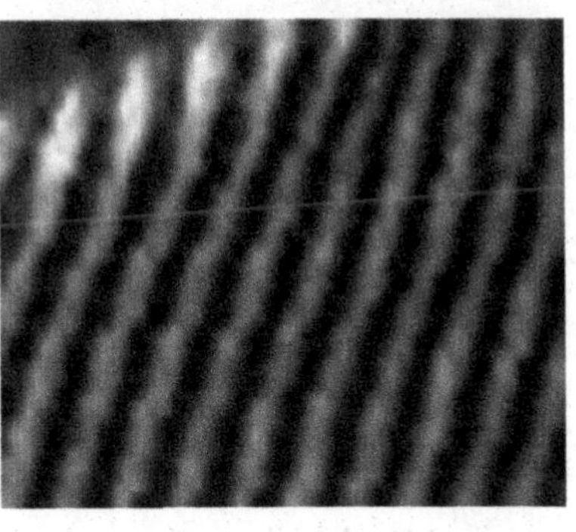

Fig. 16 The part of Fig. 11

Fig. 15, Fig. 16, Fig. 17 and Fig. 18 illustrate the part of Fig. 10 and Fig. 11. Fig. 15 and Fig. 16 are the part of the scarf and Fig. 17 and Fig. 18 are the part of the back of the chair which is upper right of the image. There are differences between Fig. 15 and Fig. 16 and between Fig. 17 and Fig. 18 respectively.

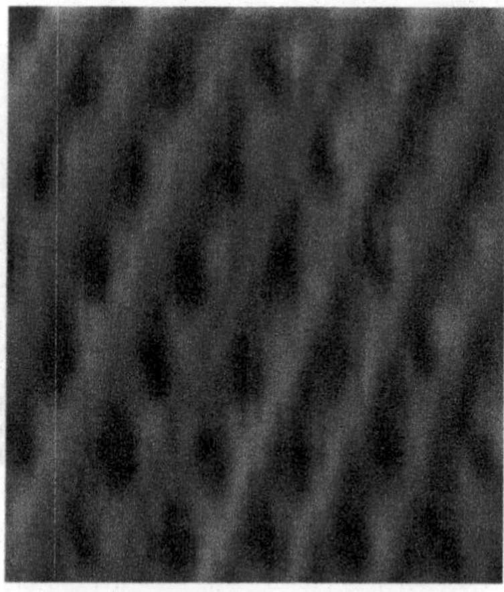

Fig. 17 The part of Fig. 10

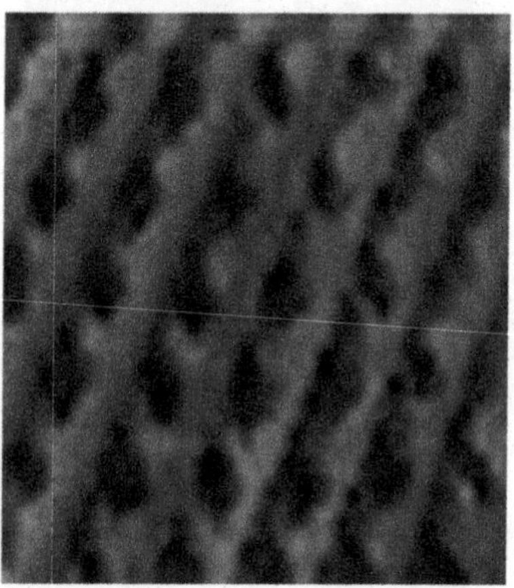

Fig. 18 The part of Fig. 11

5 Comparison with Reconstruction Super Resolution (RSR)

The main targets for the proposed method are TV and video. TV with RSR is available on the market [9][10][13]. The basic idea of RSR requires the TV to be equipped with several frame memories. Since the frame memories increase the TV cost, RSR in a frame technology for the TV application (RSRTV) was developed and RSRTV has been available on the market [12[13]]. It is not fair that the proposed method is not compared with RSRTV. Since RSRTV does not show 100% capability of RSR, we will only discuss RSR and the proposed method. The reason for it being that RSR produces the best image quality of RSRTV. RSR requires several low resolution images to reconstruct just one high resolution (HR) image [2]. The low resolution images are derived from one HR image and the sampling phase of the low resolution (LR) images is different. This is the essential condition for the reconstruction type SR.

If we assume to use this technology to improve video, we will face several issues. Video consists of frames and frames consist of fields. Each field is different due to objects moving. The field images are the LR images and the frames are HR images. However, the field images cannot become the LR images due to the objects moving. The only condition for the LR image is that each filed shakes vertically in a continuous manner up and down such as a head motion to express 'Yes'. We may improve the resolution if we can detect the sub-pixel precision motion vectors to adjust the objects displacement in different fields However, though it is very difficult, it can be done in certain situations. We are supposed to say that we cannot improve the horizontal resolution due to the relationship between the field LR images and the frame HR images if the sub-pixel motion vector cannot be detected accurately.

If we detect the motion vector precisely, we can improve the SR in very limited sequences such as a head motion expressing 'No' in a continuous manner. For other, bigger objects moving horizontally such as cars and so on, we will have to use a conventional technology such as image resolution improvement with motion vector to decrease the interline flicker, which is not a SR technology.

6 Conclusion

A new signal processing method with a high pass filter and the absolute function is proposed. The proposed method creates the components exceeding the Nyquist frequency that cannot be produced using conventional enhancers. The important point of this method is that it improves the image quality and creates the components exceeding the Nyquist frequency using a single frame of the video image.

The proposed algorithm can be housed in a compact hardware device and can work in a real time machine in TV sets.

Appendix A

Using Mathematica^{TM}, the series of |sin(x)| can be obtained. Although it becomes the infinite series, only the first five terms are shown due to space limitations. The first term of it is cos(2pi x). It has a frequency 2pi times higher than the original The other terms have harmonic frequencies of the original signal. According to this calculation, the absolute function creates the high frequencies that exceed the Nyquist frequency.

```
In[1]=<<Calculus'FourierTransform'
In[2]=FourierTrigSeries[Abs[Sin[x]],x,5]
```

Out[1]=

$$\frac{8\,\mathrm{Cos}[\frac{1}{4}]^2\,\mathrm{Cos}[2\pi\,x]}{1-4\pi^2}+\frac{8\,\mathrm{Cos}[\frac{1}{4}]^2\,\mathrm{Cos}[6\pi\,x]}{1-36\pi^2}+\frac{8\,\mathrm{Cos}[\frac{1}{4}]^2\,\mathrm{Cos}[10\pi\,x]}{1-100\pi^2}+4\,\mathrm{Sin}\left[\frac{1}{4}\right]^2+\frac{8\,\mathrm{Cos}[4\pi\,x]\,\mathrm{Sin}[\frac{1}{4}]^2}{1-16\pi^2}+\frac{8\,\mathrm{Cos}[8\pi\,x]\,\mathrm{Sin}[\frac{1}{4}]^2}{1-64\pi^2}$$

References

1. Subhasis Chaudhuri, "Super-Resolution Imaging", Kluwer Academic Publishers, ISBN978-0-7923-7471-8
2. Sina Farsiu etal, "Fast and Robust Mutiframe Super Resolution", IEEE Transaction on Image Processing, Vol.13, No.10, October, 2004
3. Hideaki Kawamura etal, "Edge detection and digital television", Japanese Patent No. 2001-292341 in Japanese
4. http://homepages.inf.ed.ac.uk/rbf/HIPR2/unsharp.htm
5. http://www.engadgethd.com/2007/10/05/jvc-victor-exhibits-4k-x-2k-d-ila-projector-at-ceatec/
6. http://www.informationdisplay.org/article.cfm?year=2008%26issue=04%26file=art6
7. http://insightmedia.info/emailblasts/ces2007rodneyawards.htm
8. Aggelos Katssaggelos, Rafael Molina, Javier Mateos "Super Resolution of Image and Video" Morgan&Claypool Publishers, 2007
9. http://www.toshiba.co.jp/rdc/rd/fields/07_e01_e.htm
10. http://www.toshiba.co.jp/tech/review/2009/high2009/high2009pdf/0902.pdf
11. D. Glasner, S. Bagon, and M. Irani, "Super-Resolution from a Single Image", International Conference on Computer Vision (ICCV), October 2009.
12. Nobuyuki Matsumoto, Takashi Ida," A Study on One Frame Reconstruction-based Super-resolution Using Image Segmentation", SIP2008-6, IE2008-6, IEICE Tech. Rep., vol. 108, no. 4, IE2008-6, pp. 31-36, April 2008 (in Japanese)
13. http://www.toshiba.co.jp/regza/detail/superresolution/resolution.html (in Japanese)

Applications

A Novel UEP Scheme for Scalable Video Transmission Over MIMO Systems

Chao Zhou, Xinggong Zhang, and Zongming Guo

Abstract In this paper, we propose a novel unequal error protection (UEP) scheme to improve the system performances for scalable video transmission over MIMO wireless networks, in which antenna selection, modulation, and channel coding are jointly optimized. We formulate the proposed scheme as an optimization problem and an efficient heuristic algorithm is proposed to solve it. By analyzing the dependency among antenna selection, modulation and channel coding, we determine the three vectors sequentially that antenna selection is heuristically implemented according to the order of subchannel's SNR strength, the best modulation levels are selected by maximizing the good throughput, and based on the optimal antenna selection and modulation level vectors, the channel coding rate vector is determined to lower the packet error ratio (PER) as much as possible under bandwidth constraint. Experimental results show that the proposed algorithm achieves nearly the same optimal PSNR performance based on exhaustive search. By comparing with other transmission schemes, our proposed scheme and algorithm significantly improve the system performance.

Keywords MIMO • SVC • UEP • Antenna selection • Modulation adaptation • Dynamic channel coding

1 Introduction

Advances in video coding technology and standardization [1] along with the rapid development and improvement of wireless network infrastructures, storage capacity, and computing power are enable an increasing number of video applications over

C. Zhou • X. Zhang • Z. Guo (✉)
Institute of Computer Science and Technology, Peking University, Beijing 100871, P.R. China
e-mail: guozongming@icst.pku.edu.cn

J.S. Jin et al., *The Era of Interactive Media*,
DOI 10.1007/978-1-4614-3501-3_50,

wireless networks. However, the inherently limited channel bandwidth and the unpredictability of the propagation channel become significant obstacles for wireless communication providers to offer high quality multimedia services. Meanwhile, multiple antennas system with multiple transmit antennas and multiple receive antennas, called multiple-input and multiple-output (MIMO) system, has been shown to be an effective way to transmit high data rates over wireless channels [2–4]. In this paper, we attempt to combine antenna selection, modulation and channel coding to improve the performance of scalable video transmission over MIMO wireless networks.

MIMO can be used to provide unequal error protection (UEP) for video transmission as MIMO wireless channel can be decomposed into independent equivalent parallel subchannels. However, the subchannels' heterogeneity in channel condition, combining with the unequal priorities and diverse bit rates of SVC video layers, make it challenging to map each video layer to a appropriate antenna. Furthermore, modulation and channel coding are also very crucial for video transmission. Generally, there is a tradeoff between the transmission rate and reliability. High level modulations generally provide high bandwidth with low transmission reliability, and vice versa. Besides, by means of channel coding, parity bits can be used to correct bit errors and improve the transmission reliability, but additional bandwidth is consumed at the same time. So, how to select the best modulation level and channel coding rate is also challenging.

Some research works about UEP for video communication over MIMO systems have been proposed. However, most of them assume that the estimated channel state information (CSI) is available at the transmitter. In [5], ACS-MIMO is proposed and the UEP is automatically achieved by scheduling the video layers to different transmit antennas according to the ordering of each sub-channel's SNR strength. An unequal power allocation scheme for transmission of JPEG compressed images over MIMO system is proposed in literature [6], in which the power is allocated unequally according to the importance of data. But the modulation level is fixed in these schemes. Under power and bit error ratio (BER) constraint, adaptive M-ary QAM is adopted in [7] by reallocating the surplus power to some sub-channels, but the modulation level for the most important layer is fixed. UEP is also achieved in [8, 9] by unequal power allocation, unequally channel coding, JSCC or cross-layer optimization.

In this paper, we propose a novel UEP scheme to improve the performances of scalable video transmission over MIMO wireless networks. In this proposed scheme, antenna selection, modulation, and channel coding are jointly optimized to provide different levels of error protection for the video layers. We formulate it as an optimization problem, and it can be solved by the method of exhaustive search, which has the highest accuracy level and computational complexity. In order to lower the complexity and make it suitable for practical implementation, we present an efficient heuristic algorithm. By analyzing the dependency among antenna selection vector, modulation level vector and channel coding rate vector, we determine the there vectors sequentially that antenna selection is heuristically implemented according to the order of subchannel's SNR strength, the best modulation levels are selected by maximizing the effective throughput, and based on the optimal antenna selection and modulation level vectors, the channel coding rates are determined to lower the packet error ratio (PER) as much as possible under bandwidth constraint. The algorithm is shown to be efficient, and the performance deterioration is neglectable compared with the exhaustive algorithm. As compared with some existing schemes, the experimental results demonstrate significant improvement in our proposed scheme and heuristic algorithm.

Compared with the existing works, we differ here in several major ways. Firstly, our paper provides more general formulation with antenna selection, modulation and channel coding consideration and UEP is achieved. Furthermore, we propose an efficient low-complexity heuristic algorithm to solve the above optimization problem. Our approach, optimizing the three variables sequentially, is efficient and achieves PSNR performance close to exhaustive search.

The rest of the paper is organized as follows. Section 2 describes the MIMO wireless system infrastructure for scalable video transmission. In Sect. 3, we formulate the proposed UEP scheme as an optimization problem, and an efficient low-complexity heuristic algorithm is presented to solve it. The experimental results and conclusion are presented in Sects. 4 and 5, respectively.

2 System Structure

In this section, we briefly describe the infrastructure of the proposed MIMO wireless system with M_{tx} transmit antennas and M_{rx} receive antennas. An example of 3 ×3 MIMO system is described as Fig. 1 shows. Without loss of generality, it is commonly assumed that the channel is block fading [10], and we also assume that the duration of each block is T. In the following of this paper, all the description is restricted in a certain block. The system equation is written as

$$\mathbf{Y} = \sqrt{\frac{E_s}{M_{tx}}}\mathbf{H}\mathbf{S} + \mathbf{W} \tag{1}$$

where $\mathbf{H}$ is the complex channel matrix with size $M_{rx} \times M_{tx}$, $\mathbf{S}$ is the $M_{tx} \times 1$ transmitted signal vector, $\mathbf{Y}$ is the $M_{rx} \times 1$ received signal vector, $\mathbf{W}$ is the $M_{rx} \times 1$ noise vector from i.i.d. Gaussian distribution with zero mean, independent real and imaginary parts, with variance σ^2, and E_s is the total average energy available at the transmitter over a symbol period having removed losses due to propagation and shadowing.

At the encoder side, the input video sequence is pre-coded by the latest scalable video coding (SVC) technology. For illustration purpose, one base layer and two enhancement layers are generated after SVC encoding. With the feedback channel

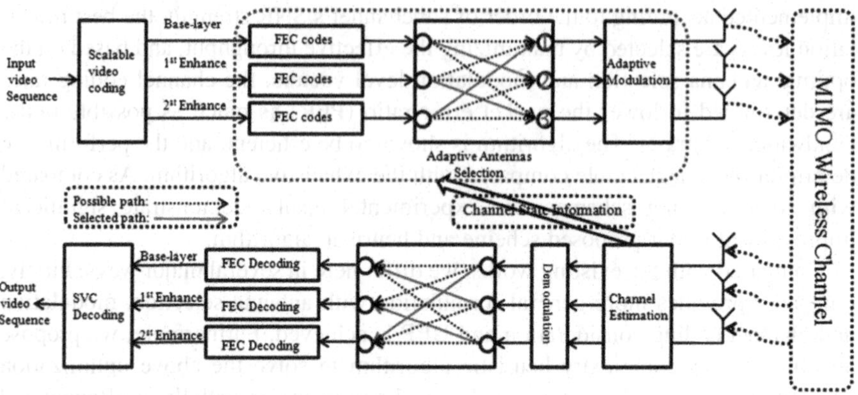

Fig. 1 Proposed system framework

state information (CSI), adaptive antenna selection, modulation, and dynamic channel coding are cooperatively optimized to provide different levels of error protection for the video layers and improve the system performance. The adaptive antenna selection is achieved according to the ordering of each subchannel's SNR strength, which is calculated from the feedback CSI. For example, if the ordering of SNR strength is "2, 3, 1," the bit loading of each layer bit stream is therefore described as Fig. 1 shows. Meanwhile, in order to further minimize the end-to-end video transmission distortion, appropriate modulation level and channel coding rate are jointly selected under the temporal fairness constraint. At the receiver side, the SNR of each subchannel is estimated using pilot symbols and sent back to the transmitter as CSI [11]. After demodulation, the bit layer streams are unloaded to the proper subchannel buffers, bit errors are corrected by channel coding, and finally the transmitted video sequences are reconstructed.

3 The Proposed UEP Transmission Scheme

The input video sequence is pre-coded into one base layer and several enhancement layers by the latest scalable video coding (SVC) technique. Since the video layers have different importance to the video quality, more important layers should be transmitted with more protection from errors as compared with less important layers. In order to improve the system performance, adaptive antenna selection, modulation, and dynamic channel coding are jointly optimized to provide different levels of error protection for different video layers over MIMO wireless networks. To account for this, a novel UEP scheme is proposed, which aims to minimize the expected end-to-end video transmission distortion. We formulate this optimization problem and a low complexity algorithm is proposed to solve it in this section.

3.1 Problem Formulation

The input video sequence is encoded L layers: one base layer and $L-1$ enhancement layers. In order to maintain the temporal fairness, the transmission is subject to the temporal constraint that the normalization transmission time for each layer should not exceed a threshold τ. Considering the different importance of video layers, we adopt the distortion model proposed in [12] to describe the end-to-end distortion over MIMO system. The predicted peak signal-to-noise ratio (PSNR) for a certain block can be represented as follows:

$$S(\mathbf{P}) = P_1 d_{EC} + (1 - P_1)d_1 + \sum_{i=2}^{L} \prod_{j=1}^{i} (1 - P_j)(d_i - d_{i-1}) \quad (2)$$

where L is the number of the video layers, d_{EC} is the PSNR due to the error concealment mismatch, d_i corresponds to the video PSNR achieved by decoding layers 1 to i, and $\mathbf{P} = P_1, P_2 \ldots P_L$ is the packet error (PER) rate vector. It is worth noting that d_{EC} and d_i are only depending on the encoder parameters and can be easily derived [12], and we aim to minimize the end-to-end distortion through optimizing PER vector $\mathbf{P}$, which is achieved by selecting optimal antenna selection vector $\mathbf{A}^*$, modulation level vector $\mathbf{M}^*$, and channel coding rate vector $\mathbf{R}^*$. We use Θ to denote the dependency among them and it is presented as $\mathbf{P}\Theta\{\mathbf{A}^*, \mathbf{M}^*, \mathbf{R}^*\}$.

For a rectangular constellation and a Gaussian channel, the bit-error probability of M-QAM is given by [13]

$$\rho_b \approx \frac{2(K-1)}{K \log_2 K} K\left(\sqrt{\left(\frac{3 \log_2 K}{K^2 - 1}\right) \frac{2E_b}{N_0}}\right) \quad (3)$$

where $M = 2^q, K = \sqrt{M}$ and q is the number of information bits per symbol and is even. It clearly shows the uncoded bit error probability is depending on the SNR strength and modulation level M, which can be further presented as $\rho_b\Theta\{SNR, M\}$ and M is the modulation level.

With the feedback CSI, we derive the SNR of each subchannel, so the SNR of each video layer is decided by antenna selection. And then the uncoded bit-error probability vector can be further rewritten as

$$\mathbf{P}_b = \left[\rho_b^1, \rho_b^2 \ldots \rho_b^L\right] \Theta \{\mathbf{A}, \mathbf{M}\} \quad (4)$$

where $\mathbf{A}$ and $\mathbf{M}$ are the antenna selection vector and modulation vector respectively. Moreover, channel coding is carried out to correct the transmission errors and RS codes is implemented. The source bits and parity bits of wth layer are denoted by $R_{s,w}$

and $R_{c,w}$ respectively. The source bits and the redundancy bits are distributed into v_w transport packets with channel coding rate r_w. Then the coded PER in wth layer is

$$p_w = 1 - \sum_{i=0}^{t_w} \binom{N}{i} \left(\rho_b^w\right)^i \left(1 - \rho_b^w\right)^{N-i} \tag{5}$$

where N is the packet size, $t_w = N \times (1 - r_w)$, $\rho_b{}^w$, which is the uncoded bit error probability of wth video layer, is depending on the antenna selection vector and modulation level vector, and $w = 1, 2...L$. After taking the video layer's dependency into consideration that the loss of a frame in lower layers affects the frames in higher layers, we can derive P_w from p_w as follows

$$P_w = \begin{cases} p_1 \\ p_w + P_w\,(1 - p_w) \end{cases} \tag{6}$$

In order to maintain temporal fairness, the transmission is subject to the temporal constraint that the normalization transmission time should not exceed the threshold τ in a certain block:

$$\tau_w = \frac{R_{s,w} + R_{c,w}}{q_w R_s} < \tau \tag{7}$$

where q_w is the number of information bits per symbol of M-QAM for wth layer and R_s is the symbol rate. The above optimization problem is formulated as

$$\begin{aligned} \{\mathbf{A}^*, \mathbf{M}^*, \mathbf{R}^*\} &= \underset{\{\mathbf{A},\mathbf{M},\mathbf{R}\}}{\arg\max}\, S(\mathbf{P}) \\ &\textit{Subject to} \\ &\frac{R_{s,w} + R_{c,w}}{q_w R_s} < \tau, \forall\, 1 \le w \le L \end{aligned} \tag{8}$$

and the vector **P** can be easily derived from vector **A**, **M** and **R** according to formula (3)–(6).

3.2 Solution to the Optimization Problem

The above optimization problem needs to determine three vectors and it is too complex to solve this problem by traditional exhaustive algorithm. In this subsection, we propose a low complexity heuristic algorithm to solve this problem.

As the video sequence are encoded into several layers with different priority, more important layers should be transmitted over the antennas with better quality, i.e., the antennas with higher SNR. So, the antenna selection vector $\mathbf{A}^*$ is heuristically derived according to the ordering of each subchannel's SNR strength. After antenna selection, the base layer is launched to the subchannel with highest SNR strength, first enhancement layer is mapped to the subchannel with second highest SNR strength, and so on.

According to the antenna selection vector $\mathbf{A}^*$, the video layers are mapped to appropriate transmit antennas. Then, for each transmit antenna, the best modulation level and channel coding rate need to be determined to further minimize the end-to-end distortion. While in an actual system, the available modulation levels and channel coding rates are discrete. Combining with the distortion model and antenna selection vector, the best modulation level and channel coding rates can be derived by the exhaustive algorithm. However, this kind of algorithm may lead to high delay and it is not suitable for real time video transmission. In the following of this subsection, a low-complexity algorithm is designed for this sub-optimization problem, which aims to select the best modulation level and channel coding rate to minimize the end-to-end video transmission distortion.

Formula (3)–(5) shows that the uncoded bit error probability is depending on the modulation level M and SNR strength. Given the SNR strength, which is only depending on the antenna selection vector after receiving the feedback CSI, we can further rewrite the uncoded error bit probability for wth layer as

$$\rho_b^w \Theta\{M_w\} \tag{9}$$

On the other hand, the essence of channel coding is to add some redundant bits to the source bits. In general, when given the channel condition and source bit rate, the more redundant bits, the lower coded PER can be derived. In our proposed system, the source bit rate and channel condition is constant in a certain block, and we can get all these information according to the feedback CSI and antenna selection vector. Then, in order to add as much as possible redundant bits to lower the coded PER, the sub-optimization problem can be transformed into maximizing the effective throughput, which denotes the expected correctly received bits at the receiver. And for wth video layer, the effective throughput can be presented as

$$\Psi_w = R_s q_w \left(1 - \rho_b^w\right) \tag{10}$$

where Ψ_w denotes the effective throughput for wth video layer with modulation level M_w. From (9) and (10), we can find that

$$\Psi_w \Theta\{M_w\} \tag{11}$$

Moreover, the transmission time should not exceed the constraint τ, so

$$R_{c,w} \leq q_w R_s \tau - R_{s,w} \tag{12}$$

and it also indicates that

$$\left(R_{c,w}\right)_{\max} \Theta\left\{q_w\right\} \Theta\{M_w\} \tag{13}$$

From the above analysis, we can see that the main challenge is to select the best modulation level, because when given the modulation level, the maximal number of redundant bits can be easily determined. However, in order not to add too much redundant bits and waste the bandwidth, the channel coding rate for wth video layer can be determined as

$$r_w = \max\left\{\arg\max_{r \in \Xi} r | P_w \leq 0, \frac{R_{s,w}}{R_{s,w} + \max R_{c,w}}\right\} \tag{14}$$

and Ξ denotes the set of the discrete achievable channel coding rate. The formula indicates that if the bandwidth is not high enough, we will add as much redundant bits as possible to lower the PER. Otherwise, the channel coding rate, r_w, is selected to guarantee that each packet can be transmitted accurately, which can be derived easily by setting $P_w = 0$. It is worth noting that the channel coding rates are discrete in actual system, if the above selected rate is not available, the channel coding rate, which is the closest to the above selected rate but lower than the above selected rate, is selected.

The above analysis shows that when given the modulation level M_w, the best coding rate r_w can be easily determined. So the main challenge is to select the best modulation level. Though the modulation level is discrete, we assume that the modulation level used for wth video layer is continuous and denoted as $\hat{M}_w$, then combining with the antenna selection vector and above analysis, $\hat{M}_w$ can be easily determined by solving the following equation

$$\frac{d\Psi_w(\hat{M}_w)}{d\hat{M}_w} = 0 \tag{15}$$

Generally, the optimal modulation level $\hat{M}_w$ is continuous. Then, the modulation level points M'_w and M''_w, which are discrete achievable modulation levels adjacent to $\hat{M}_w$ are selected from Ω, such that $\left\{M'_w \leq \hat{M}_w \leq M''_w,\ M'_w, M''_w \in \Omega\right\}$, and Ω is the set of available modulation levels. At last, according to the antenna selection vector and the method used to choose the channel coding rate, which are mentioned above, the best modulation level for wth video layer is selected

$$M_w = \arg\max_{\{M'_w, M''_w\}} S(\mathbf{P}) \tag{16}$$

and the optimization modulation vector $\mathbf{M}^* = [M_1, M_2 \ldots M_L]$ is derived, so as the channel coding rate vector $\mathbf{R}^* = [r_1, r_2 \ldots r_L]$.

According to the above analysis, the antenna selection vector, modulation level vector and channel coding rate vector are sequentially determined in our proposed suboptimization algorithm. This greatly reduces the complexity of the optimization problem and its effectiveness is demonstrated in the next section.

4 Experimental Evaluation and Results

The experiments in this section are to demonstrate the effectiveness of our proposed UEP scheme for scalable video transmission over MIMO wireless system. We use a 3×3 MIMO system as Fig. 1 shows under independent Rayleigh fading. The set, Ω, includes four available modulation levels: {4-QAM, 16-QAM, 64-QAM, 256-QAM}, and Ξ includes nine available rates: {1/16, 2/16. . . 9/16}. The temporal constraint τ is set to 0.15 and T is set to 0.5, that the CSI is estimated and feedback to the transmitter per 0.5 s. Four video sequences, "Football," "City," "Mobile," and "Foreman" are examined. All test sequences contain 150 frames with a frame rate of 30 fps and are encoded by JSVM reference encoder to generate one base layer and two enhancement layers. We present the PER and effective throughput results as well as the PSNR performance of the reconstructed video sequences of different schemes. In traditional parallel transmission MIMO (PT-MIMO) [14], the unequal importance of the video layers is not taken into consideration. All the video layers are transmitted with the same priority and fixed modulation level. Its performance is much worse than ACS-MIMO [5]. In this work, we modify the traditional PT-MIMO by adding adaptive modulation (AM) at the transmitter. In order to evaluate the proposed scheme's performance, modified PT-MIMO and ACS-MIMO are implemented for comparison and the modulation level is fixed to 4-QAM for ACS-MIMO.

In our system, the video layers are transmitted simultaneously from multiple transmit antennas. Figure 2 illustrates the uncoded PER performance of all the schemes. The results show that UEP is automatically achieved through antenna selection both in ACS-MIMO and our proposed scheme, while in modified PT-MIMO, all the video layers are treated equally and having nearly the same average PER. Moreover, it is worth noting that the PER performance of our proposed scheme is a little worse than ACS-MIMO, this is mainly because adaptive modulation level is implemented in the proposed scheme, while in ACS-MIMO, the most robust modulation level, 4-QAM is implement all the time.

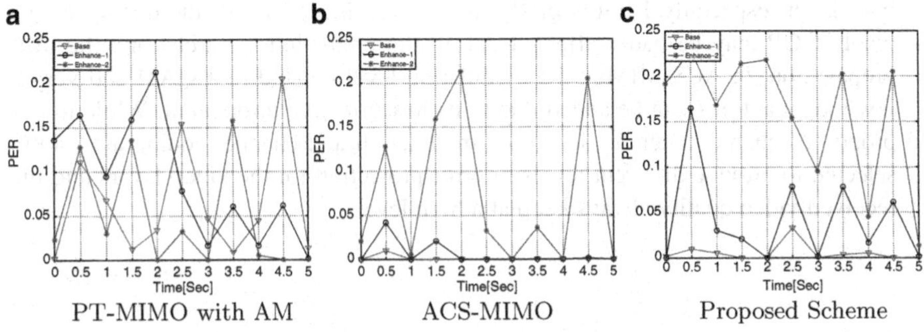

Fig. 2 The uncoded PER performance of different schemes

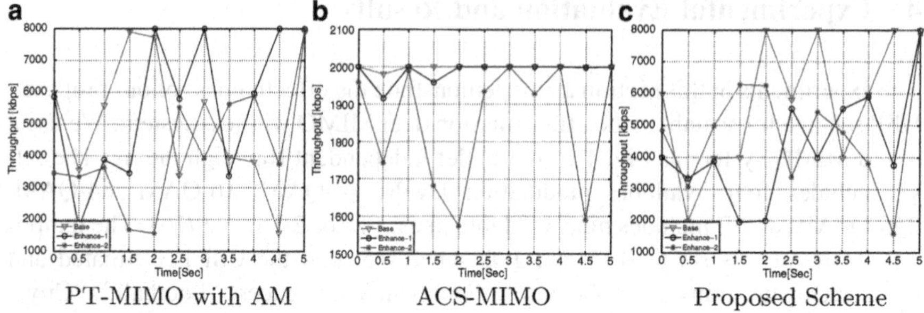

Fig. 3 The effective throughput of different schemes

Table 1 PSNR performance summary

	PT-MIMO with AM (dB)	ACS-MIMO (dB)	Proposed (dB)	Exhaustive algorithm (dB)
Foreman	34.029	35.193	38.623	38.756
City	30.111	34.270	38.224	38.571
Football	28.795	32.196	37.720	38.013
Mobile	29.156	33.156	38.056	38.224

Though through fixing the modulation level in a low level, ACS-MIMO has better PER performance than modified PT-MIMO and our proposed scheme, its effective throughput is much lower as Fig. 3 shows. So in modified PT-MIMO and our proposed scheme, much more redundant bits can be added to the source bits and the PER is greatly decreased after channel decoding, which has been analyzed in Sect. 3.2.

At last, we compare the PSNR of the reconstructed video sequences of different schemes and four video sequences are examined. Table 1 shows that our proposed scheme is efficient, and compared with the exhaustive algorithm,the performance deterioration is neglectable. The performance loss of modified PT-MIMO is mainly because that it does not consider the unequal importance of the video layers. If the base layer, especially I frame or P frame's base layer, is lost, the quality of the whole GOP may be badly affected due to the prediction hierarchy and the drift propagation. In ACS-MIMO, the modulation level is fixed to 4-QAM and very a few redundant bits can be added due to its low effective throughput. While in our proposed scheme, antennas selection, modulation and channel coding are jointly selected to provide different levels of error protection for the video layers and the received video quality always keep at a high level.

5 Conclusion

In this paper, we have proposed a novel unequal error protection video transmission scheme, which aims to minimize the end-to-end distortion for scalable video transmission over MIMO wireless networks. We formulate this UEP scheme as an optimization problem, which jointly optimize antenna selection, modulation, and channel coding in order to provide different levels of error protection for the video layers. Furthermore, a low complexity suboptimization algorithm is proposed to determine the above there vectors sequentially that antenna selection is heuristically implemented according to the order of subchannel's SNR strength, the best modulation levels are selected by maximizing the effective throughput, and based on the optimal antenna selection and modulation level vectors, the channel coding rates are determined to lower the packet error ratio (PER) as much as possible under bandwidth constraint. Experimental results show that our approach is efficient and achieves performance close to exhaustive search.

Acknowledgements This work is supported by National Development and Reform Commission High-tech Program of China under Grant No. [2010]3044 and National Natural Science Foundation of China under contract No. 60902004.

References

1. T. Wiegand, G. J. Sullivan, G. Bjontegaard, and A. Luthra, "Overview of the H.264/AVC video coding standard," *IEEE Trans. Circuits. Syst. Video Technol.*, vol. 13, no. 7, pp. 560–575, Jul. 2003.
2. S. Alamouti, "A simple transmit diversity technique for wireless communications," *IEEE J. Sel. Areas Commun.*, vol. 16, no. 8, pp. 1451–1458, Oct. 1998.
3. N. Chiurtu, B. Rimoldi, and E. Telatar, "On the capacity of multi-antenna Gaussian channels," *IEEE Int. Symp. Inf. Theory*, p. 53, 2001.
4. P. Wolniansky, G. Foschini, G. Golden, and R. Valenzuela, "V-BLAST: an architecture for realizing very high data rates over the rich-scattering wireless channel," *IEEE Int. Symp. Signals, Syst. Electron.*, pp. 295–300, Sep. 1998.
5. D. Song and C. W. Chen, "Scalable H.264/AVC Video Transmission Over MIMO Wireless Systems With Adaptive Channel Selection Based on Partial Channel Information," *IEEE Trans. Circuits. Syst. Video Technol.*, vol. 17, no. 9, pp. 1218–1226, Sep. 2007.
6. M. Sabir, A. Bovik, and R. Heath, "Unequal Power Allocation for JPEG Transmission Over MIMO Systems," *IEEE Trans. Image Process.*, vol. 19, no. 2, pp. 410–421, Feb. 2010.
7. D. Song and C. W. Chen, "QoS Guaranteed SVC-based Video Transmission over MIMO Wireless Systems with Channel State Information," *IEEE Int. Conf. Image Process.*, pp. 3057–3060, Oct. 2006.
8. S. Zhao, M. You, and L. Gui, "Scalable video delivery over MIMO OFDM wireless systems using joint power allocation and antenna selection," *IEEE Int. Conf. Multimedia Signal Process.*, pp. 1–6, Oct. 2009.
9. J. Xu, R. Hormis, and X. Wang, "MIMO video broadcast via transmit-precoding and SNR-scalable video coding," *IEEE J. Sel. Areas Commun.*, vol. 28, no. 3, pp. 456–4661, Apr. 2010.
10. E. Biglieri, J. Proakis, and S. Shamai, "Fading channels: information-theoretic and communications aspects," *IEEE Trans. Inf. Theory*, vol. 44, no. 6, pp. 2619–2692, Oct. 1998.

11. K. Lee and J. Chun, "On the interference nulling operation of the V-BLAST under channel estimation errors," *IEEE Veh. Technol. Conf.*, vol. 4, pp. 2131–2135, Jul. 2002.
12. H. Mansour, Y. Fallah, P. Nasiopoulos, and V. Krishnamurthy, "Dynamic Resource Allocation for MGS H.264/AVC Video Transmission Over Link-Adaptive Networks," *IEEE Trans. Multimedia*, vol. 11, no. 8, pp. 1478–1491, Dec. 2009.
13. B. Sklar, *Digital communications - fundamentals and applications*. Prentice Hall, NJ, 2001.
14. H. Zheng and K. Liu, "Space-time diversity for multimedia delivery over wireless channels," *IEEE Int. Conf. Circuits Syst.*, vol. 4, pp. 285–288, May. 2000.

Framework of Contour Based Depth Map Coding System

Minghui Wang, Xun He, Xin Jin, and Satoshi Goto

Abstract As conventional video coding standards such as H.264, Multiview Video Coding (MVC) adopts a strategy of "block based prediction" to achieve high compression ratio (such as JMVC). In order to improve the coding efficiency of MVC system, Depth Image Based Rendering (DIBR) is proposed. Depth map is introduced to represent the information of "another dimension". Comparing with texture map (2D), depth map indicates much more spatial continuity. In this work, Contour Based Depth map Coding (CBDC) is proposed to take the place of the conventional block based code structure. Framework of whole system is illustrated. Especially, details about the contour coding module are introduced in this paper. Experimental result shows that the bit cost of propose method (when DLP between 8 and 16) is equivalent to JMVC when QP between 12 and 16. Although the reconstructed frame lost some detail of texture in painting, the PSNR of synthesized view is competitive.

Keyword DIBR • Contour coding • MVC • Depth map

1 Introduction

Multiview Video Coding (MVC) is a hot topic in video coding field. To meet the requirement of coding efficiency, Depth Image Based Rendering (DIBR) is proposed [1]. Compared with simulcast coding [2], only basic views and depth maps are coded in DIBR. It saves computation of codec and bandwidth as well. Depth map is a new coding object that involved in DIBR system (Fig. 1) against the traditional 2D video coding. To be compatible with simulcast coding, depth

M. Wang (✉) • X. He • S. Goto
Graduate School of Information Productionand System, Waseda University, Fukuoka, Japan
e-mail: wmh.vip@gmail.com

X. Jin
Information Technology Research Organization, Waseda University, Fukuoka, Japan

J.S. Jin et al., *The Era of Interactive Media*,
DOI 10.1007/978-1-4614-3501-3_51,

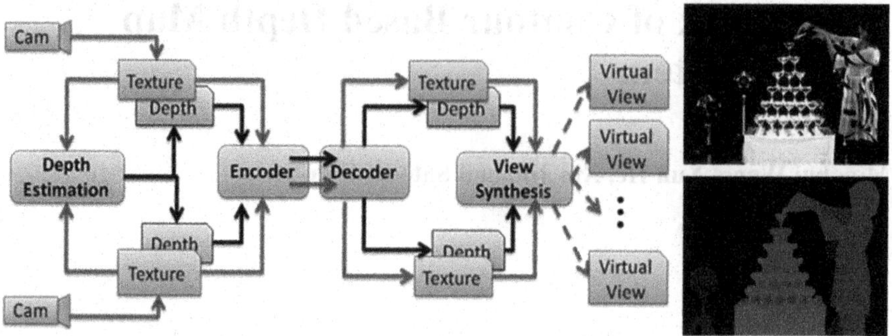

Fig. 1 DIBR system: On the *left side* is the system overview of DIBR. As a traditional way, both depth and texture map are encoded and decoded in same encoder and decoders. The *right side* images show a frame of texture map and its corresponding depth map

map estimation is introduced. Currently, the depth which is estimated from texture view shows more practicability than captured depth video [3]. In decoder side, view synthesis is introduced, after the basic view and depth view are decoded, to synthesize virtual views. Since the quality of virtual view is sensitive with depth view, depth plays a very important role. Errors in depth map causes distortion in synthesized virtual views. Some previous works [4] show that depth errors on object's edge take more influence in view synthesis than other errors. As a result, it is necessary to protect edge more than other parts in depth map.

In block based coding system, each macroblock (MB) is equally coded. It means that MBs on edges have the same probabilities to have distortion, and the distortion is even higher after quantization. Some edge-aware strategies [5, 6] are proposed to enhance the quality of synthesized view according to edge information. The quality of synthesized view is improved.

Depth view is essentially different from texture view (basic view). In texture view, value of a pixel denotes the luminance (chrominance) intensity in its position. It is affected by some luminance fluctuation from environment and different responding of camera sensors. As a result, the spatial and temporal continuity is relatively poor in texture maps. In depth map, value of pixel denotes the distance between the object and the camera. The granularity is relatively large (always several centimeters or more) in depth map. As a result, in the depth-camera-capture cases, tiny shake in video capturing process does not affect the value of pixels. In depth-estimation cases, some strategies are adopted to improve the continuation of depth maps. Furthermore, the geometric surface of a real object is "less complex" than its texture in most cases. Therefore depth map always shows good spatial and temporal continuity. The energy is gathered in edges in depth map, while in texture map it is gathered not only in edges, but also in high contrast texture (Fig. 1 right).

Considering the aforementioned features of depth map, an edge oriented coding strategy is proposed, which is regarded as Contour Based Depth Coding (CBDC). To guarantee the quality of object edges, a vector based lossless coding strategy is introduced. Edges and inside part are coded in different modules. The contours are coded in lossless way, and the inside is coded in lossy way. In CBDC, depth pixels with similar depth value are grouped into a region. Contours between adjacent regions are coded as vector graph. Each pixel on contours is exactly rebuilt in decoder. Inside of regions are rebuilt by painting the space between contours. Painting mode and coefficients are coded. This coding strategy has some features in the following aspects:

- **Accurate contour**. Since the coordinate of pixels in object edges are coded in lossless way (no approximation, no quantization), edges in rebuilt depth map is guaranteed to be exactly the same with original depth map.
- **Separately make the tradeoff of "Bitrate and PSNR"**. Unlike block based coding strategies, CBDC costs bits mainly in a contour coding module (coordinates of points on contours always cost much more bits than painting parameters) and the PSNR depends on the painting module (contour coding is a lossless coding).
- **Easy to zoom in or zoom out**. Since adopting vector graph to describe depth maps, zooming is easy to perform. The zooming result is better than bitmap based upsample/downsample way. On the other hand, for some downsample based fast coding strategy [7], this coding structure is supposed to give a better performance.
- **Parallel computing (high data dependency)**. In the proposed work, it codes a frame in three levels: frame coding, layer coding and region coding. In each level, the processing can be paralleled.

This is not the first work to introduce contour based method in video/image coding. TureType font in computer operating system is a successful application of contour coding. It adopts Bezier Curves to describe the contour of character, instead of recording a bitmap. Comparing to TureType, contours are more complex in CBDC, and cannot be modified by codec. Many works use straight line fit to code digital contour or curve [8, 9]. In their works, linear regression is adopted to find straight lines in contour. Thus these algorithms are lossy coding, which do not meet the requirement for depth map coding. In MPEG4 related research, to achieve object oriented coding, contour coding is adopted to improve the performance [10, 11]. Some smooth parts are rebuilt by painting, instead of intra prediction.

The rest of this paper will be organized as: Sect.2 gives a system overview of proposed CBDC. Sects.3 and 4 introduced the encoder and decoder part of the CBDC respectively. The experimental result is shown in Sect.5. A conclusion is given in Sect.6.

2 System Overview

Against the block-based code structure, the proposed work introduces a contour based code structure. Some terms are defined as follows before illustrating the whole system:

- **Depth map**: One frame of depth video, which represents the depth information of the scene.

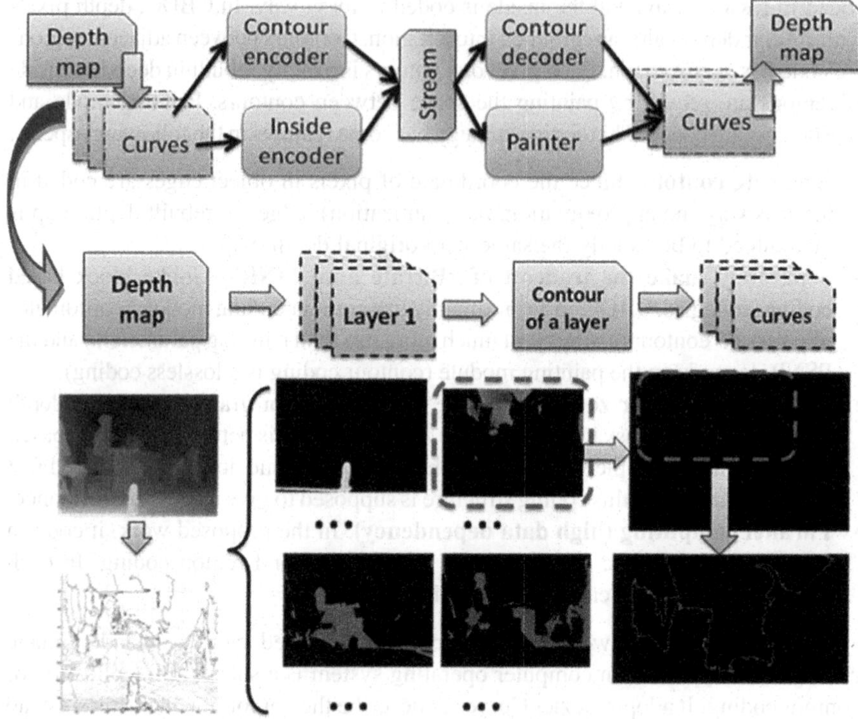

Fig. 2 System architecture of CBDC

- **Texture map**: One frame of texture/color video, or called conventional 2D video. Represent luminance and chrominance information of the scene.
- **Layer**: In one layer, it only contains pixels whose depth value is in the depth interval of that layer. A depth map can be divided into several layers. The depth interval length is regarded as "depths per layer" or DPL
- **Region**: Inside one layer, if we can find a set of pixels that no other pixel is connecting pixels of the set and all pixels in the set are connected, then the set is called a region.
- **Contour**: The one-pixel-width edge of a region is called the contour of that region.
- **Curve**: a subset of pixels in contour. Every pixel connects at least another one pixel in this subset.
- **Inside of region**: A set of pixels, belongs to a region, but not belongs to the contour of the region.
- **Paint**: Calculate the depth value of each pixel in the inside of region with a formula. The coefficients in that formula are calculated in the encoder.

System architecture of CBDC is illustrated in Fig. 2. There are two functional modules in the encoder and two in the decoder. They are contour encoder, inside encoder, contour decoder and painter. Encoding is a single-pass process without inter-frame prediction. Painting for inside part is regarded as intra-frame prediction. In the encoder side, a depth map is divided into several layers at first. It is further segmented into unconnected regions. Contours of these regions are loaded into contour encoder sequentially. "Texture" of a region is loaded in to inside encoder at the same time. Inside encoder determines the optimal painting mode, and painting coefficients. Output of the encoders contains contours in the form of points (vectors) list, painting mode and painting coefficients for each region, and also semantic information (such as headers). In decoder side, contours are rebuilt first. Painter fills the inside part according to painting mode and parameters of each region. After that, the whole frame is fully reconstructed.

3 Encoder Side

3.1 Dataflow

Traditional video coding method divides a frame into MBs to process. In CBDC, depth maps are first divided into different layers by depth value interval. The length of the depth interval is fixed after coding starts. Note that more layers result in more bits and higher quality of reconstructed depth map, we compare 16 layers (16 depth values per layer or "DPL =16 ") case and 32 layers (eight depth values per layer or "DPL = 8") case in this work, since simulation result shows these two cases are similar with block based coding method in term of the tradeoff of Bitrate-PSNR. In this work, coding process of each layer is independent. In each layer, connecting pixels group regions. There is no connection between regions in a layer. Each region has a close curve as its contour. All these contours form the contour of one layer.

In a frame, layers are coded sequentially or in parallel. In a layer, regions and contours are coded sequentially or in parallel. For each region and contour, contour coding and inside coding can be taken simultaneously. The architecture of the encoder is illustrated in Fig. 3.

3.2 From Depth Map to Regions

In conventional bock based coding structure, the frame segmentation performs in spatial domain. Note that spatial continuity is stronger in depth map than in texture map. Thus we do not segment a frame in spatial domain. Instead of that, we divide the depth into several layers in depth domain (Fig. 2).

Depth map is recoded as a 256-level gray map. It is natural to equally divide it into 2^n layers. In this work, it is set 16 layers and 32 layers. Therefore, every 16/8

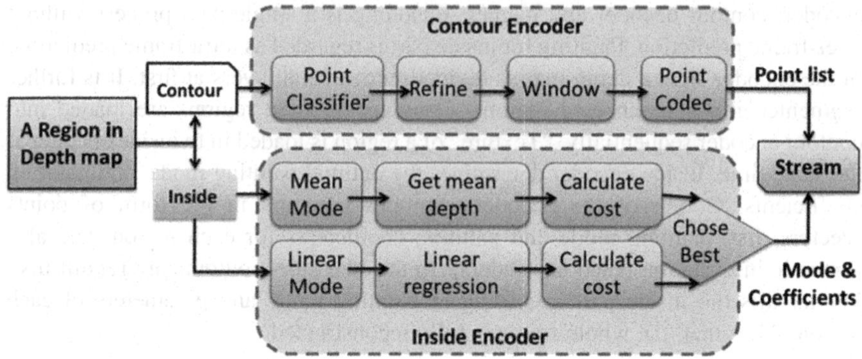

Fig. 3 Contour encoder and inside encoder

gray levels group a layer. For the *i*th layer, the depth value is from ((i–1)*16) to (i*16–1) or ((i–1)*8) to (i*8–1). The *i*th layer is defined as (1):

$$Layer(x, y, i) = \begin{cases} depth(x, y), & if \quad depth(x, y) \in [step^*(i-1), step^*i-1], \\ 0, & Others \end{cases} \tag{1}$$

Layer(x,y,i) is the depth value of point *(x,y)* in layer *i* (index start from 1), *depth (x,y)* is the depth value in point *(x,y)* in original depth map. *Step* represents the depth interval length of each layer (DLP). DLP is 16 or 8 in this work.

In a layer, "Erase-inside" method is adopted to get the contour of regions. A point is removed from a layer if it matches any one situation in the following:

1. A point with eight neighbours
2. A point with seven neighbours, and a "corner neighbour" is blank
3. A point with only one neighbour

After removal, only contour pixels are left in the map. It is followed by contour segment, in which the "scan-and-update" strategy is adapted to segment contour into curves. First the contour map is scanned line by line. If a new contour point is found, check the neighbour points of it. If all neighbour points have not been scanned before, give current point a new index (one larger than last used index). If one or more neighbour points already have an index, then:

1. If the neighbour points have the same index, then the current point also use this index
2. If the neighbour points have different indies (for example k1, k2, k3), then use the minimum one (for example k1) to mark current point, and change all other neighbours' index to this minimum one, and all points who have these index also change. (All points with k2 and k3 change index to k1).

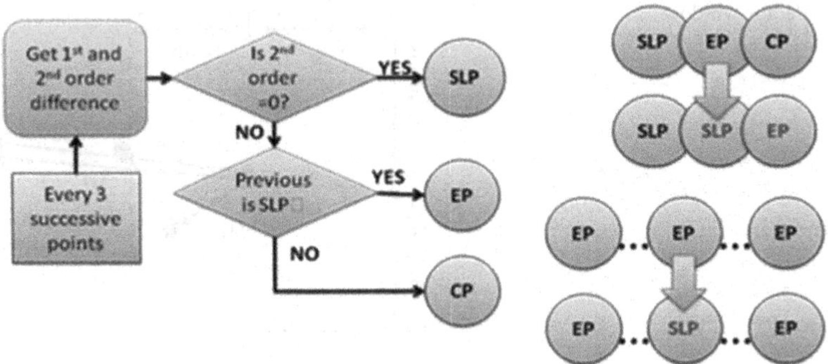

Fig. 4 Initial point classify (*left*) and refinement (*right*)

Table 1 SLP rate in different sequences

Seq.	Balloons	Book_arrival	Lovebird1	Champagne tower
SLP/ALL	83.1%	82.5%	86.7%	93.5%

After scanning, connected contour points are marked as same index, unconnected points are marked as different index. Therefore, different curves are distinguished by the index.

3.3 Contour Code

To code curves in a contour, second-order-difference based method is adopt as the classifier to initial the point type. There are three types: Straight Line Point (SLP), straight line End Point (EP) and Curve Point (CP). Points are first classified by the second order difference as shown in Fig. 4.

After initial classifying, two steps of refinement are taken to further distinguish the SLP:

- Change SLP-EP-CP type chain into SLP-SLP-EP
- If EP is periodic appears, middle EP can be changed to SLP

More points are marked as SLP after these refinements. For each point, we recode its coordinate and type (SLP, EP or CP). Therefore the straight line is denoted by its first SLP and EP, and other parts on the curve are denoted by CPs. In all of our test depth sequences SLP occupy a high percentage (more than 80%) among all points on contour curves (Table 1). Note that only two end points are required to represent a straight line, and all online points are required for a curve, it is quite important for us to detect as much SLP as possible.

Except the first point on the curve, all points are recoded as a vector, pointing from last point to itself. In order to limit the bit cost for each point, a vector window

Fig. 5 Vector window

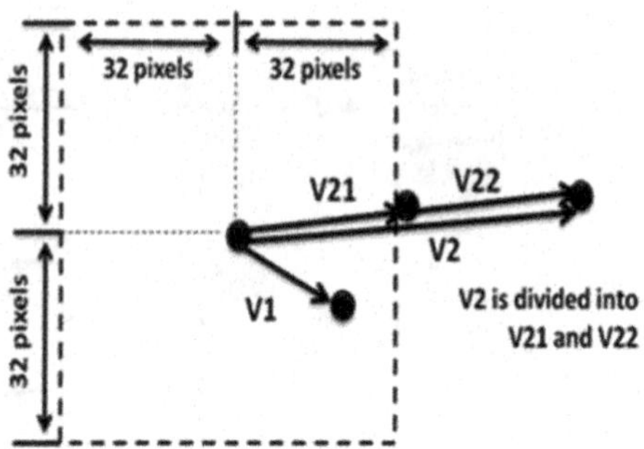

Table 2 State transfer of point types

		Current state		
	Code of type	SLP	EP	CP
Option 1	0	SLP	SLP	SLP
Option 2	1	EP	CP	CP

is set. In this work the search window is fixed to 32 (Fig. 5). Vectors "longer" than the window will be divided.

Each point (SLP, EP, and CP) cost 13 bits (X and Y coordinate of the vector cost 6 bits respectively, type cost 1 bit). For point types, we only recode the "change" of the type. There are only two options of the point type when the type of previous point is known (Table 2).

3.4 Inside Coding

In the inside paint module, two painting modes, mean paint and linear paint, are available. The choice is made by automatic judgment. Distortion cost in term of SAD (Sum of Absolute Difference) is calculated after painting finished under each mode, and then the one with less cost wins.

The mean paint denotes painting whole region with the mean depth of this region. Only the mean depth value is recode in the output stream.

Linear paint denotes painting a region as a flat surface. Several points (4 points are selected in this work, which are the middle of the most up, most down, most left and most right in the contour) are selected as samples in a region. In the encoder, for sample points, if *depth* $(x_i,y_i) = d_i$ $(i = 1,2,3,4)$, we can calculate coefficient vector A by regression:

$$Find\ A = (a_1, a_2, a_3)^T,\ s.t.\ \begin{bmatrix} d_1 \\ d_2 \\ d_3 \\ d_4 \end{bmatrix} \approx \begin{bmatrix} x_1 & y_1 & 1 \\ x_2 & y_2 & 1 \\ x_3 & y_3 & 1 \\ x_4 & y_4 & 1 \end{bmatrix} * A \tag{2}$$

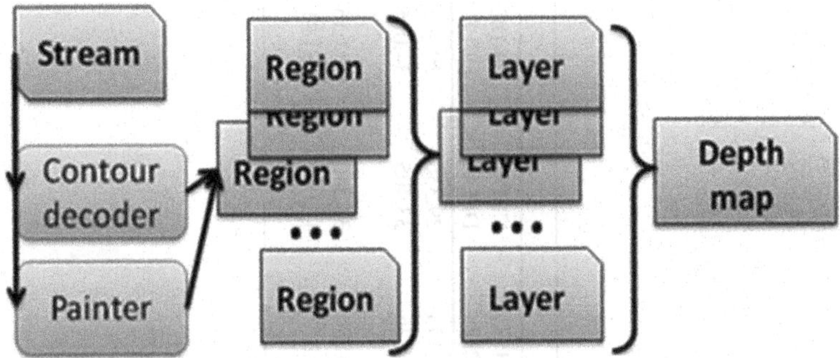

Fig. 6 Contour painter and painter

This information is written into output stream together with contour point list of this region. In decoder side, when we reconstruct the region, the depth will be calculated by (3):

$$d(x,y) = a_1x + a_2y + a_3 \tag{3}$$

4 Decoder Side

Figure 6 illustrates the flow chart of the contour decoder and painter. For each contour, the decoder reconstructs straight lines and curve points according to the start coordinate and vectors. Headers include some flags to distinguish inside and outside. Then painter fill the inside part of each curve, under a certain mode and follow the plane function if linear painting mode is chosen. Regions are rebuilt after curve and inside decoding are finished. Finally the rebuilt regions form layer, layers form a reconstructed frame.

5 Experimental Result

To evaluate the proposed coding system, we compare it with JMVC. For JMVC, CABAC is off, Intra prediction only, QP = 12, 16. For our proposed CBDC, depth per layer (DPL) is set to 8 and 16. After getting reconstructed depth videos from JMVC and CBDC respectively, we use VSRS to synthesize the virtual views (mid-view). Reconstructed depth videos (left and right) and original texture video (left and right views, without encode-decode) are used to make synthesis. Finally we calculate the PSNR by comparing original mid-view and virtual view. Table 3 shows the sum of bit cost per frame of two texture views, and the PSNR of the virtual views.

An important feature of the proposed CBDC is that bit cost is mainly depends on the contour coding and PSNR is mainly depends on painting. From the view of

Table 3 Compare JMVC and proposed CBDC

Bit cost per frame of depth video					PSNR of virtual view				
Depth	JMVC QP16	JMVC QP12	CBDC DPL16	CBDC DPL8	Virtual view	JMVC QP16	JMVC QP12	CBDC DPL16	CBDC DPL8
Love view6&8	207k	250k	195k	408k	view7	29.196	29.196	29.336	29.405
Tower view37&39	418k	519k	313k	586k	view38	34.140	34.126	33.405	34.015
Book view8&10	615k	855kk	650k	1328k	view9	33.846	33.880	33.246	33.936
Balloons view3&5	386k	518k	403k	851k	view4	18.059	18.057	18.068	18.081

Bitrate, the proposed algorithm is equivalent to JMVC when QP is between 12 and 16 (Less bits when DLP = 16 and more bits when DLP = 8). Note that currently CBDC directly transform the semantic information into binary bits. There is no entropy coding actually. The bitrate can be further reduced by 20% approximately if CABAC-like entropy code module is introduced. The PSNR of synthesized view shows the painting method competitive with JMVC's results.

6 Conclusion

This work introduces a contour based coding strategy to remain the quality of edges in depth map as much as possible. The contour coding is a lossless process. Inside painting can reduce a lot of special redundancy while keeping the quality of the synthesized view. The coding efficiency is close to the conventional block based coding method (such as JMVC) in high quality cases.

References

1. Fehn, C.: Depth-image-based rendering (DIBR), compression and transmission for a new approach on 3D-TV. In: Proceedings of SPIE Stereoscopic Displays and Virtual Reality Systems XI, vol. 5291 pp. 93–104 (2004)
2. Shimizu, S., Kitahara, M., Kimata, H., Kamikura, K., Yashima, Y.: View Scalable Multiview Video Coding Using 3-D Warping With Depth Map. In: Circuits and Systems for Video Technology, IEEE Transactions, 2007. vol. 17 (11) pp. 1485–1495 (2007)
3. Kim, S.Y., Lee, E.K., Ho, Y.S.: Generation of ROI Enhanced Depth Maps Using Stereoscopic Cameras and a Depth Camera. In: Broadcasting, IEEE Transactions, 2008, vol. 54 (4) pp. 732–740 (2008)
4. Yea, S., Vetro, A.: Multi-layered coding of depth for virtual view synthesis. In: Picture Coding Symposium, Chicago (2009)
5. Ekmekcioglu, E., Mrak, M., Worrall, S., Kondoz, A.: Utilisation of edge adaptive upsampling in compression of depth map videos for enhanced free-viewpoint rendering. In: 16th IEEE International Conference on Image Processing (ICIP), pp. 733–736 (2009)
6. Zhao, Y., Chen, Z., Tian D., Zhu, C., Yu, L.: Suppressing texture-depth misalignment for boundary noise removal in view synthesis. In: 28th Picture Coding Symposium (PCS), Nagoya (2010)
7. Ekmekcioglu, E., Worrall, S.T., Kondoz, A.M.: Bit-Rate Adaptive Downsampling for the Coding of Multi-View Video with Depth Information. In: 3DTV Conference: The True Vision - Capture, Transmission and Display of 3D Video, pp. 137–140 (2008)
8. Jordan, L.B., Ebrahimi, T.: Progressive polygon encoding of shape contours. In: Sixth International Conference on Image Processing and Its Applications, vol. 1, pp.17–21 (1997)
9. Pinheiro, A., Ghanbari, M.: Piecewise Approximation of Contours Through Scale-Space Selection of Dominant Points. In: IEEE Transactions on Image Processing, 2010 vol. 19 (6) pp. 1442 – 1450 (2010)
10. Liu, D., Sun, X., Wu, F.: Intra Prediction via Edge-Based Inpainting. In: Data Compression Conference, DCC 2008, pp. 282–291 (2008)
11. Liu, D., Sun, X., Wu, F.: Edge-Based Inpainting and Texture Synthesis for Image Compression. In: IEEE International Conference on Multimedia and Expo, 2007, pp. 1443–1446 (2007)

An Audiovisual Wireless Field Guide

Ruben Gonzalez and Yongsheng Gao

Abstract This paper describes our work on developing a multimedia wireless field guide platform (WFG) for both fully automatic and assisted identification of different fauna and flora species. Built using a smart-client and server model it supports both visual and acoustic capture of individual specimen samples with optional graphical annotation for posing queries alongside more traditional searching and browsing query interfaces. The WFG assists the user to iteratively converge on a correct match by seeking additional information required to resolve class uncertainty.

1 Introduction

Over the last decade technological advances have radically increased the availability of data processing. Once confined to offices and laboratories, there is now sufficient computing power in a typical mobile telephone handset to rival that of computer workstations from some years ago. This ability to undertake data processing in the field is greatly enhanced by wireless communication capabilities that provide remote access to a virtually unlimited amount of remote computing resources and data. Thus computing can now be applied in new ways to challenging problems that previously would have been impractical.

One such area is species identification in the field that, in the case of some species, can be a difficult task for biologists let alone the general public. Field guides that can automatically identify or interpret data for different species would

R. Gonzalez (✉) • Y. Gao
Queensland Research Laboratory, National ICT Australia, QLD 4072, Australia

Institute for Integrated and Intelligent Systems, Griffith University, Australia
e-mail: r.gonzalez@gu.edu.au

J.S. Jin et al., *The Era of Interactive Media*,
DOI 10.1007/978-1-4614-3501-3_52, © Springer Science+Business Media, LLC 2013

provide a significant benefit to field workers in areas of conservation of threatened species, biosecurity with regard to pests and invasive species, and other key areas.

Current paper field guides are being gradually replaced with their digital counterparts that can be accessed using electronic devices such as handheld computers [1]. These require users to locate information about different species by searching through scientific or common names, or by browsing through pictures using tools similar to Photomesa [2]. There are also extensive efforts to digitise and catalogue taxonomic and biodiversity information regarding different species and other efforts within the scientific communities to ensure interoperability between these databases by various organisations such as the Global Biodiversity Information Facility [3], the Biodiversity Information Standards (TDWG) group [4] and the National Biological Information Infrastructure (NBII) [5]. Given that there are nearly two million identified species representing a total of less than 10% of the total number of species on earth [6] the large amount of data only compounds the problem of identifying an unknown species.

One solution used by computer-based guides such as Lucid [7], DiscoverLife [8] and Delta [9] permits filters to be applied to various observable or deductible properties to narrow down the search such as selecting all birds with red wings and long beaks. This approach doesn't provide automated species classification or recognition but, rather, guides the user to possible species. It relies on ordering the distinguishing characteristics of each species in databases so as to most rapidly converge on a particular species using principles derived empirically from experts (and not by the use of technologies such as Decision Trees [10] to automatically order the discriminating features).

Alternatively one could make use of Pattern Recognition and Machine Learning algorithms to automatically identify species and interpret information collected in the field, in situ. These can either require little or no domain knowledge such as those used in generic content-based retrieval [11], or, be highly domain specific such those used to identify specific leaf shapes of terrestrial [12] or aquatic plants [13]. If successful, these approaches return a ranked short-list of potential matches for users to choose from as the most likely identification.

The content-based retrieval methods return matching images based on statistical similarity of pixel data and don't work very well in distinguishing images with similar statistical distributions but different local or structural features such as differences in the shape of a wing shape for example. Alternatively, domain specific methods ignore the bulk statistical properties and look for the fine discriminating details in the data, which if not found, or if they don't conform within an expected range prohibits the matching process from continuing.

One of the problems with the application of Pattern Recognition techniques to identification is that success is highly dependent on whether key discriminating features have been captured with sufficient quality. If they have not low quality matches will be presented to the user. Hence instead of just short-listing potential matches and leaving it up to the user to decide which was the correct one, we wanted to use automatic pattern recognition to interactively assist users in choosing the correct match if the WFG system was not able to confidently identify a species on its own. The remainder of this paper describes the design of a WFG and its approach to automatic species identification including its query interface and system architecture.

2 Query Interface

The WFG supports three primary query interfaces; searching by browsing, searching through text and key matching and query by example. For text and key based searching the WFG backend essentially operates as a proxy for existing taxonomic databases. Browsing type queries are performed through a visual taxonomic hierarchy. Users are initially presented with a pictorial representation of the top-level of this hierarchy, consisting of selected phyla and they can navigate down through the various taxonomic ranks by clicking on images at each level.

In the case of query by example the query data is first captured using an appropriate capture device connected to the WFG client device such as digital microscopes, cameras and microphones. Once the relevant data has been captured it can be manually annotated or cropped to identify specific regions of interest using the built-in tools as is depicted in Fig. 1. It can then be submitted for identification by one of an arbitrary number of server side automatic identification modules (AIMs). The captured data and annotations are forwarded to the processing server that passes it on to the appropriate AIM. If identification can be successfully performed, the module returns a resulting identifier, which is typically the entity's scientific name, to the server that then uses it as a text search key for a relevant taxonomic database.

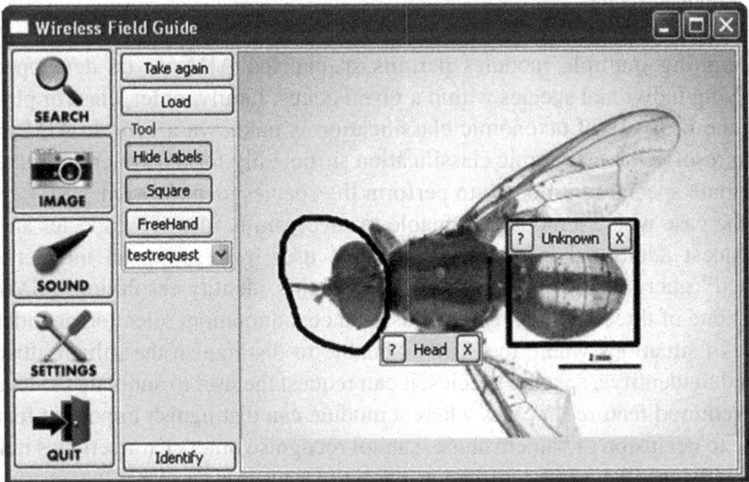

Fig. 1 (**a**) Image capture and annotation screen (fruit fly). (**b**) Image query interaction process

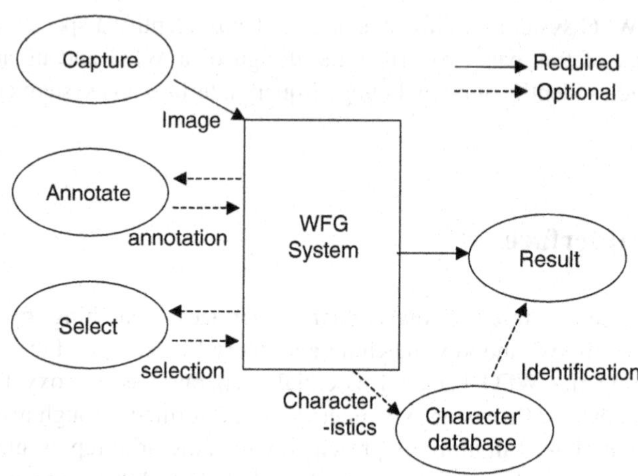

Fig. 1 (continued)

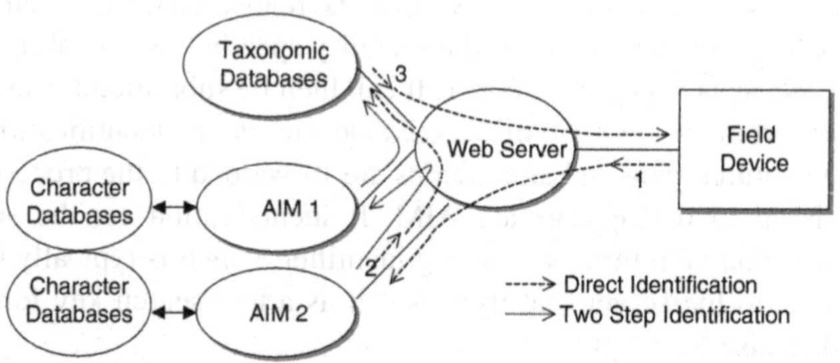

Fig. 2 Information flow

Supporting multiple modules permits specialised AIMs to be developed for identifying individual species within a given genus, family, order, class or phylum. When the broad level taxonomic classification is unknown a generic AIM is first used to resolve the taxonomic classification sufficiently for the system to select the appropriate specialised module to perform the species identification.

In the case where a module is unable to successfully identify a species an AIM can request additional information from the user by creating an interactive or "assisted" query session to help guide it towards identity resolution. AIMs can request one of three different types of assistance; annotation, selection and identification. In situations where the AIM is unable to distinguish the salient attributes required to identify a specific species, it can request the user to annotate the location of the required feature. In cases where a module can distinguish important features but due to occlusion or camera angle, cannot recognise other characteristics it needs to uniquely resolve identity it can request the end user to select the appropriate characteristic from a set of candidates. As a trivial example it may present to the user a selection of wing shapes.

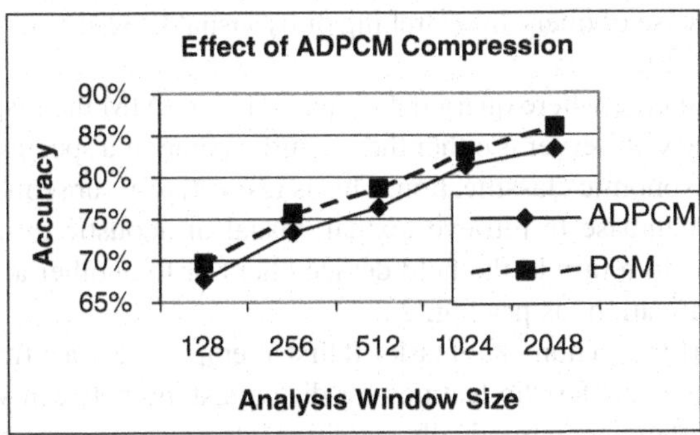

Fig. 3 Compressed audio classification performance

Once an AIM has successfully isolated the characteristic features of a specimen it can either identify the species directly itself or it can pass the features to a character database for identification. These options and the interaction process of a query are shown in Fig. 3.

3 System Architecture

Unlike other efforts that focus on taxonomic or character database architectures [14], our approach primarily focuses on providing a flexible platform for capturing specimen data and automatically extracting and recognising their features either directly or by leveraging existing taxonomic and biodiversity databases. We also wanted the WFG system to be transparently upgradeable to identify additional species from additional phyla or to make use different identification techniques without requiring any alterations to software on the field devices. Other requirements were to make the WFG system ubiquitously accessible using as wide a range of wireless client devices as possible. This included devices with an inbuilt ability to natively capture images and sound and as those without and to also support the use of other capture devices such as microscopes.

Currently supported field devices for the WFG include an N97 that uses the Nokia Symbian 6.0 platform and a Viliv S5 handheld computer running Microsoft Windows. WFG smart client software running on these devices provides audio, image and location (GPS coordinates) capture and graphical annotation functions and xHTML forms support for framing queries that are submitted to the server over HTTP 1.1. It also displays responses from the server using a version of XHTML basic 1.1.

The WFG server is predominantly a two-tier architecture. The first tier contains the presentation and high-level application logic. The second tier consists of AIMs and various databases. The web server in the first tier is responsible for communicating with the client and deciding whether to pass query data to selected taxonomic databases in the case of query by searching or by visual browsing or alternatively to an appropriate AIM.

In the simplest case where query data is passed to an AIM the response provided by the AIM to the web server is either the scientific name of a species or the name of a higher order taxonomic classification. This is respectively subsequently submitted to a taxonomic database to retrieve textual, visual or acoustic information of the identified species to return to the field device client or to another appropriate AIM for further identification, as per Fig. 2 .

Each AIM performs a number of tasks. It first attempts to extract from the query by example data the characteristic features for distinguishing between various species. If it is successful these are individually classified into one of various potential classes using machine-learning techniques. Each class corresponds to different characteristics that differentiate various species. The name of the species that matches the specific combination of these characteristics is the result returned to the server. In performing these tasks the AIM must communicate with a database containing feature vectors for each characteristic of known species. This database can be embedded within the AIM, or it can be external to the module as a separate database.

The AIMs themselves are executable objects that are invoked by the server. Once AIMs are invoked by a new query they persist through a user session until the query is resolved or until they time out. AIMs communicate with the server using a library of software routines (WFGLib) that manage the data exchange and encode and decode any image, audio or annotation data appropriately. AIMs can be added or deleted transparently from the WFG system via a simple web interface. Thus AIM developers can focus on implementing identification algorithms rather than communication and system integration issues. The next sections discuss some the methods used by generic AIMs for species identification.

4 Audio Identification

Automatic identification of animals by their calls has been an area of study over the last decade. This includes identification of bird and frog calls [15–18], bat echolocation calls [19, 20] and insects such as grasshoppers and cicadas [21]. These studies have made use of a variety of machine learning techniques such as C4.5 decision trees [22], as well as Neural Networks [23] and classification methods including k-Nearest Neighbour, Gaussian Mixture Models and Support Vector Machines (SVM) [15, 24].

Audio classification approaches typically use a combination of temporal features and spectral features [25] derived from the short term Fourier transform or Mel-Frequency Cepstral Coefficients (MFCCs) [26]. Some of the more common temporal features include the signal bandwidth (BW), spectral centroid (SC), short-term energy (E), energy flux (F), Zero Crossing Rate (ZCR), and pitch (P) by means of subharmonic summation [27]. The most common spectral features are the first six MFCCs, which are calculated as the cepstrum of the mel-warped spectrum.

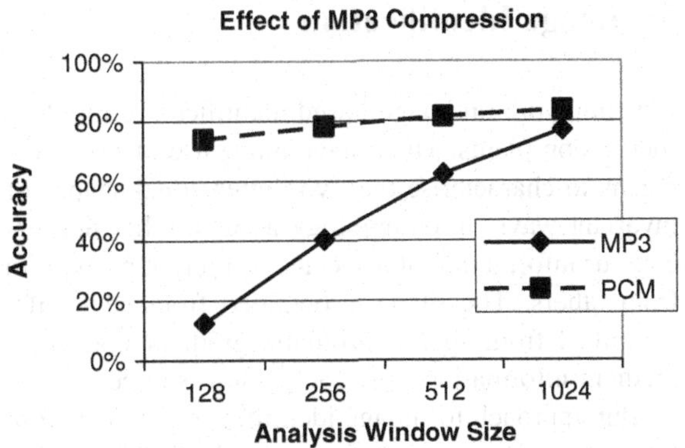

Fig. 4 MP3 compressed classification performance

Generic audio AIMs in the WFG currently utilise this set of features and a k-NN classifier which while being relatively simple can perform within a few percent of the more sophisticated classifiers. For evaluation we have used a database of 1,629 recordings of seventy four different species of native Australian frogs from the Myobatrachidae family (Southern Frogs). Using tenfold cross validation we achieved over 90% correct classification with single and multiple calls in the laboratory. We also used a database of sounds from 381 different species of insects with which we were able to also achieve a correct classification into insect families of over 90%.

In practice the identification of single isolated animal calls under ideal conditions is fairly easy and close to 90% correct performance can be achieved. In the field, with high levels of background noise, compounded by simultaneous calls from different species [22] identification is less successful. In one study, a success rate of only about 60% was achieved [28] in the in-field identification of twenty different species of frogs. This is further compounded in the case of the WFG since in the interests of reducing network latency and other costs the captured audio data will typically be compressed before being communicated to the server for identification. While the effects of background noise on the classification performance are variable the effects of audio compression is more predictable. To determine what effect audio compression has on identification accuracy we performed some experiments using both the ADPCM [29] and MP3 algorithms as being representative of a range of audio compression methods as is reported in [30]. We discovered as is shown in Fig. 3 that using ADPCM encoding with 4 bits per sample resulting in a consistent drop of about 3% in classification accuracy irrespective of analysis window size. This drop is due to the introduction of quantization noise.

In the case of the MP3 compression identification performance was notably worse and varied depending on the analysis window size used for extracting classification features as is shown in Fig. 4 .

5 Image Identification

Existing work on image-based identification for electronic field guides has largely focused on plants. These have made use of Fourier Shape Descriptions [31] other means to characterise the two dimensional shapes of leaves in rotation and scale invariant ways. In entomology as with other fields within zoology the shape and contour information of a species is often of primary importance in differentiating it from others. The shape is obtained from edge information that can be directly computed from spatio-chromatic gradient operators or indirectly via combining gradient information from each colour source.

Our approach for image identification is to analyse the colour or texture related features in annotated regions together with the local shape of the object. We represent the shape using line edge maps [32] that are created from edge contours using the Canny Edge Detector. This permits shape similarity to be measured using a modified Hausdorff Distance. This shape information is combined with micro-pattern representations of image texture defined by the Local Derivative Pattern (LDP) [33]. The LDP encodes the higher-order derivative texture pattern which contains more detailed information than that the first-order Local Binary Pattern (LBP) [34] can extract. The *n*th -order LDP is a sequence of binary digits encoding derivative changes in a local region of (*n*-1)th -order derivative images $I_\alpha^{n-1}(Z)$ as

$$LDP_\alpha^n(Z_0) = \{f(I_\alpha^{n-1}(Z_0), I_\alpha^{n-1}(Z_1)), f(I_\alpha^{n-1}(Z_0), I_\alpha^{n-1}(Z_2)), \cdots, f(I_\alpha^{n-1} \times (Z_0), I_\alpha^{n-1}(Z_8))\}, \tag{1}$$

where $I_\alpha^{n-1}(Z_0)$ denotes the (*n*-1)th-order derivative in *a* direction at $Z = Z_0$. $f(I_\alpha^{n-1}(Z_0), I_\alpha^{n-1}(Z_i))$ encodes the (*n*-1)th order gradient changes into a binary digit as follows:

$$f(I_\alpha^{n-1}(Z_0), I_\alpha^{n-1}(Z_i)) = \begin{cases} 0, & \text{if } I_\alpha^{n-1}(Z_i) \cdot I_\alpha^{n-1}(Z_0) > 0 \\ i = 1, 2, \cdots 8. & \\ 1, & \text{if } I_\alpha^{n-1}(Z_i) \cdot I_\alpha^{n-1}(Z_0) \leq 0 \end{cases} \tag{2}$$

This binarization creates an additional order of texture information within the neighbourhood. The texture-pattern representation of each region of interest in the captured images is then classified against known micro-patterns that are particular to specific species.

6 Conclusions and Further Work

This paper has described our work on developing a multimedia wireless field guide that provides automatic acoustic as well as visual identification. Unlike conventional image based approaches that attempt to identify an image of a specimen as a single class in a multidimensional feature space following the classical image content-based retrieval model our approach leverages existing character databases model where the identification is based on classifying individual visual distinguishing characteristics of specimens. As this approach requires such characteristics to be visible in query images the query interface supports the notion of an assisted query session whereby the user can be prompted to provide additional information that may be not be apparent in the query image but is necessary for correct identification. Our initial focus is visual identification of insects and acoustic identification of frogs.

Since our approach leverages existing character databases our focus has been on the processing model and software architecture to facilitate ubiquitous mobile access. The processing model revolves around the need for specialized automatic identification modules (AIM) for different taxonomic groups since different characteristics are required for identifying species belonging to different groups. Since the appropriate AIM for an identification query may be unknown a hierarchical process of incremental refinement is pursued utilizing high-level classification AIMs to converge on the final identification.

While the WFG system implementation is complete further work is required on developing the individual AIMs. For the acoustic AIMs this includes investigating ways to improve performance in the field by reducing noise sensitivity and resolving simultaneous call confusion. For the visual identification AIMs further work involves modeling and implementing AIMs for locating the visual characteristics in different query images classes from which to extract LDPs and LEMs for classification.

Acknowledgements The authors would like to acknowledge the assistance NICTA for providing funding for this work and the efforts of Steven Tucker, Craig Hume and Coby Chapple in the development of the WFG client-server software.

References

1. Stevenson, R. D., W. A. Haber, and R. A. Morris. 2003. "Electronic field guides and user communities in the eco-informatics revolution." Conservation Ecology 7(1): 3. [online] URL: http://www.consecol.org/vol7/iss1/art3/
2. White, S., Marino, D., and Feiner, S., "Designing a Mobile User Interface for Automated Species" Identification, Proc. ACM CHI 2007, April 28–May 3, 2007, pp. 291–294.
3. Global Biodiversity Information Facility, http://www.gbif.org [accessed 2010].
4. Biodiversity Information Standards, http://www.tdwg.org/ [accessed 2010]
5. National Biological Information Infrastructure, http://www.nbii.gov [accessed 2010].

6. May, R. M. (1990). How many species? Philosophical Trans. of the Royal Society of London. B, 330, 293–304.
7. http://www.lucidcentral.com/ [accessed 2010].
8. http://www.discoverlife.org/ [accessed 2010].
9. Dallwitz, M. J. 1980. A general system for coding taxonomic descriptions. Taxon 29: 41–6.
10. J. R. Quinlan, Learning decision tree classifiers, ACM Computing Surveys (CSUR), v. 28 n. 1, p.71–72, March 1996
11. Datta, Ritendra; Dhiraj Joshi, Jia Li, James Z. Wang (2008). "Image Retrieval: Ideas, Influences, and Trends of the New Age". ACM Computing Surveys 40: 1–60.
12. Agarwal, G., Belhumeur, P., Feiner, S., Jacobs, D., Kress, W.J., Ramamoorthi, R., Bourg, N., Dixit, N., Ling, H., Mahajan, D., Russell, R., Shirdhonkar, S., Sunkavalli, K., and White, S. "First Steps Toward an Electronic Field Guide for Plants. Taxon, Journal of the International Assoc. for Plant Taxonomy", 55(3), August 2006, pp. 597–610
13. Park J-K., Hwang E., "Implementation of an Aquatic Plant Information Bank" Proceedings of the 2007 Frontiers in the Convergence of Bioscience and Information Technologies, pp. 861–866, ISBN:978–0–7695–2999–8
14. R.A. Morris, R.D. Stevenson and W.Haber "An architecture for electronic field guides", Journal of Intelligent Information Systems, V.29, No.1, August, 2007 pp.97–110
15. M.A. Acevedoa, C.J. Corrada-Bravoc, H. Corrada-Bravob, L. J. Villanueva-Riverad and T. Mitchell Aidea, "Automated classification of bird and amphibian calls using machine learning: A comparison of methods" Ecological Informatics, Vol. 4, Issue 4, Sept. 2009, Pages 206–214.
16. Mills H. 1995. Automatic detection and classification of nocturnal migrant bird calls. J Acoust Soc Amer. 97: 3370–3371.
17. H.Wang, J.Elson, L.Girod, D.Estin and K.Yao, "Target Classification and Localization in Habitat Monitoring", In Proc. of IEEE International Conference on Acoustics, Speech, and Signal Processing (ICASSP 2003) Hong Kong.
18. Darren Moore. "Demonstration of bird species detection using an acoustic wireless sensor network." 33rd IEEE International Conference on Local Computer Networks (LCN 2008): SenseApp 2008; Montreal, Que. IEEE; 2008: 730–731. ISBN: 9781424424122
19. Parsons S. 2001. Identification of New Zealand bats in flight from analysis of echolocation calls by artificial neural networks. J Zool London 253: 447–456.
20. Vaughan N, Jones G and Harris S.1997. Identification of British bat species by multivariate analysis of echolocation call parameters. Bioacoustics 7: 189–207.
21. Ohya Eand Chesmore ED.2003. Automated identifica-tion of grasshoppers by their songs. Iwate University, Morioka, Japan: Annual Meeting of the Japanese Society of Applied Entomology and Zoology.
22. A.Taylor, G.Watson, G.Grigg and H.McCallum, "Monitoring Frog Communities: An application of Machine Learning", in the Proceedings of 8th innovative applications of AI conference (IAAI) Portland, Oregon 1996, pp. 1564–1569
23. Yen, Gary G.; Fu, Qiang, "Automatic frog call monitoring system: a machine learning approach" Proc. SPIE Vol. 4739, p. 188–199, *Applications and Science of Computational Intelligence* V, Kevin L. Priddy; Paul E. Keller; Peter J. Angeline; Eds, 2002
24. Chenn-Jung Huang, Yi-Ju Yang, Dian-Xiu Yang, "Frog classification using machine learning techniques", Expert Systems with Applications: An International Journal Volume 36, Issue 2 (March 2009) Pages 3737–3743 ISSN:0957–4174
25. R. Gonzalez, "Better than MFCC Audio Classification Features" Submitted to The 2011 Pacific-Rim Conference on Multimedia (PCM 2011) December 20–22, Sydney, Australia
26. Peltonen, V. Tuomi, J. Klapuri, A. Huopaniemi, J. Sorsa, T., "Computational auditory scene recognition", Proceeding of. International Conference on Acoustics, Speech, and Signal Processing, (ICASSP 2002). IEEE, May 13–17, 2002, Orlando, FL, USA, vol.2, pp. 1941–1944

27. D.J.Hermes, “Measurement of pitch by subharmonic summation” J. Acoust. Soc. Am. Volume 83, Issue 1, pp. 257–264 (January 1988)
28. Ning-Han Liu, Chen-An Wu and Shu-Ju Hsieh, Long-Term Animal Observation by Wireless Sensor Networks with Sound Recognition, WASA 2009, LNCS 5682, p.1–11, 5th Aug 2009
29. ITU Recommendation G.726, “40, 32, 24, 16 kbit/s Adaptive Differential Pulse Code Modulation (ADPCM)”
30. R.Gonzalez, “Effects of Compression and Window Size on Remote Acoustic Identification using Sensor Networks” Proceedings of ICSPCS’2010. pp.
31. Belhumeur, P.N., Chen, D., Feiner, S., Jacobs, D.W., Kress, W.J., Ling, H.B., Lopez, I., Ramamoorthi, R., Sheorey, S., White, S., Zhang, L., “Searching the World’s Herbaria: A System for Visual Identification of Plant Species,” Proceedings of the 10th European Conference on Computer Vision, Marseille, France, October 12–18, 2008 (ECCV 2008, IV: 116–129)..
32. Y. Gao and M. Leung, “Face Recognition Using Line Edge Map”, IEEE Transactions on Pattern Analysis and Machine Intelligence, Vol. 24, No.6, pp. 764–779, 2002.
33. B. Zhang, Y. Gao, S. Zhao and J. Liu, “Local Derivative Pattern versus Local Binary Pattern: Face Recognition with High-Order Local Pattern Descriptor”, IEEE Transactions on Image Processing, Vol. 19, No. 2, pp. 533–544, 2010.
34. T. Ojala, M. Pietikäinen, and T. Mäenpää, “Multiresolution Gray-Scale and Rotation Invariant Texture Classification with Local Binary Patterns,” TPAMI, 24(7): 971–987, 2002.

CDNs with DASH and iDASH Using Priority Caching

Cornelius Hellge, Yago Sánchez, Thomas Schierl, Thomas Wiegand, Danny De Vleeschauwer, Dohy Hong, and Yannick Le Louédec

Abstract Global Internet traffic shows an upward trend mainly driven by the increasing demand for video services. In addition the further spread of mobile Internet leads to an increased diversification of access data rates and internet terminals. In such a context, Content Delivery Networks (CDNs) are forced to offer content in multiple versions for different resolutions. Moreover multiple bitrates are needed, such that emerging adaptive streaming technologies are enabled to adapt to network congestion. This enormous proliferation of the multimedia content becomes more and more a challenge for the efficiency of existing network and caching infrastructure. Dynamic Adaptive Streaming over HTTP (DASH) is an emerging standard which enables adaptation of the media bitrate to varying throughput conditions by offering multiple representations of the same content. The combination of Scalable Video Coding (SVC) with DASH, called improved DASH (iDASH) consists basically of relying on SVC to provide the different representations. This paper shows how prioritized caching strategies can improve the caching performance of (i)DASH services. Results obtained from statistics of a

C. Hellge (✉) • Y. Sánchez • T. Schierl • T. Wiegand
Fraunhofer HHI and Berlin Institute of Technology, Berlin, Germany
e-mail: cornelius.hellge@hhi.fraunhofer.de; yago.sanchez@hhi.fraunhofer.de; thomas.schierl@hhi.fraunhofer.de; thomas.wiegand@hhi.fraunhofer.de

D. De Vleeschauwer
Bell Labs – Alcatel Lucent, Antwerp, Belgium
e-mail: danny.de_vleeschauwer@alcatel-lucent.com

D. Hong
N2N Soft, Fontenay-sous-Bois, France
e-mail: dohy.hong@n2nsoft.com

Y. Le Louédec
Orange-FT, Lannion, France
e-mail: yannick.lelouedec@orange.com

J.S. Jin et al., *The Era of Interactive Media*,
DOI 10.1007/978-1-4614-3501-3_53,

real world CDN deployment and a simple revenue model show a clear benefit in revenue for content providers when priority caching is used especially in combination with iDASH.

Keywords HTTP • CDN • SVC • Cache • DASH • iDASH

1 Introduction

In today's global Internet, traffic has been increasing with up to 50% per year. Moreover, the proportion in the total amount of traffic of the video streaming and downloads keeps on growing and is beginning to take a larger share of bandwidth [1]. In such a context, it is important for Internet Service Providers (ISPs) to build and dimension the future Content Delivery Network (CDN) infrastructure based on the right video revenue models.

Typical CDN solutions deployed in the ISP's network (also referred to as a Telecommunication Company (TELCO) CDN) are designed for a capacity determined by the maximum throughput of the transit link from the TELCO CDN to the open internet. However, for economic reasons the network may still be under dimensioned and hence, during peak hours, the overall bitrate of requested services may exceed the capacity of the system design resulting in congestion on the transit link. One solution to reduce the congestion on the transit link is to implement local caches within the CDN network closer to the end user. Caching reduces the traffic on the transit link by serving popular content directly from local network caches [2]. The caching efficiency depends on the available storage capacity, the implemented caching algorithm, and the statistics of the user requests [3]. The use of local caches increases the overall CDN's capacity but does not prevent from congestion in busy hours.

Adaptive Hyper Text Transfer Protocol (HTTP) video streaming has been gaining popularity within recent years. A clear evidence of it is the standardization processes lead by different standardization organizations, such as in 3GPP [4], OIPTV [5], or MPEG [6]. Relying on HTTP/Transmission Control Protocol (TCP) allows reusing the widely deployed network caches, which reduces the amount of data that servers have to send directly to the clients. Furthermore, it resolves the common traversal issues with firewalls and Network Address Translation (NATs) typical when the data is transmitted over Real-time Transport Protocol/User Datagram Protocol (RTP/UDP). Moreover, implementation of such systems is simple, since servers are typical web servers. Due to the mentioned benefits of HTTP streaming, there has been a sharp increase in the interest of the market in adaptive HTTP streaming. The benefit of this technique can even be augmented by adopting Scalable Video Coding (SVC) [7] as the video codec for HTTP Streaming. The potential benefit of adopting SVC as the video codec in terms of caching efficiency and saved bandwidth at the server in comparison to the use of H.264/Advanced Video Coding (AVC) was already shown in [8].

The purpose of this paper is to compare the potential revenue of different delivery technologies, Dynamic Adaptive Streaming over HTTP (DASH) and improved DASH (iDASH), and caching strategies based on a simple model of content provider's revenue. We compare the impact on the revenue of the different caching strategies for adaptive HTTP streaming using H.264/AVC or SVC, where a priority based cache replacement algorithm is studied. Analysis on basis of statistical data from a real Video on Demand (VoD) system show that there is a clear benefit of implementing a SVC based solution associated to a priority based cache replacement algorithm.

The rest of the paper is organized as follows. In Sect. 2 we discuss the considered technologies. Section 3 describes the different components of the revenue model and describes the model itself. Section 4 shows the analysis of the revenue for the different models based on the request statistics of a real VoD system.

2 Considered Technologies

The aim of this work is to investigate how different technologies influence the achievable revenue of a Video on Demand (VoD) service within an existing video delivery system. The revenue model is derived from the simplified delivery architecture illustrated in Fig. 1. Users request video services from a content server in the Internet. This technique is also referred to as over the top (OTT) delivery over an ISP exploited by a TELCO. In order to alleviate its links the TELCO deploys CDN technology in its own network. The requested content is delivered at a service rate r through this CDN. The origin content server is connected to the CDN via the transit link with a maximum throughput X. In this paper we consider TELCO CDNs where the CDN and the access link are owned by the same player, but the transit link is not owned by the TELCO operator serving the customers, as is typically the case. Therefore the operator tries to minimize the amount of traffic on that transit link by serving popular content directly from the caches.

Although the use of caches in the TELCO CDNs reduces its traffic, when a lot of users request (different) content at the same time, the transit link X can be congested. To alleviate this congestion, different technologies are considered within this work: DASH (adaptability with single layer codec) and iDASH

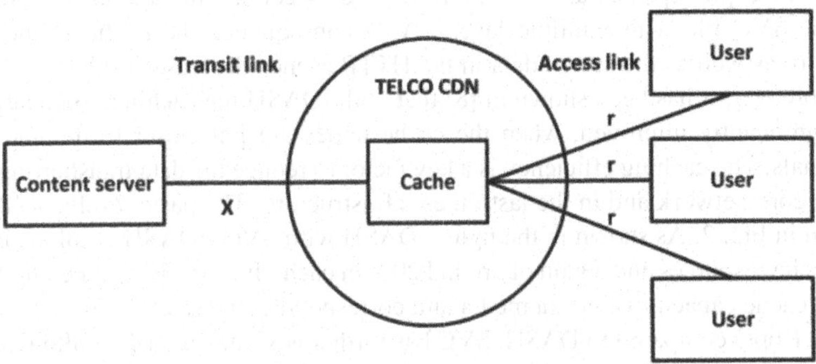

Fig. 1 Considered delivery architecture with caches deployed in the TELCO CDN

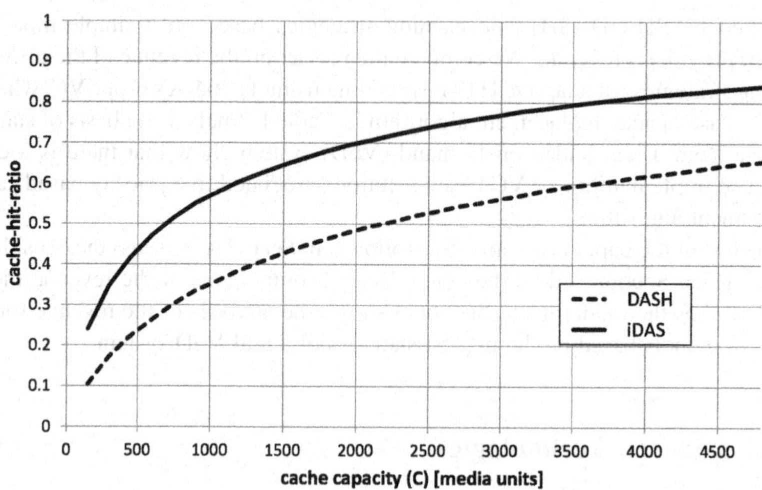

Fig. 2 Cache hit ratio over caching capacity for using DASH and iDASH [8]

(adaptability with SVC). The mentioned technologies are analyzed either in a network where local caches are implemented with a simple Least Recently Used (LRU) mechanism or in a network with local caches based on a more sophisticated priority based caching algorithm.

2.1 *DASH and iDASH*

DASH [6] is an emerging MPEG-Standard, which defines a format for multimedia delivery over HTTP. MPEG DASH also specifies the media delivery based on SVC. The combination of SVC with DASH, called in [8] iDASH consists basically of relying on SVC to provide the different representations offered by a DASH service for rate adaptation. In contrast to DASH, with iDASH multiple files on the server (as for multiple representations with a single layer codec) may be substituted by a unique SVC file with multiple layers. As a consequence the traffic in the core network as well as the stored data in the HTTP caches decreases [8].

Moreover, it has been shown in [8] that with iDASH the caching efficiency can be significantly improved, when the cache nodes are put closer to the end user terminals. The caching efficiency is a key factor to reduce the data transporting cost in the core network and in the last miles infrastructure. The basic results of [8] are shown in Fig. 2. As shown in the figure, DASH with SVC (iDASH) exploits better the cache resources and a gain of around 20% in cache-hit ratio is obtained for most of the cache capacity values (a media unit correspond to the size of a film of 90 min at 500 Kbps) compared to DASH. SVC has further advantages such as allowing for multiple Operation Points (OP) with the same bitrate in order to efficiently serve a large number of users with heterogeneous access capabilities (wired—wireless) [8] and with different terminal equipment capabilities, against a reasonable bitrate penalty of about 10% [9].

2.2 *Caching of Content*

Implementing local caches allows temporarily storing a video file in the cache. Users requesting the cached video file can be redirected to that local cache and the content can be served directly from the cache instead of transmitting it from the server over the transit link. Since the cache is usually too small to host the complete video library and the content of the origin video library often changes, it needs to be carefully chosen which video files to store in the cache at every moment. This choice is made by an appropriate caching algorithm.

There are many different cache replacement algorithms that have been proposed over the last years that optimize the caching performance based on some special criteria, as summarized in [2]. Roughly explained, the choice of which files to cache certainly depends on the (measured) file popularity: caching a file A that is requested more frequently than file B is more beneficial than vice versa (given the same file size, same bit rate and same duration), simply because caching file A saves more transmission bitrate than caching file B at the same storage cost. Thus, some scores will be given to the cached files depending on their popularity, resulting in a ranking, which will determine the cache replacement policies (cf. [3]).

The presented work is based on simple LRU caching algorithm and a modified LRU with multiple quality queues with unequal treatment also referred to as priority caching. Like similar shown in [10], with priority caching the number of queues corresponds to the number of different versions (qualities) at which each video is offered and depending on the version, which a file corresponds to, a different queue is assigned to it at the cache. A desired relation of sizes is defined between the queues and LRU is applied per quality queue. The idea behind priority caching is to give a bigger size to the queues of the lowest quality versions of the videos.

Like shown in Fig. 5 and explained later, typically the daily request pattern of a VoD service shows different activity intensity over the day: there are peak hours where many clients are requesting content at the same time and off-peak hours, where low activity is seen. At peak hours, the transit link may be congested and therefore a lower quality is provided to the clients. Whereas at off-peak hours even though providing the highest quality (bitrate) to the users the throughput of the transit link is not completely used. Therefore, the idea of the priority caching is to increase the cache efficiency for low quality versions to cope better with congestion in the transit link and be able to provide a higher quality to the users during peak hours. This comes at the cost of lower cache efficiency for high quality versions which increases the traffic over the transit link during off-peak hours, where anyway there is sufficient capacity. Figure 3 shows the cache-hit ratio for

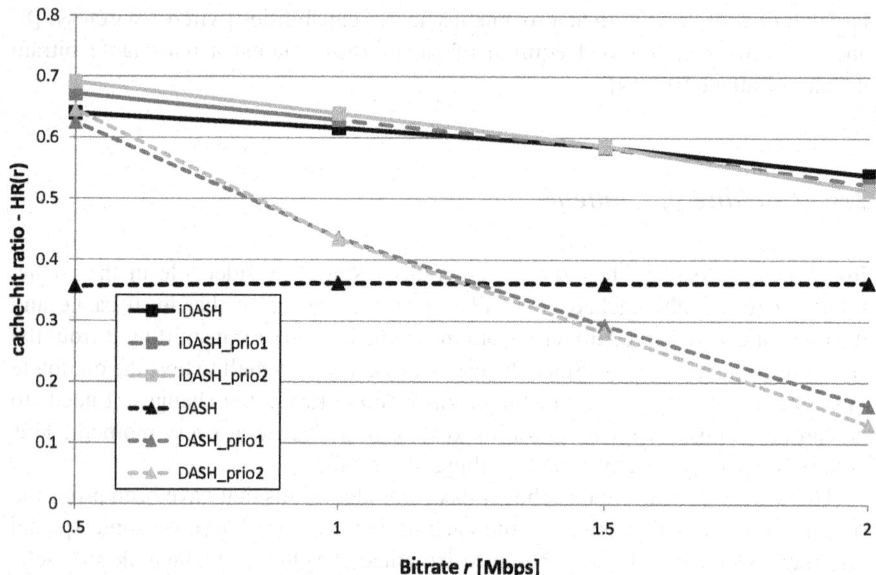

Fig. 3 Cache-Hit ratio over bitrate for DASH and iDASH implementing four adaptation points (0.5, 1, 1.5, 2 Mbps) without and with priority based caching

straightforward LRU with DASH and iDASH and priority caching of DASH and iDASH for the case that four quality versions (adaptation points) are offered per video content. For priority caching two queue size relations have been chosen: expressing queue sizes by an arbitrary size unit from the queue for the lowest quality version files to the queue for the highest quality version files, *prio1* refers to queue sizes of 4,3,2,1 and *prio2* to sizes of 12,8,5,2 used as basis also for the remainder of the paper.

For the results presented within this paper similar assumptions as in [8] have been done, i.e. a uniform request pattern is considered with a 25% request share for each quality version. However, for the use case considered here the share of requested video quality versions depends on the time of the day. The reason for that is that, as shown in Fig. 5, the number of connected users varies over the time and since the network resources are shared among the connected users, with (i) DASH high quality versions are requested when few users are connected to the system while low quality versions are requested when more users are connected. We identify four different users' density groups (different time intervals in the day with a different number of connected users) which validate the assumption regarding the 25% of request for each quality version as an average over a day. Furthermore, we consider that the caches are updated once a day over the night when the resource demand is very low.

The results in Fig. 3 show the influence of the prioritized caching on the cache-hit ratio (HR) using DASH and iDASH. With iDASH, the difference in HR of the lowest quality level (0.5 Mbps) to the highest quality level (2 Mbps) is approx. 0.15–0.18. Using DASH, this difference becomes more significant at approx. 0.5. The difference between the two queue sizes (*prio1* and *prio2*) is marginal. In general, iDASH keeps a significantly higher HR over all approaches. However, during peak hours where clients would request mainly the lowest quality, the HR value of DASH with priority caching is similar to the iDASH performance with traditional LRU.

3 Revenue Model

The target of the proposed model is to analyze the influence of the different caching strategies on the revenues of DASH and iDASH services. The basic assumption for the revenue model is, that the TELCO revenue RE_{telco} depends on the number of users n that can be served with the given network architecture and the revenue $RE_{service}$ per service. The revenue of the whole CDN service can be calculated by equation (1)

$$RE_{telco} = n * RE_{service}(r) \tag{1}$$

In the proposed model it is assumed that $RE_{service}$ directly depends on the delivered bitrate r. This assumption is a simplification, since in a real system the revenue is also influenced by the cost of delivering a service, which consists of Capital expenditures (CAPEX) and operational expenditures (OPEX). The same applies for the achievable revenue, which in a real system depends on the delivered video quality (e.g. SD or HD services) itself. However, this paper targets to give a global perspective on the potential revenue of the discussed technologies and the simplified model gives an appropriate approximation of the reality.

3.1 Components in Revenue Calculation

The impact of the caching strategy on the number of supportable users is directly obtained from the cache hit performance. Those impacts are summarized in Sect. 3.3. The increase in the supportable number of users is the result of a reduction of the traffic on the transit link. Another way of seeing the impact of the caches is that, for a same number of users the transmittable rate is higher and thereby the revenue too.

In order to compare the different caching strategies we calculate the revenue $RE_{service}$ per service in a time unit the operator receives. The revenue of the operator is calculated as follows: The revenue is associated with each flow supported by the operator, and the higher the (average) delivered bitrate r, the higher this revenue. We choose a sublinear function for this revenue RE as function of the average bitrate r (see Fig. 4). The revenue RE depends on the maximum revenue RE_{max}, the

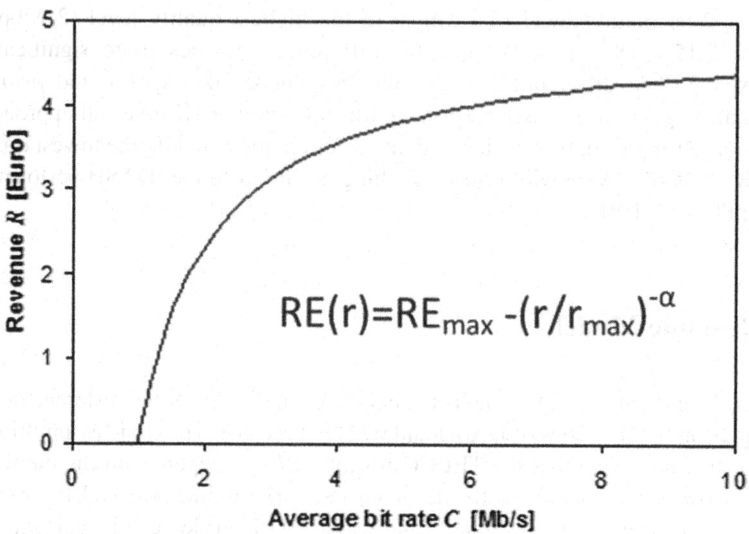

Fig. 4 Model for revenue calculation depending on the delivered video bit rate to a user

Table 1 Illustrative parameter assumptions

Transit link capacity	X	300 Mbps	–
Maximum number of users	N_{max}	1,500	–
SVC coding penalty	μ	1.1	[9]
Maximum service rate	r_{max}	2 Mbps	~ SD resolution
Minimum service rate	r_{min}	500 kbps	–
Maximum revenue	RE_{max}	3.99 €	–
–	α	0.6	–

maximum bitrate r_{max}, and the parameter α. This law of diminishing returns is inspired by the fact that in commercially deployed systems the revenue an operator gets for providing an HD video is less than the ratio of bitrates associated with HD and SD video. Consequently the parameters in Table 1 are chosen to as to express a HD video typically is sold at a price 50% higher than an SD video, while the bitrate of HD is typically 4 times higher. This is directly linked to the concavity of the Mean Opinion Score function [11].

3.2 Statistics on User Requests

The revenue calculation in Sect. 4 is based on statistics gathered from a deployed CDN system within the timeframe of a month. The derived client activity statistics are used for the results presented in following sections. Figure 5 shows the activity

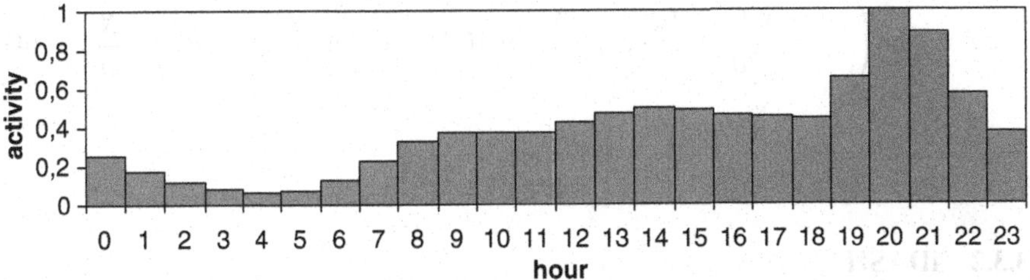

Fig. 5 Average number of active users per hour

ration, i.e. percentage of clients relative to a maximum amount of users per hour (N_{max}) that join the service, over the time within a day.

It can be seen how the activity varies for different times in the day where minimums can be seen at night around 1–6 h when most of the people are asleep (off-peak hours) and the maximum is around 20–21 h (peak hours).

3.3 Model Description

Taking the preceding discussions into account, the influence of the different technologies and caching strategies on the potential revenue depends on the number of requesting users n, the transit link capacity X, the cache-hit ratio HR, and the supportable service rate per user r. The model aims to calculate r depending on n for each scenario. With priority caching, HR depends on the delivered bitrate r as shown in Fig. 3. The only case where it can be considered to be constant is for DASH without prioritized caching, since the distribution of request for all versions is considered uniform. The revenue can then be calculated by feeding the service bitrate in the revenue model in Sect. 3.1.

3.3.1 General Approach

The average service bitrate can be calculated by Eq. (2).

$$r = \min\left(\frac{X}{n * (1 - HR(r))}, r_{max}\right) \tag{2}$$

Since *HR(r)* behaves almost linear (cf. Fig. 3), it can be calculated by:

$$HR(r) = wr + v \tag{3}$$

With w and v derived by linear interpolation from the measurement points. After rearranging Eqs. (2) and (3), Eq. (2) can be rewritten as:

$$r = \min\left(\frac{-b + \sqrt{b^2 - 4ac}}{2a}, r_{max}\right) \quad \text{with } b = 1 - w; a = -v; c = -\frac{X}{n} \tag{4}$$

3.3.2 iDASH

In case of iDASH (either without priority caching or with priority caching) the SVC coding penalty μ has to be taken into account. Derivation of the average bitrate is straight forward following Eq. (2) with the difference that the maximum rate r_{max} has to include the overhead as follows:

$$r = \min\left(\frac{X}{n * (1 - HR(r))}, \mu * r_{max}\right) \tag{5}$$

SVC has an efficiency penalty in comparison to the AVC stream with the same quality. For the revenue calculation, users pay for the quality of the service and not for the coding overhead. Therefore, the equivalent rate of an AVC stream (r_f) with the same quality is used for the revenue calculation. Equation (6) shows the relation between the SVC rate (r_{SVC}) and the AVC rate (r_f) of streams with the same quality:

$$r_{SVC} = r_{min} + \frac{\mu * r_{max} - r_{min}}{r_{max} - r_{min}}(r_f - r_{min}) \tag{6}$$

Equation (6) assumes that the overhead can be linearly interpolated from 0% overhead for the r_{min}, which is the rate of the base layer, to the maximum overhead for the rate of the higher layer $\mu * r_{max}$, being r_{max} the maximum rate of the highest quality version among the AVC streams used for DASH. Equation (7) is derived from Eq. (6) and shows how to map the received SVC rate (r_{SVC}) to the equivalent AVC rate (r_f).

$$r_f = \frac{r_{SVC} + (\beta - 1) * r_{min}}{\beta} \tag{7}$$

Where β is:

$$\beta = \frac{\mu * r_{max} - r_{min}}{r_{max} - r_{min}} \tag{8}$$

4 Analysis in a VoD System

In this section we show analytical results based on the revenue model described in Sect. 3.1, the illustrative parameters in Table 1, the request statistics derived from a real VoD system shown in Sect. 3.2, and the model in Sect. 3.3. The activity ratio (cf. Fig. 5) is mapped on the maximum number of users N_{max} and the revenue is calculated on basis of the number of users n in that hour. The cache performance data is taken from the caching efficiency analysis in Sect. 2.2 and shown in Fig. 3.

The plots in Fig. 6 show the average delivered bitrate to each client (top) and the CDN revenue (bottom) for the scenarios with and without prioritized caching. In general it can be seen, that iDASH with SVC exploits the potential revenue much better than using DASH with AVC.

Figure 6 shows how the delivered bitrate and revenue per user is increased by prioritized caching for DASH and iDASH. Espcially in peak hours (19–22), clients requesting the base layer benefit from the prioritization. The benefit of prioritized caching is summarized in Fig. 7, where the revenue per day is shown. Priority caching shows significantly higher revenue per day for DASH and iDASH. Relying on SVC (iDASH) outperforms the AVC solution (DASH) for all settings. Although, the revenue increase is not as big as for DASH, the usage of SVC (iDASH) is much more efficient than with AVC. The gain in revenue per day shows that priority caching is a useful mechanism both for DASH and iDASH.

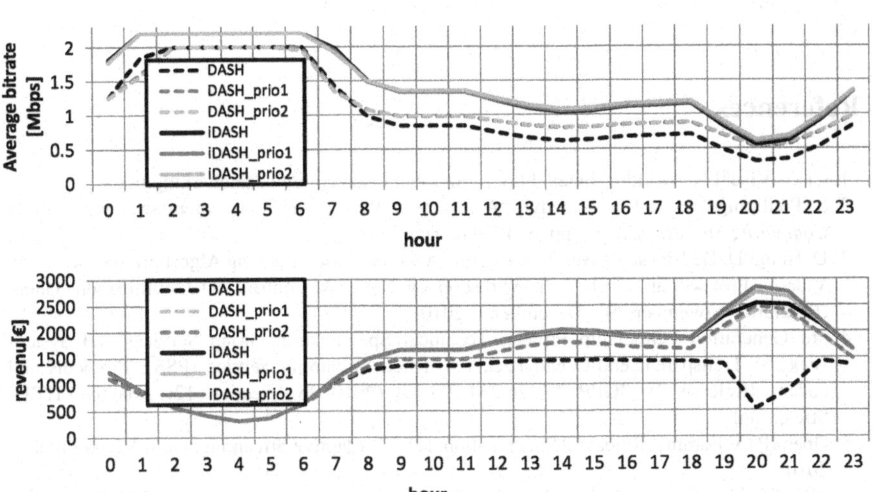

Fig. 6 Average bitrate (*top*) and revenue (*bottom*) for the systems with caching per hour based on the request statistics in Fig. 5

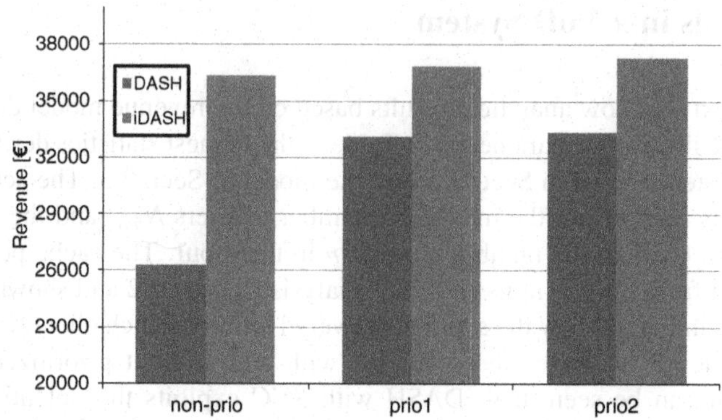

Fig. 7 Revenue per day with normal (non-prio) and priority caching (prio1, prio2)

5 Conclusion

The paper presents the benefits of prioritized caching for DASH using AVC and SVC. The potential revenue for TELCO CDNs is calculated by a simple revenue analysis. The potential revenue is compared for a CDN using dynamic adaptive streaming (DASH) with H.264/AVC or using Scalable Video Coding (SVC) in Telco CDNs. The results show the revenue using the described model for which real user statistics from a deployed VoD system are considered. The use of DASH and SVC in combination with prioritized caching outperforms the other technologies especially in busy/peak hours.

References

1. Cisco Visual Networking Index. http://newsroom.cisco.com/visualnetwrkingindex/.
2. S. Podlipnig and L. Böszörmenyi, "A survey of Web cache replacement strategies," *ACM Computing Surveys*, vol. 35, pp. 374–398, Dec. 2003.
3. D. Hong, D. De Vleeschauwer, F. Baccelli, "A Chunk-based Caching Algorithm for Streaming Video", Proceedings of the 4th Workshop on Network Control and Optimization, Ghent (Belgium), November 29 – December 1, 2010.
4. 3rd Generation Partnership Project; Technical Specification Group Services and System Aspects; Transparent end-to-end Packet-switched Streaming Service (PSS); Protocols and codecs (Release 9); 3GPP TS 26.234 V9.3.0 (2010–06), Section 12: Adaptive HTTP Streaming.
5. Open IPTV Forum – Release 2 Specification, HTTP Adaptive Streaming, Draft V0.06 - June 7, 2010.
6. ISO/IEC JTC 1/SC 29/WG 11 (MPEG), "Dynamic adaptive streaming over HTTP", w11578, CD 23001–6, Guangzhou, China, Oct 2010.
7. H. Schwarz, D. Marpe, and T. Wiegand, "Overview of the scalable video coding extension of the H.264/AVC standard," IEEE Transactions on Circuits and Systems for Video Technology, vol. 17, no.9, pp. 1103–1120, 2007.

8. Y. Sánchez, T. Schierl, C. Hellge, T. Wiegand, D. Hong, D. De Vleeschauwer, W. Van Leekwijck, Y. Le Louedec. "iDASH: improved Dynamic Adaptive Streaming over HTTP using Scalable Video Coding", Proceedings of Multimedia Systems Conference - Special Session Media Transport, San Jose, USA, February 23–25, 2011.
9. H. Schwarz and T. Wiegand, "Further results for an rd-optimized multi-loop SVC encoder", JVT-W071, JVT Meeting San Jose, USA, 2007, ftp://avguest@ftp3.itu.int/jvt-site/2007_04_SanJose/JVT-W071.zip.
10. K. Cheng and Y. Kambayashi, "Multicache-based content management for Web caching," in *Proceedings of the First International Conference on Web Information Systems Engineering, 2000*, vol. 1, pp. 42–49, 2000.
11. O. Verscheure, X. Garcia, G. Karlsson, and J.P. Hubaux, "User-Oriented QoS in Packet Video Delivery", IEEE Network, vol. 12, pp. 12–21, Dec. 1998.

A Travel Planning System Based on Travel Trajectories Extracted from a Large Number of Geotagged Photos on the Web

Kohya Okuyama and Keiji Yanai

Abstract Due to the recent wide spread of camera devices with GPS, the number of geotagged photos on the Web is increasing rapidly. Some image retrieval systems and travel recommendation systems which make use of geotagged images on the Web have been proposed so far. While most of them handle a large number of geotagged images as a set of location points, in this paper we handle them as sequences of location points. We propose a travel route recommendation system which utilizes actual travel paths extracted from a large number of photos uploaded by many people on the Web.

1 Introduction

Due to the recent spread of devices having cameras and GPSs such as iPhone, Android phones and some GPS-equipped digital cameras, we can easily record location information as well as digital photos. In general, photos with location information are called "geotagged photos." At the same time, some photo sharing Web sites which can handle geotagged photos such as Flickr[1] and Panoramio[2] have become popular, and the number of geotagged photos on these sites has been increasing rapidly. Since geotagged photos on the photo sharing sites can be gathered via Web API easily, recently, many researches on geotagged photos are being carried out in the field of multimedia and computer vision.

In this paper, we propose a travel planning system which utilizes a large number of geotagged photos on the Web and travel paths by many people extracted from

[1] http://www.flickr.com/

[2] http://www.panoramio.com/

K. Okuyama • K. Yanai (✉)
The University of Electro-Communications, Tokyo, Japan
e-mail: yanai@cs.uec.ac.jp

J.S. Jin et al., *The Era of Interactive Media*,
DOI 10.1007/978-1-4614-3501-3_54,

them. In general, the places where many photos are taken by many people mean tourist places drawing attention of many tourists such as historical architectures, monuments, and beautiful scenic places. By gathering many geotagged photos from the Web and analyzing them, we can get to know such places easily. In fact, many works to extract tourist places automatically from geotagged photos on the Web have been proposed so far [4, 7, 8, 11].

In addition, if a person travels through several tourist places continuously within a day or over several days, took geotagged photos at each of all the visited places, and upload them to the photo sharing sites such as Flickr or Panoramio, we can extract travel traces from a sequence of geotagged photos taken by the person. Using Web API provided by photo sharing sites, we can obtain user IDs as well as photo IDs and geotag information consisting of a set of values of latitude and longitude as metadata of photos. By obtaining meta data regarding a set of geotagged photos associated with a certain user ID, we can obtain a sequence of geotag locations which expresses a travel path of the user. This enables us to handle geotagged photos as not only a set of tourist places but also a set of travel paths.

Then, in this paper, we extract popular tourist places and travel paths of many Web users by analyzing a large number of geotagged photos, and propose a travel route recommendation system using the extracted travel information. Our proposed system can gather, aggregate and summarize travel route information, and recommends travel routes that many Web user's preferences reflect.

This paper is organized as follows: We describe related work in Sect. 2. In Sect. 3, we explain the overview of the proposed system and its detail. In Sect. 4, we show experiments and examples of recommended travel paths. In Sect. 5, we conclude this paper.

2 Related Work

Since there are so many geotagged photos on the Web nowadays, several researches have considered the problem of selecting representative or canonical photographs for popular locations for tourists. Jaffe et al. [4] selected a summary set of photos from a large collection of geotagged photographs based on keyword tags and geotags. Simon et al. [8] have proposed a method to select canonical views for the landmarks by clustering images based on the visual similarity between two views. Kennedy et al. [5] attempted to generate representative views for the world's landmarks based on the clustering and on the generated link structure. Zheng et al. [11] built a large-scale landmark image database including 5,314 landmarks using about one million geotagged photos and twenty million Web images.

Y. Zheng et al. [9] analyzed GPS log data recorded by handy GPS devices, and estimated popular human travel routes and places. Since their work used GPS log data, they can analyze precise human traces. However, the problem is that such data is very expensive to obtain, and large-scale analysis on GPS trace data is impossible, since carrying handy GPS during travel is not very common. Although travel paths extracted from geotagged photos are much coarser than GPS traces, we can obtain them much more than GPS traces instead.

As works on travel planning using geotagged photos on the Web, Cao et al. [2] proposed a travel planning system which recommends travel places based on user's preferences. This system recommends not routes and just only places.

On the other hand, X. Lu [6] proposed using travel traces extracted from geotagged photos on the Web for travel route recommendation. To generate travel paths, they used all the places extracted from geotagged photos. On the other hand, in our system, we use only geo-location information on popular tourist places and the order of traveling among them, which are represented as "trip models" in this paper.

Arase et al. [1] also proposed a travel recommendation system which utilizes travel routes extracted from geotagged photos. While their objective is to recommend travel plans for the users who have not decided even areas to visit, the objective of our system is to recommend travel routes within a given area for the uses who have decided the area to visit but have not decided the tourist spots to visit within the area.

Zheng et al. [10] proposed a method to extract "regions of attractions (RoA)," which mean popular tourist places, and tourist flows between RoAs. This work is one of the most similar works to ours. We propose a travel route recommendation system including extraction of representation photos on each tourist place, while they proposed just a method to analyze travel trajectories extracted geotagged photos.

3 Proposed System

3.1 Overview

In this paper, we propose a travel route planning system, which recommends several efficient travel routes so as to visit user's favorite places. We assume that users use this system before starting trips after deciding which area they are going to travel to. Here, an "area" means a regional range over which tourist places we usually visit during one trip are distributed. For example, New York, Paris, London, Kyoto and Tokyo are examples of "areas" in this paper. Our system helps us to decide the places to visit and the order of the places to visit within the given area. How to use the system is as follows:

1. The system presents popular places in the given area with representative tags and photos, and then the user selects some favorite places.
2. The system presents several recommended routes which travel through the given places, and the user selects a favorite route.
3. The system shows the selected route on the online map.

To realize this system, as offline processing, we extract representative tourist places and common travel paths within the given area from a large number of geotagged photos collected from Web photo sharing sites in advance. This offline processing consists of the following four steps: (1) data collection (2) extraction of common tourist places (3) selection of representative photos and textural tags for each tourist place and (4) extraction and modeling of travel routes,

In this section, we explain the offline processing first, and the online processing of the proposed system next.

3.2 Data Collection and Selection

As Web photo sharing sites, we use Flickr[3] since Flickr has more than one billion geotagged photos which can be searched and obtained easily via Flickr API.[4]

First of all, we obtain metadata of geotagged photos using the "flickr.photos. search" method of Flickr API. We obtain the following metadata items for each geotagged photo:

Metadata used in the proposed system

id unique ID of the photo
owner user ID who uploaded the photo
date-taken date and time of taking the photo
tags text tags for the photo
latitude, longitude geotag information
accuracy accuracy of the given geotag. Higher value means high accuracy.

Before downloading photos, we remove noise photos and select only geotagged photos suitable for extracting travel trajectories. First, we remove geotagged photos the geotag accuracy of which are less than 11. Next, to extract travel trajectories effectively, we select only the photos uploaded by the users who uploaded more than two photos taken in the same day.

Moreover, geotags of some photos are attached not by GPS but by clicking online maps, and some of them sometimes have exactly the same geotags. Such photos are also not appropriate for our work. Thus, we exclude all the pairs of the photos whose geotag locations are exactly identical but whose taken time are different by more than five minutes. As an example, we show the number of photos before and after noise removal for "user A" and "user B" in Table 1. In this example, user A is estimated to be inaccurate regarding location information, while user B is estimated to be highly accurate, and probably used GPS to attach geotags to his/her photos. For this work, user A is much more useful than user B.

---

[3] http://flickr.com/

[4] http://www.flickr.com/services/api/

Table 1 The number of photos before and after noise removal

	Number of original images	Number of images after cleaning
User A	25,189	192
User B	4,793	4,766

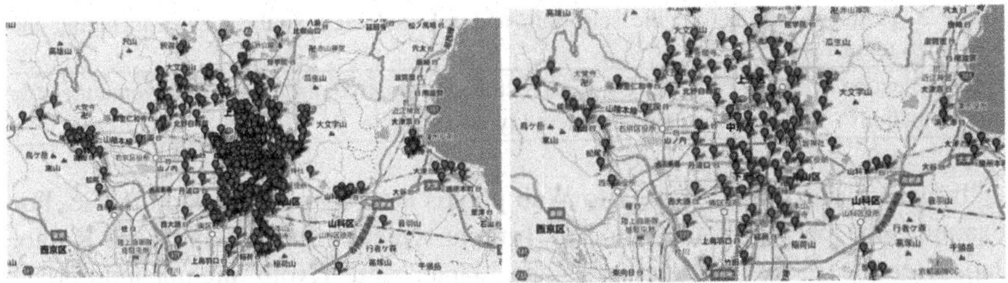

Fig. 1 (*Left*) Place clusters for the 100-m threshold. (*Right*) Place clusters for the 400-m threshold

3.3 Tourist Place Detection

To detect tourist places from geotagged photos, we apply clustering for geotags of the collected photos. As clustering methods, you use a hierarchical clustering as described as follows:

1. Initially, all the geotag locations are regarded as being cluster centers.
2. Aggregate two clusters the distance between which is the closest into one new cluster. The location of the new cluster is defined as being the average location of two points.
3. If the closest distance between any two clusters become less than the pre-defined threshold, clustering will be finished. Otherwise, repeat from Step 2.

To compute distance D between two locations, we use the spherical distance as computed in the following equation:

$$\rho = R\cos^{-1}\{\sin\delta_A \sin\delta_B + \cos\delta_A \cos\delta_B \cos(\lambda_A - \lambda_B)\} \quad (1)$$

where R represents the radius of the earth, and δ_A, λ_A, δ_B, λ_B represent latitude and longitude of place A and place B, respectively.

In Figure. 1, we show two geotag clustering results in case that the thresholds are set as 100 m and 400 m. The left of the figure shows about 400 clusters in case of the 100-m threshold, and the right shows about 100 clusters in case of the 400-m threshold.

3.4 Extraction of Representative Tags and Photos

In this subsection, we describe a method to assign representative text tags and photos to each of the common tourist clusters. Representative tags and photos are helpful to explain the places both semantically and visually.

Table 2 Frequent tags before the selection, and selected tags on the cluster including the Kinkaku temple

before selection	kinkakuji japanesebuses japan kansai kyoto ofriceandzen
after selection	kinkakuji japanesebuses

Table 3 Frequent tags before the selection, and selected tags on the cluster including the Kiyomizu temple

before selection	october japan october kyoto kiyomizudera 2009 kiyomizutemple
after selection	kiyomizudera kiyomizutemple

In general, text tags attached to Web photos are very various and diverse. For example, the photos of the Kinkaku Temple typically have "Kinkakuji, Kyoto, Japan, temple" as tags. Among these tags, "Japan" and "Kyoto" are not appropriate to explain the place since they mean broad area. "Kinkakuji" is the best tag to explain the place of "Kinkaku temple," since it is a unique tag for the place.

To select unique tags for the places, we compute a evaluation score of uniqueness of tags $score_{c,\ t}$ to the places in the following equation:

$$score_{c,t} = \frac{N_c(t)}{\sum_{c \in C} N_c(t)}$$

where C, c, t, and $N_c(T)$ represents all the clusters, a cluster, a tag, and the number of photos having tag t in cluster c, respectively. If $score_{c,\ t}$ is more than the pre-defined threshold, the tag t is regarded as being one of representative tags of the cluster c.

In Tables 2 and 3, we show two examples before and after the tag selection on the clusters including the Kinkaku temple and the Kiyomizu temple. In these examples, some tags which mean broad areas such as "japan" and "kansai" are eliminated successfully.

Next, we select some representative photos for each cluster by employing local-feature-based image analysis. We decide representative photos based on the number of matched local feature points. As local features, we use SURFSpeeded-Up Robust Features) [3]. We extract SURF descriptors from each of the photos, and search for matched local point pairs within the same cluster. We select the top five photos as representative ones in terms of the number of matched points in each cluster. Two figures in Fig. 2 show local feature matching between two photos of the Kinkaku temple taken from the different angles and between two photos of the Kinkaku temple and the Kiyomizu temple. In general, the pair of the photos of the same landmark bring much more matched points than the pair of the different landmarks. As a result, the landmark taken in many photos gathers many matched points and it is selected as representative one.

3.5 Modeling Travel Trajectories

In the proposed system, after selecting tourist place clusters and their tags and photos, we extract travel trajectories of many people from geotagged photos, and

Fig. 2 SURF point matching. (*Left*) between two photos of the Kinkaku Temple. (*Right*) between the Kinkaku and the Kiyomizu temple

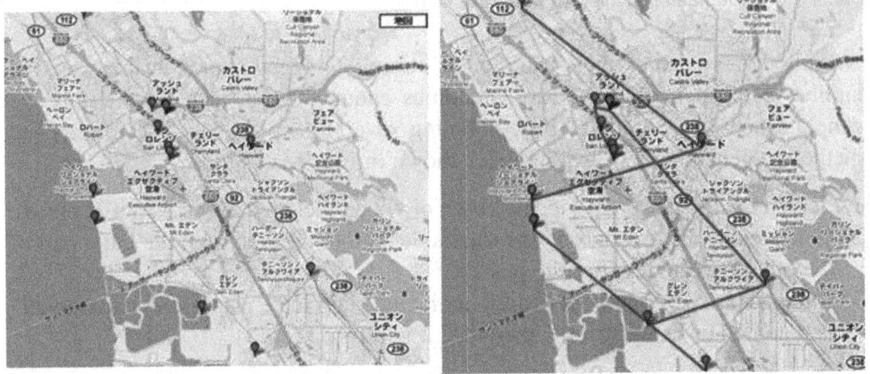

Fig. 3 (*Left*) Photo places of a certain user in a day. (*Right*) Travel sequences

generate "trip models" from them which represent canonical move sequences among tourist place clusters.

At first, we extract geotag sequences from geotagged photos taken by one user within a certain day in the time order, and gather them regarding many users and many days as a set of one-day travel trajectories. We call an one-day travel trajectory as "a trip." We show the places where a certain user took geotagged photos within the same day in the left of Fig. 3, and their travel path in the right of Fig. 3.

Some "trips" include many geotag places densely, while some "trips" include some places sparsely most of which are popular tourist places. In addition, some "trips" might include many geotag locations around the same landmarks. In this way, the resolution of geotags varies depending on users greatly. Then, to make the resolution of "trips" even and to remove redundant places, we convert a "trip" trajectory, which is a sequence of geotagged places, into a "trip model," which is a sequence of the moves between common tourist places detected in the previous section. In this paper, all the travel paths are represented as "trip models."

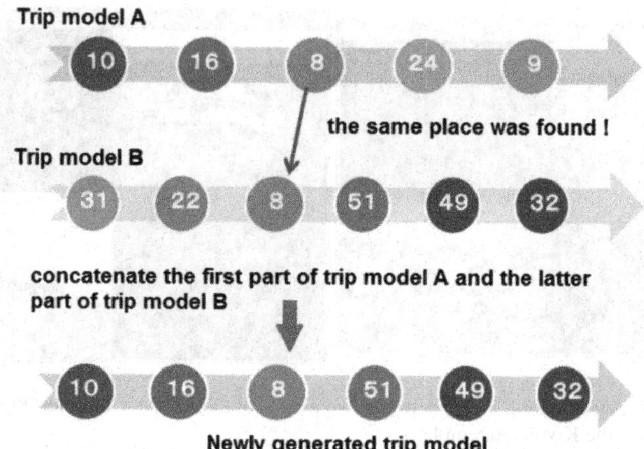

Fig. 4 An example of generating a new "trip model"

Although we can extract "trip models" from geotagged photos in this way, the number of "trip models" is not sometimes enough. Then, in the next step, we generate new "trip models" by combining several "trip models." The proposed method to generate new "trip models" shown in Fig. 4 is as follows:

1. Search for the two "trip models" both of which include the same tourist places.
2. Concatenate the first part of one trip model before the place and the latter part of the other trip model after the place.
3. If the generated "trip model" does not include duplicate places, the "trip model" is regarded as being valid. Otherwise, it will be discarded.

Note that to prevent loops from being made in trip models, we limit the same place to being included once in one "trip model."

In Fig. 4, a new "trip model" is generated by linking the first part of "trip model A" with the latter part of "trip model B." In addition, we can concatenate the first part of "trip model B" and the latter part of "trip model A."

3.6 Online System

In this subsection, we explain online processing on a route recommendation system which makes use of common tourist places and "trip models" extracted from geotagged photos. The online processing of the system consists of the following three steps:

1. Selection of tourist places where a user like to visit
2. Presenting travel route candidates and selection from them
3. Presenting the selected travel route on the map

Each of three figures in Fig. 5 corresponds to each of the above three steps.

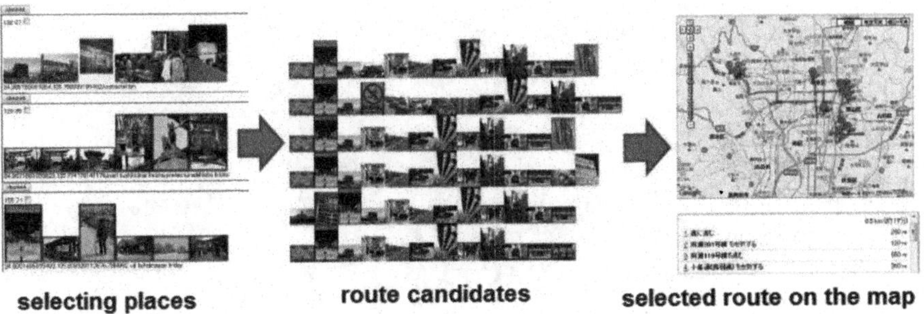

Fig. 5 Three steps in the online system

3.6.1 Selection of Places

In the first step, the system shows common tourist places with their tags and representative photos, and asks a user to select some places where he/she like to visit. As help for a user to select places, the system shows some information on each place which are obtained via Yahoo! Local Search API[5] as well.

3.6.2 Showing and Selection of "trip models"

The system searches the "trip model" database for the routes including as many tourist places the user selected as possible. To search for "trip models" quickly, we prepare an search index on "trip models" regarding each of common tourist places in advance.

3.6.3 Presenting a Travel Route on the Map

In the last step, the system shows the selected "trip model" on the map. "Trip models" do not contain road information between tourist places, but contain only information on sequences of tourist places. Then, we obtain common road routes between the tourist places by using the Directions Service of Google Maps API.[6] Using this service as well as basic function of Google Maps API, we can present the selected "trip model" on the map as shown in the right figure of Fig. 5.

[5] http://developer.yahoo.co.jp/webapi/map/localsearch/v1/localsearch.html

[6] http://code.google.com/intl/ja/apis/maps/

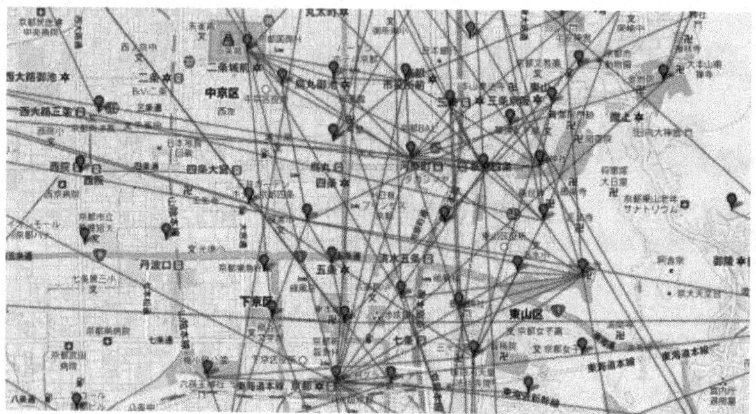

Fig. 6 Extracted common tourist places and "trip models" in "Kyoto"

4 Experiments

To gather a large number of geotagged images within areas where people travel around in one day, popular tourist areas are appropriate. As a target area in the experiment, we selected "Kyoto" which is one of the most popular tourist areas in Japan.

We gathered 20,000 geotagged photos taken in the Kyoto area from Flickr via Flickr API. After noise removal described in Sect. 3.2, we collected 1,805 geotagged photos uploaded by 162 unique users. After carrying out hierarchical clustering with the 400-m threshold in terms of the radius of clusters, we obtained 154 tourist place clusters and 18,742 "trip models," part of which are shown in Fig. 6.

Figure 7 shows a part of common tourist place candidates with representative tags and photos, and address information on the locations obtained from Yahoo! Local Search API. The tourist places are shown in the descending order of the number of the cluster members of geotagged photos, that is, in the order of popularity.

As a case study, we selected four places, "Kyoto Station," "Fushimi temple," "Uji bridge" and "Nijo castle." As route candidates that go through the given four places, three route, "Trip 1," "Trip 2" and "Trip 3," are presented in the ascending order of the total moving distance. When clicking each of route candidates, each of the three routes are displayed on the map as shown in Figs. 8–10, respectively. Table 4 shows the number of common tourist places included in the route candidates, the total moving distances and the average moving distances between the common tourist places.

From Table 4, a user who wants to move quickly between selected places will select "Trip 1" or "Trip 2," while a user who wants to visit as many tourist places as

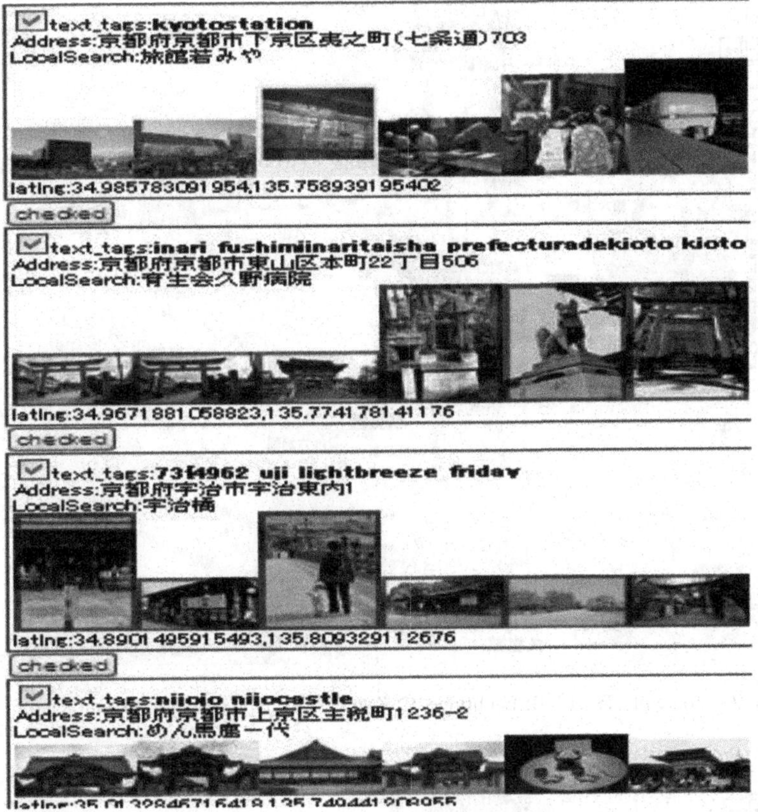

Fig. 7 Part of place candidates

possible might select "Trip 3." In this way, selection from the route candidates depends on the user's preference greatly. Thus, the important thing is presenting as many route candidates and their additional information as possible which suit user's preference conditions.

5 Conclusions

In this paper, we proposed a travel route recommendation system based on sequences of geotagged photos on the Web, which presents several travel route candidates with representative tags and photos by selecting tourist places where a user like to visit. To gather information on travel routes, we proposed "trip models"

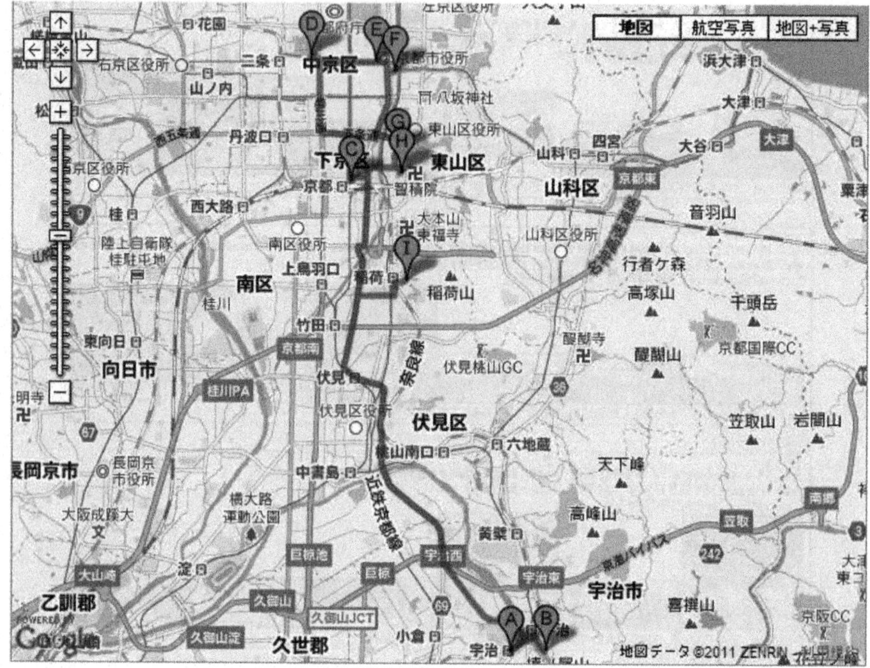

Fig. 8 The route of "Trip1." B: Uji bridge. C: Kyoto St. D: Nijo castle. I:Fushimi temple

Fig. 9 The route of "Trip2." C: Nijo castle. E: Kyoto St. H: Fushimi temple. O: Uji bridge

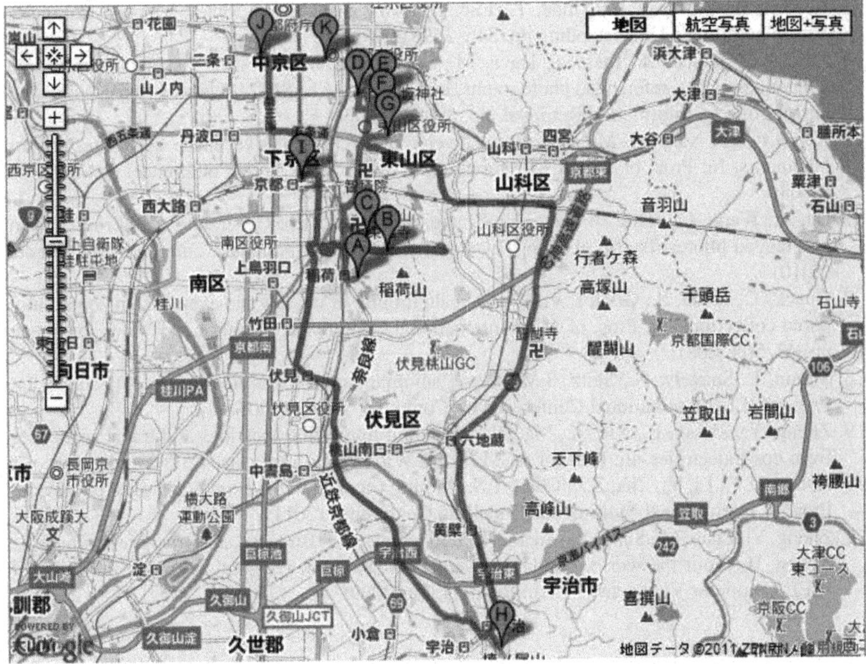

Fig. 10 The route of "Trip3." A: Fushimi temple. H: Uji bridge. I: Kyoto St. J: Nijo castle

Table 4 The number of visiting tourist places, and the total and average distances of the three routes

Route candidate	Number of places	Total distance (km)	Average distance between places (km)
Trip 1	9	29.8	3.73
Trip 2	15	52.7	3.76
Trip 3	11	54.1	5.41

represented by the order sequences of tourist places. In the experiments, we build a "trip model" database on the Kyoto area as a case study.

As future work, we plan to apply many other areas over the world than Kyoto and extend the system to recommend travel routes taking account of travel time.

References

1. Arase, Y., Xie, X., Hara, T., Nishio, S.: Mining people's trips from large scale geo-tagged photos. In: Proc. of ACM International Conference Multimedia (2010)
2. Cao, L., Luo, J., Gallagher, A., Jin, X., Han, J., Huang, T.: A worldwide tourism recommendation system based on geotagged web photos. In: Proc. of IEEE International Conference on Acoustics, Spech and Signal Processing (2010)

3. Herbert, B., Andreas, E., Tinne, T., Luc, G.: Surf: Speeded up robust features. Computer Vision and Image Understanding pp. 346–359 (2008)
4. Jaffe, A., Naaman, M., Tassa, T., Davis, M.: Generating summaries and visualization for large collections of geo-referenced photographs. In: Proc. of ACM SIGMM International Workshop on Multimedia Information Retrieval. pp. 89–98 (2006)
5. Kennedy, L., Naaman, M.: Generating diverse and representative image search results for landmarks. In: Proc. of the ACM International World Wide Web Conference. pp. 297–306 (2008)
6. Lu, X., Wang, C., Yang, J., Pang, Y., Zhang, L.: Photo2Trip: Generating travel routes from geo-tagged photos for trip planning. In: Proc. of ACM International Conference Multimedia (2010)
7. Quack, T., Leibe, B., Gool, L.V.: World-scale mining of objects and events from community photo collections. In: Proc. of ACM International Conference on Image and Video Retrieval. pp. 47–56 (2008)
8. Simon, I., Snavely, N., Seitz, S.M.: Scene summarization for online image collections. In: Proc. of IEEE International Conference on Computer Vision (2007)
9. Zheng, Y., Zhang, L., Xie, X., Ma, W.Y.: Mining interesting locations and travel sequences from gps trajectories. In: Proc. of ACM World Wide Web Conference (2009)
10. Zheng, Y.T., Li, Y., Zha, Z.J., Chua, T.S.: Mining travel patterns from gps-tagged photos. In: Proc. of International Multimedia Modelling Conference (2011)
11. Zheng, Y., Zhao, M., Song, Y., Adam, H., Buddemeier, U., Bissacco, A., Brucher, F., Chua, T., Neven, H.: Tour the world: building a web-scale landmark recognition engine. In: Proc. of IEEE Computer Vision and Pattern Recognition (2009)

A Robust Histogram Region-Based Global Camera Estimation Method for Video Sequences

Xuesong Le and Ruben Gonzalez

Abstract Global motion estimation (GME) plays an important role in video object segmentation. This paper presents a computationally efficient two stage affine GME algorithm. The key idea is to create initial matches for histogram-based image segmented regions. Then an affine motion model is estimated and refined by iteratively removing incorrect matches. Experiments with different types of video sequences are used to demonstrate the performance of the proposed approach.

Keywords Histogram-based • Affine motion estimation • Outliers removal

1 Introduction

Global motion estimation (GME) is an important task in video object segmentation. The goal is to remove the global camera motion and retain object motion. GME methods can be divided into three classes: pixel-based, block-based, and feature based. Pixel-based approaches [1] suffer from heavy computation requirements. In block-based approaches [2], working on motion vector fields requires detection and removal of outliers not belonging to global motion. The third approach is to establish correspondences of features in frames and then estimate a transformation model from those matches. Various feature based algorithms have been surveyed in [3–5]. In this work, we are particularly interested in region-based feature matching algorithms. Compared to other methods [6, 7] where several hundreds of points are detected for matching, region based methods require only a small number of matches to estimate motion parameters.

X. Le (✉) • R. Gonzalez
School of Information, communication, and Technology, Griffith University,
Parklands Drive, Southport QLD 4222, Australia
e-mail: x.le@griffith.edu.au

J.S. Jin et al., *The Era of Interactive Media*,
DOI 10.1007/978-1-4614-3501-3_55,

To estimate global motion between two images in a video sequence, a number of segmentation techniques have been proposed. Flusser [8] proposed to detect regions bounded by closed edges as features. Goshtasby [9] iteratively split entire image into regions recursively until the variation of gray-level histogram in each sub-region is small. Dai [10] produces a number of boundary contours by detecting edges with Laplacian of Gaussian filter and a seven-dimensional invariant-moment feature vector for each region is extracted in matching. Though much progress has been made, these methods are still not widely used in video motion estimation due to the computational complexity of the post-processing requirements such as edge linking or boundary closing. This paper presents a computational efficient and robust region-based feature matching approach for video sequences that undergo affine transformations.

The main contributions in this work are: (a) a simple multi-level thresholding method is proposed to create initial regions; (b) an efficient and fast variance-cut classification algorithm is proposed to perform initial matching on extracted region descriptors; (c) an outlier removal algorithm is proposed to reduce incorrect matches.

2 A Two Stage GME Algorithm

In this section we first introduce a region based feature detector. A two-stage algorithm for determining correspondences between two sets of feature vectors is then presented.

2.1 Region Based Detection Algorithm

Typically, a histogram-based image segmentation method comprises three stages: recognizing the modes of the histogram, finding the valleys between the identified modes and finally applying thresholds to the image based on the valleys. The common solution to the histogram valley detection is to use a 1D convolution kernel to smooth samples iteratively until all abrupt changes disappear. Then each valley in smoothed histogram is assigned with a unique label. The disadvantage of this histogram-seeking method is that it may be difficult to identify significant peaks and valleys in an over-smoothed histogram. In Fig. 1, there is only one valley be found after smoothing original histogram 20 times, with 1D averaging kernel K. As a consequence, most of the objects in the scene have been classified as background.

The proposed solution to the over-smoothing problem is an extension of OTSU's bi-level thresholding method [11] to a multi-level thresholding method. We assume that there are M-1 thresholds, $\{t_1, t_2, \ldots, t_{M-1}\}$, which divide the original image into M classes: C_1 for $[0, \ldots, t_1]$, C_2 for $[t_1+1, \ldots, t_2]$, …, C_i for $[t_{i-1}+1, \ldots, t_i]$, …,

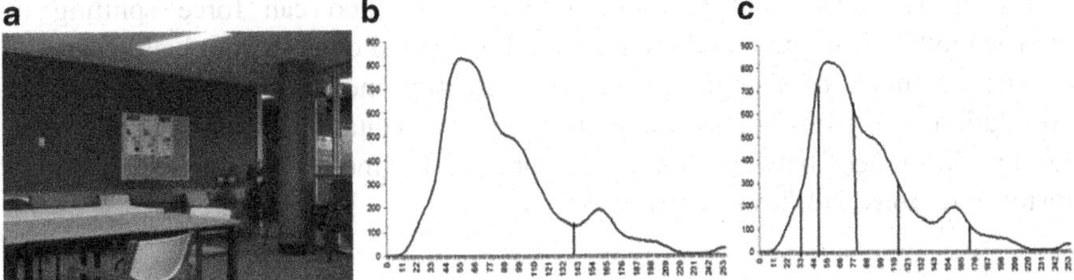

Fig. 1 (**a**) Original image, (**b**) Valley Based Thresholding (**c**) Clustering Based Thresholding

and C_M for $[t_{M-1}+1, \ldots, 255]$. The cumulative probabilities, ω_k, mean, μ_k, and total variance, σ_k^2, mean for each class C_k is defined as:

$$\omega_k = \sum_{i=C_k} p_i, \mu_k = \sum_{i=C_k} ip_i/\omega_k, \sigma_k^2 = \sum_{i=C_k} (i - \mu_k)^2 p_i/\omega_k \tag{1}$$

In [11], the optimal threshold t in any class C_i for $[t_{i-1}+1, \ldots, t_i]$ is the maximum between class variance,σ_B^2:

$$\sigma_B^2 = \omega_1\omega_2(\mu_1 - \mu_2)^2. \tag{2}$$

Where $\omega_1 = \sum_{j=t_{i-1}}^{t} p_j$; $\omega_2 = \sum_{j=t+1}^{t_i} p_j$; $\mu_1 = \sum_{j=t_{i-1}}^{t} jp_j/\omega_1$ and $\mu_2 = \sum_{j=t+1}^{t_i} jp_j/\omega_2$.

The search for the optimal multi-level thresholds is a divisive approach. It starts with a single class and recursively splits the single class into M classes. This algorithm is described as following:

1. Start with a single class C0 which has all intensity levels $t = 0 \ldots 255$ and add it to a list C with count $m = 0$.
2. Compute the total variance σ_0^2 in class C_0 with Eq. (1) and the optimal threshold t with Eq. (2).
3. Search each candidate class c_i in list C and find the class c_s, which has the largest total variance σ_i^2 and the optimal threshold t_i. The intensity gray levels in class c_s range from t_s to t_{s+1}, where $0 \leq t_1 < \ldots < t_s < t_{s+1} < \ldots < L$
4. Split class C_s into two new classes C_m, and C_n. The intensity gray levels in class c_m range from t_s to t_i. And the intensity gray levels in class c_n range from $t_i + 1$ to t_{s+1}.
5. Compute total variance σ_m^2, σ_n^2 and the optimal thresholds, t_m, and t_n for two classes.
6. If any new created class c_j has satisfied the criteria $\sigma_j^2 < \sigma_{\min}^2 \vee size(c_j) < \min\_size$, classify this class as a none-divisible class. Otherwise this class is assigned as a candidate class.
7. Remove c_s from list C and add two split classes c_m and c_n to list C. Increment number of classes m by 1.
8. If the number of classes including all none-divisible classes and candidate classes has reached maximum threshold M or the largest variance is below some threshold, then stop, else go back to step 3.

Figure 1c shows that proposed clustering method can force splitting in over-smoothed histogram and separate the foreground objects from background.

The advantage of histogram based segmentation methods is that there is high correlation of regions across frames in video segmentation which typically have limited differences between frames. In contrast, the methods discussed in [8–10] result in regions with lower correlation.

2.2 *Region: Descriptor Selections*

For this work, we use three features, the mean of gray levels in a region, h_r, the contrast of gray levels in a region c_r and the compactness of a region, defined as:

$$Rad\_comp = \left(\sum_{i=1}^{k} Rad_j / k \right)^2 / n \tag{3}$$

Each radius Rad_j is calculated as the distance between the gravity center C_R and every region boundary point counted along vectors centered at C_R and at angle, θ, where θ, is in steps of (360/k) degrees from 0° to 360°.

The mean, contrast, and compactness are easy to compute features that are independent of each other and invariant to affine transformations. Each region of an image must next be matched with the corresponding regions in the second image. This is performed using the classification algorithm as described in Sect. 2.2.

2.3 *Initial Feature Vectors Classification*

Similar to the one dimensional multi-level clustering algorithm proposed in 2.1, a multi-dimensional multi-level clustering (MDMLC) method is developed for initial feature vectors matching. It also starts with a single class and recursively splits the single class into M classes. The only difference is that the selection of which class to split requires a search for the maximum class variance across all dimensions. If the feature vector space is implemented in a binary tree data structure, the amount of computation needed to build the binary tree for N feature vectors is only $O(2N \log_2 N)$. Given an input feature vector, searching for classes which may contain its close matches requires $O(\log_2 C \times N)$ complexity, where C is a constant. This MDMLC method makes use of a recursive search to find feature vectors and is described as following:

Procedure: search_Vectors(Node currentNode, Vector f, List l)

c: a feature class which currentNode refers to

1. If currentNode is a leaf node, add all the feature vectors in class c to l, else call **find_Search_Direction** to find how to continue the search.
2. If f is not in the left or right branch, then stop search and return not_found.
3. Call **search_Vectors** with left or right branch as required.

Procedure: find_Search_Direction(Node cNode, Vector v)

c: a feature class that cNode refers to, **left_c**: a feature class that the left child of cNode refers to, **right_c**: a feature class that the right child of cNode refers to, **w:** some predefined threshold.

1. Find the kth dimension, which has the largest variance, $\sigma_{l,c}^2$ in class c among all dimensions. If the following criteria are satisfied: $\sigma_{l,c}^2 < \min\_t$ and size(c)<min_size, then return search_Left_And_Right.
2. Find the mean of elements at kth dimension of feature vectors in the class that the left node refers to, $\overline{x_{l,left\_c}}$, and the mean of elements at kth dimension of feature vectors in the class that the right node refers to, right_c, $\overline{x_{l,right\_c}}$.
3. Find the element of feature vector v, at kth dimension, v_l If $\left|v_l - \overline{x_{l,left\_c}}\right| < w^* \sigma_{l,left\_c}^2$, return search_Left.
4. If $\left|v_l - \overline{x_{l,right\_c}}\right| < w^* \sigma_{l,right\_c}^2$, return search_Right.

This initial classification produces a list of potential close matching regions in the current image for each region in the next image. From this list, we select the best candidate match using a custom outlier removal procedure.

2.4 *Affine Parameter Derivation*

In order to select the best match, we first need to calculate the set of potential transformation parameters derived from the initial matches found in Sect. 2.3. Each image has a set consisting of the centres of gravity for each region in the image. Set P consists of m points extracted from the first image, where $P = \{p_0, p_1, p_2, \ldots, p_{m-1}\}$, and set Q consists of n feature points, where $Q = \{q_0, q_1, q_2, \ldots, q_{n-1}\}$. The purpose of matching is to find a correspondence between a point p_i in P and a point q_a in Q that makes this corresponding pair consistent under an affine transformation registration. From the list of potential matches, we first calculate all the possible affine transformation parameters.

Notations and Theorems:

The 2D affine transformation can be modelled as composite matrix operation of translation, scaling, and rotation, which maps a point $p = (x_p, y_p)^T$ to a point $q = (x_q, y_q)^T$ as follows:

$$\begin{bmatrix} x_q \\ y_q \\ 1 \end{bmatrix} = \begin{bmatrix} 1 & 0 & x_c \\ 0 & 1 & y_c \\ 0 & 0 & 1 \end{bmatrix} * \begin{bmatrix} 1 & 0 & t_x \\ 0 & 1 & t_y \\ 0 & 0 & 1 \end{bmatrix} * \begin{bmatrix} \cos\theta & -\sin\theta & 0 \\ -\sin\theta & \cos\theta & 0 \\ 0 & 0 & 1 \end{bmatrix}$$
$$* \begin{bmatrix} s & 0 & 0 \\ 0 & s & 0 \\ 0 & 0 & 1 \end{bmatrix} * \begin{bmatrix} 1 & 0 & -x_c \\ 0 & 1 & -y_c \\ 0 & 0 & 1 \end{bmatrix} * \begin{bmatrix} x_p \\ y_p \\ 1 \end{bmatrix} \tag{4}$$

where x_c and y_c are the coordinate center of the image and θ is the rotation angle, and s_i is the scaling and tx and ty are the translation in x and y direction respectively.

Theorem 1: *Let (p_i, p_j) and (q_a, q_b) be two pairs in P and Q. If $p_i \neq p_j$ and $q_a \neq q_b$, and a unique registration G_r exists between p_i and q_a pair, and p_j and q_b pair, that makes $q_a = G(p_i)$, $q_b = G_r(p_j)$, where $r = (tx, ty, s, \theta)$, The scaling factor s, here is calculated as:*

$$s_{\overrightarrow{q_a,q_b}\ \overrightarrow{p_i,p_j}} = \left|\overrightarrow{q_aq_b}\right| / \left|\overrightarrow{p_ip_j}\right|. \tag{5}$$

The magnitude, $|\theta|$ of rotation angle θ, is calculated as:

$$\left|\theta_{\overrightarrow{q_a,q_b}\ \overrightarrow{p_i,p_j}}\right| = \arccos\left(\left(\overrightarrow{q_aq_b} \bullet \overrightarrow{p_ip_j}\right) / \left(\left|\overrightarrow{q_aq_b}\right|\left|\overrightarrow{p_ip_j}\right|\right)\right) \tag{6}$$

The sign of rotation angle, θ, is calculated as the value of cross product from vector $\overrightarrow{q_aq_b}$ and $\overrightarrow{p_ip_j}$ along the z-axis which is perpendicular to the x-y plane as following:

$$z_{\overrightarrow{q_a,q_b}\ \overrightarrow{p_i,p_j}} = \left|\overrightarrow{q_aq_b}\right| \times \left|\overrightarrow{p_ip_j}\right| \tag{7}$$

$$\theta_{\overrightarrow{q_a,q_b}\ \overrightarrow{p_ip_j}} = \begin{cases} \theta_{\overrightarrow{q_aq_b}\ \overrightarrow{p_ip_j}} & \text{if } (z \geq 0), \text{clockwise} \\ -\theta_{\overrightarrow{q_aq_b}\ \overrightarrow{p_ip_j}} & \text{otherwise, anti} - \text{clockwise} \end{cases} \tag{8}$$

Calculation of translation parameters, tx and ty between pair $p = (x_p, y_p)^T$ and $q = (x_q, y_q)$ is:

$$tx = \left(x_q - x_c + \frac{s * (x_c - x_p)}{\cos\theta} + \frac{\sin^2\theta(x_q - x_c)}{\cos^2\theta} + \frac{\sin\theta * s(y_p - y_c)}{\cos^2\theta}\right) \Big/ \left(1 + \frac{\sin^2\theta}{\cos^2\theta}\right) \tag{9}$$

$$ty = \left(y_q - y_c + \frac{s * (y_c - y_p)}{\cos\theta} + \frac{\sin^2\theta(y_q - y_c)}{\cos^2\theta} + \frac{\sin\theta * s(x_p - x_c)}{\cos^2\theta}\right) \Big/ \left(1 + \frac{\sin^2\theta}{\cos^2\theta}\right) \tag{10}$$

The set of potential transformation parameters obtained for all potential matches must now be refined using outlier removal to converge on the most likely solution.

2.5 Stage 2: Outlier Removal

Most outlier removal methods work well for large sample size. In our case, we need one that can operate correctly with small sample sizes. The proposed method carries out the affine-parameter refinement in several iterations. The assumption is that the initially obtained transformation model is not always accurate, but it still includes a considerable number of inliers. The model parameters are adapted to the newly obtained set of inliers and the number of inliers increase over iterations.

The algorithm is stated as follows:

1. Calculate ranges of possible transformation parameters from match list.
2. Update match list.
3. If threshold is within the minimal acceptable range or the maximum iteration number has been reached, stop, else reduce threshold weighting, w, decrement iteration counter and go back to step 1.

2.5.1 Affine Transformations Bound Calculation

We first estimate the Probability Density Function (PDF) of scaling, $S_c = \{s_{0,c}, s_{i,c}, . s_{k-1,c}\}$ in all matched pairs during iteration c. From the estimated PDF, we pick the following values:

- Median of the scaling ratio, $\mathrm{med}_{s,c}$
- Arithmetic mean of the scaling ratio, $\mathrm{mean}_{s,c}$
- Standard deviation of the scaling ratio, $\mathrm{std}_{s,c}$
- Skew of the scaling ratio, $\mathrm{sk}_{s,c}$: is approximated as absolute difference between $\mathrm{mean}_{s,c}$ and $\mathrm{med}_{s,c}$.

$$sk_{s,c} = \left|mean_{s,c} - med_{s,c}\right| \tag{11}$$

The choice of whether using $\mathrm{med}_{s,c}$ or $\mathrm{mean}_{s,c}$ as the center of distribution, $\mathrm{center}_{s,c}$ depends on $\mathrm{sk}_{s,c}$:

$$center_{s,c} = \begin{cases} mean_{s,c} & if(sk_{s,c} < std_{s,c}) \\ median_{s,c} & else \end{cases} \tag{12}$$

The minimum and maximum acceptable scale ratio $\mathrm{s}_{\{\max,c,\min,c\}}$ is defined as:

$$s_{\{\max,c,\min,c\}} = center_{s,c} \pm w * std_{s,c} \tag{13}$$

where w is the constant weighting factor in current iteration.

The same procedure is applied to find the possible ranges of rotation angles, $\theta_{\{\max,c,\min,c\}}$ and translations $\mathrm{tx}_{\{\max,c,\min,c\}}$, $\mathrm{ty}_{\{\max,c,\min,c\}}$ except that the calculation

Fig. 2 (**a**) Car-park (**b**) Hall (**c**) Lounge

of maxima and minima in translations is after centres of scaling distribution rotation distribution have been determined.

After calculation of possible ranges, each match (i_q,j_p) in current matching list is said to be consistent if the associated transformation parameters $m_c = \{tx_{i,j}, ty_{i,j}, s_{i,j}, \theta_{i,j}\}$ are within given ranges:

$$tx_{\max,c} < \left|tx_{i,j} - center_{tx,c}\right| < tx_{\max,c} \wedge ty_{\max,c} < \left|ty_{i,j} - center_{ty,c}\right| < ty_{\max,c} \wedge$$
$$s_{\max,c} < \left|s_{i,j} - center_{s,c}\right| < s_{\max,c} \wedge \theta_{\max,c} < \left|\theta_{i,j} - center_{\theta,c}\right| < \theta_{\max,c}. \tag{14}$$

2.5.2 Update Match List

Each matched pair (i_q,j_p) can be interpreted that feature $a_{q,i}$ in set A_q is matched with another feature vector $b_{p,j}$ in set B_p and $a_{q,i}$ is associated with a subset of feature vectors, $E_p = \{e_{0,p}, ..e_{t-l,p}\}$ in set B_p. If the transformation associated with match pair (i_q,j_p) is not within affine parameter ranges, a search for the remaining candidate $e_{l,p}$ in associated set $E_p = \{e_{0,p}, e_{l,p}, ..e_{t-1,p}\}$ is performed.

2.5.3 Reduce Thresholds on Ranges and Decrement Iteration Count

In this step, the weighting w is reduced by predefined amount which is based on the assumption that transformation parameters have adapted to the newly obtained set of inliers and bounds decrease.

After all outliers are removed, then we use any calculated affine transformation parameters within one standard deviation distance from the mean and recalculate the average of those inliers as final affine transformation parameters (Fig. 2).

3 Experiment Results

To test performance of the proposed algorithm under different scenes, various video sequences in Fig. 3 are used in experiments. Each type has been further tested under varying scaling, rotation, and translation camera transformations.

3.1 Computation Time Test on Feature Detection

Our histogram region based feature detection method is compared with SIFT method [7] and Harris [6] in terms of computation complexity. It runs much faster than both SIFT and Harris on a PC with 3.00 GHZ Intel Pentium 4 CPU and 1G Memory. Table 1 shows that the running time on above video sequences among three detectors.

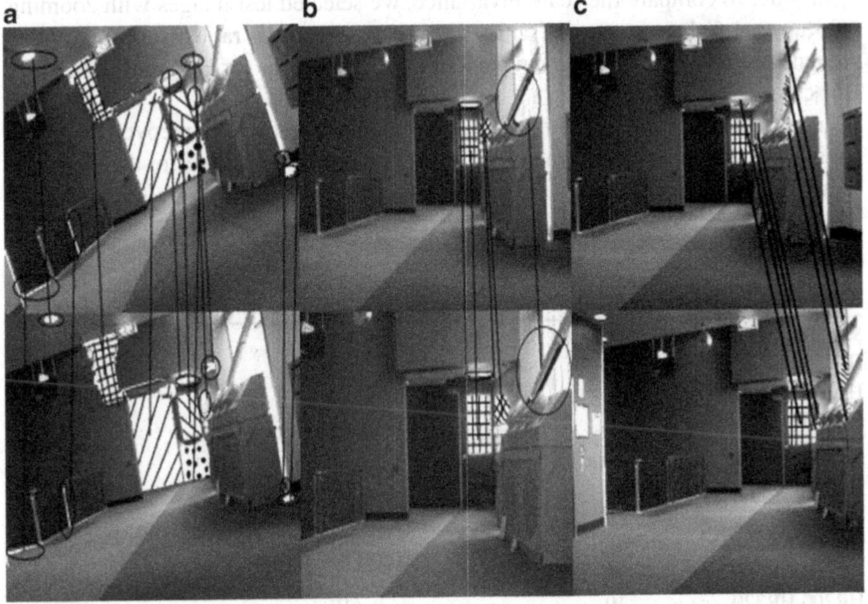

Fig. 3 (**a**) Matching under rotation (**b**) Matching under translation (**c**) Matching under scaling

Table 1 Complexity comparison results

Comp. time (ms)	Histogram-based	Harris	SIFT
Carpark	240	1,108	3,052
Hall	275	1,123	3,808

3.2 Matching Precision Test

To test transformation robustness over a range of images, we evaluated the performance of matching over different frame intervals. We use the first frame as reference frame and evaluate matching performance between the chosen reference frame and successive frames and determine the accuracy of matches in each pair. The accuracy is determined as per Eq. (28) and number of correct matches in each test pair is manually counted as the ground truth data.

Testing images for rotation tests were selected every 20 frames from the input video sequence. The maximum frame interval range is 100 frames, approximating 10° rotations which are reasonable in video sequence. Images in translation tests were selected every 20 frames among 100 frames as well. The horizontal translation was measured as percentage of amount of translation over the image width. The maximum translation range in the testing sequence was 15%. Figure 3a shows 12 pairs of matched regions for Hall sequence under camera rotations between 200th frame and 400th frame. Figure 3b shows five pairs of matched regions for Hall sequence under camera translation between 200th frame and 280th frame.

In order to compare the scale invariance, we selected test images with zooming ratio up to 1.5 that covers the range of expected zooming ratios in normal video sequences. Figure 3c shows seven pairs of matched regions for Hall sequence under 1.5 scaling.

In all test cases, we found that proposed method was able to recover the affine parameters correctly 93% of the time for the Hall video and 100% for the other test sequences in Table 1.

Table 2 Feature matching results

Hall	#Detected matches	#Correct matches	Precision
Scaling			
HS26-HS27	10	10	100%
HS26-HS28	7	7	100%
HS26-HS29	8	8	100%
HS26-HS30	9	7	78%
HS26-HS31	9	9	100%
Rotation			
HR200-HR240	10	10	100%
HR200-HR280	10	10	100%
HR200-HR320	10	10	100%
HR200-HR360	10	10	100%
HR200-HR400	11	11	100%
Translation			
HT200-HT220	9	9	100%
HT200-HT240	6	6	100%
HT200-HT260	9	9	100%
HT200-HT280	5	5	100%

4 Conclusion

This paper has presented an original algorithm for global motion estimation in video sequences. Designed for low computation requirements, it is faster than conventional methods while providing high accuracy. Future work involves extending this method for robust real time moving object extracting and tracking in video sequences (Table 2).

References

1. D.J. Fleet and Y. Weiss, Optical Flow Estimation. In Paragios et al.. Handbook of Mathematical Models in Computer Vision, (2006).
2. L. M. Po and W. C. Ma, A novel four-step search algorithm for fast block motion estimation, IEEE Trans. Circuits Syst. Video Technol. vol. 6, pp. 313–317, June 1996.
3. L.G.Brown, A survey of image registration techniques, ACM Computing Surveys 24(4), pp. 325–376, December 1992.
4. B. Zitová, Jan Flusser: Image registration methods: a survey. Image Vision Comput. 21(11): 977–1000 (2003).
5. J. B. A. Maintz and M. A. Viergever, A survey of medical image registration, Medical Image Analysis 2(1), 1998.
6. C. Harris and M. Stephens, A Combined Corner and Edge Detector, Proc. Alvey Vision Conf., Univ. Manchester, pp. 147–151, 1988.
7. Lowe, D. G., Distinctive Image Features from Scale-Invariant Key Points, International Journal of Computer Vision, 60, pp. 91–110, 2004
8. J.Flusser, T. Suk, A Moment-based Approach to Registration of Images with affine Geometric Distortion.", IEEE Trans on Geoscience and Remote Sensing, Vol 32. No.2 March, 1994.
9. A. Goshtasby, G. C. Stockman, and C. V. Page, A region-based approach to digital image registration with subpixel accuracy, IEEE Trans. Geosci. Remote Sensing, vol. 24, no. 3, pp. 390–399, 1986.
10. X. Dai and S. Khorram, A feature-based image registration algorithm using improved chain-code representation combined with invariant moments, IEEE Trans. Geosci. Remote Sensing, vol.37, Sept. 1999.
11. N. Otsu, A threshold selection method from gray-level histograms, IEEE Transactions on Systems Man Cybernet SMC-9 1979, pp. 62–66.